Who's Who

of

NASA

Astronauts

Lee Ellis

Americana Group Publishing

Who's Who of NASA Astronauts

by Lee Ellis

Americana Group Publishing
54 Woodridge Drive West
River Falls, WI 54022
e-mail at: american@pressenter.com
Telephone: 715-425-9653
Fax: 715-425-5347

ISBN: 0966796144

0 9 8 7 6 5 4 3 2

Published February, 2001
Second Printing January, 2002

Printed and bound in the United States of America

p. 481 cm.

$39.95

Cover photograph courtesy of Johnson Space Center Digital Image Collection

About the Author

Lee Ellis started writing books about autograph collecting more than 10 years ago. He is an avid autograph collector and specializes in collecting NASA astronaut signatures. His research into the biographies of astronauts and space flight information has led to the creation and publication of "Who's Who of NASA Astronauts." Mr. Ellis received his bachelor of science degree from the University of Wisconsin and lives in River Falls, WI, with his wife, Shirley. When Mr. Ellis is not working on a book he enjoys fishing western Wisconsin's trout streams and has pastimes of photography and traveling.

Acknowledgements

Many individuals contributed in some way or another to the completion of this book. The people at River Valley Printing gave their technical advice and expertise, which was invaluable in the production of this book. The crew at Americana Group Publishing guided the path of this book and made it a reality. Most importantly, I wish to thank my family, who gave me the support and encouragement to seek the rewards of this project.

"Who's Who of NASA Astronauts" is a compilation of data received from many sources. I am grateful to the NASA astronauts who participated in the interviews that made up a large portion of this book. I also want to thank NASA and its agencies for their cooperation in my search for astronaut information. Among the agencies I wish to thank are; Johnson Space Center Astronaut Office, Kennedy Space Center Media Resources and the NASA History Office in Washington, DC.

Editor: Lee Ellis
Assistant Editor: Kathryn Clark
Book Design: Americana Group Publishing
Index: Multiplex Inc.
Technical Support: Michael Ellis

Table of Contents

Chapter One:

NASA Astronaut

Training & Selection

The 21st century promises the challenge for humans to live and work in space. The achievements of scientists, engineers, technicians, and specialists who will build and operate the Space Station are the legacy of the National Aeronautics and Space Administration's (NASA's) many years experience in selecting and training astronauts to work on the frontier of space.

History of Astronaut Selection

Man's scope of space exploration has broadened since the first U.S. manned space flight in 1961. But the Nation can never forget the original seven space pilots who focused our vision on the stars. In 1959, NASA asked the U.S. military services to list their members who met specific qualifications. In seeking its first astronauts, NASA required jet aircraft flight experience and engineering training. Height could be no more than 5 feet 11 inches because of limited cabin space available in the Mercury space capsule being designed. After many series of intense physical and psychological screenings, NASA selected seven men from an original field of 500 candidates. They were Air Force Captains L. Gordon Cooper, Jr., Virgil "Gus" Grissom, and Donald K. "Deke" Slayton; Marine Lieutenant Colonel John H. Glenn, Jr., Navy Lieutenant M. Scott Carpenter and Navy Lieutenant Commanders Walter M. Schirra, Jr., and Alan B. Shepard, Jr. Each man flew in Project Mercury except Slayton, who was grounded for medical reasons. Sixteen years later, Slayton was an American crew member of the Apollo-Soyuz Test Project, the world's first international manned space flight. Nine pilot astronauts were chosen in September 1962, and fourteen more were selected in October 1963. By then, prime emphasis had shifted away from flight experience and toward superior academic qualifications. In October 1964, applications were invited on the basis of educational background alone. These were the scientist astronauts, so called because the 400-plus applicants who met minimum requirements had a doctorate or equivalent experience in the natural sciences, medicine or engineering. Of these 400 applicants, six were selected in June 1965. In April 1966, 19 pilot astronauts were named and in August 1967, 11 scientist astronauts were addedto the program. When the Air Force Manned Orbiting Laboratory program was canceled in mid-1969, seven astronaut trainees transferred to NASA.

Shuttle Era Astronaut Candidate Recruiting

The first group of astronaut candidates for the space shuttle program was selected in January 1978. In July of that year, the 35 candidates began a rigorous training and evaluation period at NASA's Johnson Space Center (JSC), Houston, Texas, to qualify for subsequent assignment for future space shuttle flight crews. This group of 20 mission scientist astronauts and 15 pilots completed training and went from astronaut candidate status to astronaut (active status) in August 1979. Six of the 35 were women and four were minorities. Ten groups of pilots and mission specialists have been added since then: 19 in 1980, 17 in 1984, 13 in 1985, 15 in 1987, 23 in 1990, 19 in 1992, 19 in 1995, 35 in 1996, 25 in 1998 and 17 in 2000.

Selection and Training for the Future

In the future, the United States with its international partners Japan, Canada, Russia and the European Space Agency, will operate a man-tended space station. From that orbiting depot, humans will continue their journeys to the Moon and Mars. As these plans become reality, the need for qualified space flight professionals will increase. To respond to these needs, NASA accepts applications for the Astronaut Candidate Program on a continuous basis. Candidates are selected as needed, normally every two years, for pilot and mission specialist categories. Both civilian and military personnel are considered for the program. Civilians may apply at any time. Military personnel must apply through their parent service and be nominated by their service to NASA. The astronaut candidate selection process was developed to select highly qualified individuals for human space programs. For mission specialists and pilot astronaut candidates, the education and experience requirements are at least a bachelor's degree from an accredited institution in engineering, biological science, physical science, or mathematics. For mission specialist applicants, three years of related, progressively responsible professional experience must follow the degree. An advanced degree is desirable and may be substituted for all or part of the experience requirement (i.e., master's degree = 1 year of work experience, doctoral degree = 3 years of experience). Pilot astronaut applicants must also meet the following requirements prior to submitting an application: At least 1,000 hours pilot-in-command time in jet aircraft; flight test experience is highly desirable. Ability to pass a NASA Class I space physical, which is similar to a military or civilian Class I flight physical, and includes the following specific standards: for vision-distance visual acuity - 20/70 or better uncorrected, correctable to 20/20, each eye. For Blood Pressure-140/90 measured in a sitting position. Height between 64 and 76 inches. Mission specialists have similar requirements to pilot astronauts, except that the qualifying physical is a NASA Class II space physical, which is similar to a military of civilian Class II flight physical and includes the following specific standards: for vision-distance visual acuity - 20/200 or better uncorrected, correctable to 20/20, each eye. For Blood pressure-Same as for Pilots. Height requirements for mission specialists are between 58.5 and 76 inches. The application package may be obtained by writing to the Astronaut Selection Office, Mail Code AHX, Johnson Space Center, Houston, TX 77058-3696. Applicants who meet the basic qualifications are evaluated by discipline panels. Those selected as finalists are screened during a week-long process of personal interviews, thorough medical evaluations, and orientation. The Astronaut Selection Board's recommendations are based on the applicant's education, training, and experience as well as unique qualifications and skills. Because several hundred applicants fulfill the requirements, the final selection is based largely on personal interviews. Astronauts are expected to be team players and highly skilled generalists with just the right amount of individuality and self-reliance to be effective crew members. Selected applicants are designated astronaut candidates and assigned to the astronaut office at the Johnson Space Center for a 1 to 2 year training and evaluation program. Civilian candidates who successfully complete the training and evaluation and are selected astronauts are expected to remain with NASA for at least 5 years. Successful military candidates are detailed to NASA for a specified tour of duty. Salaries for civilian astronaut candidates are based on the Federal Government's General Schedule pay scales for grades GS-11 through GS-14, and are set in accordance with each individual's academic achievements and experience.

Space Shuttle Crew Positions

Commander/Pilot astronauts : Pilot astronauts serve as both space shuttle commanders and pilots. During flight, the commander has onboard responsibility for the vehicle, crew, mission success, and safety of flight. The pilot assists the commander in controlling and operating the vehicle and may assist in the deployment and retrieval of satellites using the remote manipulator system (RMS), referred to as the robot arm or mechanical arm.

Mission Specialist Astronauts: Mission specialist astronauts work with the commander and the pilot and have overall responsibility for coordinating shuttle operations in the following areas: Shuttle systems, crew activity planning, consumables usage, and experiment/payload operations. Mission specialists are trained in the details of the Orbiter onboard systems, as well as the operational characteristics, mission requirements/ objectives, and supporting equipment/systems for each of the experiments conducted on their assigned missions. Mission specialists perform extravehicular activities (EVAs), or space walks, operate the remote manipulator system, and are responsible for payloads and specific experiment operations.

Payload Specialists: Payload specialists are persons other than NASA astronauts (including foreign nationals) who have specialized onboard duties; they may be added to shuttle crews if activities that have unique requirements are involved and more than the minimum crew size of five is needed. First consideration for additional crew members is given to qualified NASA mission specialists. When payload specialists are required they are nominated by NASA, the foreign sponsor, or the designated payload sponsor. In the case of NASA or NASA-related payloads, the nominations are based on the recommendations of the appropriate Investigator Working Group (IWG). Although payload specialists are not part of the Astronaut Candidate Program, they must have the appropriate education and training related to the payload or experiment. All applicants must meet certain physical requirements and must pass NASA space physical examinations with varying standards depending on classification.

Astronaut Candidate Training

Astronaut candidates receive training at JSC near Houston, Texas. They attend classes on shuttle systems, in basic science and technology: mathematics, geology meteorology, guidance and navigation, oceanography, orbital dynamics, astronomy, physics, and materials processing are among the subjects. Candidates also receive training in land and sea survival training, scuba diving, and space suits.

As part of the Astronaut Candidate training program, Astronaut Candidates are required to complete military water survival prior to beginning their flying syllabus, and become SCUBA qualified to prepare them for the extravehicular activity training. Consequently, all Astronaut Candidates will be required to pass a swimming test during their first month of training. They must swim 3 lengths of a 25M pool in a flight suit and tennis shoes. The strokes allowed are freestyle, breast, and sidestroke. There is no time limit. They must also tread water continuously for 10 minutes.

Candidates are also exposed to the problems associated with high (hyperbaric) and low (hypobaric) atmospheric pressures in the altitude chambers and learn to deal with emergencies associated with these conditions.

In addition, astronaut candidates are given exposure to the microgravity of space flight. A modified KC-135 jet aircraft produces periods of weightlessness for 20 seconds. During this brief period, astronauts experience the feeling of microgravity. The aircraft then returns to the original altitude and the sequence is repeated up to 40 times in a day.

Pilot astronauts maintain flying proficiency by flying 15 hours per month in NASA's fleet of 2-seat T-38 jets; they build up jet aircraft hours and also practice Orbiter landings in the Shuttle Training Aircraft, a modified corporate jet aircraft. Mission specialist astronauts fly a minimum of 4 hours per month.

Astronaut Formal Training

The astronauts begin their formal space transportation system training program during their year of candidacy by reading manuals and by taking computer-based training lessons on the various Orbiter systems ranging from propulsion to environmental control.

The next step in the training process is the single systems trainer (SST). Each astronaut is accompanied by an instructor who helps in the learning process about the operations of each Orbiter subsystem using checklists similar to those found on a mission. The checklists contain information on normal system operations and corrective actions for malfunctions. The astronauts are trained in the SSTs to operate each system, to recognize malfunctions, and to perform corrective actions.

Following the SST portion of the training program, the astronauts begin training in the complex Shuttle Mission Simulators (SMSs). The SMS provides training in all areas of shuttle vehicle operations and in all systems tasks associated with the major flight phases: prelaunch, ascent, orbit operations, entry and landing. The orbit training includes payload operation, payload deployment and retrieval, maneuvers, and rendezvous. Two additional simulators, a fixed base and a motion base, are used to train the astronauts.

The fixed base crew station is used for both specific mission/payload training and launch descent and landing training. It is the only trainer with complete fore and aft consoles, including an RMS console. A digital image generation system provides visual cues for out-the-window scenes of the entire mission, e.g., the Earth, stars, payloads and the landing runway. Missions can be simulated literally from launch to landing.

The motion base crew station is used to train pilots and commanders in the mission phases of launch, descent, and landing. Motion cues are provided by the 6-degrees-of-freedom motion system which also allows the flight deck to be rotated 90 degrees to simulate lift-off and ascent. Astronauts begin their training in the SMS using generic training software until they are assigned to a particular mission, approximately 10 months before flight. Once they are assigned to a flight, astronauts train on a flight simulator with actual flight-specific training software.

During this last 11 weeks, the astronauts also train with the flight controllers in the Mission Control Center (MCC). The SMS and MCC are linked by computer in the same way the Orbiter and MCC are linked during an actual mission. The astronauts and flight controllers learn to work as a team, solving problems and working nominal and contingency mission timelines. Total hours in the SMS for the astronauts, after flight assignment, is about 300 hours.

In parallel with the SMS training there are several other part-task trainers that are used to prepare astronauts for shuttle missions. These trainers are in varying degrees of fidelity and each serve a particular purpose.

The Sonny Carter Training Facility, or Neutral Buoyancy Laboratory (NBL), provides controlled neutral buoyancy operations in the facility water tank to simulate the zero-g or weightless condition which is experienced by the spacecraft and crew during space flight. It is an essential tool for the design, testing and development of the space station and future NASA programs. For the astronaut, the facility provides important pre-flight training in becoming familiar with planned crew activities and with the dynamics of body motion under weightless conditions. Several full-scale mockups and trainers are also used to train astronauts. The full fuselage trainer is a full-sized plywood Orbiter mockup with nonfunctional mid-deck and flight deck, and full-scale payload bay. It is used for onboard systems orientation and habitability training. Astronauts practice meal preparation, equipment stowage, trash management, use of cameras, and experiment familiarization. This trainer is also used for emergency egress training after shuttle landings. The crew compartment trainer is a mockup of the forward section of the Orbiter crew station, without a payload bay, that can be tilted vertically. It is used to train for on-orbit habitability procedures and also emergency pad egress and bailout operations. The crew stations of both trainers are similar. The manipulator development facility is a full-scale mockup of the payload bay with full-scale hydraulically operated RMS, the mechanical arm on the Orbiter which is used to move payloads in and out of the payload bay. Mission specialists use this trainer to practice deploying and reberthing of payloads into the Orbiter.

Pilots training for a specific mission receive more intensive instruction in Orbiter approach and landing in Shuttle Training Aircraft (STA), which are four Gulfstream II business jets modified to perform like the Orbiter during landing. Because the Orbiter approaches landings at such a steep angle (17-20 degrees) and high speed (over 300 miles per hour), the STA approaches with its engines in reverse thrust and main landing gear down to increase drag and duplicate the unique glide characteristics of the Orbiter. Assigned pilots receive about 100 hours of STA training prior to a flight, which is equivalent to 600 shuttle approaches. In between training sessions, the crew members continue to keep themselves up-to-date on the status of the space craft and payloads for their assigned mission. In addition, the astronauts study flight rules and flight data file procedures, and participate in mission-related technical meetings. They also participate in test and checkout activities at the NASA Kennedy Space Center in Florida, the launch site for the space shuttle.

The months of preparation pay off and the mission is a success; the actual mission will have far fewer contingencies than were practiced for. The accuracy of the simulations and training is remarkable. Astronauts often comment that only the noise and vibration of launch and the experience of weightlessness are missing from the practice sessions; everything else in training accurately duplicates the space experience. Astronauts who participate in the Russian Space Station Mir program receive Russian language training before transferring to the Yuri Gagarin Cosmonaut Training Center for approximately 13 months. Four weeks prior to the shuttle launch that will deliver them to Mir, the astronaut returns to JSC to train and integrate as part of the shuttle crew during the final phase. Russian language courses continue at the Gagarin Training Center until the astronaut reaches the level required to begin technical training. The Russian technical training includes theoretical training on the Russian vehicles design and systems, EVA training, scientific investigations and experiments, and biomedical training. The astronauts' mission continues even after the Orbiter has returned. The crew will spend several days in medical testing and debriefing, recounting their experiences for the benefit of future crews to assist in future training and to add to the space flight knowledge base. Members of the media also receive a detailed post-flight briefing by the crew. Then, the studies and training that may eventually lead to another space flight are resumed.

Chapter Two:

Current

NASA

Astronauts

NAME: Scott D. Altman (Commander, USN)
NASA Astronaut

PERSONAL DATA: Born August 15, 1959 in Lincoln, Illinois. Married to the former Jill Shannon Loomer of Tucson, Arizona. They have three children. Enjoys classic automobiles, flying and computers. Avid reader and sports fan/participant. Hometown is Pekin, Illinois, where his parents, Fred and Sharon Altman, currently reside.

EDUCATION: Graduated from Pekin Community High School, Pekin, Illinois in 1977; received bachelor of science degree in aeronautical and astronautical engineering from the University of Illinois in May 1981, and a master of science degree in aeronautical engineering from the Naval Postgraduate School in June 1990.

ORGANIZATIONS: University of Illinois Alumni Association, Sigma Chi Alumni Association, life member Association of Naval Aviation and Military Order of the World Wars, full member Society of Experimental Test Pilots.

SPECIAL HONORS: Navy Strike/Flight Air Medal, Navy Commendation Medal, Navy Achievement Medal, 1987 Award winner for Outstanding Achievement in Tactical Aviation as selected by the Association of Naval Aviation.

EXPERIENCE: Altman was commissioned an Ensign in the United States Navy following completion of Aviation Reserve Officer Candidate School in Pensacola, Florida, in August 1981. Following training in Florida and Texas, he received his Navy wings of gold in February 1983 and was ordered to NAS Miramar in San Diego, California, to fly the F-14. Attached to Fighter Squadron 51, Altman completed two deployments to the Western Pacific and Indian Ocean. In August 1987, he was selected for the Naval Postgraduate School-Test Pilot School Coop program and graduated with Test Pilot School Class 97 in June 1990 as a Distinguished Graduate. After graduation, he spent the next two years as a test pilot working on various F-14 projects such as the air to ground separation effort, and aft center of gravity flying qualities evaluation, as well as the Navy evaluation of the Air Force F-15 S/MTD technology demonstrator. Selected to help take the new F-14D on its first operational deployment, his next assignment was to VF-31 at NAS Miramar where he served as Maintenance Officer and later Operations Officer. Altman was awarded the Navy Air Medal for his role as a strike leader flying over Southern Iraq in support of Operation Southern Watch. Shortly following his return from this six month deployment, he was selected for the astronaut program. He has logged over 4000 flight hours in more than 40 types of aircraft.

NASA EXPERIENCE: Selected as an astronaut candidate by NASA in December 1994, Altman reported to the Johnson Space Center in March 1995. He completed a year of training and was initially assigned to work technical aspects of orbiter landing and roll out issues for the Astronaut Office Vehicle Systems Branch. Twice flown, Altman has logged over 664 hours in space. He was the pilot on STS-90 in 1998, and STS-106 in 2000.

SPACE FLIGHT EXPERIENCE: STS-90 Neurolab (April 17 to May 3, 1998). During the 16-day Spacelab flight the seven person crew aboard Space Shuttle Columbia served as both experiment subjects and operators for 26 individual life science experiments focusing on the effects of microgravity on the brain and nervous system. The STS-90 flight orbited the Earth 256 times, and covered 6.3 million miles in over 381. STS-106 Atlantis (September 8-20, 2000). During the 12-day mission, the crew successfully prepared the International Space Station for the arrival of the first permanent crew. The five astronauts and two cosmonauts delivered more than 6,600 pounds of supplies and installed batteries, power converters, a toilet and a treadmill on the Space Station. Altman was one of two operators of the robot arm transporting the EVA crew during the spacewalk. Additionally, he handflew two complete flyarounds of the station after performing the undocking from the station. STS-106 orbited the Earth 185 times, and covered 4.9 million miles in 11 days, 19 hours, and 10 minutes.

NAME: Clayton C. Anderson
NASA Astronaut (Mission Specialist Candidate)

PERSONAL DATA: Born February 23, 1959 in Omaha, Nebraska. He considers Ashland, Nebraska to be his hometown. Married to the former Susan Jane Harreld of Elkhart, Indiana. They have one child, a son, Clayton "Cole." His mother, Alice J. Anderson, resides in Ashland, Nebraska. His father, John T. Anderson, is deceased. Her parents are Jack and Mary Harreld of Anderson, Missouri. Recreational interests include officiating College and High School basketball; participation in all sports; flying; reading; writing music; playing the piano/organ and vocal performance. As an undergraduate he competed on the football, basketball and track teams.

EDUCATION: Graduated from Ashland-Greenwood High School, Ashland, Nebraska, 1977; received a bachelor of science degree in Physics from Hastings College, Nebraska in 1981 and a master of science degree in Aerospace Engineering from Iowa State University in 1983.

ORGANIZATIONS: Southwest Basketball Officials Association; Men's College Basketball Official: Red River Athletic, Southern Collegiate Athletic, Heart of Texas, Lone Star, and Texas/New Mexico Junior College Athletic Conferences; Aircraft Owners and Pilots Association (AOPA); Johnson Space Center Employee Activities Association: Vice President of Athletics (1987-1992); Clear Lake Optimist Club Past President and Vice President. SPECIAL HONORS: NASA Quality and Safety Achievement Recognition (QASAR) Award 1998; NCAA National Christian College Basketball Championships Official (1997, 1998); JSC Certificate of Commendation (1993); Outstanding Young Man of America (1981, 1985, 1987); Bronco Award Winner, Hastings College (1981).

NASA EXPERIENCE: Anderson joined the Johnson Space Center in 1983 in the Mission Planning and Analysis Division where he performed rendezvous and proximity operations trajectory designs for early Space Shuttle and Space Station missions. In 1988 he moved to the Mission Operations Directorate (MOD) as a Flight Design Manager leading the trajectory design team for the Galileo planetary mission (STS-34) while serving as the backup for the Magellan planetary mission (STS-31). He was later assigned the Gamma Ray Observatory (STS-37) and Tethered Satellite/EURECA (STS-46) missions. In 1989, Anderson was chosen as the supervisor of the MOD Ascent Flight Design Section and, following a reorganization, the Flight Design Engineering Office of the Flight Design and Dynamics Division. In 1993 hewas named the Chief of the Flight Design Branch. From 1996 until his selection Anderson held the post of Manager, Emergency Operations Center, NASA Johnson Space Center, Houston, Texas. Selected by NASA in June 1998, he reported for training in August 1998. Astronaut Candidate Training includes orientation briefings and tours, numerous scientific and technical briefings, intensive instruction in Shuttle and International Space Station systems, physiological training and ground school to prepare for T-38 flight training, as well as learning water and wilderness survival techniques. Anderson is currently assigned to the Astronaut Office Shuttle Operations Branch. He will serve in technical assignments until assigned to a space flight.

NAME: Michael P. Anderson (Lieutenant Colonel, USAF)
NASA Astronaut

PERSONAL DATA: Born December 25, 1959, in Plattsburgh, New York. Considers Spokane, Washington, to be his hometown. Married. Enjoys photography, chess, computers, and tennis.

EDUCATION: Graduated from Cheney High School in Cheney, Washington, in 1977. Bachelor of science degree in physics/astronomy from University of Washington, 1981. Master of science degree in physics from Creighton University, 1990.

SPECIAL HONORS: Distinguished graduate USAF Communication Electronics Officers course. Recipient of the Armed Forces Communication Electronics Associations Academic Excellence Award 1983. Received the USAF Undergraduate Pilot Training Academic Achievement Award for Class 87-08 Vance AFB. Awarded the Defense Superior Service Medal, the USAF Meritorious Service Medal, and the USAF Achievement Medal with one oak leaf cluster.

EXPERIENCE: Anderson graduated form the University of Washington in 1981 and was commissioned a second lieutenant. After completing a year of technical training at Keesler AFB Mississippi he was assigned to Randolph AFB Texas. At Randolph he served as Chief of Communication Maintenance for the 2015 Communication Squadron and later as Director of Information System Maintenance for the 1920 Information System Group. In 1986 he was selected to attend Undergraduate Pilot Training at Vance AFB, Oklahoma. Upon graduation he was assigned to the 2nd Airborne Command and Control Squadron, Offutt AFB Nebraska as an EC 135 pilot, flying the Strategic Air Commands airborne command post code-named "Looking Glass". From January 1991 to September 1992 he served as an aircraft commander and instructor pilot in the 920th Air Refueling Squadron, Wurtsmith AFB Michigan. From September 1992 to February 1995 he was assigned as an instructor pilot and tactics officer in the 380 Air Refueling Wing, Plattsburgh AFB New York. Anderson has logged over 3000 hours in various models of the KC-135 and the T-38A aircraft.

NASA EXPERIENCE: Selected by NASA in December 1994, Anderson reported to the Johnson Space Center in March 1995. He completed a year of training and evaluation, and is qualified for flight crew assignment as a mission specialist. Anderson was initially assigned technical duties in the Flight Support Branch of the Astronaut Office. Most recently, he flew on the crew of STS-89. In completing his first space flight Anderson has logged over 211 hours in space. Anderson is assigned to the crew of STS-107 scheduled to launch in 2001.

NAME: Lee Joseph Archambault (Lieutenant Colonel, USAF)
NASA Astronaut (Pilot Candidate)

PERSONAL DATA: Born August 25, 1960 in Oak Park, Illinois, but considers Bellwood, Illinois to be his hometown. Married to the former Kelly Renee Raup. They have three children. Recreational interests include weight lifting, golf, running, and ice hockey. His parents, Lee and Mary Ann Archambault, reside in Addison, Illinois. Her parents, Linda Post and Henry Raup reside in Royal, Illinois and Tavares, Florida, respectively.

EDUCATION: Graduated from Proviso West High School, Hillside, Illinois in 1978. Earned Bachelor of Science and Master of Science degrees in Aeronautical/ Astronautical Engineering from the

University of Illinois-Urbana, in 1982 and 1984, respectively.

ORGANIZATIONS: Society of Experimental Test Pilots, Order of Daedalians (fraternity of military pilots), University of Illinois Alumni Association, University of Illinois Aeronautical/Astronautical Engineering Department Academic Advisory Committee.

AWARDS: Military decorations include the Distinguished Flying Cross, Meritorious Service Medal (1st Oak Leaf Cluster), Air Medal (2nd Oak Leaf Cluster), Aerial Achievement Medal (4th Oak Leaf Cluster), Commendation Medal (1st Oak Leaf Cluster), Air Force Achievement Medal, Combat Readiness Medal, Southwest Asia Service Medal, Kuwaiti Liberation Medal, and various other service awards.

SPECIAL HONORS: Distinguished Graduate and Liethen-Tittle Award (top graduate) from the U.S. Air Force Test Pilot School. Distinguished Graduate from the U.S. Air Force Officer Training School. Graduated with Honors from the University of Illinois. University of Illinois Aeronautical/Astronautical Engineering Outstanding Recent Alumnus.

EXPERIENCE: Archambault received his commission as a Second Lieutenant in the United States Air Force from the Air Force Officer Training School at Lackland Air Force Base (AFB), Texas, in January 1985. Upon completion, he attended the Euro-Nato Joint Jet Pilot Training Program at Sheppard AFB, Texas, and earned his pilot wings in April 1986. He then reported to Cannon AFB, New Mexico, where he served as a combat ready F-111D pilot in the 27th Tactical Fighter Wing until April 1990. In May 1990, he transitioned to the F-117A Stealth Fighter in the 37th Tactical Fighter Wing at Nellis AFB/Tonopah Test Range, Nevada. From November 1990 through April 1991, he deployed to Saudi Arabia in support of Operation Desert Shield/Desert Storm and flew twenty-two combat missions in the F-117A during the Gulf War. He served a second F-117A tour in Saudi Arabia from August 1991 through December 1991 in support of post-Desert Storm peacekeeping efforts. In August 1992, Archambault was reassigned to Holloman AFB, New Mexico, where he served as an F-117A instructor pilot and operational test pilot for the 57th Wing. Archambault attended the U.S. Air Force Test Pilot School at Edwards AFB, California, from July 1994 until June 1995. In July 1995, he was assigned to the 46th Test Wing at the Air Force Development Test Center, Eglin AFB, Florida. There, he performed weapons developmental flight tests in all models of the F-16. Archambault was the assistant operations officer for the 39th Flight Test Squadron when he was selected for the astronaut program. He has logged over 3000 flight hours in more than 30 different aircraft.

NASA EXPERIENCE: Selected by NASA in June 1998, he reported for training in August 1998. Astronaut Candidate Training includes orientation briefings and tours, numerous scientific and technical briefings, intensive instruction in Shuttle and International Space Station systems, physiological training and ground school to prepare for T-38 flight training, as well as learning water and wilderness survival techniques. He is currently assigned to the Astronaut Office Shuttle Operations Branch, working on flight instrument upgrades for the Space Shuttle Cockpit Council. He will maintain a technical assignment until assigned to a space flight.

NAME: Jeffrey S. Ashby (Captain, USN)
NASA Astronaut

PERSONAL DATA: Born June 16, 1954 in Dallas, Texas. Raised in the Colorado mountains. Married. Recreational interests include skiing, backpacking, fly fishing.

EDUCATION: Graduated from Evergreen High School, Evergreen, Colorado in 1972. Bachelor of science degree in mechanical engineering from the University of Idaho, 1976. Master of science degree in aviation systems from the University of Tennessee, 1993.

SPECIAL HONORS: Distinguished Flying Cross, Meritorious Service Medal, Navy Air Medals (4), Navy Commendation Medals (2), Navy Achievement Medal, and numerous Unit decorations. Navy Attack Aviator of the Year, 1991.

EXPERIENCE: Ashby has accumulated over 6000 flight hours and 1000 carrier landings. He is a graduate of the Naval Test Pilot School (1988) and the Naval Fighter Weapons School (Top Gun, 1986). During his 16 year tenure as a fleet Navy pilot, Ashby completed five carrier deployments, flying A-7E and FA-18 aircraft from the USS CONSTELLATION, USS CORAL SEA, USS MIDWAY, and USS ABRAHAM LINCOLN. He has flown missions in support of Operations Desert Shield, Desert Storm, and Southern Watch in Iraq, and Operation Continue Hope in Somalia. Ashby successfully completed 33 combat missions in the FA-18 during Operation Desert Storm. As a Navy test pilot, Ashby participated in the early development of the FA-18 aircraft, directing and flying tests of its smart weapons systems and electronic warfare suite. He has flown test flights for over 80 projects including carrier suitability, ordnance release, and flying qualities of the Night attack and reconnaissance versions of the Hornet. In his final operational Navy tour, Ashby served as the Commanding Officer of Strike Fighter Squadron 94.

NASA EXPERIENCE: Selected by NASA in December 1994, Ashby reported to the Johnson Space Center in March 1995. Ashby completed his first space flight as pilot for STS-93 (Columbia) from July 22-27, 1999. The 5-day mission featured the deployment of the Chandra X-Ray Observatory. Designed to conduct comprehensive studies of the universe, the telescope will enable scientists to study exotic phenomena such as exploding stars, quasars, and black holes. In completing his first mission Ashby logged 118 hours and 50 minutes in space.

Ashby is assigned as pilot on STS-100/ISS Assembly Flight 6A scheduled for launch in 2001.

NAME: Ellen S. Baker (M.D., M.P.H.)
NASA Astronaut

PERSONAL DATA: Born April 27, 1953, in Fayetteville, North Carolina, but considers New York City her hometown. Married to Kenneth J. Baker. They have two daughters. She enjoys swimming, skiing, running, movies, music, and reading Ellen's parents, Dr. & Mrs. Melvin Shulman, reside in Beechhurst, New York. Ken's parents, Mr. & Mrs. James Baker, reside in Columbus, Ohio.

EDUCATION: Graduated from Bayside High School, New York, New York, in 1970; received a bachelor of arts degree in geology from the State University of New York at Buffalo in 1974, a doctorate of medicine degree from Cornell University in 1978, and a masters in public health from University of Texas School of Public Health in 1994.

EXPERIENCE: After completing medical school, Dr. Baker trained in internal medicine at the University of Texas Health Science Center, San Antonio, Texas. In 1981, after three years of training, she was certified by the American Board of Internal Medicine.

NASA EXPERIENCE: In 1981, following her residency, Dr. Baker joined NASA as a medical officer at the Lyndon B. Johnson Space Center. That same year, she graduated from the Air Force Aerospace Medicine Course at Brooks Air Force Base, San Antonio, Texas. Prior to her selection as an astronaut candidate she served as a physician in the Flight Medicine Clinic at the Johnson Space Center. Selected by NASA in May 1984, Dr. Baker became an astronaut in June 1985. Since then, she has worked a variety of jobs at NASA in support of the Space Shuttle program and Space Station development. A veteran of three space flights, Dr. Baker has logged over 686 hours in space. She was a mission specialist on STS-34 in 1989, STS-50 in 1992, and STS-71 in 1995.

SPACE FLIGHT EXPERIENCE: STS-34 Atlantis (October 18-23, 1989) launched from the Kennedy Space Center in Florida, and landed at Edwards Air Force Base in California. During the mission, the crew successfully deployed the Galileo to explore Jupiter, operated the Shuttle Solar Backscatter Ultraviolet Instrument (SSBUV) to map atmospheric ozone, conducted several medical experiments, and numerous scientific experiments. Mission objectives were accomplished in 79 orbits of the Earth, traveling 1.8 million miles in 119 hours and 41 minutes. STS-50 Columbia (June 25-July 9, 1992) launched and landed at the Kennedy Space Center in Florida. STS-50 was the first flight of the United States Microgravity Laboratory and the first Extended Duration Orbiter flight. Over a two-week period, the crew conducted scientific experiments involving crystal growth, fluid physics, fluid dynamics, biological science, and combustion science. Mission objectives were accomplished in 221 orbits of the Earth, traveling 5.7 million miles in 331 hours 30 seconds and 4 minutes in space. STS-71 Atlantis (June 27-July 7, 1995) launched from the Kennedy Space Center with a seven-member crew and returned there with an eight-member crew. STS-71 was the first Space Shuttle mission to dock with the Russian Space Station Mir, and involved an exchange of crews. The Atlantis Space Shuttle was modified to carry a docking system compatible with the Russian Mir Space Station. It also carried a Spacelab module in the payload bay in which the crew performed various life sciences experiments and data collections. Mission accomplished in 153 orbits of the Earth, traveling 4.1 million miles in 235 hours and 23 minutes.

NAME: Michael A. Baker (Captain, USN)
NASA Astronaut

PERSONAL DATA: Born October 27, 1953, in Memphis, Tennessee, but considers Lemoore, California, to be his hometown. Married to the former Deidra A. Mudurian of San Francisco, California. Two children. He enjoys tennis, swimming, hiking, and running. His parents, Mr. & Mrs. Clyde E. Baker, reside in Lemoore, California. Her mother, Mrs. Patricia TeStruth, resides in San Jose, California. Her father, Mr. Myron Mudurian, resides in Akron, Ohio.

EDUCATION: Graduated from Lemoore Union High School, Lemoore, California, in 1971; received a bachelor of science degree in aerospace engineering from the University of Texas in 1975.

ORGANIZATIONS: Member of the Society of Experimental Test Pilots, Association of Naval Aviation, the Tailhook Association, Association of Space Explorers, National Aeronautic Association, Sierra Club, and Veterans of Foreign Wars. Member of the Advisory Committee to the University of Texas College of Engineering, Aerospace Engineering Department.

SPECIAL HONORS: Awarded the Defense Superior Service Medal, 2 Defense Meritorious Service Medals, the Distinguished Flying Cross, the Navy Unit Commendation, 3 Meritorious Unit Commendations, the Battle "E" Award, NASA Distinguished Service Medal, NASA Outstanding Leadership Medal, NASA Exceptional Service Medal, 4 NASA Space Flight Medals, 3 Navy Expeditionary Medals, the National Defense Medal, 2 Sea Service Awards, and the Overseas Service Award. Named 1993 Outstanding University of Texas Alumni.

EXPERIENCE: After graduation from the University of Texas, Baker completed flight training and earned his Wings of Gold at Naval Air Station Chase Field, Beeville, Texas, in 1977. In 1978, he was assigned to Attack Squadron 56, embarked in the USS Midway, homeported in Yokosuka, Japan, where he flew the A-7E Corsair II. In late 1980 he was assigned to Carrier Air Wing 30 as the air wing landing signal officer. He attended the U.S. Naval Test Pilot School in 1981 and, after graduation, was assigned to the Carrier Suitability Branch of the Strike Aircraft Test Directorate. While there, Baker conducted carrier suitability structural tests, aircraft carrier catapult and arresting gear certification tests, and automatic carrier landing system certification and verification tests on the various aircraft carriers of the Navy's fleet in the A-7 aircraft. In 1983, he returned to the U.S. Naval Test Pilot School as an instructor. He was then assigned as the U.S. Navy exchange instructor at the Empire Test Pilots School in Boscombe Down, England, teaching performance, flying qualities and systems flight test techniques. He has logged over 5,400 hours flying time in approximately 50 different types of airplanes, including tactical jets, VSTOL, multi-engine transport and rotary wing aircraft, and has over 300 carrier landings to his credit.

NASA EXPERIENCE: Selected by NASA in June 1985, Baker became an astronaut in July 1986 upon completion of a one-year training and evaluation program. Following the Challenger accident, from January 1986 to December 1987, Baker was assigned as a member of the team that was pursuing redesign, modification and improvements to the Shuttle Landing and Deceleration Systems, including nosewheel steering, brakes, tires, and drag chute, in an effort to provide greater safety margins during landing and rollout. He was then assigned to the Shuttle Avionics Integration Laboratory (SAIL), where he was involved in the checkout and verification of the computer software and hardware interfaces for STS-26 (the return-to-flight mission) and subsequent flights. Baker then served as an ascent, entry and orbit spacecraft communicator (CAPCOM) for STS-27, STS-29, STS-30, STS-28, STS-34, STS-33, STS-32, STS-36, STS-31, STS-38, and STS-35. In this capacity his duties included communication with the Shuttle crew during simulations and actual missions, as well as working procedural problems and modifications between missions. He served as the leader of the Astronaut Support Personnel team at the Kennedy Space Center for Shuttle Missions STS-44, STS-42 and STS-45. From December 1992 to January 1994 he was assigned as the Flight Crew Operations Directorate Representative to the Space Shuttle Program Office. From March to October 1995 he served as the Director of Operations for NASA at the Gagarin Cosmonaut Training Center in Star City, Russia. He was responsible for the coordination and implementation of mission operation activities in the Moscow region for the joint U.S./Russian Shuttle/Mir program. A veteran of four space flights, Baker has logged 965 hours in space. He served as pilot on STS-43 (August 2-11, 1991) and STS-52 (October 22 to November 1, 1992), and was the mission commander on STS-68 (September 30 to October 11, 1994) and STS-81 (January 12-22, 1997).

CURRENT ASSIGNMENT: He is currently assigned as the Assistant Director of Johnson Space Center (JSC) for Human Space Flight Programs, Russia, responsible for implementation and integration of NASA's human space flight programs in Russia. These activities include International Space Station (ISS) training, operations, technical liaison, logistics and personnel administration support. He also serves as the NASA JSC representative to the Russian Space Agency, Gagarin Cosmonaut Training Center, Star City; Mission Control Center-Moscow, Energia Rocket and Spacecraft Corporation, Krunichev State Scientific and Production Space Center and other Russian government agencies and manufacturers involved in the ISS program.

SPACEFLIGHT EXPERIENCE: STS-43 Space Shuttle Atlantis launched from the Kennedy Space Center, Florida, on August 2, 1991. During the flight, crew members deployed the fifth Tracking and Data Relay Satellite (TDRS-E), in addition to conducting 32 physical, material, and life science experiments, mostly relating to the Extended Duration Orbiter and Space Station Freedom. After 142 orbits of the Earth, the 9-day mission concluded with a landing on Runway 15 at the Kennedy Space Center on August 11, 1991. Mission duration was 213 hours, 21 minutes, 25 seconds. STS-52 Space Shuttle Columbia launched from the Kennedy Space Center, Florida, on October 22, 1992. During the mission crew members deployed the Italian Laser Geodynamic Satellite (LAGEOS) which will be used to measure movement of the Earth's crust, and operated the U.S. Microgravity Payload 1 (USMP-1). Additionally, the Space Vision System (SVS) developed by the Canadian Space Agency was tested by the Canadian payload specialist and the crew using a small target assembly which was released from the remote manipulator system. The SVS will be used for Space Station construction. These three primary payloads together with numerous other payloads operated by the crew encompassed geophysics, materials science, biological research and applied research for Space Station Freedom. Following 159 orbits of the Earth, the 10-day mission concluded with a landing on Runway 33 at the Kennedy Space Center on November 1, 1992. Mission duration was 236 hours, 56 minutes, 13 seconds. STS-68 Space Shuttle Endeavour launched from the Kennedy Space Center, Florida, on September 30, 1994. This flight was the second flight of the Space Radar Laboratory (SRL) comprised of a large radar called SIR-C/X-SAR (Shuttle Imaging Radar-C/X-Band Synthetic Aperture Radar) and MAPS (Measurement of Air Pollution from Satellites). As part of NASA's Mission to Planet Earth, SRL was an international, multidisciplinary study of global environmental change, both natural and man-made. The primary objective was to radar map the surface of the Earth to help us understand the contributions of ecology, hydrology, geology, and oceanography to changes in our Planet's environment. Real-time crew observations of environmental conditions, along with over 14,000 photographs, aided in interpretation of the radar images. This SRL mission was a highly successful test of technology intended for long-term environmental and geological monitoring of planet Earth. Following 183 orbits of the Earth, the eleven-day mission concluded with a landing on Runway 22 at Edwards Air Force Base, California, on October 11, 1994. Mission duration was 269 hours, 46 minutes, 10 seconds. STS-81 Space Shuttle Atlantis launched from the Kennedy Space Center, Florida on January 12, 1997. STS-81 was the fifth in a series of joint missions between the U.S. Space Shuttle and the Russian Space Station Mir and the second one involving an exchange of U.S. astronauts. In five days of docked operations more than three tons of food, water,experiment equipment and samples were moved back and forth between the two spacecraft. Following 160 orbits of the Earth the STS-81 mission concluded with a landing on Kennedy Space Center's Runway 33 ending a 3.9 million mile journey. Mission duration was 244 hours, 56 minutes.

NAME: Daniel T. Barry (M.D., Ph.D.)
NASA Astronaut

PERSONAL DATA: Born December 30, 1953, in Norwalk, Connecticut, but considers South Hadley, Massachusetts, to be his hometown. Enjoys flying, tennis, running.

EDUCATION: Graduated from Bolton High School, Alexandria, Louisiana, in 1971; received a bachelor of science degree in electrical engineering from Cornell University in 1975; a master of engineering degree and a master of arts degree in electrical engineering/computer science from Princeton University in 1977; a doctorate in electrical engineering/computer science from Princeton University in 1980; and a doctorate in medicine from the University of Miami in 1982.

ORGANIZATIONS: Institute of Electrical and Electronic Engineers (IEEE); American Association of Electrodiagnostic Medicine (AAEM); American Academy of Physical Medicine and Rehabilitation (AAPMR); Association of Academic Physiatrists (AAP); Sigma Xi; Association of Space Explorers, United States Tennis Association.

SPECIAL HONORS: 1971 McMullen Engineering Award. 1979 NSF National Needs Fellow. 1984 Young Investigator Award, American Association of Electrodiagnostic Medicine (AAEM). 1985-1990 Clinical Investigator Development Award, National Institutes of Health. 1990 Silver Crutch Teaching Award, University of Michigan. 1992-1996 Trustee, Albert and Ellen Grass Foundation. 1996 Honorary 2-Dan, Nihon Kiin, Japan. 1996, 1999 NASA Space Flight Medals. 1996 Honorary Doctor of Science, St. Louis University. 1998 Vladimir Komarov Diploma, Federation Aeronautique Internationale. 1999 Honorary Life Member, United States Tennis Association. 1999 Stuart Reiner Award, AAEM.

EXPERIENCE: Following graduate school at Princeton University, Dr. Barry was an National Science Foundation postdoctoral fellow in physics at Princeton. He then attended the University of Miami Medical School, graduating in 1982. He completed an internship and a Physical Medicine and Rehabilitation residency at the University of Michigan in 1985. He was appointed as an assistant professor in the Department of Physical Medicine and Rehabilitation and in the Bioengineering Program at the University of Michigan in 1985, and his tenure was approved by the Regents in 1992. He spent the summers of 1985-87 at the Marine Biological Laboratory in Woods Hole, Massachusetts, supported by the Grass Foundation for work in skeletal muscle physiology and as the Associate Director of the Grass Foundation Fellowship Program (1986-87). His research primarily involves biological signal processing, including signal processing theory, algorithms, and applications to specific biological systems. The applications include acoustic signals generated by contracting skeletal muscle, electrical signals from muscle, and heart sounds. He has also worked in prosthetic design. Dr. Barry's work has been supported by the National Institutes of Health, the National Science Foundation, the Grass Foundation, and the American Heart Association of Michigan. He has five patents, over 50 articles in scientific journals, and has served on two scientific journal editorial boards.

NASA EXPERIENCE: Selected by NASA in March 1992, Dr. Barry reported to the Johnson Space Center in August 1992. He completed one year of training and qualified for assignment as a mission specialist on Space Shuttle flight crews. Dr. Barry has worked on primary payload development, the Shuttle Avionics Integration Laboratory (SAIL), portable computing issues for Space Shuttle, Chief of Astronaut Appearances, and as a source board member for the NASA Space Biomedical

Research Institute (NSBRI). He flew on STS-72 in 1996 and STS-96 in 1999 and has logged over 449 hours in space, including two spacewalks totaling 14 hours and 8 minutes.

SPACE FLIGHT EXPERIENCE: STS-72 Endeavour (January 11-20, 1996) was a 9-day flight during which the crew retrieved the Space Flyer Unit (launched from Japan 10-months earlier), deployed and retrieved the OAST-Flyer, and Dr. Barry performed a 6 hour, 9 minute spacewalk designed to demonstrate and evaluate techniques to be used in the assembly of the International Space Station. Mission duration was 142 Earth orbits, traveling 3.7 million miles in 214 hours and 41 seconds. STS-96 Discovery (May 27 to June 6, 1999) was a 10-day mission during which the crew delivered 4 tons of logistics and supplies to the International Space Station in preparation for the arrival of the first crew to live on the station early next year. The mission was accomplished in 153 Earth orbits, traveling 4 million miles in 235 hours and 13 minutes. Dr. Barry performed a spacewalk of 7 hours and 55 minute duration.

NAME: Michael J. Bloomfield (Lieutenant Colonel, USAF)
NASA Astronaut

PERSONAL DATA: Born March 16, 1959, in Flint, Michigan. Considers Lake Fenton, Michigan, to be his hometown. Married to the former Lori Miller. They have two children He enjoys reading, gardening, all sporting activities including running, softball, skiing, and any activity with his children His parents, Rodger and Maxine Bloomfield, reside in Linden, Michigan. Her parents, Dave and Donna Miller, reside in Albuquerque, New Mexico.

EDUCATION: Graduated from Lake Fenton High School, Fenton, Michigan, in 1977. Bachelor of science degree in engineering mechanics from the U.S. Air Force Academy, 1981. Master of science degree in engineering management from Old Dominion University, 1993.

ORGANIZATIONS: Member of the United States Air Force Academy Association of Graduates, and the Air Force Association.

SPECIAL HONORS: Captain, 1980 United States Air Force Academy Falcon Football Team. Voted to the 1980 WAC All-Academic Football Team. Commanders Trophy winner as top graduate from Air Force Undergraduate Pilot Training (1983). Distinguished Graduate of USAF Test Pilot School Class 92A. Awarded the Air Force Meritorious Service Medal, the Air Force Commendation Medal, and the Air Force Aerial Achievement Medal.

EXPERIENCE: Bloomfield graduated from the USAF Academy in 1981. He completed Undergraduate Pilot Training at Vance Air Force Base (AFB), Oklahoma, in 1983, and was selected to fly the F-15. From 1983 until 1986, he served as a combat ready pilot and instructor pilot in the F-15 at Holloman AFB, New Mexico. In 1987, Bloomfield was re-assigned to Bitburg Air Base, Germany, where he served as an F-15 instructor pilot and completed the United States Fighter Weapons Instructor Course. In 1989 he was subsequently assigned to the 48th Fighter Interceptor Squadron at Langley AFB, Virginia. serving as an F-15 squadron weapons officer until 1992, when he was selected for the USAF Test Pilot School. Honored as a distinguished graduate in 1992, Bloomfield remained at Edwards AFB, California, where he conducted tests in all models of the F-16. While a member of the 416th Flight Test Squadron, Bloomfield served as squadron safety officer and as squadron flight commander. In March 1995, he was assigned to NASA as an astronaut candidate.

NASA EXPERIENCE: Selected by NASA in December 1994, Bloomfield reported to the Johnson Space Center in March 1995, has completed a year of training and evaluation, and is currently qualified for assignment as a shuttle pilot. He has worked technical issues for the Operations Planning Branch, and has worked as Chief of Safety for the Astronaut Office. A veteran of two space flights, STS-86 in 1997 and STS-97 in 2000, he has logged over 494 hours in space.

SPACE FLIGHT EXPERIENCE: STS-86 Atlantis (September 25 to October 6, 1997) was the seventh mission to rendezvous and dock with the Russian Space Station Mir. Highlights included the exchange of U.S. crew members Mike Foale and David Wolf, a spacewalk by two crew members to retrieve four experiments first deployed on Mir during the STS-76 docking mission, the transfer to Mir of 10,400 pounds of science and logistics, and the return of experiment hardware and results to Earth. Mission duration was 169 orbits in 10 days, 19 hours and 21 minutes, and covered more than 2.2 million miles. STS-97 Endeavour (November 30 to December December 11, 2000) was the fifth Space Shuttle mission dedicated to the assembly of the International Space Station. While docked to the Station, the crew installed the first set of U.S. solar arrays, performed three space walks, in addition to delivering supplies and equipment to the station's first resident crew. Mission duration was 10 days, 19 hours, 57 minutes, and traveled 4.47 million miles.

NAME: Kenneth D. Bowersox (Captain, USN)
NASA Astronaut

PERSONAL DATA: Born November 14, 1956, in Portsmouth, Virginia, but considers Bedford, Indiana, to be his hometown.

EDUCATION: Graduated from Bedford High School, Bedford, Indiana, in 1974; received a bachelor of science degree in aerospace engineering from the United States Naval Academy in 1978, and a master of science degree in mechanical engineering from Columbia University in 1979.

EXPERIENCE: Bowersox received his commission in the United States Navy in 1978 and was designated a Naval Aviator in 1981. He was then assigned to Attack Squadron 22, aboard the USS Enterprise, where he served as a Fleet A-7E pilot, logging over 300 carrier arrested landings. Following graduation from the United States Air Force Test Pilot School at Edwards Air Force Base, California, in 1985, he moved to the Naval Weapon Center at China Lake, California, where he spent the next year and a half as a test pilot flying A-7E and F/A-18 aircraft until advised of his selection to the astronaut program.

NASA EXPERIENCE: Selected as an astronaut candidate by NASA in June 1987, Bowersox completed a one-year training and evaluation program in August 1988. He has held a variety of assignments since then including: flight software testing in the Shuttle Avionics Integration Laboratory (SAIL); Technical Assistant to the Director of Flight Crew Operations; Astronaut Office representative for Orbiter landing and rollout issues; Chief of the Astronaut Office Safety Branch; Chairman of the Spaceflight Safety Panel; during several Shuttle missions he served as a spacecraft communicator (CAPCOM) in the Houston Mission Control Center. A four flight veteran, Bowersox has logged over 50 days in space. He flew as pilot on STS-50 in 1992 and STS-61 in 1993, and was the spacecraft commander on STS-73 in 1995 and STS-82 in 1997. Bowersox is currently in training as back-up to the first International Space Station crew, targeted for launch in early 2000.

SPACE FLIGHT EXPERIENCE: STS-50, June 25-July 9, 1992, was the first flight of the United States Microgravity Laboratory and the first Extended Duration Orbiter flight. Over a two-week period, the STS-50 flight crew aboard Space Shuttle Columbia conducted a wide variety of experiments relating to materials processing and fluid physics in a microgravity environment. STS-61, December 2-13, 1993, was the Hubble Space Telescope (HST) servicing and repair mission. During the 11-day flight, the HST was captured and restored to full capacity through a record five space walks by four astronauts. STS-73, Oct. 20 to Nov. 5, 1995, was the second flight of the United States Microgravity Laboratory. The mission focused on materials science, biotechnology, combustion science, the physics of fluids, and numerous scientific experiments housed in the pressurized Spacelab module. STS-82, Feb. 11-21, 1997, was the second Hubble Space Telescope (HST) maintenance mission. During the flight, the crew retrieved and secured the HST in Discovery's payload bay. In five space walks, two teams installed two new spectrometers and eight replacement instruments, as well as replacing insulation patches over three compartments containing key data processing, electronics and scientific instrument telemetry packages. Following completion of upgrades and repairs, HST was boosted to a higher orbit and redeployed.

NAME: Charles E. Brady, Jr. (Captain, USN)
NASA Astronaut

PERSONAL DATA: Born August 12, 1951, in Pinehurst, North Carolina, but considers Robbins, North Carolina, to be his hometown. He maintains a home on Ben Ure Island, Oak Harbor, Washington. He enjoys canoeing, kayaking, tennis, biking, amateur radio operator. His father, Dr. Charles E. Brady, Sr., is deceased. His mother, Mrs. Ann Maness Brady, resides in Robbins, North Carolina. One sister, Jerry Ann Kennedy, her husband Clifford, and two children Mark and Mary Jayne live in Burlington, North Carolina.

EDUCATION: Graduated from North Moore High School, Robbins, North Carolina, in 1969; was pre-med at University of North Carolina at Chapel Hill, 1969-1971; received a doctorate in medicine from Duke University in 1975.

ORGANIZATIONS: Association of Military Surgeons of the United States, Society of U.S. Naval Flight Surgeons, Aerospace Medical Association and Space Medicine Branch, Phi Beta Kappa, and Phi Eta Sigma.

SPECIAL HONORS: Eagle Scout; recipient of the Fox Flag for highest academic achievement at Naval Aerospace Medical Institute; Richard E. Luehrs Memorial Award for Navy Operational Flight Surgeon of the Year (1987); Flight Surgeon for the "Blue Angels" Navy Flight Demonstration Squadron (1989-1990); Physician Coordinator for Operation Raleigh-USA (a British-sponsored international youth leadership program selected by the U.S. Department of Defense); Defense Superior Service Medal; Navy Commendation Medal with Gold Star; Navy Achievement Medal; Meritorious Unit Commendation, Battle E; NASA Space Flight Medal; National Defense Medal; Armed Forces Expeditionary Service Medal; Sea Service Ribbon.

EXPERIENCE: Following graduation in 1969, Brady attended the University of North Carolina at Chapel Hill, majoring in pre-med. He was accepted into medical school at Duke University in Durham, North Carolina, in 1971 and graduated in 1975. From Duke, he went to the University of Tennessee Hospital in Knoxville for his internship. In 1978 Brady worked as the team physician in sports medicine for Iowa State University in Ames. He continued in sports medicine and family practice for the next seven years working as a team physician at the University of North Carolina at Chapel Hill and East Carolina University in Greenville, North Carolina. He joined the Navy in 1986 receiving training as a flight surgeon at the Naval Aerospace Medical Institute at Naval Air Station Pensacola, Florida. In June 1986 he reported to Carrier Air Wing Two on board the aircraft carrier USS Ranger (CV 61). He was assigned to the attack wing including Attack Squadron 145 (VA-145) and Aviation Electronic Countermeasures Squadron 131 (VAQ-131). Brady was selected for the Navy Flight Demonstration Squadron "Blue Angels" in 1988 and served with them through 1990. He was serving in Tactical Electronic Warfare Squadron 129 when selected for the astronaut program.

NASA EXPERIENCE: Brady was selected by NASA in March 1992, and reported to the Johnson Space Center in August 1992. He is qualified for selection as a mission specialist on future Space Shuttle flight crews. Assignments to date include: working technical issues for the Astronaut Office Mission Development Branch; flight software testing in the Shuttle Avionics Integration Laboratory (SAIL); astronaut representative to the Human Research Policy and Procedures Committee; deputy chief for Space Shuttle astronaut training; and chief for Space Station astronaut training in the Mission Operations Division. He flew on STS-78 in 1996 and has logged over 405 hours in space.

SPACE FLIGHT EXPERIENCE: STS-78 launched June 20, 1996 and landed July 7, 1996 becoming the longest Space Shuttle mission to date. The Life and Microgravity Spacelab mission served as a model for future studies onboard the International Space Station. The mission included studies sponsored by ten nations, five space agencies, and the crew included a Frenchman, a Canadian, a Spaniard and an Italian.

NAME: Curtis L. Brown, Jr. (Colonel, USAF)
NASA Astronaut

PERSONAL DATA: Born March 11, 1956, in Elizabethtown, North Carolina. Unmarried. One son. He enjoys water and snow skiing, scuba diving, air racing, restoring old cars, sailing, aerobatic flying. His mother, Mrs. Rachel H. Brown, resides in Elizabethtown, North Carolina. His father, Mr. Curtis L. Brown, Sr., is deceased.

EDUCATION: Graduated from East Bladen High School, Elizabethtown, North Carolina, in 1974; received a bachelor of science degree in electrical engineering from the Air Force Academy in 1978.

ORGANIZATIONS: Member, United States Air Force Association, United States Air Force Academy Association of Graduates, Experimental Aircraft Association and Classic Jet Aircraft Association.

SPECIAL HONORS: Defense Superior Service Medal, Defense Meritorious Service Medal (2), Air Force Meritorious Service Medal, Air Force Commendation Medal, Air Force Achievement Medal, NASA Space Flight Medal (6).

EXPERIENCE: Brown was commissioned a second lieutenant at the United States Air Force Academy, Colorado Springs, in 1978, and completed undergraduate pilot training at Laughlin Air Force Base, Del Rio, Texas. He graduated in July 1979 and was assigned to fly A-10 aircraft at Myrtle Beach Air Force Base, South Carolina, arriving there in January 1980 after completing A-10 training at Davis-Monthan Air Force Base, Arizona. In March 1982, he was reassigned to Davis-Monthan Air Force Base as an instructor pilot in the A-10. In January 1983, he attended USAF Fighter Weapons

School at Nellis Air Force Base and returned to Davis-Monthan Air Force Base as an instructor in A-10 weapons and tactics. In June 1985, he attended USAF Test Pilot School at Edwards Air Force Base, California. Upon graduation in June 1986, Brown was assigned to Eglin Air Force Base, Florida, where he served as a test pilot in the A-10 and F-16 aircraft until his selection for the astronaut program. He has logged over 6,000 hours flight time in jet aircraft.

NASA EXPERIENCE: Selected as an astronaut candidate by NASA in June 1987, Brown completed a one-year training and evaluation program in August 1988, and is qualified for flight assignment as a pilot. Technical assignments have included: involvement in the upgrade of the Shuttle Mission Simulator (SMS); development of the Flight Data File (FDF); lead of the astronaut launch support team responsible for crew ingress/strap-in prior to launch and crew egress after landing; monitored the refurbishment of OV-102 and OV-103 during ground turnaround processing; lead spacecraft communicator (CAPCOM); Astronaut Office Lead of Shuttle Operations; Deputy Director, Flight Crew Operations Directorate. A veteran of six space flights, Brown has logged over 1,383 hours in space. He was the pilot on STS-47 in 1992, STS-66 in 1994 and STS-77 in 1996, and was spacecraft commander on STS-85 in 1997, STS-95 in 1998, and STS-103 in 1999.

SPACE FLIGHT EXPERIENCE: STS-47 Spacelab-J (September 12-20, 1992) was an eight-day cooperative mission between the United States and Japan focused on life science and materials processing experiments in space. After completing 126 orbits of the Earth, the mission ended with Space Shuttle Endeavour landing at Kennedy Space Center, Florida. Mission duration was 190 hours, 30 minutes, 23 seconds. STS-66 (November 3-14, 1994) was the Atmospheric Laboratory for Applications and Science-3 (ATLAS-3) mission. ATLAS-3 was part of an ongoing program to determine the Earth's energy balance and atmospheric change over an 11-year solar cycle. Following 175 orbits of the Earth, the 11-day mission ended with the Shuttle Atlantis landing at Edwards Air Force Base, California. Mission duration was 262 hours and 34 minutes. STS-77 (May 19-29, 1996) was a ten-day mission aboard Space Shuttle Endeavour. The crew performed a record number of rendezvous sequences (one with a SPARTAN satellite and three with a deployed Satellite Test Unit) and approximately 21 hours of formation flying in close proximity of the satellites. During the flight the crew also conducted 12 materials processing, fluid physics and biotechnology experiments in a Spacehab Module. STS-77 deployed and retrieved a SPARTAN satellite, which carried the Inflatable Antenna Experiment designed to test the concept of large, inflatable space structures. A small Satellite Test Unit was also deployed to test the concept of self-stabilization by using aerodynamic forces and magnetic damping. The mission was concluded in 160 Earth orbits, traveling 4.1 million miles in 240 hours and 39 minutes. STS-85 (August 7-19, 1997) was a 12-day mission during which the crew deployed and retrieved the CRISTA-SPAS payload, operated the Japanese Manipulator Flight Demonstration (MFD) robotic arm, studied changes in the Earth's atmosphere and tested technology destined for use on the future International Space Station. The mission was accomplished in 189 Earth orbits, traveling 4.7 million miles in 284 hours and 27 minutes. STS-95 (October 29 to November 7, 1998) was a 9-day mission during which the crew supported a variety of research payloads including deployment of the Spartan solar-observing spacecraft, the Hubble Space Telescope Orbital Systems Test Platform, and investigations on space flight and the aging process. The mission was accomplished in 134 Earth orbits, traveling 3.6 million miles in 213 hours and 44 minutes. STS-103 (December 19-27, 1999) was an 8-day mission during which the crew successfully installed new instruments and upgraded systems on the Hubble Space Telescope (HST). Enhancing HST scientific capabilities required three space walks. The STS-103 mission was accomplished in 120 Earth orbits, traveling 3.2 million miles in 191 hours and 11 minutes.

NAME: David M. Brown (Captain, USN)
    NASA Astronaut

PERSONAL DATA: Born April 16, 1956 in Arlington, Virginia. Single. Enjoys flying and bicycle tour-ing. Was a four year collegiate varsity gymnast. While in college he performed in the Circus King-dom as an acrobat, 7 foot unicyclist and stilt walker. His parents, Paul and Dorothy Brown, reside in Washington, Virginia.

EDUCATION: Graduated from Yorktown High School, Arlington, Virginia, in 1974; received bach-elor of science degree in biology from the College of William and Mary in 1978 and a doctorate in medicine from Eastern Virginia Medical School in 1982.

ORGANIZATIONS: Past President, International Association of Military Flight Surgeon Pilots. Asso-ciate Fellow, Aerospace Medical Association. Society of U.S. Naval Flight Surgeons.

SPECIAL HONORS: Navy Operational Flight Surgeon of the Year in 1986, Meritorious Service Medal, Navy Achievement Medal.

EXPERIENCE: Brown joined the Navy after his internship at the Medical University of South Carolina. Upon completion of flight surgeon training in 1984, he reported to the Navy Branch Hospital in Adak, Alaska, as Director of Medical Services. He was then assigned to Carrier Airwing Fifteen which deployed aboard the USS Carl Vinson in the western Pacific. In 1988, he was the only flight surgeon in a ten year period to be chosen for pilot training. He was ultimately designated a naval aviator in 1990 in Beeville, Texas, ranking number one in his class. Brown was then sent for train-ing and carrier qualification in the A-6E Intruder. In 1991 he reported to the Naval Strike Warfare Center in Fallon, Nevada, where he served as a Strike Leader Attack Training Syllabus Instructor and a Contingency Cell Planning Officer. Additionally, he was qualified in the F-18 Hornet and deployed from Japan in 1992 aboard the USS Independence flying the A-6E with VA-115. In 1995, he reported to the U.S. Naval Test Pilot School as their flight surgeon where he also flew the T-38 Talon. Brown has logged over 2,700 flight hours with 1,700 in high performance military aircraft. He is qualified as first pilot in NASA T-38 aircraft.

NASA EXPERIENCE: Selected by NASA in April 1996, Brown reported to the Johnson Space Center in August 1996. Having completed two years of training and evaluation, he is eligible for flight as-signment as a mission specialist. He was initially assigned to support payload development for the International Space Station, followed by the astronaut support team responsible for orbiter cockpit setup, crew strap-in, and landing recovery. He is currently assigned to the crew of STS-107 sched-uled to launch in 2001.

NAME: Daniel C. Burbank (Lieutenant Commander, USCG)
    NASA Astronaut

PERSONAL DATA: Born July 27, 1961 in Manchester, Connecticut, but considers Tolland, Connecti-cut, to be his hometown. Married. Two children. Enjoys running, skiing, hiking, sailing, amateur astronomy, playing guitar. His parents, Daniel and Joan Burbank, reside in Tolland, Connecticut. His sister, Suzanne Burbank, resides in Colorado Springs, Colorado.

EDUCATION: Graduated from Tolland High School, Tolland, Connecticut, in 1979; received a bachelor of science degree in electrical engineering from the U.S. Coast Guard Academy in 1985, and a master of science degree in aeronautical science from Embry-Riddle Aeronautical University in 1990.

ORGANIZATIONS: National Space Society; Order of Daedalians; U.S. Coast Guard Pterodactyls; U.S. Coast Guard Academy Alumni Association.

AWARDS: Air Medal, 2 Coast Guard Commendation Medals, Coast Guard Achievement Medal, 2 Coast Guard Commandant's Letter of Commendation Ribbons, 3 Coast Guard Meritorious Team Commendations, National Defense Service Medal, Humanitarian Service Medal, various other service awards.

SPECIAL HONORS: Awarded the Orville Wright Achievement Award and honorary membership in the Order of Daedalians as the top naval flight training graduate during the period January 1 to June 30, 1988. Awarded Texas Society of the Daughters of the American Revolution Achievement Award as the top Coast Guard graduate of flight training for the year 1988.

EXPERIENCE: Burbank received his commission from the U.S. Coast Guard Academy in May 1985, and was assigned to the Coast Guard Cutter Gallatin (WHEC 721) as Deck Watch Officer and Law Enforcement/Boarding Officer. In January 1987, he reported to naval flight training at Pensacola, Florida, and graduated in February 1988. Burbank was then assigned to Coast Guard Air Station Elizabeth City, North Carolina, where he became an Aircraft Commander in the HH-3F Pelican and then an Aircraft Commander/Instructor Pilot in the HH-60J Jayhawk. While at Elizabeth City, he completed training in Aviation Maintenance/Administration in preparation for assignment as an Aeronautical Engineering Officer. He also earned a master's degree in aeronautical science. In July 1992, Burbank was assigned to Coast Guard Air Station Cape Cod, Massachusetts, as the Rotary Wing Engineering Officer and HH-60J Aircraft Commander/Instructor Pilot. In May 1995, he was assigned to Coast Guard Air Station Sitka, Alaska, as the Aeronautical Engineering Officer and HH-60J Aircraft Commander. Burbank has logged over 3,000 flight hours, primarily in Coast Guard helicopters, and has flown more than 1,800 missions including over 300 search and rescue missions.

NASA EXPERIENCE: Selected by NASA in April 1996, Burbank reported to the Johnson Space Center in August 1996. Having completed two years of training and evaluation, he is qualified for flight assignment as a mission specialist. Burbank has worked technical issues for the Astronaut Office Operations Planning Branch, and the International Space Station. He flew as a mission specialist on STS-106 and has logged over 283 hours in space.

SPACE FLIGHT EXPERIENCE: STS-106 Atlantis (September 8-20, 2000). During the 12-day mission, the crew successfully prepared the International Space Station for the arrival of the first permanent crew. The five astronauts and two cosmonauts delivered more than 6,600 pounds of supplies and installed batteries, power converters, oxygen generation equipment and a treadmill on the Space Station. Two crew members performed a space walk in order to connect power, data and communications cables to the newly arrived Zvesda Service Module and the Space Station. STS-106 orbited the Earth 185 times, and covered 4.9 million miles in 11 days, 19 hours, and 10 minutes.

NAME: Daniel W. Bursch (Captain, USN)
NASA Astronaut

PERSONAL DATA: Born July 25, 1957, in Bristol, Pennsylvania, but considers Vestal, New York, to be his hometown. Married to the former Roni J. Patterson of Modesto, California. Four children. He enjoys tennis, softball, windsurfing, skiing, and woodworking. His father, Dudley Bursch, resides in Stuart, Florida. His mother, Betsy Bursch, is deceased. Roni's mother, Gayle Hutcheson, resides in Modesto California. Her father, Jack Patterson, resides in Truckee, California.

EDUCATION: Graduated from Vestal Senior High School, Vestal, New York, in 1975; received a bachelor of science degree in physics from the United States Naval Academy in 1979, and a master of science degree in engineering science from the Naval Postgraduate School in 1991.

ORGANIZATIONS: Member of the U.S. Naval Academy Alumni Association.

SPECIAL HONORS: Awarded the Defense Superior Service Medal, NASA Space Flight Medals, the Navy Commendation Medal and the Navy Achievement Medal. Distinguished graduate, U.S. Naval Academy and U.S. Naval Test Pilot School.

EXPERIENCE: Bursch graduated from the U.S. Naval Academy in 1979, and was designated a naval flight officer in April 1980 at Pensacola, Florida. After initial training as an A-6E Intruder bombardier/navigator (B/N), he reported to Attack Squadron 34 in January 1981, and deployed to the Mediterranean aboard the USS John F. Kennedy, and to the North Atlantic and Indian Oceans aboard the USS America. He attended the U.S. Naval Test Pilot School in January 1984. Upon graduation in December he worked as a project test flight officer flying the A-6 Intruder until August 1984, when he returned to the U.S. Naval Test Pilot School as a flight instructor. In April 1987, Bursch was assigned to the Commander, Cruiser-Destroyer Group 1, as Strike Operations Officer, making deployments to the Indian Ocean aboard the USS Long Beach and the USS Midway. Redesignated an Aeronautical Engineering Duty officer (AEDO), he attended the Naval Postgraduate School in Monterey, California, from July 1989 until his selection to the astronaut program. He has over 2,900 flight hours in more than 35 different aircraft.

NASA EXPERIENCE: Selected by NASA in January 1990, Bursch became an astronaut in July 1991. His technical assignments to date include: Astronaut Office Operations Development Branch, working on controls and displays for the Space Shuttle and Space Station; Chief of Astronaut Appearances; spacecraft communicator (CAPCOM) in mission control. A veteran of three space flights, Bursch has logged over 746 hours in space. He served as a mission specialist on STS-51 in 1993, STS-68 in 1994 and STS-77 in 1996. Bursch is assigned to the fourth crew scheduled to live on the International Space Station (ISS-4). He will launch aboard a Space Shuttle in late 2001 and return aboard a Space Shuttle 4-months later. The crew of three (two American astronauts and one Russian cosmonaut) will perform flight tests of the station hardware, conduct internal and external maintenance tasks, and develop the capability of the station to support the addition of science experiments.

SPACE FLIGHT EXPERIENCE: STS-51 launched from the Kennedy Space Center, Florida, on September 12, 1993. During the ten-day mission the crew of five aboard the Shuttle Discovery deployed the U.S. Advanced Communications Technology Satellite (ACTS), and the Shuttle Pallet Satellite (SPAS) with NASA and German scientific experiments aboard. Following a spacewalk by two crew members to evaluate Hubble Space Telescope repair tools, the crew initiated rendezvous burns and Bursch recovered the SPAS using the Remote Manipulator System (RMS). The mission concluded on September 22, 1993, with the first night landing at the Kennedy Space Center. Mission duration was 236 hours and 11 minutes. STS-68, Space Radar Lab-2 (SRL-2), launched from the Kennedy Space Center, Florida, on September 30, 1994. As part of NASA's Mission to Planet Earth, SRL-2 was the second flight of three advanced radars called SIR-C/X-SAR (Spaceborne Imaging Radar-C/X-Band Synthetic Aperture Radar), and a carbon-monoxide pollution sensor, MAPS (Measurement of Air Pollution from Satellites). SIR-C/X-SAR and MAPS operated together in Endeavour's cargo bay to study Earth's surface and atmosphere, creating radar images of Earth's surface environment and mapping global production and transport of carbon monoxide pollution. Real-time crew observations of environmental conditions, along with over 14,000 photographs aided the science team in interpreting the SRL data. The SRL-2 mission was a highly successful test of technology intended for long-term environmental and geological monitoring of planet Earth. Following 183 orbits of the Earth, the eleven-day mission ended with Space Shuttle Endeavour landing at Edwards Air Force Base, California, on October 11, 1994. Mission duration was 269 hours and 46 minutes. STS-77 launched from the Kennedy Space Center on May 19, 1996. It included the fourth Spacehab module flight as a scientific laboratory, designated SPACEHAB-4. It consisted of 12 separate materials processing, fluid physics and biotechnology experiments, with an emphasis on commercial space product development. STS-77 completed a record four rendezvous in support of two satellites sponsored by the Goddard Space Flight Center, and the SPARTAN 207/Inflatable Antenna Experiment (IAE) and the Passive Aerodynamically-stabilized Magnetically-damped Satellite/Satellite Test Unit (PAMS/STU). Following 160 orbits of the Earth, the ten-day mission ended with Space Shuttle Endeavour landing at the Kennedy Space Center on May 29, 1996. Mission duration was 240 hours and 39 minutes.

NAME: Robert D. Cabana (Colonel, USMC)
NASA Astronaut

PERSONAL DATA: Born January 23, 1949, in Minneapolis, Minnesota, where his parents still reside. Married to the former Nancy Joan Shimer of Cortland, New York. Three children, Jeffrey, Christopher and Sarah. He enjoys jogging, cycling, softball, sailing, and woodworking.

EDUCATION: Graduated from Washburn High School, Minneapolis, Minnesota, in 1967; received a bachelor of science degree in mathematics from the United States Naval Academy in 1971.

ORGANIZATIONS: Member of the Association of Space Explorers and Associate Fellow in the Society of Experimental Test Pilots.

SPECIAL HONORS: Recipient of The Daughters of the American Revolution Award for the top Marine to complete naval flight training in 1976. Distinguished Graduate, U.S. Naval Test Pilot School. Awarded the De La Vaulx medal by the Federation Aeronautique Internationale in 1994. Personal decorations include the Defense Superior Service Medal, the Distinguished Flying Cross, the Defense Meritorious Service Medal, the Meritorious Service Medal, the National Intelligence Medal of Achievement, the NASA Distinguished Service Medal, two NASA Medals for Outstanding Leadership, two NASA Exceptional Service Medals, and four NASA Space Flight Medals.

EXPERIENCE: After graduation from the Naval Academy, Cabana attended the Basic School in Quantico, Virginia, and completed naval flight officer training in Pensacola, Florida, in 1972. He served as an A-6 bombardier/navigator with Marine Air Wings in Cherry Point, North Carolina, and

Iwakuni, Japan. He returned to Pensacola in 1975 for pilot training and was designated a naval aviator in September 1976. He was then assigned to the 2nd Marine Aircraft Wing in Cherry Point, North Carolina, where he flew A-6 Intruders. He graduated from the U.S. Naval Test Pilot School in 1981, and served at the Naval Air Test Center in Patuxent River, Maryland, as the A-6 program manager, X-29 advanced technology demonstrator project officer, and as a test pilot for flight systems and ordnance separation testing on A-6 and A-4 series aircraft. Prior to his selection as an astronaut candidate he was serving as the Assistant Operations Officer of Marine Aircraft Group Twelve in Iwakuni, Japan. He has logged over 6,000 hours in 34 different kinds of aircraft.

NASA EXPERIENCE: Selected by NASA in June 1985, Cabana completed initial astronaut training in July 1986, qualifying for assignment as a pilot on future Space Shuttle flight crews. His initial assignment was as the Astronaut Office Space Shuttle flight software coordinator until November 1986. At that time he was assigned as the Deputy Chief of Aircraft Operations for the Johnson Space Center where he served for 2-1/2 years. He then served as the lead astronaut in the Shuttle Avionics Integration Laboratory (SAIL) where the Orbiter's flight software is tested prior to flight. Cabana has served as a spacecraft communicator (CAPCOM) in Mission Control during Space Shuttle missions, and as Chief of Astronaut Appearances. Prior to his assignment to command STS-88, Cabana served three years as the Chief of NASA's Astronaut Office. Following STS-88, Cabana served as the Deputy Director of Flight Crew Operations. In October of 1999, he was assigned as the Manager for International Operations, International Space Station Program where he is currently serving. A veteran of four space flights, Cabana has logged over 1,010 hours in space. He served as pilot on STS-41 (October 6-10, 1990) and STS-53 (December 2-9, 1992), and was mission commander on STS-65 (July 8-23, 1994) and STS-88 (December 4-15, 1998) the first International Space Station assembly mission.

SPACEFLIGHT EXPERIENCE: STS-41 Discovery launched on October 6, 1990 from the Kennedy Space Center, Florida, and landed at Edwards Air Force Base, California, on October 10, 1990. During 66 orbits of the Earth, the five-man crew successfully deployed the Ulysses spacecraft, starting the interplanetary probe on its four-year journey, via Jupiter, to investigate the polar regions of the Sun; operated the Shuttle Solar Backscatter Ultraviolet instrument (SSBUV) to map atmospheric ozone levels; activated a controlled "fire in space" experiment (the Solid Surface Combustion Experiment [SSCE]); and conducted numerous other middeck experiments involving radiation measurements, polymer membrane production, and microgravity effects on plants. STS-53 Discovery launched from the Kennedy Space Center, Florida, on December 2, 1992. The crew of five deployed the classified Department of Defense payload DOD-1 and then performed several Military-Man-in-Space and NASA experiments. After completing 115 orbits of the Earth in 175 hours, Discovery landed at Edwards Air Force Base, California, on December 9, 1992. STS-65 Columbia launched from the Kennedy Space Center, Florida, on July 8, 1994, returning to Florida on July 23, 1994. The STS-65 crew conducted the second International Microgravity Laboratory (IML-2) mission utilizing the long spacelab module in the payload bay. The flight consisted of 82 experiments from 15 countries and six space agencies from around the world. During the record setting 15-day flight, the crew conducted experiments which focused on materials and life sciences research in a microgravity environment paving the way for future operations and cooperation aboard International Space Station. The mission was accomplished in 236 orbits of the Earth in 353 hours and 55 minutes. STS-88 Endeavour (December 4-15, 1998) was the first International Space Station assembly mission. During the 12-day mission, Unity, the U.S. built node, was mated with Zarya, the Russian built Functional Cargo Block (FGB). Two crew members performed three space walks to connect umbilicals and attach tools/hardware in the assembly and outfitting of the station.

Additionally, the crew performed the initial activation and first ingress of the International Space Station preparing it for future assembly missions and full time occupation. The crew also performed IMAX Cargo Bay Camera (ICBC) operations, and deployed two satellites, Mighty Sat 1 built by the USAF Phillips Laboratory and SAC-A the first successful launch of an Argentine satellite. The mission was accomplished in 185 orbits of the Earth in 283 hours and 18 minutes.

NAME: Yvonne Darlene Cagle (M.D.)
NASA Astronaut

PERSONAL DATA: Born April 24, 1959 in West Point, New York, but considers Novato, California, to be her hometown. Enjoys jigsaw puzzles, juggling, skating, hiking, music, writing, public speaking, historical novels.

EDUCATION: Novato High School Novato, California, in 1977; received a bachelor of arts degree in biochemistry from San Francisco State University in 1981, and a doctorate in medicine from the University of Washington in 1985. Internship at Transitional Highland General Hospital, Oakland, California, in 1985. Received certification in Aerospace Medicine from the School of Aerospace Medicine at Brooks Air Force Base, Texas, in 1988. Completed residency in family practice and GHENTFP at Eastern Virginia Medical School in 1992. Received certification as a senior aviation medical examiner from the Federal Aviation Administration in 1995.

ORGANIZATIONS: Boys and Girls Club; Aerospace Medical Association; Third Baptist Church. American Academy of Family Physicians.

AWARDS: Outstanding Young Women of America; National Defense Service Medal; Air Force Achievement Medal; United States Air Force (USAF) Air Staff Exceptional Physician Commendation; National Technical Association Distinguished Scientist Award; Commendation Marin County Board of Supervisors; Commendation Novato School Board.

EXPERIENCE: Dr. Cagle's medical training was sponsored by the Health Professions Scholarship Program, through which she received her commission as a reserve officer with the United States Air Force, and subsequently was awarded her board certification in family practice. During her initial active duty tour at Royal Air Force Lakenheath, United Kingdom, she was selected to attend the School of Aerospace Medicine at Brooks Air Force Base, Texas. In April 1988, she became certified as a flight surgeon logging numerous hours in a diversity of aircraft. She was actively involved in mission support of aircraft providing medical support and rescue in a variety of aeromedical missions. From 1994 to 1996, Dr. Cagle served as the Deputy Project Manager for Kelsey-Seybold Clinics, practicing as an occupational physician at the NASA-JSC Occupational Health Clinic. In addition to conducting job-related exams, routine health screenings, and providing acute care for on-site injuries and illness, she designed the medical protocols and conducted the screenings for select NASA remote duty operations. Dr. Cagle is a certified FAA Senior Aviation Medical Examiner, is ACLS Instructor qualified, teaches fitness courses. Dr. Cagle is a Clinical Assistant Professor at UTMB, Galveston. She has served on the Volunteer Family Practice Clinical Faculty at the University of California, Davis, California. While a USAF reservist, she was assigned to the Pentagon Flight Medicine/Special Mission Clinic.

NASA EXPERIENCE: During May 1989, while a flight surgeon assigned to the 48th Tactical Hospital, United Kingdom, Dr. Cagle volunteered to serve as the Air Force Medical Liaison Officer for the

STS-30 Atlantis Shuttle Mission to test the Magellan Spacecraft. She was assigned to the Trans Atlantic (TAL) Landing site at Banjul, West Africa, to provide emergency rescue and evacuation of the shuttle crew should it be required. Dr. Cagle has contributed on-going data to the Longitudinal Study on Astronaut Health, and has served as a consultant for space telemedicine. She was a member of the NASA Working Group and traveled to Russia to establish international medical standards and procedures for astronauts. She also conducted health screenings of Mir-18 consultants from the Russian Federation. Selected by NASA in April 1996, Dr. Cagle reported to the Johnson Space Center in August 1996. Having completed two years of training and evaluation, she is qualified for flight assignment as a mission specialist. Currently, Dr. Cagle is assigned technical duties in the Astronaut Office Operations Planning Branch, supporting Shuttle and Space Station.

NAME: Fernando (Frank) Caldeiro
      NASA Astronaut

PERSONAL DATA: Born June 12, 1958 in Buenos Aires, Argentina, but considers Merritt Island, Florida, to be his hometown. Married to the former Donna Marie Emero of Huntington Beach, California. They have one child. He enjoys building, flying and racing his own experimental aircraft, snorkeling, amateur radio (KE4RFI). His parents reside in Flushing, New York. Her parents reside in Fountain Valley, California.

EDUCATION: Graduated from W.C. Bryant High School, Long Island City, New York, in 1976; received an associate degree in applied science in Aerospace Technology from the State University of New York at Farmingdale in 1978, a bachelor of science degree in mechanical engineering from the University of Arizona in 1984, and a master of science degree in engineering management from the University of Central Florida in 1995.

ORGANIZATIONS: Experimental Aircraft Association, Aircraft Owners and Pilots Association.

AWARDS: Kennedy Space Center (KSC) Technical Leadership Certificate; Rockwell Certificate of Commendation; Group Achievement Awards (9); KSC Center Director Round Table Award; KSC Superior Performance Awards (2); KSC Public Affairs Certificate of Appreciation for Service.

EXPERIENCE: From 1985-1988, Caldeiro worked as a test director during the production and flight test of the Rockwell/USAF B-1B Bomber. In 1988, he was transferred by Rockwell to the Kennedy Space Center as a space shuttle main propulsion system specialist. In this capacity he was the Rockwell design center representative for the ground processing and launch of the Orbiter Discovery.

NASA EXPERIENCE: He was hired by NASA KSC in 1991 as a cryogenics and propulsion systems expert for the safety and mission assurance office. Selected by NASA as an astronaut candidate in April 1996, Caldeiro reported to the Johnson Space Center in August 1996. Having completed two years of training and evaluation, he is qualified for flight assignment as a mission specialist. Currently, Caldeiro is assigned technical duties in the Astronaut Office Operations Planning Branch.

NAME: Tracy E. Caldwell (Ph.D.)
NASA Astronaut (Mission Specialist Candidate)

PERSONAL DATA: Born August 14, 1969 in Arcadia, California. Recreational interests include running, weight training, hiking, softball, basketball, and auto repair/maintenance. She also enjoys spending time with family. As an undergraduate, she competed in intercollegiate athletics on CSUF's track team as both a sprinter and long jumper. Her parents, James H. and Mary Ellen Caldwell, reside in Cherry Valley, California. Her sister, Stacy H. Caldwell-Tockerman, and nephew, James F. Tockerman, reside in Beaumont, California.

EDUCATION: Graduated from Beaumont High School, Beaumont, California in 1987; received a bachelor of science degree in chemistry from the California State University at Fullerton in 1993 and a doctorate in physical chemistry from the University of California at Davis in 1997.

ORGANIZATIONS: Sigma Xi Research Society, American Chemical Society, American Vacuum Society, American Institute of Physics, American Association of University Women.

SPECIAL HONORS: Camille and Henry Dreyfus Postdoctoral Fellowship in Environmental Science (1997). National Research Council Associateship Award, NIST (1997, declined). Outstanding Doctoral Student Award in Chemistry from the University of California Davis (1997). American Vacuum Society - Nellie Yeoh Whetten Award (1996). American Vacuum Society Graduate Research Award (1996). Pro Femina Research Consortium Graduate Research Award (1996). Pro Femina Research Consortium Graduate Award for Scientific Travel (1996). University of California, Davis Graduate Research Award (1996). University of California, Davis Graduate Student Award for Scientific Travel (1994). Patricia Roberts Harris Graduate Fellowship in Chemistry (1993-1997). Lyle Wallace Award for Service to the Department of Chemistry, California State University Fullerton (1993). National Science Foundation Research Experience for Undergraduates Award, (1992). Council of Building & Construction Trades Scholarship (1991 and 1992). Parents' Association Scholarship (1990 and 1991). Big West Scholar Athlete (1989-1991).

EXPERIENCE: As an undergraduate researcher at the California State University, Fullerton (CSUF), Dr. Caldwell designed, constructed and implemented electronics and hardware associated with a laser-ionization, time-of-flight mass spectrometer for studying atmospherically-relevant gas-phase chemistry. Also at CSUF, she worked for the Research and Instructional Safety Office as a lab assistant performing environmental monitoring of laboratories using hazardous chemicals and radioactive materials, as well as calibrating survey instruments and helping to process chemical and radioactive waste. During that time (and for many years prior) she also worked as an electrician/inside wireman for her father's electrical contracting company doing commercial and light industrial type construction. At the University of California, Davis, Dr. Caldwell taught general chemistry laboratory and began her graduate research. Her dissertation work focused on investigating molecular-level surface reactivity and kinetics of metal surfaces using electron spectroscopy, laser desorption, and Fourier transform mass spectrometry techniques. She also designed and built peripheral components for a variable temperature, ultra-high vacuum scanning tunneling microscopy system. In 1997, Dr. Caldwell received the Camille and Henry Drefus Postdoctoral Fellowship in Environmental Science to study atmospheric chemistry at the University of California, Irvine. There she investigated reactivity and kinetics of atmospherically relevant systems using atmospheric pressure ionization mass spectrometry, Fourier transform infrared and ultraviolet absorption spectroscopies. In addition, she developed methods of chemical ionization for spectral interpretation of trace compounds. Dr. Caldwell has published and presented her work in numerous papers at technical conferences and in scientific journals. Dr. Caldwell is a private pilot and also fluent in American Sign Language (ASL) as well as conversational in Russian and Spanish.

NASA EXPERIENCE: Selected by NASA in June 1998, Dr. Caldwell reported for training in August 1998. Astronaut Candidate Training includes orientation briefings and tours, numerous scientific and technical briefings, intensive instruction in Shuttle and International Space Station systems, physiological training and ground school to prepare for T-38 flight training, as well as learning water and wilderness survival techniques. Dr. Caldwell is currently assigned to the Astronaut Office Shuttle Operations Branch. She will serve in technical assignments until assigned to a space flight.

NAME: Charles J. Camarda (Ph.D.)
NASA Astronaut

PERSONAL DATA: Born May 8, 1952, in Queens, New York. Single. He has one child. He enjoys racquetball, running, weightlifting, boxing. His parents, Ray and Jack Camarda, reside in Queens, New York. His brother, Barney Camarda, and his family reside in Valley Stream, Long Island.

EDUCATION: Graduated from Archbishop Molloy High School, Jamaica, New York, in 1970; received a bachelor of science degree in aerospace engineering from Polytechnic Institute of Brooklyn in 1974; a master of science degree in engineering science from George Washington University in 1980; and a doctorate in aerospace engineering from Virginia Polytechnic Institute and State University in 1990.

ORGANIZATIONS: Associate Fellow, American Institute of Aeronautics and Astronautics.

AWARDS: NASA Certificates of Recognition (10); Sustained Superior Performance Awards (2); Special Achievement Awards (2); Technology Commercialization Awards (2); Research and Development 100 Award from Industrial Research Magazine for one of the top 100 technical innovations in 1983 - A Heat-Pipe-Cooled Sandwich Panel.

NASA EXPERIENCE: Upon completing his B.S. degree from the Polytechnic Institute of Brooklyn, Camarda began work for NASA's Langley Research Center, Hampton, Virginia, in 1974. He was a research scientist in the Thermal Structures Branch of the Structures and Materials Division and was responsible for demonstrating the feasibility of a heat-pipe-cooled leading edge for Space Shuttle by analysis, laboratory experiments, and aerothermal testing in Langley's 8-foot High Temperature Tunnel. He conducted analytical and experimental research in heat pipes, structural mechanics and dynamics, heat transfer, and numerical optimization for aircraft, spacecraft, and space launch vehicles. While at Langley, Camarda earned his masters degree from George Washington University in Engineering Science with emphasis on mechanics of composite structures at elevated temperature and his doctorate degree from Virginia Polytechnic Institute and State University with emphasis on the development of advanced modal methods for efficiently predicting transient thermal and structural performance. In 1989, Camarda was selected to lead the Structures and Materials Technology Maturation Team for the National Aero-Space Plane (NASP) program which was responsible for maturing materials and structures technologies necessary to enable the development of an airbreathing hypersonic vehicle capable of horizontal take-off to orbit. Camarda was selected to head the Thermal Structures Branch (TSB) in 1994 with responsibility for a research engineering staff, two major focused programs (the high-speed research (HSR) and reusable launch vehicle (RLV) programs), and several structural test facilities including the Thermal Structures Laboratory. Some of the primary responsibilities of the TSB is the development of durable, lightweight metallic thermal protection systems (TPS), reusable cryogenic tank systems, and graphite-composite primary structure for RLV. Camarda has received over 18 NASA awards for technical innovations and accomplishments. He also received a Research and Development 100 award from Industrial Research Magazine for one of the top 100 technical innovations of 1983 entitled "Heat-Pipe-Cooled Sandwich Panel." He holds four patents and has two patents pending. Selected as an astronaut candidate by NASA in April 1996, Dr. Camarda reported to the NASA Johnson Space Center in August 1996. Having completed two years of training and evaluation, he is qualified for flight assignment as a mission specialist. Currently, Dr. Camarda is assigned technical duties in the Astronaut Office Spacecraft Systems/Operations Branch.

NAME: Duane G. "Digger" Carey (Lieutenant Colonel, USAF)
NASA Astronaut

PERSONAL DATA: Born April 30, 1957 in St. Paul, Minnesota. Married to the former Cheryl Ann Tobritzhofer of St. Paul, Minnesota. They have two children. He enjoys motorcycle travel, racing motocross, camping, home-schooling his children, and reading science fiction. His parents reside in Minneapolis, Minnesota. Her mother resides in St. Paul Minnesota. Her father is deceased.

EDUCATION: Graduated from Highland Park High School, St. Paul, Minnesota in 1975; received a Bachelor of Science degree in Aerospace Engineering and Mechanics and a Master of Science degree in Aerospace Engineering from the University of Minnesota-Minneapolis in 1981 and 1982, respectively.

ORGANIZATIONS: National Space Society, American Motorcyclist Association, Air Force Association.

SPECIAL HONORS: Awarded the Distinguished Flying Cross and three Air Medals.

EXPERIENCE: Carey received his commission from the Reserve Officer Training Corps in 1981 and graduated from Undergraduate Pilot Training in 1983. He flew the A-10A during tours at England Air Force Base, Louisiana, and Suwon Air Base, Republic of Korea. He completed F-16 training in 1988 and was assigned to Torrejon Air Base, Spain. In 1991, he was selected to attend the United States Air Force Test Pilot School at Edwards Air Force Base, California. After graduation in 1992, he worked as an F-16 experimental test pilot and System Safety Officer at Edwards Air Force Base.

NASA EXPERIENCE: Carey was selected as an astronaut candidate by NASA in April 1996. He reported to the NASA Johnson Space Center in August 1996. Having completed two years of training and evaluation, he is qualified for flight assignment as a pilot. Currently, Carey is assigned technical duties in the Astronaut Office Spacecraft Systems/Operations Branch.

NAME: Gregory Errol Chamitoff (Ph.D.)
NASA Astronaut (Mission Specialist Candidate)

PERSONAL DATA: Born August 6, 1962 in Montreal, Canada. Has lived in the U.S. since 1974, and considers San Jose, California, to be his hometown. He is married to A. Chantal Caviness, M.D., of Boston, Massachusetts. His mother, Shari J. Chamitoff, resides in Discovery Bay, California. His father, Ashley M. Chamitoff, is deceased. Her parents are Madeline Caviness, Ph.D., and Verne Caviness, M.D., of Boston, Massachusetts. Recreational interests include scuba diving, flying, backpacking, skiing, racquetball, aikido, and guitar.

EDUCATION: Graduated from Blackford High School, San Jose, California, in 1980; received a bachelor of science degree in electrical engineering from the California Polytechnic State University (Cal Poly), San Luis Obispo, California, in 1984; a master of science degree in aeronautical engineering from the California Institute of Technology (Caltech), Pasadena, California, in 1985; and a doctorate in aeronautics and astronautics from the Massachusetts Institute of Technology (MIT), Cambridge, Massachusetts, in 1992.

ORGANIZATIONS: Senior Member, American Institute of Aeronautics & Astronautics (AIAA), Institute of Electrical & Electronic Engineers (IEEE), Eta Kappa Nu Honor Society, Tau Beta Pi Engineering Society, Phi Kappa Phi Honor Society, National Space Society (NSS).

HONORS: AIAA Technical Excellence Award (1998); NASA Silver Snoopy Award (1997); NASA/USA Space Flight Awareness Award (1997); C.S. Draper Laboratory Graduate Fellowship (1985-92); IEEE Graduate Fellowship (1985); Tau Beta Pi Fellowship (1984); Applied Magnetics Scholarships (1982, 83, 84); Academic Excellence Award (Cal Poly, 1984); Most Outstanding Senior Award (Cal Poly, 1984); President's Honor List (Cal Poly, 1981-84); Degree of Excellence and California Statewide Speech Finalist (National Forensic League, 1980); Eagle Scout (Boy Scouts of America, 1980).

EXPERIENCE: As an electrical engineering student at Cal Poly, Chamitoff worked summers as a student engineer at Four Phase Systems, Atari, Northern Telecom, and IBM. He was also a lab course instructor for analog and digital circuit design. His undergraduate thesis was on the development and construction of a self-guided robot. While at MIT and Draper Labs (1985-91) Chamitoff worked on a variety of NASA projects. He performed stability analyses of shuttle attitude control for the initial release of the Hubble Space Telescope, developed flight control upgrades for redundancy in the Space Shuttle autopilot, and constructed models for vehicle design and trajectory optimization of the National Aerospace Plane. In his doctoral thesis, Chamitoff developed a new robust intelligent flight control approach for hypersonic single-stage-to-orbit launch vehicles. After graduation, he remained at Draper Labs on a team that developed an incremental attitude control system for Space Station Freedom. In 1993, Chamitoff became a visiting professor at the University of Sydney, Australia. There he led a research group in the development of autonomous flight control systems and taught courses in flight dynamics and control theory. In 1995, Chamitoff joined the International Space Station Motion Control Systems group in the Mission Operations Directorate at JSC (as a Rockwell employee). In that position, he led the development of several applications for the automation of spacecraft attitude control monitoring, prediction, analysis, and maneuver optimization. Chamitoff has published numerous papers on aircraft and spacecraft guidance and control, trajectory optimization, parameter estimation, and in-situ resource utilization on Mars.

NASA EXPERIENCE: Selected by NASA in June 1998, he reported for training in August 1998. Astronaut CandidateTraining includes orientation briefings and tours, numerous scientific and technical briefings, intensive instruction in Shuttle and International Space Station systems, physiological training and ground school to prepare for T-38 flight training, as well as learning water and wilderness survival techniques. Chamitoff is currently assigned to the Astronaut Office Space Station Operations Branch. He will serve in technical assignments until assigned to a space flight.

NAME: Franklin R. Chang-Dìaz (Ph.D.)
NASA Astronaut

PERSONAL DATA: Born April 5, 1950, in San Josè, Costa Rica, to the late Mr. Ramòn A. Chang-Morales and Mrs. Marìa Eugenia Dìaz De Chang. Married to the former Peggy Marguerite Doncaster of Alexandria, Louisiana. Four children. He enjoys music, glider planes, soccer, scuba-diving, and hiking. His mother, brothers and sisters still reside in Costa Rica.

EDUCATION: Graduated from Colegio De La Salle in San Josè, Costa Rica, in November 1967, and from Hartford High School in Hartford, Connecticut, in 1969; received a bachelor of science degree in mechanical engineering from the University of Connecticut in 1973 and a doctorate in applied plasma physics from the Massachusetts Institute of Technology (MIT) in 1977.

SPECIAL HONORS: Recipient of the University of Connecticut's Outstanding Alumni Award (1980); 6 NASA Space Flight Medals (1986, 1989, 1992, 1994, 1996, 1998); 2 NASA Distinguished Service Medals (1995, 1997), and 3 NASA Exceptional Service Medals (1988, 1990, 1993). In 1986, he received the Liberty Medal from President Ronald Reagan at the Statue of Liberty Centennial Celebration in New York City, and in 1987 the Medal of Excellence from the Congressional Hispanic Caucus. He received the Cross of the Venezuelan Air Force from President Jaime Lusinchi during the 68th Anniversary of the Venezuelan Air Force in Caracas, Venezuela (1988), and the Flight Achievement Award from the American Astronautical Society (1989). Recipient of four Doctorates "Honoris Causa" (Doctor of Science from the Universidad Nacional de Costa Rica; Doctor of Science from the University of Connecticut, Doctor of Law from Babson College, and Doctor of Science from the Universidade de Santiago de Chile. He is Honorary faculty at the College of Engineering, University of Costa Rica. In April 1995, the government of Costa Rica confered on him the title of "Honorary Citizen." This is the highest honor Costa Rica confers to a foreign citizen, making him the first such honoree who was actually born there.

EXPERIENCE: While attending the University of Connecticut, he also worked as a research assistant in the Physics Department and participated in the design and construction of high energy atomic collision experiments. Following graduation in 1973, he entered graduate school at MIT, becoming heavily involved in the United States' controlled fusion program and doing intensive research in the design and operation of fusion reactors. He obtained his doctorate in the field of applied plasma physics and fusion technology and, in that same year, joined the technical staff of the Charles Stark Draper Laboratory. His work at Draper was geared strongly toward the design and integration of control systems for fusion reactor concepts and experimental devices, in both inertial and magnetic confinement fusion. In 1979, he developed a novel concept to guide and target fuel pellets in an inertial fusion reactor chamber. More recently he has been engaged in the design of a new concept in rocket propulsion based on magnetically confined high temperature plasmas. As a visiting scientist with the M.I.T. Plasma Fusion Center from October 1983 to December 1993, he led the plasma propulsion program there to develop this technology for future human missions to Mars. In December 1993, Dr. Chang-Dìaz was appointed Director of the Advanced Space Propulsion Laboratory at the Johnson Space Center where he continues his research on plasma rockets. He is an Adjunct Professor of Physics at Rice University and the University of Houston and has presented numerous papers at technical conferences and in scientific journals. In addition to his main fields of science and engineering, he worked for 2-1/2 years as a house manager in an experimental community residence for de-institutionalizing chronic mental patients, and was heavily involved as an instructor/advisor with a rehabilitation program for hispanic drug abusers in Massachusetts.

NASA EXPERIENCE: Selected by NASA in May 1980, Dr. Chang-Dìaz became an astronaut in August 1981. While undergoing astronaut training he was also involved in flight software checkout at the Shuttle Avionics Integration Laboratory (SAIL), and participated in the early Space Station design studies. In late 1982 he was designated as support crew for the first Spacelab mission and, in November 1983, served as on orbit capsule communicator (CAPCOM) during that flight. From October 1984 to August 1985 he was leader of the astronaut support team at the Kennedy Space Center. His duties included astronaut support during the processing of the various vehicles and payloads, as well as flight crew support during the final phases of the launch countdown. He has logged over 1,800 hours of flight time, including 1,500 hours in jet aircraft. Dr. Chang-Dìaz was instrumental in implementing closer ties between the astronaut corps and the scientific community. In January 1987, he started the Astronaut Science Colloquium Program and later helped form the Astronaut Science Support Group, which he directed until January 1989. A veteran of six space flights (STS 61-C in 1986, STS-34 in 1989, STS-46 in 1992, STS-60 in 1994, STS-75 in 1996, and STS-91 in 1998), he has logged over 1,269 hours in space.

SPACE FLIGHT EXPERIENCE: STS 61-C (January 12-18, 1986), was launched from the Kennedy Space Center, Florida, on the Space Shuttle Columbia. STS 61-C was a 6-day flight during which Dr. Chang-Díaz participated in the deployment of the SATCOM KU satellite, conducted experiments in astrophysics, and operated the materials processing laboratory MSL-2. Following 96 orbits of the Earth, Columbia and her crew made a successful night landing at Edwards Air Force Base, California. Mission duration was 146 hours, 3 minutes, 51 seconds. On STS-34 (October 18-23, 1989), the crew aboard Space Shuttle Atlantis successfully deployed the Galileo spacecraft on its journey to explore Jupiter, operated the Shuttle Solar Backscatter Ultraviolet Instrument (SSBUV) to map atmospheric ozone, and performed numerous secondary experiments involving radiation measurements, polymer morphology, lightning research, microgravity effects on plants, and a student experiment on ice crystal growth in space. STS-34 launched from Kennedy Space Center, Florida, and landed at Edwards Air Force Base, California. Mission duration was 119 hours and 41 minutes and was accomplished in 79 orbits of the Earth. STS-46 (July 31-August 8, 1992), was an 8-day mission during which crew members deployed the European Retrievable Carrier (EURECA) satellite, and conducted the first Tethered Satellite System (TSS) test flight. Mission duration was 191 hours, 16 minutes, 7 seconds. Space Shuttle Atlantis and her crew launched and landed at the Kennedy Space Center, Florida, after completing 126 orbits of the Earth in 3.35 million miles. STS-60 (February 3-11, 1994), was the first flight of the Wake Shield Facility (WSF-1), the second flight of the Space Habitation Module-2 (Spacehab-2), and the first joint U.S./Russian Space Shuttle mission on which a Russian Cosmonaut was a crew member. During the 8-day flight, the crew aboard Space Shuttle Discovery conducted a wide variety of biological materials science, earth observation, and life science experiments. STS-60 launched and landed at Kennedy Space Center, Florida. The mission achieved 130 orbits of Earth in 3,439,705 miles. STS-75 (February 22 to March 9, 1996), was a 15-day mission with principal payloads being the reflight of the Tethered Satellite System (TSS) and the third flight of the United States Microgravity Payload (USMP-3). The TSS successfully demonstrated the ability of tethers to produce electricity. The TSS experiment produced a wealth of new information on the electrodynamics of tethers and plasma physics before the tether broke at 19.7 km, just shy of the 20.7 km goal. The crew also worked around the clock performing combustion experiments and research related to USMP-3 microgravity investigations used to improve production of medicines, metal alloys, and semiconductors. The mission was completed in 252 orbits covering 6.5 million miles in 377 hours and 40 minutes. STS-91 Discovery (June 2-12, 1998) was the 9th and final Shuttle-Mir docking mission and marked the conclusion of the highly successful joint U.S./Russian Phase I Program. The crew, including a Russian cosmonaut, performed logistics and hardware resupply of the Mir during four docked days. They also conducted the Alpha Magnetic Spectrometer experiment, which involved the first of its kind research of antimatter in space. Mission duration was 235 hours, 54 minutes.

NAME: Kalpana Chawla (Ph.D.)
NASA Astronaut

PERSONAL DATA: Born in Karnal, India. Kalpana Chawla enjoys flying, hiking, back-packing, and reading. She holds Certificated Flight Instructor's license with airplane and glider ratings, Commercial Pilot's licenses for single- and multi-engine land and seaplanes, and Gliders, and instrument rating for airplanes. She enjoys flying aerobatics and tail-wheel airplanes.

EDUCATION: Graduated from Tagore School, Karnal, India, in 1976. Bachelor of science degree in aeronautical engineering from Punjab Engineering College, India, 1982. Master of science degree in aerospace engineering from University of Texas, 1984. Doctorate of philosophy in aerospace engineering from University of Colorado, 1988.

EXPERIENCE: In 1988, Kalpana Chawla started work at NASA Ames Research Center in the area of powered-lift computational fluid dynamics. Her research concentrated on simulation of complex air flows encountered around aircraft such as the Harrier in "ground-effect." Following completion of this project she supported research in mapping of flow solvers to parallel computers, and testing of these solvers by carrying out powered lift computations. In 1993 Kalpana Chawla joined Overset Methods Inc., Los Altos, California, as Vice President and Research Scientist to form a team with other researchers specializing in simulation of moving multiple body problems. She was responsible for development and implementation of efficient techniques to perform aerodynamic optimization. Results of various projects that Kalpana Chawla participated in are documented in technical conference papers and journals.

NASA EXPERIENCE: Selected by NASA in December 1994, Kalpana Chawla reported to the Johnson Space Center in March 1995 as an astronaut candidate in the 15th Group of Astronauts. After completing a year of training and evaluation, she was assigned as crew representative to work technical issues for the Astronaut Office EVA/Robotics and Computer Branches. Her assignments included work on development of Robotic Situational Awareness Displays and testing space shuttle control software in the Shuttle Avionics Integration Laboratory. In November, 1996, Kalpana Chawla was assigned as mission specialist and prime robotic arm operator on STS-87 (November 19 to December 5, 1997). STS-87 was the fourth U.S Microgravity Payload flight and focused on experiments designed to study how the weightless environment of space affects various physical processes, and on observations of the Sun's outer atmospheric layers. Two members of the crew performed an EVA (spacewalk) which featured the manual capture of a Spartan satellite, in addition to testing EVA tools and procedures for future Space Station assembly. In completing her first mission, Kalpana Chawla traveled 6.5 million miles in 252 orbits of the Earth and logged 376 hours and 34 minutes in space. In January, 1998, Kalpana Chawla was assigned as crew representative for shuttle and station flight crew equipment. Subsequently, she was assigned as the lead for Astronaut Office's Crew Systems and Habitability section. She is currently assigned to the crew of STS-107 scheduled for launch in 2001.

NAME: Leroy Chiao (Ph.D.)
NASA Astronaut

PERSONAL DATA: Born August 28, 1960, in Milwaukee, Wisconsin, but considers Danville, California, to be his hometown. Single. He enjoys flying, basketball, racquetball, and skiing.

EDUCATION: Graduated from Monte Vista High School, Danville, California, in 1978; received a bachelor of science degree in chemical engineering from the University of California, Berkeley, in 1983, and a master of science degree and a doctorate in chemical engineering from the University of California, Santa Barbara, in 1985 and 1987, respectively.

SPECIAL HONORS: Invited to give technical seminars on honeycomb material and bonded panels, and cure modeling of aerospace composite materials, at the Beijing Institute of Aeronautical Materials, and at the Changsha Institute of Technology, 5th Department, in the Peoples Republic of China. Invited contributor to the International Encyclopedia of Composite Materials. Listed in Who's Who in Science and Engineering. Recipient of Distinguished Alumni Award from University of California, Santa Barbara. Keynote Commencement Speaker for the Departments of Engineering at the University of California at Berkeley, and at Santa Barbara, in 1996.

EXPERIENCE: Dr. Chiao graduated in 1987 from the University of California at Santa Barbara, and joined the Hexcel Corporation in Dublin, California. He worked for Hexcel until 1989, during which time he was involved in process, manufacturing, and engineering research on advanced aerospace materials; worked on a joint NASA-JPL/Hexcel project to develop a practical, optically correct, precision segment reflector, made entirely of advanced polymer composite materials, for future space telescopes; as well as working on cure modeling and finite element analysis. In January of 1989 Dr. Chiao joined the Lawrence Livermore National Laboratory in Livermore, California, where he was involved in processing research for fabrication of filament-wound and thick-section aerospace composites. Dr. Chiao also developed and demonstrated a mechanistic cure model for graphite fiber/epoxy composite material. An instrument-rated pilot, Dr. Chiao has logged over 2000 flight hours in a variety of aircraft.

NASA EXPERIENCE: Selected by NASA in January 1990, Dr. Chiao became an astronaut in July 1991. He is qualified for flight assignment as a mission specialist. His technical assignments to date include: Space Shuttle flight software verification in the Shuttle Avionics Integration Laboratory (SAIL); crew equipment, Spacelab, Spacehab and payloads issues for the Astronaut Office Mission Development Branch; Training and Flight Data File issues; EVA issues for the EVA Branch. A veteran of three space flights, he flew as a mission specialist on STS-65 in 1994, STS-72 in 1996 and STS-92 in 2000. Dr. Chiao has logged a total of 36 days, 12 hours, 36 minutes and 5 seconds in space, including over 26 EVA hours in four space walks.

SPACE FLIGHT EXPERIENCE: STS-65 Columbia (July 8-23, 1994) launched from and returned to land at the Kennedy Space Center, Florida, setting a new flight duration record for the Space Shuttle program at that time. The STS-65 mission flew the second International Microgravity Laboratory (IML-2). During the 15-day flight the seven-member crew conducted more than 80 experiments focusing on materials and life sciences research in microgravity. The STS-65 mission was accomplished in 236 orbits of the Earth, traveling 6.1 million miles in 353 hours and 55 minutes. STS-72 Endeavour (January 11-20, 1996) was a 9-day mission during which the crew retrieved the Space Flyer Unit (launched from Japan 10-months earlier), and deployed and retrieved the OAST-Flyer. Dr. Chiao performed two spacewalks designed to demonstrate tools and hardware, and evaluate techniques to be used in the assembly of the International Space Station. In completing this mission, Dr. Chiao logged a total of 214 hours and 41 seconds in space, including just over 13 EVA hours, and traveled 3.7 million miles in 142 orbits of the Earth. STS-92 Discovery (October 11-24, 2000) was launched from the Kennedy Space Center, Florida and returned to land at Edwards Air Force Base, California. During the 13-day flight, the seven member crew attached the Z1 Truss and Pressurized Mating Adapter 3 to the International Space Station using Discovery's robotic arm and performed four space walks to configure these elements. This expansion of the ISS opened the door for future assembly missions and prepared the station for its first resident crew. Dr. Chiao totaled 13 hours and 16 minutes of EVA time in two space walks. The STS-92 mission was accomplished in 202 orbits, traveling 5.3 million miles in 12 days, 21 hours, 40 minutes and 25 seconds.

NAME: Jean-Loup J.M. Chrétien (Brigadier-General, French Air Force)
NASA Mission Specialist Astronaut

PERSONAL DATA: Born August 20, 1938, in the town of La Rochelle, France. Married to Amy Kristine Jensen of New Canaan, Connecticut. Five children (one deceased). Hobbies include skiing in Winter and sailing in Summer. He also enjoys golf, wind-surfing, car-rallying and woodworking. In addition, he plays the church organ, and took an electric one with him during his first stay in Star City, Russia. His father, Jacques, was a Navy sailor, and his mother, the former Marie-Blanche Coudurier, was a housewife. Her parents, Nels and Betty Jensen, reside in Tarpon Springs, Florida.

EDUCATION: Chrétien was educated at L'Ecole communale a Ploujean, the College Saint-Charles a Saint-Brieuc, and the Lycee de Morlaix. He entered L'Ecole de l'Air (the French Air Force Academy) at Salon deProvence in 1959, and graduated in 1961, receiving a master's degree in aeronautical engineering.

ORGANIZATIONS: Member of the board of the Accademie de l'Air et de l'Espace, and the French Air and Space Museum. Former Counselor for Space Activities (Manned) to the President of Dassault Aviation. Member of the American Institute of Aeronautics and Astronautics, the International Academy of Astronautics, and the Association of Space Explorers. Member of the Board of BRIT AIR, an airline in his hometown, Morlaix.

SPECIAL HONORS: Awarded the title of Hero of the Soviet Union. Recipient of the Order of Lenin; the Order of the Red Banner of Labor; Commandeur de la Légion d'Honneur (Commander of the Order of the Legion of Honor); Chevalier de l'Ordre National du Mérite (Knight of the National Order of Merit); Titulaire de la Médaille de l'Aéronautique (Holder of the Aeronautics Medal), and honorary citizenship of Arkalyk.

EXPERIENCE: Chrétien received his fighter pilot/pilot-engineer wings in 1962, after one year of training on Mystere-4's. He was promoted to Lieutenant, and joined the 5th Fighter Squadron in in the Southeast of France, where he served for seven years as a fighter pilot in an operational squadron flying Super-Mystere B2's and then Mirage III interceptors. In 1970, he was assigned to the French test pilots school, EPNER (Ecole du Personnel Navigant d'Essais et de Réception), then served as a test pilot at the Istres Flight Test Center for seven years. During that time he was responsible for supervising the flight test program for the Mirage F-1 fighter. In 1977-78, he was appointed Deputy Commander of the South Air Defense Division in Aix en Provence, and he served in this position until his selection as a cosmonaut in June 1980. Chrétien remained a French Air Force officer but was placed on detachment to CNES for his space flight activities ensuring his availability for future flights with the Shuttle (NASA), Mir (Soviet Union) or Spacelab (ESA). He has accumulated over 8000 hours of flying time in various aircraft, including Russia's Tupolev 154, MIG 25, and Sukoi 26 and 27. A veteran of three space flights, Chrétien was the 10th Intercosmos cosmonaut, and has spent a total of 43 days, 11 hours, 18 minutes, 42 seconds in space, including an EVA of 5 hours, 57 minutes. In April 1979, the Soviet Union offered France the opportunity to fly a cosmonaut on board a joint Soviet-French space flight, along the same lines as the agreement to fly non-Soviet cosmonauts from member countries of the Intercosmos program. The offer was accepted, and France began a cosmonaut selection program in September 1979. Chrétien was one of two finalists named on June 12, 1980. He started training at the Yuri Gagarin Cosmonaut Training Center in September 1980. The following year he was named as the research-cosmonaut for the prime crew of the Soyuz T-6 mission. Soyuz T-6 was launched on June 24, 1982, and Chrétien, Dzhanibekov and Ivanchenkov linked up with Salyut 7 and joined the crew of Berezovoi and Lebedev already on board. They spent nearly seven days carrying out a program of joint Soviet-French experiments, including a series of French echography cardiovascular monitoring system experiments, before returning to Earth after a flight lasting 7 days, 21 hours, 50 minutes, 42 seconds. This flight made him the first Western non-American to go to space, as well as the first Western European. Following the mission he was appointed Chief, CNES Astronaut Office. Chrétien was selected as the back-up payload specialist for STS-51G. During 1984-85, he participated in mission training at the Johnson Space Center. Chrétien made his second space flight as a research-cosmonaut on board Soyuz TM-7, which launched on November 26, 1988. Together with Volkov and Krikalev, he linked up with Mir 1 and joined the crew of Titov Manarov and Polyakov already on board. They spent 22 days carrying out a program of joint Soviet-French experiments, including a 5 hour 57 minute EVA by Volkov and Chrétien during which the two men installed the French ERA experimental deployable structure and a panel of material samples. In making the EVA, he became the first non-American and non-Soviet cosmonaut to walk in space. In addition, he was the first non-Soviet cosmonaut to make a second space flight aboard a Soviet spacecraft. The mission lasted 24 days, 18 hours, 7 minutes. During 1990-93, Chrétien participated in Buran spacecraft pilot training at the Moscow Joukovski Institute. He has also flown the Tupolev 154 and MIG 25 aircraft, flying simulators equivalent to the Shuttle Training Aircraft (STA). Chrétien is fluent in English and Russian.

NASA EXPERIENCE: Chrétien attended ASCAN Training at the Johnson Space Center during 1995. He was initially assigned to work technical issues for the Operations Planning Branch of the Astronaut Office. He served on the crew of STS-86 Atlantis (September 25 to October 6, 1997) the seventh mission to rendezvous and dock with the Russian Space Station Mir. Highlights included the delivery of a Mir attitude control computer, the exchange of U.S. crew members Mike Foale and David Wolf, a spacewalk by Scott Parazynski and Vladimir Titov to retrieve four experiments first deployed on Mir during the STS-76 docking mission, the transfer to Mir of 10,400 pounds of science and logistics, and the return of experiment hardware and results to Earth. Mission duration was 10 days, 19 hours, 21 minutes.

NAME: Laurel Blair Salton Clark, M.D. (Commander, USN)
NASA Astronaut

PERSONAL DATA: Born March 10, 1961 in Ames, Iowa, but considers Racine, Wisconsin, to be her hometown. Married to Jonathan B. Clark (Captain, USN). They have one child. She enjoys scuba diving, hiking, camping, biking, parachuting, flying, traveling. Her mother and step-father, Dr. and Mrs. R.J.C. Brown, reside in Racine, Wisconsin. Her father and step-mother, Mr. and Mrs. Robert Salton, reside in Albuquerque, New Mexico. His parents, Colonel (ret) & Mrs. E.B. Clark III, reside in Alexandria, Virginia.

EDUCATION: Graduated from William Horlick High School, Racine Wisconsin in 1979; received bachelor of science degree in zoology from the University of Wisconsin-Madison in 1983 and doctorate in medicine from the same school in 1987.

ORGANIZATIONS: Aerospace Medical Association, Society of U.S. Naval Flight Surgeons.

AWARDS: Navy Commendation Medals (3); National Defense Medal, and Overseas Service Ribbon.

EXPERIENCE: During medical school she did active duty training with the Diving Medicine Department at the Naval Experimental Diving Unit in March 1987. After completing medical school, Dr. Clark underwent postgraduate Medical education in Pediatrics from 1987-1988 at Naval Hospital Bethesda, Maryland. The following year she completed Navy undersea medical officer training at the Naval Undersea Medical Institute in Groton Connecticut and diving medical officer training at the Naval Diving and Salvage Training Center in Panama City, Florida, and was designated a Radiation Health Officer and Undersea Medical Officer. She was then assigned as the Submarine Squadron Fourteen Medical Department Head in Holy Loch Scotland. During that assignment she dove with US Navy divers and Naval Special Warfare Unit Two Seals and performed numerous medical evacuations from US submarines. After two years of operational experience she was designated as a Naval Submarine Medical Officer and Diving Medical Officer. She underwent 6 months of aeromedical training at the Naval Aerospace Medical Institute in Pensacola, Florida and was designated as a Naval Flight Surgeon. She was stationed at MCAS Yuma, Arizona and assigned as Flight Surgeon for a Marine Corps AV-8B Night Attack Harrier Squadron (VMA 211). She made numerous deployments, including one overseas to the Western Pacific, and practiced medicine in austere environments, and flew on multiple aircraft. Her squadron won the Marine Attack Squadron of the year for its successful deployment. She was then assigned as the Group Flight Surgeon for the Marine Aircraft Group (MAG 13). Prior to her selection as an astronaut candidate she served as a Flight Surgeon for the Naval Flight Officer advanced training squadron (VT-86) in Pensacola, Florida. LCDR Clark is Board Certified by the National Board of Medical Examiners and holds a Wisconsin Medical License. Her military qualifications include Radiation Health Officer, Undersea Medical Officer, Diving Medical Officer, Submarine Medical Officer, and Naval Flight Surgeon. She is a Basic Life Support Instructor, Advanced Cardiac Life Support Provider, Advanced Trauma Life Support Provider, and Hyperbaric Chamber Advisor.

NASA EXPERIENCE: Selected by NASA in April 1996, Dr. Clark reported to the Johnson Space Center in August 1996. After completing two years of training and evaluation, she was qualified for flight assignment as a mission specialist. From July 1997 to August 2000 Dr. Clark worked in the Astronaut Office Payloads/Habitability Branch. She is currently assigned to the crew of STS-107 scheduled for launch in 2001.

NAME: Jean-François Clervoy
ESA Astronaut

PERSONAL DATA: Born November 19, 1958, in Longeville-les-Metz, France, but considers Toulouse, France, to be his hometown. Married to the former Laurence Boulanger. They have two children. He enjoys racquet sports, skill games, canyoning, skiing, and flying activities such as boomerang, frisbee, kites. His father, Jean Clervoy (French Air Force, Ret.), and his mother, Mireille Clervoy, reside in Franconville, France. Her parents, Robert and Juliette Boulanger, reside in Le Perreux-sur-Marne, France.

EDUCATION: Received his baccalauréat from Collège Militaire de Saint Cyr l' Ecole in 1976; passed Math. Sup. and Math. Spé. M' at Prytanée Militaire, La Flèche in 1978. Graduated from Ecole Polytechnique, Paris, in 1981; graduated from Ecole Nationale Supérieure de l' Aéronautique et de l' Espace, Toulouse, in 1983; graduated as a Flight Test Engineer from Ecole du Personnel Navigant d' Essais et de Réception, Istres, in 1987.

ORGANIZATIONS: Member, Association of Space Explorers. Honorary member of the French Aeronautics and Astronautics Association.

SPECIAL HONORS: NASA Space Flight Medal. Chevalier de l' Ordre National du Mérite. Chevalier de l' Ordre National de la Légion d' Honneur. Komarov Award. NASA Exceptional Service Medal.

EXPERIENCE: Clervoy was seconded from the Délégation Générale pour L' Armement (DGA) to CNES (French Space Agency) in 1983, where he worked on automatics and attitude control systems for several satellite projects. He was selected in the second group of French astronauts in 1985 and subsequently undertook intensive Russian language training. After graduating as a flight test engineer in 1987, he spent the next five years part-time at the Flight Test Center, Brétigny-sur-Orge, as Chief Test Director of the Parabolic Flight Program, responsible for testing and qualifying the Caravelle aircraft for microgravity, and part-time at the Hermes Crew Office, Toulouse, where he supported the European Manned Space Programs in the fields of extravehicular activity, rendezvous and docking, robotic arm, and man machine interface. In 1991, he trained in Star City, Moscow, on the Soyuz and Mir systems. In 1992, he was selected to join the astronaut corps of the European Space Agency (ESA). He holds military and civilian parachuting licenses, military and civilian diving licenses, and private pilot license. From 1983 to 1987, Clervoy was also a lecturer in signal processing and general mechanics at the Ecole Nationale Supérieure de l' Aéronautique et de l' Espace, Toulouse. Jean-François holds a commission as Ingénieur en Chef de l' Armement in the DGA.

NASA EXPERIENCE: Clervoy reported to the Johnson Space Center in August 1992. Following one year of training he qualified as a mission specialist for Space Shuttle flights. Clervoy was initially assigned to the Astronaut Office MissionDevelopment Branch where he designed a new concept of robotic steering displays. After his first space mission he was assigned as flight software verification lead in the Shuttle Avionics Integration Laboratory (SAIL) and was responsible for designing the International Space Station (ISS) robotics displays for the Astronaut Office Mission Support Branch. Following his second space mission, he served as ISS displays integration lead for the Astronaut Office Computer Support Branch. A veteran of three space flights, Clervoy has logged over 674 hours in space. He served as a mission specialist on STS-66 in 1994, was the Payload Commander on STS-84 in 1997, and again served as a mission specialist on STS-103 in 1999.

Clervoy currently leads the crew interface and software section for the Astronaut Office Space Station Branch.

SPACE FLIGHT EXPERIENCE: STS-66 Atlantis (November 3-14, 1994), the Atmospheric Laboratory for Applications and Science-3 (ATLAS-3) mission was part of an ongoing program to determine the Earth's energy balance and atmospheric change over an eleven-year solar cycle. Clervoy used the robotic arm to deploy the CRISTA-SPAS atmospheric research satellite 20 hours after lift-off, and logged 262 hours and 34 minutes in space and 175 orbits of the Earth. STS-84 Atlantis (May 15-24, 1997), was NASA's sixth Shuttle mission to rendezvous and dock with the Russian Space Station Mir. Clervoy's primary tasks were the coordination of the execution of more than 20 experiments, the operation of the docking system and the double module SPACEHAB, and the transfer of 4 tons of equipment between Atlantis and Mir. He was also trained as a contingency spacewalker on this mission. STS-84 was accomplished in 144 Earth orbits, traveling 3.6 million miles in 221 hours and 20 minutes. STS-103 Discovery (December 19-27, 1999) was an 8-day mission during which the crew successfully installed new instruments and upgraded systems on the Hubble Space Telescope (HST). Clervoy was the flight engineer for ascent and entry. He used the robot arm to capture and deploy the telescope, and to maneuver the suited astronauts during 3 eight hour long spacewalks required to repair and upgrade the telescope. The STS-103 mission was accomplished in 120 Earth orbits, traveling 3.2 million miles in 191 hours and 11 minutes.

NAME: Kenneth D. Cockrell (Mr.)
       NASA Astronaut

PERSONAL DATA: Born April 9, 1950, in Austin, Texas. Two children. He enjoys sport flying, snow skiing, water skiing, tennis. His parents, Dale and Jewell Cockrell, reside in Westminster, South Carolina.

EDUCATION: Graduated from Rockdale High School, Rockdale, Texas, in 1968; received a bachelor of science degree in mechanical engineering from University of Texas in 1972, and a master of science degree in aeronautical systems from the University of West Florida in 1974.

ORGANIZATIONS: Member, Society of Experimental Test Pilots (SETP), and Association of Space Explorers (ASE).

SPECIAL HONORS: Awarded the Armed Forces Meritorious Service Medal, the Navy Commendation Medal, the Armed Forces Expeditionary Medal, and the Humanitarian Service Medal. Received the Alcoa Foundation Scholarship upon graduating from high school.

EXPERIENCE: Cockrell received his commission through the Naval Aviation Reserve Officer Candidate Program at Naval Air Station Pensacola, Florida, in December 1972. He was designated a Naval Aviator in August 1974 at Naval Air Station Pensacola. Following type training in the A-7 aircraft, he flew the Corsair II from 1975 to 1978 aboard the USS Midway in the Western Pacific and Indian Oceans. In 1978 he reported to the United States Naval Test Pilot School at Patuxent River, Maryland. After graduation in 1979, he remained at the Naval Air Test Center conducting a variety of flight tests on the A-4, A-7, F-4, and F/A-18 aircraft through mid-1982. He then reported to Naval Station, San Diego, for duty as a staff officer for the Commander of the USS Ranger and subsequently the USS Kitty Hawk Battle Groups. Cockrell was then assigned as a pilot in an operational F/A-18 squadron and made two cruises on the USS Constellation in 1985 and 1987. He resigned his commission in 1987 and accepted a position at the Aircraft Operations Division of the Johnson Space Center. Cockrell retired from the Naval Reserve in June 1999. He has logged over 7,500 flying hours and 650 carrier landings.

NASA EXPERIENCE: From November 1987 to July 1990, Cockrell worked as an aerospace engineer and research pilot at Ellington Field, Houston. He was an instructor pilot and functional check pilot in NASA T-38 aircraft. He conducted air sampling and other high altitude research while piloting the WB-57 and was an aircraft commander in the Gulfstream I administrative transport aircraft. Selected by NASA in January 1990, Cockrell became an astronaut in July 1991. His technical assignments to date include: duties in the Astronaut Office Operations Development Branch, working on landing, rollout, tires and brakes issues; CAPCOM in Mission Control for ascent and entry; Astronaut Office representative for Flight Data File, the numerous books of procedures carried aboard Shuttle flights. He served as Assistant to the Chief of the Astronaut Office for Shuttle operations and hardware, and has served as Chief of the Astronaut Office Operations Development Branch. A veteran of three space flights, he has logged over 906 hours in space. He served as a mission specialist on STS-56 (April 8-17, 1993), was the pilot on STS-69 (September 7-18, 1995), and was the mission commander on STS-80 (November 19 to December 7, 1996). He presently serves as Chief of the Astronaut Office. Cockrell is assigned to command the crew of STS-98 that will continue the task of building and enhancing the International Space Station by delivering the U.S. laboratory module. The Shuttle will spend six days docked to the station while the laboratory is attached and three spacewalks are conducted to complete its assembly. The STS-98 mission will occur while the first station crew is aboard the new spacecraft. Launch is targeted for 2001.

SPACEFLIGHT EXPERIENCE: STS-56, carrying ATLAS-2 was a nine-day mission during which the crew of Discovery conducted atmospheric and solar studies in order to better understand the effect of solar activity on the Earth's climate and environment. STS-56 launched April 8, 1993, and landed April 17, 1993. Mission duration was 9 days, 6 hours, 9 minutes, 21 seconds. The primary objective of STS-69 (September 7-18, 1995) was the successful deployment and retrieval of a SPARTAN satellite and the Wake Shield Facility (WSF). The WSF is designed to evaluate the effectiveness of using a free-flying platform to grow semiconductors, high temperature superconductors and other materials using the ultra-high vacuum created behind the spacecraft. Mission duration was 10 days, 20 hours, 28 minutes. During STS-80 (November 19 to December 7, 1996) the crew deployed and retrieved the Wake Shield Facility (WSF) and the Orbiting Retrievable Far and Extreme Ultraviolet Spectrometer (ORFEUS) satellites. The ORFEUS instruments, mounted on the reusable Shuttle Pallet Satellite, studied the origin and makeup of stars. Mission duration was a record breaking 17 days, 15 hours, 53 minutes.

NAME: Catherine G. "Cady" Coleman, Ph.D. (Lieutenant Colonel, USAF)
NASA Astronaut

PERSONAL DATA: Born December 14, 1960, in Charleston, South Carolina. Married to glass artist Josh Simpson. She enjoys flying, scuba diving, sports, music. As an undergraduate, she competed in intercollegiate athletics on MIT's crew team. Her father, James J. Coleman, resides in Vancouver, Washington. Her mother, Ann L. Doty, resides in Westerly, Rhode Island.

EDUCATION: Graduated from W.T. Woodson High School, Fairfax, Virginia, in 1978; received a bachelor of science degree in chemistry from the Massachusetts Institute of Technology in 1983, and a doctorate in polymer science and engineering from the University of Massachusetts in 1991.

ORGANIZATIONS: Member of the American Chemical Society, the Society for Photo-Optical Instrumentation Engineers (SPIE), the American Association of University Women, and the International Womens' Air and Space Museum.

EXPERIENCE: Coleman was commissioned as a 2nd lieutenant in the Air Force in 1983 and began graduate work at the University of Massachusetts. Her research focused on polymer synthesis using the olefin metathesis reaction, and polymer surface modification. In 1988, Coleman entered active duty and was assigned to Wright-Patterson Air Force Base. As a research chemist at the Materials Directorate of the Wright Laboratory, she synthesized model compounds to investigate the use of organic polymers for third-order nonlinear optical applications such as advanced computers and data storage. Coleman also acted as a surface analysis consultant for the Long Duration Exposure Facility (launched from STS 41-C in 1984 and retrieved during STS-32 in 1990). In addition to assigned duties, Coleman was a volunteer test subject for the centrifuge program at the Crew Systems Directorate of the Armstrong Aeromedical Laboratory. She set several endurance and tolerance records during her participation in physiological and new equipment studies.

NASA EXPERIENCE: Coleman was selected by NASA in March 1992 and reported to the Johnson Space Center in August 1992. Initially assigned to the Astronaut Office Mission Support Branch and detailed to flight software verification in the Shuttle Avionics Integration Laboratory, Coleman subsequently served as the special assistant to the Center Director, Johnson Space Center. She served in the Astronaut Office Payloads and Habitability Branch, working with experiment designers to insure that payloads can be operated successfully in the microgravity environment of low earth orbit. As the lead astronaut for long term space flight habitability issues, she led the effort to label the Russian segments of the International Space Station in English and also tracked issues such as accoustics and living accommodations aboard the station. A veteran of two space missions, Coleman has logged over 500 hours in space. She was a mission specialist on STS-73, trained as a backup mission specialist for an injured crew member on STS-83, and was lead mission specialist on STS-93.

SPACE FLIGHT EXPERIENCE: STS-73 Columbia (October 20 to November 5, 1995), was the second United States Microgravity Laboratory mission. The mission focused on materials science, biotechnology, combustion science, the physics of fluids, and numerous scientific experiments housed in the pressurized Spacelab module. In completing her first space flight, Coleman orbited the Earth 256 times, traveled over 6 million miles, and logged a total of 15 days, 21 hours, 52 minutes and 21 seconds in space. STS-93 Columbia (July 22-27, 1999) was a 5-day mission during which Coleman was the lead mission specialist for the deployment of the Chandra X-Ray Observatory. Designed to conduct comprehensive studies of the universe, the telescope will enable scientists to study exotic phenomena such as exploding stars, quasars, and black holes. Mission duration was 118 hours and 50 minutes.

NAME: Eileen Marie Collins (Colonel, USAF)
NASA Astronaut

PERSONAL DATA: Born November 19, 1956, in Elmira, New York. Married to Pat Youngs, originally from San Antonio, Texas. They have one child. She enjoys running, golf, hiking, camping, reading, photography, astronomy. Her parents are James and Rose Marie Collins, from Elmira, New York. His parents are Pat and Jackie Youngs, from San Antonio, Texas.

EDUCATION: Graduated from Elmira Free Academy, Elmira, New York, in 1974; received an associate in science degree in mathematics/science from Corning Community College in 1976; a bachelor of arts degree in mathematics and economics from Syracuse University in 1978; a master of science degree in operations research from Stanford University in 1986; and a master of arts degree in space systems management from Webster University in 1989.

ORGANIZATIONS: Member of the Air Force Association, Order of Daedalians, Women Military Aviators, U.S. Space Foundation, the American Institute of Aeronautics and Astronautics, and the Ninety-Nines.

SPECIAL HONORS: Awarded the Defense Superior Service Medal, the Air Force Meritorious Service Medal with one oak leaf cluster, the Air Force Commendation Medal with one oak leaf cluster, the Armed Forces Expeditionary Medal for service in Grenada (Operation Urgent Fury, October 1983), and the NASA Space Flight Medal.

EXPERIENCE: Collins graduated in 1979 from Air Force Undergraduate Pilot Training at Vance AFB, Oklahoma, where she was a T-38 instructor pilot until 1982. From 1983 to 1985, she was a C-141 aircraft commander and instructor pilot at Travis AFB, California. She spent the following year as a student with the Air Force Institute of Technology. From 1986 to 1989, she was assigned to the U.S. Air Force Academy in Colorado, where she was an assistant professor in mathematics and a T-41 instructor pilot. She was selected for the astronaut program while attending the Air Force Test Pilot School at Edwards AFB, California, from which she graduated in 1990. She has logged over 5,000 hours in 30 different types of aircraft.

NASA EXPERIENCE: Selected by NASA in January 1990, Collins became an astronaut in July 1991. Initially assigned to Orbiter engineering support, she has also served on the astronaut support team responsible for Orbiter prelaunch checkout, final launch configuration, crew ingress/egress, landing/recovery, worked in Mission Control as a spacecraft communicator (CAPCOM) for numerous shuttle missions, and served as the Astronaut Office Spacecraft Systems Branch Chief. A veteran of three space flights, Collins has logged over 537 hours in space. She served as pilot on STS-63 (February 2-11, 1995) and STS-84 (May 15-24, 1997), and was the first woman Shuttle commander on STS-93 (July 22-27, 1999).

SPACE FLIGHT EXPERIENCE: STS-63 (February 2-11, 1995) was the first flight of the new joint Russian-American Space Program. Mission highlights included the rendezvous with the Russian Space Station Mir, operation of Spacehab, the deployment and retrieval of an astronomy satellite, and a space walk. Collins' first mission was accomplished in 129 orbits, traveling over 2.9 million miles in 198 hours, 29 minutes. She was the first woman pilot of a Space Shuttle. STS-84 (May 15-24, 1997) was NASA's sixth Shuttle mission to rendezvous and dock with the Russian Space Station Mir. During the flight, the crew conducted a number of secondary experiments and transferred nearly 4 tons of supplies and experiment equipment between Atlantis and the Mir station. In completing this 9-day mission, she traveled 3.8 million miles in 145 orbits of the Earth logging a total of 221 hours and 20 minutes in space. STS-93 Columbia (July 22-27, 1999) was the first Shuttle mission to be commanded by a woman. STS-93 highlighted the deployment of the Chandra X-Ray Observatory. Designed to conduct comprehensive studies of the universe, the telescope will enable scientists to study exotic phenomena such as exploding stars, quasars, and black holes. Mission duration was 118 hours and 50 minutes.

NAME: Timothy J. (TJ) Creamer (Lieutenant Colonel, USA)
NASA Astronaut (Mission Specialist Candidate)

PERSONAL DATA: Born November 15, 1959 in Ft. Huachuca, Arizona, but considers Upper Marlboro, Maryland, to be his hometown. Married to the former Margaret E. Hammer. They have two children. A vegetarian, his interests also include tennis, running, reading, SCUBA, and information technologies. His mother, Mary E. Creamer, resides in Upper Marlboro, Maryland. His father, Edmund J. Creamer, Jr., is deceased.

EDUCATION: Bishop McNamara High School, Forestville, Maryland, 1978. B.S., Chemistry, Loyola College, Baltimore, Maryland, 1982. M.S., Physics, Massachusetts Institute of Technology, 1992.

ORGANIZATIONS: Member of Alpha Sigma Nu, Phi Kappa Phi, Sigma Pi Sigma, Army Aviation Association of America, Association of the United States Army, and the British-American Project.

SPECIAL HONORS: Meritorious Service Medal (2nd Oak Leaf Cluster); Army Achievement Medal (1st Oak Leaf Cluster); National Defense Service Medal; Senior Army Aviator; Senior Parachutist; Distinguished Graduate of the U.S. Army Aviation School.

EXPERIENCE: Creamer graduated from Loyola College in May 1982, and was commissioned through the ROTC program as a Second Lieutenant in the U.S. Army. He entered the U.S. Army Aviation School in December 1982, and was designated as an Army Aviator in August 1983, graduating as the Distinguished Graduate from his class. He was subsequently assigned to the 1st Armored Division as a section leader, platoon leader, flight operations officer, and as a personnel staff officer for the 501st Attack Helicopter Battalion. In 1987, he was assigned to the 82nd Airborne Division as a commander of an air cavalry troop in the 17th Cavalry, and later as the personnel officer of the 82nd Aviation Brigade. Following this assignment, he completed a Master of Science degree in physics at MIT in 1992, and was subsequently assigned to the Department of Physics at the United States Military Academy as an Assistant Professor. Other military schools include Army Parachutist Course, Army Jumpmaster Course, the Combined Arms Services Staff School, and the Command and General Staff College. Most recently, he had been working as a Space Operations Officer, with the Army Space Command, stationed in Houston, Texas.

NASA EXPERIENCE: Creamer was assigned to NASA at the Johnson Space Center in July 1995 as a Space Shuttle vehicle integration test engineer. His duties primarily involved engineering liaison for launch and landing operations of the Space Shuttle. He was actively involved in the integrated tests of the systems for each Orbiter for its preparations for its next flight, and directly supported eight Shuttle missions as a vehicle integration test team lead. Additionally, he focused his efforts in coordinating the information technologies for the Astronaut Office to aid personnel in their electronic communications both on JSC as well as through their travels to other Centers. Selected by NASA in June 1998, Creamer reported for Astronaut Candidate Training in August 1998. Having completed two years of intensive Space Shuttle and Space Station training, he has been assigned technical duties in the Space Station Branch of the Astronaut Office, where his primary focus involves the command and control computers on Space Station, as well as the office automation support computers, and the operational Local Area Network encompassing all international partners and modules.

NAME: Frank L. Culbertson, Jr. (Captain, USN, ret.)
   NASA Astronaut

PERSONAL DATA: Born May 15, 1949, in Charleston, South Carolina, but considers Holly Hill to be his hometown. Married, June 1987, to the former Rebecca Ellen Dora of Vincennes, Indiana. Five children. He enjoys flying, bicycling, squash, running, golf, camping, photography, music, and water sports. Member of varsity rowing and wrestling teams at USNA. His parents, Dr. and Mrs. Frank Culbertson, Sr., reside in Holly Hill, South Carolina. Her mother, Mrs. Avanelle Vincent Dora, resides in Vincennes, Indiana. Her father, Mr. Robert E. Dora, is deceased.

EDUCATION: Graduated from Holly Hill High School, Holly Hill, South Carolina, in 1967; received a bachelor of science degree in aerospace engineering from the U.S. Naval Academy in 1971.

ORGANIZATIONS: Member of the American Institute of Aeronautics and Astronautics, the Association of Naval Aviators, Aircraft Owners & Pilots Association, the U.S. Naval Institute, the Aviation Boatswains Mate's Association, and the Association of Space Explorers.

SPECIAL HONORS: Awarded the Navy Flying Cross, the Defense Superior Service Medal, the NASA Outstanding Leadership Medal, NASA Space Flight Medals, Navy Commendation Medal, Air Force Commendation Medal, Navy Unit Commendation, 3 Meritorious Unit Commendations, the Armed Forces Expeditionary Medal, the Humanitarian Services Medal, and various other unit and service awards. Distinguished graduate, U.S. Naval Test Pilot School. Awarded Honorary Doctor of Science Degree, College of Charleston, 1994.

EXPERIENCE: Culbertson graduated from Annapolis in 1971 and served aboard the USS Fox (CG-33) in the Gulf of Tonkin for six months prior to reporting to flight training in Pensacola, Florida. After designation as a Naval Aviator at Beeville, Texas, in May 1973, he received training as an F-4 Phantom pilot at VF-121, NAS Miramar, California. From March 1974 to May 1976, he was assigned to VF-151 aboard the USS Midway (CV-41), permanently homeported in Yokosuka, Japan. He subsequently was assigned as an exchange pilot with the USAF at Luke Air Force Base, Arizona, where he served as Weapons and Tactics Instructor flying F-4C's with the 426th TFTS until September 1978. Culbertson then served as the Catapult and Arresting Gear Officer for the USS John F. Kennedy (CV-67) until May 1981 when he was selected to attend the U.S. Naval Test Pilot School, Patuxent River, Maryland. Following graduation with distinction in June 1982, he was assigned to the Carrier Systems Branch of the Strike Aircraft Test Directorate where he served as Program Manager for all F-4 testing and as a test pilot for automatic carrier landing system tests in the F-4S, and carrier suitability in the F-4S and the OV-10A. He was engaged in fleet replacement training in the F-14A Tomcat at VF-101, NAS Oceana, Virginia, from January 1984 until his selection for the astronaut candidate program. He has logged over 5,000 hours flying time in 40 different types of aircraft, and 350 carrier landings.

NASA EXPERIENCE: Selected as a NASA astronaut candidate in May 1984, Culbertson completed basic astronaut training in June 1985 and is qualified for flight assignment as a pilot. Technical assignments since then include: member of the team that redesigned and tested the Shuttle nose-wheel steering, tires, and brakes, to provide more safety margin during landing rollout; member of the launch support team at Kennedy Space Center for Shuttle flights 61-A, 61-B, 61-C, and 51-L; participated in the preparations for the proposed launch at Vandenberg Air Force Base, California, in 1986; worked at the NASA Headquarters Action Center in Washington, D.C., assisting with the

Challenger accident investigations conducted by NASA, the Presidential Commission, and Congress; lead astronaut at the Shuttle Avionics Integration Laboratory (SAIL), involved in the checkout and verification of the computer software and hardware interfaces for STS-26 and subsequent flights; lead of the First Emergency Egress Team, which conducts periodic tests of improvements to the Shuttle ground egress systems; member of the Astronaut Office Safety Branch; lead spacecraft communicator (CAPCOM) in the Mission Control Center for seven missions (STS-27, 29,30, 28, 34, 33, and 32), where his duties included communications with the Shuttle crew during ascent and entry and during simulations, in addition to serving on the panel which dealt with procedural problems and flight technique issues between missions; following his first flight, he served as the Deputy Chief of the Flight Crew Operations Space Station Support Office as well as the lead astronaut for Space Station Safety, where he supervised the engineers and astronauts evaluating the design, safety, and operational capabilities of Space Station Freedom; while assigned to STS-51, was also a member of the team evaluating the proposed mission to dock with the Russian Space Station Mir; Chief of the Astronaut Office Mission Support Branch; Chief of the Johnson Space Center Russian Projects Office; Program Manager, Phase 1 Shuttle/Mir, a program consisting of at least seven Shuttle docking missions to the Russian Space Station Mir, five astronauts spending at least 22 months cumulatively on-board the Mir, and all the associated science and docking hardware to ensure the success of the joint program, a precursor to the building of the joint International Space Station. A veteran of two space flights, Culbertson has logged over 344 hours in space. He was the pilot on STS-38 in 1990, and was the crew commander on STS-51 in 1993. Culbertson is currently in training to command the Expedition-3 crew on a future mission aboard the International Space Station.

SPACE FLIGHT EXPERIENCE: STS-38 Atlantis (November 15-20, 1990) was a five-day mission during which the crew conducted Department of Defense operations. It also was the first Shuttle recovery in Florida since 1985. The mission concluded after 80 orbits of the Earth in 117 hours, 54 minutes, 28 seconds. STS-51 Discovery (September 12-22, 1993) was a ten day mission during which the crew deployed the U.S. Advanced Communications Technology Satellite (ACTS/TOS), and the Shuttle Pallet Satellite (ORFEUS/SPAS) carrying U.S. and German scientific experiments, including an ultraviolet spectrometer. On flight day five, a seven-hour EVA was conducted to evaluate Hubble Space Telescope repair tools and methods. After the SPAS spacecraft had completed six days of free flight some 40 miles from Discovery, the crew completed a successful rendezvous and recovered the SPAS with the Shuttle's robot arm. The mission concluded with the first night landing at the Kennedy Space Center. Mission duration was 158 Earth orbits in 236 hours and 11 minutes.

NAME: Robert L. Curbeam, Jr., (Commander, USN)
NASA Astronaut

PERSONAL DATA: Born March 5, 1962, in Baltimore, Maryland. Married to the former Julie Dawn Lein; they have two children. He enjoys weightlifting, biking, and family activities.

EDUCATION: Graduated from Woodlawn High School, Baltimore County, Maryland, 1980. Bachelor of science degree in aerospace engineering from the United States Naval Academy, 1984. Master of science degree in aeronautical engineering from the Naval Postgraduate School, 1990. Degree of aeronautical & astronautical engineering from the Naval Postgraduate School, 1991.

ORGANIZATIONS: Member of the U.S. Naval Academy Alumni Association and the Association of Old Crows.

SPECIAL HONORS: Fighter Wing One Radar Intercept Officer of the Year for 1989, U.S. Naval Test Pilot School Best Developmental Thesis (DT-II) Award, two Navy Commendation Medals, the Navy Meritorious Unit Commendation, the Armed Forces Expeditionary Medal, the National Defense Service Medal, the Navy Battle Efficiency Award, and the Sea Service Deployment Ribbon.

EXPERIENCE: Upon graduation from the U.S. Naval Academy, Curbeam commenced Naval Flight Officer training in 1984. In 1986 he reported to Fighter Squadron 11 (VF-11) and made overseas deployments to the Mediterranean and Caribbean Seas, and the Arctic and Indian Oceans on board the USS Forrestal (CV-59). During his tour in VF-11, he also attended Navy Fighter Weapons School (Topgun). Upon completion of Test Pilot School in December 1991, he reported to the Strike Aircraft Test Directorate where he was the project officer for the F-14A/B Air-to-Ground Weapons Separation Program. In August 1994, he returned to the U.S. Naval Academy as an instructor in the Weapons and Systems Engineering Department.

NASA EXPERIENCE: Selected by NASA in December 1994, Curbeam reported to the Johnson Space Center in March 1995. He completed a year of training and evaluation and was assigned to the Computer Support Branch of the Astronaut Office. In 1997 he flew as a mission specialist on STS-85. In completing his first flight Curbeam logged 284 hours and 27 minutes in space. More recently, he served as a spacecraft communicator (CAPCOM) responsible for relaying all voice communication between Mission Control and crews aboard the Space Shuttle. Currently, Curbeam is assigned to STS-98, Space Station Assembly Mission 5A, targeted for launch in 2001. The STS-98 crew will deliver the U.S. Laboratory Module to the Space Station, and Curbeam will help install the Lab with a series of three spacewalks. The STS-98 mission will provide the station with science research facilities and expand its power, life support and control capabilities.

SPACE FLIGHT EXPERIENCE: STS-85 (August 7-19, 1997) was a 12-day mission during which the crew deployed and retrieved the CRISTA-SPAS payload, operated the Japanese Manipulator Flight Demonstration (MFD) robotic arm, studied changes in the Earth's atmosphere and tested technology destined for use on the future International Space Station. The mission was accomplished in 189 Earth orbits, traveling 4.7 million miles in 284 hours and 27 minutes.

NAME: Nancy Jane Currie, Ph.D. (Lieutenant Colonel, USA)
NASA Astronaut

PERSONAL DATA: Born December 29, 1958, in Wilmington, Delaware, but considers Troy, Ohio, to be her hometown. Married to David W. Currie. They have one daughter. She enjoys weight lifting, running, swimming, scuba diving, and skiing.

EDUCATION: Graduated from Troy High School, Troy, Ohio, in 1977; received a bachelor of arts degree in biological science from Ohio State University, Columbus, Ohio, in 1980, a master of science degree in safety from the University of Southern California in 1985, and a doctorate in industrial engineering from the University of Houston in 1997.

ORGANIZATIONS: Member of Army Aviation Association of America, Phi Kappa Phi, Ohio State University and ROTC Alumni Associations, Institute of Industrial Engineers, and Human Factors and Ergonomics Society.

SPECIAL HONORS: Arts and Sciences Award for Scholarship, Ohio State University (1980), Distinguished Graduate of the Army Air Defense Artillery Officer Basic Course (1981), Honor Graduate of the Army Rotary Wing Aviator Course (1982), Honor Graduate of the Army Aviation Officer Advanced Course (1986), NASA Flight Simulation Engineering Award (1988), NASA Space Flight Medal (1993, 1995, 1998), Defense Superior Service Medal (1993), Ohio Veteran's Hall of Fame (1994), Troy, Ohio Hall of Fame (1996), Ohio State University Army ROTC Hall of Fame (1996), Silver Order of St. Michael, Army Aviation Award (1997).

EXPERIENCE: Following graduation, Nancy served as a neuropathology research assistant at the Ohio State University College of Medicine. She was commissioned as a second lieutenant in the U.S. Army in July 1981, and attended the Air Defense Officer Basic Course and the United States Army Aviation School. Following flight training she was assigned to Fort Rucker, Alabama as a helicopter instructor pilot. She also served as a section leader, platoon leader, and brigade flight standardization officer for all phases of rotary wing flight, including combat skills and night vision goggle operations. A Master Army Aviator, she has logged 3,900 flying hours in a variety of rotary wing and fixed wing aircraft.

NASA EXPERIENCE: Currie was assigned to NASA Johnson Space Center in September 1987 as a flight simulation engineer on the Shuttle Training Aircraft, a complex airborne simulator which models flight characteristics of the Orbiter. Selected by NASA in January 1990, she became an astronaut in July 1991. Her technical assignments within the Astronaut Office have included flight crew representative for crew equipment; lead for the Remote Manipulator System (RMS), and spacecraft communicator (CAPCOM), providing a communications interface between ground controllers and flight crews. A veteran of three space flights, she has logged over 737 hours in space. She was a mission specialist on STS-57 in 1993, STS-70 in 1995, and STS-88 in 1998 (the first International Space Station assembly mission). She currently serves as Chief of the Astronaut Office Robotics Branch.

SPACE FLIGHT EXPERIENCE: On her first spaceflight, STS-57, Dr. Currie served as the flight engineer. This mission launched from the Kennedy Space Center, Florida, on June 21, 1993, and returned on July 1, 1993. The primary objective of this flight was the retrieval of the European Retrievable Carrier satellite (EURECA) using the RMS. Additionally, this mission featured the first flight of Spacehab, a commercially-provided middeck augmentation module for the conduct of microgravity experiments, as well as a spacewalk by two crew members, during which Currie operated the Shuttle's robotic arm. Spacehab carried 22 individual flight experiments in materials and life sciences research. The STS-57 mission was accomplished in 155 orbits of the Earth in 239 hours. Currie also served as the flight engineer on STS-70, which launched from the Kennedy Space Center, Florida, on July 13, 1995, and returned July 22, 1995. The five-member crew aboard Space Shuttle Discovery deployed the final NASA Tracking and Data Relay Satellite to complete the constellation of NASA's orbiting communication satellite system. The crew also conducted a myriad of biomedical and remote sensing experiments. During this 8 day 22 hour mission, the crew completed 142 orbits of the Earth, traveling 3.7 million miles. In December 1998, Currie served as the flight engineer on STS-88, the first International Space Station assembly mission. The primary objective of this 12-day mission was to mate the first American-made module, Unity, to the first Russian-made module, Zarya. Dr. Currie's primary role was to operate the Shuttle's 50-foot robotic arm to retrieve Zarya and connect the first two station segments. Two crewmembers performed a series of three space walks to connect electrical umbilicals and to attach hardware to the exterior structure for use during future EVA's. Dr. Currie also operated the robot arm during the space walks. During the mission the STS-88 crew ingressed the International Space Station to complete systems activation and installation of communication's equipment. They also deployed two satellites, Mighty Sat 1 and SAC-A. The mission was achieved in 185 orbits of the Earth in 283 hours and 18 minutes.

NAME: N. Jan Davis (Ph.D.)
NASA Astronaut

PERSONAL DATA: Born November 1, 1953, at Cocoa Beach, Florida, but considers Huntsville Alabama, to be her hometown. She enjoys flying, ice skating, snow skiing, water sports, and needlepoint.

EDUCATION: Graduated from Huntsville High School in 1971; received bachelor of science degrees in applied biology from Georgia Institute of Technology and in mechanical engineering from Auburn University in 1975 and 1977, respectively; received a master of science degree and a doctorate in mechanical engineering from University of Alabama in Huntsville, in 1983 and 1985, respectively.

ORGANIZATIONS: Fellow, American Society of Mechanical Engineers. Member, Tau Beta Pi, Omicron Delta Kappa, Pi Tau Sigma, and Sigma Gamma Tau honoraries, and Alpha Xi Delta social sorority.

SPECIAL HONORS: NASA Outstanding Leadership Medal (1998), NASA Exceptional Service Medal (1995), NASA Space Flight Medal (1992, 1994, 1997), Marshall Space Flight Center Director's Commendation (1987), NASA Fellowship for Full-Time Study (1983), ASME National Old Guard Prize (1978), and Alpha Xi Delta Woman of Distinction (1993).

EXPERIENCE: After graduating from Auburn University in 1977, Dr. Davis joined Texaco in Bellaire, Texas, working as a petroleum engineer in tertiary oil recovery. She left there in 1979 to work for NASA's Marshall Space Flight Center as an aerospace engineer. In 1986, she was named as team leader in the Structural Analysis Division, and her team was responsible for the structural analysis and verification of the Hubble Space Telescope (HST), the HST maintenance mission, and the Advanced X-Ray Astrophysics Facility. In 1987, she was also assigned to be the lead engineer for the redesign of the solid rocket booster external tank attach ring. Dr. Davis did her graduate research at the University of Alabama in Huntsville, studying the long-term strength of pressure vessels due to the viscoelastic characteristics of filament-wound composites. She holds one patent, has authored several technical papers, and is a Registered Professional Engineer. Dr. Davis became an astronaut in June 1987. Her initial technical assignment was in the Astronaut Office Mission Development Branch, where she provided technical support for Shuttle payloads. She then served as a CAPCOM in Mission Control communicating with Shuttle crews for seven missions. After her first space flight, Dr. Davis served as the Astronaut Office representative for the Remote Manipulator System (RMS), with responsibility for RMS operations, training, and payloads. After her second space flight, she served as the Chairperson of the NASA Education Working Group and as Chief for the Payloads Branch, which provided Astronaut Office support for all Shuttle and Space Station payloads. A veteran of three space flights, Dr. Davis has logged over 673 hours in space. She flew as a mission specialist on STS-47 in 1992 and STS-60 in 1994, and was the payload commander on STS-85 in 1997. After her flight on STS-85, Dr. Davis was assigned to NASA Headquarters as the Director of the Human Exploration and Development of Space (HEDS), Independent Assurance Office for the Office of Safety and Mission Assurance. In that position, Dr. Davis managed and directed independent assessments for the programs and projects assigned to the HEDS enterprise. In July 1999, she was named the Deputy Director of the Flight Projects Directorate at the Marshall Space Flight Center.

SPACE FLIGHT EXPERIENCE: STS-47, Spacelab-J, was the 50th Space Shuttle mission. Launched on September 12, 1992, this cooperative venture between the United States and Japan, conducted 43 experiments in life sciences and materials processing. During the eight-day mission, she was responsible for operating Spacelab and its subsystems and performing a variety of experiments. After completing 126 orbits of the Earth, STS-47 Endeavour landed at Kennedy Space Center on September 20, 1992. STS-60 was the second flight of Spacehab (Space Habitation Module) and the first flight of the Wake Shield Facility (WSF). Launched on February 3, 1994, this flight was the first Space Shuttle flight on which a Russian Cosmonaut was a crew member. During the eight-day mission, her prime responsibility was to maneuver the WSF on the RMS, to conduct thin film crystal growth and she was also responsible for performing scientific experiments in the Spacehab. The STS-60 Discovery landed at Kennedy Space Center on February 11, 1994, after completing 130 orbits of the Earth. Dr. Davis was the payload commander for STS-85, which was launched on Discovery on August 7, 1997. During this 12-day mission, Dr. Davis deployed and retrieved the CRISTA-SPAS payload, and operated the Japanese Manipulator Flight Demonstration (MFD) robotic arm. The mission also included several other scientific payloads for the conduct of research on astronomy, Earth sciences, life sciences, and materials science. The mission was accomplished in 189 Earth orbits, traveling 4.7 million miles. The STS-85 Discovery landed at Kennedy Space Center on August 19, 1997.

NAME: Takao Doi (Ph.D.)
NASDA Astronaut

PERSONAL DATA: Born September 18, 1954 in Minamitama, Tokyo, Japan. Married to the former Hitomi Abe of Toukamachi, Niigata, Japan. He enjoys flying, soaring, playing tennis, jogging, soccer, and observing stars as an amateur astronomer.

EDUCATION: Graduated from Ousaka-phu, Mikunigaoka High School in 1973. Bachelor of engineering degree from University of Tokyo, 1978. Master of engineering degree from University of Tokyo, 1980. Doctorate in aerospace engineering from University of Tokyo, 1983.

ORGANIZATIONS: The Japan Society of Microgravity Application, the Japan Society for Aeronautical and Space Science, American Institute of Aeronautics and Astronautics.

SPECIAL HONORS: Received Minister of State for Science and Technology's Commendation, Science Council of Japan's Special Citation, and National Space Development Agency of Japan's Outstanding Service Award in 1992.

PUBLICATIONS: Published over 40 papers in the areas of chemical propulsion systems, electric propulsion systems, fluid dynamics, and microgravity science and technology.

EXPERIENCE: Takao Doi studied space propulsion systems as a research student in the Institute of Space and Astronautical Science in Japan from 1983 to 1985. He worked for the National Aeronautics and Space Administration (NASA) Lewis Research Center as a National Research Council research associate in 1985. He joined the National Space Development Agency (NASDA) of Japan in

1985 and has been working in the Japanese manned space program since then. He conducted research on microgravity fluid dynamics at the University of Colorado from 1987 to 1988, and at National Aerospace Laboratory in Japan in 1989 as a visiting scientist. In 1992, he served as a backup payload specialist for the Spacelab Japan mission (STS-47). In 1994, he worked as a project scientist on the International Microgravity Laboratory 2 mission (STS-65).

NASA EXPERIENCE: Dr. Doi was selected by NASDA in 1985. He participated in payload specialist training from 1990 to 1992 in preparation for the Spacelab Japan mission. He reported to the Johnson Space Center in March 1995. On completing a year of training and evaluation he was assigned technical duties in the Vehicle Systems/Operations Branch of the Astronaut Office. Dr. Doi was a mission specialist on STS-87 (November 19 to December 5, 1997) and is the first Japanese astronaut to perform an EVA (spacewalk). In completing his first mission, Dr. Doi logged 376 hours and 34 minutes in space, including 2 spacewalks totaling 12 hours and 43 minutes.

SPACE FLIGHT EXPERIENCE: STS-87 was the fourth U.S Microgravity Payload flight and focused on experiments designed to study how the weightless environment of space affects various physical processes, and on observations of the Sun's outer atmospheric layers. Dr. Doi and Navy Captain Scott performed two EVA's (spacewalks). The first, a 7 hour and 43 minute spacewalk featured the manual capture of a Spartan satellite, in addition to testing EVA tools and procedures for future Space Station assembly. The second spacewalk lasted 5 hours and also featured space station assembly tests. The mission was accomplished in 252 Earth orbits, traveling 6.5 million miles in 376 hours and 34 minutes.

NAME: Brian Duffy (Colonel, USAF)
NASA Astronaut

PERSONAL DATA: Born June 20, 1953, in Boston, Massachusetts. Married to the former Janet M. Helms of West Lafayette, Indiana. They have two children. He enjoys golf, running, and reading. His mother, Mrs. Anne C. Duffy, resides in Hingham, Massachusetts. His father, Mr. Daniel E. Duffy, is deceased. Her father, John J. Helms, resides in Ft. Myers, Florida. Her Mother, Mary Helms, is deceased.

EDUCATION: Graduated from Rockland High School, Rockland, Massachusetts, in 1971; received a bachelor of science degree in mathematics from the United States Air Force (USAF) Academy in 1975, and a master of science degree in systems management from the University of Southern California in 1981.

ORGANIZATIONS: Member of the United States Air Force Academy Association of Graduates, the Air Force Association, and the Association of Space Explorers.

SPECIAL HONORS: Distinguished Graduate of USAF Undergraduate Pilot Training where he was awarded the UPT Flying Training Award. Distinguished Graduate of USAF Test Pilot School Class 82B. Awarded the Distinguished Flying Cross, Defense Meritorious Service Medal, Defense Superior Service Medal, Air Force Meritorious Service Medal, Air Force Commendation Medal, and NASA Space Flight Medals.

EXPERIENCE: Duffy graduated from the USAF Academy in 1975. He completed Undergraduate Pilot Training at Columbus Air Force Base, Mississippi, in 1976, and was selected to fly the F-15. He was stationed at Langley Air Force Base, Virginia, until 1979. At the end of 1979 he transferred to Kadena Air Base, Okinawa, Japan. He flew F-15's there until 1982 when he was selected to attend the U.S. Air Force Test Pilot School. Following graduation, he served as the Director of F-15 Tests at Eglin Air Force Base, Florida. He has logged over 5,000 hours of flight time in more than 25 different aircraft.

NASA EXPERIENCE: Selected by NASA in June 1985, Duffy became an astronaut in July 1986. Since then, he has participated in the development and testing of displays, flight crew procedures, and computer software to be used on Shuttle flights. He served as spacecraft communicator (CAPCOM) in Mission Control during numerous Space Shuttle missions. He also served as Assistant Director (Technical) and as Deputy Director (Acting) of the Johnson Space Center. In this role he assisted the Center Director in the direction and management of JSC's resources, functions, programs, and projects assigned to the Center. A veteran of four space flights, he has logged a total of 40 days, 17 hours, 34 minutes and 59 seconds in space. Duffy was the pilot on STS-45 Atlantis (March 24 to April 2, 1992), the first of the ATLAS series of missions to address the atmosphere and its interaction with the Sun. He also was the pilot on STS-57 Endeavour (June 21 to July 1, 1993). Mission highlights included retrieval of the European Retrievable Carrier with the Shuttle's robotic arm, a spacewalk by two crew members, and an assortment of experiments in the first flight of the Spacehab middeck augmentation module. Duffy next commanded a six-man crew on STS-72 Endeavour (January 11-20, 1996). During the 9-day flight the crew retrieved the Space Flyer Unit (launched from Japan 10-months earlier), deployed and retrieved the OAST-Flyer, and conducted two spacewalks to demonstrate and evaluate techniques to be used in the assembly of the International Space Station. Most recently, Duffy commanded a crew of seven on STS-92 Discovery (October 11-24, 2000). During the 13-day flight, the seven member crew attached the Z1 Truss and Pressurized Mating Adapter 3 to the International Space Station using Discovery's robotic arm and performed four space walks to configure these elements. This expansion of the ISS opened the door for future assembly missions and prepared the station for its first resident crew.

NAME: Bonnie J. Dunbar (Ph.D.)
NASA Astronaut

PERSONAL DATA: Born March 3, 1949, in Sunnyside, Washington.

EDUCATION: Graduated from Sunnyside High School, Sunnyside, Washington, in 1967; received bachelor of science and master of science degrees in ceramic engineering from the University of Washington in 1971 and 1975, respectively; and a doctorate in Mechanical/Biomedical Engineering from the University of Houston, 1983.

ORGANIZATIONS: Member of the American Ceramic Society (ACS), the National Institute of Ceramic Engineers (NICE), Keramos Honorary, the Society of Biomedical Engineering, American Association for the Advancement of Science, Tau Beta Pi, Materials Research Society (MRS); Board of Directors, Arnold Air Society and Angel Flight, International Academy of Astronautics (IAF), Experimental Aircraft Association (EAA), Society of Women Engineers (SWE), Association of Space Explorers (ASE).

SPECIAL HONORS: American Ceramics Society James I. Mueller Award, Cocoa Beach, Florida. (2000). Inducted into the Women in Technology International (WITI) Hall of Fame in 2000, one of five women in the world so honored. Selected as one of the top 20 women in technology in Houston, Texas (2000). NASA Space Flight Medals (1985, 1990, 1992, 1995 and 1998). Superior

Accomplishment Award (1997). Member, National Science Foundation (NSF) Engineering Advisory Board, 1993 - present. NASA Exceptional Achievement Medal(1996). NASA Outstanding Leadership Award (1993). Fellow of American Ceramic Society (1993). Design News Engineering Achievement Award (1993). IEEE Judith Resnik Award (1993). Society of Women Engineers Resnik Challenger Medal (1993). Boeing Corporation Pathfinder Award (1992). AAES National Engineering Award (1992). NASA Exceptional Service Award (1991). University of Houston Distinguished Engineering Alumna (1991). M.R.S. President's Award (1990). ACS Schwaltzwalder P.A.C.E. Award (1990). University of Washington Engineering Alumni Achievement (1989). NASA Exceptional Service Medal (1988). ACS Life Membership (1986). General Jimmy Doolittle Fellow of the Aerospace Education Foundation (1986). Evergreen Safety Council Public Service in Space Award (1986). American Ceramic Society (ACS) Greaves-Walker Award (1985). Rockwell International Engineer of the Year in 1978. Graduated Cum Laude from the University of Washington in 1975.

EXPERIENCE: Following graduation in 1971, Dr. Dunbar worked for Boeing Computer Services for two years as a systems analyst. From 1973 to 1975, she conducted research for her master's thesis in the field of mechanisms and kinetics of ionic diffusion in sodium beta-alumina. In 1975, she was invited to participate in research at Harwell Laboratories in Oxford, England, as a visiting scientist. Her work there involved the wetting behavior of liquids on solid substrates. Following her work in England, she accepted a senior research engineer position with Rockwell International Space Division in Downey, California. Her responsibilities there included developing equipment and processes for the manufacture of the Space Shuttle thermal protection system in Palmdale, California. She also represented Rockwell International as a member of the Dr. Kraft Ehricke evaluation committee on prospective space industrialization concepts. Dr. Dunbar completed her doctorate at the University of Houston in Houston, Texas. Her multi-disciplinary dissertation (materials science and physiology) involved evaluating the effects of simulated space flight on bone strength and fracture toughness. These results were correlated to alterations in hormonal and metabolic activity. Dr. Dunbar has served as an adjunct assistant professor in Mechanical Engineering at the University of Houston. She is a private pilot with over 200 hours in single engine land aircraft, has logged more than 700 hours flying time in T-38 jets as co-pilot, and has over 100 hours as co-pilot in a Cessna Citation Jet.

NASA EXPERIENCE: Dr. Dunbar accepted a position as a payload officer/flight controller at the Lyndon B. Johnson Space Center in 1978. She served as a guidance and navigation officer/flight controller for the Skylab reentry mission in 1979 and was subsequently designated project officer/payload officer for the integration of several Space Shuttle payloads. Dr. Dunbar became a NASA astronaut in August 1981. Her technical assignments have included assisting in the verification of Shuttle flight software at the Shuttle Avionics Integration Laboratory (SAIL), serving as a member of the Flight Crew Equipment Control Board, participation as a member of the Astronaut Office Science Support Group, supporting operational development of the remote manipulator system (RMS). She has served as chief of the Mission Development Branch, as the Astronaut Office interface for "secondary" payloads, and as lead for the Science Support Group. In 1993, Dr. Dunbar served as Deputy Associate Administrator, Office of Life and Microgravity Sciences, NASA Headquarters, Washington, D.C. In February 1994, she traveled to Star City, Russia, where she spent 13-months training as a back-up crew member for a 3-month flight on the Russian Space Station, Mir. In March 1995, she was certified by the Russian Gagarin Cosmonaut Training Center as qualified to fly on long duration Mir Space Station flights. From October 1995 to November 1996, she was detailed to the NASA JSC Mission Operations Directorate as Assistant Director where she was responsible for chairing the International Space Station Training Readiness Reviews, and facilitating Russian/

American operations and training strategies. Currently, Dr. Dunbar serves as Assistant Director to the NASA Johnson Space Center (JSC) with a focus on University Research. A veteran of five space flights, Dr. Dunbar has logged more than 1,208 hours (50 days) in space. She served as a mission specialist on STS 61-A in 1985, STS-32 in 1990, and STS-71 in 1995, and was the Payload Commander on STS-50 in 1992, and STS-89 in 1998.

SPACE FLIGHT EXPERIENCE: STS 61-A Challenger (October 30-November 6, 1985), was the West German D-1 Spacelab mission. It was the first to carry eight crew members, the largest to fly in space, and was also the first in which payload activities were controlled from outside the United States. More than 75 scientific experiments were completed in the areas of physiological sciences, materials science, biology, and navigation. During the flight, Dr. Dunbar was responsible for operating Spacelab and its subsystems and performing a variety of experiments. Her mission training included six months of experiment training in Germany, France, Switzerland, and The Netherlands. STS 61-A launched from the Kennedy Space Center, Florida, and returned to land at Edwards Air Force Base, California. Mission duration was 7 days, 44 minutes 51 seconds, traveling 2.5 million miles in 111 orbits of the Earth. STS-32 Columbia (January 9-20, 1990), launched from the Kennedy Space Center, Florida, and returned to a night landing at Edwards Air Base in California. During the flight, the crew successfully deployed the Syncom IV-F5 satellite, and retrieved the 21,400-pound Long Duration Exposure Facility (LDEF) using the RMS. They also operated a variety of middeck experiments including the Microgravity Disturbance Experiment (MDE) using the Fluids Experiment Apparatus (FEA), Protein Crystal Growth (PCG), American Flight Echocardiograph (AFE), Latitude/Longitude Locator (L3), Mesoscale Lightning Experiment (MLE), Characterization of Neurospora Circadian Rhythms (CNCR),and the IMAX Camera. Dr. Dunbar was principal investigator for the MDE/FEA Experiment. Additionally, numerous medical test objectives, including in-flight lower body negative pressure (LBNP), in-flight aerobic exercise and muscle performance were conducted to evaluate human adaptation to extended duration missions. Mission duration was 10 days, 21 hours, 01 minute, 38 seconds, traveling 4.5 million miles in 173 orbits of the Earth. STS-50 Columbia (June 25 to July 9, 1992). Dr. Dunbar was the Payload Commander on STS-50, the United States Microgravity Lab-1 mission which was dedicated to microgravity fluid physics and materials science. Over 30 experiments sponsored by over 100 investigators were housed in the "Spacelab" in the Shuttle's Payload Bay. A payload crew of four operated around-the-clock for 13 days performing experiments in scientific disciplines such as protein crystal growth, electronic and infrared detector crystal growth, surface tension physics, zeolite crystal growth, and human physiology. Mission duration was 13 days, 19 hours, 30 minutes and 4 seconds, traveling 5.7 million miles in 221 orbits of the Earth. STS-71 Atlantis (June 27 to July 7, 1995), was the first Space Shuttle mission to dock with the Russian Space Station Mir, and involved an exchange of crews. The Atlantis was modified to carry a docking system compatible with the Russian Mir Space Station. Dr. Dunbar served as MS-3 on this flight which also carried a Spacelab module in the payload bay in which the crew performed medical evaluations on the returning Mir crew. These evaluations included ascertaining the effects of weightlessness on the cardio/vascular system, the bone/muscle system, the immune system, and the cardio/pulmonary system. Mission duration was 9 days, 19 hours, 23 minutes and 8 seconds, traveling 4.1 million miles in 153 orbits of the earth. STS-89 Endeavour (January 22-31, 1998), was the eighth Shuttle-Mir docking mission during which the crew transferred more than 9,000 pounds of scientific equipment, logistical hardware and water from Space Shuttle Endeavour to Mir. In the fifth and last exchange of a U.S. astronaut, STS-89 delivered Andy Thomas to Mir and returned with David Wolf. Mission duration was 8 days, 19 hours and 47 seconds, traveling 3.6 million miles in 138 orbits of the Earth. Dr. Dunbar was the Payload Commander, responsible for all payload activities including the conduct of 23 technology and science experiments.

NAME: Pedro Duque
ESA Astronaut

PERSONAL DATA: Born March 14, 1963 in Madrid, Spain. Enjoys diving, swimming and cycling.

EDUCATION: Received a degree in Aeronautical Engineering from the Escuela Técnica Superior de Ingenieros Aeronáuticos, Universidad Politécnica, Madrid, Spain, in 1986.

SPECIAL HONORS: Awarded the "Order of Friendship" by President Yeltsin of the Russian Federation (March 1995).

EXPERIENCE: During Duque's studies, he worked on a flight simulator project in the laboratory of Flight Mechanics on a fellowship, and on the computation of environmental torques on spacecraft, under ESA contract. He joined GMV (Grupo Mecánica del Vuelo) in 1986, and in the same year he became the technical leader in a helicopter rotor simulation project. At the end of 1986, Duque was sent as contracted staff to ESA's European Space Operations Center (ESOC) in Darmstadt Germany, to work within the Precise Orbit Determination Group. From 1986 to 1992, he worked on the development of models for orbit determination, algorithms and implementation of orbit computation software. He was also part of the Flight Control Team (Orbit Determination) of ESA's ERS-1 and EURECA satellites. In May 1992, Duque was selected to join the Astronaut Corps of the European Space Agency (ESA) based at the European Astronauts Centre (EAC) in Cologne, Germany. In 1992 he completed the Introductory Training Program at EAC and a four-week training program at TsPK (the Russian Astronauts Training Centre) in Star City, Russia, with a view to future ESA-Russian collaboration on the Mir Space Station. From January to July 1993, he performed Basic Training at EAC. In August 1993, Duque returned to TsPK to train in preparation for the joint ESA-Russian EUROMIR 94 mission. Training led to qualification as Research Astronaut for Soyuz and Mir. In May 1994, he was selected as member of crew 2 (backup) joining Yuri Gidzenko and Sergeij Avdeev. During the EUROMIR 94 mission which took place from October 3, 1994 to November 4, 1994, Duque was the prime Crew Interface Coordinator in the Russian Mission Control Centre (TsUP). In January 1995, Duque began an extended training course on Russian space systems in Star City and supported the second joint ESA-Russian mission, EUROMIR 95.

NASA EXPERIENCE: In May, 1995, Duque was selected as an Alternate Payload Specialist astronaut for the Life and Microgravity Spacelab (LMS) mission, STS-78, flown in June-July, 1996. During this seventeen day mission Duque worked with the Crew Interface Coordinators as the interface between the investigators on ground and the crew onboard Columbia for all experiment related issues. ESA had five major facilities on the flight and was responsible for more than half of the experiments performed. In July 1996 he was selected by ESA to attend NASA Astronaut Candidate Training. Duque reported to the Johnson Space Center in August 1996 for two years of training and evaluation. He was initially assigned to the Computer Support Branch of the Astronaut Office, supporting Space Shuttle and International Space Station Programs and advanced technology development. In 1998 he flew as a mission specialist on STS-95 and haslogged over 213 hours in space.

SPACE FLIGHT EXPERIECE: STS-95 Discovery (October 29 to November 7, 1998) was a 9-day mission during which the crew supported a variety of research payloads including deployment of the Spartan solar-observing spacecraft, the Hubble Space Telescope Orbital Systems Test Platform, and investigations on space flight and the aging process.

NAME: Léopold Eyharts (Colonel, French Air Force)
ESA Astronaut (Mission Specialist Candidate)

PERSONAL DATA: Born April 28, 1957, in Biarritz, France. He is married and has one child His hobbies are reading, computers and sport.

EDUCATION: Graduated as an engineer from the French Air Force Academy of Salon-de-Provence in 1979.

SPECIAL HONORS: Léopold Eyharts has been decorated with the French Légion d'Honneur, the Ordre National du Mérite and Médaille d'Outre Mer, and the Russian medals of Friendship and Courage.

EXPERIENCE: He joined the French Air Force Academy of Salon-de-Provence in 1977 and was graduated as an aeronautical engineer in 1979. In 1980, he became a fighter pilot and was assigned to an operational Jaguar squadron in Istres Air Force Base (France). In 1985, he was assigned as a wing commander in Saint-Dizier Air Force base. In 1988, he was graduated as a test pilot in the French test pilot school (EPNER) and was assigned to Bretigny flight test center near Paris. He then flew on different types of military and civilian aircraft including Mirage 2000, Alpha-jet, Mirage 3, Caravelle, C-160 mainly involved in radar and equipment testing. He has logged 3500 flight hours as a fighter and test pilot in 40 different aircraft types, 21 parachute jumps including one ejection. In 1990, Léopold Eyharts was selected as an astronaut by CNES (Center National d'Etudes Spatiales) and assigned to support the Hermes spaceplane program managed by the Hermes Crew office in Toulouse. He became also one of the test pilots in charge of the CNES parabolic flights program, an experimental aircraft (Caravelle) managed by Bretigny Flight Test Center to provide a microgravity laboratory to the scientific community. In 1994, he was in charge of parabolic flight testing of the Caravelle replacement, an Airbus A300 which become operational in 1995. In 1992, Léopold Eyharts participated in the second European Space Agency astronaut selection. At the end of the same year, he took part in an ESA evaluation of Russian "Bouran" Space Shuttle training in Moscow, where he flew in the Tupolev 154 Bouran in-flight simulator. He also participated in two additional short-duration spaceflight training courses in Star City, Moscow--6-weeks in 1991 and 2-weeks in 1993. Léopold Eyharts was assigned to full spaceflight training in January 1995. He trained as a back-up cosmonaut for the Cassiopeia French-Russian space mission, which took place in August 1996. He was the prime cosmonaut for the follow-on CNES scientific space mission called "Pégase." He flew in the Mir Space Station in February 1998. During the three week Pégase mission he performed various French experiments in the area of medical research, neuroscience, biology, fluid physics and technology. In completing his first space mission, he has logged 20 days, 18 hours and 20 minutes in space.

NASA EXPERIENCE: In August 1998, Léopold Eyharts was assigned by the European Space Agency to train at NASA's Johnson Space Center in Houston, Texas. As part of the international astronauts of the 1998 class, he attended Astronaut Candidate Training which included orientation briefings and tours, numerous scientific and technical briefings, intensive instruction in Shuttle and International Space Station systems, physiological training and ground school to prepare for T-38 flight training, as well as learning water and wilderness survival techniques. Léopold Eyharts is currently assigned to the Astronaut Office Space Station Operations Branch. He will serve in technical assignments until assigned to a space flight.

NAME: Christopher J. Ferguson (Commander, USN)
NASA Astronaut (Pilot Candidate)

PERSONAL DATA: Born September 1, 1961 in Philadelphia, Pennsylvania. Married to the former Sandra A. Cabot. They have three children. Recreational interests include golf, woodworking, running, music, and weight lifting. His mother, Mary Ann Pietras and stepfather, Norman Pietras, reside in Bensalem, Pennsylvania. Sandra's mother, Trudy, resides in Norristown, PA. His father, Ian A. Ferguson, is deceased.

EDUCATION: Graduated from Archbishop Ryan High School, Philadelphia, Pennsylvania, 1979; received a bachelor of science degree in Mechanical Engineering from Drexel University, 1984 and a master of science in Aeronautical Engineering from the Naval Postgraduate School, 1991.

ORGANIZATIONS: Society of Experimental Test Pilots, Pi Tau Sigma Engineering Honor Society

AWARDS: Navy Strike/Flight Air Medal, Navy Commendation Medal (3), Navy Achievement Medal, various other service awards/citations.

EXPERIENCE: Ferguson was commissioned from the NROTC program after completion of a 5 year cooperative education curriculum at Drexel University. He was temporarily assigned to the Naval Test Pilot School at Naval Air Station (NAS) Patuxent River, Maryland prior to commencing flight school in Pensacola, Florida in November 1984. Following flight training in Florida and Texas, he received his Navy wings and was ordered to the F-14 replacement training squadron in Virginia Beach, Virginia, where, after a nine month period of instruction, he joined the 'Red Rippers' of VF-11. With VF-11 he made deployments to the North Atlantic, Mediterranean and Indian Ocean on board the USS Forrestal (CV-59). While with VF-11 he also attended the Navy Fighter Weapon School (TOPGUN). He was selected for the Naval Postgraduate/Test Pilot School program in 1989 and graduated with class 101. From July 1992 through June 1994 he was assigned to the Ordnance Branch of the Strike Aircraft Test Directorate at NAS Patuxent River. There he served as the project officer for the F-14D weapon separation program where he became the first to release numerous air-to-ground stores from both the A and D model of the Tomcat. In July 1994, he was chosen to instruct at the Naval Test Pilot School which he did so until July 1995. After a brief retraining period he joined the 'Checkmates' of VF-211 where he completed a deployment to the Western Pacific/Persian Gulf aboard the Nimitz (CVN-68) in support Operation Southern Watch and contingency operations off the coast of Taiwan. He briefly served as the F-14 Class Desk Officer for the Commander Naval Air Force, Atlantic Fleet prior to his selection to the space program.

NASA EXPERIENCE: Selected by NASA in June 1998, Ferguson reported to the Johnson Space Center in August 1998. Having completed two years of training and evaluation, he is qualified for flight assignment as a pilot. Currently, he is assigned technical duties in the Astronaut Office Spacecraft Systems/Operations Branch involving the Shuttle Main Engine, External Tank, Solid Rocket Boosters and Shuttle Software.

NAME: Edward Michael "Mike" Fincke (Major, USAF)
NASA Astronaut

PERSONAL DATA: Born March 14, 1967 in Pittsburgh, Pennsylvania, but considers Emsworth, Pennsylvania to be his hometown. Married to the former Renita Saikia of Houston, Texas. He is the oldest of 9 children. Enjoys hiking, flying, travel, Geology, Astronomy, learning new languages, and reading. Major Fincke is conversant in Japanese and Russian. His parents, Edward and Alma Fincke reside in Emsworth, Pennsylvania. Renita's parents, Rupesh and Probha Saikia formerly of Assam, India reside in Huntsville, Alabama.

EDUCATION: Graduated from Sewickley Academy, Sewickley, Pennsylvania in 1985. He attended the Massachusetts Institute of Technology (MIT) on an Air Force ROTC scholarship and graduated in 1989 with a bachelor of science in Aeronautics and Astronautics as well as a bachelor of science in Earth, Atmospheric and Planetary Sciences. He then received a master of science in Aeronautics and Astronautics from Stanford University in 1990.

ORGANIZATIONS: Geological Society of America (GSA).

SPECIAL HONORS: Recipient of two United States Air Force Commendation Medals, the United States Air Force Achievement Medal, and various unit and service awards. Distinguished graduate from the United States Air Force ROTC, Squadron Officer School and Test Pilot School Programs. Recipient of the United States Air Force Test Pilot School Colonel Ray Jones Award as the top Flight Test Engineer/Flight Test Navigator in class 93B.

EXPERIENCE: Major Mike Fincke graduated from MIT in 1989, and immediately attended a Summer exchange program with the Moscow Aviation Institute in the former Soviet Union, where he studied Cosmonautics. After graduation from Stanford University in 1990, Major Fincke entered the United States Air Force where he was assigned to the Air Force Space and Missiles Systems Center, Los Angeles Air Force Base, California. There he served as a Space Systems Engineer and a Space Test Engineer. In 1994, upon completion of the United States Air Force Test Pilot School, Edwards Air Force Base, California, Major Fincke joined the 39th Flight Test Squadron, Eglin Air Force Base, Florida, where he served as a Flight Test Engineer working on a variety of flight test programs, flying the F-16 and F-15 aircraft. In January of 1996, he reported to the Gifu Test Center, Gifu Air Base, Japan where he was the United States Flight Test Liaison to the Japanese/United States XF-2 fighter program. Major Fincke has over 750 flight hours in more than 30 different aircraft types.

NASA EXPERIENCE: Selected by NASA in April 1996, Major Fincke reported to the Johnson Space Center in August 1996. Having completed two years of training and evaluation, he was assigned technical duties in the Astronaut Office Station Operations Branch serving as an International Space Station Spacecraft Communicator (ISS CAPCOM), a member of the Crew Test Support Team in Russia and as the ISS crew procedures team lead. In July 1999, Major Fincke was assigned as backup crewmember for the International Space Station Expedition 4 crew, which is due to launch in 2001. This assignment will be followed by a subsequent assignment to a prime International Space Station crew.

NAME: Anna L. Fisher, (M.D.)
NASA Astronaut

PERSONAL DATA: Born August 24, 1949, in New York City, New York, but considers San Pedro, California, to be her hometown. Married to Dr. William F. Fisher of Dallas, Texas. They have two children. She enjoys snow and water skiing, jogging, flying, scuba diving, reading, photography, and spending time with her daughters. Her mother, Mrs. Riley F. Tingle, resides in San Pedro, California. Father, deceased, July 3, 1982. His mother, Mrs. Russell F. Fisher, resides in Winter Park, Florida. His father is deceased.

EDUCATION: Graduated from San Pedro High School, San Pedro, California, in 1967; received a bachelor of science in Chemistry and a doctor of Medicine from the University of California, Los Angeles, in 1971 and 1976, respectively; completed a 1-year internship at Harbor General Hospital in Torrance, California, in 1977; received a master of science in Chemistry from the University of California, Los Angeles, in 1987.

SPECIAL HONORS: Awarded a National Science Foundation Undergraduate Research Fellowship in 1970, 1971. Graduated from UCLA cum laude and with honors in chemistry. Recipient of: NASA Space Flight Medal; Lloyd's of London Silver Medal for Meritorious Salvage Operations; Mother of the Year Award 1984; UCLA Professional Achievement Award, UCLA Medical Professional Achievement Award. NASA Exceptional Service Medal, 1999.

EXPERIENCE: After graduating from UCLA in 1971, Dr. Fisher spent a year in graduate school in chemistry at UCLA working in the field of x-ray crystallographic studies of metallocarbonanes. She co-authored 3 publications relating to these studies for the Journal of Inorganic Chemistry. She began medical school at UCLA in 1972 and, following graduation in 1976, commenced a 1-year internship at Harbor General Hospital in Torrance, California. After completing that internship, she specialized in emergency medicine and worked in several hospitals in the Los Angeles area.

NASA EXPERIENCE: Dr. Fisher was selected as an astronaut candidate by NASA in January 1978. In August 1979, she completed a one year training and evaluation period, making her eligible for assignment as a mission specialist on future Space Shuttle flight crews. Following the one-year basic training program Dr. Fisher's early NASA assignments (pre-STS-1 through STS-4) included the following: Crew representative to support development and testing of the Remote Manipulator System (RMS); Crew representative to support development and testing of payload bay door contingency EVA procedures, the extra-small Extravehicular Mobility Unit (EMU), and contingency on-orbit TPS repair hardware and procedures; Verification of flight software at the Shuttle Avionics Integration Laboratory (SAIL) -- in that capacity she reviewed test requirements and procedures for ascent, on-orbit, and RMS software verification -- and served as a crew evaluator for verification and development testing for STS-2, 3 and 4. For STS-5 through STS-7 Dr. Fisher was assigned as a crew representative to support vehicle integrated testing and payload testing at KSC. In addition, Dr. Fisher supported each Orbital Flight Test (STS 1-4) launch and landing (at either a prime or backup site) as a physician in the rescue helicopters, and provided both medical & operational inputs to the development of rescue procedures. Dr. Fisher was also an on-orbit CAPCOM for the STS-9 mission. Dr. Fisher was a mission specialist on STS-51A which launched from Kennedy Space Center, Florida, on November 8, 1984. She was accompanied by Captain Frederick (Rick) Hauck (spacecraft commander), Captain David M. Walker (pilot), and fellow mission specialists, Dr. Joseph P. Allen, and Commander Dale H. Gardner. This was the second flight of the orbiter Discovery.

During the mission the crew deployed two satellites, Canada's Anik D-2 (Telesat H) and Hughes' LEASAT-1 (Syncom IV-1), and operated the Radiation Monitoring Equipment (RME) device, and the 3M Company's Diffusive Mixing of Organic Solutions (DMOS) experiment. In the first space salvage mission in history the crew also retrieved for return to earth the Palapa B-2 and Westar VI satellites. STS-51A completed 127 orbits of the Earth before landing at Kennedy Space Center, Florida, on November 16, 1984. With the completion of her first flight, Dr. Fisher has logged a total of 192 hours in space. Dr. Fisher was assigned as a mission specialist on STS-61H prior to the Challenger accident. Following the accident she worked as the Deputy of the Mission Development Branch of the Astronaut Office, and as the astronaut office representative for Flight Data File issues. In that capacity she served as the crew representative on the Crew Procedures Change Board. Dr. Fisher served on the Astronaut Selection Board for the 1987 class of astronauts. Dr. Fisher also served in the Space Station Support Office where she worked part-time in the Space Station Operations Branch. She was the crew representative supporting space station development in the areas of training, operations concepts, and the health maintenance facility. Dr. Fisher returned to the Astronaut Office in 1996 after an extended leave of absence to raise her family (1989-1996). When she first returned to the Astronaut Office, she was assigned to the Operations Planning Branch to work on the Operational Flight Data File (procedures) and training issues in support of the International Space Station. She served as the Branch Chief of the Operations Planning Branch from June 1997-June 1998. Following a reorganization of the Astronaut office, she was assigned as the Deputy for Operations/Training of the Space Station Branch from June 1998-June 1999. In that capacity, she had oversight responsibility for Astronaut Office inputs to the Space Station Program on issues regarding operations, procedures, and training for the ISS. She currently serves as the Chief of the Space Station Branch of the Astronaut Office and has oversight responsibility for 40-50 astronauts and support engineers. In that capacity, she coordinates all astronaut inputs to the Space Station Program Office on issues regarding the design, development, and testing of space station hardware. Additionally, she coordinates all Astronaut Office inputs to Space Station operations, procedures, and training and works with the International Partners to negotiate common design requirements and standards for displays and procedures. As Chief of the Space Station Branch, she serves as the Astronaut Office representative on numerous Space Station Program Boards and Multilateral Boards. Following completion of this assignment, she looks forward to assignment as either a Space Shuttle crewmember on a Space Station assembly mission or as a crewmember aboard the International Space Station.

NAME: C. Michael Foale (Ph.D.)
NASA Astronaut

PERSONAL DATA: Born January 6, 1957, in Louth, England, but considers Cambridge, England, to be his hometown. Married to the former Rhonda R. Butler of Louisville, Kentucky. They have two children. He enjoys many outdoor activities, particularly wind surfing. Private flying, soaring, and project scuba diving have been his other major sporting interests. He also enjoys exploring theoretical physics and writing children's software on a personal computer. His parents, Colin and Mary Foale, reside in Cambridge, England. Her parents, Reed & Dorothy Butler, reside in Louisville, Kentucky.

EDUCATION: Graduated from Kings School, Canterbury, in 1975. He attended the University of Cambridge, Queens' College, receiving a bachelor of arts degree in Physics, Natural Sciences Tripos, with 1st class honors, in 1978. While at Queens' College, he completed his doctorate in Laboratory Astrophysics at Cambridge University in 1982.

EXPERIENCE: While a postgraduate at Cambridge University, Foale participated in the organization and execution of scientific scuba diving projects. Pursuing a career in the U.S. Space Program, Foale moved to Houston, Texas, to work on Space Shuttle navigation problems at McDonnell Douglas Aircraft Corporation. In June 1983, Foale joined NASA Johnson Space Center in the payload operations area of the Mission Operations Directorate. In his capacity as payload officer in the Mission Control Center, he was responsible for payload operations on Space Shuttle missions STS-51G, 51-I, 61-B and 61-C.

NASA EXPERIENCE: Selected as an astronaut candidate by NASA in June 1987. Before his first flight he flew the Shuttle Avionics Integration Laboratory (SAIL) simulator to provide verification and testing of the Shuttle flight software, and later developed crew rescue and integrated operations for International Space Station Alpha. Foale has served as Deputy Chief of the Mission Development Branch in the Astronaut Office, and Head of the Astronaut Office Science Support Group. In preparation for a long-duration flight on the Russian Space Station Mir, Foale trained at the Cosmonaut Training Center, Star City, Russia. A veteran of five space flights, Foale has logged over 168 days in space including three space walks totaling 18 hours and 49 minutes. He was a mission specialist on STS-45, STS-56, STS-63 and STS-103, and served as Board Engineer 2 on Mir 24 (ascent on STS-84 and return on STS-86). He currently serves as Chief of the Astronaut Office Expedition Corps, while continuing his duties as Assistant Director (Technical), Johnson Space Center.

SPACEFLIGHT EXPERIENCE: STS-45 (March 24 to April 2, 1992) was the first of the ATLAS series of missions to address the atmosphere and its interaction with the Sun. STS-56 (April 9-17, 1993) carried ATLAS-2 and the SPARTAN retrievable satellite which made observations of the solar corona. STS-63 (February 2-11, 1995) was the first rendezvous with the Russian Space Station Mir. During the flight he made a space walk (extravehicular activity) for 4 hours, 39 minutes, evaluating the effects of extremely cold conditions on his spacesuit, as well as moving the 2800-pound Spartan satellite as part of a mass handling experiment. Foale next spent 4-½ months aboard the Russian Space Station Mir. He launched with the crew of STS-84 aboard Space Shuttle Atlantis on May 15, 1997. Following docking, he joined the crew aboard Mir on May 17, 1997. Foale spent the following 134 days conducting various science experiments and helping the crew resolve and repair numerous malfunctioning systems. On September 6, 1997 he and Commander Anatoly Solovyev conducted a 6-hour EVA to inspect damage to the station's Spektr module caused by the June 25 collision with a Progress resupply ship. Foale returned on October 6, 1997 with the crew of STS-86 aboard Space Shuttle Atlantis. Most recently he served aboard STS-103 (December 19-27, 1999), an 8-day mission during which the crew successfully installed new instruments and upgraded systems on the Hubble Space Telescope (HST). During an 8 hours and 10 minute EVA, Foale and Nicollier replaced the telescope's main computer and Fine Guidance Sensor. The STS-103 mission was accomplished in 120 Earth orbits, traveling 3.2 million miles in 191 hours and 11 minutes.

NAME: Michael J. Foreman (Commander, USN)
NASA Astronaut (Mission Specialist Candidate)

PERSONAL DATA: Born March 29, 1957 in Columbus, Ohio. His hometown is Wadsworth, Ohio. Married to the former Lorrie Lee Dancer of Oklahoma City, Oklahoma. They have three children. Recreational interests include golf, running, skiing, home repair/improvement and spending time with his family. His mother, Nancy C. Foreman, resides in Wadsworth, Ohio. His father, James W. Foreman, is deceased. Her parents, Jim and Pat Dancer, reside in Tulsa, Oklahoma.

EDUCATION: Graduated from Wadsworth High School, Wadsworth, Ohio in 1975; received a bachelor of science degree in aerospace engineering from the U.S. Naval Academy in 1979 and a master of science degree in aeronautical engineering from the U.S. Naval Postgraduate School in 1986.

ORGANIZATIONS: Society of Experimental Test Pilots, Association of Naval Aviation, United States Naval Academy Alumni Association.

AWARDS: Meritorious Service Medal, Navy Commendation Medal; Navy Achievement Medal and various other service awards. NASA Certificate of Recognition for Technical Brief (1987).

SPECIAL HONORS: Graduated with Distinction, U.S. Naval Postgraduate School; Admiral William Adger Moffett Aeronautics Award, U.S. Naval Postgraduate School; Distinguished Graduate, U.S. Naval Test Pilot School; Empire Test Pilots School-sponsored award for best final report (DT-IIA), U.S. Naval Test Pilot School.

EXPERIENCE: Foreman graduated from Annapolis in May 1979 and was commissioned as an Ensign in the United States Navy. He went on to pilot training in Pensacola, Florida and Corpus Christi, Texas and was designated a Naval Aviator in January 1981. After initial training in the P-3 Orion aircraft in Jacksonville, Florida, he was assigned to Patrol Squadron Twenty-Three at NAS Brunswick, Maine. He made deployments to Rota, Spain; Keflavik, Iceland; Lajes, Azores; Sigonella, Sicily; Bermuda and Panama. Following this tour he attended the U.S. Naval Postgraduate School in Monterey, California where he earned a Master of Science degree in Aeronautical Engineering in 1986. As a graduate student, Foreman conducted his thesis research at the NASA Ames Research Center in Mountainview, California. Following graduation he was assigned as the Assistant Air Operations Officer in USS CORAL SEA (CV-43) homeported in Norfolk, Virginia. In addition to his Air Operations duties, he flew as an E-2 pilot with VAW-120 and VAW-127. Upon selection to the U.S. Naval Test Pilot School (USNTPS) in 1989 he moved to NAS Patuxent River, Maryland. He graduated from USNTPS in June 1990 and was then assigned to the Force Warfare Aircraft Test Directorate at Patuxent River as the P-7 Project Officer. In 1991 he was reassigned as a flight instructor and the Operations Officer at USNTPS. During his tenure there he instructed in the F-18, P-3, T-2, T-38, U-21, U-6 and X-26 glider. In 1993, Foreman was assigned to the Naval Air Systems Command in Crystal City, Virginia, first as the deputy, and then as the Class Desk Officer for the T-45 Goshawk aircraft program. Following that tour he was again assigned to NAS Patuxent River, this time as the Military Director for the Research and Engineering Group of the Naval Air Warfare Center Aircraft Division. In addition to his duties at Patuxent River, he was assigned as the Navy liaison to the Advanced Orbiter Cockpit Project at the Johnson Space Center. Foreman was working as the technical lead for the Advanced Orbiter Cockpit Project team when he was selected for the astronaut program. He has logged over 3,000 hours in more than 50 different aircraft.

NASA EXPERIENCE: Selected by NASA in June 1998, he reported for training in August 1998. Astronaut Candidate Training includes orientation briefings and tours, numerous scientific and technical briefings, intensive instruction in Shuttle and International Space Station systems, physiological training and ground school to prepare for T-38 flight training, as well as learning water and wilderness survival techniques. Foreman is currently assigned as the Astronaut Office representative on Space Station Training issues. He will serve in technical assignments until assigned to a space flight.

NAME: Patrick G. Forrester (Lieutenant Colonel, USA)
NASA Astronaut

PERSONAL DATA: Born March 31, 1957 in El Paso, Texas. Married to the former Diana Lynn Morris of Springfield, Virginia. They have two children. He enjoys baseball, running, and coaching youth sports. His parents, Colonel (ret.) Redmond V. and Patsy L. Forrester, reside in Fort Walton Beach, Florida. Her father, Colonel (ret.) Lurie J. Morris, resides in Prattville, Alabama. Her mother, Bettye Morris, is deceased.

EDUCATION: Graduated from West Springfield High School, Springfield, Virginia in 1975; received a bachelor of science degree in applied sciences and engineering from the United States Military Academy, West Point, New York, in 1979, and a master of science degree in mechanical and aerospace engineering from the University of Virginia in 1989.

ORGANIZATIONS: Society of Experimental Test Pilots; Army Aviation Association of America; American Helicopter Society; United States Military Academy Association of Graduates; West Point Society of Greater Houston.

AWARDS: Meritorious Service Medal (2nd Oak Leaf Cluster); Army Commendation Medal; Army Achievement Medal; National Defense Service Medal; Expert Infantryman Badge.

SPECIAL HONORS: The Jack Northrop Award for most outstanding presentation at the 26th Annual Society of Experimental Test Pilots Symposium (1996). The Lyndon B. Johnson Space Center Certificate of Commendation (1995).

EXPERIENCE: Forrester graduated from West Point in June 1979 and was commissioned as a Second Lieutenant in the U.S. Army. He entered the U.S. Army Aviation School in 1979 and was designated an Army aviator in September 1980. He was subsequently assigned as an instructor pilot at the Aviation School and as the Aide-de-Camp to the Deputy Commanding General of the U.S. Army Aviation Center. In 1984, he was assigned to the 25th Infantry Division (Light), Schofield Barracks, Hawaii, where he served as a platoon leader, aviation company operations officer, and an assault helicopter battalion operations officer. After completing a master of science degree at the University of Virginia in 1989, he was assigned as a flight test engineer and as the research and development coordinator with the Army Aviation Engineering Flight Activity at Edwards Air Force Base, California. In June 1992, he graduated from the U.S. Naval Test Pilot School and was designated an experimental test pilot. In 1992, he was assigned as an engineering test pilot at the U.S. Army Aviation Technical Test Center, Fort Rucker, Alabama. Other military schools include the Army Parachutist Course, U.S. Army Ranger School, the Combined Arms Services Staff School, and the Command and General Staff College. Master Army Aviator, he has logged over 3100 hours in 49 different aircraft.

NASA EXPERIENCE: Forrester was assigned to NASA at the Johnson Space Center as an aerospace engineer in July 1993. His technical assignments within the Astronaut Office Operations Development Branch have included: flight software testing with the Shuttle Avionics Integration Laboratory (SAIL); astronaut office representative for Landing/Rollout issues, Multi-function Electronic Display System (MEDS) upgrade of the Orbiter fleet, and the Portable In-flight Landing Operations Trainer (PILOT). He has also served as the crew representative for robotics development for the International Space Station.Forrester was selected as an astronaut candidate by NASA in May 1996.

Having completed two years of training and evaluation, he is qualified for flight assignment as a mission specialist. Initially, Forrester was assigned to duties at the Kennedy Space Center as a member of the astronaut support team, responsible for Shuttle prelaunch vehicle checkout, crew ingress and strap-in, and crew egress after landing. He next served as an assistant to the Director, Flight Crew Operations. Currently, Forrester is assigned to STS-105 scheduled for launch in 2001.

NAME: Michael E. Fossum
NASA Astronaut (Mission Specialist Candidate)

PERSONAL DATA: Born December 19, 1957 in Sioux Falls, South Dakota, and grew up in McAllen, Texas. Married to the former Melanie J. London. They have 4 children. He enjoys family activities, jogging, fishing, and backpacking. His mother, Patricia A. Fossum, resides in McAllen, Texas. His father, Merlyn E. Fossum, is deceased.

EDUCATION: McAllen High School, McAllen, Texas, 1976. B.S., Mechanical Engineering, Texas A&M University, 1980. M.S., Systems Engineering , Air Force Institute of Technology, 1981. M.S., Physical Science (Space Science), University of Houston-Clear Lake, 1997.

SPECIAL HONORS: Distinguished Military Graduate from Texas A&M University. Awarded the USAF Meritorious Service Medal with one Oak Leaf Cluster and various other service awards. Distinguished Graduate from the USAF Test Pilot School, Class 85A.

EXPERIENCE: Fossum received his commission in the US Air Force from Texas A&M University in May 1980. After completing his graduate work at the Air Force Institute of Technology in 1981, he was detailed to NASA-Johnson Space Center where he supported the development of Space Shuttle flight procedures. He was selected for Air Force Test Pilot School at Edwards Air Force Base, California, where he graduated in 1985. After graduation, Fossum served at Edwards AFB as a Flight Test Engineer in the F-16 Test Squadron, working on a variety of airframe, avionics, and armament development programs. From 1989 to 1992, he served as a Flight Test Manager at Detachment 3, Air Force Flight Test Center. Fossum resigned from active duty in 1992 in order to work for NASA. He has logged over 800 hours in 34 different aircraft.

NASA EXPERIENCE: In January 1993, Fossum was employed by NASA as a systems engineer. His primary responsibilities were to evaluate the Russian Soyuz spacecraft for use as an emergency escape vehicle for the new space station. Later in 1993, Fossum was selected to represent the Flight Crew Operations Directorate in an extensive redesign of the International Space Station. After this, he continued work for the crew office and Mission Operations Directorate in the area of assembly operations. In 1996, Fossum supported the Astronaut Office as a Technical Assistant for Space Shuttle, supporting design and management reviews. In 1997, he served as a Flight Test Engineer on the X-38, a prototype crew escape vehicle for the new Space Station, which is under development in-house by the Engineering Directorate at NASA-JSC and being flight tested at NASA-Dryden. Selected by NASA in June 1998, he reported for training in August 1998. Astronaut Candidate Training includes orientation briefings and tours, numerous scientific and technical briefings, intensive instruction in Shuttle and International Space Station systems, physiological training and ground school to prepare for T-38 flight training, as well as learning water and wilderness survival techniques. Fossum is currently assigned to the Astronaut Office Space Station Operations Branch. He will serve in technical assignments until assigned to a space flight.

NAME: Stephen N. Frick (Lieutenant Commander, USN)
NASA Astronaut

PERSONAL DATA: Born September 30, 1964, in Pittsburgh, Pennsylvania. Married. He enjoys skiing, biking, hiking, and camping.

EDUCATION: Graduated from Richland High School, Gibsonia, Pennsylvania in 1982; received a bachelor of science degree in aerospace engineering from the US Naval Academy in 1986; master of science degree in aeronautical engineering from the U.S. Naval Postgraduate School in 1994.

ORGANIZATIONS: Society of Experimental Test Pilots, Association of Naval Aviators, U.S. Naval Academy Alumni Association.

SPECIAL HONORS: Air Medal with 2 Strike-Flight awards; 3 Navy Commendation Medals, one with Combat V; Navy Unit Commendation; National Defense Service Medal; Sea Service Deployment Ribbon, 2 Southwest Asia Service Medals; and various other service awards.

EXPERIENCE: Frick was commissioned upon graduation from the U.S. Naval Academy in May 1986. After being designated as a Naval Aviator in February 1988, he reported to Strike Fighter Squadron 106 at Naval Air Station Cecil Field, Florida, for transition to the F/A-18 Hornet. Upon completion of training, he reported to Strike Fighter Squadron 83 also at Cecil Field, and deployed to the Mediterranean Sea and Red Sea onboard the USS Saratoga (CV-60). During the 8 month deployment, he participated in Operation Desert Shield and Desert Storm, flying 26 combat missions from the Red Sea to targets in Iraq and Kuwait. He was also designated an airwing qualified landing signals officer. After leaving Strike Fighter Squadron 83 in December 1991, Frick participated in a cooperative program consisting of 15 months at the Naval Postgraduate School in Monterey, California, and 1 year with the Naval Test Pilot School at Naval Air Station Patuxent River, Maryland. Upon graduation in June 1994, he was assigned as a project officer and test pilot to the Carrier Suitability Department of the Strike Aircraft Test Squadron also located at Patuxent River. While there, he conducted shore-based and shipboard testing of the F/A-18 Hornet. Frick was assigned to Strike Fighter Squadron 125 in Lemoore, California, preparing for return to a deployed F/A-18 squadron when selected for the astronaut program in April 1996. Frick Has logged over 1,800 flight hours in 27 different aircraft, and has over 370 carrier landings.

NASA EXPERIENCE: Selected by NASA in April 1996, Frick reported to the Johnson Space Center in August 1996. Having completed two years of training and evaluation, he is qualified for flight assignment as a pilot. Currently, Frick is assigned technical duties in the Astronaut Office Spacecraft Systems/Operations Branch.

NAME: Christer Fuglesang
ESA Astronaut

PERSONAL DATA: Born March 18, 1957 in Stockholm, Sweden. Married to the former Elisabeth Walldie. They have three children. Enjoys sports, sailing, skiing, frisbee, traveling, games, reading.

EDUCATION: Graduated from Bromma Gymnasium, Stockholm, Sweden, in 1975; received a master of science degree in Engineering Physics from the Royal Institute of Technology (KTH), Stockholm, Sweden, in 1981; received a doctorate in Experimental Particle Physics from the University of

Stockholm in 1987. He became a Docent in Particle Physics at the University of Stockholm in 1991.

ORGANIZATIONS: Member, Swedish Physics Society.

EXPERIENCE: As a graduate student, Fuglesang worked at the CERN Research Laboratory outside Geneva on the UA5 experiment, which studied proton-antiproton collisions. In 1988, he became a Fellow of CERN, where he worked with the CPLEAR experiment, studying the subtle CP-violation of Kaon-particles. After a year at CERN he became Senior Fellow and was head of the particle identification subdetector. In November 1990, Fuglesang obtained a position at the Manne Siegbahn Institute of Physic, Stockholm, but remained stationed at CERN in Geneva working towards the new LHC project (Large Hadron Collider). In August 1991 he moved back to Stockholm. Since 1980, when stationed in Sweden, Fuglesang taught Mathematics at KTH. In May 1992, Fuglesang was selected to join the Astronaut Corps of the European Space Agency (ESA) based at the European Astronauts Centre (EAC) in Cologne, Germany. In 1992, he completed the introductory Training Programme at EAC and a four-week training Program at TsPK (Cosmonauts Training Centre) in Star City, Russia, with a view to future ESA-Russian collaboration in the Mir Space Station. From January to July 1993, he performed Basic Training at EAC. In May 1993, Fuglesang and fellow ESA astronaut, Thomas Reiter, of Germany were selected for the EUROMIR 95 mission. In August 1993, the two astronauts started training at TsPK in preparation for their board-engineer tasks, extra vehicular activities (spacewalks) and operations of the Soyuz transportation system. The EUROMIR 95 experiment training was organized and mainly carried out at the European Astronaut Centre. On March 17, 1995, he was selected as a member of the backup crew for the EUROMIR mission joining Genadi Manakov and Pavel Vinogradov. During the ESA's EUROMIR 95 mission (September 3, 1995 to February 29, 1996), Fuglesang was the prime Crew Interface Coordinator (CIC). From the Russian Mission Control Centre (TsUP) in Kaliningrad, he was the main contact of Thomas Reiter in Mir and acted as a coordinator between Mir and the EUROMIR 95 Payloads Operations Control Centre (SCOPE) located in Oberpfaffenhofen, Germany and the project management. Fuglesang continued with some of his scientific work and is presently involved in the SilEye (Silicon Eye) experiment on board Mir. SilEye studies the light flashes which occasionally occur on orbit in the eyes of astronauts. In July 1996, he was selected by the European Space Agency to attend NASA's Astronaut Candidate Training.

NASA EXPERIENCE: Fuglesang reported to the Johnson Space Center in August 1996. Having completed two years of training and evaluation, he is qualified for flight assignment as a mission specialist. Currently, Fuglesang is assigned technical duties in the Astronaut Office Computer Support Branch.

NAME: Marc Garneau (Ph.D.)
CSA Astronaut

PERSONAL DATA: Born February 23, 1949, in Quebec City, Canada. Married to the former Pamela Soame of Ottawa, Canada. Three children. He enjoys flying, scuba diving, squash, tennis, car mechanics, and home repairs. In 1969 and again in 1970, he sailed across the Atlantic in a 59-foot yawl with 12 other crewmen. His parents, Jean and Andre Garneau, reside in Ottawa, Canada. Her parents, Diana and James Soame, reside in Ottawa, Canada.

EDUCATION: Attended primary and secondary schools in Quebec City & Saint-Jean, Quebec, and in London, England. Received a bachelor of science degree in engineering physics from the Royal Military College of Kingston in 1970, and a doctorate in electrical engineering from the Imperial College of Science and Technology, London, England, in 1973. Attended the Canadian Forces Command and Staff College of Toronto in 1982-83.

ORGANIZATIONS: Honorary Fellow of the Canadian Aeronautics and Space Institute. Member of the Association of Professional Engineers of Nova Scotia, and the Navy League of Canada. In 1988, he was named Honorary Member of the Canadian Society of Aviation Medicine.

SPECIAL HONORS: Recipient of the NASA Exceptional Service Medal (1997); NASA Space Flight Medals (1996, 1984); the Canadian Decoration (military) (1980); the Athlone Fellowship (1970); and the National Research Council (NRC) Bursary (1972). Awarded Honorary Doctorates by the University of Ottawa (1997); the Collège militaire royal de Saint-Jean (1990); the Université Laval, Québec (1985); the Technical University of Nova Scotia (1985); and the Royal Military College, Kingston, Ontario (1985). Appointed as an Officer of the Order of Canada in 1984. Co-recipient of the F.W. (Casey) Baldwin Award in 1985 for the best paper in the Canadian Aeronautics and Space Journal.

EXPERIENCE: Dr. Garneau was a combat systems engineer in HMCS Algonquin, 1974-76. While serving as an instructor in naval weapon systems at the Canadian Forces Fleet School in Halifax, 1976-77, he designed a simulator for use in training weapons officers in the use of missile systems aboard Tribal class destroyers. He served as project engineer in naval weapon systems in Ottawa from 1977 to 1980. He returned to Halifax with the Naval Engineering Unit which troubleshoots and performs trials on ship-fitted equipment, and helped develop an aircraft-towed target system for the scoring of naval gunnery accuracy. Promoted to Commander in 1982 while at Staff College, he was transferred to Ottawa in 1983 and became design authority for naval communications and electronic warfare equipment and systems. In January 1986, he was promoted to Captain. He retired from the Navy in 1989. He is one of six Canadian astronauts selected in December 1983. He was seconded to the Canadian Astronaut Program from the Department of National Defence in February 1984 to begin astronaut training. He flew as a payload specialist on Shuttle Mission 41-G, October 5-13, 1984. He was named Deputy Director of the Canadian Astronaut Program in 1989, providing technical and program support in the preparation of experiments to fly during future Canadian missions. He was selected for astronaut candidate training in July 1992.

NASA EXPERIENCE: Dr. Garneau reported to the Johnson Space Center in August 1992. He completed a one-year training and evaluation program and is qualified for flight assignment as a mission specialist. Dr. Garneau initially worked technical issues for the Astronaut Office Robotics Integration Team. He subsequently served as spacecraft communicator (CAPCOM) in Mission Control during Shuttle flights. A veteran of three space flights (STS-41G in 1984, STS-77 in 1996 and STS-97 in 2000), Dr. Garneau has logged over 677 hours in space.

SPACE FLIGHT EXPERIENCE:
STS-41G (October 5-13, 1984) was an eight-day mission aboard Space Shuttle Challenger. Dr. Garneau was the first Canadian to fly on NASA's first mission to carry a seven-person crew. During 133 orbits of the earth in 3.4 million miles, the crew deployed the Earth Radiation Budget Satellite, conducted scientific observations of the earth with the OSTA-3 pallet and Large Format Camera (LFC), performed numerous in-cabin experiments, activated eight "Getaway Special" canisters, and

demonstrated potential satellite refueling with an EVA and associated hydrazine transfer. Mission duration was 197 hours 23 minutes. STS-77 (May 19-29, 1996) was a ten-day mission aboard Space Shuttle Endeavour. During 160 orbits of the earth in 4.1 million miles, the crew deployed two satellites (the SPARTAN satellite which carried the Inflatable Antenna Experiment designed to test the concept of large, inflatable space structures, and the small Satellite Test Unit designed to test the concept of self-stabilization by using aerodynamic forces and magnetic damping, conducted twelve materials processing, fluid physics and biotechnology experiments in the Spacehab laboratory module carried in Endeavour's payload bay. Mission duration was 240 hours and 39 minutes. STS-97 Endeavour (November 30 to December December 11, 2000) was the fifth Space Shuttle mission dedicated to the assembly of the International Space Station. While docked to the Station, the crew installed the first set of U.S. solar arrays, performed three space walks, in addition to delivering supplies and equipment to the station's first resident crew. Mission duration was 10 days, 19 hours, 57 minutes, and traveled 4.47 million miles.

NAME: Michael L. Gernhardt (Ph.D.)
NASA Astronaut

PERSONAL DATA: Born May 4, 1956, in Mansfield, Ohio. Single. He enjoys running, swimming, flying, fishing, and scuba diving. His father, George M. Gernhardt, resides in Marco Island, Florida. His mother, Suzanne C. Winters, resides in Whitestone, Virginia.

HONORS: NASA Space Flight Medals (3); Exceptional Service Medals (2); Exceptional Achievement Medal (1).

EDUCATION: Graduated from Malabar High School, Mansfield, Ohio, in 1974; received a bachelor of science degree in physics from Vanderbilt University in 1978; master of science degree and a doctorate in bioengineering from University of Pennsylvania, in 1983 and 1991, respectively.

ORGANIZATIONS: American Institute of Aeronautics and Astronautics (AIAA); Undersea and Hyperbaric Medical Society; Sea Space Symposium; Aerospace Medical Association.

EXPERIENCE: From 1977 to 1984, Gernhardt worked as a professional deep sea diver and project engineer on a variety of subsea oil field construction and repair projects around the world. He has logged over 700 deep sea dives and has experience in air, mixed gas, bounce bell and saturation diving. During his diving career Gernhardt attended graduate school at the University of Pennsylvania and developed a new theoretical decompression model based on tissue gas bubble dynamics. He then participated in the development and field implementation of a variety of new decompression tables. From 1984 to 1988, Gernhardt worked as Manager and then Vice President of Special Projects for Oceaneering International. During this time he led the development of a telerobotic system for subsea platform cleaning and inspection as well as a variety of new diver and robot tools. In 1988 he founded Oceaneering Space Systems, a wholly owned subsidiary of Oceaneering International. From 1988 until his selection by NASA in 1992, he worked on the development of new astronaut and robot-compatible tools for performing maintenance on Space Station Freedom. He also worked on the development of new portable life support systems and decompression procedures for extravehicular activity.

NASA EXPERIENCE: Dr. Gernhardt was selected by NASA in March 1992, and reported to the Johnson Space Center in August 1992. Technical assignments to date include: flight software verification in the Shuttle Avionics Integration Laboratory (SAIL); development of nitrox diving to support training for the Hubble Space Telescope repair and on a variety of Space Station EVA developments; member of the astronaut support team at Kennedy Space Center, Florida, responsible for Shuttle prelaunch vehicle checkout, crew ingress/egress; spacecraft communicator (CAPCOM) at Mission Control Center, Houston, during various Shuttle missions; currently leading an international effort to develop new prebreathe procedures for future spacewalks from an International Space Station. A three flight veteran, Dr. Gernhardt has logged over 931 hours in space, including 6 hours and 46 minutes of EVA. He was a mission specialist on STS-69 (September 7-18, 1995), STS-83 (April 4-8, 1997) and STS-94 (July 1-17, 1997). Dr. Gernhardt is assigned to STS-104, where he will perform three spacewalks related to the assembly of the International Space Station (ISS). Launch is targeted for 2001.

SPACE FLIGHT EXPERIENCE: STS-69's prime objective was the successful deployment and retrieval of a SPARTAN satellite and the Wake Shield Facility (WSF). The WSF is designed to evaluate the effectiveness of using this free-flying experiment to grow semiconductors, high temperature superconductors and other materials using the ultra-high vacuum created behind the spacecraft near the experiment package. Dr. Gernhardt was one of two astronauts to perform a spacewalk to evaluate future Space Station tools and hardware, logging 6 hours and 46 minutes of EVA. Mission duration was 260 hours, 29 minutes, and 8 seconds, traveling 4.5 million miles in 171 orbits of the Earth. STS-83, the Microgravity Science Laboratory (MSL-1) Spacelab mission, was cut short because of problems with one of the Shuttle's three fuel cell power generation units. Mission duration was 95 hours and 12 minutes, traveling 1.5 million miles in 63 orbits of the Earth. STS-94 was a reflight of the Microgravity Science Laboratory (MSL-1) Spacelab mission, and focused on materials and combustion science research in microgravity. Mission duration was 376 hours and 45 minutes, traveling 6.3 million miles in 251 orbits of the Earth.

NAME: Linda M. Godwin (Ph.D.)
NASA Astronaut

PERSONAL DATA: Born July 2, 1952, in Cape Girardeau, Missouri. Her hometown is Jackson, Missouri. Married to Steven R. Nagel of Houston, Texas. Two daughters. She enjoys playing saxophone and clarinet, reading, and flying. Her father, Mr. James M. Godwin, resides in Oak Ridge, Missouri. His parents, Mr. and Mrs. Ivan R. Nagel, reside in Canton, Illinois.

EDUCATION: Graduated from Jackson High School in Jackson, Missouri, in 1970; received a bachelor of science degree in mathematics and physics from Southeast Missouri State in 1974, and a master of science degree and a doctorate in physics from the University of Missouri in 1976 and 1980.

ORGANIZATIONS: Member of the American Physical Society, Space City Chapter of the Ninety-Nines, Inc., Association of Space Explorers, Aircraft Owners and Pilots Association.

SPECIAL HONORS: Recipient of NASA Outstanding Performance Rating, Sustained Superior Performance Award, and Outstanding Leadership Award.

EXPERIENCE: After completing undergraduate studies in physics and mathematics at Southeast Missouri State University, Dr. Godwin attended graduate school at the University of Missouri in

Columbia, Missouri. During that time she taught undergraduate physics labs and was the recipient of several research assistantships. She conducted research in low temperature solid state physics, including studies in electron tunneling and vibrational modes of absorbed molecular species on metallic substrates at liquid helium temperatures. Results of her research have been published in several journals. Dr. Godwin is an instrument rated private pilot.

NASA EXPERIENCE: Dr. Godwin joined NASA in 1980, in the Payload Operations Division, Mission Operations Directorate, where she worked in payload integration (attached payloads and Spacelabs), and as a flight controller and payloads officer on several Shuttle missions. Selected by NASA as an astronaut candidate in June 1985, Dr. Godwin became an astronaut in July 1986. Her technical assignments have included working with flight software verification in the Shuttle Avionics Integration Laboratory (SAIL), and coordinating mission development activities for the Inertial Upper Stage (IUS), deployable payloads, and Spacelab missions. She also has served as Chief of Astronaut Appearances, Chief of the Mission Development Branch of the Astronaut Office and as the astronaut liaison to its Educational Working Group, Deputy Chief of the Astronaut Office, and Deputy Director, Flight Crew Operations Directorate. A veteran of three space flights, Dr. Godwin has logged over 633 hours in space, including a 6-hour spacewalk. In 1991 she served as a Mission Specialist on STS-37, was the Payload Commander on STS-59 in 1994, and in 1996 was on the crew of STS-76, a Mir docking mission.

SPACE FLIGHT EXPERIENCE: STS-37 Atlantis (April 5-11, 1991) was launched from the Kennedy Space Center, Florida, and returned to land at Edwards Air Force Base, California. During the 93 orbits of the mission, the crew deployed the Gamma Ray Observatory (GRO) to study gamma ray sources in the universe. GRO, at almost 35,000 pounds, was the heaviest payload deployed to date by the Shuttle Remote Manipulator System (RMS). The crew also conducted an unscheduled space walk to free the GRO high gain antenna, and conducted the first scheduled extravehicular activity in 5-1/2 years to test concepts for moving about large space structures. Several middeck experiments and activities were conducted including test of elements of a heat pipe to study fluid transfer processed in microgravity environments (SHARE), a chemical processing apparatus to characterize the structure of biologicalmaterials (BIMDA), and an experiment to grow larger and more perfect protein crystals than can be grown on the ground (PCG II). Atlantis carried amateur radio equipment for voice contact, fast scan and slow scan TV, and packet radio. Several hundred contacts were made with amateur radio operators around the world. Mission duration was 143 hours, 32 minutes, 44 seconds. STS-59 Endeavour (April 9-20, 1994) was the Space Radar Laboratory (SRL) mission. SRL consisted of three large radars, SIR-C/X-SAR (Shuttle Imaging Radar C/X-Band Synthetic Aperture Radar), and a carbon monoxide sensor that were used to enhance studies of the Earth's surface and atmosphere. The imaging radars operated in three frequencies and four polarizations. This multispectral capability of the radars provided information about the Earth's surface over a wide range of scales not discernible with previous single-frequency experiments. The carbon monoxide sensor MAPS (Measurement of Air Pollution by Satellite) used gas filter radiometry to measure the global distribution of CO in the troposphere. Real-time crew observations of surface phenomena and climatic conditions augmented with over 14,000 photographs aided investigators in interpretation and calibration of the data. The mission concluded with a landing at Edwards AFB after orbiting the Earth 183 times in 269 hours, 29 minutes. STS-76 Atlantis (March 22-31, 1996) was the third docking mission to the Russian space station Mir. Following rendezvous and docking with Mir, transfer of a NASA astronaut to Mir for a 5-month stay was accomplished to begin a continuous presence of U.S. astronauts aboard Mir for the next two year period. The crew also transferred 4800 pounds of science and mission hardware, food, water and air to Mir and returned over 1100 pounds of U.S. and ESA science and Russian hardware. Dr. Godwin performed a six-hour spacewalk, the first while docked to an orbiting space station, to mount experiment packages on the Mir docking module to detect and assess debris and contamination in a space station environment. The packages will be retrieved by a future shuttle mission. The Spacehab module carried in the Shuttle payload bay was utilized extensively for transfer and return stowage of logistics and science and also carried Biorack, a small multipurpose laboratory used during this mission for research of plant and animal cellular function. This mission was also the first flight of Kidsat, an electronic camera controlled by classroom students via a Ku-band link between JSC Mission Control and the Shuttle, which uses digitized photography from the Shuttle for science and education. The STS-76 mission was accomplished in 145 orbits of the Earth, traveling 3.8 million miles in 221 hours and 15 minutes.

NAME: Dominic L. Pudwill Gorie (Captain, USN)
NASA Astronaut

PERSONAL DATA: Born May 2, 1957, in Lake Charles, Louisiana. Married to Wendy Lu Williams of Midland, Texas. They have two children. He enjoys skiing, bicycling, fishing, and golf with his family.

EDUCATION: Graduated from Miami Palmetto High School, Miami, Florida, in 1975. Bachelor of Science degree in ocean engineering from the U.S. Naval Academy in 1979. Master of science degree in aviation systems from the University of Tennessee in 1990.

SPECIAL HONORS: Distinguished Flying Cross with Combat "V", Joint Meritorious Service Medal, Air Medal (2), Space Flight Medal, Navy Commendation Medal with Combat "V" (2), Navy Achievement Medal, 1985 Strike Fighter Wing Atlantic Pilot-of-the-Year.

EXPERIENCE: Designated a Naval Aviator in 1981. Flew the A-7E Corsair with Attack Squadron 46 aboard the USS America from 1981 to 1983. Transitioned to Strike Fighter Squadron 132 in 1983, flying the F/A-18 Hornet aboard the USS Coral Sea until 1986. Attended the U.S. Naval Test Pilot School in 1987 and served as a Test Pilot at the Naval Air Test Center from 1988 to 1990. Then was assigned to Strike Fighter Squadron 87 flying the F/A-18 aboard the USS Roosevelt until 1992. Participated in Operation Desert Storm, flying 38 combat missions. In 1992 received orders to U.S. Space Command in Colorado Springs for two years before reporting to Strike Fighter Squadron 106 for F/A-18 refresher training. Was enroute to his command tour of Strike Fighter Squadron 37 when selected as an Astronaut Candidate. Gorie has accumulated over 4700 hours in more than 30 aircraft and has over 600 carrier landings.

NASA EXPERIENCE: Selected as an astronaut candidate by NASA in December 1994, Gorie reported to the Johnson Space Center in March 1995. He completed a year of training and evaluation and then was initially assigned to work safety issues for the Astronaut Office. Gorie next served as a spacecraft communicator (CAPCOM) in Mission Control for numerous Space Shuttle flights. A veteran of two space flights, Gorie has logged 504 hours and 32 minutes in space. He served as pilot aboard STS-91 in 1998 and STS-99 in 2000.

SPACE FLIGHT EXPERIENCE: STS-91 Discovery (June 2-12, 1998) was the 9th and final Shuttle-Mir docking mission, concluding the joint U.S./Russian Phase I Program. The STS-91 mission was accomplished in 154 Earth orbits, traveling 3.8 million miles in 235 hours and 54 seconds.

STS-99 (February 11-22, 2000) was an 11-day flight during which the international crew aboard Space Shuttle Endeavour worked dual shifts to support payload operations. The Shuttle Radar Topography Mission mapped more than 47 million miles of the Earth's land surface. The STS-99 mission was accomplished in 181 Earth orbits, traveling over 4 million miles in 268 hours and 38 minutes.

NAME: John M. Grunsfeld (Ph.D.)
     NASA Astronaut

PERSONAL DATA: Born October 10, 1958, in Chicago, Illinois. Married to the former Carol E. Schiff. They have two children. He enjoys mountaineering, flying, sailing, bicycling, and music. His parents, Ernest and Sally Grunsfeld, reside in Highland Park, Illinois. Her parents, David and Ruth Schiff, reside in Highland Park, Illinois.

EDUCATION: Graduated from Highland Park High School, Highland Park, Illinois, in 1976; received a bachelor of science degree in physics from the Massachusetts Institute of Technology in 1980; a master of science degree and a doctor of philosophy degree in physics from the University of Chicago in 1984 and 1988, respectively.

ORGANIZATIONS: American Astronomical Society.

SPECIAL HONORS: W.D. Grainger Fellow in Experimental Physics, 1988-89. NASA Graduate Student Research Fellow, 1985-87. NASA Space Flight Medals (1995, 1997, 1999). NASA Exceptional Service Medals (1997, 1998).

EXPERIENCE: Dr. Grunsfeld's academic positions include that of Visiting Scientist, University of Tokyo/Institute of Space and Astronautical Science (1980-81); Graduate Research Assistant, University of Chicago (1981-85); NASA Graduate Student Fellow, University of Chicago (1985-87); W.D. Grainger Postdoctoral Fellow in Experimental Physics, University of Chicago (1988-89); and Senior Research Fellow, California Institute of Technology (1989-92). Dr. Grunsfeld's research has covered x-ray and gamma-ray astronomy, high energy cosmic ray studies, and development of new detectors and instrumentation. Dr. Grunsfeld studies binary pulsars and energetic x-ray and gamma-ray sources using the NASA Compton Gamma Ray Observatory, x-ray astronomy satellites, radio telescopes, and optical telescopes.

NASA EXPERIENCE: Dr. Grunsfeld was selected by NASA in March 1992, and reported to the Johnson Space Center in August 1992. He completed one year of training and is qualified for flight selection as a mission specialist. Dr. Grunsfeld was initially detailed to the Astronaut Office Mission Development Branch. Following his first flight, he led a team of engineers and computer programmers tasked with defining and producing the crew displays for command and control of the International Space Station (ISS). As part of this activity he directed an effort combining the resources of the Mission Control Center (MCC) Display Team and the Space Station Training Facility. The result was the creation of the Common Display Development Facility (CDDF), responsible for the onboard and MCC displays for the ISS, using object-oriented programming techniques. Following his second flight he was assigned as Chief of the Computer Support Branch in the Astronaut Office supporting Space Shuttle and International Space Station Programs and advanced technology development. A veteran of three space flights, STS-67 in 1995, STS-81 in 1997, and STS-103 in 1999, Grunsfeld has logged over 835 hours in space, including two space walks totaling 16 hours and 23 minutes. He is currently assigned to upgrade and service the Hubble Space Telescope during the STS-109 mission scheduled for launch in 2001 .

SPACE FLIGHT EXPERIENCE: STS-67 Astro-2 (March 2-18,1995) was the second flight of the Astro observatory, a unique complement of three telescopes. During this record-setting 16-day mission, the crew conducted observations around the clock to study the far ultraviolet spectra of faint astronomical objects and the polarization of ultraviolet light coming from hot stars and distant galaxies. Mission duration was 399 hours and 9 minutes. STS-81 (January 12-22, 1997) was a ten-day mission, the fifth to dock with Russia's Space Station Mir, and the second to exchange U.S. astronauts. The mission also carried the Spacehab double module providing additional middeck locker space for secondary experiments. In five days of docked operations more than three tons of food, water, experiment equipment and samples were moved back and forth between the two spacecraft. Following 160 orbits of the Earth the STS-81 mission concluded with a landing on Kennedy Space Center's Runway 33 ending a 3.9 million mile journey. Mission duration was 244 hours, 56 minutes. STS-103 (December 19-27, 1999) was an 8-day mission during which the crew successfully installed new instruments and upgraded systems on the Hubble Space Telescope (HST). Enhancing HST scientific capabilities required three space walks (EVA). Grunsfeld performed two space walks totaling 16 hours and 23 minutes. The STS-103 mission was accomplished in 120 Earth orbits, traveling 3.2 million miles in 191 hours and 11 minutes.

NAME: Umberto Guidoni (Ph.D.)
ESA Astronaut

PERSONAL DATA: Born August 18, 1954, in Rome, Italy. Married to Mariarita Bartolacci of Milan, Italy. They have one child named Luca. His parents, Pietro Guidoni and Giuseppina Cocco-Guidoni, reside in Rome, Italy.

EDUCATION: Graduated from Classic Lyceum "Gaio Lucilio" in Rome, Italy, in 1973; received his B.S. degree in physics and Ph.D. in Astrophysics (Summa Cum Laude) from University of Rome in 1978.

ORGANIZATIONS: Member of the Italian Space Society (ISS).

SPECIAL HONORS: Received a National Committee for Nuclear Energy (CNEN) Post-Doctoral Fellowship (1979-80) in the thermonuclear fusion field. Dr. Guidoni was awarded the NASA Space Flight Medal in 1996.

MILITARY STATUS: Reserve Officer of the Italian Air Force.

SCIENTIFIC EXPERIENCE: In 1983, as a staff scientist in the Solar Energy Division of the National Committee for Renewable Energy (ENEA), Dr. Guidoni was responsible for developing new techniques to characterize solar panels. In 1984, he became a permanent researcher of the Space Physics Institute (IFSI-CNR) and was involved as co-investigator in the Research on Electrodynamic Tether Effects (RETE) experiment, one of the payloads selected for the Tethered Satellite System (TSS-1). From 1985 to 1988 he supervised the design and testing of the RETE experiment. He also collaborated to the realization of a plasma chamber at IFSI, for laboratory simulations of electrodynamics tether phenomena and for characterization of plasma contactors in ionospheric environment. In 1988, Dr. Guidoni was appointed Project Scientist of RETE. In this capacity he was responsible for the integration of the experiment with the Tethered Satellite System. In 1989, he was selected by the Italian Space Agency (ASI) to be one of the two Italian scientists to be trained as payload specialists for the TSS-1 mission. In 1990 he joined ASI and started the training as Alternate Payload Specialist (APS) for the STS-46/TSS-1 mission. For the duration of the flight (July 31 to August 8, 1992) he assisted the Science Team for on-orbit operations at the Payload Operations Control Center (POCC) at the Johnson Space Center in Houston.

NASA EXPERIENCE: In 1994, he was assigned to serve as a payload specialist on the crew of STS-75/TSS-1R. Selected by ASI to attend NASA Astronaut Candidate Training, Dr. Guidoni reported to the Johnson Space Center in August 1996. Having completed two years of training and evaluation, he is qualified for flight assignment as a mission specialist. In August 1998, Dr. Guidoni joined the Astronaut Corps of the European Space Agency (ESA) based at the European Astronauts Center (EAC) in Cologne, Germany. Dr. Guidoni is currently assigned technical duties in the Astronaut Office Robotics Branch, in addition to training for STS-100 scheduled for launch in 2001.

SPACE FLIGHT EXPERIENCE: Dr. Guidoni made his first flight as Payload Specialist on STS-75 (February 22 to March 9, 1996) on the Shuttle Columbia. This was a 16-day mission whose principal payloads were the reflight of the Tethered Satellite System (TSS) and the third flight of the United States Microgravity Payload (USMP-3). The TSS successfully demonstrated the ability of tethers to produce electricity. The TSS experiment produced a wealth of new information on the electrodynamics of tethers and plasma physics before the tether broke at 19.7 km, just shy of the 20.7 km goal. The crew also worked around the clock performing combustion experiments and research related to USMP-3 microgravity investigations. The mission was completed in 252 orbits covering 6.5 million miles in 377 hours and 40 minutes.

NAME: Chris A. Hadfield (Colonel, CAF)
CSA Astronaut

PERSONAL DATA: Born August 29, 1959, in Sarnia, Ontario, Canada, and grew up in Milton, Ontario. Married to Helene Hadfield (née Walter). They have three children. He enjoys skiing, volleyball, guitar, singing, riding, writing, soccer. His parents, Roger and Eleanor Hadfield, reside near Milton. Her mother, Gwendoline Walter, resides in Victoria, B.C. Her father, Erhard Walter, is deceased.

EDUCATION: Received a bachelor degree in mechanical engineering (honours), Royal Military College, Kingston, Ontario, Canada, in 1982; post-graduate research at University of Waterloo, Ontario, Canada, in 1982; and a master of science degree in aviation systems, University of Tennessee, in 1992.

ORGANIZATIONS: Royal Military College Club; Society of Experimental Test Pilots; Canadian Aeronautics and Space Institute; Mensa.

SPECIAL HONORS: Recipient of the 1988 Liethen-Tittle Award (given to the top pilot graduate of the USAF Test Pilot School, Hadfield is the third foreign student to win the award in the history of the school); U.S. Navy Test Pilot of the Year (1991) - (for overall achievement at the Naval Air Test Center, Patuxent River, Maryland, and for work done on National Aerospace Plane propulsion, and F/A-18 out-of-control testing); awarded an honourary doctorate of engineering from the Royal Military College, Kingston, Ontario, Canada (1996); member of the Order of Ontario (1996); Honourary Doctorate of Laws from Trent University (1999).

EXPERIENCE: Hadfield was raised on a corn farm in southern Ontario. He taught skiing and ski racing part- and full-time for 10 years. He was an Air Cadet, and won a glider pilot scholarship at age 15, and a powered pilot scholarship at age 16. He graduated as an Ontario scholar from Milton District High School in 1977, and joined the Canadian Armed Forces in May 1978. He spent the next two years at Royal Roads Military College, Victoria, B.C., followed by two years at Royal Military College, Kingston, Ontario, from where he graduated with honors in mechanical engineering. He was top pilot at basic flying training, Portage La Prarie, Manitoba, in 1980, and was overall top graduate at Basic Jet Training, Moose Jaw, Saskatchewan, in 1982-1983. Fighter and CF-18 training was done in Cold Lake, Alberta, in 1984-1985. For the next three years he was with 425 Squadron, flying CF-18s for NORAD. In June 1985 Hadfield flew the first CF-18 intercept of Soviet "Bear" aircraft. He attended the USAF Test Pilot School, Edwards Air Force Base, California, Course 88A. Upon graduation he served as an exchange officer with the U. S. Navy at Strike Test Directorate, Patuxent River Naval Air Station. His accomplishments during 1989-1992 included: testing the F/A-18 and A-7 aircraft; performing research work with NASA on pitch control margin simulation and flight; the first military flight of F/A-18 enhanced performance engines; the first flight test of the National Aerospace Plane (NASP) external burning hydrogen propulsion; developing a new handling qualities rating scale for high angle-of-attack test; and the F/A-18 out-of-control recovery test program. Hadfield was selected as one of four Canadian astronauts from a field of 5,330 in June 1992.

NASA EXPERIENCE: Hadfield reported to the Johnson Space Center in August 1992. His technical assignments have included technical and safety issues for the Astronaut Office Operations Development Branch, Shuttle glass cockpit development, and launch support at Kennedy Space Center, Florida. In November 1995 Hadfield served as a missionspecialist on STS-74, NASA's second Space Shuttle mission to rendezvous and dock with the Russian Space Station Mir. During the 8-day flight the crew aboard Space Shuttle Atlantis successfully attached a permanent docking module to Mir and transferred over 2,000 pounds of food, water and scientific supplies for use by the cosmonauts. Hadfield flew as the first Canadian mission specialist, the first Canadian to operate the Canadarm in orbit, and the only Canadian to ever visit Mir. The STS-74 mission was accomplished in 129 orbits of the Earth, traveling 3.4 million miles in 196 hours, 30 minutes, 44 seconds. Hadfield currently works as NASA's Chief CAPCOM, the voice of mission control to Shuttles in orbit, and is the Chief Astronaut for the Canadian Space Agency. In 2001 Hadfield will fly on STS-100, International Space Station assembly Flight 6A. The primary purpose of the flight is to deliver and install the new Canadian Robot Arm (Space Station Remote Manipulator System), as well as an Italian-made resupply Logistics Module. During the flight two spacewalks are planned, which will make Hadfield the first Canadian to ever leave a spacecraft, and float free in space.

NAME: James Donald Halsell, Jr., (Colonel, USAF)
NASA Astronaut

PERSONAL DATA: Born September 29, 1956, in West Monroe, Louisiana, where his parents, Don and Jean Halsell, reside. Married to the former Kathy D. Spooner of Merritt Island, Florida, where her parents, Charles and Lynn Spooner, reside. They have one son. He enjoys snow skiing, water skiing, light aircraft flying and racquetball.

EDUCATION: Graduated from West Monroe High School, West Monroe, Louisiana, in 1974; received a bachelor of science degree in engineering from the United States Air Force (USAF) Academy in 1978, a master of science degree in management from Troy University in 1983, and a master of science degree in space operations from the Air Force Institute of Technology in 1985.

ORGANIZATIONS: Member of the Society of Experimental Test Pilots.

SPECIAL HONORS: Graduated first in test pilot school class and awarded the Liethen/Tittle Trophy for the Best Overall Record for Flying and Academic Performance (1986). Recipient of the Defense Meritorious Service Medal (1995), the Defense Superior Service Medal (1996), the Distinguished Flying Cross (1998), and the NASA Space Flight Medal (1994, 1995, 1997, 2000).

AIR FORCE EXPERIENCE: Halsell graduated from the USAF Academy in 1978, and from Undergraduate Pilot Training at Columbus Air Force Base, Mississippi, in 1979. An F-4 pilot qualified in conventional and nuclear weapons deliveries, he served at Nellis Air Force Base, Las Vegas, Nevada, from 1980-1981, and Moody Air Force Base, Valdosta, Georgia, from 1982-1984. In 1984-1985, he was a graduate student at the Air Force Institute of Technology, Wright-Patterson Air Force Base, Dayton, Ohio. He then attended the Air Force Test Pilot School at Edwards Air Force Base, California, and during the next four years he performed test flights in the F-4, the F-16, and the SR-71 aircraft.

NASA EXPERIENCE: Selected by NASA in January 1990, Halsell became an astronaut in July 1991. A five flight veteran, Halsell has logged over 1,250 hours in space. He was the pilot on STS-65 (July 8-23, 1994) and STS-74 (November 12-20, 1995), and was mission commander on STS-83 (Apr 4-8, 1997), STS-94 (July 1-17, 1997) and STS-101 (May 19-29, 2000). From February-August 1998, he served as NASA Director of Operations at the Yuri Gagarin Cosmonaut Training Center, Star City, Russia. Halsell's current assignment is Manager, Shuttle Launch Integration, Kennedy Space Center, Florida.

ADDITIONAL MISSION DETAILS: STS-65 flew the second International Microgravity Laboratory (IML-2). During the 15-day flight the crew conducted more than 80 experiments focusing on materials and life sciences research in microgravity. The mission was accomplished in 236 orbits of the Earth, traveling 6.1 million miles in 353 hours and 55 minutes. STS-74 was NASA's second Space Shuttle mission to rendezvous and dock with the Russian Space Station Mir. During the 8-day flight the Atlantis crew successfully attached a permanent docking module to Mir and transferred over 2,000 pounds of food, water and scientific supplies for use by the cosmonauts. The STS-74 mission was accomplished in 129 orbits of the Earth, traveling 3.4 million miles in 196 hours, 30 minutes, 44 seconds. STS-83, the Microgravity Science Laboratory (MSL-1) Spacelab mission, was cut short because of problems with one of the Shuttle's three fuel cell power generation units. Mission duration was 95 hours and 12 minutes, traveling 1.5 million miles in 63 orbits of the Earth. STS-94, a re-flight of the Microgravity Science Laboratory (MSL-1) Spacelab mission, focused on materials and combustion science research in microgravity. Mission duration was 376 hours and 45 minutes, traveling 6.3 million miles in 251 orbits of the Earth. STS-101 was the third Shuttle mission devoted to International Space Station (ISS) construction. Objectives included transporting and installing over 5,000 pounds of equipment and supplies, and conducting a space walk. The mission was accomplished in 155 orbits of the Earth, traveling 4.1 million miles in 236 hours and 9 minutes.

NAME: Kenneth T. Ham (Lieutenant Commander, USN)
NASA Astronaut (Pilot Candidate)

PERSONAL DATA: Born December 12, 1964 in Plainfield, New Jersey. Married to the former Linda J. Hautzinger of Salem, Wisconsin. They have two children, Ryan and Randy. Recreational interests include running, weight lifting, general aviation, snow and water skiing, and sky and scuba diving.

EDUCATION: Arthur L. Johnson Regional High School, Clark, New Jersey, 1983. B.S., Aerospace Engineering, U.S. Naval Academy, 1987. M.S., Aeronautical Engineering, Naval Postgraduate School, 1996.

ORGANIZATIONS: Society of Experimental Test Pilots, U.S. Naval Academy Alumni Association.

SPECIAL HONORS: Distinguished Graduate U.S. Naval Test Pilot School.

EXPERIENCE: Ken received his commission as an ensign in the United States Navy from the United States Naval Academy in May 1987. He was temporarily assigned to the NASA-JSC zero-g office at Ellington Field, Houston where he flew as a crew member on the NASA zero-g research aircraft. He was designated a Naval Aviator in October 1989 after completing flight training in the T-34C, T-2C, and TA-4J aircraft at NAS Corpus Christi and NAS Beeville, Texas. Ken reported to NAS Cecil Field, Florida for F/A-18 training and subsequent operational assignments with the Privateers of VFA-132 and the Gunslingers of VFA-105. He completed two deployments to the Mediterranean Sea including combat missions over North Iraq and Bosnia. During these tours, he served as an air wing strike leader, F/A-18 demonstration pilot, and night vision goggle instructor. Ken was selected for the Naval Postgraduate School/Test Pilot School cooperative program where he studied aeronautical engineering for 18 months in Monterey California followed by 12 months of test pilot training at NAS Patuxent River Maryland. He was selected as a team member of the F/A-18E/F Super Hornet Integrated Test Team as one of five Navy pilots responsible for developing a new fleet aircraft. This duty involved envelope expansion flight test in arrested landings, catapult assisted takeoffs, weapon separation, propulsion stability, performance, and general flying qualities. Ken was serving as the F/A-18E/F lead carrier suitability test pilot when he was selected for the astronaut program. He has logged over 2,500 flight hours in more than 40 different aircraft and has over 300 shipboard, and 300 land based arrested landings.

NASA EXPERIENCE: Selected by NASA in June 1998, he reported for training in August 1998. Astronaut Candidate Training includes orientation briefings and tours, numerous scientific and technical briefings, intensive instruction in Shuttle and International Space Station systems, physiological training and ground school to prepare for T-38 flight training, as well as learning water and wilderness survival techniques. Currently, Ken is currently assigned to the Astronaut Office Shuttle Operations Branch. He will serve in technical assignments until assigned to a space flight.

NAME: Gregory J. Harbaugh (Mr.)
NASA Astronaut

PERSONAL DATA: Born April 15, 1956, in Cleveland, Ohio. Willoughby, Ohio, is his hometown. Married. Three children. Enjoys building his own airplane, golf, flying, basketball, running, and snow skiing.

EDUCATION: Graduated from Willoughby South High School in 1974; received a bachelor of science degree in aeronautical and astronautical engineering from Purdue University in 1978, and a master of science degree in physical science from University of Houston-Clear Lake in 1986.

ORGANIZATIONS: Member, Sigma Chi Fraternity, Omicron Delta Kappa, Sigma Gamma Tau.

SPECIAL HONORS: Recipient of the NASA Distinguished Service Medal, four NASA Space Flight Medals, the NASA Exceptional Service Medal, the NASA Exceptional Achievement Medal, the 1999 Rotary National Award for Space Achievement- "Stellar" Award for Outstanding Leadership, the 1995 American Astronautical Society Flight Achievement Award, the Johns Hopkins University Presidential Medal, the Purdue University Outstanding Aerospace Engineer and Astronaut Alumnus Awards, Aviation Week and Space Technology Laurels for 1991 (STS 39) and 1995 (STS 71), and the Sigma Chi Fraternity Significant Sig Award.

NASA EXPERIENCE: Mr. Harbaugh came to NASA's Johnson Space Center after graduation from Purdue University. Since 1978 he has held engineering and technical management positions in Space Shuttle flight operations. Mr. Harbaugh supported Shuttle flight operations from Mission Control for most of the flights from STS-1 through STS 51-L. He served as Lead Data Processing Systems (DPS) Officer for STS-9 (Spacelab-1) and STS 41-D, Orbit DPS for STS 41-B and STS 41-C, and Ascent/Entry DPS for STS 41-G. Harbaugh also served as a senior flight controller addressing issues requiring real-time resolution, for several flights from STS 51-A through STS 51-L. Mr. Harbaugh has a commercial pilot's license with instrument rating, and over 1600 hours total flying time. Selected by NASA in June 1987, Mr. Harbaugh became an astronaut in August 1988. His technical assignments to date have included work in the Shuttle Avionics Integration Laboratory (SAIL), the Shuttle Remote Manipulator System (RMS), telerobotics systems development for Space Station, the Hubble Space Telescope servicing mission development, spacecraft communicator (CAPCOM) in Mission Control, and extravehicular activity (EVA) for the International Space Station (ISS). He was assigned as the backup EVA crew member and capsule communicator (Capcom) for STS-61, the first Hubble Space Telescope servicing mission. A veteran of four space flights, Mr. Harbaugh has logged a total of 818 hours in space, including 18 hours, 29 minutes EVA. He served aboard STS-39 (April 28 through May 6, 1991), STS-54 (January 13-19, 1993), STS-71 (June 27 to July 7, 1995) and STS-82 (February 11-21, 1997). Since 1997 Mr. Harbaugh has served as Manager of the Extravehicular Activity Project Office, with program management responsibility for all aspects of NASA's spacewalk industry, including spacesuits, tools, training, tasks and operations for the Space Shuttle, the International Space Station, and future planetary missions.

SPACE FLIGHT EXPERIENCE: STS-39 Discovery (April 28 through May 6, 1991) was an eight- eight-day unclassified Department of Defense mission involving research for the Strategic Defense Initiative. Mr. Harbaugh flew as a mission specialist and was responsible for operation of the RMS and the Infrared Background Signature Survey (IBSS) spacecraft, and he was one of two crewmen trained for EVA in the event of a contingency requiring a space walk. Mission duration was 199 hours, 22 minutes. STS-54 Endeavour (January 13-19, 1993) was a six-day mission which featured the deployment of TDRS-F, and a 4-hour 28-minute space walk by Mr. Harbaugh. Mission duration was 143 hours 38 minutes. STS-71 Atlantis (June 27 to July 7, 1995) was the first docking.mission with the Russian Space Station Mir, and involved an exchange of crews. On this mission, .Mr. Harbaugh served as the Flight Engineer (Mission Specialist) on a seven-member (up) eight-member (down) crew. Space Shuttle Atlantis was modified to carry a docking system compatible with the Russian Mir Space Station, and Mr. Harbaugh was responsible for the inflight operation of the docking system. He was also assigned to perform any contingency EVA. Mission duration was 235 hours, 23 minutes. STS-82 Discovery (February 11-21, 1997) the second Hubble Space Telescope (HST) servicing mission . It was a night launch and landing flight. During the 10-day mission, the crew retrieved and secured the HST in Discovery's payload bay. In five spacewalks, two teams installed two new spectrometers and eight replacement instruments, and placed insulation patches over several compartments containing key data processing, electronics and scientific instrument telemetry packages. Mr. Harbaugh participated in two space walks, totaling 14 hours and 01 minute. Following completion of upgrades and repairs, HST was redeployed and boosted to its highest orbit ever. Mission duration was 239 hours, 37 minutes.

NAME: Steven A. Hawley (Ph.D.)
NASA Astronaut

PERSONAL DATA: Born December 12, 1951, in Ottawa, Kansas, but considers Salina, Kansas, to be his hometown. Married to the former Eileen M. Keegan of Redondo Beach, California. He enjoys basketball, softball, golf, running, playing bridge, and umpiring. His parents, Dr. and Mrs. Bernard Hawley, reside in Surprise, Arizona. Her mother, Mrs. Jo Keegan, resides in Houston, Texas.

EDUCATION: Graduated from Salina (Central) High School, Salina, Kansas, in 1969; received bachelor of arts degrees in physics and astronomy (graduating with highest distinction) from the University of Kansas in 1973, and a doctor of philosophy in astronomy and astrophysics from the University of California in 1977.

ORGANIZATIONS: Member of the American Astronomical Society, the Astronomical Society of the Pacific, the American Institute of Aeronautics and Astronautics, Sigma Pi Sigma, and Phi Beta Kappa.

SPECIAL HONORS: Evans Foundation Scholarship, 1970; University of Kansas Honor Scholarship, 1970; Summerfield Scholarship, 1970-1973; Veta B. Lear Award, 1970; Stranathan Award, 1972; Outstanding Physics Major Award, 1973; University of California Regents Fellowship, 1974; Group Achievement Award for software testing at the Shuttle Avionics Integration Laboratory, 1981; NASA Outstanding Performance Award, 1981; NASA Superior Performance Award, 1981; Group Achievement Award for Second Orbiter Test and Checkout at Kennedy Space Center, 1982; Quality Increase, 1982; NASA Space Flight Medal (1984, 1986, 1990, 1997, 1999); Group Achievement Award for JSC Strategic Planning, 1987; NASA Exceptional Service Medal (1988, 1991); Special Achievement Award, 1988; Exceptional Service Medal for Return to Flight, 1988; Outstanding Leadership Medal, 1990; Special Achievement Award, 1990; Haley Flight Achievement Award, 1991; Kansan of the Year Award, 1992; Group Achievement Award for ESIG 3000 Integration Project, 1994; Presidential Rank Award (1994, 1999); Group Achievement Award for Space Shuttle Program Functional Workforce Review, 1995; Group Achievement Award for SFOC Contract Acquisition, 1997; Kansas Aviation Hall of Fame, 1997; Kansas University Distinguished Service Citation, 1998; NASA Distinguished Service Medal (1998, 2000); Aviation Week and Space Technology Laurel Citation for Space, 1998.

EXPERIENCE: Hawley attended the University of Kansas, majoring in physics and astronomy. He spent three summers employed as a research assistant: 1972 at the U.S. Naval Observatory in Washington, D.C., and 1973 and 1974 at the National Radio Astronomy Observatory in Green Bank, West Virginia. He attended graduate school at Lick Observatory, University of California, Santa Cruz. His research involved spectrophotometry of gaseous nebulae and emission-line galaxies with particular emphasis on chemical abundance determinations for these objects. The results of his research have been published in major astronomical journals. Prior to his selection by NASA in 1978, Hawley was a post-doctoral research associate at Cerro Tololo Inter-American Observatory in La Serena, Chile.

NASA EXPERIENCE: Dr. Hawley was selected as a NASA astronaut in January 1978. Prior to STS-1, he served as a simulator pilot for software checkout at the Shuttle Avionics Integration Laboratory (SAIL). For STS-2, STS-3, and STS-4, he was a member of the astronaut support crew at Kennedy Space Center, Florida, for Orbiter test and checkout, and also served as prime close-out crewman for STS-3 and STS-4. During 1984-1985, he was Technical Assistant to the Director, Flight Crew Operations. From 1987-1990, he was the Deputy Chief of the Astronaut Office. In June 1990, he left the Astronaut Office to assume the post of Associate Director of NASA's Ames Research Center in California. In August 1992, he returned to the Johnson Space Center as Deputy Director of Flight Crew Operations. Dr. Hawley was returned to astronaut flight status in February 1996. He served on the second Hubble Space Telescope mission and returned to duty as Deputy Director, Flight Crew Operations. A veteran of five space flights (STS-41D in 1984, STS-61C in 1986, STS-31 in 1990, STS-82 in 1997 and STS-93 in 1999), Dr. Hawley has logged 32 days in space.

SPACE FLIGHT EXPERIENCE: A veteran of five space flights, Dr. Hawley has logged a total of 770 hours and 27 minutes in space. He served as a mission specialist on STS-41D in 1984, STS-61C in 1986, STS-31 in 1990, STS-82 in 1997 and STS-93 in 1999. STS-41D (August 30 to September 5, 1984) was launched from the Kennedy Space Center, Florida, and returned to land at Edwards Air Force Base, California. This was the maiden flight of the Space Shuttle Discovery. During the 7-day mission the crew successfully activated the OAST-1 solar cell wing experiment, deployed the SBS-D, SYNCOM IV-2, and TELSTAR 3-C satellites, operated the CFES-III experiment, the student crystal growth experiment, as well as photography experiments using the IMAX motion picture camera. The mission was completed in 96 orbits of the Earth in 144 hours and 57 minutes. STS-61C (January 12-18, 1986) was launched from the Kennedy Space Center, Florida, and returned to a night landing at Edwards Air Force Base, California. During the 6-day flight of Columbia the crew deployed the SATCOM KU satellite and conducted experiments in astrophysics and materials processing. Mission duration was 146 hours and 03 minutes. STS-31 (April 24-29, 1990) was launched from the Kennedy Space Center in Florida, and also returned to land at Edwards Air Force Base, California. During the 5-day mission, the crew deployed the Hubble Space Telescope, and conducted a variety of middeck experiments involving the study of protein crystal growth, polymer membrane processing, and the effects of weightlessness and magnetic fields on an ion arc. They also operated a variety of cameras, including both the IMAX in-cabin and cargo bay cameras, for Earth observations from their record-setting altitude of 380 miles. The mission was completed in 76 orbits of the earth in 121 hours. STS-82 (February 11-21, 1997) the second Hubble Space Telescope (HST) maintenance mission, was launched at night and returned to a night landing at Kennedy Space Center, Florida. During the flight, Dr. Hawley's primary role was to operate the Shuttle's 50-foot robot arm to retrieve and redeploy the HST following completion of upgrades and repairs. Dr. Hawley also operated the robot arm during five space walks in which two teams installed two new spectrometers and eight replacement instruments. They also replaced insulation patches over three compartments containing key data processing, electronics and scientific instrument telemetry packages. HST was then redeployed and boosted to a higher orbit. The flight was completed in 149 orbits covering 3.8 million miles in 9 days, 23 hours, 37 minutes. STS-93 Columbia (July 22-27, 1999) was launched from the Kennedy Space Center on a 5-day mission returning to KSC for the 12th night landing in the Shuttle Program's history. Dr. Hawley served as Columbia's flight engineer. The primary mission objective was the successful deployment of the Chandra X-ray Observatory, the third of NASA's Great Observatories after Hubble Space Telescope and the Compton Gamma Ray Observatory. Dr. Hawley also served as the primary operator of a second telescope carried in the crew module which was used for several days to make broadband ultraviolet observations of a variety of solar system objects. The mission completed 79 orbits in 4 days, 22 hours, and 50 minutes.

NAME: Susan J. Helms (Colonel, USAF)
NASA Astronaut

PERSONAL DATA: Born February 26, 1958, in Charlotte, North Carolina, but considers Portland, Oregon, to be her hometown. She enjoys piano and other musical activities, jogging, traveling, reading, computers, and cooking. Plays keyboard for MAX-Q, a rock-n-roll band. Her parents, Lt. Col. (Ret., USAF) Pat and Dori Helms, reside in Albuquerque, New Mexico.

EDUCATION: Graduated from Parkrose Senior High School, Portland, Oregon, in 1976; received a bachelor of science degree in aeronautical engineering from the U.S. Air Force Academy in 1980, and a master of science degree in aeronautics/astronautics from Stanford University in 1985.

ORGANIZATIONS: Women Military Aviators; U.S. Air Force Academy Association of Graduates; Stanford Alumni Association; Association of Space Explorers, Sea/Space Symposium, Chi Omega Alumni.

SPECIAL HONORS: Recipient of the Distinguished Superior Service Medal, the Defense Meritorious Service Medal, the Air Force Meritorious Service Medal, the Air Force Commendation Medal, NASA Space Flight Medals, and the NASA Outstanding Leadership Medal. Named a Distinguished Graduate of the USAF Test Pilot School, and recipient of the R.L. Jones Award for Outstanding Flight Test Engineer, Class 88A. In 1990, she received the Aerospace Engineering Test Establishment Commanding Officer's Commendation, a special award unique to the Canadian Forces. Named the Air Force Armament Laboratory Junior Engineer of the Year in 1983.

EXPERIENCE: Helms graduated from the U.S. Air Force Academy in 1980. She received her commission and was assigned to Eglin Air Force Base, Florida, as an F-16 weapons separation engineer with the Air Force Armament Laboratory. In 1982, she became the lead engineer for F-15 weapons separation. In 1984, she was selected to attend graduate school. She received her degree from Stanford University in 1985 and was assigned as an assistant professor of aeronautics at the U.S. Air Force Academy. In 1987, she attended the Air Force Test Pilot School at Edwards Air Force Base, California. After completing one year of training as a flight test engineer, Helms was assigned as a USAF Exchange Officer to the Aerospace Engineering Test Establishment, Canadian Forces Base, Cold Lake, Alberta, Canada, where she worked as a flight test engineer and project officer on the CF-18 aircraft. She was managing the development of a CF-18 Flight Control System Simulation for the Canadian Forces when selected for the astronaut program. As a flight test engineer, Helms has flown in 30 different types of U.S. and Canadian military aircraft.

NASA EXPERIENCE: Selected by NASA in January 1990, Helms became an astronaut in July 1991. A veteran of four space flights, Helms has logged over 1,096 hours in space. She flew on STS-54 in 1993, STS-64 in 1994, STS-78 in 1996, and most recently on STS-101. Helms is assigned as a member of the second crew to inhabit the International Space Station (ISS-2), scheduled for launch in February 2001, and composed of a 3 member crew (2 American astronauts and one Russian cosmonaut). The crew will install and conduct tests on the Canadian made Space Station Robotic arm (SSRMS), unload the Italian made Logistics module, conduct internal and external maintenance tasks, conduct medical and science experiments. During her stay onboard the Space Station, STS-104 will bring up the Airlock which will be added to the Space Station. Helms will be the SSRMS operator taking the Airlock from the Shuttle and will berth the Airlock to the Space Station. After approximately 5 months, the ISS-2 crew will return onboard a Space Shuttle that will transport their replacement crew.

SPACE FLIGHT EXPERIENCE: STS-54 Endeavour, January 13-19, 1993. The primary objective of this mission was the deploy of a $200-million NASA Tracking and Data Relay Satellite (TDRS-F). A Diffuse X-Ray Spectrometer (DXS) carried in the payload bay, collected over 80,000 seconds of quality X-ray data that will enable investigators to answer questions about the origin of the Milky Way galaxy. The crew demonstrated the physics principles of everyday toys to an interactive audience of elementary school students across the United States. A highly successful Extravehicular Activity (EVA) resulted in many lessons learned that will benefit Space Station Freedom assembly. Mission duration was 5 days, 23 hours, 38 minutes, 17 seconds. STS-64 Discovery, September 9-20, 1994. On this flight, Helms served as the flight engineer for orbiter operations and the primary RMS operator aboard Space Shuttle. The major objective of this flight was to validate the design and operating characteristics of Lidar in Space Technology Experiment (LITE) by gathering data about the Earth's troposphere and stratosphere. Additional objectives included the deploy and retrieval of SPARTAN-201, a free-flying satellite that investigated the physics of the solar corona, and the testing of a new EVA maneuvering device. The Shuttle Plume Impingement Flight Experiment (SPIFEX) was used to collect extensive data on the effects of jet thruster impingement, in preparation for proximity tasks such as space station docking. Mission duration was 10 days, 22 hours, 51 minutes. STS-78 Columbia, June 20 to July 7, 1996, Helms was the payload commander and flight engineer aboard Columbia, on the longest Space Shuttle mission to date. The mission included studies sponsored by ten nations and five space agencies, and was the first mission to combine both a full microgravity studies agenda and a comprehensive life science investigation. The Life and Microgravity Spacelab mission served as a model for future studies on board the International Space Station. Mission duration was 16 days, 21 hours, 48 minutes. STS-101 Atlantis, May 19-29, 2000, was a mission dedicated to the delivery and repair of critical hardware for the International Space Station. Helms prime responsibilities during this mission were to perform critical repairs to extend the life of the Functional Cargo Block (FGB). In addition, she had prime responsibility of the onboard computer network and served as the mission specialist for rendezvous with the ISS. Mission duration was 9 days, 20 hours and 9 minutes.

NAME: John Bennett Herrington (Commander, USN)
NASA Astronaut

PERSONAL DATA: Born September 14, 1958 in Wetumka, Oklahoma. He grew up in Colorado Springs, Colorado, Riverton, Wyoming, and Plano, Texas. Married to the former Debra Ann Farmer of Colorado Springs, Colorado. They have two children. He enjoys rock climbing, snow skiing, running, cycling. His parents, Mr. and Mrs. James E. Herrington, reside in Spicewood, Texas. His brother, James E. Herrington, Jr., resides in Fort Collins, Colorado. His sister, Jennifer D. Monshaugen, resides in Austin, Texas.

EDUCATION: Graduated from Plano Senior High School, Plano, Texas, in 1976; received a bachelor of science degree in applied mathematics from the University of Colorado at Colorado Springs, in 1983, and a master of science degree in aeronautical engineering from the U.S. Naval Postgraduate School in 1995.

ORGANIZATIONS: Life member of the Association of Naval Aviation, University of Colorado at Colorado Springs Alumni Association. Sequoyah Fellow, American Indian Science and Engineering Society.

SPECIAL HONORS: Distinguished Naval Graduate from Aviation Officer Candidate School, Pensacola, Florida, in 1984. Awarded Navy Commendation Medal, Navy Meritorious Unit Commendation, Coast Guard Meritorious Unit Commendation, Coast Guard Special Operations Service Ribbon, National Defense Medal, Sea Service Deployment Ribbons (3), and various other service awards.

EXPERIENCE: Herrington received his commission from Aviation Officer Candidate School in March 1984 and was designated a Naval Aviator in March 1985. He reported to Patrol Squadron Thirty-One (VP-31) at the Moffett Field Naval Air Station, Mountain View, California for initial training in the P-3C Orion. His first operational assignment was with Patrol Squadron Forty-Eight (VP-48) where he made three operational deployments, two to the Northern Pacific based from Naval Air Station Adak, Alaska and one to the Western Pacific based from the Naval Air Station Cubi Point, Republic of the Philippines. While assigned to VP-48, Herrington was designated a Patrol Plane Commander, Mission Commander, and Patrol Plane Instructor Pilot. Following completion of his first operational tour, Herrington then returned to VP-31 as a Fleet Replacement Squadron Instructor Pilot. While assigned to VP-31 he was selected to attend the U.S. Naval Test Pilot School in Patuxent River, Maryland in January 1990. After graduation in December, 1990, he reported to the Force Warfare Aircraft Test Directorate as a project test pilot for the Joint Primary Aircraft Training System. Herrington conducted additional flight test assignments flying numerous variants of the P-3 Orion as well as the T-34C and the DeHavilland Dash 7. Following his selection as an Aeronautical Engineering Duty Officer, Herrington reported to the U.S. Naval Postgraduate School where he completed a master of science degree in aeronautical engineering in June 1995. Herrington was assigned as a special projects officer to the Bureau of Naval Personnel Sea Duty Component when selected for the astronaut program. He has logged over 2,900 flight hours in over 30 different types of aircraft.

NASA EXPERIENCE: Selected by NASA in April 1996, Herrington reported to the Johnson Space Center in August 1996. Having completed two years of training and evaluation, he is qualified for flight assignment as a mission specialist. Currently, Herrington is assigned to the Flight Support Branch of the Astronaut Office where he serves as a member of the Astronaut Support Personnel team responsible for Shuttle launch preparations and post-landing operations.

NAME: Joan E. Higginbotham
NASA Astronaut

PERSONAL DATA: Born August 3, 1964 in Chicago, Illinois. She enjoys body building (weightlifting), cycling, music, motivational speaking.

EDUCATION: Graduated from Whitney M. Young Magnet High School, Chicago, Illinois, in 1982; received a bachelor of science degree electrical engineering from Southern Illinois University at Carbondale, in 1987, and masters of management and space systems from Florida Institute of Technology in 1992 and 1996, respectively.

ORGANIZATIONS: Delta Sigma Theta Sorority, Inc., Bronze Eagles.

AWARDS: NASA Exceptional Service Medal; Keys to the Cities of Cocoa and Rockledge, Florida; Group Achievement Award for STS-26 Return to Flight; Kennedy Space Center Public Affairs Certificate of Appreciation for Service; Commendation of Merit for Service to the Department of Defense (DOD) Missions; Presidential Sports Award in bicycling and weight training; Outstanding Woman of the Year Award; Outstanding Performance 1992, 1993, 1995; National Technical Association's 50 Distinguished Scientists and Engineers; Florida Institute of Technology's Distinguished Alumni for 1997; Southern Illinois University's Distinguished Alumni.

NASA EXPERIENCE: Joan Higginbotham began her career in 1987 at the Kennedy Space Center (KSC), Florida, as a Payload Electrical Engineer in the Electrical and Telecommunications Systems Division. Within six months she became the lead for the Orbiter Experiments (OEX) on OV-102, the Space Shuttle Columbia. She later worked on the Shuttle payload bay reconfiguration for all Shuttle missions and conducted electrical compatibility tests for all payloads flown aboard theShuttle. She was also tasked by KSC management to undertake several special assignments where she served as the Executive Staff Assistant to the Director of Shuttle Operations and Management, led a team of engineers in performing critical analysis for the Space Shuttle flow in support of a simulation model tool, and worked on an interactive display detailing the Space Shuttle processing procedures at Spaceport USA (Kennedy Space Center's Visitors Center). Higginbotham then served as backup orbiter project engineer for OV-104, Space Shuttle Atlantis, where she participated in the integration of the orbiter docking station (ODS) into the space shuttle used during Shuttle/Mir docking missions. Two years later, she was promoted to lead orbiter project engineer for OV-102, Space Shuttle Columbia. In this position, she held the technical lead government engineering position in the firing room where she supported and managed the integration of vehicle testing and troubleshooting. She actively participated in 53 space shuttle launches during her 9 year tenure at Kennedy Space Center. Selected as an astronaut candidate by NASA in April 1996 Joan Higginbotham reported to the Johnson Space Center in August 1996. Since that time, she had been assigned technical duties in the Payloads & Habitability Branch, the Shuttle Avionics & Integration Laboratory (SAIL), and the Kennedy Space Center (KSC) Operations (Ops) Support Branch. In her previous assignment with the KSC Ops Support Branch, she tested various modules of the International Space Station for operability, compatibility, and functionality prior to launch. Currently, Joan Higginbotham is assigned technical duties in the Astronaut Office CAPCOM (Capsule Communicator) Branch. Having completed two years of training and evaluation, she is qualified for flight assignment as a mission specialist.

NAME: Patricia Hilliard Robertson (M.D.)
NASA Astronaut (Mission Specialist Candidate)

PERSONAL DATA: Born March 12, 1963 in Indiana, Pennsylvania. Her hometown is Homer City, Pennsylvania. Her parents are Ilse Hilliard and the late Harold Hilliard of Homer City, Pennsylvania. Married to Scott Robertson. Patricia enjoys flying, windsurfing, hiking and cooking.

EDUCATION: Graduated from Homer Center High School, Homer City, Pennsylvania In 1980; received a bachelor of science degree in biology from Indiana University of Pennsylvania in 1985, and a medical degree from the Medical College of Pennsylvania in 1989. Completed a three year residency in Family Medicine in 1992 and was certified by the American Board of Family Practice in the same year. Completed a two year fellowship in Space Medicine at the University of Texas Medical Branch and NASA Johnson Space Center in 1997, which included the Aerospace Medicine Primary Course at Brooks Air Force Base.

ORGANIZATIONS: Aerospace Medicine Association, American Association of Family Practice, Experimental Aircraft Association, International Aerobatic Club, Aircraft Owners and Pilot's Association.

SPECIAL HONORS: NASA Performance Award, Young Investigator Award Finalist (Aerospace Medicine Association).

EXPERIENCE: After completing her training in Family Medicine in 1992, Dr. Robertson joined a group practice in Erie, Pennsylvania. She was on the staff of St. Vincent hospital for three years where she served as the clinical coordinator for medical student training, and also provided training and supervision for resident physicians. In 1995 Dr. Robertson was one of two fellows selected to study aerospace medicine at the University of Texas Medical Branch (UTMB), Galveston, and at the Johnson Space Center, Houston. While enrolled as a Space Medicine Fellow, Dr. Robertson completed a research project where she studied eccentric and concentric resistive exercise countermeasures for space flight. Dr. Robertson also served as a member of the faculty at UTMB in the Departments of Family Medicine and Emergency Medicine. In 1997, Dr. Robertson joined the Flight Medicine Clinic at Johnson Space Center, where she provided health care for astronauts and their families, and served as Chairman of the Bone, Muscle, and Exercise Integrated Product Team. Dr. Robertson is a multiengine rated flight instructor and avid aerobatic pilot. In her free time, she enjoys flight instructing, aerobatics, and flying with her husband. She has accumulated over 1500 hours of flight time.

NASA EXPERIENCE: Selected by NASA in June 1998, Dr. Robertson reported for training in August 1998. Astronaut Candidate Training included orientation briefings and tours, numerous scientific and technical briefings, intensive instruction in Shuttle and International Space Station systems, physiological training and ground school to prepare for T-38 flight training, as well as learning water and wilderness survival techniques. Technical assignments to date include serving as the office representative for the Crew Healthcare System (CHeCS), and as Crew Support Astronaut (CSA) for the ISS Expedition 2 Crew.

NAME: Kathryn P. (Kay) Hire (Commander, U.S. Naval Reserve)
NASA Astronaut

PERSONAL DATA: Born August 26, 1959, in Mobile, Alabama. She enjoys competitive sailing, snow skiing, scuba diving, and fishing.

EDUCATION: Graduated from Murphy High School, Mobile, Alabama, in 1977. Bachelor of science degree in engineering and management from the U.S. Naval Academy, 1981. Master of science degree in space technology from Florida Institute of Technology, 1991.

ORGANIZATIONS: Association of Naval Aviation, American Institute of Aeronautics and Astronautics, Institute of Navigation, Society of Women Engineers, U.S. Sailing Association.

SPECIAL HONORS: National Defense Service Medal, Coast Guard Special Operations Service Ribbon, Navy and Marine Corps Overseas Service Ribbon, Space Coast Society of Women Engineers Distinguished New Woman Engineer for 1993.

EXPERIENCE: After earning her Naval Flight Officer Wings in October 1982, Hire conducted worldwide airborne oceanographic research missions with Oceanographic Development Squadron Eight (VXN-8) based at NAS Patuxent River, Maryland. She worked as Oceanographic Project Coordinator, Mission Commander and Detachment Officer-in-Charge on board the specially configured P-3 aircraft.

Hire instructed student naval flight officers in the classroom, simulator, and on board the T-43 aircraft at the Naval Air Training Unit on Mather Air Force Base, California. She progressed from Navigation Instructor through Course Manager to Curriculum Manager and was awarded the Air Force Master of Flying Instruction. In January 1989, Hire joined the Naval Air Reserve at NAS Jacksonville, Florida. Her tours of duty included Squadron Augment Unit VP-0545 and Anti-submarine Warfare Operations Center 0574 and 0374. Hire became the first female in the United States assigned to a combat aircrew when she reported to Patrol Squadron Sixty-Two (VP-62) on May 13, 1993. As a Patrol Plane Navigator/Communicator she deployed to Iceland, Puerto Rico and Panama. Hire later served at NAS Joint Reserve Base New Orleans with CV-63 USS Kittyhawk 0482 and Tactical Support Center 0682. Presently she is a member of the Naval Reserve, Commander Seventh Fleet Detachment 111 at Naval Air Station Dallas, Texas. Hire began work at the Kennedy Space Center in May 1989, first as an Orbiter Processing Facility 3 Activation Engineer with EG&G and later as a Space Shuttle Orbiter Mechanical Systems Engineer for Lockheed Space Operations Company. In 1991 she certified as a Space Shuttle Test Project Engineer (TPE). From the TPE computer console position in the Launch Control Center, she integrated all technical aspects of Space Shuttle turnaround maintenance from landing through next launch. Additionally, she headed the checkout of the Extravehicular Mobility Units (spacesuits) and Russian Orbiter Docking System. Hire was assigned Supervisor of Space Shuttle Orbiter Mechanisms and Launch Pad Swing Arms in 1994.

NASA EXPERIENCE: Selected by NASA in December 1994, Hire reported to the Johnson Space Center in March 1995, and completed a year of training and evaluation. She has worked in mission control as a spacecraft communicator (CAPCOM) since April 1996. Most recently, she served as Mission Specialist 2 on STS-90 Neurolab (April 17 to May 3, 1998). During the 16-day Spacelab flight the seven person crew aboard Space Shuttle Columbia served as both experiment subjects and operators for 26 individual life science experiments focusing on the effects of microgravity on the brain and nervous system. The STS-90 flight orbited the Earth 256 times, covered 6.3 million miles, and logged her over 381 hours inspace.

NAME: Charles Owen Hobaugh (Major, USMC)
NASA Astronaut

PERSONAL DATA: Born November 5, 1961 in Bar Harbor, Maine. Married to the former Corinna Lynn Leaman of East Petersburg, Pennsylvania. They have four children. He enjoys weight lifting, volleyball, boating, water skiing, snow skiing, soccer, bicycling, running, rowing, triathlons. His parents, Jimmie and Virginia Hobaugh, reside in Sault Ste. Marie, Michigan. Her parents, Jerry and Dottie Leaman, reside in East Petersburg, Pennsylvania.

EDUCATION: Graduated from North Ridgeville High School, North Ridgeville Ohio, in 1980; received a Bachelor of Science degree Aerospace Engineering from the U.S. Naval Academy in 1984.

ORGANIZATIONS: U.S. Naval Academy Alumni Association.

SPECIAL HONORS: Distinguished Graduate U.S. Naval Academy, Joe Foss Award for Advanced Jet Training, Graduated with Distinction U.S. Naval Test Pilot School. Awarded the Strike/Flight Air Medal, Navy and Marine Corps Achievement Medal, Combat Action Ribbon, Navy Unit Commendation, and various other service awards.

EXPERIENCE: Hobaugh received his commission as a Second Lieutenant in the United States Marine Corps from the United States Naval Academy in May 1984. He graduated from the Marine Corps Basic School in December 1984. After a six month temporary assignment at the Naval Air Systems Command, he reported to Naval Aviation Training Command and was designated a Naval Aviator in February 1987. He then reported to Marine V/STOL Attack Squadron VMAT-203 for initial AV-8B Harrier Training. Upon completion of this training, he was assigned to Marine Attack Squadron VMA-331 and made overseas deployments to the Western Pacific at MCAS Iwakuni Japan and flew combat missions in the Persian Gulf during Desert Shield/Desert Storm embarked aboard the USS Nassau. While assigned to VMA-331, he attended Marine Aviation Warfare and Tactics Instructor Course and was subsequently assigned as the Squadron Weapons and Tactics Instructor. Hobaugh was selected for U.S. Naval Test Pilot School and began the course in June 1991. After graduation in June 1992, he was assigned to the Strike Aircraft Test Directorate as an AV-8 Project Officer and as the ASTOVL/JAST/JSF Program Officer. While there, he flew the AV-8B, YAV-8B (VSRA) and A-7E. In July 1994, he went back to the Naval Test Pilot School as an Instructor in the Systems Department, where he flew the F-18, T-2, U-6A and gliders. Hobaugh was assigned to the U.S. Naval Test Pilot School when he was selected for the astronaut program. He has logged over 3,000 flight hours in more than 40 different aircraft and has over 200 V/STOL shipboard landings.

NASA EXPERIENCE: Selected by NASA in April 1996, Hobaugh reported to the Johnson Space Center in August 1996. Having completed two years of training and evaluation, he is qualified for flight assignment as a pilot. Hobaugh was initially assigned technical duties in the Astronaut Office Spacecraft Systems/Operations Branch. He is currently assigned to serve as pilot on STS-104/ISS Assembly Flight 7A scheduled for launch in 2001.

NAME: Scott J. "Doc" Horowitz, Ph.D. (Colonel, USAF)
NASA Astronaut

PERSONAL DATA: Born March 24, 1957, in Philadelphia, Pennsylvania, but considers Thousand Oaks, California, to be his hometown. Married to the former Lisa Marie Kern. They have one child. He enjoys designing, building, and flying home-built aircraft, restoring automobiles, and running. His father, Seymour B. Horowitz, resides in Thousand Oaks, California. His mother, Iris D. Chester, resides in Santa Monica, California. Her parents, Frank and Joan Ecker, reside in Jensen Beach, Florida.

EDUCATION: Graduated from Newbury Park High School, Newbury Park, California, in 1974; received a bachelor of science degree in engineering from California State University at Northridge in 1978; a master of science degree in aerospace engineering from Georgia Institute of Technology in 1979; and a doctorate in aerospace engineering from Georgia Institute of Technology in 1982.

SPECIAL HONORS: NASA Exceptional Service Medal (1997), Defense Meritorious Service Medal (1997), NASA Space Flight Medals (STS-75 1996, STS-82 1997, STS-101 2000), Defense Superior Service Medal (1996), USAF Test Pilot School Class 90A Distinguished Graduate (1990); Combat Readiness Medal (1989); Air Force Commendation Medals (1987, 1989); F-15 Pilot, 22TFS, Hughes Trophy (1988); F-15 Pilot, 22TFS, CINCUSAFE Trophy; Mission Ready in the F-15 Eagle at Bitburg Air Base (1987); Systems Command Quarterly Scientific & Engineering Technical Achievement Award (1986); Master T-38 Instructor Pilot (1986); Daedalean (1986); 82nd Flying Training Wing Rated Officer of the Quarter (1986); Outstanding Young Men In America (1985); Outstanding T-38 Instructor Pilot (1985); Outstanding Doctoral Research Award for 1981-82 (1982); Sigma Xi Scientific Research Society (1980); Tau Beta Pi Engineering Honor Society (1978); 1st Place ASME Design Competition.

EXPERIENCE: Following graduation from Georgia Tech in 1982, Scott worked as an associate scientist for the Lockheed-Georgia Company, Marietta, Georgia, where he performed background studies and analyses for experiments related to aerospace technology to validate advanced scientific concepts. In 1983, he graduated from Undergraduate Pilot Training at Williams Air Force Base, Arizona. From 1984 to 1987, he flew as a T-38 instructor pilot and performed research and development for the Human Resources Laboratory at Williams Air Force Base. The following two years were spent as an operational F-15 Eagle Fighter Pilot in the 22nd Tactical Fighter Squadron stationed at Bitburg Air Base in Germany. In 1990, Scott attended the United States Air Force Test Pilot School at Edwards Air Force Base, California, and was subsequently assigned as a test pilot flying A-7s and T-38s for the 6512th Test Squadron at Edwards. Additionally, from 1985 to 1989, Scott served as an adjunct professor at Embry Riddle University where he conducted graduate level courses in aircraft design, aircraft propulsion and rocket propulsion. In 1991, as a professor for California State University, Fresno, he conducted graduate level courses in mechanical engineering including advanced stability and control. Scott has logged more than 5,000 hours in over 50 different aircraft.

NASA EXPERIENCE: Selected as a pilot by NASA in March 1992, Scott reported to the Johnson Space Center in August 1992. He successfully completed a year of initial training and assignments since then include: working technical issues for the Astronaut Office Operations Development Branch; support crew at the Kennedy Space Center for Shuttle launches and landings. A veteran of three space flights, Scott has logged over 853 hours in space. He served as pilot on STS-75 (1996), STS 82 (1997), and STS-101 (2000). He is assigned to command the crew of STS-105 scheduled for launch in 2001.

SPACE FLIGHT EXPERIENCE: STS-75 Columbia (February 22 - March 9, 1996) was launched from and return to land at the Kennedy Space Center, Florida. Principal payloads on STS-75 were the reflight of Tethered Satellite System (TSS) and the third flight of the United States Microgravity Payload (USMP-3). The TSS successfully demonstrated the ability of tethers to produce electricity. The TSS experiment produced a wealth of new information on the electrodynamics of tethers and plasma physics before the tether broke at 19.7 km, just shy of the 20.7 km goal. The crew also worked around the clock performing combustion experiments and research related to USMP-3 microgravity investigations used to improve production of medicines, metal alloys, and semiconductors. The STS-75 mission was completed in 252 orbits covering 6.5 million miles in 377 hours and 40 minutes. STS-82 Discovery (February 11-21, 1997) was the second Hubble Space Telescope (HST) maintenance mission. STS-82 was launched at night and returned to a night landing at Kennedy Space Center, Florida. During the flight, the crew retrieved and secured the HST in Discovery's payload bay. In five space walks, two teams installed two new spectrometers and eight replacement instruments, as well as replacing insulation patches over three compartments containing key data processing, electronics and scientific instrument telemetry packages. Following completion of upgrades and repairs, HST was redeployed and boosted to a higher orbit. The STS-82 mission was completed in 149 orbits covering 3.8 million miles in 9 days, 23 hours, and 37 minutes. STS-101 Atlantis (May 19-29, 2000) was the third Shuttle mission devoted to International Space Station (ISS) construction. Objectives included transporting and installing over 5,000 pounds of equipment and supplies, and one space walk. The STS-101 mission was accomplished in 155 orbits of the Earth, traveling 4.1 million miles in 236 hours and 9 minutes.

NAME: Rick Douglas Husband (Lieutenant Colonel, USAF)
NASA Astronaut

PERSONAL DATA: Born July 12, 1957, in Amarillo, Texas. Married. Two children. He enjoys singing, water and snow skiing, cycling, and spending time with his family.

EDUCATION: Graduated from Amarillo High School, Amarillo, Texas, in 1975. Received a bachelor of science degree in mechanical engineering from Texas Tech University in 1980, and a master of science degree in mechanical engineering from California State University, Fresno, in 1990.

ORGANIZATIONS: Member of the Society of Experimental Test Pilots, Tau Beta Pi, Air Force Association, and the Texas Tech Ex-Students Association.

SPECIAL HONORS: Distinguished Graduate of AFROTC, Undergraduate Pilot Training, Squadron Officers School, F-4 Instructor School, and USAF Test Pilot School; Outstanding Engineering Student Award, Texas Tech University, 1980; F-4 Tactical Air Command Instructor Pilot of the Year (1987); named a 1997 Distinguished Engineer of the College of Engineering, Texas Tech University. Military decorations include the Meritorious Service Medal with two Oak Leaf Clusters, the Aerial Achievement Medal, the Air Force Commendation Medal, the National Defense Service Medal, two NASA Group Achievement Awards for work on the X-38 Development Team and the Orbiter Upgrade Definition Team.

EXPERIENCE: After graduation from Texas Tech University in May 1980, Husband was commissioned a second lieutenant in the USAF and attended pilot training at Vance Air Force Base (AFB), Oklahoma. He graduated in October 1981, and was assigned to F-4 training at Homestead AFB, Florida. After completion of F-4 training in September 1982, Husband was assigned to Moody AFB, Georgia flying the F-4E. From September to November 1985, he attended F-4 Instructor School at Homestead AFB and was assigned as an F-4E instructor pilot and academic instructor at George AFB, California in December 1985. In December 1987, Husband was assigned to Edwards AFB, California, where he attended the USAF Test Pilot School. Upon completion of Test Pilot School, Husband served as a test pilot flying the F-4 and all five models of the F-15. In the F-15 Combined Test Force, Husband was the program manager for the Pratt & Whitney F100-PW-229 increased performance engine, and also served as the F-15 Aerial Demonstration Pilot. In June 1992, Husband was assigned to the Aircraft and Armament Evaluation Establishment at Boscombe Down, England, as an exchange test pilot with the Royal Air Force. At Boscombe Down, Husband was the Tornado GR1 and GR4 Project Pilot and served as a test pilot in the Hawk, Hunter, Buccaneer, Jet Provost, Tucano, and Harvard. He has logged over 3800 hours of flight time in more than 40 different types of aircraft.

NASA EXPERIENCE: Husband was selected as an astronaut candidate by NASA in December 1994. He reported to the Johnson Space Center in March 1995 to begin a year of training and evaluation. Upon completion of training, Husband was named the Astronaut Office representative for Advanced Projects at Johnson Space Center, working on Space Shuttle Upgrades, the Crew Return Vehicle (CRV) and studies to return to the Moon and travel to Mars. Most recently, he served as Chief of Safety for the Astronaut Office. He flew as pilot on STS-96 in 1999, and has logged 235 hours and 13 minutes in space. Husband is assigned to command the crew of STS-107 scheduled for launch in 2001.

SPACE FLIGHT EXPERIENCE: STS-96 Discovery (May 27 to June 6, 1999) was a 10-day mission during which the crew performed the first docking with the International Space Station and delivered 4 tons of logistics and supplies in preparation for the arrival of the first crew to live on the station early next year. The mission was accomplished in 153 Earth orbits, traveling 4 million miles in 9 days, 19 hours and 13 minutes.

NAME: Marsha S. Ivins
NASA Astronaut

PERSONAL DATA: Born April 15, 1951, in Baltimore, Maryland. She enjoys flying, baking. Her parents, Dr. and Mrs. Joseph L. Ivins, reside in Wallingford, Pennsylvania.

EDUCATION: Graduated from Nether Providence High School, Wallingford, Pennsylvania, in 1969; received a bachelor of science degree in aerospace engineering from the University of Colorado in 1973.

NASA EXPERIENCE: Ms. Ivins has been employed at the Lyndon B. Johnson Space Center since July 1974, and until 1980, was assigned as an engineer, Crew Station Design Branch, working on Orbiter Displays and Controls and Man Machine Engineering. Her major assignment in 1978 was to participate in development of the Orbiter Head-Up Display (HUD). In 1980 she was assigned as a flight engineer on the Shuttle Training Aircraft (Aircraft Operations) and a co-pilot in the NASA administrative aircraft (Gulfstream-1). Ms. Ivins holds a multi-engine Airline Transport Pilot License with Gulfstream-1 type rating, single engine airplane, land, sea, and glider commercial licenses, and airplane, instrument, and glider flight instructor ratings. She has logged over 5,700 hours in civilian and NASA aircraft. Ms. Ivins was selected in the NASA Astronaut Class of 1984 as a mission specialist. Her technical assignments to date include: crew support for Orbiter launch and landing operations; review of Orbiter safety and reliability issues; avionics upgrades to the Orbiter cockpit; software verification in the Shuttle Avionics Integration Laboratory (SAIL); Capsule Communicator (CAPCOM) in Mission Control; crew representative for Orbiter photographic system and procedures; crew representative for Orbiter flight crew equipment issues; Lead of Astronaut Support Personnel team at the Kennedy Space Center in Florida, supporting Space Shuttle launches and landings; crew representative for Space Station storage logistics transfer issues. A veteran of four space flights, (STS-32 in 1990, STS-46 in 1992, STS-62 in 1994, and STS-81 in 1997), Ms. Ivins has logged over 1009 hours in space. Ms. Ivins is assigned to STS-98. The crew will continue the task of building and enhancing the International Space Station by delivering the U.S. laboratory module. The Shuttle will spend six days docked to the station while the laboratory is attached and three spacewalks are conducted to complete its assembly. The STS-98 mission will occur while the first station crew is aboard the new spacecraft. Launch is targeted for 2001.

SPACE FLIGHT EXPERIENCE: STS-32 (January 9-20, 1990) launched from the Kennedy Space Center, Florida, on an eleven-day flight, during which crew members on board the Orbiter Columbia successfully deployed a Syncom satellite, and retrieved the 21,400 pound Long Duration Exposure Facility (LDEF). Mission duration was 261 hours, 1 minute, and 38 seconds. Following 173 orbits of the Earth and 4.5 million miles, Columbia returned with a night landing at Edwards Air Force Base, California. STS-46 (July 31-August 8, 1992) was an 8-day mission, during which crew members deployed the European Retrievable Carrier (EURECA) satellite, and conducted the first Tethered Satellite System (TSS) test flight. Mission duration was 191 hours, 16 minutes, and 7 seconds. Space Shuttle Atlantis and her crew launched and landed at the Kennedy Space Center, Florida, completing 126 orbits of the Earth in 3.35 million miles. STS-62 (March 4-18, 1994) was a 14-day mission for the United States Microgravity Payload (USMP) 2 and Office of Aeronautics and Space Technology (OAST) 2 payloads. These payloads studied the effects of microgravity on materials sciences and other space flight technologies. Other experiments on board included demonstration of advanced teleoperator tasks using the remote manipulator system, protein crystal growth, and dynamic behavior of space structures. Mission duration was 312 hours, 23 minutes, and 16 seconds. Space Shuttle Columbia launched and landed at the Kennedy Space Center, Florida, completing 224 orbits in 5.82 million miles. STS-81 (January 12-22, 1997) was a 10-day mission, the fifth to dock with Russia's Space Station Mir, and the second to exchange U.S. astronauts. The mission also carried the Spacehab double module providing additional middeck locker space for secondary experiments. In five days of docked operations more than three tons of food, water, experiment equipment and samples were moved back and forth between the two spacecraft. Following 160 orbits of the Earth the STS-81 mission concluded with a landing on Kennedy Space Center's Runway 33 ending a 3.9 million mile journey. Mission duration was 244 hours, 56 minutes.

NAME: Tamara E. Jernigan (Ph.D.)
NASA Astronaut

PERSONAL DATA: Born May 7, 1959, in Chattanooga, Tennessee. She enjoys volleyball, racquetball, softball, and flying. As an undergraduate, she competed in intercollegiate athletics on Stanford's varsity volleyball team. Her father, Mr. Terry L. Jernigan, resides in Chattanooga, Tennessee. Her mother, Mrs. Mary P. Jernigan, resides in Hesperia, California.

EDUCATION: Graduated from Santa Fe High School, Santa Fe Springs, California, in 1977; received a bachelor of science degree in physics (with honors), and a master of science degree in engineering science from Stanford University in 1981 and 1983, a master of science degree in astronomy from the University of California-Berkeley in 1985, and a doctorate in space physics and astronomy from Rice University in 1988.

ORGANIZATIONS: Member of the American Astronomical Association, the American Physical Society, the United States Volleyball Association, and a Lifetime Member of Girl Scouts.

AWARDS: Distinguished Service Medal (1997); Outstanding Leadership Medal (1996); Exceptional Service Medal (1993); NASA Space Flight Medal (1991, 1992, 1995, 1996).

EXPERIENCE: After graduating from Stanford University, Jernigan served as a research scientist in the Theoretical Studies Branch at NASA Ames Research Center from June 1981 until July 1985. Her research interests have included the study of bipolar outflows in regions of star formation, gamma ray bursters, and shock wave phenomena in the interstellar medium.

NASA EXPERIENCE: Selected as an astronaut candidate by NASA in June 1985, Dr. Jernigan became an astronaut in July 1986. Her assignments since then have included: software verification in the Shuttle Avionics Integration Laboratory (SAIL); operations coordination on secondary payloads; spacecraft communicator (CAPCOM) in Mission Control for STS-30, STS-28, STS-34, STS-33, and STS-32; lead astronaut for flight software development; Chief of the Astronaut Office Mission Development Branch; Deputy Chief of the Astronaut Office. Prior to STS-96 she served as the Assistant for Station to the Chief of the Astronaut Office, directing crew involvement in the development and operation of the Station. A veteran of five space flights, Dr. Jernigan has logged over 1,512 hours in space, including an EVA totaling 7 hours and 55 minutes. She was a mission specialist on STS-40 (June 5-14, 1991) and STS-52 (October 22-November 1, 1992), was the payload commander on STS-67 (March 2-18, 1995), and again served as a mission specialist on STS-80 (November 19 to December 7, 1996) and STS-96 (May 27 to June 6, 1999).

SPACE FLIGHT EXPERIENCE: STS-40 Spacelab Life Sciences (SLS-1) was a dedicated space and life sciences mission aboard Space Shuttle Columbia. During the nine-day flight crew members performed experiments which explored how humans, animals and cells respond to microgravity and readapt to Earth's gravity on return. Other payloads included experiments designed to investigate materials science, plant biology and cosmic radiation. Mission duration was 218 hours, 14 minutes, 20 seconds. Landing was at Edwards Air Force Base, California. STS-52 was also launched aboard Space Shuttle Columbia. During the ten-day flight, the crew deployed the Italian Laser Geodynamic Satellite (LAGEOS) which will be used to measure movement of the Earth's crust, and operated the U.S. Microgravity Payload 1 (USMP-1). Also, the Space Vision System (SVS), developed by the Canadian Space Agency, was tested by the crew using a small target assembly which was released from the remote manipulator system. The SVS will be used for Space Station construction. In addition, numerous other experiments were performed by the crew encompassing the areas of geophysics, materials science, biological research and applied research for Space Station. Mission duration was 236 hours, 56 minutes 13 seconds. Landing was at Kennedy Space Center, Florida. STS-67 Astro-2 mission aboard the Space Shuttle Endeavour was the second flight of the Astro observatory, a unique complement of three telescopes. During this record-setting 16-day mission, the crew conducted observations around the clock to study the far ultraviolet spectra of faint astronomical objects and the polarization of ultraviolet light coming from hot stars and distant galaxies. Mission duration was 399 hours and 9 minutes. Landing was at Edwards Air Force Base in California. On STS-80 the crew aboard Space Shuttle Columbia successfully deployed and retrieved the Wake Shield Facility (WSF) and the Orbiting Retrievable Far and Extreme Ultraviolet Spectrometer (ORFEUS) satellites. The free-flying WSF created a super vacuum in its wake and grew thin film wafers for use in semiconductors and other high-tech electrical components. The ORFEUS instruments, mounted on the reusable Shuttle Pallet Satellite, studied the origin and makeup of stars. Her two planned spacewalks were lost due to a jammed outer hatch on the airlock. Mission duration was a record breaking 423 hours, 53 minutes. STS-96 Discovery (May 27 to June 6, 1999) was a 10-day mission during which the crew performed the first docking to the International Space Station, and delivered 4 tons of logistics and supplies in preparation for the arrival of the first crew to live on the station early next year. The mission was accomplished in 153 Earth orbits, traveling 4 million miles in 235 hours and 13 minutes, during which Dr. Jernigan performed an EVA of 7 hours and 55 minute duration.

NAME: Brent W. Jett, Jr. (Commander, USN)
NASA Astronaut

PERSONAL DATA: Born October 5, 1958, in Pontiac, Michigan, but considers Ft. Lauderdale, Florida, to be his hometown. Married to Janet Leigh Lyon of Patuxent River, Maryland. He enjoys water and snow skiing, board sailing, boating, running, basketball, squash. His parents, Mr. & Mrs. Brent W. Jett, Sr., reside in Ft. Lauderdale, Florida. Her mother, Mrs.Mary Patricia Lyon, resides in Fredericksburg, Virginia. Her father, Mr. James Richard Lyon, Sr., is deceased.

EDUCATION: Graduated from Northeast High School, Oakland Park, Florida, in 1976; received a bachelor of science degree in aerospace engineering from the U.S. Naval Academy in 1981; a master of science degree in aeronautical engineering from the U.S. Naval Postgraduate School in 1989.

ORGANIZATIONS: Society of Experimental Test Pilots, Association of Naval Aviation, U.S. Naval Academy Alumni Association, Association of Space Explorers.

SPECIAL HONORS: Graduated first of 976 in the Class of 1981 at U.S. Naval Academy; Distinguished Graduate U.S. Naval Test Pilot School Class 95. Awarded the Department of Defense Superior Service Medal, DOD Exceptional Service Medal, the Navy Commendation Medal, NASA Exceptional Service Medal, 2 NASA Space Flight Medals, and various otherservice awards.

EXPERIENCE: Jett received his commission from the U.S. Naval Academy in May 1981 and was designated a Naval Aviator in March 1983. He then reported to Fighter Squadron 101 at Naval Air Station Oceana, Virginia Beach, Virginia, for initial F-14 Tomcat training. Upon completion of this training, he was assigned to Fighter Squadron 74 and made overseas deployments to the Mediterranean Sea and Indian Ocean aboard the USS Saratoga (CV-60). While assigned to Fighter Squadron 74, he was designated as an airwing qualified landing signal officer (LSO) and also attended the Navy Fighter Weapons School (Topgun). Jett was selected for the Naval Postgraduate School - Test Pilot School Cooperative Education Program in July 1986, and completed 15 months of graduate work at Monterey, California, before attending the U.S. Naval Test Pilot School in June 1989. After graduation in June 1990, he worked as a project test pilot at the Carrier Stability Department of the Strike Aircraft Test Directorate, Naval Air Test Center, flying the F-14A/B/D, T-45A, and A-7E. Jett returned to the operational Navy in September 1991 and was again assigned to Fighter Squadron 74, flying the F-14B aboard the USS Saratoga (CV-60). Jett was deployed with VF-74 to the Mediterranean Sea when selected for the astronaut program. He has logged over 3,500 flight hours in more than 30 different aircraft and has over 450 carrier landings.

NASA EXPERIENCE: Selected by NASA in March 1992, Jett reported to the Johnson Space Center in August 1992. After 2-years of various technical assignments in the Astronaut Office, Jett was assigned to his first mission as the pilot of STS-72. A year later he again served as pilot on STS-81. From June 1997 to February 1998, he served as NASA Director of Operations at the Yuri Gagarin Cosmonaut Training Center, Star City, Russia. More recently, Jett was the Crew Commander on STS-97. A veteran of three space missions, he has traveled over 12.1 million miles, and logged a total of 699 hours, 15 minutes and 57 seconds in space.

SPACE FLIGHT EXPERIENCE: STS-72 Endeavour (January 11-20, 1996) was a 9-day flight during which the crew retrieved the Space Flyer Unit (launched from Japan 10-months earlier), deployed and retrieved the OAST-Flyer, and conducted two spacewalks to demonstrate and evaluate techniques to be used in the assembly of the International Space Station. STS-81 Atlantis (January 12-22, 1997) was the fifth in a series of joint missions between the U.S. Space Shuttle and the Russian Space Station Mir and the second one involving an exchange of U.S. astronauts. In five days of docked operations more than three tons of food, water, experiment equipment and samples were moved back and forth between the two spacecraft. STS-97 Endeavour (November 30 to December 2, 2000) was the fifth American mission to build and enhance the capabilities of the International Space Station. STS-97 delivered the first set of U.S.-provided solar arrays and batteries as well as radiators to provide cooling. Three spacewalks were conducted to complete assembly operations while the arrays were attached and unfurled. A communications system for voice and telemetry was also installed.

NAME: Gregory C. Johnson (Mr.)
NASA Astronaut (Pilot Candidate)

PERSONAL DATA: Born July 30, 1954 in Seattle, Washington. Married to the former Christine R. Scott. They have 2 children, Scott (21) and Kent (18). Recreational interests include running, cycling and auto repair. His father, Raleigh O. Johnson, resides in Everett, Washington. His mother, Mary Ann Johnson, is deceased. Her parents are Earl and Patricia Scott of Seattle, Washington.

EDUCATION: West Seattle High School, Seattle, Washington, 1972. B.S., Aerospace Engineering, University of Washington, 1977.

ORGANIZATIONS: Society of Experimental Test Pilots; American Institute of Aeronautics and Astronautics; Tau Beta Pi Honorary Engineering Society; Naval Reserve Association.

SPECIAL HONORS: NASA William A. Korkowski Excellence in Achievement Award, VA-128 Attack Pilot of the Year, Carrier Airwing Fifteen Top Ten Tailhook Pilot, Carrier Airwing Fourteen Top Ten Tailhook Pilot, Navy Commendation Medals (3), Navy Achievement Medal, Armed Forces Expeditionary Medal, Humanitarian Service Medal and numerous other USN decorations.

EXPERIENCE: Johnson received his commission through the Naval Aviation Officer Candidate Program at Naval Air Station Pensacola, Fl. in September 1977. He received his Naval Aviator wings in December 1978 and following training was designated an instructor pilot in TA-4J aircraft. In 1980 he transitioned to A-6E aircraft completing 2 deployments in the Western Pacific and Indian Oceans. In 1984 he reported to the United States Air Force Test Pilot School at Edwards Air Force Base, CA. After graduation he reported to the Naval Weapons Center, China lake CA. performing flight test in A-6 and F/A-18 aircraft. Following his flight test tour he reported to Naval Air Station Whidbey Island, WA, as the maintenance deartment head in an operational A-6 squadron. During this tour he completed another western Pacific and Indian Ocean deployment as well as a Northern Pacific deployment. He resigned his commission in 1990 and accepted a position at the NASA JSC Aircraft Operations Division. Johnson is a Captain in the United States Naval Reserve and has served as the commanding officer of three Naval Reserve units. He is the current Commanding Officer of Naval Research Lab 510 in Houston, TX. He has logged over 7,400 flying hours in 50 aircraft and 500 carrier landings.

NASA EXPERIENCE: In April 1990, Johnson was accepted as an aerospace engineer and research pilot at the NASA JSC Aircraft Operations Division, Ellington Field, TX. He qualified as a T-38 instructor, functional check flight and examiner pilot, as well as Gulfstream I aircraft commander, WB-57 high altitude research pilot and KC-135 co-pilot. Additionally, he conducted flight test programs in the T-38 aircraft including JET-A airstart testing, T-38N avionics upgrade testing and the first flight of the T-38 inlet redesign aircraft. In 1994 he assumed duties as the Chief, Maintenance & Engineering Branch responsible for all maintenance and engineering modifications on NASA JSC aircraft. Selected by NASA in June 1998, he reported for training in August 1998. Astronaut Candidate Training includes orientation briefings and tours, numerous scientific and technical briefings, intensive instruction in Shuttle and International Space Station systems, physiological training and ground school to prepare for T-38 flight training, as well as learning water and wilderness survival techniques. Johnson is currently assigned to KSC Operations Support . He will serve in technical assignments until assigned to a space flight.

NAME: Gregory H. Johnson (Lieutenant Colonel, USAF)
NASA Astronaut (Pilot Candidate)

PERSONAL DATA: Born on May 12, 1962 in Upper Ruislip, Middlesex, United Kingdom. Married to the former Cari M. Harbaugh of Lubbock, Texas. They have three children: Matthew, Joseph and Rachel. Recreational interests include traveling, biking, golfing, music, duplicate bridge, and woodworking. His father, Harold C. Johnson, resides in Traverse City, Michigan. His mother, Marion F. Johnson, is deceased. Cari's mother, Beverly S. Harbaugh, resides in Lubbock, Texas. Her father and stepmother, George R. and Arlene Harbaugh, also reside in Lubbock.

EDUCATION: Park Hills High School, Fairborn, Ohio, 1980. B.S., Aeronautical Engineering, United States Air Force Academy, 1984. M.S., Flight Structures Engineering, Columbia University, 1985.

SPECIAL HONORS: 1996 Lieutenant General Bobby Bond Award – Top USAF test pilot, Distinguished Graduate USAF Test Pilot School Class 94A, Onizuka "Prop Wash" Award (94A), 1985 Guggenheim Fellowship to Columbia University, Distinguished Graduate with Honors – USAF Academy Class of 1984, Valedictorian – Park Hills High School Class of 1980, Eagle Scout. Military decorations include Distinguished Flying Cross, Meritorious Service Medal, Air Medals (4), Aerial Achievement Medals (3), Air Force Commendation Medal, Air Force Achievement Medals (2), and various others.

EXPERIENCE: Johnson received his commission from the United States Air Force Academy in May 1984 and was designated an Air Force pilot in May 1986 at Reese Air Force Base, Texas. He was retained as a T-38A instructor pilot at Reese until 1989, when he was selected for an F-15E Eagle assignment. After completing initial F-15E training, Johnson was assigned to the 335th Fighter Squadron, at Seymour Johnson Air Force Base, North Carolina. In December 1990, Johnson deployed to Al Kharj, Saudi Arabia, flying 34 combat missions in support of Operation Desert Storm. In December 1992, he was again deployed to Saudi Arabia for three months, flying an additional 27 combat missions in support of Operation Southern Watch. In 1993, he was selected for Air Force Test Pilot School at Edwards Air Force Base, California, graduating in December 1994. After graduation, he was assigned to the 445th Flight Test Squadron at Edwards, where he flew and tested F-15C/E, NF-15B, and T-38A/B aircraft. In August 1997, he was assigned to Maxwell Air Force Base, Alabama, to attend Air Command and Staff College. He has logged over 3,000 flight hours in more than 30 different aircraft.

NASA EXPERIENCE: Selected by NASA in June 1998, he reported for training in August 1998. Astronaut Candidate Training includes orientation briefings and tours, numerous scientific and technical briefings, intensive instruction in Shuttle and International Space Station systems and operations, physiological training, and flight training in T-38N and Gulfstream II aircraft. Following initial training and evaluation, astronaut candidates receive technical assignments within the Flight Crew Operations Directorate before being assigned to a space flight. Johnson is currently assigned to the Shuttle cockpit upgrade council - redesigning cockpit displays for future Space Shuttle missions.

NAME: Thomas D. Jones (Ph.D.)
NASA Astronaut

PERSONAL DATA: Born January 22, 1955, in Baltimore, Maryland. Enjoys baseball, hiking, biking, camping, skiing, and recreational flying. An avid reader, his favorite subjects are aviation and military history, particularly the American Civil War.

EDUCATION: Graduated from Kenwood Senior High School, Essex, Maryland, in 1973; received a bachelor of science degree in basic sciences from the United States Air Force (USAF) Academy in Colorado Springs in 1977, and a doctorate in planetary science from the University of Arizona in Tucson in 1988.

ORGANIZATIONS: Member of the American Astronomical Society (Division for Planetary Sciences), and the American Geophysical Union.

SPECIAL HONORS: NASA Exceptional Service Award, 1997. NASA Outstanding Leadership Medal, 1995. Komarov Diploma, Federation Aéronautique Internationale, 1997 and 1995. NASA Space Flight Medal, 1996 and 1994. Phi Beta Kappa, University of Arizona, 1988. NASA Graduate Student Research Fellow, 1987. Air Force Commendation Medal, 1983. Distinguished Graduate and Outstanding Graduate in Basic Sciences, USAF Academy, 1977. National Merit Scholar, 1973. Eagle Scout, 1969.

EXPERIENCE: A Distinguished Graduate of the USAF Academy, Dr. Jones served on active duty as an Air Force officer for 6 years. After pilot training in Oklahoma, he flew strategic bombers at Carswell Air Force Base, Texas. As pilot and aircraft commander of a B-52D Stratofortress, he led a combat crew of six, accumulating over 2,000 hours of jet experience before resigning as a captain in 1983. From 1983 to 1988 he worked toward a Ph.D. at the University of Arizona in Tucson. His research interests included the remote sensing of asteroids, meteorite spectroscopy, and applications of space resources. From 1989 to 1990, he was a program management engineer in Washington, D.C., at the CIA's Office of Development and Engineering. In 1990 he joined Science Applications International Corporation in Washington, D.C. as a senior scientist. Dr. Jones performed advanced program planning for NASA's Solar System Exploration Division, investigating future robotic missions to Mars, asteroids, and the outer solar system. After a year of training following his selection by NASA in January 1990, Dr. Jones became an astronaut in July 1991. In 1994 he flew as a mission specialist on successive flights of space shuttle Endeavour. First, in April 1994, he ran science operations on the "night shift" during STS-59, the first flight of the Space Radar Laboratory (SRL-1). Then, in October 1994, he was the payload commander on the SRL-2 mission, STS-68. Dr. Jones next flew in late 1996 on Columbia. Mission STS-80 successfully deployed and retrieved 2 science satellites, ORFEUS/SPAS and the Wake Shield Facility. While helping set a Shuttle endurance record of nearly 18 days in orbit, Dr. Jones used Columbia's robot arm to release the Wake Shield satellite and later grapple it from orbit. Dr. Jones has logged over 40 days (963 hours) in space. Dr. Jones is currently training full-time for the Space Station Assembly Mission 5A, STS-98, targeted for launch in 2001. Dr. Jones' crew will deliver the U.S. Laboratory Module to the Space Station, and he will help install the Lab with a series of three spacewalks. The STS-98 mission will provide the station with science research facilities and expand its power, life support and control capabilities.

NAME: Janet Lynn Kavandi (Ph.D.)
NASA Astronaut

PERSONAL DATA: Born in Springfield, Missouri. Married to John Kavandi. They have two children. She enjoys snow skiing, hiking, camping, horseback riding, windsurfing, flying, scuba diving, piano. Her parents, William and Ruth Sellers of Cassville, Missouri, are deceased.

EDUCATION: Graduated from Carthage Senior High School, Carthage Missouri, in 1977; received a bachelor of science degree in chemistry from Missouri Southern State College - Joplin in 1980; master of science degree in chemistry from the University of Missouri - Rolla in 1982; doctorate in analytical chemistry from the University of Washington - Seattle in 1990.

SPECIAL HONORS: Elected to the National Honor Society, 1977. Valedictorian of Carthage Senior High School, 1977. Awarded Presidential Scholarship from Missouri Southern State College, 1977. Graduated magma cum laude from Missouri Southern State College, 1980. Elected to Who's Who Among Students in American Universities and Colleges, 1980; Who's Who of Emerging Leaders in America, 1989-90, 1991-92; and Who's Who in the West, 1987-88. Awarded certificates for Team Excellence and Performance Excellence from Boeing Missile Systems, 1991.

EXPERIENCE: Following graduation in 1982, Dr. Kavandi accepted a position at Eagle-Picher Industries in Joplin, Missouri, as an engineer in new battery development for defense applications. In 1984, she accepted a position as an engineer in the Power Systems Technology Department of the Boeing Aerospace Company. During her ten years at Boeing, Kavandi supported numerous programs, proposals and red teams in the energy storage systems area. She was lead engineer of secondary power for the Short Range Attack Missile II, and principal technical staff representative involved in the design and development of thermal batteries for Sea Lance and the Lightweight Exo-Atmospheric Projectile. Other programs she supported include Space Station, Lunar and Mars Base studies, Inertial Upper Stage, Advanced Orbital Transfer Vehicle, Get-Away Specials, Air Launched Cruise Missile, Minuteman, and Peacekeeper. In 1986, while still working for Boeing, she was accepted into graduate school at the University of Washington, where she began working toward her doctorate in analytical chemistry. Her doctoral dissertation involved the development of a pressure-indicating coating that uses oxygen quenching of porphyrin photoluminescence to provide continuous surface pressure maps of aerodynamic test models in wind tunnels. Her work on pressure indicating paints has resulted in two patents. Dr. Kavandi has also published and presented several papers at technical conferences and in scientific journals.

NASA EXPERIENCE: Dr. Kavandi was selected as an astronaut candidate by NASA in December 1994 and reported to the Johnson Space Center in March 1995. Following an initial year of training, she was assigned to the Payloads and Habitability Branch where she supported payload integration for the International Space Station. A veteran of two space flights, Dr. Kavandi has logged over 503 hours in space. Dr. Kavandi served as a mission specialist on STS-91 (June 2-12, 1998) the 9th and final Shuttle-Mir docking mission, concluding the joint U.S./Russian Phase 1 program. Most recently, she served aboard STS-99 (February 11-22, 2000) the Shuttle Radar Topography Mission which mapped more than 47 million miles of the Earth's land surface to provide data for a three-dimensional topographical map. Betweenflights, Dr. Kavandi has served in the Robotics Branch and as a CAPCOM (spacecraft communicator) in NASA's Mission Control Center. Dr. Kavandi is currently assigned to the crew of STS-104/ISS Assembly Flight 7A scheduled for launch in 2001.

NAME: James M. Kelly (Lieutenant Colonel, USAF)
NASA Astronaut

PERSONAL DATA: Born May 14, 1964 in Burlington, Iowa. Married to the former Dawn Renee Timmerman of Burlington, Iowa. They have four children. He enjoys family activities, biking, softball, reading, music. Jim's mother, Mary Ann Kelly, resides in Texas. His father, William Kelly, is deceased. Dawn's mother and step father, Kathleen and Russ Williams, reside in Iowa. Her father, Gerald Timmerman, is deceased.

EDUCATION: Graduated from Burlington Community High School, Burlington, Iowa, in 1982; received a bachelor of science degree in astronautical engineering from the U.S. Air Force Academy in 1986; a master of science degree in aerospace engineering from the University of Alabama in 1996.

ORGANIZATIONS: U.S. Air Force Academy Association of Graduates.

SPECIAL HONORS: Distinguished Graduate in the class of 1986 at the U.S. Air Force Academy, with honors; Distinguished Graduate of Undergraduate Pilot Training at Euro-NATO Joint Jet Pilot Training at Sheppard Air Force Base, Wichita Falls, Texas; Top Gun at F-15 initial training at Luke Air Force Base, Phoenix, Arizona; Distinguished Graduate and Liethen-Tittle award for the Outstanding Graduate of the Air Force Test Pilot School, class 93B; Meritorious Service Medal, Air Force Commendation Medals (2), Outstanding Unit Awards (2), Combat Readiness Medals (2), and various other service awards.

EXPERIENCE: Kelly received his commission from the U.S. Air Force Academy in May 1986 and was designated an Air Force Pilot in October 1987. He then reported to the 426th F-15 Replacement Training Unit at Luke Air Force Base, Phoenix, Arizona for initial F-15 Eagle training. After completion, he was assigned to the 67th Fighter Squadron, 18th Fighter Wing at Kadena Air Base in Okinawa, Japan. During his tour in Japan, he was designated as an instructor pilot, evaluator pilot, and mission commander. He was reassigned in April 1992 to Otis Air National Guard Base in Cape Cod, Massachusetts, as part of Project TOTAL FORCE, where he continued flying the F-15 as an instructor and mission commander. He was selected for Air Force Test Pilot School at Edwards Air Force Base, Edwards, California, where he graduated in June 1994. After graduation, he was assigned to the Air Force Flight Test Center detachment at Nellis Air Force Base in Las Vegas, Nevada, where he was a project test pilot and assistant operations officer. He was at Nellis when selected for the astronaut program. He has logged over 1,500 flight hours in more than 35 different aircraft.

NASA EXPERIENCE: Selected by NASA in April 1996, Kelly reported to the Johnson Space Center in August 1996. Having completed two years of training and evaluation, he is qualified for selection as a pilot on a Space Shuttle flight crew. Initially, Kelly was assigned to the Astronaut Office Flight Support Branch where he served as a member of the Astronaut Support Personnel team responsible for shuttle launch preparation. Kelly is assigned to serve as pilot on the STS-102 mission, scheduled for launch in 2001.

NAME: Mark E. Kelly (Lieutenant Commander, USN)
NASA Astronaut

PERSONAL DATA: Born February 21, 1964 in Orange, New Jersey, but considers West Orange, New Jersey, to be his hometown. Married to the former Amelia Victoria Babis of Roscommon, Michigan. They have two children. He enjoys running, weightlifting, basketball, golf. His parents, Richard and Patricia Kelly, reside in Flagler Beach, Florida.

EDUCATION: Graduated from Mountain High School, West Orange, New Jersey, in 1982; received a bachelor of science degree in marine engineering and nautical science (with highest honors) from the U.S. Merchant Marine Academy in 1986, and a master of science degree in aeronautical engineering from the U.S. Naval Postgraduate School in 1994.

ORGANIZATIONS: U.S. Merchant Marine Academy Alumni Association.

AWARDS: Awarded four Air Medals (2 individual/2 strike flight) with Combat "V," Navy Commendation Medal with "V," Navy Achievement Medal, two Southwest Asia Service Medals, Navy Expeditionary Medal, two Sea Service Deployment Ribbons, Overseas Service Ribbon, and various other unit awards.

EXPERIENCE: Kelly received his commission from the U.S. Merchant Marine Academy in June 1986, and was designated a Naval Aviator in December 1987. He then reported to Attack Squadron 128 at Naval Air Station (NAS) Whidbey Island, Oak Harbor, Washington, for initial training in the A-6E Aircraft. Upon completion of this training, he was assigned to Attack Squadron 115 based in Atsugi, Japan. While assigned to Attack Squadron 115 he made two deployments to the Persian Gulf aboard the USS Midway. During his second deployment he flew 39 combat missions in Operation Desert Storm. During this tour he was designated an Airwing Qualified Landing Signals Officer (LSO). Kelly was selected for the Naval Post Graduate School/Test Pilot School Cooperative Education Program in July 1991. He completed 15 months of graduate work at Monterey, California, before attending the U.S. Naval Test Pilot School in June 1993. After graduating in June 1994, he worked as a project test pilot at the Carrier Suitability Department of the Strike Aircraft Test Squadron, Naval Air Warfare Center, Patuxent River, Maryland, flying the A-6E, EA-6B and F-18 aircraft. Kelly was assigned to the U.S. Naval Test Pilot School as an instructor pilot in the F-18, T-38 and T-2 aircraft when selected for the astronaut program. He has logged over 2,000 flight hours in more than 40 different aircraft and has over 375 carrier landings.

NASA EXPERIENCE: Selected by NASA in April 1996, Kelly reported to the Johnson Space Center in August 1996. Having completed two years of training and evaluation, he is qualified for flight assignment as a pilot. Currently, Kelly is assigned technical duties in the Astronaut Office Computer Support Branch.

NAME: Scott J. Kelly (Lieutenant Commander, USN)
NASA Astronaut

PERSONAL DATA: Born February 21, 1964 in Orange, New Jersey. Married to the former Leslie S. Yandell of Atlanta, Georgia. They have one child. His parents, Richard and Patricia Kelly, reside in Flagler Beach, Florida. Enjoys running and weightlifting.

EDUCATION: Graduated from Mountain High School, West Orange, New Jersey, in 1982; received a bachelor of science degree in electrical engineering from the State University of New York Maritime College in 1987, and a master of science degree in aviation systems from the University of Tennessee, Knoxville, in 1996.

ORGANIZATIONS: Member, Society of Experimental Test Pilots.

AWARDS: Navy Commendation Medal, Navy Achievement Medal, 2 Navy Unit Commendations, National Defense Service Medal, Southwest Asia Service Medal, Defense of Kuwait Medal, Sea Service Deployment Ribbon.

EXPERIENCE: Kelly received his commission from the State University of New York Maritime College in May 1987, and was designated a naval aviator in July 1989 at Naval Air Station (NAS) Beeville, Texas. He then reported to Fighter Squadron 101 at NAS Oceana, Virginia Beach, Virginia, for initial F-14 Tomcat training. Upon completion of this training, he was assigned to Fighter Squadron 143 and made overseas deployments to the North Atlantic, Mediterranean Sea, Red Sea and Persian Gulf aboard the USS Dwight D. Eisenhower (CVN-69). Kelly was selected to attend the U.S. Naval Test Pilot School in January 1993 and completed training in June 1994. After graduation, he worked as a test pilot at the Strike Aircraft Test Squadron, Naval Air Warfare Center, Aircraft Division, Patuxent River, Maryland, flying the F-14A/B/D, F/A-18A/B/C/D and KC-130F. Kelly was the first pilot to fly an F-14 with an experimental digital flight control system installed and performed subsequent high angle of attack and departure testing. Kelly has logged over 2,500 flight hours in more than 30 different aircraft and has over 250 carrier landings.

NASA EXPERIENCE: Selected by NASA in April 1996, Kelly reported to the Johnson Space Center in August 1996. On completion of training, he was assigned technical duties in the Astronaut Office Spacecraft Systems/Operations Branch. Most recently, Kelly was the pilot aboard STS-103 Discovery (December 19-27, 1999), an 8-day mission during which the crew successfully installed new instruments and upgraded systems on the Hubble Space Telescope (HST). Enhancing HST scientific capabilities required three space walks space walks. The STS-103 mission was accomplished in 120 Earth orbits, traveling 3.2 million miles in 191 hours and 11 minutes.

NAME: Susan Still-Kilrain (Lieutenant Commander, USN)
NASA Astronaut

PERSONAL DATA: Born October, 24, 1961, in Augusta, Georgia. Married to Colin James Kilrain of Braintree, Massachusetts. She enjoys triathlons, martial arts, and playing the piano. Her parents, Joe and Sue Still, reside in Martinez, Georgia. Colin's mother, Mrs. Terry Kilrain, resides in Braintree, Massachusetts.

EDUCATION: Graduated from Walnut Hill High School, Natick, Massachusetts, in 1979. Master of science degree in aerospace engineering from Georgia Institute of Technology, 1985.

ORGANIZATIONS: Association of Naval Aviation. Association of Space Explorers. The Georgia Tech Foundation.

SPECIAL HONORS: Distinguished Naval Graduate of Aviation Officer Candidate School; Distinguished Graduate of the United States Naval Test Pilot School, Class 103; Awarded the Defense Superior Service Medal, Navy Meritorious Service Medal, Navy Commendation Medal, Navy Achievement Medal, NASA Space Flight Medals (2), and the National Defense Service Medal. Ten Outstanding Young Americans Award by the United States Junior Chamber of Commerce. Good Scout Award, 1997.

EXPERIENCE: After graduating from undergraduate school, Susan worked as a Wind Tunnel Project Officer for Lockheed Corporation in Marietta, Georgia and earned her graduate degree. She was commissioned in 1985 and designated a naval aviator in 1987. Still was selected to be a flight instructor in the TA-4J Skyhawk. She later flew EA-6A Electric Intruders for Tactical Electronic Warfare Squadron 33 in Key West, Florida. After completing Test Pilot School, she reported to Fighter Squadron 101 in Virginia Beach, Virginia for F-14 Tomcat training. She has logged over 3,000 flight hours in more than 30 different aircraft.

NASA EXPERIENCE: Susan reported to the Johnson Space Center in March 1995. Following a year of training, she worked technical issues for the Vehicle Systems and Operations Branch of the Astronaut Office. She also served as spacecraft communicator (CAPCOM) in mission control during launch and entry for numerous missions. A veteran of two space flights, she has logged over 471 hours in space. She flew as pilot on STS-83 (April 4-8, 1997) and STS-94 (July 1-17, 1997). She currently detailed to the Office of Space Flight, NASA Headquarters, Washington, D.C.

SPACE FLIGHT EXPERIENCE: Her first mission, STS-83 (April 4-8, 1997), was cut short because of problems with one of the Shuttle's three fuel cell power generation units. Mission duration was 95 hours and 12 minutes, traveling 1.5 million miles in 63 orbits of the Earth. STS-94 (July 1-17, 1997) was a re-flight of the Microgravity Science Laboratory (MSL-1) Spacelab mission, and focused on materials and combustion science research in microgravity. Mission duration was 376 hours and 45 minutes, traveling 6.3 million miles in 251 orbits of the Earth.

NAME: Kevin R. Kregel
NASA Astronaut

PERSONAL DATA: Born September 16, 1956. Grew up in Amityville, New York. Married to the former Jeanne F. Kammer of Farmingdale, New York. They have four children. His parents, Alfred H. Kregel Jr., and Frances T. Kregel, are deceased.

EDUCATION: Graduated from Amityville Memorial High School, Amityville, New York, in 1974; received a bachelor of science degree in astronautical engineering from the U.S. Air Force Academy in 1978; master's degree in public administration from Troy State University in 1988.

SPECIAL HONORS: Defense Meritorious Service Medal; Air Force Meritorious Service Medal; Air Force Commendation Medal; Navy Commendation Medal; four NASA Space Flight Medals; NASA Exceptional Service Medal.

EXPERIENCE: Kregel graduated from the U.S. Air Force Academy in 1978, and earned his pilot wings in August 1979 at Williams Air Force Base, Arizona. From 1980 to 1983 he was assigned to F111 aircraft at RAF Lakenheath. While serving as an exchange officer flying A-6E aircraft with the U.S. Navy at NAS Whidbey Island, Seattle, and aboard the USS Kitty Hawk, Kregel made 66 carrier landings during a cruise of the Western Pacific. His next assignment was an exchange tour at the U.S. Naval Test Pilot School at Patuxent River, Maryland. Upon graduation he was assigned to Eglin AFB, Florida, conducting weapons and electronic systems testing on the F111, F15, and the initial weapons certification test of the F15E aircraft. Kregel resigned from active duty in 1990 in order to work for NASA. He has logged over 5,000 flight hours in 30 different aircraft.

NASA EXPERIENCE: In April 1990, Kregel was employed by NASA as an aerospace engineer and instructor pilot. Stationed at Ellington Field, Houston, Texas, his primary responsibilities included flying as an instructor pilot in the Shuttle Training Aircraft (STA) and conducting the initial flight test of the T38 avionics upgrade aircraft. Selected by NASA in March 1992, Kregel reported to the Johnson Space Center in August 1992. He completed one year of training and is qualified for assignment as a pilot on future Space Shuttle flight crews. Additional duties have included: Astronaut Support Personnel team at the Kennedy Space Center in Florida supporting Space Shuttle launches and landings; CAPCOM in Mission Control. A veteran of four space flights, Kregel has logged 52 days, 17 hours, 20 minutes and 5 seconds in space. He was the pilot on STS 70 (July 13-22, 1995) and STS-78 (June 20 to July 7, 1996), and was the spacecraft commander on STS-87 (November 19 to December 5, 1997) and STS-99 (February 11-22, 2000).

SPACE FLIGHT EXPERIENCE: STS-70 Discovery (July 13-22, 1995) was a 9-day mission during which the crew performed a variety of experiments in addition to deploying the sixth and final NASA Tracking and Data Relay Satellite. The mission was completed in 142 orbits of the Earth, traveling 3.7 million miles in 214 hours, 20 minutes. STS-70 was the first mission controlled from the new combined control center. STS-78 Columbia (June 20 to July 7, 1996) was a 16-day Life and Microgravity Spacelab mission. It included studies sponsored by ten nations and five space agencies, was the first mission to combine both a full microgravity studies agenda and a comprehensive life science investigation, and served as a model for future studies on board the International Space Station. STS-78 orbited the Earth 271 times, covering 7 million miles in 405 hours, 48 minutes. STS-87 Columbia (November 19 to December 5, 1997) was the fourth U.S Microgravity Payload flight and focused on experiments to study how the weightless environment of space affects various physical processes, and observations of the Sun's outer atmospheric layers. Two members of the crew performed an EVA (spacewalk) which featured the manual capture of a Spartan satellite and also tested EVA tools and procedures for future Space Station assembly. The mission was accomplished in 252 Earth orbits during which the crew traveled 6.5 million miles in 376 hours, 34 minutes. STS-99 (February 11-22, 2000) was an 11-day mission during which the international crew aboard Space Shuttle Endeavour worked dual shifts to support payload operations. The Shuttle Radar Topography Mission mapped more than 47 million miles of the Earth's land surface. The STS-99 mission was accomplished in 181 Earth orbits, traveling over 4 million miles in 268 hours and 38 minutes.

NAME: Wendy B. Lawrence (Commander, USN)
NASA Astronaut

PERSONAL DATA: Born July 2, 1959, in Jacksonville, Florida. She enjoys running, rowing, triathlons and gardening. Her father, Vice Admiral William P. Lawrence (USN, retired), resides in Crownsville, Maryland. Her mother, Anne Haynes, resides in Alvadore, Oregon.

EDUCATION: Graduated from Fort Hunt High School, Alexandria, Virginia, in 1977; received a bachelor of science degree in ocean engineering from U.S Naval Academy in 1981; a master of science degree in ocean engineering from Massachusetts Institute of Technology (MIT) and the Woods Hole Oceanographic Institution (WHOI) in 1988.

ORGANIZATIONS: Phi Kappa Phi; Association of Naval Aviation; Women Military Aviators; Naval Helicopter Association.

SPECIAL HONORS: Awarded the Defense Superior Service Medal, the NASA Space Flight Medal, the Navy Commendation Medal and the Navy Achievement Medal. Recipient of the National Navy League's Captain Winifred Collins Award for inspirational leadership (1986).

EXPERIENCE: Lawrence graduated from the United States Naval Academy in 1981. A distinguished flight school graduate, she was designated as a naval aviator in July 1982. Lawrence has more than 1,500 hours flight time in six different types of helicopters and has made more than 800 ship-board landings. While stationed at Helicopter Combat Support Squadron SIX (HC-6), she was one of the first two female helicopter pilots to make a long deployment to the Indian Ocean as part of a carrier battle group. After completion of a master's degree program at MIT and WHOI in 1988, she was assigned to Helicopter Anti-Submarine Squadron Light THIRTY (HSL-30) as officer-in-charge of Detachment ALFA. In October 1990, Lawrence reported to the U.S. Naval Academy where she served as a physics instructor and the novice women's crew coach.

NASA EXPERIENCE: Selected by NASA in March 1992, Lawrence reported to the Johnson Space Center in August 1992. She completed one year of training and is qualified for assignment as a mission specialist on future Space Shuttle missions. Her technical assignments within the Astronaut Office have included: flight software verification in the Shuttle Avionics Integration Laboratory (SAIL); Astronaut Office Assistant Training Officer. She flew as the ascent/entry flight engineer and blue shift orbit pilot on STS-67 (March 2-18, 1995). She next served as Director of Operations for NASA at the Gagarin Cosmonaut Training Center in Star City, Russia, with responsibility for the coordination and implementation of mission operations activities in the Moscow region for the joint U.S./Russian Shuttle/Mir program. In September 1996 she began training for a 4-month mission on the Russian Space Station Mir, but in July 1997 NASA decided to replace Lawrence with her back-up, Dr. David Wolf. This decision enabled Wolf to act as a backup crew member for spacewalks planned over the next several months to repair the damaged Spektr module on the Russian outpost. Because of her knowledge and experience with Mir systems and with crew transfer logistics for the Mir, she flew with the crew of STS-86 (September 25 to October 6, 1997). A veteran of three space flights, she has logged 894 hours in space.

SPACEFLIGHT EXPERIENCE: STS-67 Endeavour (March 2-18, 1995) was the second flight of the ASTRO observatory, a unique complement of three telescopes. During this 16-day mission, the crew conducted observations around the clock to study the far ultraviolet spectra of faint astronomical objects and the polarization of ultraviolet light coming from hot stars and distant galaxies. Mission duration was 399 hours and 9 minutes. STS-86 Atlantis (September 25 to October 6, 1997) was the seventh mission to rendezvous and dock with the Russian Space Station Mir. Highlights included the exchange of U.S. crew members Mike Foale and David Wolf, a spacewalk by two crew members to retrieve four experiments first deployed on Mir during the STS-76 docking mission, the transfer to Mir of 10,400 pounds of science and logistics, and the return of experiment hardware and results to Earth. Mission duration was 259 hours and 21 minutes. STS-91 Discovery (June 2-12, 1998) was the 9th and final Shuttle-Mir docking mission and marked the conclusion of the joint U.S./Russian Phase I Program. Mission duration was 235 hours, 54 minutes.

NAME: Mark C. Lee (Colonel, USAF)
NASA Astronaut

PERSONAL DATA: Born August 14, 1952, in Viroqua, Wisconsin. Married to the former Paula Marie Simon of Chicago, Illinois. They have two boys, Erik and Matthew. He enjoys jogging, swimming, carpentry, furniture refinishing, and farming. His parents, Charles M. and Ruth Lee, reside in Viroqua, Wisconsin.

EDUCATION: Graduated from Viroqua High School, Viroqua, Wisconsin, in 1970; received a bachelor of science degree in civil engineering from the U.S. Air Force Academy in 1974, and a master of science degree in mechanical engineering from Massachusetts Institute of Technology in 1980.

ORGANIZATIONS: Registered professional engineer in the State of Colorado. Member of the American Angus Association and the Fraternal Order of Eagles.

SPECIAL HONORS: Distinguished Flying Cross, Defense Superior Service Medal, Defense Meritorious Service Medal, Air Force Meritorious Service Medal, 2 Air Force Commendation Medals, 4 NASA Space Flight Medals, NASA Distinguished Service Medal, NASA Outstanding Leadership Medal, NASA Public Service Group Achievement Award, and 2 NASA Exceptional Service Medals.

EXPERIENCE: Following pilot training at Laughlin Air Force Base, Texas, and F-4 upgrade at Luke Air Force Base, Arizona, Lee spent 2-1/2 years at Okinawa Air Base, Japan, flying F-4's in the 25th Tactical Fighter Squadron. Following this assignment, he began his studies at MIT in 1979 specializing in graphite/epoxy advanced composite materials. After graduation in 1980, he was assigned to Hanscom Air Force Base, Massachusetts, in the Airborne Warning and Control System (AWACS) Program Office, as the operational support manager. His responsibilities included resolving mechanical and material deficiencies which affected the mission readiness of the AWACS aircraft. In 1982 he returned to flying, upgrading in the F-16 and serving as executive officer for the 388th

Tactical Fighter Wing Deputy Commander for Operations, and as flight commander in the 4th Tactical Fighter Squadron at Hill Air Force Base, Utah, until his selection as an astronaut candidate. He has logged 4,500 hours flying time, predominantly in the T-38, F-4 and F-16 aircraft.

NASA EXPERIENCE: Lee was selected as an astronaut candidate by NASA in May 1984. In June 1985, he completed a one-year training and evaluation program, qualifying him for assignment as a mission specialist on future Space Shuttle flight crews. His technical responsibilities within the Astronaut Office have included extravehicular activity (EVA), the inertial upper stage (IUS), Spacelab and Space Station systems. Lee has also served as a spacecraft communicator (CAPCOM) in the Mission Control Center, as Lead "Cape Crusader" at the Kennedy Space Center, Chief of Astronaut Appearances, Chief of the Astronaut Office Mission Development Branch, Chief of the EVA Robotics Branch, and Chief of the EVA Branch. He is currently working Space Station assembly issues for the Astronaut Office. A veteran of four space flights, Lee has traveled over 13 million miles going around the world 517 times and spending 33 days in orbit. He flew as a mission specialist on STS-30 (May 4-8, 1989) and STS-64 (September 9-20, 1994), and was the Payload Commander on STS-47 (September 12-20, 1992), and STS-82 (February 11-21, 1997). During STS-64, he logged EVA hours totaling 6 hours and 51 minutes. During STS-82 he logged 19 hours and 10 minutes in 3 EVAs.

SPACE FLIGHT EXPERIENCE: STS-30 Atlantis was launched from Kennedy Space Center, Florida, on May 4, 1989. During this four-day mission, the crew successfully deployed the Magellan Venus-exploration spacecraft, the first U.S. planetary science mission launched since 1978, and the first planetary probe to be deployed from the Shuttle. Magellan arrived at Venus in August 1990, and mapped over 95% of the surface of Venus. Magellan has been one of NASA's most successful scientific missions and has provided us with valuable information about the Venetian atmosphere and magnetic field. In addition, the crew also worked on secondary payloads involving life sciences and crystals. Following 64 orbits of the Earth, the STS-30 mission concluded with a landing at Edwards Air Force Base, California, on May 8, 1989. STS-47 Endeavour, Spacelab-J, was launched from the Kennedy Space Center on September 12, 1992, and landed at the same location on Runway 33 eight days later. Lee was the payload commander on this mission with overall crew responsibility for the planning, integration, and on-orbit coordination of payload/Space Shuttle activities. This cooperative mission between the United States and Japan included 44 Japanese and U.S. life science and materials processing experiments. STS-64 Discovery, was launched from the Kennedy Space Center on September 9, 1994 and landed eleven days later at Edwards Air Force Base, California. Mission highlights included: first use of lasers for environmental research; deployment and retrieval of a solar science satellite; robotic processing of semiconductors; use of RMS boom for jet thruster research; first untethered spacewalk in 10 years to test a self-rescue jetpack, during which Lee logged 6 hours and 51 minutes of EVA. STS-82 Discovery, was the second Hubble Space Telescope maintenance mission. STS-82 launched at night on February 11 and returned to a night landing at Kennedy Space Center on February 21, 1997. Lee again served as payload commander. During the flight, the crew retrieved and secured the HST in Discovery's payload bay. In five space walks, two teams installed two new spectrometers and eight replacement instruments, as well as replacing insulation patches over three compartments containing key data processing, electronics and scientific instrument telemetry packages. Lee conducted three space walks totaling 19 hours and 10 minutes. Following completion of upgrades and repairs, HST was redeployed and boosted to a higher orbit. The flight was completed in 149 orbits covering 3.8 million miles in 9 days, 23 hours, 37 minutes.

NAME: David C. Leestma (Captain, USN, Ret.)
NASA Astronaut

PERSONAL DATA: Born May 6, 1949, in Muskegon, Michigan. Married to the former Patti K. Opp of Dallas, Texas. They have six children. He enjoys golfing, tennis, flying, and fishing. His parents, Dr. and Mrs. Harold F. Leestma, reside in San Clemente, California. Her parents, Mr. and Mrs. Robert L. Opp, reside in Wimberley, Texas.

EDUCATION: Graduated from Tustin High School, Tustin, California, in 1967; received a bachelor of science degree in aeronautical engineering from the United States Naval Academy in 1971, and a master of science degree in aeronautical engineering from the U.S. Naval Postgraduate School in 1972.

ORGANIZATIONS: Associate Fellow, American Institute of Astronautics and Aeronautics (AIAA); Life Member, Association of Naval Aviation.

SPECIAL HONORS: The Distinguished Flying Cross, Legion of Merit, Defense Superior Service Medal, Defense Meritorious Service Medal, Navy Commendation Medal, Navy Achievement Medal, Meritorious Unit Commendation (VX-4), National Defense Service Medal, Battle "E" Award (VF-32), the Rear Admiral Thurston James Award (1973), the NASA Space Flight Medal (1984, 1989, 1992), the NASA Exceptional Service Medal (1985, 1988, 1991, 1992), and the NASA Outstanding Leadership Medal (1993, 1994).

EXPERIENCE: Leestma was graduated first in his class from the U.S. Naval Academy in 1971. As a first lieutenant afloat, he was assigned to USS Hepburn (DE-1055) in Long Beach, California, before reporting in January 1972 to the U.S. Naval Postgraduate School. He completed flight training and received his wings in October 1973. He was assigned to VF-124 in San Diego, California, for initial flight training in the F-14A Tomcat and then transferred to VF-32 in June 1974 and was stationed at Virginia Beach, Virginia. Leestma made three overseas deployments to the Mediterranean/North Atlantic areas while flying aboard the USS John F. Kennedy. In 1977, he was reassigned to Air Test and Evaluation Squadron Four (VX-4) at Naval Air Station Point Mugu, California. As an operational test director with the F-14A, he conducted the first operational testing of new tactical software for the F-14 and completed the follow-on test and evaluation of new F-14A avionics, including the programmable signal processor. He also served as fleet model manager for the F-14A tactical manual. He has logged over 3,500 hours of flight time, including nearly 1,500 hours in the F-14A.

NASA EXPERIENCE: Selected to become an astronaut in 1980. Following his first flight Leestma served as a capsule communicator (CAPCOM) for STS-51C through STS-61A. He was then assigned as the Chief, Mission Development Branch, responsible for assessing the operational integration requirements of payloads that will fly aboard the Shuttle. From February 1990 to September 1991, when he started training for his third space mission, Leestma served as Deputy Director of Flight Crew Operations. Following this flight, he served as Deputy Chief and acting Chief of the Astronaut Office. Leestma was selected as the Director, Flight Crew Operations Directorate, in November 1992. As Director, FCOD, he had overall responsibility for the Astronaut Office and for JSC Aircraft Operations. During his tenure as Director, 41 Shuttle flights and 7 Mir missions were successfully flown. He was responsible for the selection of Astronaut Groups 15, 16 and 17. While director, he oversaw the requirements, development modifications of the T-38A transition to the T-38N avionics upgrades. A veteran of three space flights, Leestma has logged a total of 532.7 hours in space.

He served as a mission specialist on STS-41G (October 5-13, 1984), STS-28 (August 8-13, 1989), and STS-45 (March 24 to April 2, 1992). In September 1998, Leestma was reassigned as the Deputy Director, Engineering, in charge of the management of Johnson Space Center Government Furnished Equipment (GFE) Projects.

SPACE FLIGHT EXPERIENCE: STS-41G Challenger, launched from Kennedy Space Center, Florida, on October 5, 1984. It was the sixth flight of the Orbiter Challenger and the thirteenth flight of the Space Shuttle system. The seven-person crew also included two payload specialists: one from Canada, and one a Navy oceanographer. During the mission the crew deployed the ERBS satellite using the remote manipulator system (RMS), operated the OSTA-3 payload (including the SIR-B radar, FILE, and MAPS experiments) and the Large Format Camera (LFC), conducted a satellite refueling demonstration using hydrazine fuel with the Orbital Refueling System (ORS), and conducted numerous in-cabin experiments as well as activating eight "Getaway Special" canisters. Dave Leestma and Kathryn Sullivan successfully conducted a 3-1/2 hour extravehicular activity (EVA) to demonstrate the feasibility of actual satellite refueling. STS-28 Columbia, launched from Kennedy Space Center, Florida, on August 8, 1989. The mission carried Department of Defense payloads and a number of secondary payloads. After 80 orbits of the Earth, this five-day mission concluded with a lakebed landing on Runway 17 at Edwards Air Force Base, California, on August 13, 1989. STS-45 Atlantis, launched from the Kennedy Space Center, Florida on March 24, 1992. During the nine-day mission the crew operated the twelve experiments that constituted the ATLAS-1 (Atmospheric Laboratory for Applications and Science) cargo. ATLAS-1 obtained a vast array of detailed measurements of atmospheric, chemical and physical properties, which will contribute significantly to improving our understanding of our climate and atmosphere. STS-45 landed on April 2, 1992 on Runway 33 at the Kennedy Space Center, Florida, after completing 142 orbits of the Earth.

NAME: Steven W. Lindsey (Lieutenant Colonel, USAF)
   NASA Astronaut

PERSONAL DATA: Born August 24, 1960, in Arcadia, California. Considers Temple City, California, to be his hometown. Married to the former Diane Renee Trujillo. They have three children. He enjoys reading, water and snow skiing, scuba diving, windsurfing, camping, running, and racket sports. His parents, Arden and Lois Lindsey, reside in Arcadia, California. Her parents, Gene and Marcene Trujillo, reside in Temple City, California.

EDUCATION: Graduated from Temple City High School, Temple City, California, in 1978; received a bachelor of science degree in engineering sciences from the U.S. Air Force Academy in 1982, and a master of science degree in aeronautical engineering from the Air Force Institute of Technology in 1990.

ORGANIZATIONS: Member, Society of Experimental Test Pilots, USAF Academy Association of Graduates.

SPECIAL HONORS: Distinguished Graduate Air Force Undergraduate Pilot Training (1983). Distinguished Graduate and recipient of the Liethen-Tittle Award as the outstanding test pilot of the USAF Test Pilot School Class 89A (1989). Awarded Department of Defense Superior Service Medal, 2 NASA Space Flight Medals, Air Force Meritorious Service Medal, Air Force Commendation Medal, Air Force Achievement Medal and Aerial Achievement Medal.

EXPERIENCE: Lindsey was commissioned a second lieutenant at the United States Air Force Academy, Colorado Springs, Colorado, in 1982. In 1983, after receiving his pilot wings at Reese Air Force Base, Texas, he qualified in the RF-4C Phantom II and was assigned to the 12th Tactical Reconnaissance Squadron at Bergstrom Air Force Base, Texas. From 1984 until 1987, he served as a combat-ready pilot, instructor pilot, and academic instructor at Bergstrom. In 1987, he was selected to attend graduate school at the Air Force Institute of Technology, Wright-Patterson Air Force Base, Ohio, where he studied aeronautical engineering. In 1989, he attended the USAF Test Pilot School at Edwards Air Force Base, California. In 1990, Lindsey was assigned to Eglin Air Force Base, Florida, where he conducted weapons and systems tests in F-16 and F-4 aircraft. While a member of the 3247th Test Squadron, Lindsey served as the deputy director, Advanced Tactical Air Reconnaissance System Joint Test Force and as the squadron's F-16 Flight Commander. In August of 1993 Lindsey was selected to attend Air Command and Staff College at Maxwell Air Force Base, Alabama. Upon graduation in June of 1994 he was reassigned to Eglin Air Force Base, Florida as an Integrated Product Team leader in the USAF SEEK EAGLE Office where he was responsible for Air Force weapons certification for the F-16, F-111, A-10, and F-117 aircraft. In March of 1995 he was assigned to NASA as an astronaut candidate. He has logged over 3800 hours of flying time in 50 different types of aircraft.

NASA EXPERIENCE: Selected by NASA in December 1994, Lindsey became an astronaut in May 1996, qualified for flight assignment as a pilot. Initially assigned to flight software verification in the Shuttle Avionics Integration Laboratory (SAIL), Lindsey also served as the Astronaut Office representative working on the Multifunction Electronic Display System (MEDS) program, a glass cockpit Space Shuttle upgrade program, as well as a number of other advanced upgrade projects. Lindsey also served as Deputy for Shuttle Operations and Co-Chairman of the Space Shuttle Cockpit Council, responsible for designing and implementing an advanced Shuttle cockpit. In between flights he worked as the Shuttle Landing and Rollout representative responsible for training flight crews and testing orbiter landing techniques and flying qualities. He flew as pilot on STS-87 in 1997 and STS-95 in 1998, and has logged over 589 hours in space. Lindsey will command the crew of Atlantis on STS-104, scheduled for launch in 2001. The primary objective of STS-104 is to deliver and install the joint airlock on the International Space Station.

SPACE FLIGHT EXPERIENCE: STS-87 (November 19 to December 5, 1997) was the fourth U.S Microgravity Payload flight and focused on experiments designed to study how the weightless environment of space affects various physical processes, and on observations of the Sun's outer atmospheric layers. Two members of the crew performed an EVA (spacewalk) which featured the manual capture of a Spartan satellite, and tested EVA tools and procedures for future Space Station assembly. During the EVA, Lindsey piloted the first flight of the AERCam Sprint, a free-flying robotic camera. The mission was accomplished in 252 orbits of the Earth, traveling 6.5 million miles in 376 hours and 34 minutes. STS-95 (October 29 to November 7, 1998) was a 9-day mission during which the crew supported a variety of research payloads including deployment of the Spartan solar-observing spacecraft, the Hubble Space Telescope Orbital Systems Test Platform, and investigations on space flight and the aging process. The mission was accomplished in 134 Earth orbits, traveling 3.6 million miles in 213 hours and 44 minutes.

NAME: Richard M. Linnehan (DVM)
NASA Astronaut

PERSONAL DATA: Born in Lowell, Massachusetts. Raised by his paternal grandparents, Henry and Mae Linnehan. Single. He enjoys various sports, outdoor activities and natural history. His sister, Colleen, resides in Nevada.

EDUCATION: Attended Alvirne High School, Hudson, New Hampshire from 1971-1974. Graduated from Pelham High School, Pelham, New Hampshire, in 1975. attended Colby College in Waterville, Maine and the University of New Hampshire in Durham, New Hampshire. Graduated from the University of New Hampshire in 1980 with a bachelor of science degree in Animal Sciences with a minor in Microbiology. Received the degree of Doctor of Veterinary Medicine from The Ohio State University College of Veterinary Medicine in 1985.

ORGANIZATIONS: Member of the American Veterinary Medical Association, the American Association of Zoo Veterinarians, and the International Association of Aquatic Animal Medicine. Faculty member at the North Carolina State University College of Veterinary Medicine in Raleigh-Durham, North Carolina. Board member of the Tulane/Xavier/NASA Astrobiology Center, New Orleans, Louisiana.

SPECIAL HONORS: Navy Group Achievement Award, Navy Commendation Medal, two NASA Space Flight Medals (1996, 1998), NASA Outstanding Leadership Medal (1999), AVMA President's Award, The OSU College of Veterinary Medicine Alumni Award, and The University of New Hampshire Distinguished Alumni Award.

EXPERIENCE: After graduating from The Ohio State University College of Veterinary Medicine in June 1985, Dr. Linnehan entered private veterinary practice and was later accepted to a 2-year joint internship in zoo animal medicine and comparative pathology at the Baltimore Zoo and The Johns Hopkins University. After completing his internship Dr. Linnehan was commissioned as a Captain in the U.S. Army Veterinary Corps and reported for duty in early 1989 at the Naval Ocean Systems Center, San Diego, California, as chief clinical veterinarian for the U.S. Navy's Marine Mammal Program. During his assignment at the Naval Ocean Systems Center Dr. Linnehan initiated and supervised research in the areas of cetacean and pinniped anesthesia, orthopedics, drug pharmacokinetics and reproduction in direct support of U.S. Navy mobile marine mammal systems stationed in California, Florida, and Hawaii.

NASA EXPERIENCE: Selected by NASA in March 1992, Dr. Linnehan reported to the Johnson Space Center in August 1992 where he completed one year of Astronaut Candidate training qualifying him for Space Shuttle flight assignments as a mission specialist. Dr. Linnehan was initially assigned to flight software verification in the Shuttle Avionics Integration Laboratory (SAIL). He was subsequently assigned to the Astronaut Office Mission Development Branch, working on payload development, and mission development flight support for future Space Shuttle missions. A veteran of two space flights, Dr. Linnehan has logged over 787 hours in space. He first flew as a mission specialist in 1996 on STS-78, the Life Sciences and Microgravity Spacelab (LMS) mission. In 1998, he served as the payload commander on the STS-90 Neurolab mission. He is currently assigned to upgrade and service the Hubble Space Telescope as a member of the 4 man EVA crew on STS-109 scheduled for launch in late 2001.

SPACE FLIGHT EXPERIENCE: STS-78 Life and Microgravity Spacelab (June 20 to July 7, 1996) was the longest Space Shuttle mission to date. The 17-day mission included studies sponsored by ten nations and five space agencies, and was the first mission to combine both a full microgravity studies agenda and a comprehensive life sciences payload. STS-78 orbited the Earth 271 times, covered 7 million miles and logged him 405 hours in space. STS-90 Neurolab (April 17 to May 3, 1998) was his second Spacelab mission. During the 16-day flight the seven person crew aboard Space Shuttle Columbia served as both experiment subjects and operators for 26 individual life science experiments focusing on the effects of microgravity on the brain and nervous system. STS-90 orbited the Earth 256 times, covered 6.3 million miles, and logged him an additional 381 hours in space. Both missions served as a model for future life sciences studies on board the International Space Station.

NAME: Paul S. Lockhart (Lieutenant Colonel, USAF)
NASA Astronaut

PERSONAL DATA: Born April 28, 1956 in Amarillo, Texas, to Mr. and Mrs. Charles W. Lockhart. Married to the former Mary Theresa Germaine of Boston, Massachusetts, where her parents, Mr. and Mrs. Joseph R. Germaine, still reside. His mother and stepfather, Joy and Leo Wiley, continue to reside in Amarillo. He enjoys all outdoor sports, including hunting and camping.

EDUCATION: Graduated from Tascosa High School, Amarillo, Texas, in 1974; received a bachelor of arts degree in mathematics from Texas Tech University in 1978, and a master of science degree in aerospace engineering from the University of Texas in 1981. Studied at the University of Innsbruck and the University of Vienna Summer School from 1978-79 on a Rotarian Fellowship. Has also completed aerospace related courses from Syracuse University and the University of Florida.

ORGANIZATIONS: Society of Experimental Test Pilots, Order of Daedalians (Fraternal Order of Military Pilots).

AWARDS: Recipient of Air Force Aerial Achievement Medal, Commendation Medal, Outstanding Unit Award with Valor, National Defense Service Medal, Achievement Medal, and numerous other service recognitions and ribbons. A distinguished graduate of both ROTC and the Air Force Squadron Officer School, Lockhart is also a member of Outstanding Young Men of America and Who's Who in American Colleges.

EXPERIENCE: Lockhart was commissioned a 2nd Lieutenant in the USAF in 1981. Upon graduation from pilot training in 1983, he was assigned to the 49th Fighter Interceptor Squadron flying T-33s. In 1986, he transitioned to the F-4 and flew operationally with U.S. Air Forces, Europe (in Germany) from 1987-1990 as an instructor pilot for F-4 and F-16 aircrew in the tactics of surface-to-air missile suppression. In 1991 he reported to Edwards Air Force Base for year long training as a test pilot in high performance military aircraft. Upon graduation, he was assigned to the Test Wing at the Air Force Developmental Test Center at Eglin Air Force Base, Florida, performing weapons testing for the F-16 aircraft. During his 4-1/2 year tour at Eglin, he was selected as the Operations Officer for the 39th Flight Test Squadron. Much of America's state-of-the-art weaponry was first tested under his guidance at the 39th Flight Test Squadron. He has logged over 3,000 hours in more than 30 different aircraft.

NASA EXPERIENCE: Selected by NASA in April 1996, Lockhart reported to the Johnson Space Center in August 1996. Having completed two years of training and evaluation, he is qualified for flight assignment as a pilot. Currently, Lockhart is assigned technical duties in the Astronaut Office Spacecraft Systems/Operations Branch.

NAME: Michael E. Lopez-Alegria (Commander, USN)
NASA Astronaut

PERSONAL DATA: Born May 30, 1958, in Madrid, Spain. Considers both Madrid, and Mission Viejo, California, to be his hometowns. Married to the former Daria Robinson of Geneva, Switzerland. They have one son. Michael enjoys sports, traveling, cooking. His father, Eladio Lopez-Alegria, resides in Madrid. His mother, Louise Lopez-Alegria, is deceased. Her parents, Professor Stuart and Margareta Robinson, reside in Geneva.

EDUCATION: Graduated from Mission Viejo High School, Mission Viejo, California, in 1976; received a bachelor of science degree in systems engineering from the U.S. Naval Academy in 1980; a master of science degree in aeronautical engineering from the U.S. Naval Postgraduate School in 1988.

ORGANIZATIONS: Member, Society of Experimental Test Pilots; Association of Naval Aviation.

EXPERIENCE: Following flight training, Lopez-Alegria was designated a Naval Aviator on September 4, 1981. He then served as a flight instructor in Pensacola, Florida, until March 1983. His next assignment was to a fleet electronic reconnaissance squadron in Rota, Spain. There he served as a pilot and mission commander aboard EP-3E aircraft, flying missions in the Mediterranean Sea, North Atlantic, Baltic Sea and Central America. In 1986 he was assigned to a two year cooperative program between the Naval Postgraduate School in Monterey, California, and the U.S. Naval Test Pilot School in Patuxent River, Maryland. His final tour before being assigned to NASA was at the Naval Air Test Center as an engineering test pilot and program manager. He has accumulated 4,000 pilot hours in over 30 different aircraft types.

NASA EXPERIENCE: Selected by NASA in March 1992, Lopez-Alegria reported for training to the Johnson Space Center in August 1992. Following one year of training and designation as an astronaut, he was assigned as the Astronaut Office technical point of contact to the Space Shuttle Orbiter, Main Engine, Solid Rocket Booster and External Tank projects. He was subsequently assigned to the Kennedy Space Center where he provided crew representation on orbiter processing issues and provided direct crew support during launches and landings. Following his first space flight he served as NASA Director of Operations at the Yuri Gagarin Cosmonaut Training Center, Star City, Russia. A veteran of two space flights, STS-73 in 1995 and STS92 in 2000, Lopez-Alegria has logged a total of 27 days, 43 hours, 32 minutes and 46 seconds in space, including 14 hours and 3 minutes in two space walks.

SPACE FLIGHT EXPERIENCE: STS-73 Columbia (October 20 to November 5, 1995) was launched from and returned to land at the Kennedy Space Center, Florida. STS-73 was the second United States Microgravity Laboratory mission and focused on materials science, biotechnology, combustion science, the physics of fluids, and numerous scientific experiments housed in the pressurized Spacelab module. Lopez-Alegria served as the flight engineer during the ascent and entry phases of flight, and was responsible for all operations of the "blue" shift on orbit. The STS-73 mission was completed in 15 days, 21 hours, 52 minutes and 21 seconds and traveled over 6 million miles in 256 Earth orbits. STS-92 Discovery (October 11-24, 2000) was launched from the Kennedy Space Center, Florida and returned to land at Edwards Air Force Base, California. During the 13-day flight, the seven member crew attached the Z1 Truss and Pressurized Mating Adapter 3 to the International Space Station using Discovery's robotic arm and performed four space walks to configure these elements. This expansion of the ISS opened the door for future assembly missions and prepared the station for its first resident crew. Lopez-Alegria totaled 14 hours and 3 minutes of EVA time in two space walks. TheSTS-92 mission was accomplished in 202 orbits, traveling 5.3 million miles in 12 days, 21 hours, 40 minutes and 25 seconds.

NAME: Christopher J. "Gus" Loria (Major, USMC)
NASA Astronaut

PERSONAL DATA: Born July 9, 1960 in Newton, Massachusetts. Considers Belmont, Massachusetts, his hometown. Married to the former Sandra Lee Sullivan, R.N., of Oklahoma City, Oklahoma. They have two children. He enjoys running, cycling, weight training, sailing, hiking, fishing, hunting. His mother, Joan Loria, resides in Belmont, Massachusetts. His father, Robert L. Loria, is deceased.

EDUCATION: Graduated from Belmont High School in 1978, and from the US Naval Academy Prepatory School in 1979. Bachelor of science degree in general engineering from the U.S. Naval Academy in 1983. Currently completing his thesis for a master of science degree in aeronautical engineering from the Florida Institute of Technology.

ORGANIZATIONS: Society of Experimental Test Pilots, Safari Club International, Experimental Aircraft Association, Aircraft Owners & Pilots Association, U.S. Naval Academy Alumni Association, Marine Corps Aviation Association, National Rifle Association.

SPECIAL HONORS: Naval Test Wing Atlantic Test Pilot of the Year 1995-1996. Who's Who in the World 1995, Who's Who in the American West 1994. Graduated first in all phases of flight training, Commodore's List with Distinction. Personal awards include the Meritorious Service Medal, 2 Navy Commendation Medals (1 with "V"), 2 Air Medals (both with "V"), 4 Strike Flight Air Medals, Navy Achievement Medal.

EXPERIENCE: Loria received his commission from the Naval Academy in 1983, and was designated a Naval Aviator in July 1988. He transitioned to the F/A-18 Hornet with Strike Fighter Squadron 125 (VFA-125) at Naval air Station Lemoore, California, during August 1988 through August 1989. His next assignment was with Marine Fighter Attack Squadron 314 (VMFA-314) the "Black Knights" at Marine Corps Air Station El Toro, California, where he served as squadron pilot and performed collateral duties as the Quality Assurance Officer and Assistant Maintenance Officer in the squadron aircraft maintenance department. While assigned to the Black Knights he deployed to Bahrain for Operations Desert Shield and Desert Storm where he flew 42 combat missions in support of allied operations. In 1992, while assigned as an instructor pilot to Marine Fighter Attack Training Squadron 101 (VMFAT-101) he was selected for the United States Air Force Test Pilot School at Edwards Air Force Base, California. January 1994 to July 1996, he was assigned to the Strike Aircraft Test Squadron, Naval Air Station Patuxent River, Maryland, as an experimental test pilot. Loria distinguished himself in the areas of high angle of attack flight test, aircraft departure and spin testing, ordnance, flight controls and aircraft flying qualities testing for the F/A-18 Hornet. He has almost 2,000 hours of flight time and had flown over 35 different aircraft.

NASA EXPERIENCE: Previous NASA experience includes assignment as test pilot and Project Officer for the Department of the Navy on the X-31 Program at the NASA Dryden Flight Research Facility, Edwards AFB, CA from July 1994 to June 1995. Also test pilot on Dryden's F/A-18 High Alpha Research Vehicle or "HARV" during March of 1995, conducting spin testing and the first successful excitation of the Hornet Falling Leaf out of control mode during flight test. Participated in physiology testing of the prototype High Altitude & G System (or HAGS) which is a combination g-suit and partial pressure suit for NASA Dryden's F-16XL Program. Lead Department of the Navy test pilot on the prestigious NASA/U.S. Navy/Industry Aircraft Control Power Working Group. Selected by NASA in April 1996, Loria reported to the Johnson Space Center in August 1996. Having completed two years of training and evaluation, he is qualified for flight assignment as a pilot. Currently, Loria is assigned technical duties in the Astronaut Office Spacecraft Systems/Operations Branch.

NAME: Stanley G. Love (Ph.D.)
NASA Astronaut (Mission Specialist Candidate)

PERSONAL DATA: Born June 8, 1965 in San Diego, California, but considers Eugene, Oregon to be his hometown. Married. Two children. Recreational interests include flying, alpine hiking, bicycling, snorkeling, alternative music, and animation. His parents, Glen A. and Rhoda M. Love, reside in Oregon.

EDUCATION: Graduated from Winston Churchill High School, Eugene, Oregon, in 1983; received a bachelor of science degree in physics from Harvey Mudd College, Claremont, California, in 1987; received master of science and doctor of philosophy degrees in astronomy from the University of Washington in 1989 and 1993, respectively.

ORGANIZATIONS: American Astronomical Society; American Geophysical Union; American Institute of Aeronautics and Astronautics; Astronomical Society of the Pacific; Harvey Mudd College Alumni Association; Meteoritical Society.

AWARDS: NOVA Award, Jet Propulsion Laboratory (1998). O.K. Earl Prize Postdoctoral Fellowship, California Institute of Technology (1995). Dean's List Distinction, Harvey Mudd College (1985, 1986, 1987).

EXPERIENCE: Worked summers at the University of Oregon in Eugene, as a computer programming instructor (1984) and as an assistant in physics and chemistry laboratories (1985-1987). As a graduate teaching assistant at the University of Washington in Seattle beginning in 1987, he taught and led laboratory sections for undergraduate courses in general, and for planetary astronomy. He worked as a graduate research assistant at the University of Washington from 1989 to 1993 on a variety of projects including space propulsion and energy storage, stellar photometry and spectroscopy, analysis of space-exposed surfaces, hypervelocity impact and particle capture, atmospheric entry heating of micrometeoroids, infrared imaging of the zodiacal light, and electron microscopy of interplanetary dust particles. Moved to the University of Hawaii in Honolulu in 1994 for a postdoctoral research appointment modeling the formation of meteoritic chondrules and the collisional evolution of asteroids, and investigating the possibility of meteorites from the planet Mercury. Awarded a prize postdoctoral fellowship at the California Institute of Technology in 1995: work there included computational fluid dynamic simulations of asteroid collisions, calibration of the Cassini spacecraft dust particle impact detector, and experimental shock compression of the mineral calcite. Transferred to the Jet Propulsion Laboratory as a staff engineer in 1997 to work on computer models and simulations of spacecraft optical instrument systems and to participate in a Laboratory-wide process re-engineering effort.

NASA EXPERIENCE: Selected by NASA in June 1998, he reported for training in August 1998. Astronaut CandidateTraining includes orientation briefings and tours, numerous scientific and technical briefings, intensive instruction in Shuttle and International Space Station systems, physiological training and ground school to prepare for T-38 flight training, as well as learning water and wilderness survival techniques. Dr. Love currently serves as a CAPCOM (spacecraft communicator) in Mission Control during International Space Station missions. He will serve in technical assignments until assigned to a space flight.

NAME: Edward Tsang Lu (Ph.D.)
NASA Astronaut

PERSONAL DATA: Born July 1, 1963, in Springfield, Massachusetts. Considers Honolulu, Hawaii, and Webster, New York, to be his hometowns. Unmarried. He enjoys aerobatic flying, coaching wrestling, piano, tennis, surfing, skiing, travel. His parents, Charlie and Snowlily Lu, reside in Fremont, California.

EDUCATION: Graduated from R.L. Thomas High School, Webster, New York, in 1980. Bachelor of science degree in electrical engineering from Cornell University, 1984. Doctorate in applied physics from Stanford University, 1989.

ORGANIZATIONS: American Astronomical Society, Aircraft Owners and Pilots Association, Experimental Aircraft Association.

SPECIAL HONORS: Cornell University Presidential Scholar, Hughes Aircraft Company Masters Fellow.

EXPERIENCE: Since obtaining his Ph.D., Dr. Lu has been a research physicist working in the fields of solar physics and astrophysics. He was a visiting scientist at the High Altitude Observatory in Boulder, Colorado, from 1989 until 1992, the final year holding a joint appointment with the Joint Institute for Laboratory Astrophysics at the University of Colorado. From 1992 until 1995, he was a postdoctoral fellow at the Institute for Astronomy in Honolulu, Hawaii. Dr. Lu has developed a number of new theoretical advances which have provided for the first time a basic understanding of the underlying physics of solar flares. He has published articles on a wide range of topics including solar flares, cosmology, solar oscillations, statistical mechanics, and plasma physics. He holds a commercial pilot certificate with instrument andmulti-engine ratings, and has over 1000 hours of flying time.

NASA EXPERIENCE: Selected by NASA in December 1994, Dr. Lu reported to the Johnson Space Center in March 1995, has completed a year of training and evaluation, and is qualified for assignment as a mission specialist. Among technical assignments held since then Dr. Lu has worked in the astronaut office computer support branch, and has served as lead astronaut for Space Station training issues. Dr. Lu flew as a mission specialist on STS-84 in 1997, and was a mission specialist and payload commander on STS-106 in 2000. Twice flown, Dr. Lu has logged over 504 hours in space, and an EVA (spacewalk) totalling 6 hours and 14 minutes.

SPACE FLIGHT EXPERIENCE: STS-84 Atlantis (May 15-24, 1997), was NASA's sixth Shuttle mission to rendezvous and dock with the Russian Space Station Mir. In completing this 9-day mission, Dr. Lu traveled 3.6 million miles in 144 orbits of the Earth logging a total of 221 hours and 20 minutes in space. STS-106 Atlantis (September 8-20, 2000). During the 12-day mission, the crew successfully prepared the International Space Station for the arrival of the first permanent crew. The five astronauts and two cosmonauts delivered more than 6,600 pounds of supplies and installed batteries, power converters, life support, and exercise equipment on the Space Station. Ed Lu and Yuri Malenchenko performed a 6 hour and 14 minute space walk in order to connect power, data and communications cables to the newly arrived Zvezda Service Module and the Space Station. STS-106 orbited the Earth 185 times, and covered 4.9 million miles in 11 days, 19 hours, and 10 minutes.

NAME: Shannon W. Lucid (Ph.D.)
NASA Astronaut

PERSONAL DATA: Born January 14, 1943, in Shanghai, China, but considers Bethany, Oklahoma, to be her hometown. Married to Michael F. Lucid of Indianapolis, Indiana. They have two daughters and one son. She enjoys flying, camping, hiking, and reading. Her parents, Mr. and Mrs. Joseph O. Wells, are deceased.

EDUCATION: Graduated from Bethany High School, Bethany, Oklahoma, in 1960; received a bachelor of science degree in chemistry from the University of Oklahoma in 1963, and master of science and doctor of philosophy degrees in biochemistry from the University of Oklahoma in 1970 and 1973, respectively.

SPECIAL HONORS: The recipient of numerous awards, Dr. Lucid most recently was awarded the Congressional Space Medal of Honor by the President of the United States. She is the first and only woman to have earned this prestigious award. Dr. Lucid was also awarded the Order of Friendship Medal by Russian President Boris Yeltsin. This is one of the highest Russian civilian awards and the highest award that can be presented to a non-citizen.

EXPERIENCE: Dr. Lucid's experience includes a variety of academic assignments, such as teaching assistant at the University of Oklahoma's Department of Chemistry from 1963 to 1964; senior laboratory technician at the Oklahoma Medical Research Foundation from 1964 to 1966; chemist at Kerr-McGee, Oklahoma City, Oklahoma, 1966 to 1968; graduate assistant at the University of Oklahoma Health Science Center's Department of Biochemistry and Molecular Biology from 1969 to 1973; and research associate with the Oklahoma Medical Research Foundation in Oklahoma City, Oklahoma, from 1974 until her selection to the astronaut candidate training program. Dr. Lucid is a commercial, instrument, and multi-engine rated pilot.

NASA EXPERIENCE: Selected by NASA in January 1978, Dr. Lucid became an astronaut in August 1979. She is qualified for assignment as a mission specialist on Space Shuttle flight crews. Some of her technical assignments have included: the Shuttle Avionics Integration Laboratory (SAIL); the Flight Software Laboratory, in Downey, California, working with the rendezvous and proximity operations group; Astronaut Office interface at Kennedy Space Center, Florida, participating in payload testing, Shuttle testing, and launch countdowns; spacecraft communicator (CAPCOM) in the JSC Mission Control Center during numerous Space Shuttle missions; Chief of Mission Support; Chief of Astronaut Appearances. A veteran of five space flights, Dr. Lucid has logged 5,354 hours (223 days) in space. She served as a mission specialist on STS-51G (June 17-24, 1985), STS-34

(October 18-23, 1989), STS-43 (August 2-11, 1991), STS-58 (October 18 to November 1, 1993), and most recently served as a Board Engineer 2 on Russia's Space Station Mir (launching March 22, 1996 aboard STS-76 and returning September 26, 1996 aboard STS-79). Dr. Lucid holds an international record for the most flight hours in orbit by any non-Russian, and holds the record for the most flight hours in orbit by any woman in the world.

SPACE FLIGHT EXPERIENCE: STS-51G Discovery (June 17-24, 1985) was a 7-day mission during which crew deployed communications satellites for Mexico (Morelos), the Arab League (Arabsat), and the United States (AT&T Telstar). They used the Remote Manipulator System (RMS) to deploy and later retrieve the SPARTAN satellite which performed 17 hours of x-ray astronomy experiments while separated from the Space Shuttle. In addition, the crew activated the Automated Directional Solidification Furnace (ADSF), six Getaway Specials, and participated in biomedical experiments. The mission was accomplished in 112 orbits of the Earth, traveling 2.5 million miles in 169 hours and 39 minutes. Landing was at Edwards Air Force Base (EAFB), California. STS-34 Atlantis (October 18-23, 1989) was a 5-day mission during which the deployed the Galileo spacecraft on its journey to explore Jupiter, operated the Shuttle Solar Backscatter Ultraviolet Instrument (SSBUV) to map atmospheric ozone, and performed numerous secondary experiments involving radiation measurements, polymer morphology, lightning research, microgravity effects on plants, and a student experiment on ice crystal growth in space. The mission was accomplished in 79 orbits of the Earth, traveling 1.8 million miles in 119 hours and 41 minutes. Landing was at Edwards Air Force Base, California. STS-43 Atlantis (August 2-11, 1991) was a nine-day mission during which the crew deployed the fifth Tracking and Data Relay Satellite (TDRS-E). The crew also conducted 32 physical, material, and life science experiments, mostly relating to the Extended Duration Orbiter and Space Station Freedom. The mission was accomplished in 142 orbits of the Earth, traveling 3.7 million miles in 213 hours, 21 minutes, 25 seconds. STS-43 Atlantis was the eighth Space Shuttle to land at KSC.STS-58 Columbia (October 18 to November 1, 1993). This record duration fourteen-day mission was recognized by NASA management as the most successful and efficient Spacelab flight flown by NASA. The STS-58 crew performed neurovestibular, cardiovascular, cardiopulmonary, metabolic, and musculoskeletal medical experiments on themselves and 48 rats, expanding our knowledge of human and animal physiology both on earth and in space flight. In addition, they performed 16 engineering tests aboard the Orbiter Columbia and 20 Extended Duration Orbiter Medical Project experiments. The mission was accomplished in 225 orbits of the Earth, traveling 5.8 million miles in 336 hours, 13 minutes, 01 seconds. Landing was at Edwards Air Force Base, California. In completing this flight Dr. Lucid logged 838 hours, 54 minutes in space making her America's female space traveler with the most hours in space. Dr. Lucid currently holds the United States single mission space flight endurance record on the Russian Space Station Mir. Following a year of training in Star City, Russia, her journey started with liftoff at Kennedy Space Center, Florida, on March 22, 1996 aboard STS-76 Atlantis. Following docking, she transferred to the Mir Space Station. Assigned as a Board Engineer 2, she performed numerous life science and physical science experiments during the course of her stay aboard Mir. Her return journey to KSC was made aboard STS-79 Atlantis on September 26, 1996. In completing this mission Dr. Lucid traveled 75.2 million miles in 188 days, 04 hours, 00 minutes, 14 seconds.

NAME: Steven (Steve) Glenwood MacLean (Ph.D.)
CSA Astronaut

PERSONAL DATA: Born December 14, 1954, in Ottawa, Ontario. Married to Nadine Wielgopolski of Hull, Quebec. They have three children. He enjoys hiking, canoeing, flying, parachuting, gymnastics.

EDUCATION: Attended primary and secondary schools in Ottawa. Received a Bachelor of Science degree in Honors Physics in 1977 and a Doctorate in Physics in 1983 from York University in Toronto, Ontario.

ORGANIZATIONS: Honorary Fellow of Norman Bethune College of York University (1988). President of the Board of Directors for the Mont Megantic Observatory project.

SPECIAL HONORS: In 1977, he received the President's Award at York University (Murray G. Ross Award). He is recipient of a Natural Sciences and Engineering Research Council Post Graduate Scholarship in 1980, two Ontario Graduate Scholarships, one in 1981 and the other in 1982, and a Natural Sciences and Engineering Research Council Postdoctoral Fellowship in 1983. In 1993, he received a doctorate (Honoris causa) from the Collège militaire royal de Saint-Jean in Quebec, a Doctorate of Science (Honoris causa) from York University in Toronto, and a Doctorate of Science (Honoris causa) from Acadia University in Halifax.

EXPERIENCE: In 1974-76, Dr. MacLean worked in sports administration and public relations at York University. In 1976-77, he was a member of the Canadian National Gymnastics Team. He taught part-time at York University from 1980-83. In 1983, he became a visiting scholar at Stanford University under Nobel Laureate A.L. Shalow. He is a laser-physicist, and his research has included work on electro-optics, laser-induced fluorescence of particles and crystals and multi-photon laser spectroscopy. In December 1983, Dr. MacLean was one of six astronauts selected by the Canadian Space Agency (CSA). He began astronaut training in February 1984 and, in December 1985, was designated as the Canadian Payload Specialist to fly with the CANEX-2 set of Canadian experiments in space. His mission, STS-52, took place October 22 to November 1, 1992. From 1988 to 1991, he was Astronaut Adviser to the Strategic Technologies in Automation & Robotics Program (STEAR). From 1987 to 1993, he was Program Manager of the Advanced Space Vision System (SVS). In July 1992, NASA agreed to outfit the shuttle fleet with an operational version of the Orbiter Space Vision System (OSVS) which will give eyes to the Canadarm on board the space shuttle, and the Advanced Vision Unit (AVU) which will be used with the Mobile Servicing System (MSS). The MSS is Canada's contribution to the International Space Station. He was Program Manager for the OSVS until his interim assignment, in July 1993, to a collateral duty as Science Advisor for the International Space Station. In 1993, he became an adjunct professor at the University of Toronto Institute for Aerospace Studies. In April 1994, he was appointed Acting Director-General of the Canadian Astronaut Program. In July 1996 he was selected to attend NASA's Astronaut Candidate Training at Johnson Space Center, Houston, Texas. Having completed two years of training and evaluation, he is qualified for flight assignment as a mission specialist. Currently, MacLean is assigned technical duties in the Astronaut Office Robotics Branch.

NAME: Sandra H. Magnus (Ph.D.)
     NASA Astronaut

PERSONAL DATA: Born October 30, 1964 in Belleville, Illinois. Enjoys soccer, reading, travel, water activities .

EDUCATION: Graduated from Belleville West High School, Belleville, Illinois, in 1982; received a bachelor degree in physics and a master degree in electrical engineering from the University of Missouri-Rolla in 1986 and 1990, respectively, and a doctorate from the School of Material Science and Engineering at the Georgia Institute of Technology in 1996.

ORGANIZATIONS: ASM/TMS (Metallurgical/Material Society), Material Research Society.

SPECIAL HONORS: Outstanding Graduate Teaching Assistant Award (1994 and 1996), Saturn Team Award (1994), Performance Bonus Award (1989).

EXPERIENCE: During 1986 to 1991, Magnus worked for McDonnell Douglas Aircraft Company as a stealth engineer where she worked on internal research and development studying the effectiveness of RADAR signature reduction techniques. She was also assigned to the Navy's A-12 Attack Aircraft program primarily working on the propulsion system until the program was cancelled. From 1991 to 1996, Magnus completed her thesis work which was supported by NASA-Lewis Research Center through a Graduate Student Fellowship and involved investigations on materials of interest for "Scandate" thermionic cathodes. Thermodynamic equilibria studies along with conductivity and emission measurements on compounds in the Ba O.SC2O3.WO3 ternary system were conducted to identify compounds with potential use in these types of cathodes.

NASA EXPERIENCE: Selected by NASA in April 1996, Dr. Magnus reported to the Johnson Space Center in August 1996. Having completed two years of training and evaluation, she is qualified for flight assignment as a mission specialist. From January 1997 through May 1998 Dr. Magnus worked in the Astronaut Office Payloads/Habitability Branch. Her duties involved working with ESA, NASDA and Brazil on science freezers, glove boxes and other facility type payloads. In May 1998 Dr. Magnus was assigned as a "Russian Crusader" which involves travel to Russia in support of hardware testing and operational products development.

NAME: Michael J. Massimino (Ph.D.)
     NASA Astronaut

PERSONAL DATA: Born August 19, 1962 in Oceanside, New York. His hometown is Franklin Square, New York. Married. He enjoys basketball, running, weightlifting, and camping.

EDUCATION: Graduated from H. Frank Carey High School, Franklin Square, New York, in 1980; received a bachelor of science degree in industrial engineering with honors from Columbia University in 1984; master of science degrees in mechanical engineering and in technology and policy, the degree of mechanical engineer, and a doctorate in mechanical engineering from the Massachusetts Institute of Technology (MIT) in 1988, 1990, and 1992, respectively.

ORGANIZATIONS: MIT Alumni Association, and Columbia University Alumni Association.

SPECIAL HONORS: NASA Graduate Student Researchers Program Fellowship, U.S. Air Force Office of Scientific Research Travel Prize to Japan, Best Paper Award at the 5th IFAC Symposium on Man-Machine Systems, Gold Medal in the Student Paper Contest at the 41st Congress of the International Astronautical Federation, and MIT Zakhartchenko Fellowship.

EXPERIENCE: Upon completing his B.S. degree from Columbia University, Massimino worked for IBM as a systems engineer in New York City from 1984 until 1986. In 1986 he entered graduate school at the Massachusetts Institute of Technology where he conducted research on human operator control of space robotics systems in the MIT Mechanical Engineering Department's Human-Machine Systems Laboratory. His work resulted in the awarding of two patents. While a student at MIT he worked during the Summer of 1987 as a general engineer at NASA Headquarters in the Office of Aeronautics and Space Technology, during the summers of 1988 and 1989 as a research fellow in the Man-Systems Integration Branch at the NASA Marshall Spaceflight Center, and during the summer of 1990 as a visiting research engineer at the German Aerospace Research Establishment (DLR) in Oberpfaffenhofen, Germany. After graduating from MIT in 1992, Massimino worked at McDonnell Douglas Aerospace in Houston, Texas as a research engineer where he developed laptop computer displays to assist operators of the Space Shuttle remote manipulator system. These displays included the Manipulator Position Display, which was evaluated on STS-69. From 1992 to 1995 he was also an adjunct assistant professor in the Mechanical Engineering & Material Sciences Department at Rice University, where he taught feedback control of mechanical systems. In September, 1995 Massimino joined the faculty of the Georgia Institute of Technology as an assistant professor in the School of Industrial and Systems Engineering. At Georgia Tech he taught human-machine systems engineering classes and conducted research on human-machine interfaces for space and aircraft systems in the Center for Human-Machine Systems Research. He has published papers in technical journals and in the proceedings of technical conferences.

NASA EXPERIENCE: Selected as an astronaut candidate by NASA in May 1996, Massimino reported to the Johnson Space Center in August 1996. Having completed two years of training and evaluation, he is qualified for flight assignment as a mission specialist. Massimino was initially assigned technical duties in the Astronaut Office Robotics Branch. He is currently assigned to upgrade and service the Hubble Space Telescope during the STS-109 mission scheduled for launch in 2001.

NAME: Richard A. "Rick" Mastracchio
NASA Astronaut

PERSONAL DATA: Born February 11, 1960 in Waterbury, Connecticut. Married to the former Candace L. Stolfi of Waterbury, Connecticut. They have three children. He enjoys flying, baseball, basketball, swimming, wood working, spending time with his family. His parents, Ralph and Georgiana Mastracchio, reside in Waterbury, Connecticut. Her mother, Helen Cooke, resides in Cheshire, Connecticut.

EDUCATION: Graduated from Crosby High School, Waterbury, Connecticut, in 1978; received a bachelor of science degree in electrical engineering/computer science from the University of Connecticut in 1982, a master of science of degree in electrical engineering from Rensselaer Polytechnic Institute in 1987, and a master of science degree in physical science from the University of Houston-Clear Lake in 1991.

ORGANIZATIONS: Member, Institute of Electrical and Electronics Engineers.

EXPERIENCE: Rick Mastracchio worked for Hamilton Standard in Connecticut as an engineer in the system design group from 1982 until 1987. During that time, he participated in the development of high performance, strapped-down inertial measurement units and flight control computers.

NASA EXPERIENCE: In 1987, Mastracchio moved to Houston, Texas, to work for the Rockwell Shuttle Operations Company at the Johnson Space Center. In 1990, he joined NASA as an engineer in the Flight Crew Operations Directorate. His duties included the development of space shuttle flight software requirements, the verification of space shuttle flight software in the Shuttle Avionics Integration Laboratory, and the development of ascent and abort crew procedures for the Astronaut Office. From 1993 until 1996, he worked as an ascent/entry Guidance and Procedures Officer (GPO) in Mission Control. An ascent/entry GPO has both pre-mission and real time Space Shuttle support responsibilities in the areas of onboard guidance, navigation, and targeting. During that time, he supported seventeen missions as a flight controller. In April 1996, Mastracchio was selected as an Astronaut Candidate and started training in August 1996. Having completed two years of training and evaluation, he is qualified for flight assignment as a mission specialist. Mastracchio has worked technical issues for the Astronaut Office Computer Support Branch, for Space Station Operations, and the EVA Branch. He flew as a mission specialist on STS-106 and has logged over 283 hours in space.

SPACE FLIGHT EXPERIENCE: STS-106 Atlantis (September 8-20, 2000). During the 12-day mission, the crew successfully prepared the International Space Station for the arrival of the first permanent crew. The five astronauts and two cosmonauts delivered more than 6,600 pounds of supplies and installed batteries, power converters, a toilet and a treadmill on the Space Station. Two crew members performed a space walk in order to connect power, data and communications cables to the newly arrived Zvezda Service Module and the Space Station. Mastracchio was the ascent/entry flight engineer, the primary robotic arm operator, and responsible for the transfer of items from the Space Shuttle to the Space Station. STS-106 orbited the Earth 185 times, and covered 4.9 million miles in 11 days, 19 hours, and 10 minutes.

NAME: William Surles "Bill" McArthur, Jr., (Colonel, USA)
NASA Astronaut

PERSONAL DATA: Born July 26, 1951, in Laurinburg, North Carolina. His hometown is Wakulla, North Carolina. Married to the former Cynthia Kathryn Lovin of Red Springs, North Carolina. They have two daughters. He enjoys basketball, running, and working with personal computers. Bill's stepfather, Mr. Weldon C. Avant, resides in Red Springs. His parents, Brigadier General William S. McArthur and Mrs. Edith P. Avant, are deceased. Cynthia's mother, Mrs. A.K. Lovin, resides in Red Springs, North Carolina.

EDUCATION: Graduated from Red Springs High School, Red Springs, North Carolina, in 1969; received a bachelor of science degree in applied science and engineering from the United States Military Academy, West Point, New York, in 1973, and a master of science degree in aerospace engineering from the Georgia Institute of Technology in 1983.

ORGANIZATIONS: Member of the American Institute of Aeronautics & Astronautics (AIAA), the Army Aviation Association of America, the Association of the United States Army, the United States

Military Academy Association of Graduates, the West Point Society of Greater Houston, MENSA, Phi Kappa Phi, and the Association of Space Explorers.

SPECIAL HONORS: Recipient of the Defense Superior Service Medal, the Defense Meritorious Service Medal, the Meritorious Service Medal (First Oak Leaf Cluster), the Army Commendation Medal, the NASA Space Flight Medal, and the NASA Exceptional Service Medal. Distinguished Graduate of the U.S. Army Aviation School. Honorary Doctor of Science degree from the University of North Carolina at Pembroke. Recipient of the Order of the Long Leaf Pine, North Carolina's highest civilian award. Member of the Georgia Tech Academy of Distinguished Engineering Alumni. 1996 American Astronautical Society Flight Achievement Award. Recipient of the Ellis Island Medal of Honor.

EXPERIENCE: McArthur graduated from West Point in June 1973 and was commissioned as a Second Lieutenant in the U.S. Army. Following a tour with the 82nd Airborne Division at Fort Bragg, North Carolina, he entered the U.S. Army Aviation School in 1975. He was the top graduate of his flight class and was designated an Army aviator in June 1976. He subsequently served as an aeroscout team leader and brigade aviation section commander with the 2nd Infantry Division in the Republic of Korea. In 1978 he was assigned to the 24th Combat Aviation Battalion in Savannah, Georgia, where he served as a company commander, platoon leader, and operations officer. After completing studies at Georgia Tech, he was assigned to the Department of Mechanics at West Point as an assistant professor. In June 1987, he graduated from the U.S. Naval Test Pilot School and was designated an experimental test pilot. Other military schools completed include the Army Parachutist Course, the Jumpmaster Course, and the Command and General Staff Officers' Course. A Master Army Aviator, he has logged over 4000 flight hours in 37 different aircraft.

NASA EXPERIENCE: McArthur was assigned to NASA at the Johnson Space Center in August 1987 as a Space Shuttle vehicle integration test engineer. Duties involved engineering liaison for launch and landing operations of the Space Shuttle. He was actively involved in the integrated test of the flight control system for each Orbiter for its return to flight and was a member of the Emergency Escape and Rescue Working Group. Selected by NASA in January 1990, McArthur became an astronaut in July 1991. Since then, McArthur has held various assignments within the Astronaut Office including: working issues relating to the solid rocket booster, redesigned solid rocket motor, and the advanced solid rocket motor. Most recently, he served as Chief of the Astronaut Office Flight Support Branch, supervising astronaut support of the Mission Control Center, prelaunch Space Shuttle processing, and launch and landing operations. A veteran of three space flights, McArthur has logged 35 days, 2 hours, 25 minutes and 10 seconds in space, including 13 hours and 16 minutes of EVA time in two space walks. .

SPACE FLIGHT EXPERIENCE: STS-58 Columbia (October 18 - November 1, 1993) was launched from the Kennedy Space Center, Florida, and returned to land at Edwards Air Force Base, California. During the mission the crew performed neurovestibular, cardiovascular, cardiopulmonary, metabolic, and musculoskeletal medical experiments on themselves and 48 rats, expanding our knowledge of human and animal physiology both on earth and in space flight. In addition, the crew performed 16 engineering tests aboard the Orbiter Columbia and 20 Extended Duration Orbiter Medical Project experiments. Additionally, the crew made extensive contacts with school children and amateur radio operators around the world through the Shuttle Amateur Radio experiment. The STS-58 mission was accomplished in 225 orbits of the Earth in 336 hours, 13 minutes, 01 second.STS-74 Atlantis (November 12-20, 1995) was NASA's second Space Shuttle mission to rendezvous and dock with the Russian Space Station Mir. STS-74 was launched from and returned to land at the Kennedy Space Center in Florida. During the 8-day flight the crew successfully attached a permanent docking module to Mir, conducted experiments on anumber of secondary payloads, and transferred one and a half tons of supplies between Atlantis and Mir. The STS-74 mission was accomplished in 129 orbits of the Earth, traveling 3.4 million miles in 196 hours, 30 minutes, 44 seconds. STS-92 Discovery (October 11-24, 2000) was launched from the Kennedy Space Center, Florida and returned to land at Edwards Air Force Base, California. During the 13-day flight, the seven member crew attached the Z1 Truss and Pressurized Mating Adapter 3 to the International Space Station using Discovery's robotic arm and performed four space walks to configure these elements. This expansion of the ISS opened the door for future assembly missions and prepared the station for its first resident crew. McArthur's EVA time totaled 13 hours and 16 minutes. The STS-92 mission was accomplished in 202 orbits, traveling 5.3 million miles in 12 days, 21 hours, 40 minutes and 25 seconds.

NAME: William C. McCool (Commander, USN)
NASA Astronaut

PERSONAL DATA: Born September 23, 1961 in San Diego, California. Married. He enjoys running, mountain biking, back country hiking/camping, swimming, playing guitar, chess.

EDUCATION: Graduated from Coronado High School, Lubbock, Texas, in 1979; received a bachelor of science degree in applied science from the US Naval Academy in 1983, a master of science degree in computer science from the University of Maryland in 1985, and a master of science degree in aeronautical engineering from the US Naval Postgraduate School in 1992.

ORGANIZATIONS: U.S. Naval Academy Alumni Association.

SPECIAL HONORS: Eagle Scout; graduated second of 1,083 in the Class of 1983 at the US Naval Academy; presented "Outstanding Student" and "Best DT-II Thesis" awards as graduate of U.S. Naval Test Pilot School, Class 101; awarded Navy Commendation Medals (2), Navy Achievement Medals (2), and various other service awards.

EXPERIENCE: McCool completed flight training in August 1986 and was assigned to Tactical Electronic Warfare Squadron 129 at Whidbey Island, Washington, for initial EA-6B Prowler training. His first operational tour was with Tactical Electronic Warfare Squadron 133, where he made two deployments aboard USS CORAL SEA (CV-43) to the Mediterranean Sea, and received designation as a wing qualified landing signal officer (LSO). In November 1989, he was selected for the Naval Postgraduate School/Test Pilot School (TPS) Cooperative Education Program. After graduating from TPS in June 1992, he worked as TA-4J and EA-6B test pilot in Flight Systems Department of Strike Aircraft Test Directorate at Patuxent River, Maryland. He was responsible for the management and conduct of a wide variety of projects, ranging from airframe fatigue life studies to numerous avionics upgrades. His primary efforts, however, were dedicated to flight test of the Advanced Capability (ADVCAP) EA-6B. Following his Patuxent River tour, McCool returned to Whidbey Island, and was assigned to Tactical Electronic Warfare Squadron 132 aboard USS ENTERPRISE (CVN-65). He served as Administrative and Operations Officer with the squadron through their work-up cycle, receiving notice of NASA selection while embarked on ENTERPRISE for her final pre-deployment at-sea period. McCool has over 2,800 hours flight experience in 24 aircraft and over 400 carrier arrestments.

NASA EXPERIENCE: Selected by NASA in April 1996, McCool reported to the Johnson Space Center in August 1996. He completed two years of training and evaluation, and is qualified for flight assignment as a pilot. Initially assigned to the Computer Support Branch, McCool also served as Technical Assistant to the Director of Flight Crew Operations, and worked Shuttle cockpit upgrade issues for the Astronaut Office. He is assigned as pilot on STS-107 scheduled for launch in 2001.

NAME: Pamela Ann Melroy (Lieutenant Colonel, USAF)
NASA Astronaut

PERSONAL DATA: Born September, 17, 1961, in Palo Alto, California. Considers Rochester, New York, to be her hometown. Married to Christopher Wallace of Wilton, Connecticut. She enjoys theatre, tap and jazz dancing, reading, cooking, flying. Her parents, David and Helen Melroy, reside in upstate New York.

EDUCATION: Graduated from Bishop Kearney High School, Rochester, New York, in 1979. Bachelor of science degree in physics and astronomy from Wellesley College, 1983. Master of science degree in earth & planetary sciences from Massachusetts Institute of Technology, 1984.

ORGANIZATIONS: Member of the Society of Experimental Test Pilots, the Order of Daedalians, and the 99s.

SPECIAL HONORS: Recipient of the Air Force Meritorious Service Medal, First Oak Leaf Cluster; Air Medal, First Oak Leaf Cluster; Aerial Achievement Medal, First Oak Leaf Cluster; and Expeditionary Medal, First Oak Leaf Cluster.

EXPERIENCE: Melroy was commissioned through the Air Force ROTC program in 1983. After completing a masters degree, she attended Undergraduate Pilot Training at Reese Air Force Base in Lubbock, Texas and was graduated in 1985. She flew the KC-10 for six years at Barksdale Air Force Base in Bossier City, Louisiana, as a copilot, aircraft commander and instructor pilot. Melroy is a veteran of JUST CAUSE and DESERT SHIELD/DESERT STORM, with over 200 combat and combat support hours. In June 1991, she attended the Air Force Test Pilot School at Edwards Air Force Base, California. Upon her graduation, she was assigned to the C-17 Combined Test Force, where she served as a test pilot until her selection for the astronaut program. She has logged over 5,000 hours flight time in over 45 different aircraft.

NASA EXPERIENCE: Selected as an astronaut candidate by NASA in December 1994, Melroy reported to the Johnson Space Center in March 1995. She completed a year of training and evaluation and is qualified for flight assignment as a shuttle pilot. Initially assigned to astronaut support duties for launch and landing, she has also worked Advanced Projects for the Astronaut Office. Most recently, Melroy served as pilot on STS-92 Discovery (October 11-24, 2000). STS-92 was launched from the Kennedy Space Center, Florida and returned to land at Edwards Air Force Base, California. During the 13-day flight, the seven member crew attached the Z1 Truss and Pressurized Mating Adapter 3 to the International Space Station using Discovery's robotic arm and performed four space walks to configure these elements. This expansion of the ISS opened the door for future assembly missions and prepared the station for its first resident crew. The STS-92 mission was accomplished in 202 orbits, traveling 5.3 million miles in 12 days, 21 hours, 40 minutes and 25 seconds.

NAME: Leland D. Melvin (Mr.)
NASA Astronaut (Mission Specialist Candidate)

PERSONAL DATA: Born February 15, 1964 in Lynchburg, Virginia. Unmarried. Recreational interests include piano, reading, music, cycling, tennis, and snowboarding. Chosen by the Detroit Lions in the 11th round of the 1986 NFL college draft. Also participated in the Toronto Argonauts and Dallas Cowboys football training camps. His parents Deems and Grace Melvin, reside in Lynchburg, Virginia.

EDUCATION: Graduated from Heritage High School, Lynchburg, Virginia, in 1982; received a bachelor of science degree in chemistry from the University of Richmond, Richmond, Virginia in 1986; and a master of science degree in materials science engineering from the University of Virginia in 1991.

ORGANIZATIONS: National Technical Association (Hampton Roads Chapter Secretary 1993), American Chemical Society, The Society for Experimental Mechanics.

SPECIAL HONORS/AWARDS: Invention Disclosure Award for Lead Insensitive Fiber Optic Phase Locked Loop Sensor, NASA Outstanding Performance Awards (8), NASA Superior Accomplishment Award (2), Key to the City of Lynchburg, Virginia, NCAA Division I Academic All American, University of Richmond Athletic Hall of Fame Inductee.

NASA EXPERIENCE: Mr. Melvin began working in the Fiber Optic Sensors group of the Nondestructive Evaluation Sciences Branch at NASA Langley Research Center in 1989 where he conducted research in the area of physical measurements for the development of advanced instrumentation for Nondestructive Evaluation (NDE). His responsibilities included using optical fiber sensors to measure strain, temperature, and chemical damage in both composite and metallic structures. Additional projects included developing optical interferometric techniques for quantitative determination of damage in aerospace structures and materials. In 1994 Mr. Melvin was selected to lead the Vehicle Health Monitoring (VHM) team for the cooperative Lockheed/NASA X-33 Reuseable Launch Vehicle (RLV) program. The team developed distributed fiber optic strain, temperature and hydrogen sensors for the reduction of vehicle operational costs and to monitor composite liquid oxygen tank and cryogenic insulation performance. In 1996 Mr. Melvin codesigned and monitored construction of an optical NDE facility capable of producing in-line fiber optic Bragg grating strain sensors at rates in excess of 1000 per hour. This facility will provide a means for performing advanced sensor and laser research for development of aerospace and civil health monitoring systems. Selected by NASA JSC in June 1998, he reported for training in August 1998. Astronaut Candidate Training includes orientation briefings and tours, numerous scientific and technical briefings, intensive instruction in Shuttle and International Space Station systems, physiological training and ground school to prepare for T-38 flight training, as well as learning water and wilderness survival techniques. Mr. Melvin is currently assigned to the Astronaut Office Space Station Operations Branch. He will serve in technical assignments until assigned to a space flight.

NAME: Mamoru Mohri
NASDA Astronaut

PERSONAL DATA: Born January 29, 1948, in Yoichi, Hokkaido, Japan. Married to the former Akiko Naka of Sapporo, Japan. They have three children. He enjoys snow skiing, tennis, baseball, table tennis, ice skating, scuba diving, squash, aerobics.

EDUCATION: Graduated from Hokkaido Yoichi High School in 1966; received bachelor and master of science degree in Chemistry from Hokkaido University, in 1970 and 1972, respectively, and a doctorate in Chemistry from Flinders University of South Australia, in 1976.

ORGANIZATIONS: Member of The Japan Society of Applied Physics, The Chemical Society of Japan, The Surface Science Society of Japan, The Japan Society of Microgravity Application, The Japan Society for Aeronautical and Space Sciences, and The Japanese Rocket Society.

PUBLICATIONS: Has published over 100 papers in the diverse fields of material and vacuum sciences.

SPECIAL HONORS: Fifth Kumagai Memorial Award for the Best Science Paper in Vacuum Science (1980). Honorary doctorate degree from Flinders University of South Australia (1991). Special awards from the Prime Minister of Japan, the Minister of Science and Technology of Japan, and the Government of Hokkaido (1992). Diplome pilote-cosmonaute de l' URSS V.M. Komarov and Japan Society of Aeronautical and Space Sciences Commendation for Technology (1993). Special award for Contributions to the Japan Society of Microgravity Application (1994). Distinguished Achievement Award in Space Biology from the Japanese Society for Space Biology, and the Space Engineering Award from the Japan Society of Mechanical Engineering (1995).

EXPERIENCE: Dr. Mohri joined the Faculty of Hokkaido University, Department of Nuclear Engineering in 1975, where over the next ten years he rose to the position of Associate Professor and conducted research in the fields of surface physics and chemistry, high energy physics, ceramic and semi-conductor thin films, environmental pollution, catalysis, and application of spectroscopy to biomaterials. He was involved in Plasma-Surface interactions in a Japanese nuclear fusion project for eight years and has experience working on large scale experimental systems for plasma confinement as well as small devices which he designed and built in his laboratory. In 1980 he was selected to participate in the first group of exchange scientists under the U.S./Japan Nuclear Fusion Collaboration Program which led to the publication of an irradiation damage study of nuclear fusion materials using a linear ion accelerator at the Physics Division of the Argonne National Laboratories, USA. In 1985, Dr. Mohri was selected by the National Space Development Agency of Japan (NASDA) as a payload specialist for the First Material Processing Test project (Spacelab-J). In 1987, he was appointed as an adjunct professor of physics and worked in the center for Microgravity and Materials Research, at the University of Alabama in Huntsville, for two years where he was concerned with mass spectroscopy of high temperature vapors for space experiment applications. He also conducted microgravity experiments in alloy solidification and immiscible liquid behavior using a drop tower facility at Marshall Space Flight Center and the KC-135 aircraft. Dr. Mohri was assigned as a prime payload specialist on STS-47, Spacelab-J in 1990. This cooperative mission between the United States and Japan, to conduct experiments in materials processing and life sciences, was launched in September 1992. Dr. Mohri performed 43 Spacelab experiments with NASA astronauts aboard the Space Shuttle Endeavor during the 8 day mission. His performance in the space classroom became a popular nationwide event. Dr. Mohri was assigned as the first general manager of the NASDA Astronaut Office in Tsukuba Science City, Japan, established in October 1992. In that capacity he worked as an expert in manned space experiments at NASDA developing the new astronaut office for the space station project. In July 1996, he was selected by NASDA to attend NASA's Astronaut Candidate Training.

NASA EXPERIENCE: Dr. Mohri reported to the Johnson Space Center in August 1996. He completed two years of training and evaluation, and is qualified for flight assignment as a mission specialist. Dr. Mohri was initially assigned to the Astronaut Office Payloads and Habitability Branch where he supported integration of the Japanese Experiment Module (JEM) payload for the International Space Station. A veteran of two space flights, Dr. Mohri has logged over 459 hours in space. He flew as a payload specialist on STS-47 in 1992, and was a mission spcialist on STS-99 in 2000.

SPACE FLIGHT EXPERIENCE: STS-47, Spacelab-J (September 12-20, 1992) was a cooperative venture between the United States and Japan. During the 8-day flight, the crew conducted 44 experiments in life sciences and materials processing. The STS-47 mission was accomplished in 127 Earth orbits, traveling 3.3 million miles in 190 hours, 30 minutes, 23 seconds. STS-99 (February 11-22, 2000) was an 11-day flight during which the international crew aboard Space Shuttle Endeavour worked dual shifts to support payload operations. The Shuttle Radar Topography Mission mapped more than 47 million miles of the Earth's land surface. The STS-99 mission was accomplished in 181 Earth orbits, traveling over 4 million miles in 268 hours and 38 minutes.

NAME: Barbara R. Morgan
NASA Astronaut (Mission Specialist Candidate)

PERSONAL DATA: Born November 28, 1951, in Fresno, California. Married to writer Clay Morgan of McCall, Idaho. They have two sons. She is a classical flutist who also enjoys jazz, literature, hiking, swimming, cross-country skiing, and her family. Her parents are Dr. and Mrs. Jerry Radding. Her parents-in-law are Dr. and Mrs. Clay Morgan.

EDUCATION: Hoover High School, Fresno, California, 1969. B.A., Human Biology, Stanford University, 1973 (with distinction). Teaching Credential, College of Notre Dame, Belmont, California, 1974.

ORGANIZATIONS: Idaho Education Association; National Council of Teachers of Mathematics; National Science Teachers Association; International Reading Association; International Technology Education Association; Challenger Center for Space Science Education.

SPECIAL HONORS: Phi Beta Kappa (1973), NASA Headquarters Special Service Award (1987), NASA Public Service Group Achievement Award (1988). Other awards include Idaho Fellowship Award (1998), University of Idaho President's Medallion Award (1998), International Technology Education Association Lawrence Prakken Professional Cooperation Award (1996), Challenger Center for Space Science Education Challenger 7 Award (1995), National Space Society Space Pioneer Award for Education (1992), Los Angeles Chamber of Commerce Wright Brothers "Kitty Hawk Sands of Time" Education Award (1991), Women in Aerospace Education Award (1991), National PTA Honorary Lifetime Member (1986), and USA Today Citizens of the Year (1986).

EXPERIENCE: Morgan began her teaching career in 1974 on the Flathead Indian Reservation at Arlee Elementary School in Arlee, Montana, where she taught remedial reading and math. From 1975-1978, she taught remedial reading/math and second grade at McCall-Donnelly Elementary School in McCall, Idaho. From 1978-1979, Morgan taught English and science to third graders at Colegio Americano de Quito in Quito, Ecuador. From 1979-1998, she taught second, third, and fourth grades at McCall-Donnelly Elementary School.

NASA EXPERIENCE: Morgan was selected as the backup candidate for the NASA Teacher in Space Program on July 19, 1985. From September 1985 to January 1986, Morgan trained with Christa McAuliffe and the Challenger crew at NASA's Johnson Space Center, Houston, Texas. Following the Challenger accident, Morgan assumed the duties of Teacher in Space Designee. From March 1986 to July 1986, she worked with NASA, speaking to educational organizations throughout the country. In the fall of 1986, Morgan returned to Idaho to resume her teaching career. She taught second and third grades at McCall-Donnelly Elementary and continued to work with NASA's Education Division, Office of Human Resources and Education. Her duties as Teacher in Space Designee included public speaking, educational consulting, curriculum design, and serving on the National Science Foundation's Federal Task Force for Women and Minorities in Science and Engineering. Selected by NASA in January 1998 as the first Educator Mission Specialist, she reported for training in August 1998. Astronaut Candidate Training includes orientation briefings and tours, numerous scientific and technical briefings, intensive instruction in Shuttle and International Space Station systems, physiological training, and ground school to prepare for T-38 flight training, as well as learning water and wilderness survival techniques. Morgan is currently assigned to the Astronaut Office Space Station Operations Branch. She will serve in technical assignments until assigned to a space flight.

NAME: Lee M.E. Morin, M.D., Ph.D. (Commander, USN)
NASA Astronaut

PERSONAL DATA: Born September 9, 1952 in Manchester, New Hampshire. Married. Two children. Two grandchildren. An amateur machinist, he enjoys math, jogging.

EDUCATION: Graduated from the Western Reserve Academy, Hudson, Ohio in 1970; received a bachelor of science degree in mathematical/electrical science from the University of New Hampshire in 1974; a master of science degree in biochemistry from New York University in 1978, a doctorate of medicine and microbiology degrees from New York University in 1981 and 1982, respectively, and a Master of Public Health degree from the University of Alabama at Birmingham in 1988.

ORGANIZATIONS: Aerospace Medical Association, Force Recon Association, Undersea and Hyperbaric Medical Society, Society of United States Naval Flight Surgeons.

AWARDS: Meritorious Service Medal, Navy Commendation Medal, Navy Achievement Medal, Navy Unit Commendation, Meritorious Unit Commendation (two awards), Overseas Service Ribbon, National Defense Medal, Liberation of Kuwait Medal, Southwest Asia Medal, and both Expert Pistol and Expert Rifle Medals.

SPECIAL HONORS: Recipient of the 1994 Chairman of the Joint Chiefs of Staff Award for Excellence in Military Medicine (also known as the Fisher Award), a finalist of the 1995 Innovations in American Government Award from the John F. Kennedy School of Government at Harvard University and Ford Foundation, and received the 1996 Sustaining Membership Lecture Award from the Association of Military Surgeons of the United States.

EXPERIENCE: After graduating from the University of New Hampshire in 1974, Morin worked at the Massachusetts Institute of Technology in the laboratory now known as the Media Lab. Morin matriculated at New York University School of Medicine in 1974, received a Master of Science in Biochemistry in 1978, an M.D. in 1981, and a Ph.D. in Microbiology in 1982. He then completed two years of residency training in General Surgery at the Bronx Municipal Hospital Center and at the Montefiore Hospital Medical Center in New York City. In 1982, Morin received a Direct Commission in the Naval Reserve. In 1983, he entered active duty and attended the Naval Undersea Medical Institute in Groton, Connecticut. He was designated as an Undersea Medical Officer in 1983. He joined the crew of the USS HENRY M. JACKSON (SSBN-730) Precommissioning Unit at the Electric Boat Company Shipyards in Groton. He remained aboard as Medical Officer for both Blue and Gold crews until 1985 when the ship arrived at its homeport in Bangor, Washington. During his tour aboard the USS HENRY M. JACKSON, Morin qualified as Diving Medical Officer, and also received his "Dolphins" as a qualified Submarine Medical Officer. Morin then entered Flight Surgeon training at the Naval Aerospace Medical Institute (NAMI) in Pensacola, Florida. He received his "Wings of Gold" as a Naval Flight Surgeon in 1986, and remained on the staff at NAMI as Flight Surgeon/Diving Medal Officer until 1989. While at NAMI, he received his Masters of Public Health degree from the University of Alabama at Birmingham. He then left active duty and entered private practice in occupational medicine in Jacksonville, Florida. He remained in the Naval Reserve, and drilled with the United State Marine Corps with the Third Force Reconnaissance Company in Mobile, Alabama. In August 1990, he was recalled to active duty during Operation Desert Shield, when he was assigned to Branch Clinic, Naval Air Station Pensacola as a Flight Surgeon. Morin volunteered to reenter active duty, and was assigned to Administrative Support Unit, Bahrain, as Diving Medical Officer/Flight Surgeon during Operation Desert Storm and during the post-war build-down period. In 1992, Morin rejoined the staff at NAMI, initially as Special Projects Officer. He was named the Director of Warfare Specialty Programs when NAMI became Naval Aerospace and Operational Medical Institute (NAOMI). In 1995, Morin entered the Residency in Aerospace Medicine at the Naval Aerospace and Operational Medical Institute. He completed the residency in 1996.

NASA EXPERIENCE: Selected as an astronaut candidate by NASA in April 1996, Morin reported to the Johnson Space Center in August 1996. Having completed two years of training and evaluation, he is qualified for flight assignment as a mission specialist. Currently, Morin is assigned technical duties in the Astronaut Office Computer Support Branch.

NAME: Paolo Angelo Nespoli
ESA Astronaut (Mission Specialist Candidate)

PERSONAL DATA: Born April 6, 1957 in Milan, Italy. His hometown is Verano Brianza, Milan, Italy, where his mother Maria, father Luigi, brother Raoul and sisters Antonella and Lia live. He is single. Recreational interests include SCUBA diving, aircraft piloting, assembly of computer hardware and electronic equipment, computer software.

EDUCATION: In 1977, he graduated from the Liceo Scientifico Statale Paolo Frisi of Desio, Milano, Italy. In 1988, he received a Bachelor of Science in Aerospace Engineering from the Polytechnic University of New York and, in 1989, received a Master of Science in Aeronautics and Astronautics from the same institution. In 1990, the Università degli Studi di Firenze, Italy, recognized a Laurea in Ingegneria Meccanica.

QUALIFICATIONS - LICENSES: Civilian: Professional Engineer, Private Pilot, Advanced SCUBA Diver, NitrOx diver. Military: Master Parachutist, Parachutist Instructor, Jump Master, High Altitude Low Opening, Demolition expert, Special Forces operator.

AWARDS: Team Achievement Awards for: Space Mission Mir97 (German Space Agency), Space Mission EUROMIR 95 (European Space Agency), NASA-Mir Program (National Aeronautics and Space Administration), Space Mission EUROMIR 94 (European Space Agency), Bed Rest Experiment (European Space Agency – French Space Agency), Columbus Utilization Simulation (European Space Agency).

EXPERIENCE: Nespoli was drafted by the Italian Army in 1977, and became a non-commissioned officer working as a parachute instructor at the Scuola Militare di Paracadutismo of Pisa. In 1980, he joined the 9° Btg d'Assalto "Col Moschin" of Livorno where he became a Special Forces operator. From 1982 to 1984, he was assigned to the Italian contingent of the Multinational Peacekeeping Force in Beirut, Lebanon. Following his return to Italy, he was appointed an officer and continued working as a Special Forces operator. He resumed college studies in 1985. Nespoli left Army active duty in 1987. In 1988 and 1989, he obtained a BS and an MS from the Polytechnic University of New York. He returned to Italy in 1989 to work as a design engineer for Proel Tecnologie in Florence, where he conducted mechanical analysis and supported the qualification of the flight units of the Electron Gun Assembly, one of the main parts of the Italian Space Agency's Tethered Satellite System (TSS). In 1991, he joined the Astronaut Training Division , European Astronaut Centre, European Space Agency (ESA), Cologne, Germany. As an astronaut training engineer, he contributed to the preparation and implementation of European astronaut basic training and he was responsible for the preparation and management of astronaut proficiency maintenance. He was also responsible for the Astronaut Training Database, a software system used for the preparation and management of astronaut training. In 1995, he was detached to ESA's EUROMIR Project in the European Space Technology Centre, Noordwijk, The Netherlands, where he was responsible for the team that prepared, integrated and supported the Payload and Crew Support Computer used on the Russian space station Mir. Detached to NASA's Johnson Space Center, Houston, Texas in 1996, he worked in the Spaceflight Training Division on the preparation of training for the ground and in-orbit crew of the International Space Station. Following his selection in July 1998 by the Italian Space Agency, he was sent to the European Space Agency where he joined the European Astronaut Corps.

NASA EXPERIENCE: In August 1998, he reported to the Johnson Space Center to attend Astronaut Candidate Training which includes orientation briefings and tours, numerous scientific and technical briefings, intensive instruction in Shuttle and International Space Station systems, physiological training and ground school to prepare for T-38 flight training, as well as learning water and wilderness survival techniques. Nespoli is currently assigned to the Astronaut Office Space Station Operations Branch. He will serve in technical assignments until assigned to a space flight.

NAME: James H. Newman (Ph.D)
NASA Astronaut

PERSONAL DATA: Born October 16, 1956, in the Trust Territory of the Pacific Islands, but considers San Diego, California, to be his hometown. Married to Mary Lee Pieper. Two children. He enjoys hiking, soccer, softball, squash, and soaring. His mother, Ms. Ruth Hansen, and his father, Dr. William Newman, are both residents of San Diego. Her parents, Mr. & Mrs. Wylie Bernard Pieper, reside in Houston, Texas.

EDUCATION: Graduated from La Jolla High School, San Diego, California in 1974; received a bachelor of arts degree in physics (graduated cum laude) from Dartmouth College in 1978, a master of arts degree and a doctorate in physics from Rice University in 1982 and 1984, respectively.

ORGANIZATIONS: Member of the American Physical Society and Sigma Xi.

SPECIAL HONORS: Awarded a Citation in Senior Thesis Research from Dartmouth College in 1978. Elected to Sigma Xi in 1980. Recipient of 1982-83 Texaco Fellowship, the Sigma Xi Graduate Merit Award in 1985, and 1988 NASA Superior Achievement Award. Selected by NASA JSC to attend the 1989 summer session of the International Space University in Strasbourg, France. 1996 NASA Exceptional Service Medal. Institute of Navigation 1995 Superior Achievement Award (1996).

EXPERIENCE: After graduating from Rice University in 1984, Dr. Newman did an additional year of post-doctoral work at Rice. His research interests are in atomic and molecular physics, specifically medium to low energy collisions of atoms and molecules of aeronomic interest. His doctoral work at Rice University was in the design, construction, testing, and use of a new position-sensitive detection system for measuring differential cross sections of collisions of atoms and molecules. In 1985, Dr. Newman was appointed as adjunct professor in the Department of Space Physics and Astronomy at Rice University. That same year he came to work at NASA's Johnson Space Center, where his duties included responsibility for conducting flight crew and flight control team training for all mission phases in the areas of Orbiter propulsion, guidance, and control. He was working as a simulation supervisor when selected for the astronaut program. In that capacity, he was responsible for a team of instructors conducting flight controller training. Selected by NASA in January 1990, Dr. Newman began astronaut training in July 1990. His technical assignments since then include: Astronaut Office Mission Support Branch where he was part of a team responsible for crew ingress/strap-in prior to launch and crew egress after landing; Mission Development Branch working on the Shuttle on-board laptop computers; Chief of the Computer Support Branch in the Astronaut Office, responsible for crew involvement in the development and use of computers on the Space Shuttle and Space Station. He flew as a mission specialist on STS-51 (1993), STS-69 (1995) and STS-88 (1998) A veteran of three space flights, Dr. Newman has logged over 779 hours in space, including four spacewalks totaling 28 hours, 27 minutes. Detailed to the Orbiter Program Office in March 1999 for a one to two year tour of duty, Newman served as the RMS Integration

Manager responsible for the Orbiter robotic arm and the Space Vision System. He is currently assigned to upgrade and service the Hubble Space Telescope during the STS-109 mission scheduled for launch in 2001.

SPACE FLIGHT EXPERIENCE: STS-51 Discovery, was launched from Kennedy Space Center, Florida, on September 12, 1993. During the ten-day flight, the crew of five deployed the Advanced Communications Technology Satellite (ACTS) and the Orbiting and Retrievable Far and Extreme Ultraviolet Spectrometer on the Shuttle Pallet Satellite (ORFEUS/SPAS). Newman was responsible for the operation of the SPAS, was the backup operator for the RMS, and on flight day five conducted a seven-hour, five minute spacewalk with Carl Walz. The extravehicular activity (EVA) tested tools and techniques for use on future missions. In addition to working with numerous secondary payloads and medical test objectives, the crew successfully tested a Global Positioning System (GPS) receiver to determine real-time Shuttle positions and velocities and completed a test routing Orbiter data to on-board laptop computers. After 158 orbits of the Earth in 236 hours, 11 minutes, the mission concluded on September 22, 1993, with the first night landing at the Kennedy Space Center, Florida. STS-69 Endeavour (September 7-18, 1995), was an eleven-day mission during which the crew successfully deployed and retrieved a SPARTAN satellite and the Wake Shield Facility (WSF). Also on board was the International Extreme Ultraviolet Hitchhiker payload, numerous secondary payloads, and medical experiments. Newman was responsible for the crew's science involvement with the WSF and was also the primary RMS operator on the flight, performing the WSF and EVA RMS operations. He also operated the on-orbit tests of the Ku-band Communications Adaptor, the Relative GPS experiment, and the RMS Manipulator Positioning Display. The mission was accomplished in 171 orbits of the Earth in 260 hours, 29 minutes. STS-88 Endeavour (December 4-15, 1998), was the first International Space Station assembly mission. During the twelve-day mission the Unity module was mated with Zarya module. Newman performed three spacewalks with Jerry Ross, totaling 21 hours, 22 minutes. The primary objective of the spacewalks was to connect external power and data umbilicals between Zarya and Unity. Other objectives include setting up the Early Communication antennas, deploying antennas on Zarya that had failed to deploy as expected, installing a sunshade to protect an external computer, installing translation aids, and attaching tools/hardware for use in future EVA's. The crew also performed IMAX Cargo Bay Camera (ICBC) operations, and deployed two satellites, Mighty Sat 1, sponsored by the Air Force, and SAC-A, from Argentina. The mission was accomplished in 185 orbits of the Earth in 283 hours and 18 minutes.

NAME: Claude Nicollier
ESA Astronaut

PERSONAL DATA: Born September 2, 1944, in Vevey, Switzerland. Married to the former Susana Perez of Monterrey, Mexico. They have two daughters, Maya and Marina. He enjoys mountain climbing, flying, and photography. His father, Mr. Georges Nicollier, resides in La Tour de Peilz, Switzerland.

EDUCATION: Graduated from Gymnase de Lausanne (high school), Lausanne, Switzerland, in 1962; received a bachelor of science in physics from the University of Lausanne in 1970 and a master of science degree in astrophysics from the University of Geneva in 1975. Also graduated as a Swiss Air Force pilot in 1966, an airline pilot in 1974, and a test pilot in 1988.

ORGANIZATIONS: Member of the Swiss Astronomical Society, the Astronomical Society of the Pacific, the Swiss Air Force Officers Society (AVIA), and the Swiss Academy of Engineering Sciences. Fellow of the British Interplanetary Society. Honorary member of the Swiss Aero Club, and the Swiss Society of Engineers and Architects.

SPECIAL HONORS: Four NASA Space Flight Medals (1992, 1993, 1996, 1999), Prix d'honneur de la Fondation Pro Aero, Switzerland (1992), Yuri Gagarin Gold Medal from the International Aeronautical Federation (1994), Silver Medal from the Académie Nationale de l'Air et de l'Espace, France (1994), Collier Trophy (awarded to the crew of STS-61) from the National Aeronautics Association (1994), Prix de l'Université de Lausanne (1994), honorary doctorates from the Swiss Federal Institute of Technology, Lausanne, and the Geneva University (both in 1994). Appointed professor at the Swiss Federal Institute of Technology, Lausanne, in November 1994.

EXPERIENCE: From 1970 to 1973, Claude worked as a graduate scientist with the Institute of Astronomy at Lausanne University and at the Geneva Observatory. He then joined the Swiss Air Transport School in Zurich and was assigned as a DC-9 pilot for Swissair, concurrently participating part-time in research activities of the Geneva Observatory. At the end of 1976 he accepted a Fellowship at the European Space Agency's (ESA) Space Science Department at Noordwijk, Netherlands,where he worked as a research scientist in various airborne infrared astronomy programs. In July 1978 he was selected by ESA as a member of the first group of European astronauts. Under agreement between ESA and NASA he joined the NASA astronaut candidates selected in May 1980 for astronaut training as a mission specialist. His technical assignments in the Astronaut Office have included flight software verification in the Shuttle Avionics Integration Laboratory (SAIL), participation in the development of retrieval techniques for the Tethered Satellite System (TSS), Remote Manipulator System (RMS), and International Space Station (ISS) robotics support. From the Spring of 1996 to the end of 1998, he was Head of the Astronaut Office Robotics Branch. During 1988 he attended the Empire Test Pilot School in Boscombe Down, England, from where he graduated as a test pilot in December 1988. Claude holds a commission as captain in the Swiss Air Force. He has logged 5,500 hours flying time - including 3,900 hours in jet aircraft. A veteran of four space flights, Claude has logged more than 1,000 hours in space including 1 space walk totaling 8 hours and 10 minutes. He served on STS-46 in 1992, STS-61 in 1993, STS-75 in 1996, and STS-103 in 1999.

SPACE FLIGHT EXPERIENCE: STS-46 Atlantis (July 31-August 8, 1992), was an 8-day mission during which crew members deployed the European Retrievable Carrier (EURECA) science platform, and conducted the first Tethered Satellite System (TSS) test flight. Mission duration was 191 hours, 16 minutes, 7 seconds. STS-46 was launched from and returned to land at Kennedy Space Center, Florida. The mission was accomplished in 126 orbits of the Earth and traveled 3.35 million miles in 191hours, 16 minutes and 7 seconds. STS-61 Endeavour was the first Hubble Space Telescope (HST) servicing and repair mission. STS-61 launched at night from the Kennedy Space Center, Florida, on December 2, 1993. During the 11-day flight, the HST was captured and restored to full capacity through a record five space walks by four astronauts. After having traveled 4,433,772 miles in 163 orbits of the Earth in 259 hours, 59 minutes. STS-75 Columbia (February 22 to March 9, 1996) was a 15-day flight, with principal payloads being the reflight of the Tethered Satellite System (TSS) and the third flight of the United States Microgravity Payload (USMP-3). The TSS successfully demonstrated the ability of tethers to produce electricity. The TSS experiment produced a wealth of new information on the electrodynamics of tethers and plasma physics before the tether broke at 19.7 km, just shy of the 20.7 km goal. The crew also worked around the clock performing combustion experiments and research related to USMP-3 microgravity investigations used to improve production of medicines, metal alloys, and semiconductors. The mission was completed in 252 orbits covering 6.5 million miles in 377 hours and 40 minutes. STS-103 Discovery (December 19-27, 1999) was an 8-day mission during which the crew successfully installed new instruments and upgraded systems on the Hubble Space Telescope (HST). Enhancing HST scientific capabilities required three space walks (EVA) totaling 24 hours and 33 minutes. The STS-103 mission was accomplished in 120 Earth orbits, traveling 3.2 million miles in 191 hours and 11 minutes.

NAME: Soichi Noguchi
NASDA Astronaut

PERSONAL DATA: Born April 15,1965 in Yokohama, Kanagawa, Japan. Considers Chigasaki, Kanagawa, Japan, to be his hometown. Married. Two children. Enjoys jogging, basketball, skiing, camping.

EDUCATION: Graduated from Chigasaki-Hokuryo High School, Chigasaki, in 1984; received a bachelor of engineering degree in aeronautical engineering from the University of Tokyo in 1989, and a master of engineering degree in aeronautical engineering from the University of Tokyo in 1991.

ORGANIZATIONS: Member of the Japan Society for Aeronautical and Space Sciences.

EXPERIENCE: Noguchi joined Ishikawajima-Harima Heavy Industries Co., Ltd. (IHI) in April 1991. He completed a training course in the Manufacturing Department, and then he was assigned to the Aerodynamics Group, Research and Development Department, Aero-Engine and Space Operations, IHI. He was involved in the aerodynamic design of commercial aero-engines, planning and successful completion of the component tests of aero-engines, and the research of compressor aerodynamic performance. He was selected by the National Space Development Agency of Japan (NASDA) in June 1996.

NASA EXPERIENCE: Noguchi reported to the Johnson Space Center in August 1996. Having completed two years of training and evaluation, he is qualified for flight assignment as a mission specialist. Currently, Noguchi is assigned technical duties in the Astronaut Office Payloads/Habitability Branch.

NAME: Carlos I. Noriega (Lieutenant Colonel, USMC)
NASA Astronaut

PERSONAL DATA: Born October 8, 1959, in Lima, Peru. Considers Santa Clara, California, to be his hometown. Married to the former Wendy L. Thatcher. They have five children. He enjoys flying, running, snow skiing, racquetball, and spending time with his children. His parents, Rodolfo and Nora Noriega, reside in Gilbert, Arizona. Her parents, John and Elizabeth Thatcher, reside in Honolulu, Hawaii.

EDUCATION: Graduated from Wilcox High School, Santa Clara, California, in 1977. Bachelor of science degree in computer science from University of Southern California, 1981. Master of science degree in computer science from the Naval Postgraduate School, 1990. Master of science degree in space systems operations from the Naval Postgraduate School, 1990.

SPECIAL HONORS: Defense Superior Service Medal, Defense Meritorious Service Medal, Air Medal with Combat Distinguishing Device, Air Medal (Strike Flight Award), Navy Achievement Medal, NASA Space Flight Medal.

EXPERIENCE: Noriega was a member of the Navy ROTC unit and received his commission in the United States Marine Corps at the University of Southern California in 1981. Following graduation from flight school, he flew CH-46 Sea Knight helicopters with HMM-165 from 1983 to 1985 at Marine Corps Air Station (MCAS) Kaneohe Bay, Hawaii. Noriega made two 6-month shipboard deployments in the West Pacific/Indian Ocean including operations in support of the Multi-National Peacekeeping Force in Beirut, Lebanon. He completed his tour in Hawaii as the Base Operations Officer for Marine Air Base Squadron 24. In 1986, he was transferred to MCAS Tustin, California, where he served as the aviation safety officer and instructor pilot with HMT-301. In 1988, Noriega was selected to attend the Naval Postgraduate School in Monterey, California, where he earned two master of science degrees. Upon graduation in September 1990, he was assigned to United States Space Command in Colorado Springs, Colorado. In addition to serving as a Space Surveillance Center Commander, he was responsible for several software development projects and was ultimately the command representative for the development and integration of the major space and missile warning computer system upgrades for Cheyenne Mountain Air Force Base. At the time of his selection, he was serving on the staff of the 1st Marine Aircraft Wing in Okinawa, Japan. He has logged approximately 2,200 flight hours in various fixed wing and rotary wing aircraft.

NASA EXPERIENCE: Selected by NASA in December 1994, Noriega reported to the Johnson Space Center in March 1995. He completed a year of training and evaluation, and was qualified for assignment as a mission specialist in May 1996. He held technical assignments in the Astronaut Office EVA/Robotics and Operations Planning Branches. Noriega flew on STS-84 in 1997 and STS-97 in 2000. He has logged over 461 hours in space including over 19 EVA hours in 3 space walks.

SPACE FLIGHT EXPERIENCE: STS-84 (May 15-24, 1997), was NASA's sixth Shuttle mission to rendezvous and dock with the Russian Space Station Mir. During this 9-day mission the crew aboard Space Shuttle Atlantis conducted a number of secondary experiments, and transferred nearly 4 tons of supplies and experiment equipment between Atlantis and the Mir station. During STS-84 Noriega logged a total of 221 hours and 20 minutes in space traveling 3.6 million miles in 144 orbits of the Earth. STS-97 Endeavour (November 30 to December December 11, 2000) was the fifth Space Shuttle mission dedicated to the assembly of the International Space Station. While docked to the Station, the crew installed the first set of U.S. solar arrays, performed three space walks, in addition to delivering supplies and equipment to the station's first resident crew. Mission duration was 10 days, 19 hours, 57 minutes, and traveled 4.47 million miles.

NAME: Lisa M. Nowak (Lieutenant Commander, USN)
NASA Astronaut

PERSONAL DATA: Born May 10, 1963, in Washington, DC. Married to Richard T. Nowak of South Burlington, Vermont. They have one child. Enjoys bicycling, running, skeet, sailing, gourmet cooking, rubber stamps, crossword puzzles and piano. As an undergraduate she competed on the track team.

EDUCATION: Graduated from C.W. Woodward High School, Rockville, Maryland, in 1981; received a bachelor of science degree in aerospace engineering from the U.S. Naval Academy in 1985; a master of science degree in aeronautical engineering and a degree of aeronautical and astronautical engineer from the U.S. Naval Postgraduate School, both in 1992.

ORGANIZATIONS: American Institute of Aeronautics and Astronautics; U.S. Naval Academy Alumni Association; Tau Beta Pi Engineering Society.

AWARD: Navy Commendation Medal; Navy Achievement Medal; various other service awards.

EXPERIENCE: Nowak received her commission from the U.S. Naval Academy in May 1985, and reported to flight school after six months of temporary duty at Johnson Space Center. She earned her wings as a Naval Flight Officer in June 1987, followed by Electronic Warfare School at Corry Station, Florida, and initial A-7 training at Naval Air Station Lemoore, California. She was assigned to Electronic Warfare Aggressor Squadron 34 at Point Mugu, California, where she flew EA-7L and ERA-3B aircraft, supporting the fleet in small and large scale exercises with jamming and missile profiles. While assigned to the squadron, she qualified as Mission Commander and EW Lead. In 1992, Nowak completed two years of graduate studies at Monterey, and began working at the Systems Engineering Test Directorate at Patuxent River, Maryland. In 1993, she was selected for both Aerospace Engineering Duty and U.S. Naval Test Pilot School. After graduation in June 1994, she stayed at Patuxent River working as an aircraft systems project officer at the Air Combat Environment Test and Evaluation Facility and at Strike Aircraft Test Squadron, flying the F/A-18 and EA-6B. Nowak was then assigned to the Naval Air Systems Command, working on acquisition of new systems for naval aircraft, when she was selected for the astronaut program. Nowak has logged over 1,100 flight hours in more than 30 different aircraft.

NASA EXPERIENCE: After receiving her commission Nowak was assigned temporary duty and from June to November 1985 she provided engineering support for the JSC's Shuttle Training Aircraft Branch at Ellington, Texas. Selected by NASA in April 1996, Nowak reported to the Johnson Space Center in August 1996. Having completed two years of training and evaluation, she is qualified for flight assignment as a mission specialist. Currently, Nowak is assigned technical duties in the Astronaut Office Operations Planning Branch.

NAME: Ellen Ochoa (Ph.D)
NASA Astronaut

PERSONAL DATA: Born May 10, 1958 in Los Angeles, California, but considers La Mesa, California, to be her hometown. Married to Coe Fulmer Miles of Molalla, Oregon. They have one son. She is a classical flutist and private pilot, and also enjoys volleyball and bicycling. Her mother, Rosanne Ochoa, resides in La Mesa. His parents, Louis and Georgia Zak, reside in Waldport, Oregon.

EDUCATION: Graduated from Grossmont High School, La Mesa, California, in 1975; received a bachelor of science degree in physics from San Diego State University in 1980, a master of science degree and doctorate in electrical engineering from Stanford University in 1981 and 1985, respectively.

ORGANIZATIONS: Member of the Optical Society of America (OSA), the American Institute of Aeronautics and Astronautics (AIAA), Phi Beta Kappa and Sigma Xi honor societies.

SPECIAL HONORS: NASA awards include the Exceptional Service Medal (1997), Outstanding Leadership Medal (1995), Space Flight Medals (1999, 1994, 1993), and two Space Act Tech Brief Awards (1992). Recipient of numerous other awards, including the Women in Aerospace Outstanding Achievement Award, The Hispanic Engineer Albert Baez Award for Outstanding Technical Contribution to Humanity, the Hispanic Heritage Leadership Award, and San Diego State University Alumna of the Year. Member of the Presidential Commission on the Celebration of Women in American History.

EXPERIENCE: As a doctoral student at Stanford, and later as a researcher at Sandia National Laboratories and NASA Ames Research Center, Dr. Ochoa investigated optical systems for performing information processing. She is a co-inventor on three patents for an optical inspection system, an optical object recognition method, and a method for noise removal in images. As Chief of the Intelligent Systems Technology Branch at Ames, she supervised 35 engineers and scientists in the research and development of computational systems for aerospace missions. Dr. Ochoa has presented numerous papers at technical conferences and in scientific journals. Selected by NASA in January 1990, Dr. Ochoa became an astronaut in July 1991. Her technical assignments to date include flight software verification, crew representative for flight software and computer hardware development, crew representative for robotics development, testing, and training, Assistant for Space Station to the Chief of the Astronaut Office, directing crew involvement in the development and operation of the Station, and spacecraft communicator (CAPCOM) in Mission Control. A veteran of three space flights, Dr. Ochoa has logged over 719 hours in space. She was a mission specialist on STS-56 in 1993, was the Payload Commander on STS-66 in 1994, and was a mission specialist and flight engineer on STS-96 in 1999. STS-56 ATLAS-2 Discovery (April 4-17, 1993) was a 9-day mission during which the crew conducted atmospheric and solar studies in order to better understand the effect of solar activity on the Earth's climate and environment. Dr. Ochoa used the Remote Manipulator System (RMS) to deploy and capture the Spartan satellite, which studied the solar corona. Dr. Ochoa was the Payload Commander on the STS-66 Atmospheric Laboratory for Applications and Science-3 mission (November 3-14, 1994). ATLAS-3 continued the series of Spacelab flights to study the energy of the Sun during an 11-year solar cycle and to learn how changes in the sun's irradiance affect the Earth's climate and environment. Dr. Ochoa used the RMS to retrieve the CRISTA-SPAS atmospheric research satellite at the end of its 8-day free flight. STS-96 Discovery (May 27 to June 6, 1999) was a 10-day mission during which the crew performed the first docking to the International Space Station, and delivered 4 tons of logistics and supplies in preparation for the arrival of the first crew to live on the station early next year. Dr. Ochoa coordinated the transfer of supplies and also operated the RMS during the 8-hour space walk. The mission was accomplished in 153 Earth orbits, traveling 4 million miles in 235 hours and 13 minutes.

NAME: William A. Oefelein (Lieutenant, USN)
NASA Astronaut (Pilot Candidate)

PERSONAL DATA: Born March 29, 1965 in Ft. Belvoir, Virginia, but considers Anchorage, Alaska to be his hometown. Married to the former Michaella Davis of Anchorage, Alaska. They have two children. Recreational interests include weight lifting, wake boarding, snow skiing, bicycling, fishing, backcountry hiking, and playing the guitar. His parents, Randall W. and Billye M. Oefelein, reside in Anchorage, Alaska. Her parents, Pat and Charlene Davis, reside in Kailua-Kona, Hawaii.

EDUCATION: West Anchorage High School, Anchorage, Alaska, 1983. B.S., Electrical Engineering, Oregon State University, 1988. M.S., Aviation Systems, University of Tennessee Space Institute, 1998.

ORGANIZATIONS: Society of Experimental Test Pilots, Seaplane Pilots Association.

SPECIAL HONORS: High Scholarship Graduate Oregon State University, McClarran Award for Strike/Fighter competition. Awarded the Strike/Flight Air Medal, Navy Commendation Medal, Navy Achievement Medal, and various other service awards.

EXPERIENCE: Oefelein received his commission as an Ensign in the United States Navy from Aviation Officer Candidate School in Pensacola, Florida in 1988. He entered flight training in Texas in 1989 and was designated a Naval Aviator in September 1990. He then reported to Marine Fighter/Attack Training Squadron 101 at Marine Corps Air Station El Toro, California for initial F/A-18 training. Upon completion of training, he was assigned to Strike Fighter Squadron 146 at Naval Air Station Lemoore, California where he made overseas deployments aboard the aircraft carrier USS Nimitz to the Pacific and Indian Oceans and the Persian Gulf in support of Operation Southern Watch. While assigned to VFA-146, he attended the US Navy Fighter Weapons School, TOPGUN, and was assigned as the Squadron Air-to-Air Weapons and Tactics Officer. Oefelein was selected for the United States Naval Test Pilot School at Naval Air Station Patuxent River, Maryland and began the course in January of 1995. After graduation in December 1995, he was assigned to Strike Aircraft Test Squadron as an F/A-18 Project Officer and Test Pilot. In February 1997, he went back to the United States Naval Test Pilot School as an Instructor flying the F/A-18, T-2, and U-6 aircraft. In February 1998, he transferred to Carrier Air Wing 8, Naval Air Station Oceana, Virginia where he was assigned duties as the Strike Operations Officer when he was selected for the astronaut program. Oefelein has logged over 2000 hours in more than 50 aircraft and has over 200 carrier arrested landings.

NASA EXPERIENCE: Selected by NASA in June 1998, he reported for training in August 1998. Astronaut Candidate Training includes orientation briefings and tours, numerous scientific and technical briefings, intensive instruction in Shuttle and International Space Station systems, physiological training and ground school to prepare for T-38 flight training, as well as learning water and wilderness survival techniques. Oefelein is currently assigned to the Astronaut Office Shuttle Operations Branch. He will serve in technical assignments until assigned to a space flight.

NAME: John D. Olivas (Ph.D.)
NASA Astronaut (Mission Specialist Candidate)

PERSONAL DATA: Born May 25, 1966 in North Hollywood, California, but considers El Paso, Texas to be his hometown. Married to the former Marie K. Schwarzkopf, also of El Paso, Texas. They have 3 children. Recreational interests include running, weightlifting, hunting, fishing, surfing, and mountain biking. His parents, Juan and Carmen Olivas, reside in El Paso, Texas. Her parents, Donald and Dorothy Schwarzkopf also reside in El Paso, Texas.

EDUCATION: Graduated from Burges High School, El Paso, Texas, in 1984; received a bachelor of science degree in mechanical engineering from the University of Texas-El Paso in 1989; a masters of science degree in mechanical engineering from the University of Houston in 1993 and a doctorate in mechanical engineering and materials science from Rice University in 1996.

ORGANIZATIONS: American Society of Materials International (ASM International), Texas Registered Professional Engineer.

AWARDS: Three U.S. Patents (pending); Four NASA Class One Tech Brief Awards (1997 and 1998); Five JPL-California Institute of Technology Novel Technology Report Recognitions (1997 and 1998); Pan American Institute Scholarship Award (1995); NASA ASEE Summer Faculty Fellowship Award (1995); Rice University Scholarship (1994); Dow Life Saving Award (1992).

EXPERIENCE: After graduating in 1989, Olivas worked until 1994 for the Dow Chemical Company in Freeport, Texas. While there, he was a mechanical/materials engineer responsible for performing equipment stress/failure analysis for the operating facilities. After completing his masters degree in 1993, Olivas pursued his doctorate while supporting engine coating evaluations for C-5 maintenance operations at Kelly Air Force Base. In the Summer of 1995, he supported the Crew and Thermal Systems Directorate at NASA Johnson Space Center, evaluating materials for application to the next generation Extravehicular Mobility Unit. Upon completing his doctorate, in the Spring of 1996, he moved to Los Angeles, California, and was offered a senior research engineer position at the Jet Propulsion Laboratory (JPL), in Pasadena, California. His research included the development of tools and methodologies for nondestructively evaluating microelectronics and structural materials subjected to space environments. He was promoted to Program Manager of the JPL Advanced Interconnect and Manufacturing Assurance Program, aimed at evaluating the reliability and susceptibility of state-of-the-art microelectronics for use in future NASA projects. Additionally, he was the JPL lead for the NASA Safety Reliability and Quality Assurance Nondestructive Evaluation (NDE) program investigating applications of NDE to microelectronics applications. Through his career, he has authored and presented numerous papers at technical conferences and in scientific journals and is principal developer of seven inventions.

NASA EXPERIENCE: Selected by NASA in June 1998, he reported for training in August 1998. Astronaut Candidate Training includes orientation briefings and tours, numerous scientific and technical briefings, intensive instruction in Shuttle and International Space Station systems, physiological training and ground school to prepare for T-38 flight training, as well as learning water and wilderness survival techniques. Olivas is currently assigned technical responsibilities within the Robotics Branch of the Astronaut Office. He serves as lead for the Special Purpose Dexterous Manipulator Robot, Mobile Transporter and Mobile Base System.

NAME: Scott E. Parazynski (M.D.)
      NASA Astronaut

PERSONAL DATA: Born July 28, 1961, in Little Rock, Arkansas. Considers Palo Alto, California, and Evergreen, Colorado, to be his hometowns. Married to the former Gail Marie Vozzella. They have two children. He enjoys mountaineering, rock climbing, flying, scuba diving, skiing, travel, wood-working and nature photography. A commercial, multi-engine, seaplane and instrument-rated pi-lot, Dr. Parazynski has logged over 1600 flight hours in a variety of aircraft.

EDUCATION: Attended junior high school in Dakar, Senegal, and Beirut, Lebanon. Attended high school at the Tehran American School, Iran, and the American Community School, Athens, Greece, graduating in 1979. He received a bachelor of science degree in biology from Stanford University in 1983, continuing on to graduate with honors from Stanford Medical School in 1989. He served his medical internship at the Brigham and Women's Hospital of Harvard Medical School (1990). He had completed 22 months of a residency program in emergency medicine in Denver, Colorado when selected to the Astronaut Corps.

ORGANIZATIONS: Member of the Aerospace Medical Association, the American Society for Gravita-tional and Space Biology, the Wilderness Medical Society, the American Alpine Club, the Associa-tion of Space Explorers, the Experimental Aircraft Association, and the Aircraft Owners and Pilots Association.

SPECIAL HONORS: National Institutes of Health Predoctoral Training Award in Cancer Biology (1983); Rhodes Scholarship finalist (1984); NASA Graduate Student Researcher's Award (1988); Stanford Medical Scholars Program (1988); Research Honors Award from Stanford Medical School (1989); NASA-Ames Certificate of Recognition (1990); Wilderness Medical Society Research Award (1991); Space Station Team Excellence Award (1996); NASA Exceptional Service Medals (1998, 1999); NASA Space Flight Medals (1994, 1997, 1998). While in medical school, he competed on the United States Development Luge Team and was ranked among the top 10 competitors in the nation dur-ing the 1988 Olympic Trials. He also served as an Olympic Team Coach for the Philippines during the 1988 Olympic Winter Games in Calgary, Canada.

EXPERIENCE: While an undergraduate at Stanford University, Dr. Parazynski studied antigenic varia-tion in African Sleeping Sickness, using sophisticated molecular biological techniques. While in medical school, he was awarded a NASA Graduate Student Fellowship and conducted research at NASA-Ames Research Center on fluid shifts that occur during human space flight. Additionally, he has been involved in the design of several exercise devices that are being developed for long-duration space flight, and has conducted research on high-altitude acclimatization. Dr. Parazynski has numerous publications in the field of space physiology, and has a particular expertise in human adaptation to stressful environments.

NASA EXPERIENCE: Selected by NASA in March 1992, Dr. Parazynski reported to the Johnson Space Center in August 1992. He completed one year of training and evaluation, and was qualified as a mission specialist. Dr. Parazynski initially served as one of the crew representatives for extrave-hicular activity (EVA) in the Astronaut Office Mission Development Branch. Following his first flight he was assigned as a backup for the third American long-duration stay aboard Russia's Space Station Mir, and was expected to serve as a prime crew member on a subsequent mission. He spent 5-months intraining at the Gargarin Cosmonaut Training Center, Star City, Russia. In October

1995, when sitting-height parameters raised concerns about his fitting safely in the Soyuz vehicle in the event of an emergency on-board the Mir station, he was deemed too tall for the mission and was withdrawn from Mir training. He served as the Astronaut Office Operations Planning Branch crew representative for Space Shuttle, Space Station and Soyuz training, was assigned to the Astronaut Office EVA Branch, helping to develop tools and procedures for the assembly of the International Space Station (ISS), and most recently served as Deputy (Operations and Training) of the Astronaut Office ISS Branch. A veteran of three space flights, STS-66 (1994), STS-86 (1997), and STS-95 (1998), Dr. Parazynski has logged over 734 hours in space including over 5 hours of EVA. Dr. Parazynski is currently assigned to STS-100/ISS Assembly Flight 6A, during which he will perform a pair of EVAs to install the Space Station robotic arm and other assembly tasks. Launch is targeted for 2001.

SPACE FLIGHT EXPERIENCE: The STS-66 Atmospheric Laboratory for Applications and Science-3 (ATLAS-3) mission was launched from Kennedy Space Center, Florida, on November 3, 1994, and returned to land at Edwards Air Force Base, California, on November 14, 1994. ATLAS-3 was part of an on-going program to determine the earth's energy balance and atmospheric change over an 11-year solar cycle, particularly with respect to humanity's impact on global-ozone distribution. Dr. Parazynski had responsibility for a number of on-orbit activities including operation of the ATLAS experiments and Spacelab Pallet, as well as several secondary experiments in the crew cabin. He and his crewmates also successfully evaluated the Interlimb Resistance Device, a free-floating exercise he developed to prevent musculoskeletal atrophy in microgravity. The Space Shuttle Atlantis circled the earth 175 times and traveled over 4.5 million miles during its 262 hour and 34 minute flight. STS-86 Atlantis (September 25 to October 6, 1997) was the seventh mission to rendezvous and dock with the Russian Space Station Mir. Highlights of the mission included the exchange of U.S. crew members Mike Foale and David Wolf, the transfer of 10,400 pounds of science and logistics, and the first Shuttle-based joint American-Russian spacewalk. Dr. Parazynski served as the flight engineer (MS2) during the flight, and was also the navigator during the Mir rendezvous. Dr. Parazynski (EV1) and Russian cosmonaut Vladimir Titov performed a 5 hour, 1 minute spacewalk during which they retrieved four experiment packages first deployed during the STS-76 Shuttle-Mir docking mission. They also deployed the Spektr Solar Array Cap, which was designed to be used in a future Mir spacewalk to seal a leak in the Spektr module's damaged hull. Other objectives of EVA included the evaluation of common EVA tools to be used by astronauts wearing either Russian or American-made spacesuits, and a systems flight test of the Simplified Aid for EVA Rescue (SAFER). The Space Shuttle Atlantis circled the earth 169 times and traveled over 4.2 million miles during its 259 hour and 21 minute flight, landing at the Kennedy Space Center. STS-95 Discovery (October 29 to November 7, 1998) was a 9-day mission during which the crew supported a variety of research payloads including deployment of the Spartan solar-observing spacecraft, and the testing of the Hubble Space Telescope Orbital Systems Test Platform. The crew also conducted investigations on the correlation between space flight and the aging process. Dr. Parazynski was the flight engineer (MS2) for the mission, as well as the navigator for the Spartan spacecraft rendezvous. During the flight, he also operated the Shuttle's robotic arm in support of the testing of several space-vision systems being considered for ISS assembly. In addition, he was responsible for monitoring several life sciences investigations, including those involving crewmate-Senator John Glenn. The mission was accomplished in 134 Earth orbits, traveling 3.6 million miles in 213 hours and 44 minutes.

NAME: Nicholas J. M. Patrick (Ph.D.)
NASA Astronaut (Mission Specialist Candidate)

PERSONAL DATA: Born on 22 March 1964 in Saltburn, North Yorkshire, United Kingdom, Nicholas considers London, England and Rye, New York and to be his hometowns. He became a US citizen in 1994. He is unmarried. His mother, Gillian A.M. Patrick, lives in South Norwalk, Connecticut; his father, C. Stewart Patrick, in Narberth, Pennsylvania; and his brother, Rupert C.M. Patrick, near New Haven, Connecticut. His recreational interests include flying, reading, automotive work, hiking, skiing, and scuba diving.

EDUCATION: Harrow School, London, England, 1978-82. B.A., Engineering, University of Cambridge, England, 1986. M.A. Cantab., Engineering, University of Cambridge, England, 1990. S.M., Mechanical Engineering, Massachusetts Institute of Technology, 1990. Ph.D., Mechanical Engineering, Massachusetts Institute of Technology, 1996.

ORGANIZATIONS: Nicholas is a member of the Aircraft Owners and Pilots Association and the National Space Society, and is registered as a Professional Engineer in Massachusetts.

SPECIAL HONORS: Entrance scholarship ('Exhibition') to the University of Cambridge (Trinity College), 1983; GE Aircraft Engines Development Program Project Award for contributions to manufacturing inventory reduction, 1988.

EXPERIENCE: While at the University of Cambridge, Nicholas learned to fly as a member of the Royal Air Force's Cambridge University Air Squadron, and spent his summers as a civil engineer in New York and Connecticut. After graduating from Cambridge, he moved to Boston, Massachusetts, where he worked for four years as an engineer for the Aircraft Engines division of GE. He then attended MIT, where he was a teaching assistant and then a research assistant in the Human-Machine Systems Laboratory in the Department of Mechanical Engineering. His research interests included telerobotics, aviation psychology, optimization, air transportation, and econometrics. While at MIT, he worked as a flight instructor at Hanscom Field's East Coast Aero Club, and as a statistician and programmer for a local medical and robotic products company, and served on the Board of Stockholders of the Harvard Cooperative Society. Upon completion of his doctorate, Nicholas joined the Boeing Commercial Airplane Group in Seattle, Washington, where he worked in Flight Deck Engineering as a Systems and Human Factors Engineer on many of Boeing's commercial aircraft models. While in Seattle, he was also a flight instructor at Boeing Field's Galvin Flying Service. Nicholas has logged 1,300 hours as a pilot - including 700 hours as a flight instructor - in more than 20 types of airplane and helicopter.

NASA EXPERIENCE: Selected by NASA in June 1998, he reported for training in August 1998. Astronaut Candidate Training includes orientation briefings and tours, numerous scientific and technical briefings, intensive instruction in Shuttle and International Space Station systems, physiological training and ground school to prepare for T-38 flight training, as well as learning water and wilderness survival techniques. Nicholas is currently assigned to the Astronaut Office Shuttle Operations Branch. He will serve in technical assignments until assigned to a space flight.

NAME: Julie Payette
Astronaut, Canadian Space Agency

PERSONAL DATA: Born October 20, 1963, in Montreal, Quebec. Enjoys running, skiing, racquet sports and scuba diving. Holds a multi-engine commercial pilot license with instrument and float ratings. Ms. Payette plays piano and has sung with the Montreal Symphonic Orchestra Chamber Choir, the Piacere Vocale in Basel, Switzerland, and with the Tafelmusik Baroque Orchestra Choir in Toronto, Canada. Fluent in French and English, and conversational in Spanish, Italian, and Russian.

EDUCATION: Primary and secondary school in Montreal, Quebec. International Baccalaureate (1982) at the United World International College of the Atlantic in South Wales, UK. Bachelor of Engineering (1986) from McGill University, Montreal and a Master of Applied Science – Computer Enginering (1990) from the University of Toronto.

ORGANIZATIONS: Member of l'Ordre des Ingénieurs du Québec. Appointed member (Governor-in-Council) of the Natural Sciences and Engineering Research Council of Canada (NSERC). Fellow of the Canadian Academy of Engineering. Les Amies d'affaire du Ritz. Honorary Life Member – Association of professional engineers of Prince-Edward-Island, Canada.

SPECIAL HONORS: Received one of six Canadian scholarships to attend the International UWC of the Atlantic in South Wales, UK (1980). Greville-Smith Scholarship (1982-1986), highest undergraduate award at McGill University. McGill Faculty Scholar (1983-1986), graduated with distinction in 1986. NSERC post-graduate Scholarship (1988-1990). Massey College Fellowship (1988-1990). Canadian Council of Professional Engineers 1994 distinction for exceptional achievement by a young engineer. Doctor of Science Honoris Causa · Queens University (1999). Doctor Honoris Causa · University of Ottawa (1999). Doctor of Laws – Simon Fraser University, BC (2000). Doctorat ès Science honorifique ·Université Laval (2000). Doctor of Laws Honoris Causa – Simon Fraser University, BC (2000). Chevalier de l'Ordre de la Pléiade de l'Assemblée Nationale du Québec (2000).

EXPERIENCE: Before joining the space program, Ms. Payette conducted research in computer systems, natural language processing, automatic speech recognition and the application of interactive technology to space: System engineer · IBM Canada (1986-88). Research Assistant · University of Toronto (1988-90). Visiting scientist · IBM Research Laboratory, Zurich, Switzerland (1991). Research engineer · Speech Research Group, Bell-Northern Research, Montreal (1992). Ms. Payette was selected as an astronaut by the Canadian Space Agency (CSA) in June 1992 and underwent training in Canada. After basic training, she worked as a technical advisor for the MSS (Mobile Servicing System), an advanced robotics system and Canada's contribution to the International Space Station. In 1993, Ms. Payette established the Human-Computer Interaction (HCI) Group at the Canadian Astronaut Program and served as a technical specialist on the NATO International Research Study Group (RSG-10) on speech processing (1993-1996). In preparation for a space assignment, Ms. Payette studied Russian and logged over 120 hours of reduced gravity flight time aboard various parabolic aircraft (KC-135, T-33, Falcon-20, DC-9). In April 1996, Ms. Payette completed a deep-sea diving hard suit training program in Vancouver BC and was certified as a one-atmosphere diving suit operator. Ms. Payette obtained her captaincy on military jet at the Canadian Air Force Base in Moose Jaw, Saskatchewan in February 1996. She has since obtained her military instrument rating and continues to fly with the training squadron. Ms.Payette has logged more than 700 hours of flight time, including 350 hours on jet aircraft.

NASA EXPERIENCE: Ms. Payette reported to the Johnson Space Center in August 1996. She completed initial astronaut training in April 1998 and was assigned to work technical issues in robotics for the Astronaut Office. Ms. Payette flew on Space Shuttle Discovery, mission STS-96 (May 27 to June 6, 1999). During the 10-day mission the crew delivered 4 tons of logistics and supplies to the International Space Station in preparation for the arrival of the first crew to live aboard the station early next year. The mission was accomplished in 153 Earth orbits, traveling 4 million miles in 235 hours and 13 minutes. Currently assigned as a member of the Crew Test Support Team (Russian Crusaders) responsible for providing crew insight and support to the development and testing of International Space Station hardware and software in Russia.

NAME: Philippe Perrin (Lieutenant Colonel, French Air Force)
CNES Astronaut

PERSONAL DATA: Born January 6, 1963, in Meknes, Morocco. Considers Avignon, Provence, to be his hometown. Married to Cecile Bosc. They have one child. He enjoys scuba diving, skiing, sailing, hiking, travel, the history of sciences. His parents, Jean and Monique Perrin reside in the south of France. Her parents, Rene and Helene Bosc, reside in Provence, France.

EDUCATION: Entered the French "Ecole Polytechnique (Paris)" in 1982. Graduated as "Ingénieur Polytechnicien" (engineering degree) in 1985. Received his Test Pilot Licence in 1993 from the Ecole du Personnel Navigant d'Essais et de Réception (EPNER), the French Test Pilot School at Istres Air Force Base. Received his Air Line Pilot Certificate in 1995.

SPECIAL HONORS: Awarded his pilot's wings "first of his class" in 1996. Recipient of two French Air Force awards for Flight Safety in 1989, the French Overseas Medal (Gulf War in 1991), and two French National Defense Medals.

EXPERIENCE: Prior to graduating from the Ecole Polytechnique, Perrin completed military duty in the French Navy, where he was trained in ship piloting and navigation, and spent 6 months at sea in the Indian Ocean. Following Ecole Polytechnique, he entered the French Air Force in 1985, was awarded his pilot's wings in 1986, and assigned to the 33rd Reconnaissance Wing at Strasbourg Air Force Base (1987-1991). He flew the Mirage F1 CR and made detachments in Africa and Saudi Arabia. Upon graduating from EPNER, the French Test Pilot School, he worked on a variety of test programs while assigned to the Bretigny Test Center. In 1992, he was temporarily detached to the French Space Agency (CNES) and sent to Star City, Russia, where he trained for two months In 1993, he reported to the 2nd Air Defense Wing of Dijon Air Force Base as Senior Operations Officer (Operation Southern Watch). In 1995, he returned to the Bretigny Test Center, as Chief Pilot Deputy, in charge of the development of the Mirage 2000-5. In July 1996, CNES announced his selection as an Astronaut and assigned him to attend NASA's Astronaut Candidate Training in Houston, Texas. Perrin has flown 26 combat missions and has logged over 2,500 flying hours in over 30 types (from jet fighters to Airbus).

NASA EXPERIENCE: Perrin reported to the Johnson Space Center in August 1996. Having completed two years of training and evaluation, he is qualified for flight assignment as a mission specialist. Currently, Perrin is assigned technical duties in the Astronaut Office Spacecraft Systems/Operations Branch.

NAME: Donald R. Pettit (Ph.D.)
   NASA Astronaut

PERSONAL DATA: Born April 20, 1955 in Silverton, Oregon. Married. He enjoys photography, and swimming.

EDUCATION: Graduated from Silverton Union High School, Silverton, Oregon, in 1973; received a bachelor of science degree in chemical engineering from Oregon State Univeristy in 1978; and a doctorate in chemical engineering from the University of Arizona in 1983.

EXPERIENCE: Staff scientist at Los Alamos National Laboratory, Los Alamos, New Mexico from 1984-1996. Projects included reduced gravity fluid flow and materials processing experiments on board the NASA KC-135 airplane, atmospheric spectroscopy measurements on noctolucent clouds seeded from sounding rocket payloads, volcano fumarole gas sampling on active volcanos, and problems in detonation physics applied to weapon systems. He was a member of The Synthesis Group, slated with assembling the technology to return to the moon and explore Mars (1990), and the Space Station Freedom re-design team (1993).

NASA EXPERIENCE: Selected by NASA in April 1996, Dr. Pettit reported to the Johnson Space Center in August 1996. Having completed two years of training and evaluation, he is qualified for flight selection as a mission specialist. Currently, Dr. Pettit is assigned technical duties in the Astronaut Office Computer Support Branch.

NAME: John L. Phillips (Ph.D.)
   NASA Astronaut

PERSONAL DATA: Born April 15, 1951 in Fort Belvoir, Virginia, but considers Scottsdale, Arizona to be his hometown. Married to the former Laura Jean Doell of Scotia, New York. They have two children. Enjoys skiing, kayaking, hiking, family recreation and various fitness activities.

EDUCATION: Graduated from Scottsdale High School, Scottsdale, Arizona, in 1966; received a bachelor of science degree in mathematics and Russian from the U.S. Naval Academy in 1972; a master of science degree in aeronautical systems from the University of West Florida in 1974; a master of science degree and a doctorate in geophysics and space physics from the University of California, Los Angeles (UCLA) in 1984 and 1987 respectively.

SPECIAL HONORS: National Merit Scholar; graduated second of 906 in the class of 1972 at U.S. Naval Academy; received 2 NASA Group Achievement Awards for contributions to the Ulysses Spacecraft Mission and the Los Alamos National Laboratory Distinguished Performance Award in 1996.

VARIOUS MILITARY AWARDS: Awarded 2 Navy Unit Commendations, the National Defense Medal, 2 Sea Service Deployment Ribbons, the Armed Forces Reserve Medal, and 2 Battle "E" Ribbons.

EXPERIENCE: Phillips received a navy commission upon graduation from the U.S. Naval Academy in 1972 and was designated a Naval Aviator in November, 1974. He trained in the A-7 Corsair Aircraft at Naval Air Station Lemoore, California and made overseas deployment with Attack Squadron 155 aboard the USS Oriskany and USS Roosevelt. Subsequent tours of duty included navy recruiting in

Albany, New York, and flying the CT-39 Sabreliner Aircraft at Naval Air Station North Island, California. After leaving the Navy in 1982, Phillips enrolled as a graduate student at UCLA. While at UCLA he carried out research involving observations by the NASA Pioneer Venus Spacecraft. Upon completing his doctorate in 1987, he was awarded A. J. Robert Oppenheimer Postdoctoral Fellowship at Los Alamos National Laboratory in New Mexico. He accepted a career position at Los Alamos in 1989. While there, Phillips performed research on the sun and the space environment. From 1993 through 1996 he was Principal Investigator for the Solar Wind Plasma Experiment aboard the Ulysses Spacecraft as it executed a unique trajectory over the poles of the sun. He has authored 156 scientific papers dealing with the plasma environments of the sun, earth, other planets, comets and spacecraft. Phillips has logged over 4,300 flight hours and 250 carrier landings. He has been a Navy reservist since 1982, serving as an A-7 pilot, and in various non-flying assignments. He holds the rank of Captain, USNR.

NASA EXPERIENCE: Selected by NASA in April 1996, Phillips reported to the Johnson Space Center in August 1996. After completing astronaut candidate training, he held various jobs in the Astronaut Office, including systems engineering and CAPCOM for the International Space Station. He is currently training as a crew member of STS-100/ISS Assembly Flight 6A scheduled for launch in 2001.

NAME: Alan G. Poindexter (Lieutenant Commander, USN)
NASA Astronaut (Pilot Candidate)

PERSONAL DATA: Born November 5, 1961 in Pasadena, California, but considers Rockville, Maryland to be his hometown. Married to the former Lisa A. Pfeiffer. They have two children. Recreational interests include running, weight lifting, water skiing, boating, hunting, and fishing. His parents, John M. and Linda A. Poindexter, reside in Rockville, Maryland. Lisa's parents live in Gulf Breeze, Florida.

EDUCATION: Graduated from Coronado High School, Coronado, California in 1979. Graduated with highest honors from Georgia Institute of Technology with a bachelor of aerospace engineering degree in 1986 and a master of science in aeronautical engineering from the Naval Postgraduate School in 1995.

ORGANIZATIONS: Society of Experimental Test Pilots, Tau Beta Pi Engineering Society.

AWARDS: Navy and Marine Corps Commendation Medal with Combat V, Navy and Marine Corps Achievement Medal, various other service awards.

SPECIAL HONORS: Naval Air Warfare Center, Aircraft Division Test Pilot of the Year 1996; Top Ten Carrier Aviator, Carrier Airwing Nine.

EXPERIENCE: Poindexter was commissioned following graduation from the Georgia Institute of Technology in 1986. After a short tour of duty at the Hypervelocity Wind Tunnel Facility, Naval Surface Weapons Center, White Oak, Maryland, Poindexter reported for flight training in Pensacola, Florida. He was designated a Naval Aviator in 1988 and reported to Fighter Squadron 124, Naval Air Station Miramar, California, for transition to the F-14 Tomcat. Following his initial training, Poindexter was assigned to Fighter Squadron 211, also at Miramar, and made two deployments to the Arabian Gulf during Operations Desert Storm and Southern Watch. While attached to VF-211,

Poindexter was designated as a Wing Qualified Landing Signal Officer. During his second deployment in 1993, he was selected to attend the Naval Postgraduate School/U.S. Naval Test Pilot School Cooperative Program. Following graduation in December 1995, Poindexter was assigned as a Test Pilot and Project Officer at the Naval Strike Aircraft Test Squadron (NSATS), Naval Air Station (NAS) Patuxent River, Maryland. While at NSATS, Poindexter was assigned as the lead test pilot for the F-14 Digital Flight Control System where he logged the first carrier landing and catapult launch of an F-14 with the upgraded flight controls. He also flew numerous high angle of attack/departure tests, weapons separation tests and carrier suitability trials. Following his tour at Patuxent River, Poindexter reported to Fighter Squadron 32, NAS Oceana, Virginia where he was serving as a department head when he was selected for Astronaut training. Poindexter has more than 2,000 hours in over 30 aircraft types and has logged over 450 carrier landings.

NASA EXPERIENCE: Selected by NASA in June 1998, he reported for training in August 1998. Astronaut Candidate Training includes orientation briefings and tours, numerous scientific and technical briefings, intensive instruction in Shuttle and International Space Station systems, physiological training and ground school to prepare for T-38 flight training, as well as learning water and wilderness survival techniques. Poindexter is currently assigned to the Astronaut Office Shuttle Operations Branch. He will serve in technical assignments until assigned to a space flight.

NAME: Mark L. Polansky
NASA Astronaut

PERSONAL DATA: Born June 2, 1956 in Paterson, New Jersey. Considers Edison, New Jersey, his hometown. Enjoys ice hockey, snow skiing, light aircraft flying, music, and the arts. His parents, Irving and Edith Polansky, reside in Edison, New Jersey.

EDUCATION: Graduated from John P. Stevens High School, Edison, New Jersey, in 1974; received a bachelor of science degree in aeronautical and astronautical engineering, and a master of science degree in aeronautics and astronautics, from Purdue University, both in 1978.

ORGANIZATIONS: Member of the Society of Experimental Test Pilots, American Institute of Aeronautics and Astronautics, and the Aircraft Owners and Pilots Association.

SPECIAL HONORS: Distinguished Graduate of the USAF Test Pilot School (1987). Distinguished Graduate of USAF Undergraduate Pilot Training (1980). Recipient of the USAF Flying Training Award (1980). Awarded Air Force Meritorious Service Medal and Air Force Commendation Medal with two Oak Leaf Clusters.

EXPERIENCE: Polansky received an Air Force commission upon graduation from Purdue University in 1978. He earned his pilot wings in January 1980 at Vance Air Force Base (AFB), Oklahoma. From 1980 to 1983, he was assigned to Langley AFB, Virginia, where he flew the F-15 aircraft. In 1983, Polansky transitioned to the F-5E aircraft and served as an Aggressor Pilot, where he trained tactical aircrews to defeat enemy aircraft tactics. He was assigned in this capacity to Clark Air Base, Republic of the Philippines, and Nellis AFB, Nevada, until he was selected to attend USAF Test Pilot School, Edwards AFB, California, in 1986. Upon graduation, he was assigned to Eglin AFB, Florida, where he conducted weapons and systems testing in the F-15, F-15E, and A-10 aircraft. Polansky left active duty in 1992 to pursue a career at NASA. He has logged over 5,000 flight hours in over 30 different aircraft.

NASA EXPERIENCE: Polansky joined NASA in August 1992, as an aerospace engineer and research pilot. He was assigned to the Aircraft Operations Division of the Johnson Space Center. His primary responsibilities involved teaching the astronaut pilots Space Shuttle landing techniques in the Shuttle Trainer Aircraft and instructing astronaut pilots and mission specialists in the T-38 aircraft. Polansky also conducted flight testing of the NASA T-38 avionics upgrade aircraft. Selected by NASA in April 1996, Polansky reported to the Johnson Space Center in August 1996. Having completed two years of training and evaluation, he was assigned as a member of the Astronaut Support Personnel team at the Kennedy Space Center, supporting Space Shuttle launches and landings. Polansky is currently assigned as pilot on STS-98. The crew will continue the task of building and enhancing the International Space Station by delivering the U.S. laboratory module. The Shuttle will spend six days docked to the station while the laboratory is attached and three spacewalks are conducted to complete its assembly. The STS-98 mission will occur while the first station crew is aboard the new spacecraft. Launch is targeted for 2001.

NAME: Marcos C. Pontes (Major, Brazil Air Force)
BSA Astronaut (Mission Specialist Candidate)

PERSONAL DATA: Born March 11, 1963 in Bauru, Sao Paulo, Brazil. Married to the former Francisca de Fatima Cavalcanti of Angicos, Rio Grande do Norte, Brazil. They have two children. Recreational interests include weight lifting, soccer, guitar and piano, sketching, watercolor painting. His parents, Vergilio and Zuleika Pontes, reside in Bauru, Sao Paulo, Brazil. Her father, Praxedes Cavalcanti, resides in Angicos, Rio Grande do Norte, Brazil. Her mother, Maria Emilia Cavalcanti, is deceased.

EDUCATION: Graduated from Liceu Noroeste High School, Bauru, Sao Paulo in 1980; received a bachelor of science in aeronautical technology from the Brazil Air Force Academy, Pirassununga, Sao Paulo in 1984, a bachelor of science in aeronautical engineering, from the Instituto Tecnologico de Aeronautica, Sao Jose dos Campos, Sao Paulo in 1993, and a master of science degree in Systems Engineering from Naval Postgraduate School, Monterey, California in 1998.

AWARDS: Air Force Meritorious Service Medal.

SPECIAL HONORS: Graduated with Distinction Instituto Technologico de Aeronautica; received the Space and Aeronautics Institute Award and the EMBRAER (Empresa Brasileira de Aeronautica) Award in 1994 for Test Pilot Training. Air Force University Award in 1995. Graduated with Distinction Naval Postgraduate School.

EXPERIENCE: Pontes graduated as a military pilot from the Brazil Air Force Academy, Pirassununga, Sao Paulo, in 1984. After one year of advanced jet training at the 2/5 Instruction Aviation Group, Natal, Rio Grande do Norte, he was assigned to 3/10 Strike Aviation Group, Santa Maria, Rio Grande do Sul. As a military pilot, he was qualified as an instructor for Ground Attack missions and Attack's Advanced Air Controlling. As a Flight Safety Officer, his work experience included 4 years in aeronautical accident investigation. From 1989 to 1993 he attended Aeronautical Engineering course, followed by a one year Test Pilot course. As a test pilot he worked on weapons development, missile tests and aircraft evaluation. He has logged over 1,700 flight hours in more than 20 different aircraft, including F-15, F-16, F18 and MIG-29. In 1996, he was assigned to the Naval Postgraduate School. Pontes graduated from Naval Postgraduate School when he was selected for the astronaut program.

NASA EXPERIENCE: In August 1998, he reported to the Johnson Space Center to attend Astronaut Candidate Training which includes orientation briefings and tours, numerous scientific and technical briefings, intensive instruction in Shuttle and International Space Station systems, physiological training and ground school to prepare for T-38 flight training, as well as learning water and wilderness survival techniques. Pontes is currently assigned to the Astronaut Office Space Station Operations Branch. He will serve in technical assignments until assigned to a space flight.

NAME: Charles J. Precourt (Colonel, USAF, Ret.)
NASA Astronaut

PERSONAL DATA: Born June 29, 1955, in Waltham, Massachusetts, but considers Hudson, Massachusetts, to be his hometown. Married to the former Lynne Denise Mungle of St. Charles, Missouri. They have three daughters, Michelle, Sarah, and Aimee. Precourt enjoys golf and flying light aircraft. He flies a Varieze, an experimental aircraft that he built. His parents, Charles and Helen Precourt, reside in Hudson. Her parents, Loyd and Jerry Mungle, reside in Streetman, Texas.

EDUCATION: Graduated from Hudson High School, Hudson, Massachusetts, in 1973; received a bachelor of science degree in aeronautical engineering from the United States Air Force Academy in 1977, a master of science degree in engineering management from Golden Gate University in 1988, and a master of arts degree in national security affairs and strategic studies from the United States Naval War College in 1990. While at the United States Air Force Academy, Precourt also attended the French Air Force Academy in 1976 as part of an exchange program. Fluent in French and Russian.

ORGANIZATIONS: Vice President of the Association of Space Explorers; member of the Society of Experimental Test Pilots (SETP), and the Experimental Aircraft Association.

SPECIAL HONORS: Military decorations include: the Defense Superior Service Medal (2); the Distinguished Flying Cross; the Air Force Meritorious Service Medal (2). Distinguished graduate of the United States Air Force Academy and the United States Naval War College. In 1978 he was the Air Training Command Trophy Winner as the outstanding graduate of his pilot training class. In 1989 he was recipient of the David B. Barnes Award as the Outstanding Instructor Pilot at the United States Air ForceTest Pilot School. NASA awards include: the NASA Distinguished Service Medal; the Exceptional Service Medal and Outstanding Leadership Medal; and the NASA Space Flight Medal (4

EXPERIENCE: Precourt graduated from Undergraduate Pilot Training at Reese Air Force Base, Texas, in 1978. Initially he flew as an instructor pilot in the T-37, and later as a maintenance test pilot in the T-37 and T-38 aircraft. From 1982 through 1984, he flew an operational tour in the F-15 Eagle at Bitburg Air Base in Germany. In 1985 he attended the United States Air Force Test Pilot School at Edwards Air Force Base in California. Upon graduation, Precourt was assigned as a test pilot at Edwards, where he flew the F-15E, F-4, A-7, and A-37 aircraft until mid 1989, when he began studies at the United States Naval War College in Newport, Rhode Island. Upon graduation from the War College, Precourt joined the astronaut program. His flight experience includes over 7,000 hours in over 60 types of civil and military aircraft. He holds commercial pilot, multi-engine instrument, glider and certified flight instructor ratings. Precourt retired from the Air Force on March 31, 2000.

NASA EXPERIENCE: Precourt is currently the Chief of the Astronaut Corps, responsible for the mission preparation activities of all space shuttle and future International Space Station crews and their support personnel. Selected by NASA in January 1990, Precourt became an astronaut in July 1991. His other technical assignments to date have included: Manager of ascent, entry, and launch abort issues for the Astronaut Office Operations Development Branch; spacecraft communicator (CAPCOM), providing the voice link from the Mission Control Center during launch and entry for several Space Shuttle missions; Director of Operations for NASA at the Gagarin Cosmonaut Training Center in Star City, Russia, from October 1995 to April 1996, with responsibility for the coordination and implementation of mission operations activities in the Moscow region for the joint U.S./Russian Shuttle/Mir program. He also served as Acting Assistant Director (Technical), Johnson Space Center. A veteran of four space flights, he has logged over 932 hours in space. He served as a mission specialist on STS-55 (April 26 to May 6, 1993), was the pilot on STS-71 (June 27 to July 7, 1995), and was the spacecraft commander on STS-84 (May 15-24, 1997) and STS-91 (June 2-12, 1998), the final scheduled Shuttle-Mir docking mission, concluding the joint U.S./Russian Phase I Program.

SPACE FLIGHT EXPERIENCE: STS-55 Columbia launched from Kennedy Space Center, Florida, on April 26, 1993. Nearly 90 experiments were conducted during this German-sponsored Spacelab D-2 mission to investigate life sciences, materials sciences, physics, robotics, astronomy and the Earth and its atmosphere. STS-55 also flew the Shuttle Amateur Radio Experiment (SAREX) making contact with students in 14 schools around the world. After 160 orbits of the earth in 240 flight hours, the 10-day mission concluded with a landing on Runway 22 at Edwards Air Force Base, California, on May 6, 1993. STS-71 (June 27 to July 7, 1995) was the first Space Shuttle mission to dock with the Russian Space Station Mir, and involved an exchange of crews (seven-member crew at launch, eight-member crew on return). The Atlantis Space Shuttle was modified to carry a docking system compatible with the Russian Mir Space Station. It also carried a Spacehab module in the payload bay in which the crew performed various life sciences experiments and data collections. STS-71 Atlantis launched from and returned to land at the Kennedy Space Center, Florida. Mission duration was 235 hours, 23 minutes. STS-84 Atlantis (May 15-24, 1997) carried a seven-member international crew. This was NASA's sixth Shuttle mission to rendezvous and dock with the Russian Space Station Mir. During the 9-day flight, the crew conducted a number of secondary experiments and transferred nearly 4 tons of supplies and experiment equipment between the Space Shuttle and the Mir station. STS-84 Atlantis launched from and returned to land at the Kennedy Space Center, Florida. Mission duration was 221 hours and 20 minutes. STS-91 Discovery (June 2-12, 1998) was the 9th and final Shuttle-Mir docking mission and marked the conclusion of the highly successful joint U.S./Russian Phase I Program. The crew, including a Russian cosmonaut, performed logistics and hardware resupply of the Mir during four docked days. They also conducted the Alpha Magnetic Spectrometer experiment, which involved the first of its kind research of antimatter in space. Mission duration was 235 hours, 54 minutes.

NAME: William F. Readdy (Captain, U.S. Naval Reserve)
NASA Astronaut

PERSONAL DATA: Born January 24, 1952, in Quonset Point, Rhode Island, but considers McLean, Virginia, to be his hometown. Married to Colleen Nevius. They have two sons and one daughter. He enjoys sailing, racquet sports, flying, reading. His father, Francis Readdy, resides in McLean. Her parents, William and Barbara Nevius, reside in Virginia Beach, Virginia.

EDUCATION: Graduated from McLean High School, McLean, Virginia, in 1970; received a bachelor of science degree in aerospace engineering (with honors) from the U.S. Naval Academy in 1974. Distinguished graduate, U.S. Naval Test Pilot School 1980.

ORGANIZATIONS: Associate Fellow, Society of Experimental Test Pilots; Member, American Astronautical Society, Association of Space Explorers, and Explorers Club.

SPECIAL HONORS: Recipient of the Distinguished Flying Cross, Space Flight Safety Award, NASA Outstanding Leadership Medal, two NASA Exceptional Service Medals, three NASA Space Flight Medals, the Meritorious Service Medal, the Navy Commendation Medal, Navy Achievement Medal, Navy Expeditionary medal, two National Defense Service Medals, Armed Forces Expeditionary Medal, Armed Forces Reserve Medal, and various unit and service awards. U.S. Naval Test Pilot School Instructor of the Year (1984).

EXPERIENCE: Readdy graduated from Annapolis in 1974, and was designated a naval aviator in September 1975 at Beeville, Texas. Following training in the A-6 Intruder at VA-42 Naval Air Station Oceana, Virginia, he joined Attack Squadron 85 aboard the USS Forrestal deployed to the North Atlantic and Mediterranean from 1976 until 1980. Upon completion of the U.S. Naval Test Pilot School, Patuxent River, Maryland, he served as project pilot on a variety of test programs while assigned to the Strike Aircraft Test Directorate. Following a short tour as an instructor pilot at the U.S. Naval Test Pilot School, he reported in 1984 to the USS Coral Sea, on Caribbean and Mediterranean deployments. In October 1986 Readdy accepted a Naval Reserve commission and joined NASA as a research pilot. He is affiliated with the U.S. Naval Reserve, and is assigned to the Naval Space Command. He has logged over 7,000 flying hours in over 60 types of fixed wing and helicopters and over 550 carrier landings.

NASA EXPERIENCE: Readdy joined NASA's Johnson Space Center in October 1986 as an aerospace engineer and instructor pilot at Ellington Field, Houston, Texas, where he served as program manager for the Shuttle Carrier Aircraft. Selected as an astronaut by NASA in the 1987 Group. His technical assignments to date include: Orbiter Subsystems, Orbiter Landing and Rollout; Orbiter Project Staff; SAIL; Training Officer; Safety Officer; Operations Development Branch Chief; NASA Director of Operations, Star City, Russia; and the first manager of Space Shuttle Program Development charged with upgrading the Space Shuttle to support human space flight into the next century. A veteran pilot astronaut with three space flights, STS-42 (January 22-30, 1992), STS-51 (September 12-22, 1993) and STS-79 (September 16-26, 1996), he has logged over 672 hours in space. STS-79 rendezvoused and docked with the Russian Space Station Mir, transferred over 3.5 tons of supplies to and from the Mir and exchanged U.S. astronauts on Mir for the first time -leaving John Blaha and bringing Shannon Lucid home after her record six months stay aboard Mir. Readdy is currently assigned to the Office of Space Flight at NASA Headquarters as Deputy Associate Administrator. He remains on flight status and is eligible for future space shuttle mission command.

NAME: James F. Reilly, II (Ph.D.)
   NASA Astronaut

PERSONAL DATA: Born March 18, 1954, Mountain Home Air Force Base, Idaho. Considers Mesquite, Texas, to be his hometown. Married to the former Jo Ann Strange, a native of Dallas, Texas. Three children. He enjoys flying, skiing, photography, running, soccer, hunting and fishing. His father, James F. Reilly, resides in Rockwall, Texas. His mother, Billie N. Ruether, resides in Tyler, Texas. Her parents, Robert and Mildred Strange, reside in Dallas, Texas.

EDUCATION: Graduated from Lake Highlands High School, Dallas Texas, in 1972. Bachelor of science degree in geosciences from University of Texas-Dallas, 1977. Master of science degree in geosciences from University of Texas-Dallas, 1987. Doctorate in geosciences from University of Texas-Dallas, in 1995.

ORGANIZATIONS: Member of the American Association of Petroleum Geologists, Aircraft Owners and Pilots Association, American Institute of Aeronautics and Astronautics.

SPECIAL HONORS: Awarded the Antarctic Service Medal, 1978. US Navy ROTC scholarship, 1972.

EXPERIENCE: After receiving his Bachelor of Science degree in 1977, Reilly entered graduate school and was selected to participate as a research scientist specializing in stable isotope geochronology as part of the 1977-1978 scientific expedition to Marie Byrd Land, West Antarctica. In 1979, he accepted employment as an exploration geologist with Santa Fe Minerals Inc., in Dallas, Texas. From 1980 to the time he was selected for the astronaut program, Reilly was employed as an oil and gas exploration geologist for Enserch Exploration Inc., in Dallas, Texas, rising to the position of Chief Geologist of the Offshore Region. Concurrent with his duties as an exploration geologist, he was actively involved in the application of new imaging technology for industrial applications in deep water engineering projects and biological research. As part of this work, Reilly has spent approximately 22 days in deep submergence vehicles operated by Harbor Branch Oceanographic Institution and the US Navy.

NASA EXPERIENCE: Selected by NASA in December 1994, Reilly reported to the Johnson Space Center in March 1995, has completed a year of training and evaluation, and is qualified for flight assignment as a mission specialist. He was initially assigned to work technical issues for the Astronaut Office Computer Support Branch. He flew on STS-89 and has logged over 211 hours in space. Reilly is assigned to STS-104 where he is scheduled to peform three spacewalks related to the assembly of the International Space Station (ISS). Launch is targeted for 2001.

SPACE FLIGHT EXPERIENCE: STS-89 (January 22-31, 1998), was the eighth Shuttle-Mir docking mission during which the crew transferred more than 9,000 pounds of scientific equipment, logistical hardware and water from Space Shuttle Endeavour to Mir. In the fifth and last exchange of a U.S. astronaut, STS-89 delivered Andy Thomas to Mir and returned with David Wolf. Mission duration was 8 days, 19 hours and 47 seconds, traveling 3.6 million miles in 138 orbits of the Earth.

NAME: Garrett E. Reisman (Ph.D.)
     NASA Astronaut (Mission Specialist Candidate)

PERSONAL DATA: Born February 10, 1968 in Morristown, New Jersey, but considers Parsippany, New Jersey, to be his hometown. Recreational interests include flying, skiing and snowboarding, rock climbing, mountaineering, canyoneering, and SCUBA diving. Dr. Reisman is an FAA Certified Flight Instructor. His parents, Robert and Sheila Reisman, currently reside in Palm Harbor, Florida. His sister, Lainie Reisman, is an economic development consultant and currently resides outside the United States.

EDUCATION: Parsippany High School, Parsippany, New Jersey, 1986. B.S., Economics, University of Pennsylvania, 1991. B.S., Mechanical Engineering and Applied Mechanics, University of Pennsylvania, 1991. M.S., Mechanical Engineering, California Institute of Technology, 1992. Ph.D., Mechanical Engineering, California Institute of Technology, 1997.

EXPERIENCE: From 1996 to 1998 Dr. Reisman was employed by TRW as a Spacecraft Guidance, Navigation and Control Engineer in the Space and Technology Division, Redondo Beach, California. While at TRW, he designed the thruster-based attitude control system for the NASA EOS PM-1 Spacecraft. Prior to his employment at TRW, Dr. Reisman was a Ph.D. Candidate at Caltech in the Division of Engineering and Applied Science in Pasadena, California. His multiphase fluid mechanics research provided the first experimental evidence of the presence of shock waves in unsteady cloud cavitation. For this discovery he was presented with the Bruce Chapman Award for excellence in hydrodynamics research at Caltech.

NASA EXPERIENCE: Selected by NASA in June 1998, Dr. Reisman reported for training in August 1998. Astronaut Candidate Training includes orientation briefings and tours, numerous scientific and technical briefings, intensive instruction in Shuttle and International Space Station systems, physiological training and ground school to prepare for T-38 flight training, as well as learning water and wilderness survival techniques. Dr. Reisman is currently assigned to the Astronaut Office Robotics Branch. He will serve in technical assignments until assigned to a space flight.

NAME: Stephen K. Robinson (Ph.D.)
     NASA Astronaut

PERSONAL DATA: Born October 26, 1955, in Sacramento, California. Unmarried. Enjoys flying, antique aircraft, swimming, canoeing, hiking, music, art, and stereo photography. Plays lead guitar in Max Q, a rock-n-roll band. His parents, William and Joyce Robinson, reside in Moraga, California.

EDUCATION: Graduated from Campolindo High School, Moraga, California, 1973; Bachelor of Science degree in mechanical/aeronautical engineering from University of California at Davis, 1978; Master of Science degree in mechanical engineering from Stanford University, 1985; Doctorate in mechanical engineering, with a minor in aeronautics and astronautics from Stanford University, 1990.

ORGANIZATIONS: American Institute of Aeronautics and Astronautics, Aerospace Medical Association, Experimental Aircraft Association.

SPECIAL HONORS: NASA Ames Honor Award for Scientist (1989); American Institute of Aeronautics and Astronautics Outstanding Technical Paper Award for Applied Aerodynamics (co-author) (1992); NASA/Space Club G.M. Low Memorial Engineering Fellowship (1993).

EXPERIENCE: Robinson started work for NASA in 1975 as a student co-op at NASA's Ames Research Center in Mountain View, California. After graduation from University of California at Davis, he joined NASA Ames in 1979 as a research scientist in the fields of fluid dynamics, aerodynamics, experimental instrumentation, and computational scientific visualization. While at Ames, Robinson earned masters and doctorate degrees in mechanical engineering at Stanford University, with research emphasis in turbulence physics, and additional research in human eye dynamics. In 1990, Robinson was selected as Chief of the Experimental Flow Physics Branch at NASA's Langley Research Center in Hampton, Virginia, where he led a group of 35 engineers and scientists engaged in aerodynamics and fluid physics research. In 1993, Robinson was awarded the NASA/Space Club Low Memorial Engineering Fellowship, and was assigned for 15 months to the Massachusetts Institute of Technology (MIT) as Visiting Engineer in the Man Vehicle Laboratory (MVL). As an MVL team-member, he conducted neurovestibular research on astronauts on the Spacelab Life Sciences 2 Shuttle mission (STS-58). Other MIT research included EVA dynamics for satellite capture and space construction. While in Cambridge, Massachusetts, Robinson was also a visiting scientist at the U.S. Department of Transportation's Volpe National Transportation Systems Center, doing research on environmental modeling for flight simulation, cockpit human factors for GPS-guided instrument approach procedures, and moving-map displays. Robinson returned to NASA Langley in September 1994, where he accepted a dual assignment as research scientist in the Multidisciplinary Design Optimization Branch, and as leader of the Aerodynamics and Acoustics element of NASA's General Aviation Technology program. Robinson has logged over 1400 hours in aircraft ranging from antique taildraggers to NASA jets.

NASA EXPERIENCE: Dr. Robinson was selected as an astronaut in December 1994, and reported to the Johnson Space Center in March 1995. He completed a year of training and evaluation and was assigned to test space shuttle control software in the Shuttle Avionics Integration Laboratory (SAIL). In September 1996, Dr. Robinson was assigned to begin training for shuttle mission STS-85 as Mission Specialist #3. STS-85 (August 7-19, 1997) was a 12-day mission during which the crew deployed and retrieved the CRISTA-SPAS payload, operated the Japanese Manipulator Flight Demonstration (MFD) robotic arm, studied changes in the Earth's atmosphere and tested technology destined for use on the future International Space Station. Robinson's responsibilities on STS-85 included flying both the shuttle robot arm and the experimental Japanese robot arm, and serving as a contingency EVA crewmember. The mission was accomplished in 189 Earth orbits, traveling 4.7 million miles in 284 hours and 27 minutes. In September 1997, Dr. Robinson was assigned for two months as Astronaut Office representative for flight crew equipment. Robinson was then assigned to the Computer Support Branch of the Astronaut Office, with responsibility for new projects, including a kneeboard computer for ascent/entry use. In January 1997, Robinson was assigned to mission STS-95 as Payload Commander. STS-95 (October 29 to November 7, 1998) was a 9-day science mission during which the crew supported over 80 payloads, including deployment of the Spartan solar-observing spacecraft, the Hubble Space Telescope Orbital Systems Test Platform, and investigations on space flight and the aging process with crew member John Glenn. As prime operator of the shuttle's robot arm, Robinson deployed and retrieved the Spartan satellite. The mission was accomplished in 134 Earth orbits, traveling 3.6 million miles in 213 hours and 44 minutes. In February 1999, Robinson was assigned as the Astronaut Office representative for the Space Station Robot Arm and also as a Capcom (Capsule Communicator), functioning as the voice link between space shuttle crews and Mission Control. In July 1999, Robinson was assigned as backup crew member for the Space Station Expedition 4 crew, which is due to launch in early 2001. This assignment will be followed by a subsequent assignment to a prime International Space Station crew. Flying on STS-85 in 1997 and STS-95 in 1998, Dr. Robinson has logged over 497 hours in space.

NAME: Kent V. Rominger (Captain, USN)
NASA Astronaut

PERSONAL DATA: Born August 7, 1956, in Del Norte, Colorado. Married to the former Mary Sue Rule. One child. He enjoys snow skiing, water skiing, horseback riding, and running. His parents, Mr. & Mrs. R. Vernon Rominger, reside in Del Norte, Colorado. Her parents, Mr. & Mrs. Delbert Rule, of Durango, Colorado, are deceased.

EDUCATION: Graduated from Del Norte High School, Del Norte, Colorado, in 1974; received a bachelor of science degree in civil engineering from Colorado State University in 1978; a master of science degree in aeronautical engineering from the U.S. Naval Postgraduate School in 1987.

ORGANIZATIONS: Association of Space Explorers, Society of Experimental Test Pilots, American Institute of Aeronautics and Astronautics, Association of Naval Aviation, and Chi Epsilon Civil Engineering Society.

SPECIAL HONORS: Defense Superior Service Medal. Distinguished Flying Cross. Defense Meritorious Service Medal. NASA Distinguished Service Medal. Distinguished Graduate, U.S. Naval Test Pilot School. Naval Air Test Center Test Pilot of the Year (1988). Society of Experimental Test Pilots Ray E. Tenhoff Award (1990) and Jack Northrop Award 1996). Colorado State University Distinguished Service Award (1997). West Coast Tomcat Fighter Pilot of the Year (1992). Top Ten Carrier Landing Distinction in Airwings Two and Nine.

EXPERIENCE: Rominger received his commission through the Aviation Reserve Officer Candidate (AVROC) Program in 1979, and was designated a Naval Aviator in September 1980. Following training in the F-14 Tomcat, he was assigned to Fighter Squadron Two (VF-2) from October 1981 to January 1985 aboard the USS Ranger and USS Kitty Hawk. While assigned to VF-2 Rominger attended the Navy Fighter Weapons School (Topgun). In 1987 he completed the Naval Postgraduate School/Test Pilot School Cooperative Program, and was assigned as F-14 Project Officer to the Carrier Suitability Branch of the Strike Aircraft Test Directorate at Patuxent River, Maryland. During his tour of duty Rominger completed the initial carrier suitability sea trials of the F-14B, logging the first aircraft carrier arrestment and catapult launch in the upgraded Tomcat. In September 1990 he reported to Fighter Squadron Two Hundred Eleven (VF-211) where he served as Operations Officer and completed a Desert Storm Deployment to the Arabian Gulf aboard USS Nimitz. He has logged over 5,000 flying hours in over 35 types of aircraft and 685 carrier landings.

NASA EXPERIENCE: Selected by NASA in March 1992, Rominger reported to the Johnson Space Center in August 1992. He completed one year of training and is qualified for assignment as a pilot on future Space Shuttle flight crews. Rominger was initially assigned to work technical issues for the Astronaut Office Operations Development Branch. He also served as Chief of the Astronaut Office Shuttle Operations Branch. A veteran of four space flights, Rominger has logged over 1,325 hours in space. He flew as pilot on STS-73 in 1995, STS-80 in 1996 and STS-85 in 1997, and was crew commander on STS-96 in 1999. Rominger will serve as Crew Commander on STS-100/ISS Assembly Flight 6A scheduled for launch in 2001.

SPACE FLIGHT EXPERIENCE: STS-73 Columbia (October 20 to November 5, 1995) was the second United States Microgravity Laboratory mission. The mission focused on materials science, biotechnology, combustion science, the physics of fluids, and numerous scientific experiments housed in the pressurized Spacelab module. In completing his first space flight, Rominger orbited the earth 256 times, traveled over 6 million miles, and logged a total of 15 days, 21 hours, 52 minutes and 21 seconds in space. STS-80 Columbia (November 19 to December 7, 1996) was a 17-day mission during which the crew deployed and retrieved the Wake Shield Facility (WSF) and the Orbiting Retrievable Far and Extreme Ultraviolet Spectrometer (ORFEUS) satellites. The free-flying WSF created a super vacuum in its wake and grew thin film wafers for use in semiconductors and other high-tech electrical components. The ORFEUS instruments, mounted on the reusable Shuttle Pallet Satellite, studied the origin and makeup of stars. In completing his second space flight, Rominger orbited the earth a record 278 times, traveled over 7 million miles and logged 17 days, 15 hours and 53 minutes in space. STS-85 Discovery (August 7-19, 1997) was a 12-day mission during which the crew deployed and retrieved the CRISTA-SPAS satellite, operated the Japanese Manipulator Flight Demonstration (MFD) robotic arm, studied changes in the Earth's atmosphere and tested technology destined for use on the future International Space Station. The mission was accomplished in 189 Earth orbits, traveling 4.7 million miles in 11 days, 20 hours and 27 minutes. STS-96 Discovery (May 27 to June 6, 1999) was a 10-day mission during which the crew delivered 4 tons of logistics and supplies to the International Space Station in preparation for the arrival of the first crew to live on the station. The mission included the first docking of a Space Shuttle to the International Space Station and was accomplished in 153 Earth orbits, traveling 4 million miles in 9 days, 19 hours and 13 minutes.

NAME: Jerry L. Ross (Colonel, USAF, Ret.)
NASA Astronaut

PERSONAL DATA: Born January 20, 1948, in Crown Point, Indiana. Married to the former Karen S. Pearson of Sheridan, Indiana. They have two children. He enjoys genealogy, stained glass, racquetball, woodworking, photography, model rocketry, and flying. His mother, Mrs. Phyllis E. Ross, resides in Crown Point. His father, Donald J. Ross, is deceased. Her parents, Mr. and Mrs. Morris D. Pearson, reside in Sheridan, Indiana.

EDUCATION: Graduated from Crown Point High School, Crown Point, Indiana, in 1966; received bachelor of science and master of science degrees in Mechanical Engineering from Purdue University in 1970 and 1972, respectively.

ORGANIZATIONS: Lifetime Member of the Association of Space Explorers, and the Purdue Alumni Association.

SPECIAL HONORS: Awarded the Defense Superior Service Medal with one Oak Leaf, the Air Force Legion of Merit, the Defense Meritorious Service Medal with 3 Oak Leaf Clusters, the Air Force Meritorious Service Medal with one Oak Leaf. Named a Distinguished Graduate of the USAF Test Pilot School and recipient of the Outstanding Flight Test Engineer Award, Class 75B. Recipient of 13 NASA Medals. Awarded the American Astronautical Society, Victor A. Prather Award (1985, 1990, 1999), and Flight Achievement Award (1992, 1996, 1999). Honorary Doctor of Science, Purdue University.

EXPERIENCE: Ross, an Air Force ROTC student at Purdue University, received his commission upon graduation in 1970. After receiving his master's degree from Purdue in 1972, he entered active duty with the Air Force and was assigned to the Ramjet Engine Division of Air Force Aero-Propulsion Laboratory at Wright-Patterson Air Force Base, Ohio. He conducted computer-aided design studies on ramjet propulsion systems, served as the project engineer for captive tests of a supersonic ramjet missile using a rocket sled track, and as the project manager for preliminary configuration development of the ASALM strategic air-launched missile. From June 1974 to July 1975, he was the Laboratory Executive Officer and Chief of the Management Operations Office. Ross graduated from the USAF Test Pilot School's Flight Test Engineer Course in 1976 and was subsequently assigned to the 6510th Test Wing at Edwards Air Force Base, California. While on assignment to the 6510th's Flight Test Engineering Directorate, he was project engineer on a limited flying qualities evaluation of the RC-135S aircraft and, as lead B-1 flying qualities flight test engineer, was responsible for the stability and control and flight control system testing performed on the B-1 aircraft. He was also responsible, as chief B-1 flight test engineer, for training and supervising all Air Force B-1 flight test engineer crew members and for performing the mission planning for the B-1 offensive avionics test aircraft. Ross has flown in 21 different types of aircraft, holds a private pilot's license, and has logged over 3,400 flying hours, the majority in military aircraft. He retired from the Air Force on March 31, 2000.

NASA EXPERIENCE: In February 1979, Ross was assigned to the Payload Operations Division at the Lyndon B. Johnson Space Center as a payload officer/flight controller. In this capacity, he was responsible for the flight operations integration of payloads into the Space Shuttle. Ross was selected as an astronaut in May 1980. His technical assignments since then have included: EVA, RMS, and chase team; support crewman for STS 41-B, 41-C and 51-A; spacecraft communicator (CAPCOM) during STS 41-B, 41-C, 41-D, 51-A and 51-D; Chief of the Mission Support Branch; member of the 1990 Astronaut Selection Board; Acting Deputy Chief of the Astronaut Office, and Chief of the Astronaut Office EVA and Robotics Branch. Ross flew as a mission specialist on STS 61-B (1985), STS-27 (1988) and STS-37 (1991), was the Payload Commander on STS-55/Spacelab-D2 (1993), and again served as a mission specialist on the second Space Shuttle to rendezvous and dock with the Russian Space Station Mir, STS-74 (1995) and the first International Space Station assembly mission, STS-88 (1998). A veteran of six space flights, Ross has over 1,133 hours in space, including 44 hours, 9 minutes on seven spacewalks. He is currently the Astronaut Office Branch Chief for Kennedy Space Center Operations Support.

SPACE FLIGHT EXPERIENCE: STS 61-B was launched at night from Kennedy Space Center (KSC), Florida, on November 26, 1985. During the mission the crew deployed the MORELOS-B, AUSSAT II, and SATCOM Ku-2 communications satellites, and operated numerous other experiments. Ross conducted two 6-hour space walks to demonstrate Space Station construction techniques with the EASE/ACCESS experiments. After completing 108 orbits of the Earth in 165 hours, 4 minutes, 49 seconds STS 61-B Atlantis landed on Runway 22 at Edwards Air Force Base, California, on December 3, 1985. STS-27 Atlantis, launched from the Kennedy Space Center, Florida, on December 2, 1988. The mission carried a Department of Defense payload, as well as a number of secondary payloads. After 68 orbits of the earth in 105 hours, 6 minutes, 19 seconds, the mission concluded with a dry lakebed landing on Runway 17 at Edwards Air Force Base, California, on December 6, 1988. STS-37 Atlantis, launched from KSC on April 5, 1991, and deployed the 35,000 pound Gamma Ray Observatory. Ross performed two space walks totaling 10 hours and 49 minutes to manually deploy the stuck Gamma Ray Observatory antenna and to test prototype Space Station Freedom hardware. After 93 orbits of the Earth in 143 hours, 32 minutes, 44 seconds, the mission concluded with a landing on Runway 33, at Edwards Air Force Base, on April 11, 1991. From April 26, 1993 through May 6, 1993, Ross served as Payload Commander/Mission Specialist on STS-55 aboard the Orbiter Columbia. The mission launched from Kennedy Space Center and landed at Edwards Air Force Base, Runway 22, after 160 orbits of the Earth in 239 hours and 45 minutes. Nearly 90 experiments were conducted during the German-sponsored Spacelab D-2 mission to investigate life sciences, material sciences, physics, robotics, astronomy, and the Earth and its atmosphere. STS-74 Atlantis, was NASA's second Space Shuttle mission to rendezvous and dock with the Russian Space Station Mir. STS-74 launched on November 12, 1995, and landed at Kennedy Space Center on November 20, 1995. During the 8 day flight the crew aboard Space Shuttle Atlantis attached a permanent docking module to Mir, conducted a number of secondary experiments, and transferred 1-1/2 tons of supplies and experiment equipment between Atlantis and the Mir station. The STS-74 mission was accomplished in 129 orbits of the Earth, traveling 3.4 million miles in 196 hours, 30 minutes, 44 seconds. STS-88 Endeavour (December 4-15, 1998) was the first International Space Station assembly mission. During the 12-day mission the US-built Unity module was mated with the Russian Zarya module. Ross performed three spacewalks totaling 21 hours 22 minutes to connect umbilicals and attach tools/hardware. The crew also deployed two satellites, Mighty Sat 1 and SAC-A. The mission was accomplished in 185 orbits of the Earth in 283 hours and 18 minutes.

NAME: Mario Runco, Jr.
NASA Astronaut

PERSONAL DATA: Mario was born in the Bronx, New York on January 26, 1952. Raised in the Highbridge section of the Bronx near Yankee Stadium, he considers this to be his hometown.. He is married to the former Susan Kay Friess of Sylvania, Ohio; they have two children. He enjoys ice hockey, baseball, softball, camping, model railroads, toy train collecting, and astronomy among other interests. He played intercollegiate ice hockey on the City College of New York and Rutgers University teams. Mario's parents Mario & Filomena Ragusa Runco reside in Yonkers, New York and Sue's parents, Fredrick and Margaret Bidlack Friess, reside in Sylvania, Ohio.

EDUCATION: Graduated from Sacred Heart School, Bronx, New York, in 1966 and Cardinal Hayes High School Bronx, New York, in 1970; received a bachelor of science degree in meteorology and physical oceanography from the City College of New York in 1974, a master of science degree in meteorology from Rutgers University, New Brunswick, New Jersey, in 1976 and a doctorate in Earth Science from the City College of New York in 1999.

SPECIAL HONORS: Awarded the Defense Superior Service, Defense Meritorious Service, NASA Exceptional Service, Navy Achievement and Navy Pistol Expert Medals. Also awarded three NASA Space Flight Medals (STS-44, STS-54 and STS-77), two Navy Sea Service Deployment Ribbons (USS Nassau and USNS Chauvenet), and the Navy Battle Efficiency Ribbon (USS Nassau). Mario was also the recipient of the City College of New York's Townsend Harris Medal (1993), and the Cardinal Hayes High School John Cardinal Spellman Award (1993). As an undergraduate, he was awarded the City College of New York Class of 1938 Athletic Service Award.

EXPERIENCE: After graduating from Rutgers University, Mario worked for a year as a research hydrologist conducting ground water surveys for the U.S. Geological Survey on Long Island, New York. In 1977, he joined the New Jersey State Police and, after completing training at the New Jersey State Police Academy, he worked as a New Jersey State Trooper until he entered the Navy in

June 1978. Upon completion of Navy Officer Candidate School in Newport, Rhode Island, in September 1978, he was commissioned and assigned to the Navy Oceanographic and Atmospheric Research Lab in Monterey, California, as a research meteorologist. From April 1981 to December 1983, he served as the Meteorological Officer aboard the Amphibious Assault Ship USS Nassau (LHA-4). It was during this tour of duty that he earned his designation as a Naval Surface Warfare Officer Officer. From January 1984 to December 1985, he worked as a laboratory instructor at the Naval Postgraduate School in Monterey, California. From December 1985 to December 1986, he served as Commanding Officer of the Naval Survey Vessel USNS Chauvenet (T-AGS 29), and conducted hydrographic and oceanographic surveys of the Java Sea and Indian Ocean. His last assignment within the Navy was as Fleet Environmental Services Officer, Pearl Harbor, Hawaii. Mario joined NASA in 1987.

NASA EXPERIENCE: Selected by NASA as an astronaut candidate in June 1987, Mario qualified for assignment as an astronaut mission specialist in August of 1988. His technical assignments to date include having served in Operations Development, where he assisted in the design, development and testing of the Space Shuttle crew escape system; in Mission Support, at the Software Avionics Integration Laboratory (SAIL), where he performed test and evaluation of Space Shuttle mission-specific flight software; at the Kennedy Space Center, as astronaut support, where he assisted in preparing, Space Shuttle missions for launch, and in the Mission Control Center as a Capsule Communicator (CAPCOM). A veteran of three space flights, STS-44 in 1991, STS-54 in 1993 and STS-77 in 1996, Mario has logged over 551 hours in space. Runco is currently assigned as a Spacecraft Communicator (CAPCOM from the anachronistic term Capsule Communicator) in the Mission Control Center. He is also working in conjunction with the International Space Station (ISS) Program Office on the development of optical quality windows for the ISS. In this capacity he is also working on the development of the Window Observational Research Facility (WORF), an ISS facility that will be used to perform Earth science and remote sensing research.

SPACE FLIGHT EXPERIENCE: On his first flight, Runco served on the crew of STS-44 aboard the Space Shuttle Atlantis which launched on the night of November 24, 1991. The primary mission objective was accomplished with the successful deployment of a Defense Support Program (DSP) satellite. In addition, the crew conducted two Military Man-in-Space experiments, three radiation monitoring experiments, and numerous medical tests in support of long duration space flights. The mission concluded after completing 110 orbits of the Earth. Atlantis returned to a landing on the lakebed at Edwards Air Force Base, California, on December 1, 1991. Mission duration was 6 days, 22 hours and 50 minutes. Mario next served as a mission specialist on the crew of STS-54 aboard the Space Shuttle Endeavour. STS-54 (January 13-19, 1993) launched and landed at the Kennedy Space Center in Florida. The six-day mission featured the deployment of a NASA Tracking and Data Relay Satellite (TDRS-F). Also carried in the payload bay was the Diffuse X-Ray Spectrometer (DXS). This astronomical instrument scanned the local vicinity of our Milky Way galaxy and recorded the low-energy X-ray emanations believed to originate from the plasma remnants of an ancient supernova. The data collected by DXS will help scientists better understand stellar evolution. Crewmate Greg Harbaugh and Mario also became the 47th and 48th Americans to walk in space during a 4.5-hour space walk designed to evaluate the limits of human performance during extravehicular activities (EVA). In what was called the "Physics of Toys", which has since become a popular children's educational video, the crew also demonstrated how everyday toys behave in space to an interactive audience of elementary school students across the United States. Mission duration was 5 days, 23 hours and38 minutes. Mario most recently served as a mission specialist on the crew of STS-77 aboard the Space Shuttle Endeavour (May 19-29, 1996). STS-77 carried a number of technology development experiments as well as a suite of microgravity science experiments. The technology development experiments included two deployable satellites both of which were deployed by Runco. For the deploy of the Spartan/Inflatable Antenna Experiment Runco was the Remote Manipulator System operator. The other deployable was a small Satellite Test Unit (STU) which used residual atmospheric drag and the Earth's magnetic field for attitude stabilization. STS-77 also featured the fourth flight of a SpaceHab module as an experiment laboratory. Mission duration was 10 days and 39 minutes.

NAME: Hans Schlegel
ESA Astronaut (German), (Mission Specialist Candidate)

PERSONAL DATA:Born August 3, 1951 in Überlingen, Germany, but considers Aachen to be his hometown. He has five children. Recreational interests include skiing, scuba diving and flying. He also enjoys reading, and being a handyman.

EDUCATION: 1957-70 Attended schools in Refrath, Bensberg and Cologne, Germany. 1968-69 American Field Service (AFS) exchange student. Graduated from Lewis Central High School, Council Bluffs, Iowa. 1970 Graduated from Hansa Gymnasium (secondary school emphasizing mathematics & science), Cologne, Germany.1972-79 Studied at the University of Aachen, Germany, graduated with a Diploma in Physics.

ORGANIZATIONS: Deutsche Physikalische Gesellschaft (German Physical Society); AFS - Interkulturelle Begegnungen (American Field Service Germany).

PUBLICATIONS: Publications and scientific reports in the field of semiconductor physics.

HONORS: Verdienstkreuz 1. Klasse des Verdienstordens der Bundesrepublik Deutschland (Federal Service Cross 1st Class, Federal Republic of Germany). Medal of Friendship of Russia.

EXPERIENCE: 1970-72 Served as a paratrooper with the Federal Armed Forces. Left with the rank of second lieutenant.1980 After several reserve trainings, appointed reserve lieutenant.1979-86 Member of the academic staff at Rheinisch Westfälische Technische Hochschule (RWTH) Aachen (University of Aachen) as an experimental Solid State Physicist. Research in the field of electronic transport properties and optical properties of semiconductors. 1986-88 Specialist in non-destructive testing methodology in the research and development department of the company "Institut Dr. Förster Gmbh & Co. KG" in Reutlingen, Germany. 1988-90 Basic Astronaut Training at the German Aerospace Research Establishment (DLR). In addition to academic education and microgravity experience on experiments (approximately 1300 parabulas on KC-135), he became a certified diver and holds a Private Pilot's license, including instrument rating and aerobatics.1990-93 Assigned as prime payload specialist for the D-2 Mission (second German Spacelab mission). Payload Training in Cologne, Germany and at the Johnson Space Center in Houston, Texas. 1995-97 Cosmonaut Training for the German-Russian MIR-'97 Mission at Yuri A. Gagarin Training Centre (Moscow). During the mission (February 10 to March 2, 1997) served as Crew Interface Coordinator. 1997-98 Additional training and certification as 2nd board engineer at Yuri A. Gagarin Training Centre.1998 Integrated into ESA's single European astronaut corps, which will be involved in the assembly and on-board operations of the International Space Station.

NASA SPACE FLIGHT EXPERIENCE: From April 26, 1993 through May 6, 1993, Schlegel served as payload specialist on STS-55 aboard Space Shuttle Columbia. Nearly 90 experiments were conducted during the German-sponsored Spacelab D-2 mission to investigate life sciences, material sciences, physics, robotics, astronomy, and the Earth and its atmosphere. In August 1998, ESA sent him to the Johnson Space Center for training as a mission specialist with the NASA Astronaut Class of '98. Since August 1999, in addition to training he is also assigned to the Station Operations Branch of the Astronaut Office working technical issues relating to mechanical and structural systems and crew equipment.

NAME: Piers J. Sellers (Ph.D.)
     NASA Astronaut

PERSONAL DATA: Born April 11, 1955 in Crowborough, Sussex, United Kingdom. Married to the former Amanda Helen Lomas from Yorkshire, United Kingdom. They have two children. He enjoys his family, flying, exercise, reading.

EDUCATION: Graduated from Cranbrook School, Cranbrook, Kent, United Kingdom, in 1973; received a bachelor of science degree in ecological science from the University of Edinburgh (Scotland) in 1976, and received a doctorate in biometeorology from Leeds University (United Kingdom) in 1981.

ORGANIZATIONS: American Geophysical Union (AGU), American Meteorology Society (AMS).

AWARDS: NASA Exceptional Scientific Achievement Award in 1994; Arthur Fleming Award in 1995; Fellow of AGU in 1996; AMS Houghton Award in 1997.

EXPERIENCE: Piers has worked on research into how the Earth's Biosphere and Atmosphere interact. His work involved computer modeling of the climate system, satellite remote sensing studies and field work utilizing aircraft, satellites and ground teams in places such as Kansas, Russia, Africa, Canada and Brazil. He has logged over 1,200 hours as pilot in command of various light piston-engined aircraft (singles and twins) which have been used in these experiments. Most of this work was done while Piers was based at or near NASA Goddard Space Flight Center.

NASA EXPERIENCE: Selected as an astronaut candidate by NASA in April 1996, Piers reported to the NASA Johnson Space Center in August 1996. Having completed two years of training and evaluation, he is qualified for flight assignment as a mission specialist. Currently, Piers is assigned technical duties in the Astronaut Office Computer Support Branch.

NAME: William M. Shepherd (Captain, USN)
     NASA Astronaut

PERSONAL DATA: Born July 26, 1949, in Oak Ridge, Tennessee, but considers Babylon, New York his hometown. Married to Beth Stringham of Houston, Texas. He enjoys sailing, swimming, and working in his garage. His mother, Mrs. Barbara Shepherd, resides in Bethesda, Maryland. His father, Mr. George R. Shepherd, is deceased.

EDUCATION: Graduated from Arcadia High School, Scottsdale, Arizona, in 1967; received a bachelor of science degree in aerospace engineering from the U.S. Naval Academy in 1971, and the degrees of ocean engineer and master of science in mechanical engineering from the Massachusetts Institute of Technology in 1978.

ORGANIZATIONS: American Institute of Aeronautics and Astronautics (AIAA).

SPECIAL HONORS: Recipient of NASA's "Steve Thorne" Aviation Award.

EXPERIENCE: Shepherd was graduated from the U.S. Naval Academy in 1971, and has served with the Navy's Underwater Demolition Team ELEVEN, SEAL Teams ONE and TWO, and Special Boat Unit TWENTY.

NASA EXPERIENCE: Selected by NASA in May 1984. He made three flights as a mission specialist on STS-27 (December 2-6, 1988), STS-41 (October 6-10, 1990) and STS-52 (October 22 - November 1, 1992), and has logged 440 hours in space. From March 1993 to January 1996, Shepherd was assigned to the Space Station Program and served in various management positions.

CURRENT ASSIGNMENT: Shepherd is currently living and working aboard the International Space Station. The Expedition-1 crew launched October 31, 2000 on a Soyuz rocket from the Baikonur launch site in Kazakhstan, and successfully docked with the station on November 2, 2000. The crew is scheduled to spend approximately 4 months aboard the station, and to return to Earth on the Shuttle Flight delivering the second Expedition crew.

NAME: Steven L. Smith
NASA Astronaut

PERSONAL DATA: Born December 30, 1958, in Phoenix, Arizona, but considers San Jose, California, to be his hometown. Married. He enjoys flying, scuba diving, basketball, camping, and traveling.

EDUCATION: Graduated from Leland High School, San Jose, California, in 1977; received a bachelor of science degree in electrical in 1981; a master of science degree in electrical engineering in 1982; and a master's degree in business administration in 1987. All three degrees are from Stanford University.

SPECIAL HONORS: NASA Space Flight Medal, NASA Exceptional Service Medal, NASA Performance Award for Excellence, IBM Outstanding Technical Achievement Award, IBM Outstanding Community Service Award. Seven-time high school and collegiate All-American in swimming and water polo. Two-time National Collegiate Athletic Association (NCAA) Champion at Stanford in water polo. Captain of the 1980 NCAA Championship team. Board Member of Texas Special Olympics.

EXPERIENCE: Steve Smith worked for IBM in the Large Scale Integration (semiconductor) Technology Group in San Jose as a technical group lead from 1982 until 1985. During that time, he was responsible for the development of electron beam chemical and lithographic processes. Following a leave to pursue graduate studies, Smith returned to IBM's Hardware and Systems Management Group as a product manager until 1989.

NASA EXPERIENCE: Steve Smith is a veteran of three space flights covering 12 million miles and five space walks totaling over 35 hours. He joined NASA in 1989 in the Mission Operations Directorate. As a payload officer, his duties included preflight payload integration and real-time flight controller support in Mission Control. He was selected as an astronaut candidate by NASA in March 1992 and reported for training in August 1992. In August 1993, Smith completed one year of astronaut candidate training. In September 1993, Smith became the first member of the 1992 astronaut class to receive a flight assignment. He has served as the Astronaut Office representative for the Space Shuttle main engines, the solid rocket boosters, the external tank, and Shuttle safety. Smith was also assigned to duties at the Kennedy Space Center for a year and a half as a member of the astronaut support team. The team was responsible for Space Shuttle prelaunch vehicle checkout, crew ingress and strap-in prior to launch, and crew egress post landing. Smith served as a mission specialist aboard the Space Shuttle Endeavour on Mission STS-68 in September 1994. Smith's responsibilities were split between Shuttle systems, Space Radar Lab 2 (SRL-2, the flight's primary payload), and several experiments in the crew cabin. Smith was one of two crewmen trained to perform a space walk had one been required. Endeavour circled Earth 183 times and traveled 4.7 million miles during the 11 day, 5 hour and 46 minute flight. Smith performed three space walks as a member of the February 1997 STS-82 Discovery crew which serviced the Hubble Space Telescope (HST). The crew completed five space walks in order to dramatically improve the scientific capability of the telescope and to replace degraded support equipment. HST's orbit was also increased 8 miles by the crew. The flight orbited the Earth 150 times covering 4.1 million miles in 9 days, 23 hours, 37 minutes and Smith's three space walks totaled 19 hours. Steve Smith was the Payload Commander for STS-103 in December 1999, the Hubble Space Telescope 3A Servicing Mission. The crew performed three space walks to return Hubble to science operations with several upgraded subsystems. Smith performed two space walks totaling 16 hours and 20 minutes. His lifetime total of 35 space walk hours places him second on the all time NASA space walk list. STS-103 orbited the Earth 120 times covering 3.2 million miles in just under 8 days. Steve Smith is currently the Deputy Chief Astronaut.

NAME: Heidemarie M. Stefanyshyn-Piper (Lieutenant Commander, USN)
NASA Astronaut

PERSONAL DATA: Born February 7, 1963 in St. Paul, Minnesota. Married to Glenn A. Piper. They have one child. She enjoys scuba diving, swimming, running, roller blading, ice skating. As an undergraduate, she competed in intercollegiate athletics on MIT's crew team. Her mother, Adelheid Stefanyshyn, resides in St. Paul, Minnesota. Her father, Michael Stefanyshyn, is deceased. His parents, Glenn & Gerry Piper, reside in Bonners Ferry, Idaho.

EDUCATION: Graduated from Derham Hall High School, St. Paul, Minnesota, in 1980; received a bachelor of science degree in mechanical engineering from Massachusetts Institute of Technology in 1984, and a master of science degree in mechanical engineering from Massachusetts Institute of Technology in 1985.

ORGANIZATIONS: American Society of Mechanical Engineers.

SPECIAL HONORS: Received "VADM C.R. Bryan Award" Class 2-88B, Engineering Duty Officer Basic Course. Awarded Meritorious Service Medal, 2 Navy Commendation Medals, 2 Navy Achievement Medals, and other service medals. "Most Valuable Player Award" MIT Women's Crew in 1982.

EXPERIENCE: Stefanyshyn-Piper received her commission from the Navy ROTC Program at MIT in June 1985. She completed training at the Naval Diving and Salvage Training Center in Panama City, Florida as a Navy Basic Diving Officer and Salvage Officer. She completed several tours of duty as an Engineering Duty Officer in the area of ship maintenance and repair. She qualified as a Surface Warfare Officer onboard USS GRAPPLE (ARS 53). In September 1994, Stefanyshyn-Piper reported to the Naval Sea Systems Command as Underwater Ship Husbandry Operations Officer for the Supervisor of Salvage and Diving. In that capacity, she advised fleet diving activities in the repair of naval vessels while waterborne. Additionally she is a qualified and experienced salvage officer. Major salvage projects include: development of salvage plan for the Peruvian Navy salvage of the Peruvian submarine PACOCHA; and de-stranding of the tanker EXXON HOUSTON, off the coast of Barber's Point, on the island of Oahu, Hawaii.

NASA EXPERIENCE: Selected as an astronaut candidate by NASA in April 1996, Stefanyshyn-Piper reported to the Johnson Space Center in August 1996. Having completed two years of training and evaluation, she is qualified for flight assignment as a mission specialist. Currently, Stefanyshyn-Piper is assigned to the Astronaut Office Flight Support Branch where she serves as a member of the Astronaut Support Personnel team at the Kennedy Space Center, supporting Space Shuttle launches and landings.

NAME: Frederick W. "Rick" Sturckow (Major, USMC)
NASA Astronaut

PERSONAL DATA: Born August 11, 1961, in La Mesa, California but considers Lakeside, California to be his hometown. Married to the former Michele A. Street of Great Mills, Maryland. He enjoys flying and physical training (PT). His father, Karl H. Sturckow, resides in Lakeside and his mother, Janette R. Sturckow, resides in La Mesa.

EDUCATION: Graduated from Grossmont High School, La Mesa, California, in 1978. Bachelor of science degree in mechanical engineering from California Polytechnic State University, 1984.

ORGANIZATIONS: Marine Corps Association (MCA). Former member of Society of Experimental Test Pilots (SETP).

SPECIAL HONORS: Single Mission Air Medal with Combat "V", Strike/Flight Air Medals (4), Navy and Marine Corps Commendation Medal, Navy and Marine Corps Achievement Medal, NASA Space Flight Medal.

EXPERIENCE: Sturckow was commissioned in December, 1984. An Honor Graduate of The Basic School, he earned his wings in April, 1987. Following initial F/A-18 training at VFA-125, he reported to VMFA-333, MCAS Beaufort, South Carolina. While assigned to VMFA-333 he made an overseas deployment to Japan, Korea, and the Philipines and was then selected to attend the Navy Fighter Weapons School (TOPGUN) in March, 1990. In August of 1990 he deployed to Sheik Isa Air Base, Bahrain for a period of eight months. Sturckow flew a total of forty-one combat missions during Operation Desert Storm and served as overall mission commander for 30-plane airstrikes into Iraq and Kuwait. In January, 1992 he attended the United States Air Force Test Pilot School at Edwards AFB, California. In 1993 he reported to the Naval Air Warfare Center- Aircraft Division, Patuxent River, Maryland for duty as the F/A-18 E/F Project Pilot. Sturckow also flew a wide variety of projects and classified programs as an F/A-18 test pilot. He has logged approximately 3,000 flight hours and has flown over 40 different aircraft.

NASA EXPERIENCE: Selected by NASA in December 1994, Sturckow reported to the Johnson Space Center in March 1995. He completed a year of training and evaluation and was assigned to work technical issues for the Vehicle Systems and Operations Branch of the Astronaut Office. He flew on STS-88 in 1998 (the first International Space Station assembly mission), and has logged over 283 hours in space. He is assigned as pilot on STS-105 scheduled for launch in 2001.

SPACE FLIGHT EXPERIENCE: STS-88 Endeavour (December 4-15, 1998) was the first International Space Station assembly mission. During the 12-day mission, Unity, the U.S. built node, was mated with Zarya, the Russian built Functional Cargo Block (FGB). Two crew members performed three space walks to connect umbilicals and attach tools/hardware in the assembly and outfitting of the station. Additionally, the crew performed the initial activation and first ingress of the International Space Station preparing it for future assembly missions and full time occupation. The crew also performed IMAX Cargo Bay Camera (ICBC) operations, and deployed two satellites, Mighty Sat 1 built by the USAF Phillips Laboratory and SAC-A the first successful launch of an Argentine satellite. The mission was accomplished in 185 orbits of the Earth in 283 hours and 18 minutes.

NAME: Steven R. Swanson
NASA Astronaut (Mission Specialist Candidate)

PERSONAL DATA: Born December 3, 1960 in Syracuse, New York, but considers Steamboat Springs, Colorado to be his hometown. Married to the former Mary Drake Young of Steamboat Springs, Colorado. They have three children. He enjoys mountain biking, basketball, skiing, weight lifting, running, wood working and spending time with his family. His parents, Stanley and June Swanson, reside in Boise, Idaho. Her parents, Chan and Martha Young, reside in Steamboat Springs, Colorado.

EDUCATION: Graduated from Steamboat Springs High School in Steamboat Springs, Colorado, in 1979; received a bachelor of science degree in engineering physics from the University of Colorado in 1983, and a master of applied science in computer systems from Florida Atlantic University in 1986, and a doctorate in computer science from Texas A&M University in 1998.

SPECIAL HONORS: Recipient of the NASA Exceptional Achievement Medal, the JSC Certificate of Accommodation, Flight Simulation Engineering Award, Phi Kappa Phi Honor Society

EXPERIENCE: Prior to coming to NASA, Steve worked for GTE in Phoenix, Arizona as a software engineer working on the real-time software of telephone system multiplexer/demultiplexers.

NASA EXPERIENCE: In 1987, Steve joined NASA as a systems engineer in the Aircraft Operations Division of JSC working on the Shuttle Training Aircraft. The Shuttle Training Aircraft (STA) is a complex airborne shuttle simulator, which models the flight characteristics of the Shuttle from 35,000 ft. to main gear touchdown. In 1989, Steve also became a flight simulation engineer on the STA. During his time with the STA, Steve worked on the improvement of the STA's navigation and control systems and the incorporation of a real-time wind determination algorithm. In May of 1998, Steve was selected as an Astronaut Candidate and started training in August of 1998. Astronaut Candidate Training includes orientation briefings and tours, numerous scientific and technical briefings, intensive instruction in Shuttle and International Space Station systems, physiological training and ground school to prepare for T-38 flight training, as well as learning water and wilderness survival techniques. Steve is currently assigned to the Astronaut Office Space Station Operations Branch. He will serve in technical assignments until assigned to a space flight.

NAME: Daniel M. Tani
NASA Astronaut

PERSONAL DATA: Born February 1, 1961 in Ridley Park Pennsylvania, but considers Lombard Illinois, to be his hometown. Married. He enjoys golf, flying, running, tennis, music, cooking. His mother, Rose Tani, resides in Lombard, Illinois. His father, Henry N. Tani, is deceased.

EDUCATION: Graduated from Glenbard East High School, Lombard, Illinois, in 1979; received a bachelor and a master of science degree in mechanical engineering from Massachusetts Institute of Technology (MIT) in 1984 and 1988, respectively.

ORGANIZATIONS: Member, Japanese American Citizens League, Alpha Delta Phi Fraternity, Aircraft Owners and Pilots Association.

AWARDS: Orbital Sciences Corporation Outstanding Technical Achievement Award, 1993.

EXPERIENCE: After Tani received his bachelor's degree from MIT, he worked at Hughes Aircraft Corporation in El Segundo, California as a design engineer in the Space and Communications group. In 1986, he returned to MIT and received his master's degree in mechanical engineering in 1988, specializing in human factors and group decision making. After graduation, Tani worked for Bolt Beranek and Newman in Cambridge, Massachusetts, in the experimental psychology department. In 1988, Tani joined Orbital Sciences Corporation (OSC) in Dulles Virginia, initially as a senior structures engineer, and then as the mission operations manager for the Transfer Orbit Stage (TOS). In that role, he served as the TOS flight operations lead, working with NASA/JSC mission control in support of the deployment of the ACTS/TOS payload during the STS-51 mission in September 1993. Tani then moved to the Pegasus program at OSC as the launch operations manager. In that capacity, he served as lead for the development of procedures and constraints for the launching of the air launched Pegasus unmanned rocket. Tani also was responsible for defining, training, and leading the team of engineers who worked in the launch and control room.

NASA EXPERIENCE: Selected as an astronaut candidate by NASA in April 1996, Tani reported to the Johnson Space Center in August 1996. Having completed two years of training and evaluation, he is qualified for flight assignment as a mission specialist. Currently, Tani is assigned technical duties in the Astronaut Office Computer Support Branch.

NAME: Joseph R. "Joe" Tanner
NASA Astronaut

PERSONAL DATA: Born January 21, 1950, in Danville, Illinois. Married Martha A. Currie. They have two children. He enjoys swimming, camping, mountaineering, and spending time with his family. Joe's parents, Dr. Bill Tanner & Dr. Megan Tanner, reside in Danville, Illinois. Martha's parents, Mr. Jack A. Currie & Mrs. Ruby S. Currie, are deceased. They were residents of Atmore, Alabama.

EDUCATION: Graduated from Danville High School, Danville, Illinois, in 1968; received a bachelor of science degree in mechanical engineering from the University of Illinois in 1973.

SPECIAL HONORS: NASA Exceptional Service Medal. NASA Space Flight Medals. NASA Stuart M. Present Flight Achievement Award. JSC Superior Achievement Award. Outstanding Alumnus of the

Department of Mechanical and Industrial Engineering, University of Illinois. Distinguished graduate from Navy Flight Training. Captain of the Swimming Team and "Top 100 Seniors" Award at University of Illinois. Eagle Scout.

EXPERIENCE: Tanner joined the Navy after graduating from the University of Illinois in 1973. He earned his Navy pilot wings in 1975 before serving as an A-7E pilot with Light Attack Squadron 94 (VA-94) aboard the U.S.S. Coral Sea. He finished his active service as an advanced jet instructor pilot with Training Squadron 4 (VT-4) in Pensacola, Florida.

NASA EXPERIENCE: Tanner started working for NASA Johnson Space Center in 1984 as an aerospace engineer and research pilot. His primary flying responsibilities involved teaching the astronaut pilots Space Shuttle landing techniques in the Shuttle Training Aircraft and instructing the pilots and mission specialists in the T-38. In addition to his flying duties, Tanner held positions as the aviation safety officer, the head of the pilot section, and the Deputy Chief of the Aircraft Operations Division (AOD). He has accumulated more than 7,500 hours in military and NASA aircraft. Selected as an astronaut candidate by NASA in March 1992, Tanner reported to the Astronaut Office in August 1992. He completed one year of initial training and worked in the Shuttle Avionics Integration Laboratory before being assigned to his first mission. Tanner also served as part of the Astronaut Support Personnel team at the Kennedy Space Center, supporting Space Shuttle launches and landings. A veteran of three space flights Tanner has logged over 742 hours in space, including over 33 EVA hours in 5 space walks. He flew on STS-66 in 1994, STS-82 in 1997 and STS-97 in 2000.

SPACE FLIGHT EXPERIENCE: Tanner flew aboard the Space Shuttle Atlantis on the STS-66, November 3-14, 1994, performing the Atmospheric Laboratory for Applications and Science-3 (ATLAS-3) mission. ATLAS-3 was the third in a series of flights to study the Earth's atmosphere composition and solar effects at several points during the Sun's 11-year cycle. The mission also carried the CRISTA-SPAS satellite that was deployed to study the chemical composition of the middle atmosphere and retrieved later in the mission. Tanner logged 262 hours and 34 minutes in space and 175 orbits of the Earth. Tanner performed two space walks as a member of the STS-82 crew to service the Hubble Space Telescope (HST) in February, 1997. The STS-82 crew of 7 launched aboard Space Shuttle Discovery on February 11 and returned to a night landing at Kennedy Space Center on February 21. During the flight the crew completed a total of 5 space walks to improve the science capability of the telescope and replace aging support equipment, restoring HST to near perfect working condition. The crew boosted HST's orbit by 8 nautical miles before releasing it to once again study the universe. Tanner's two space walks totaled 14 hours and 01 minutes. The flight orbited the earth 150 times covering 4.1 million miles in 9 days, 23 hours, 37 minutes. STS-97 Endeavour (November 30 to December December 11, 2000) was the fifth Space Shuttle mission dedicated to the assembly of the International Space Station. While docked to the Station, the crew installed the first set of U.S. solar arrays, performed three space walks, in addition to delivering supplies and equipment to the station's first resident crew. Mission duration was 10 days, 19 hours, 57 minutes, and traveled 4.47 million miles.

NAME: Gerhard P.J. Thiele
ESA Astronaut

PERSONAL DATA: Born September 2, 1953, in Heidenheim-Brenz, Germany. Considers Brühl, Nordrhein-Westfalen, to be his hometown. Married. Four children. Recreational interests include cooking, music, reading and sports, especially Badminton. He enjoys his profession, and spending time with his family.

EDUCATION: Completed final high school examination at Friedrich-Schiller-Gymnasium in Ludwigsburg; studied physics at Ludwig-Maximilians Universität in Munich, and at Ruprecht-Karls-Universität in Heidelberg,from 1976 to 1982; received his doctorate at the Institute for Environmental Physics of Heidelberg Universität, in 1985.

ORGANIZATIONS: Member of Deutsche Physikalische Gesellschaft (German Physical Society), American Geophysical Union, Weltraumforum Aachen at Rheinisch-Westfälische Technische Hochschule, Aachen and of the IAA subcommittee on Lunar Development.

SPECIAL HONORS: Research fellowship at Princeton University by the Deutsche Forschungsgemeinschaft (German Research Society) and Princeton University, Federal Service Cross, 1st Class (1993).

EXPERIENCE: Thiele served as a volunteer with the Navy of the German Federal Armed Forces. From 1972 to 1976, he served as Operations/Weapons Officer aboard fast patrol boats. From 1976 to 1982, he studied physics at Ludwig-Maximilians Universität in Munich, and Ruprecht-Karls-Universität in Heidelberg. From 1982 to 1985, while completing his doctoral thesis, Thiele was a research assistant at the Institut für Umweltphysik (Institute for Environmental Physics), Universität of Heidelberg. He then completed post-doctoral research at Princeton University from 1986 to 1987. His main interests in research activities focused on large scale ocean circulation as determined by transient tracer methods to investigate into the role of large scale ocean circulation with respect to climate changes. He has authored and coauthored publications in the field of physical and chemical oceanography. In 1988, Thiele began basic astronaut training at DLR (German Aerospace Research Establishment). Upon completion in 1990, he was assigned to the German D-2 Spacelab Mission. In 1992, he reported to the Johnson Space Center where he trained with the crew back-up Payload Specialist. During the STS-55/ Spacelab D-2 Mission (April 26 to May 6, 1993) Thiele served as Alternate Payload Specialist in the Payload Operations Control Center of DLR at Oberpfaffenhofen. In 1994, he served with the Strategic Planning Group for the Program Director of DLR. Since 1994 he also has served as an active member for the IAA (International Academy of Astronautics) Subcommittee on Lunar Development. In 1995, he was assigned to head the Crew Training Center (CTC) at DLR in Cologne. In July 1996, he was selected by DARA (German Space Agency) and DLR (German Aerospace Research Establishment) to attend NASA's Astronaut Candidate Training. In August 1998, he joined the European Space Agency (ESA).

NASA EXPERIENCE: Thiele again reported to the Johnson Space Center in August 1996. He completed two years of training and evaluation, and is qualified for flight assignment as a mission specialist. He was initially assigned technical duties in the Astronaut Office Computer Support Branch. Thiele recently completed his first mission, STS-99, and has logged over 268 hours in space.

SPACE FLIGHT EXPERIENCE: STS-99 (February 11-22, 2000) was an 11-day flight during which the international crew aboard Space Shuttle Endeavour worked dual shifts to support payload operations. The Shuttle Radar Topography Mission mapped more than 47 million miles of the Earth's land surface. The STS-99 mission was accomplished in 181 Earth orbits, traveling over 4 million miles in 268 hours and 38 minutes.

NAME: Andrew S. W. Thomas (Ph.D.)
NASA Astronaut

PERSONAL DATA: Born December 18, 1951, in Adelaide, South Australia. Single. He enjoys horse riding and jumping, mountain biking, running, wind surfing, and classical guitar playing. His father, Adrian C. Thomas, resides in Hackham, South Australia. His mother, Mary E. Thomas, resides in North Adelaide, South Australia.

EDUCATION: Received a bachelor of engineering degree in mechanical engineering, with First Class Honors, from the University of Adelaide, South Australia, in 1973, and a doctorate in mechanical engineering from the University of Adelaide, South Australia, in 1978.

ORGANIZATIONS: Member of the American Institute of Aeronautics and Astronautics.

EXPERIENCE: Dr. Thomas began his professional career as a research scientist with the Lockheed Aeronautical Systems Company, Marietta, Georgia, in 1977. At that time he was responsible for experimental investigations into the control of fluid dynamic instabilities and aircraft drag. In 1980, he was appointed Principal Aerodynamic Scientist to the company and headed a research team examining various problems in advanced aerodynamics and aircraft flight test. This was followed in 1983 by an appointment as the head of the Advanced Flight Sciences Department to lead a research department of engineers and scientists engaged in experimental and computational studies in fluid dynamics, aerodynamics and aeroacoustics. He was also manager of the research laboratory, the wind tunnels, and the test facilities used in these studies. In 1987, Dr. Thomas was named manager of Lockheed's Flight Sciences Division and directed the technical efforts in vehicle aerodynamics, flight controls and propulsion systems that supported the company's fleet of production aircraft. In 1989, he moved to Pasadena, California, to join the Jet Propulsion Laboratory (JPL) and, shortly after, was appointed leader of the JPL program for microgravity materials processing in space. This NASA-sponsored research included scientific investigations, conducted in the laboratory and in low gravity on NASA's KC-135 aircraft, as well as technology studies to support the development of the space flight hardware for future Shuttle missions.

NASA EXPERIENCE: Dr. Thomas was selected by NASA in March 1992 and reported to the Johnson Space Center in August 1992. In August 1993, following one year of training, he was appointed a member of the astronaut corp and was qualified for assignment as a mission specialist on Space Shuttle flight crews. While awaiting space flight assignment, Dr. Thomas supported shuttle launch and landing operations as an Astronaut Support Person (ASP) at the Kennedy Space Center. He also provided technical support to the Space Shuttle Main Engine project, the Solid Rocket Motor project and the External Tank project at the Marshall Space Flight Center. In June 1995 Dr. Thomas was named as payload commander for STS-77 and flew his first flight in space on Endeavour in May 1996. He next trained at the Gagarin Cosmonaut Training Center in Star City, Russia in preparation for a long-duration flight. In 1998, he served as Board Engineer 2 aboard the Russian Space Station Mir for 130 days. He is in training for the STS-102 mission, targeted for launch in 2000.

SPACE FLIGHT EXPERIENCE: STS-77 was a 10-day mission during which the crew deployed two satellites, tested a large inflatable space structure on orbit and conducted a variety of scientific experiments in a Spacehab laboratory module carried in Endeavour's payload bay. The flight was launched from the Kennedy Space Center on May 19, 1996 and completed 160 orbits 153 nautical miles above the Earth while traveling 4.1 million miles and logging 240 hours and 39 minutes in space. On January 22, 1998, Dr. Thomas launched aboard Space Shuttle Endeavour as part of the STS-89 crew to dock with the Mir Space Station. He served aboard Mir as Flight Engineer 2 and returned to earth with the crew of STS-91 aboard Space Shuttle Discovery on June 12, 1998, completing 141 days in space and 2,250 orbits of the earth.

NAME: Donald A. Thomas (Ph.D.)
NASA Astronaut

PERSONAL DATA: Born May 6, 1955, in Cleveland, Ohio. Married to the former Simone Lehmann of Göppingen, Germany. They have one son. He enjoys swimming, biking, camping, flying. His mother, Mrs. Irene M. Thomas, resides in Bloomington, Indiana. Her parents, Margrit and Gerhard Lehmann, reside in Göppingen, Germany.

EDUCATION: Graduated from Cleveland Heights High School, Cleveland Heights, Ohio, in 1973; received a bachelor of science degree in Physics from Case Western Reserve University in 1977, and a master of science degree and a doctorate in Materials Science from Cornell University in 1980 and 1982, respectively. His dissertation involved evaluating the effect of crystalline defects and sample purity on the superconducting properties of niobium.

ORGANIZATIONS: Tau Beta Pi; Association of Space Explorers (ASE).

SPECIAL HONORS: Graduated with Honors from Case Western Reserve University in 1977. Recipient of NASA Sustained Superior Performance Award, 1989. Recipient of 4 NASA Group Achievement Awards, 4 NASA Space Flight Medals, 2 NASA Exceptional Service Medals, and the NASA Distinguished Service Medal.

EXPERIENCE: Following graduation from Cornell University in 1982, Dr. Thomas joined AT&T Bell Laboratories in Princeton, New Jersey, working as a Senior Member of the Technical Staff. His responsibilities there included the development of advanced materials and processes for high density interconnections of semiconductor devices. He was also an adjunct professor in the Physics Department at Trenton State College in New Jersey. He holds two patents and has authored several technical papers. He left AT&T in 1987 to work for Lockheed Engineering and Sciences Company in Houston, Texas, where his responsibilities involved reviewing materials used in Space Shuttle payloads. In 1988 he joined NASA's Lyndon B. Johnson Space Center as a Materials Engineer. His work involved lifetime projections of advanced composite materials for use on Space Station Freedom. He was also a Principal Investigator for the Microgravity Disturbances Experiment, a middeck crystal growth experiment which flew on STS-32 in January 1990. This experiment investigated the effects of Orbiter and crew-induced disturbances on the growth of crystals in space.He is a private pilot with over 250 hours in single engine land aircraft and gliders, and over 800 hours flying as mission specialist in NASA T-38 jet aircraft.

NASA EXPERIENCE: Selected by NASA in January 1990, Dr. Thomas became an astronaut in July 1991. Dr. Thomas has served in the Safety, Operations Development, and Payloads Branches of the Astronaut Office. He was CAPCOM (spacecraft communicator) for Shuttle missions STS-47, 52 and 53. From July 1999 to June 2000 he was Director of Operations for NASA at the Gagarin Cosmonaut Training Center in Star City, Russia. A veteran of four space flights, he has logged over 1,040 hours in space. He was a mission specialist on STS-65 (July 8-23, 1994), STS-70 (July 13-22, 1995), STS-83 (April 4-8, 1997) and STS-94 (July 1-17, 1997). Currently, Dr. Thomas serves as Lead for International Space Station Expeditionary Training.

SPACE FLIGHT EXPERIENCE: STS-65 Columbia (July 8-23, 1994) set a new flight duration record for the Space Shuttle program. The mission flew the second International Microgravity Laboratory (IML-2). During the 15-day flight the crew conducted more than 80 experiments focusing on materials and life sciences research in microgravity. The mission was accomplished in 236 orbits of the Earth, traveling 6.1 million miles in 353 hours and 55 minutes. STS-70 Discovery (July 13-22, 1995). During the STS-70 mission, Dr. Thomas was responsible for the deployment of the sixth and final Tracking and Data Relay Satellite from the Space Shuttle. Mission duration was 214 hours and 20 minutes, traveling 3.7 million miles in 142 orbits of the Earth. STS-83 Columbia (April 4-8, 1997). The STS-83 Microgravity Science Laboratory (MSL-1) Spacelab mission, was cut short because of problems with one of the Shuttle's three fuel cell power generation units. Mission duration was 95 hours and 12 minutes, traveling 1.5 million miles in 63 orbits of the Earth. STS-94 Columbia (July 1-17, 1997), was a re-flight of the Microgravity Science Laboratory (MSL-1) Spacelab mission, and focused on materials and combustion science research in microgravity. Mission duration was 376 hours and 45 minutes, traveling 6.3 million miles in 251 orbits of the Earth.

NAME: Michel Tognini (Brigadier General, French Air Force)
ESA Astronaut

PERSONAL DATA: Born September 30, 1949, in Vincennes, France. Four children. Hobbies include Aeroclub, parachuting and parafoil, tennis, wind-surfing, water-skiing, snow-skiing, cross-country running, wave-surfing, microcomputers.

EDUCATION: Tognini was educated at Lycee de Cachan, Paris. Received an advanced mathematics degree in 1970 from Epa Grenoble (military school). He enrolled at Ecole de l'Air,(the French Air Force Academy), Salon de Provence, France, graduating with an engineering degree in 1973. Tognini attended the Empire Test Pilots School, Boscombe Down, United Kingdom, in 1982, and the Institut des Hautes Etudes de Defense Nationale (IHEDN) in 1993-94.

SPECIAL HONORS: French Aeronautics Medal; Chevalier de Ordre National du Mérite; Commander dans l'Ordre de la Légion d'Honneur; Soviet Order of Friendship between the People; Russian Order of Friendship between the People.

QUALIFICATIONS: Engineer from the "Ecole de l'Air." Fighter Pilot (all levels). Test Pilot. Airline Pilot. Military Technical Diploma (BTEM). Cosmonaut Diploma from the Soviet Union.

EXPERIENCE: Following graduation in 1973 from the Ecole de l'Air, Tognini was posted to advanced fighter pilot training at squadron based at Normandie-Neman where he served for one year before obtaining his advanced fighter pilot training. From 1974-1981, he served as an operational fighter pilot in French Air Force (Cambrai Air Base), at the 12th Escadre de Chasse, flying SMB2 and Mirage

F1 aircraft. During this tour of duty he served as flight leader in 1976, and flight commander in 1979. In 1982, he was admitted to the Empire Test Pilot School in Boscombe Down, United Kingdom, and later that year was awarded his test pilot diploma. He was awarded his military studies diploma in 1983. Tognini was then posted to the Cazaux Flight Test Center, France, initially as a test pilot and subsequently as chief test pilot. During his time there, he helped test a great deal of French flight hardware. He did the weapon systems testing for the Mirage 2000-C, Mirage 2000-N, Jaguar ATLIS, and FLIR aircraft, and was also responsible for flight safety for pilots, experimenters and flight engineers. In 1985, France opened a recruitment program to expand its astronaut corps, and Tognini was one of seven finalists selected in September 1985. In July 1986, he was one of four candidates to undergo medical examinations in Moscow. In August 1986, he was assigned as the back-up for the Soyuz TM-7 mission. Although Tognini remained a French Air Force officer, he was placed on detachment to CNES for his space flight activities from September 1986 onwards. In November 1986 he reported to the Yuri Gagarin Cosmonaut Training Center, Star City, Russia, for alternate astronaut training, including EVA, for the Soviet-French ARAGATZ mission. During 1989-1990 he supported the HERMES program in Toulouse, France. In 1991 he returned to Star City, Russia, to start prime crew training for the 3rd Soviet-French ANTARES mission. During his stay in Russia Tognini also gained piloting experience of BURAN simulators (MIG 25, TUPOLEV 154). Tognini has 4000 flight hours on 80 types of aircraft (mainly fighter aircraft including MIG 25, TUPOLEV 154, LIGHTNING MK 3 and MK 5, METEOR, and F 104). He is fluent in English and Russian. Tognini made his first space flight on board the Soyuz TM-15, TM-14 (July 27 to August 10, 1992). Together with Anatoly Solovyev and Sergei Avdeiev he linked up with Mir 1 (ANTARES mission) and joined the crew of Alexandre Viktorenko and Alexandre Kaleri already on board. They spent 14 days carrying out a program of joint Soviet-French experiments before returning to Earth. He returned to France following the mission. During 1993-94, he attended a training cycle of the French Institute for High Studies of National Defense (IHEDN).

PUBLICATIONS: Use of new systems for future aircraft (classified report, 70p). Boscombe Down Preview on Lightning Mk III (report, 300p). The SOYUZ spacecraft system (CNES report, 150p).

NASA EXPERIENCE: Tognini attended ASCAN Training at the Johnson Space Center during 1995. He was initially assigned to the Operations Planning Branch of the Astronaut Office working technical issues on the International Space Station. Tognini served aboard Space Shuttle Columbia on STS-93 (July 22-27, 1999). During the 5-day mission his primary task was to assist in the deployment of the Chandra X-Ray Observatory, and to conduct a spacewalk if needed. The Chandra X-Ray Observatory is designed to conduct comprehensive studies of the universe, and the telescope will enable scientists to study exotic phenomena such as exploding stars, quasars, and black holes. Mission duration was 118 hours and 50 minutes. A veteran of two space flights, Tognini has logged a total of 19 days in space.

NAME: Bjarni V. Tryggvason
Canadian Space Agency Astronaut (Mission Specialist Candidate)

PERSONAL DATA: Born September 21, 1945, in Reykjavik, Iceland, but considers Vancouver, B.C., to be his hometown. He has two children. Mr. Tryggvason has about 4,000 hours of flight experience, holds an Airline Transport Rating and has been a flight instructor for 10 years. He is currently active in aerobatic flight and is qualified as Captain in the Tutor jet trainer with the Canadian Air Force. He maintains a high level of physical fitness, enjoys scuba diving, skiing, and has made 17 parachute jumps.

EDUCATION: Attended primary schools in Nova Scotia and British Columbia; completed high school in Richmond, B.C. He received a Bachelor of Applied Science in Engineering Physics from the University of British Columbia in 1972 and did postgraduate work in engineering with specialization in applied mathematics and fluid dynamics at the University of Western Ontario.

ORGANIZATIONS: Member of the Canadian Aeronautics and Space Institute.

SPECIAL HONORS: Recipient of numerous scholarships throughout his university years.

EXPERIENCE: Worked as a meteorologist with the cloud physics group at the Atmospheric Environment Service in Toronto in 1972 and 1973. In 1974, he joined the University of Western Ontario to work as a research associate at the Boundary Layer Wind Tunnel Laboratory working on projects involving rigid and aero-elastic model studies of wind effects on structures. In 1978, he was a guest research associate at Kyoto University, Japan, followed by a similar position at James Cook University in Townsville, Australia. In late 1979, he returned to the University of Western Ontario as a lecturer in applied mathematics. In 1982, he joined the Low Speed Aerodynamics Laboratory at the National Research Council (NRC) in Ottawa. He became part of the NRC team assembled to study the sinking of the Ocean Ranger oil rig in support of the Royal Commission investigation into that tragedy. He designed and led the aerodynamics tests, which established the wind loads acting on the rig. He was one of the six Canadian astronauts selected in December 1983. He was back-up Payload Specialist to Steve MacLean for the CANEX-2 set of experiments which flew on Mission STS-52, October 22 to November 1, 1992. He was the Project Engineer for the design of the SVS target spacecraft which was deployed during that mission. He is the principal investigator in the development of the Large Motion Isolation Mount (LMIM) which has flown numerous times on NASA's KC-135 and DC-9 aircrafts. He is also the principal investigator in the development of the Microgravity vibration Isolation Mount (MIM). The MIM has been in operation on board the Russian Mir Space Station since April 1996. He led the development of a second generation MIM-2 which was tested on STS-85.He was active in supervising undergraduate student projects at several universities across Canada. Between 1982 and 1992, he was a part-time lecturer at the University of Ottawa and Carleton University, teaching graduate courses on structural dynamics and random vibrations. He also served as a Canadian Space Agency representative on the NASA Microgravity Measurement Working Group, and the International Space Station (ISS) Microgravity AIT (Analysis and Integration Team).

NASA EXPERIENCE: Tryggvason served as a Payload Specialist on STS-85 (August 7-19, 1997), a 12 day mission to study changes in the Earth's atmosphere. During the flight, he focused on testing the Microgravity Vibration Isolation Mount (MIM) and performing fluid science experiments designed to examine sensitivity to spacecraft vibrations. This work is directed at developing better understanding of the need for systems such as the MIM on the International Space Station and on the effect of vibrations on the many experiments to be performed on the ISS. The mission was accomplished in 189 Earth orbits, traveling 4.7 million miles in 284 hours and 27 minutes. In August 1998, Tryggvason again reported to the Johnson Space Center to attend Astronaut Candidate Training which includes orientation briefings and tours, numerous scientific and technical briefings, intensive instruction in Shuttle and International Space Station systems, physiological training and ground school to prepare for T-38 flight training, as well as learning water and wilderness survival techniques. Tryggvason is currently assigned to the Astronaut Office Shuttle Operations Branch. He will serve in technical assignments until assigned to a space flight.

NAME: Roberto Vittori
    ESA Astronaut (Mission Specialist Candidate)

PERSONAL DATA: Born October 15, 1964 in Viterbo, Italy. He is married to the former Valeria Nardi of Citta' di Castello, Italy. They have two children. He enjoys soccer, running and swimming.

EDUCATION: Graduated from the Italian Air Force Academy in 1989.

SPECIAL HONORS: Academic award at the Undergraduate Pilot Training, Reese Air Force Base, Texas; Honor student at the Test Pilot School, Patuxent River, Maryland; Honor student at the United States Flight Safety School, Kirtland Air Force Base, New Mexico.

EXPERIENCE: Graduated in 1989 from the Undergraduate Pilot Training, Reese Air Force Base, Texas, he flew operationally Tornado GR1 with the 155 Squadron, 50 Wing, Piacenza, Italy. Graduated from the U.S. Navy Test Pilot School in 1995, he served at the Italian Test Center as project pilot for the development of the new European aircraft, the EF2000. From 1996 he was national representative in the Beyond Visual Range Air-to-Air Missile (BVRAAM) research and development program. Graduated in 1997 from the U.S. Air Force Flight Safety School, he occupied the position of wing Flight Safety Officer at the Italian Test Center. He was a teacher of aerodynamics at the Accident Investigation Course of the Italian Air Force. He has logged over 1700 hours in over 40 different aircraft to include F-104, Tornado GR1, F-18, AMX, M-2000, G-222 and P-180.

NASA EXPERIENCE: In August 1998, he reported to the Johnson Space Center to attend Astronaut Candidate Training which includes orientation briefings and tours, numerous scientific and technical briefings, intensive instruction in Shuttle and International Space Station systems, physiological training and ground school to prepare for T-38 flight training, as well as learning water and wilderness survival techniques. Vittori is currently assigned to the Astronaut Office Shuttle Operations Branch. He will serve in technical assignments until assigned to a space flight.

NAME: James S. Voss (Colonel, USA, Ret.)
    NASA Astronaut

PERSONAL DATA: Born March 3, 1949, in Cordova, Alabama, but considers Opelika, Alabama, to be his hometown. Married to the former Suzan Curry of Birmingham, Alabama. They have one daughter. Jim enjoys woodworking, skiing, softball, racquetball, scuba diving, and flying an airplane he built himself. As an undergraduate, he participated on the Auburn University Wrestling Team.

EDUCATION: Graduated from Opelika High School, Opelika, Alabama; received a bachelor of science degree in Aerospace Engineering from Auburn University in 1972, and a master of science degree in Aerospace Engineering Sciences from the University of Colorado in 1974.

SPECIAL HONORS: NASA Outstanding Leadership Award (1996); NASA Exceptional Service Medal (1994); NASA Space Flight Medals (1992, 1993, 1995); Defense Meritorious Service Medal (1993); Defense Superior Service Medal (1992); Outstanding Student Award, USN Test Pilot School (1983); William P. Clements, Jr. Award for Excellence in Education as the outstanding Professor at the U.S. Military Academy (1982); Meritorious Service Medal (1982); NASA Summer Faculty Research Fellowship (1980); Commandant's List - Infantry Officer Advanced Course (1979); Army Commendation Medal (1978); Honor Graduate and Leadership Award - Ranger School (1975); Distinguished Infantry Officer Basic Course (1974).

EXPERIENCE: Upon graduation from Auburn and commissioning as a 2nd Lieutenant, Voss went directly to the University of Colorado to obtain his masters degree under the Army Graduate Fellowship Program. After attending the Infantry Basic Course, Airborne and Ranger schools, he served with the 2nd Battalion 48th Infantry in Germany as a platoon leader, intelligence staff officer, and company commander. On returning to the United States, he attended the Infantry Officer Advanced Course, then taught for three years in the Department of Mechanics at the U.S. Military Academy. After attending the U.S. Naval Test Pilot School and the Armed Forces Staff College, Voss was assigned to the U.S. Army Aviation Engineering Flight Activity as a Flight Test Engineer/Research and Development Coordinator. He was involved in several major flight test projects before being detailed to NASA's Lyndon B. Johnson Space Center.

NASA EXPERIENCE: Voss has been working at the Johnson Space Center since November 1984. In his capacity as a Vehicle Integration Test Engineer, he supported Shuttle and payload testing at the Kennedy Space Center for STS 51-D, 51-F, 61-C and 51-L. He participated in the STS 51-L accident investigation, and supported the resulting reviews dedicated to returning the Space Shuttle safely to flight. Selected as an astronaut candidate by NASA in June 1987, Voss completed a one year training and evaluation program in August 1988, which qualified him for assignment as a mission specialist on Space Shuttle flights. He has worked as a flight crew representative in the area of Shuttle safety, as a CAPCOM, providing a communications interface between ground controllers and flight crews during simulations and Shuttle flights, and as the Astronaut Office Training Officer. A veteran of three space flights, Voss has logged over 600 hours in space. He flew as a mission specialist on STS-44 in 1991 and STS-53 in 1992, and was the payload commander on STS-69 in 1995. On his first mission, Voss served on the crew of STS-44, aboard Space Shuttle Atlantis, which launched the night of November 24, 1991. The primary mission objective was accomplished with the successful deployment of a Defense Support Program (DSP) satellite with an Inertial Upper Stage (IUS) rocket booster. In addition, the crew also conducted two Military Man in Space experiments, three radiation monitoring experiments, and numerous medical tests to support longer duration Shuttle flights. The mission was concluded after 110 orbits of the Earth with Atlantis returning to a landing on the lakebed at Edwards Air Force Base, California, on December 1, 1991, after 166 hours in space. Voss next served on the crew of STS-53 which launched from the Kennedy Space Center, Florida, on December 2, 1992. The crew of five deployed the classified Department of Defense payload DOD-1 and also performed several Military Man in Space and NASA experiments. After completing 115 orbits of the Earth in 175 hours, Discovery landed at Edwards Air Force Base, California, on December 9, 1992. Jim's last flight was as Payload Commander on STS-69 which launched on September 7, 1995. The crew successfully deployed and retrieved a SPARTAN satellite and the Wake Shield Facility. Also on board was the International Extreme Ultraviolet Hitchhiker payload, and numerous secondary payloads and medical experiments. Jim conducted an EVA (extravehicular activity) lasting 6 hours 46 minutes to test space suit modifications and to evaluate procedures and tools to be used to construct the International Space Station. Endeavour landed at the Kennedy Space Center on September 18, 1995 after 171 orbits of the Earth and 260 hours in space. Jim served as the back-up crew member for two missions to the Russian Space Station Mir. During this time he lived and trained for 2 years at the Gagarin Cosmonaut Training Center in Star City, Russia.

CURRENT ASSIGNMENT: Voss is assigned to Shuttle mission STS-101 which will repair and provision the International Space Station. Launch is scheduled for early 2000. He is also assigned to the second crew scheduled to live on board the International Space Station. Launch is targeted for early 2001.

NAME: Janice Voss (Ph.D.)
      NASA Astronaut

PERSONAL DATA: Born October 8, 1956, in South Bend, Indiana, but considers Rockford, Illinois, to be her hometown. She enjoys reading science fiction, dancing, volleyball, flying. Her parents, Dr. & Mrs. James R. Voss, reside in Dupont, Indiana.

EDUCATION: Graduated from Minnechaug Regional High School, Wilbraham, Massachusetts, in 1972; received a bachelor of science degree in engineering science from Purdue University in 1975, a master of science degree in electrical engineering and a doctorate in aeronautics/astro-nautics from the Massachusetts Institute of Technology in 1977 and 1987, respectively. From 1973 to 1975 she took correspondence courses at the University of Oklahoma. She also did some graduate work in space physics at Rice University in 1977 and 1978.

ORGANIZATIONS: American Institute of Aeronautics and Astronautics (AIAA).

SPECIAL HONORS: NASA Space Flight Medals (1993, 1995); Zonta Amelia Earhart Fellowship (1982); Howard Hughes Fellowship (1981); National Science Foundation Fellowship (1976)

EXPERIENCE: Dr. Voss was a co-op at the NASA Johnson Space Center from 1973 to 1975. During that time she did computer simulations in the Engineering and Development Directorate. In 1977 she returned to the Johnson Space Center and, for a year, worked as a crew trainer, teaching entry guidance and navigation. She completed her doctorate in 1987 and accepted a job with Orbital Sciences Corporation. Her responsibilities there included mission integration and flight operations support for an upper stage called the Transfer Orbit Stage (TOS). TOS launched the Advanced Communications Technology Satellite (ACTS) from the Space Shuttle in September 1993, and the Mars Observer from a Titan in the Fall of 1992. Selected by NASA in January 1990, Dr. Voss became an astronaut in July 1991. She is qualified for flight assignment as a mission specialist. Her techni-cal assignments have included working Spacelab/Spacehab issues for the Astronaut Office Mission Development Branch, and robotics issues for the EVA/Robotics Branch. She served aboard STS-57 in 1993, STS-63 in 1995, STS-83 & STS-97 in 1997, and STS-99 in 2000. A veteran of five space flights, Dr. Voss has logged over 49 days in space, traveling 18.8 million miles in 779 Earth orbits.

SPACE FLIGHT EXPERIENCE: Dr. Voss first flew on STS-57 (June 21 to July 1, 1993). Mission high-lights included retrieval of the European Retrievable Carrier (EURECA) with the Shuttle's robotic arm, a spacewalk by two crew members, and an assortment of experiments in the first flight of the Spacehab middeck augmentation module. She next flew on STS-63 (February 3-11, 1995). Mission highlights included the rendezvous with the Russian Space Station, Mir, the deployment and re-trieval of Spartan 204, and the third flight of Spacehab. She also flew as payload commander on STS-83 (Apr 4-8, 1997). The STS-83 Microgravity Science Laboratory (MSL-1) Spacelab mission was cut short because of problems with one of the Shuttle's three fuel cell power generation units. The entire crew and payload reflew on STS-94 (July 1-17, 1997). The STS-94 MSL-1 Spacelab mission focused on materials and combustion science research in microgravity. Most recently she served on STS-99 (February 11-22, 2000). This was an 11-day flight during which the international crew aboard Space Shuttle Endeavour worked dual shifts to support payload operations. The Shuttle Radar Topography Mission mapped more than 47 million miles of the Earth's land surface.

NAME: Rex J. Walheim (Lieutenant Colonel, USAF)
   NASA Astronaut

PERSONAL DATA: Born October 10, 1962, in Redwood City, California, but considers San Carlos, California his hometown. Married to the former Margie Dotson of Villa Park, California. They have one child. He enjoys snow skiing, hiking, softball and football. His father, Lawrence M. Walheim, Jr., resides in Roseville, California. His mother, Avis L. Walheim is deceased.

EDUCATION: Graduated from San Carlos High School, San Carlos, California in 1980; received a bachelor of science degree in mechanical engineering from the University of California, Berkeley, in 1984, and a master of science degree in industrial engineering from the University of Houston in 1989.

SPECIAL HONORS: Distinguished Graduate, Reserve Officers Training Corps, University of California, Berkeley. Distinguished Graduate and top flight test engineer in USAF Test Pilot School Class 92A. Meritorious Service Medal, 2 Air Force Commendation Medals, Aerial Achievement Medal, and various service awards.

EXPERIENCE: Walheim was commissioned as a second lieutenant in the Air Force in May 1984. In April of 1985 he was assigned to Cavalier Air Force Station in Cavalier, North Dakota, where he worked as a missile warning operations crew commander. In October 1986, he was reassigned to the Johnson Space Center, Houston, Texas, where he worked as a mechanical systems flight controller and was the lead operations engineer for the Space Shuttle landing gear, brakes, and emergency runway barrier. Walheim was transferred to Headquarters Air Force Space Command in Colorado Springs, Colorado, in August 1989 where he was manager of a program upgrading missile warning radars. He was selected for USAF Test Pilot School in 1991, and attended the course at Edwards AFB California in 1992. Following his graduation, he was assigned to the F-16 Combined Test Force at Edwards where he was a project manager, and then commander of the avionics and armament flight. In January 1996, Walheim became an instructor at USAF Test Pilot School, where he served until he commenced astronaut training.

NASA EXPERIENCE: Walheim served as a flight controller and operations engineer at the Johnson Space Center from October 1986 to January 1989. He was selected by NASA in March 1996 and reported to the Johnson Space Center in August 1996. Having completed two years of training and evaluation, he is qualified for flight assignment as a mission specialist. Currently, Walheim is assigned technical duties in the Astronaut Office Space Station Operations Branch.

NAME: Koichi Wakata
   NASDA Astronaut

PERSONAL DATA: Born August 1, 1963, in Omiya, Saitama, Japan. Married to the former Stefanie von Sachsen-Altenburg of Bonn, Germany. They have one son. He enjoys flying, hang-gliding, baseball, tennis, and snow skiing. His mother, Mrs. Takayo Wakata, resides in Omiya, Saitama, Japan. His father, Mr. Nobutaka Wakata, isdeceased.

EDUCATION: Graduated from Urawa High School, Saitama, in 1982; received a bachelor of science degree in aeronautical engineering from Kyushu University in 1987; and a master of science degree in applied mechanics from Kyushu University in 1989.

ORGANIZATIONS: Member of the Japan Society for Aeronautical and Space Sciences, the Robotics Society of Japan, and the Japanese Society for Biological Sciences in Space.

SPECIAL HONORS: Minister of State for Science and Technology Commendation. Special awards from Saitama Prefecture and Omiya City. National Space Development Agency of Japan Outstanding Service Award (1996). Diplome pilote-cosmonaute de l' URSS V.M. Komarov(1997).

EXPERIENCE: Wakata joined Japan Airlines (JAL) in April 1989. He was assigned to the Base Maintenance Department, Narita, Chiba, where he was designated as a structural engineer. From July 1991 to May 1992, Wakata was assigned to the Airframe Group, Systems Engineering Office, Engineering Department of JAL. During his tenure with JAL, Wakata was involved in the research of structural integrity of transport aircraft, fatigue fracture, corrosion prevention program, and the environmental effects on fuselage polished aluminum skin on B-747 aircraft. He was selected as an astronaut candidate by the National Space Development Agency of Japan (NASDA) in June 1992. A multi-engine and instrument rated pilot, Wakata has logged over 1100 hours in a variety of aircraft.

NASA EXPERIENCE: Wakata reported to the NASA Johnson Space Center in August 1992. He completed one year of training and is qualified for assignment as a mission specialist on future Space Shuttle flight crews. Wakata's technical assignments to date include: payload science support for the Astronaut Office Mission Development Branch (April 1993 to February 1995); Space Shuttle flight software verification testing in the Shuttle Avionics Integration Laboratory (SAIL) (April to October 1994); Space Shuttle and Space Station Robotics for the Astronaut Office Robotics Branch (March 1996 to date). Wakata was the NASDA Assistant Payload Operation Director of the Manipulator Flight Demonstration, a robotic arm experiment for the Japanese Experiment Module of the International Space Station, on STS-85 (August 7-19, 1997).

SPACE FLIGHT EXPERIENCE: STS-72 Endeavour (January 11-20, 1996). Wakata flew as the first Japanese mission specialist on this 9-day mission during which the crew retrieved the Space Flyer Unit (launched from Japan 10-months earlier), deployed and retrieved the OAST-Flyer, and conducted two spacewalks to demonstrate and evaluate techniques to be used in the assembly of the International Space Station. The STS-72 mission was completed in 142 orbits, traveling 3.7 million miles in 8 days, 22 hours and 40 seconds. STS-92 Discovery (October 11-24, 2000) was launched from the Kennedy Space Center, Florida and returned to land at Edwards Air Force Base, California. During the 13-day flight, the seven member crew attached the Z1 Truss and Pressurized Mating Adapter 3 to the International Space Station using Discovery's robotic arm and performed four space walks to configure these elements. This expansion of the ISS opened the door for future assembly missions and prepared the station for its first resident crew. The STS-92 mission was accomplished in 202 orbits, traveling 5.3 million miles in 12 days, 21 hours, 40 minutes and 25 seconds.

NAME: Carl E. Walz (Colonel, USAF)
NASA Astronaut

PERSONAL DATA: Born September 6, 1955, in Cleveland, Ohio. Married to the former Pamela J. Glady of Lyndhurst, Ohio. They have two children. He enjoys piano and vocal music, sports, and is lead singer for MAX-Q, a rock-n-roll band.

EDUCATION: Graduated from Charles F. Brush High School, Lyndhurst, Ohio, in 1973; received a bachelor of science degree in physics from Kent State University, Ohio, in 1977, and a master of science in solid state physics from John Carroll University, Ohio, in 1979.

ORGANIZATIONS: American Legion, KSU Alumni Association.

SPECIAL HONORS: Graduated Summa Cum Laude from Kent State University. Awarded the Defense Superior Service Medal, the USAF Meritorious Service Medal with one Oak Leaf Cluster, the Defense Meritorious Service Medal with one Oak Leaf, the USAF Commendation Medal, and the USAF Achievement Medal with one Oak Leaf Cluster. Distinguished Graduate from the USAF Test Pilot School, Class 83A. Inducted into the Ohio Veterans Hall of Fame. Awarded three NASA Space Flight Medals, NASA Exceptional Service Medal. Distinguished Alumnus Award, Kent State University, 1997.

EXPERIENCE: From 1979 to 1982, Walz was responsible for analysis of radioactive samples from the Atomic Energy Detection System at the 1155th Technical Operations Squadron, McClellan Air Force Base, California. The subsequent year was spent in study as a Flight Test Engineer at the USAF Test Pilot School, Edwards Air Force Base, California. From January 1984 to June 1987, Walz served as a Flight Test Engineer to the F-16 Combined Test Force at Edwards Air Force Base, where he worked on a variety of F-16C airframe avionics and armament development programs. From July 1987 to June 1990, he served as a Flight Test Manager at Detachment 3, Air Force Flight Test Center.

NASA EXPERIENCE: Selected by NASA in January 1990, Walz is a veteran of three space flights, and has logged over 833 hours (34.5 days) in space. He served as a mission specialist on STS-51 in 1993, was the Orbiter flight engineer (MS-2) on STS-65 in 1994, and was a mission specialist on STS-79 in 1996. Walz is assigned to the fourth crew scheduled to live on the International Space Station (ISS-4). He will launch aboard a Space Shuttle in late 2001 and return aboard a Space Shuttle 4-months later. The crew of three (two American astronauts and one Russian cosmonaut) will perform flight tests of the station hardware, conduct internal and external maintenance tasks, and develop the capability of the station to support the addition of science experiments.

SPACE FLIGHT EXPERIENCE: STS-51 Discovery (September 12-22, 1993). During the mission, the five member crew deployed the U.S. Advanced Communications Technology Satellite (ACTS), and the Shuttle Pallet Satellite (SPAS) with NASA and German scientific experiments aboard. Walz also participated in a 7-hour space walk (EVA) to evaluate tools for the Hubble Space Telescope servicing mission. The mission was accomplished in 9 days, 22 hours, and 12 minutes. STS-65 Columbia (July 8-23, 1994). STS-65 flew the second International Microgravity Laboratory (IML-2) spacelab module, and carried a crew of seven. During the 15-day flight the crew conducted more than 80 experiments focusing on materials and life sciences research in microgravity. The mission completed 236 orbits of the Earth, traveling 6.1 million miles, setting a new flight duration record for the Shuttle program. STS-79 Atlantis (September 16-26, 1996). On STS-79 the six member crew aboard the Shuttle Atlantis docked with the Russian MIR station, delivered food, water, U.S. scientific experiments and Russian equipment, and exchanged NASA long duration crewmembers. During the mission, the Atlantis/Mir complex set a record for docked mass in space. STS-79 was the first flight of the double Spacehab module, and landed at KSC after 10 days 3 hours and 13 minutes.

NAME: Mary Ellen Weber, Ph.D.
     NASA Astronaut

PERSONAL DATA: Dr. Weber was born August 24, 1962 in Cleveland, Ohio; Bedford Heights, Ohio is her hometown. She is married to Dr. Jerome Elkind, who is with Texas Instruments, Inc. and originally from Bayonne, New Jersey. She is an avid skydiver and golfer, and also enjoys scuba diving. Her mother, Joan Weber, currently resides in Mentor, Ohio; her father, Andrew Weber, Jr., is deceased.

EDUCATION: Graduated from Bedford High School in 1980; received a Bachelor of Science degree in chemical engineering from Purdue University in 1984; and received a Ph.D. in physical chemistry from the University of California at Berkeley in 1988.

EXPERIENCE: During her undergraduate studies at Purdue, Dr. Weber was an engineering intern at Ohio Edison, Delco Electronics, and 3M. Following this, in her doctoral research at Berkeley, she explored the physics of gas-phase reactions involving silicon. She then joined Texas instruments to research new processes for making computer chips. TI assigned her to a consortium of semiconductor companies, SEMATECH, and subsequently to Applied Materials, to create a revolutionary reactor for manufacturing next-generation chips. She has received one patent and published eight papers in scientific journals. Dr. Weber has logged over 3,300 skydives since 1983. She received a silver medal in the U.S. National Skydiving Championships in the 20-person freefall formation event, in 1997, 1995, and 1991. She was also in the world's largest freefall formation in 1996, with 297 people. In addition, she is an instrument-rated pilot. .

NASA EXPERIENCE: In administrative assignments, Dr. Weber most recently worked with a venture capital firm to identify promising areas of space research and related companies for investment. In addition, she was the Legislative Affairs liaison at NASA Headquarters in Washington D.C., interfacing with Congress and traveling with the NASA Administrator. Prior to this appointment, she was Chairman of the procurement board for the Biotechnology Program contractor. Also, she served on a team designated to assess and revamp the Space Station research facilities. Dr. Weber's principal technical assignments within the Astronaut Office have included Shuttle launch preparations at the Kennedy Space Center, payload and science development, and development of standards and methods for crew science training. She was selected by NASA in the fourteenth group of astronauts in 1992. A veteran of two spaceflights, STS-70 and STS-101, Dr. Weber has logged over 450 hours in space.

SPACE FLIGHT EXPERIENCE: STS-101 Atlantis (May 19-29, 2000), the third Shuttle mission devoted to International Space Station construction. The crew repaired and installed a myriad of electrical and life-support components, both inside and out, and boosted the Station to a safe orbit. Dr. Weber's two primary responsibilities were flying the 60-foot robotic arm to maneuver a spacewalk crewmember along the Station surface, and directing the transfer of over three thousand pounds of equipment. The STS-101 mission was accomplished in 155 orbits of the Earth, after traveling 4.1 million miles in 236 hours and 9 minutes. STS-70 Discovery (July 13-22, 1995), a mission which successfully delivered to orbit a critical NASA communications satellite, TDRS-G. Dr. Weber's primary responsibility was checking the systems of the satellite and sending it into its 22-thousand-mile orbit above the equator. She also performed biotechnology experiments, growing colon cancer tissues never before possible. She was the primary contingency spacewalk crewmember, and the medical officer. The STS-70 mission was completed in 142 orbits of the Earth, after traveling 3.7 million miles in 214 hours and 20 minutes.

NAME: James D. Wetherbee (Captain, USN)
NASA Astronaut

PERSONAL DATA: Born November 27, 1952, in Flushing, New York. Considers his hometown to be Huntington Station, New York. Married to the former Robin DeVore Platt of Jacksonville, Florida. They have two children. He enjoys tennis, skiing, softball, running, and music. His parents, Mr. and Mrs. Dana A. Wetherbee, reside in Huntington Station, New York. Her parents, Mr. and Mrs. Harry T. Platt, Jr., reside in Jacksonville, Florida.

EDUCATION: Graduated from Holy Family Diocesan High School, South Huntington, New York, in 1970; received a bachelor of science degree in aerospace engineering from the University of Notre Dame in 1974.

ORGANIZATIONS: Member of the Society of Experimental Test Pilots.

SPECIAL HONORS: Distinguished Flying Cross; Navy Achievement Medal; two Meritorious Unit Commendations.

EXPERIENCE: Wetherbee received his commission in the United States Navy in 1975 and was designated a naval aviator in December 1976. After training in the A-7E, he was assigned to Attack Squadron 72 (VA-72) from August 1977 to November 1980 aboard the USS John F. Kennedy and logged 125 night carrier landings. After attending the U.S. Naval Test Pilot School, Patuxent River, Maryland, in 1981 he was assigned to the Systems Engineering Test Directorate. He was a project officer and test pilot for the weapons delivery system and avionics integration for the F/A-18 aircraft. Subsequently assigned to Strike Fighter Squadron 132 (VFA-132), he flew operationally in the F/A-18 from January 1984 until his selection for the astronaut candidate program. He has logged over 5,000 hours flying time and 345 carrier landings in 20 different types of aircraft.

NASA EXPERIENCE: Selected by NASA in May 1984, Wetherbee became an astronaut in June 1985. A veteran of four space flights, Wetherbee has logged over 955 hours in space. He was the pilot on STS-32 in 1990, and was the mission commander on STS-52 in 1992, STS-63 in 1995 and STS-86 in 1997. Wetherbee is Director of the Flight Crew Operations Directorate and is currently in training to command the STS-102 mission scheduled for launch in 2001.

SPACE FLIGHT EXPERIENCE: STS-32 Columbia (January 9-20, 1990) included the successful deployment of the Syncom IV-F5 satellite, and retrieval of the 21,400-pound Long Duration Exposure Facility (LDEF) using the remote manipulator system (RMS). The crew also operated a variety of middeck experiments and conducted numerous medical test objectives, including in-flight aerobic exercise and muscle performance to evaluate human adaptation to extended duration missions. Mission duration was 173 orbits in 261 hours and 01 minute. STS-52 Columbia (October 22 to November 1, 1992) successfully deployed the Laser Geodynamic Satellite (LAGEOS), a joint Italian-American project. The crew also operated the first U.S. Microgravity Payload (USMP) with French and American experiments, and successfully completed the initial flight tests of the Canadian-built Space Vision System (SVS). Mission duration was 236 hours and 56 minutes. STS-63 Discovery (February 2-11, 1995), was the first joint flight of the new Russian-American Space Program. Mission highlights included the rendezvous with the Russian Space Station, Mir, operation of Spacehab, and the deployment and retrieval of Spartan 204. The mission was accomplished in 129 orbits in 198 hours and 29 minutes. STS-86 Atlantis (September 25 to October 6, 1997) was the seventh mission to rendezvous and dock with the Russian Space Station Mir. Highlights included the delivery of a Mir attitude control computer, the exchange of U.S. crew members Mike Foale and David Wolf, a spacewalk by Scott Parazynski and Vladimir Titov to retrieve four experiments first deployed on Mir during the STS-76 docking mission, the transfer to Mir of 10,400 pounds of science and logistics, and the return of experiment hardware and results to Earth. Mission duration was 169 orbits in259 hours and 21 minutes.

NAME: Douglas H. Wheelock (Major, USA)
NASA Astronaut (Mission Specialist Candidate)

PERSONAL DATA: Born May 5, 1960 in Binghamton, New York and considers Windsor, New York to be his hometown. Married to the former Cathleen Hollen of Columbus, Georgia. They have one child. Recreational interests include coaching youth sports, baseball, hiking, flying, and collecting sports memorabilia. Doug's parents, Olin and Margaret Wheelock, reside in Windsor, New York. Cathy's parents, Jack and Judy Hollen reside in Enterprise, Alabama.

EDUCATION: Graduated from Windsor Central High School, Windsor, New York, in 1978. Received a Bachelor of Science degree in Applied Science and Engineering from the United States Military Academy, West Point, New York, in 1983, and a Master of Science degree in Aerospace Engineering from the Georgia Institute of Technology in 1992.

AWARDS: Meritorious Service Medal (1st Oak Leaf Cluster); Army Achievement Medal (2nd Oak Leaf Cluster); National Defense Service Medal; Army Good Conduct Medal; Overseas Service Ribbon; Airborne Wings; Air Assault Wings; Senior Aviator Wings.

SPECIAL HONORS: Distinguished Graduate of the U.S. Army Initial Entry Flight Training Course (1984); 25th Infantry Division Flight Safety Award (1986 and 1989); Military Nominee to the U.S. Jaycees Ten Outstanding Young Men of America (1989); Veterans of Foreign Wars Outstanding Spokesman for Freedom (1990); Team Leader of the Georgia Tech Aerial Robotics Design Team (1992); Gamble Award for excellence in experimental flight testing and technical reporting (1995); NASA Group Achievement Award (Global Positioning System) (1997).

EXPERIENCE: Wheelock received his commission as a Second Lieutenant in the United States Army from West Point in May 1983. He entered the U.S. Army Aviation School, Fort Rucker, Alabama in 1984 and graduated at the top of his flight class and was designated as an Army Aviator in September 1984. Subsequently served as a combat aviation Section Leader, Platoon Leader, Company Executive Officer, Battalion Operations Officer, and Air Cavalry Troop Commander in the Pacific Theater (Hawaii, Korea and the Philippines). Following a successful command, he was assigned to the Aviation Directorate of Combat Developments, Fort Rucker, Alabama, as a Research and Development Staff Engineer. He earned a Master of Science degree in Aerospace Engineering from the Georgia Institute of Technology in 1992, having completed graduate studies and independent research in the areas of hypersonic and high temperature gas dynamics, flight stability and control, and automatic control and robotics. He was selected as a member of Class 104 at the U.S. Naval Test Pilot School and upon completion was assigned as an Experimental Test Pilot with the U.S. Army Aviation Technical Test Center (ATTC). With ATTC, his flight testing was focused in the areas of tactical reconnaissance and surveillance systems in the OH-58D(I), RU-21H and C-23. His tour with ATTC culminated with his assignment as Division Chief for fixed wing testing of airborne signal and imagery intelligence systems in support of the National Program Office for Intelligence and Electronic Warfare. He is also a graduate of the Army Airborne and Air Assault Courses, the Aviation Advanced Course, the Material Acquisition Management Course, and the U.S. Army Command and General Staff College. A dual rated Senior Army Aviator; he has logged over 2000 flight hours in 43 different rotary and fixed wing aircraft.

NASA EXPERIENCE: Wheelock was assigned to NASA at the Johnson Space Center in August of 1996. His technical assignments with the Vehicle Integration Test Office (VITO) have included support engineer for Space Shuttle missions STS-81, STS-82, STS-94, STS-84 and STS-85 Terminal Count Demonstration Test (TCDT) and Launch Countdown (LCD) testing and vehicle preparation. He was selected as the VITO Lead Engineer for the joint U.S. Space Shuttle and Russian Space Station MIR mission STS-86, and Lead Engineer for International Space Station element-to-element hardware fit checks. Selected by NASA in June 1998, he reported for training in August 1998. Astronaut Candidate Training includes orientation briefings and tours, numerous scientific and technical briefings, intensive instruction in Shuttle and International Space Station systems, physiological training and ground school to prepare for T-38 flight training, as well as learning water and wilderness survival techniques. Wheelock is currently assigned to the Astronaut Office Space Station Operations Branch. He will serve in technical assignments until assigned to a space flight.

NAME: Peggy A. Whitson (Ph.D.)
NASA Astronaut

PERSONAL DATA: Born February 9, 1960 in Mt. Ayr, Iowa. Married to Clarence F. Sams, Ph.D. She enjoys windsurfing, biking, basketball, water skiing.

EDUCATION: Graduated from Mt. Ayr Community High School, Mt. Ayr, Iowa, in 1978; received a bachelor of science degree in biology/chemistry from Iowa Wesleyan College in 1981, and a doctorate in biochemistry from Rice University in 1985.

ORGANIZATIONS: American Society for Biochemistry and Molecular Biology.

AWARDS/HONORS: Two patents approved (1997, 1998); Group Achievement Award for Shuttle-Mir Program (1996); American Astronautical Society Randolph Lovelace II Award (1995); NASA Tech Brief Award (1995); NASA Space Act Board Award (1995, 1998); NASA Silver Snoopy Award (1995); NASA Exceptional Service Medal (1995); NASA Space Act Award for Patent Application; NASA Certificate of Commendation (1994); Submission of Patent Disclosure for "Method and Apparatus for the Collection, Storage, and Real Time Analysis of Blood and Other Bodily Fluids (1993); Selected for Space Station Redesign Team (March-June 1993); NASA Sustained Superior Performance Award (1990); Krug International Merit Award (1989); NASA-JSC National Research Council Resident Research Associate (1986-1988); Robert A. Welch Postdoctoral Fellowship (1985-1986); Robert A. Welch Predoctoral Fellowship (1982-1985), Summa Cum Laude from Iowa Wesleyan College (1981); President's Honor Roll (1978-81); Orange van Calhoun Scholarship (1980); State of Iowa Scholar (1979); Academic Excellence Award (1978).

EXPERIENCE: From 1981 to 1985, Whitson conducted her graduate work in biochemistry at Rice University, Houston, Texas, as a Robert A. Welch Predoctoral Fellow. Following completion of her graduate work she continued at Rice University as a Robert A Welch Postdoctoral Fellow until October 1986. Following this position, she began her studies at NASA Johnson Space Center, Houston, Texas, as a National Research Council Resident Research Associate. From April

1988 until September 1989, Whitson served as the Supervisor for the Biochemistry Research Group at KRUG International, a medical sciences contractor at NASA-JSC. In 1991-1997, Whitson was also invited to be an Adjunct Assistant Professor in the Department of Internal Medicine and Department of Human Biological Chemistry and Genetics at University of Texas Medical Branch, Galveston, Texas. In 1997, Whitson began a position as Adjunct Assistant Professor at Rice University in the Maybee Laboratory for Biochemical and Genetic Engineering.

NASA EXPERIENCE: From 1989 to 1993, Whitson worked as a Research Biochemist in the Biomedical Operations and Research Branch at NASA-JSC. In 1990, she gained the additional duties of Research Advisor for the National Research Council Resident Research Associate. From 1991-1993, she served as Technical Monitor of the Biochemistry Research Laboratories in the Biomedical Operations and Research Branch. From 1991-1992 she was the Payload Element Developer for Bone Cell Research Experiment (E10) aboard SL-J (STS-47), and was a member of the US-USSR Joint Working Group in Space Medicine and Biology. In 1992, she was named the Project Scientist of the Shuttle-Mir Program (STS-60,STS-63, STS-71, Mir 18, Mir 19) and served in this capacity until the conclusion of the Phase 1A Program in 1995. From 1993-1996 Whitson held the additional responsibilities of the Deputy Division Chief of the Medical Sciences Division at NASA-JSC. From 1995-1996 she served as Co-Chair of the U.S.-Russian Mission Science Working Group. In April 1996, she was selected as an astronaut candidate and started training, in August 1996. Upon completing two years of training and evaluation, she was assigned technical duties in the Astronaut Office Operations Planning Branch and served as the lead for the Crew Test Support Team in Russia from 1998-99. Whitson is currently training as a back-up crew member for third increment of the International Space Station, targeted for launch in late 2000. She is also assigned to serve as a prime crew member on Increment 5 which will launch aboard a Soyuz rocket from the Baikonur launch site in Kazakhstan.

NAME: Terrence W. Wilcutt (Colonel, USMC)
NASA Astronaut

PERSONAL DATA: Born October 31, 1949, in Russellville, Kentucky. Enjoys flying, running, weight lifting, woodworking.

EDUCATION: Graduated from Southern High School, Louisville, Kentucky in 1967; received a bachelor of arts degree in math from Western Kentucky University in 1974.

ORGANIZATIONS: Member of Society of Experimental Test Pilots (SETP).

SPECIAL HONORS: Distinguished Flying Cross, Defense Superior Service Medal,Defense Meritorious Service Medal, Pritchard Committee for Academic Excellence, NASA Space Flight Medals (4), Navy Commendation Medal, and Sea Service Deployment Ribbon. Distinguished Graduate of the United States Naval Test Pilot School.

EXPERIENCE: After graduation from college in 1974, Wilcutt taught high school math for two years prior to entering the Marine Corps. He was commissioned in 1976 and earned his wings in 1978. Following initial F-4 Phantom training in VMFAT-101, he reported to VMFA-235, Kaneohe, Hawaii. While assigned to VMFA-235, Wilcutt attended the Naval Fighter Weapons School (Topgun) and made two overseas deployments to Japan, Korea, and the Philippines. In 1983, he was selected for F/A-18 conversion training and served as an F/A-18 Fighter Weapons and Air Combat Maneuvering

Instructor in VFA-125, Lemoore, California. In 1986, Wilcutt was selected to attend the United States Naval Test Pilot School (USNTPS),where he earned the title "Distinguished Graduate." Following graduation from USNTPS he was assigned as a test pilot/project officer for Strike Aircraft Test Directorate (SATD) at the Naval Aircraft Test Center, Patuxent River, Maryland. While assigned to SATD, Wilcutt flew the F/A-18 Hornet, the A-7 Corsair II, the F-4 Phantom, and various other aircraft to test a wide variety of projects and classified programs. He has over 4,400 flight hours in more than 30 different aircraft.

NASA EXPERIENCE: Selected by NASA in January 1990, Wilcutt became an astronaut in July 1991. Technical assignments to date include: work on Space Shuttle Main Engine and External Tank issues; Astronaut Support Personnel team at the Kennedy Space Center, Florida, supporting Space Shuttle launches and landings; technical issues for the Astronaut Office Operations Development Branch; NASA Director of Operations at the Yuri Gagarin Cosmonaut Training Center, Star City, Russia; Chief of the Astronaut Office Shuttle Operations Branch. He was the pilot on STS-68 in 1994 and STS-79 in 1996, and was the mission commander on STS-89 in 1998 and STS-106 in 2000. A veteran of four space flights, Wilcutt has logged over 1,007 hours in space.

SPACE FLIGHT EXPERIENCE: STS-68 Endeavour (September 30 to October 11, 1994) was part of NASA's Mission to Planet Earth. STS-68, Space Radar Lab-2 (SRL-2), was the second flight of three advanced radars called SIR-C/X-SAR (Spaceborne Imaging Radar-C/X-Band Synthetic Aperture Radar), and a carbon-monoxide pollution sensor, MAPS (Measurement of Air Pollution from Satellites). SIR-C/X-SAR and MAPS operated together in Endeavour's cargo bay to study Earth's surface and atmosphere, creating radar images of Earth's surface environment and mapping global production and transport of carbon monoxide pollution. Real-time crew observations of environmental conditions, along with over 14,000 photographs aided the science team in interpreting the SRL data. The SRL-2 mission was a highly successful test of technology intended for long-term environmental and geological monitoring of planet Earth. STS-68 launched from Kennedy Space Center, Florida, and landed at Edwards Air Force Base, California. Mission duration was 11 days, 5 hours, 46 minutes, traveling 4.7 million miles in 183 orbits of the Earth. STS-79 Atlantis (September 16-26, 1996), the fourth in the joint American-Russian Shuttle-Mir series of missions, launched from and returned to land at Kennedy Space Center, Florida. STS-79 rendezvoused with the Russian MIR space station and ferried supplies, personnel, and scientific equipment to this base 240 miles above the Earth. The crew transferred over 3.5 tons of supplies to and from the Mir and exchanged U.S. astronauts on Mir for the first time - leaving John Blaha and bringing Shannon Lucid home after her record six months stay aboard Mir. Mission duration was 10 days, 3 hours, 18 minutes, traveling 3.9 million miles in 159 orbits of the Earth. STS-89 (January 22-31, 1998), was the eighth Shuttle-Mir docking mission during which the crew transferred more than 9,000 pounds of scientific equipment, logistical hardware and water from Space Shuttle Endeavour to Mir. In the fifth and last exchange of a U.S. astronaut, STS-89 delivered Andy Thomas to Mir and returned with David Wolf. Mission duration was 8 days, 19 hours and 47 seconds, traveling 3.6 million miles in 138 orbits of the Earth. STS-106 Atlantis (September 8-20, 2000) was a 12-day mission during which the crew successfully prepared the International Space Station for the arrival of the first permanent crew. The five astronauts and two cosmonauts delivered more than 6,600 pounds of supplies and installed batteries, power converters, life support, and exercise equipment on the Space Station. Two crew members performed a space walk in order to connect power, data and communications cables to the newly arrived Zvezda Service Module and the Space Station. STS-106 orbited the Earth 185 times, and covered 4.9 million miles in 11 days, 19 hours, and 10 minutes.

NAME: Dafydd (Dave) Rhys Williams (M.D.)
      CSA Astronaut

PERSONAL DATA: Born May 16, 1954, in Saskatoon, Saskatchewan. Married to the former Cathy Fraser of Pointe-Claire, Quebec. They have a son and a daughter. Dr. Williams enjoys flying, scuba diving, hiking, sailing, kayaking, canoeing, downhill and cross-country skiing. His mother, Isobel Williams (nee Berger), resides in Williamsburg, Ontario. His father, William Williams, is deceased. Her father, Arthur Fraser, resides in Sechelt, British Columbia. Her mother, Olga Fraser (nee Bardahl), is deceased.

EDUCATION: Attended High School in Beaconsfield, Quebec. Bachelor of science degree in biology from McGill University, Montreal, 1976.; Master of science degree in physiology, Doctorate of medicine, and Master of Surgery from McGill University, Montreal, in 1983. Completed residency in Family Practice in the Faculty of Medicine, University of Ottawa in 1985. Obtained Fellowship in Emergency Medicine from the Royal College of Physicians and Surgeons of Canada, following completion of a Residency in Emergency Medicine at the University of Toronto, 1988.

ORGANIZATIONS: Member, College of Physicians and Surgeons of Ontario, the Ontario Medical Association, the College of Family Physicians of Canada, the Royal College of Physicians and Surgeons of Canada, the Canadian Association of Emergency Physicians, the Aerospace Medical Association, the Canadian Society for Aerospace Medicine and the Canadian Aeronautics and Space Institute. Past affiliations include: the Society for Neuroscience, the New York Academy of Science and the Montreal Physiological Society.

SPECIAL HONORS: Awarded the Commonwealth Certificate of Thanks (1973) and the Commonwealth Recognition Award (1975) for his contribution to the Royal Life Saving Society of Canada. Academic awards include the A.S. Hill Bursary, McGill University, in 1980; the Walter Hoare Bursary, McGill University, in 1981; the J.W. McConnell Award, McGill University, 1981-1983. He was named Faculty Scholar, in 1982, and University Scholar, in 1983, by the Faculty of Medicine, McGill University. In 1983, he also received the Psychiatry Prize and the Wood Gold Medal from the Faculty of Medicine and was named on the Dean's Honor List by the Physiology Department, McGill University, for his postgraduate research. He was twice awarded the second prize for his participation in the University of Toronto Emergency Medicine Research Papers Program, in 1986 and 1988, and received top honors in that competition in 1987.

EXPERIENCE: Dr. Williams received postgraduate training in advanced invertebrate physiology at the Friday Harbour Laboratories, University of Washington, Seattle, Washington. Subsequently, his interests switched to vertebrate neurophysiology when, for his Master's Thesis, he became involved in basic science research on the role of adrenal steroid hormones in modifying the activity of regions within the central nervous system involved in the regulation of sleep wake cycles. While working in the Neurophysiological Laboratories at the Allan Memorial Institute for Psychiatry, he assisted in clinical studies of slow wave potentials within the central nervous system. His clinical research in Emergency Medicine has included studies evaluating the initial training and skill retention of cardiopulmonary resuscitation skills, patient survival from out-of-hospital cardiac arrest, the early identification of trauma patients at high risk and the efficacy of tetanus immunization in the elderly. In 1988, he became an Emergency Physician with the Department of Emergency Services at Sunnybrook HealthScience Centre as well as a Lecturer with the Department of Surgery, University of Toronto. He served as a member of the Air Ambulance Utilization Committee with the

Ministry of Health in Ontario, both as an academic Emergency Physician and later as a representative of community Emergency Physicians. In addition, he has trained basic ambulance attendants, paramedics, nurses, residents and practicing physicians in cardiac and trauma resuscitation as a Course Director in Advanced Cardiac Life Support with the Canadian Heart and Stroke Foundation and in Advanced Trauma Life Support with the American College of Surgeons. From 1989 to 1990, he served as an Emergency Physician with the Emergency Associates of Kitchener Waterloo andas Medical Director of the Westmount Urgent Care Clinic. In 1990, he returned to Sunnybrook as Medical Director ofthe ACLS Program and Coordinator of Postgraduate Training in Emergency Medicine. Subsequently, he became theActing Director of the Department of Emergency Services at Sunnybrook Health Science Centre, Assistant Professor of Surgery, University of Toronto and Assistant Professor of Medicine, University of Toronto. Dr. Williams was selected by the Canadian Space Agency in June 1992. He completed basic training and in May 1993 was appointed Manager of the Missions and Space Medicine Group within the Astronaut Program. His collateral dutyassignments have included supervising the implementation of Operational Space Medicine activities within the Astronaut Program, and the coordination of the Canadian Astronaut Program Space Unit Life Simulation (CAPSULS) Project. In February 1994 he participated in a 7-day space mission simulation. During this CAPSULS Project, he was the principal investigator of a study to evaluate the initial training and retention of resuscitation skills by non-medical astronauts. He was also assigned as one of the crew members and acted as the crew medical officer. He remains active in life science and space medicine research, both as a Principal Investigator and as a Co-investigator. He has recently been appointed as an Assistant Professor of Surgery, McGill University, and is participating in clinical activities at St. Mary's Hospital and at the Montreal General Hospital.

NASA EXPERIENCE: In January 1995, Dr. Williams was selected to join the 1995 international class of NASA mission specialist astronaut candidates. He reported to the Johnson Space Center in March 1995 and completed training and evaluation in May 1996. On completing basic training, he was assigned to work technical issues for the Payloads/Habitability Branch of the Astronaut Office. Most recently, Dr. Williams served as Mission Specialist 3 on STS-90 Neurolab (April 17 to May 3, 1998). During the 16-day Spacelab flight the seven person crew aboard Space Shuttle Columbia served as both experiment subjects and operators for 26 individual life science experiments focusing on the effects of microgravity on the brain and nervous system. The STS-90 flight orbited the Earth 256 times, covered 6.3 million miles, and logged him over 381 hours in space.

NAME: Jeffrey N. Williams (Lieutenant Colonel, USA)
NASA Astronaut

PERSONAL DATA: Born, January 18, 1958 in Superior, Wisconsin, but considers Winter, Wisconsin to be his hometown. Married to the former Anna-Marie Moore of Newburgh, New York. They have two children. Enjoys running, fishing, camping, skiing, scuba diving and woodworking. As a cadet at the U.S. Military Academy competed on the West Point sport parachute team and also held ratings of sport parachute jumpmaster and instructor. His parents, Lloyd D. and Eunice A. Williams, reside in Winter, Wisconsin. Her mother, Gloria M. Moore, resides in Modena, New York. Her father, S. Stevens Moore, is deceased.

EDUCATION: Graduated from Winter High School, Winter, Wisconsin, in 1976; received a bachelor of science degree in applied science and engineering from the U.S. Military Academy in 1980, a master of science degree in aeronautical engineering and the degree of aeronautical engineer from the U.S. Naval Postgraduate School, both in 1987, and a master of arts degree in National security and strategic studies from the U.S. Naval War College in 1996.

ORGANIZATIONS: Society of Experimental Test Pilots, American Helicopter Society, Army Aviation Association of America, Order of Daedalians, Officer Christian Fellowship.

SPECIAL HONORS: Graduated first in U.S. Naval Test Pilot School class 103; 1988 Admiral William Adger Moffett Award for Excellence in Aeronautical Engineering, Naval Postgraduate School; 1985 Daedalian Foundation Fellowship Award for Graduate Study in Aeronautics. Awarded 2 Meritorious Service Medals, the Army Commendation Medal, NASA Space Flight Medal, NASA Exceptional Service Medal, and various other service awards. Master Army Aviator and Parachutist badges.

EXPERIENCE: Williams received his commission as a second lieutenant from the U.S. Military Academy in May 1980 and was designated an Army aviator in September 1981. He then completed a three-year assignment in Germany where he served as an Aeroscout Platoon Leader and Operations Officer in the 3rd Armored Division's aviation battalion. Following his return to the United States, Williams completed a graduate program in aeronautical engineering, and was subsequently selected for an Army assignment at the Johnson Space Center, where he served for over 4 years. In 1992, Williams was selected for the Naval Test Pilot School. After graduation in June 1993, he served as an experimental test pilot and Flight Test Division Chief in the Army's Airworthiness Qualification Test Directorate at Edwards Air Force Base, California. In 1995, he was selected for attendance at the Naval War College command and staff course as an Army exchange officer. Williams has logged over 2,500 hours in more than 50 different aircraft.

NASA EXPERIENCE: Williams was selected for an Army assignment at Johnson Space Center in 1987. Until his transfer in 1992, he served as a Shuttle launch and landing operations engineer, a pilot in the Shuttle Avionics Integration Laboratory, and chief of the Operations Development Office, Flight Crew Operations Directorate. Selected by NASA in May 1996, Williams again reported to Johnson Space Center in August 1996. After completing two years of training and evaluation, he performed technical duties in the Spacecraft Systems Branch and later the Space Station Operations Branch. Most recently, he served as a mission specialist on STS-101. In completing his first space flight, Williams logged over 236 hours in space, including 6 hours and 44 minutes of EVA.

SPACE FLIGHT EXPERIENCE: STS-101 Atlantis (May 19-29, 2000) was the third Shuttle mission devoted to International Space Station (ISS) construction. Objectives included transporting and installing over 5,000 pounds of equipment and supplies, and included Jeff's first EVA (space walk) lasting over 6 hours. The mission was accomplished in 155 orbits of the Earth, traveling 4.1 million miles in 236 hours and 9 minutes.

NAME: Sunita L. Williams (Lieutenant Commander, USN)
NASA Astronaut (Mission Specialist Candidate)

PERSONAL DATA: Born September 19, 1965 in Euclid, Ohio, but considers Needham, Massachusetts to be her hometown. Married to Michael J. Williams. They have no children, but they have an awesome black Labrador retriever named Turbo. Recreational interests include running, swimming, biking, triathlons, windsurfing, snowboarding and bow hunting. Her parents, Deepak N. and Ursaline B. Pandya, reside in Falmouth, Massachusetts.

EDUCATION: Needham High School, Needham, Massachusetts, 1983. B.S., Physical Science, U.S. Naval Academy, 1987.M.S., Engineering Management, Florida Institute of Technology, 1995.

ORGANIZATIONS: Society of Experimental Test Pilots, Society of Flight Test Engineers, American Helicopter Association.

SPECIAL HONORS: Awarded Navy Commendation Medal (2), Navy and Marine Corps Achievement Medal, Humanitarian Service Medal and various other service awards.

EXPERIENCE: Williams received her commission as an Ensign in the United States Navy from the United States Naval Academy in May 1987. After a six-month temporary assignment at the Naval Coastal System Command, she received her designation as a Basic Diving Officer and then reported to Naval Aviation Training Command. She was designated a Naval Aviator in July 1989. She then reported to Helicopter Combat Support Squadron 3 for initial H46, Seaknight, training. Upon completion of this training, she was assigned to Helicopter Combat Support Squadron 8 in Norfolk, Virginia, and made overseas deployments to the Mediterranean, Red Sea and the Persian Gulf in support of Desert Shield and Operation Provide Comfort. In September 1992 she was the Officer-in-Charge of an H-46 detachment sent to Miami, Florida for Hurricane Andrew Relief Operations onboard USS Sylvania. Williams was selected for United States Naval Test Pilot School and began the course in January 1993. After graduation in December 1993, she was assigned to the Rotary Wing Aircraft Test Directorate as an H-46 Project Officer, and V-22 Chase Pilot in the T-2. While there she was also assigned as the squadron Safety Officer and flew test flights in the SH-60B/F, UH-1, AH-1W, SH-2, VH-3, H-46, CH-53 and the H-57. In December 1995, she went back to the Naval Test Pilot School as an Instructor in the Rotary Wing Department and the school's Safety Officer. There she flew the UH-60, OH-6 and the OH-58. From thereshe was assigned to the USS Saipan (LHA-2), Norfolk, Virginia, as the Aircraft Handler and the Assistant Air Boss. Williams was deployed onboard USS Saipan when she was selected for the astronaut program. She has logged over 2300 flight hours in more than 30 different aircraft.

NASA EXPERIENCE: Selected by NASA in June 1998, she reported for training in August 1998. Astronaut Candidate Training includes orientation briefings and tours, numerous scientific and technical briefings, intensive instruction in Shuttle and International Space Station systems, physiological training and ground school to prepare for T-38 flight training, as well as learning water and wilderness survival techniques. Williams is currently assigned to the Astronaut Office Space Station Operations Branch. She will serve in technical assignments until assigned to a space flight.

NAME: Stephanie D. Wilson
       NASA Astronaut

PERSONAL DATA: Born September 27, 1966 in Boston, Massachusetts. Married to Julius "BJ" McCurdy. Enjoys snow skiing, music, astronomy, stamp collecting, and traveling.

EDUCATION: Graduated from Taconic High School, Pittsfield, Massachusetts, in 1984; received a bachelor of science degree in engineering science from Harvard University in 1988, and a master of science degree in aerospace engineering from the University of Texas, in 1992.

ORGANIZATIONS: American Institute of Aeronautics and Astronautics.

EXPERIENCE: After graduating from Harvard in 1988, Wilson worked for 2 years for the former Martin Marietta Astronautics Group in Denver, Colorado. As a Loads and Dynamics engineer for Titan IV, Wilson was responsible for performing coupled loads analyses for the launch vehicle and payloads during flight events. Wilson left Martin Marietta in 1990 to attend graduate school at the University of Texas. Her research focused on the control and modeling of large, flexible space structures. Following the completion of her graduate work, she began working for the Jet Propulsion Laboratory in Pasadena, California, in 1992. As a member of the Attitude and Articulation Control Subsystem for the Galileo spacecraft, Wilson was responsible for assessing attitude controller performance, science platform pointing accuracy, antenna pointing accuracy and spin rate accuracy. She worked in the areas of sequence development and testing as well. While at the Jet Propulsion Laboratory, Wilson also supported the Interferometery Technology Program as a member of the Integrated Modeling Team, which was responsible for finite element modeling, controller design, and software development.

NASA EXPERIENCE: Selected by NASA in April 1996, Wilson reported to the Johnson Space Center in August 1996. Having completed two years of training and evaluation, she is qualified for flight assignment as a mission specialist. Currently, Wilson is assigned technical duties in the Astronaut Office Space Station Operations Branch.

NAME: Peter J.K. "Jeff" Wisoff (Ph.D)
       NASA Astronaut

PERSONAL DATA: Born August 16, 1958, in Norfolk, Virginia. Married to Tamara E. Jernigan. He enjoys scuba diving, racquetball, swimming, and sailing. His parents, Carl & Pat Wisoff, reside in Norfolk.

EDUCATION: Graduated from Norfolk Academy, Norfolk, Virginia, in 1976; received a bachelor of science degree in physics (with Highest Distinction) from University of Virginia in 1980, a master of science degree and a doctorate in applied physics from Stanford University in 1982 and 1986 respectively.

SPECIAL HONORS: NASA Space Flight Medals (1993, 1994, 1997); NCR Faculty Award of Excellence (1989); National Science Foundation Graduate Fellowship 1980-1983; Physics Prize and Shannon Award from the University of Virginia (1980). Selected to Phi Beta Kappa in 1979.

EXPERIENCE: After graduating from the University of Virginia in 1976, Dr. Wisoff began his graduate work on the development of short wavelength lasers at Stanford University as a National Science Foundation Graduate Fellow. Upon completing his master's and doctorate degrees at Stanford in 1986, Dr. Wisoff joined the faculty of the Electrical and Computer Engineering Department at Rice University. His research focused on the development of new vacuum ultraviolet and high intensity laser sources. In addition, he also collaborated with researchers from regional Texas Medical Centers on the applications of lasers to the reconstruction of damaged nerves. He has recently collaborated with researchers at Rice University on new techniques for growing and evaluating semiconductor materials using lasers. Dr. Wisoff has contributed numerous papers at technical conferences and in journals in the areas of lasers and laser applications.

NASA EXPERIENCE: Selected by NASA in January 1990, Dr. Wisoff became an astronaut in July 1991. He is qualified for flight assignment as a mission specialist. His technical assignments to date include: spacecraft communicator (CAPCOM) in Mission Control; flight software verification in the Shuttle Avionics Integration Laboratory (SAIL); coordinating flight crew equipment; evaluating extravehicular activity (EVA) equipment and techniques for the construction of Space Station; lead for the Payloads and Habitability Branch of the Astronaut Office. A veteran of four space flights, STS-57 in 1993, STS-68 in 1994, STS-81 in 1997 and STS-92 in 2000, Dr. Wisoff has logged a total of 42 days, 56 hours, 1 minute and 48 seconds in space, including 19 hours and 53 minutes of EVA time in three space walks.

SPACE FLIGHT EXPERIENCE: STS-57 Endeavour (June 21 to July 1, 1993) launched from and returned to land at the Kennedy Space Center, Florida. The primary objective of this flight was the retrieval of the European Retrievable Carrier satellite (EURECA) using the RMS. Additionally, this mission featured the first flight of Spacehab, a commercially-provided middeck augmentation module for the conduct of microgravity experiments. Spacehab carried 22 individual flight experiments in materials and life sciences research. During the mission Wisoff conducted a 5-hour, 50-minute spacewalk during which the EURECA communications antennas were manually positioned for latching, and various extravehicular activity tools and techniques were evaluated for use on future missions. STS-57 was accomplished in 155 orbits of the Earth in 239 hours and 45 minutes. STS-68 Endeavour (September 30 to October 11, 1994) was the Space Radar Lab-2 (SRL-2) mission. As part of NASA's Mission to Planet Earth, SRL-2 was the second flight of three advanced radars called SIR-C/X-SAR (Spaceborne Imaging Radar-C/X-Band Synthetic Aperture Radar), and a carbon-monoxide pollution sensor, MAPS (Measurement of Air Pollution from Satellites). SIR-C/X-SAR and MAPS operated together in Endeavour's cargo bay to study Earth's surface and atmosphere, creating radar images of Earth's surface environment and mapping global production and transport of carbon monoxide pollution. Real-time crew observations of environmental conditions, along with over 14,000 photographs aided the science team in interpreting the SRL data. The SRL-2 mission was a highly successful test of technology intended for long-term environmental and geological monitoring of planet Earth. Following 183 orbits of the Earth in 269 hours and 46 minutes, the eleven-day mission ended with Space Shuttle Endeavour landing at Edwards Air Force Base, California. STS-81 Atlantis (January 12-22, 1997) was a ten-day mission, the fifth to dock with Russia's Space Station Mir, and the second to exchange U.S. astronauts. The mission also carried the Spacehab double module providing additional middeck locker space for secondary experiments. In five days of docked operations more than three tons of food, water, experiment equipment and samples were moved back and forth between the two spacecraft. Following 160 orbits of the Earth in 244 hours, 55 minutes, the STS-81 mission concluded with a landing on Kennedy Space Center's Runway 33 ending a 3.9 million mile journey. STS-92 Discovery (October 11-24, 2000) was launched from the

Kennedy Space Center, Florida and returned to land at Edwards Air Force Base, California. During the 13-day flight, the seven member crew attached the Z1 Truss and Pressurized Mating Adapter 3 to the International Space Station using Discovery's robotic arm and performed four space walks to configure these elements. This expansion of the ISS opened the door for future assembly missions and prepared the station for its first resident crew. Dr. Wisoff totaled 13 hours and 16 minutes of EVA time in two space walks. The STS-92 mission was accomplished in 202 orbits, traveling 5.3 million miles in 12 days, 21 hours, 40 minutes and 25 seconds.

NAME: David A. Wolf (M.D.)
NASA Astronaut

PERSONAL DATA: Born August 23, 1956, in Indianapolis, Indiana. Single. He enjoys sport aerobatic flying, scuba diving, handball, running, and water skiing. His parents, Dr. and Mrs. Harry Wolf, reside in Indianapolis.

EDUCATION: Graduated from North Central High School, Indianapolis, Indiana, in 1974; received a bachelor of science degree in electrical engineering from Purdue University in 1978, and a doctorate of medicine from Indiana University in 1982. He completed his medical internship (1983) at Methodist Hospital in Indianapolis, Indiana, and USAF flight surgeon primary training at Brooks Air Force Base in San Antonio, Texas.

ORGANIZATIONS: Member of the Institute of Electrical and Electronics Engineers; the Aerospace Medical Association; the Experimental Aircraft Association; the International Aerobatic Club; and the Air National Guard.

SPECIAL HONORS: Recipient of the NASA Exceptional Engineering Achievement Medal (1990); NASA Inventor of the Year, 1992. Dr. Wolf graduated "with distinction" from the honors curriculum in electrical engineering at Purdue University and received an Academic Achievement Award upon graduation from medical school. He received the Carl R. Ruddell scholarship award for research in medical ultrasonic signal and image processing. He is a member of Eta Kappa Knu and Phi Eta Sigma honorary societies. Dr. Wolf has received 11 U.S. Patents and over 20 Space Act Awards for 3-dimensional tissue engineering technologies earning the Texas State Bar Patent of the Year in 1994. He has published over 40 technical papers.

EXPERIENCE: As a research scientist at the Indianapolis Center for Advanced Research from 1980 to 1983, he developed digital signal and image processing techniques utilizing matched filter detection of high time-bandwidth product transmissions producing "state of the art" high resolution medical ultrasonic images to the 100 micron level. He also developed new doppler demodulation techniques extending the range velocity product limitation of conventional pulsed doppler systems. He is a USAF senior flight surgeon in the Air National Guard (1982 to present) and is a member of the Board of Directors of the National Inventors Hall of Fame. He has logged over 2000 hours of flight time including air combat training as a weapons systems officer (F4 Phantom jet), T-38 Talon, and competition aerobatics (PITTS Special and Christen Eagle).

NASA EXPERIENCE: In 1983, Dr. Wolf joined the Medical Sciences Division, Johnson Space Center, Houston, Texas. He was responsible for development of the American Flight Echocardiograph for investigating cardiovascular physiology in microgravity. Upon completion he was assigned as chief engineer for design of the Space Station medical facility. In 1986 he was assigned to direct development of the Space Bioreactor and associated tissue engineering and cancer research applications utilizing controlled gravitational conditions. This resulted in the state of the art NASA rotating tissue culture systems. He has particular expertise in the design of real time computer process control systems, communications, bioprocessing, physiology, fluid dynamics, and aerospace medicine. Dr. Wolf is an active public speaker. Selected as a NASA astronaut in January 1990, Dr. Wolf became qualified for space flight in July 1991. His technical assignments have included Orbiter vehicle processing and test at Kennedy Space Center (1991-1992) and spacecraft communications (CAPCOM) (1994-1995). He is qualified for Extravehicular Activity (Spacewalk), Remote Manipulator System (Robot Arm), and Rendezvous. He was CAPCOM for the first and third Shuttle-Mir rendezvous. He trained at the Gagarin Cosmonaut Training Center in Star City, Russia, in preparation for a long-duration stay aboard Mir. Dr. Wolf has logged 142 days in space including a 4 hour EVA in a Russian Orlan spacesuit. He was a mission specialist on STS-58, and served as Board Engineer 2 for 119 days aboard the Russian Space Station Mir. He is currently assigned to the EVA Development Group focusing on assembly techniques for the International Space Station.

SPACEFLIGHT EXPERIENCE: STS-58 Columbia (10/16/93-11/1/93) was a 14-day dedicated Spacelab life sciences research mission. During this record length shuttle mission the crew conducted neurovestibular, cardiovascular, cardiopulmonary, metabolic, and musculoskeletal research utilizing microgravity to reveal fundamental physiology normally masked by earth gravity. Mission duration was 336 hours, 13 minutes, 01 seconds. On September 25, 1997, Dr. Wolf launched aboard Space Shuttle Atlantis as part of the STS-86 crew. Following docking, September 28, 1997 marked the official start of his 119 days aboard Mir. He returned with the crew of STS-89 aboard Shuttle Endeavour on January 31, 1998. Mission duration was 128 days.

NAME: Neil W. Woodward III (Lieutenant Commander, USN)
NASA Astronaut (Mission Specialist Candidate)

PERSONAL DATA: Born July 26, 1962 in Chicago, Illinois. Married. Enjoys reading, running, computers, sailing, music, wines and cooking. His father, Dr. Neil W. Woodward Jr., resides in Oklahoma City, Oklahoma. His mother, Aileen S. Woodward, is deceased.

EDUCATION: Putnam City High School, Oklahoma City, Oklahoma, 1980. B.S., Physics, Massachusetts Institute of Technology, 1984. M.A., Physics, University of Texas at Austin, 1988.

ORGANIZATIONS: United States Naval Institute, Tau Epsilon Phi fraternity.

AWARDS: Distinguished Graduate, US Naval Test Pilot School; Empire Test Pilot School Award for Best Developmental Test Thesis, USNTPS. Awarded Navy Commendation Medal; two Navy Achievement Medals; various other service awards.

EXPERIENCE: Woodward graduated from MIT in June, 1980, with a degree in Physics. He attended graduate school at the University of Texas at Austin, working in the Center for Relativity and then the Fusion Research Center. His thesis research involved using optical spectroscopy to investigate neoclassical plasma rotation in the Texas Experimental Tokamak fusion reactor. He received his Master's degree in 1988 and joined the US Navy, reporting to Aviation Officer Candidate School in Pensacola, Florida. He was commissioned in January 1989, and earned his wings as a Naval Flight Officer in March 1990. He reported to NAS Whidbey Island, Washington, where he completed initial Bombardier/Navigator training in the A-6E Intruder and was then assigned to the Green Lizards of

Attack Squadron 95. Woodward made two deployments with VA-95 aboard the USS Abraham Lincoln (CVN-72) in support of Operations Desert Storm (post-cease fire), Southern Watch, and Somalia. He was then assigned to the Naval Strike Warfare Center in Fallon, Nevada, where he served as Weaponeering Officer and Contingency Cell Officer. In 1995, he was selected to attend the U.S. Naval Test Pilot School at Naval Air Station Patuxent River, Maryland, and graduated with distinction in July 1996. Upon graduation, he was assigned to the Air Vehicle/Stores Compatibility Department at the Naval Strike Aircraft Test Squadron in Patuxent River. While at NSATS, he cross-trained in the F/A-18 Hornet and tested stores and systems for the F/A-18B,F/A-18D, and F/A-18F aircraft. Woodward was assigned to the Strike Aircraft Test Squadron when he was selected for the astronaut program. Woodward has logged over 1,500 flight hours in more than 25 different aircraft and has 265 arrested landings.

NASA EXPERIENCE: Selected by NASA in June 1998, he reported for training in August 1998. Astronaut Candidate Training includes orientation briefings and tours, numerous scientific and technical briefings, intensive instruction in Shuttle and International Space Station systems, physiological training and ground school to prepare for T-38 flight training, as well as learning water and wilderness survival techniques. Woodward is currently assigned to the Astronaut Office Shuttle Operations Branch. He will serve in technical assignments until assigned to a space flight.

NAME: John W. Young (Mr.)
NASA Astronaut

PERSONAL DATA: Born September 24, 1930, in San Francisco, California. Married to the former Susy Feldman of St. Louis, Missouri. Two children, two grandchildren. Enjoys wind surfing, bicycling, reading, and gardening.

EDUCATION: Graduated from Orlando High School, Orlando, Florida; received a bachelor of science degree in aeronautical engineering with highest honors from Georgia Institute of Technology in 1952.

ORGANIZATIONS: Fellow of the American Astronautical Society (AAS), the Society of Experimental Test Pilots (SETP), and the American Institute of Aeronautics and Astronautics (AIAA).

SPECIAL HONORS: Awarded the Congressional Space Medal of Honor (1981), 3 NASA Distinguished Service Medals, NASA Outstanding Leadership Medal (1992), NASA Exceptional Engineering Achievement Medal (1987), NASA Outstanding Achievement Medal (1994), Navy Astronaut Wings (1965), 2 Navy Distinguished Service Medals, 3 Navy Distinguished Flying Crosses, the Georgia Tech Distinguished Young Alumni Award (1965), Distinguished Service Alumni Award (1972), the Exceptional Engineering Achievement Award (1985), the Academy of Distinguished Engineering Alumni (1994), and the American Astronautical Society Space Flight Award (1993), Distinguished Executive Award (1998), Rotary National Space Achievement Award (2000). Inducted into the National Aviation Hall and the U.S. Astronaut Halls of Fame. Recipient of more than 80 other major awards, including 4 honorary doctorate degrees.

NAVY EXPERIENCE: Upon graduation from Georgia Tech, Young entered the United States Navy. After serving on the west coast destroyer USS LAWS (DD-558) for 1 year, he was sent to flight training. He was then assigned to Fighter Squadron 103 for 4 years, flying Cougars and Crusaders.

After test pilot training at the U.S. Navy Test Pilot School in 1959, he was assigned to the Naval Air Test Center for 3 years. His test projects included evaluations of the Crusader and Phantom fighter weapons systems. In 1962, he set world time-to-climb records to 3,000-meter and 25,000-meter altitudes in the Phantom. Prior to reporting to NASA, he was maintenance officer of Phantom Fighter Squadron 143. Young retired from the Navy as a Captain in September 1976, after completing 25 years of active military service.

NASA EXPERIENCE: In September 1962, Young was selected as an astronaut. He is the first person to fly in space six times from earth, and seven times counting his lunar liftoff. The first flight was with Gus Grissom in Gemini 3, the first manned Gemini mission, on March 23, 1965. This was a complete end-to-end test of the Gemini spacecraft, during which Gus accomplished the first manual change of orbit altitude and plane and the first lifting reentry, and Young operated the first computer on a manned spacecraft. On Gemini 10, July 18-21, 1966, Young, as Commander, and Mike Collins, as Pilot, completed a dual rendezvous with two separate Agena target vehicles. While Young flew close formation on the second Agena, Mike Collins did an extravehicular transfer to retrieve a micro meteorite detector from that Agena. On his third flight, May 18-26, 1969, Young was Command Module Pilot of Apollo 10. Tom Stafford and Gene Cernan were also on this mission which orbited the Moon, completed a lunar rendezvous, and tracked proposed lunar landing sites. His fourth space flight, Apollo 16, April 16-27, 1972, was a lunar exploration mission, with Young as Spacecraft Commander, and Ken Mattingly and Charlie Duke. Young and Duke set up scientific equipment and explored the lunar highlands at Descartes. They collected 200 pounds of rocks and drove over 16 miles in the lunar rover on three separate geology traverses. Young's fifth flight was as Spacecraft Commander of STS-1, the first flight of the Space Shuttle, April 12-14, 1981, with Bob Crippen as Pilot. The 54-1/2 hour, 36-orbit mission verified Space Shuttle systems performance during launch, on orbit, and entry. Tests of the Orbiter Columbia included evaluation of mechanical systems including the payload bay doors, the attitude and maneuvering rocket thrusters, guidance and navigation systems, and Orbiter/crew compatibility. One hundred and thirty three of the mission's flight test objectives were accomplished. The Orbiter Columbia was the first manned spaceship tested during ascent, on orbit, and entry without benefit of previous unmanned missions. Columbia was also the first winged reentry vehicle to return from space to a runway landing. It weighed about 98 tons as Young landed it on the dry lakebed at Edwards Air Force Base, California. Young's sixth flight was as Spacecraft Commander of STS-9, the first Spacelab mission, November 28-December 8, 1983, with Pilot Brewster Shaw, Mission Specialists Bob Parker and Owen Garriott, and Payload Specialists Byron Lichtenberg of the USA and Ulf Merbold of West Germany. The mission successfully completed all 94 of its flight test objectives. For ten days the 6-man crew worked 12-hour shifts around-the-clock, performing more than 70 experiments in the fields of atmospheric physics, Earth observations, space plasma physics, astronomy and solar physics, materials processing and life sciences. The mission returned more scientific and technical data than all the previous Apollo and Skylab missions put together. The Spacelab was brought back for re-use, so that Columbia weighed over 110 tons as Young landed the spaceship at Edwards Air Force Base, California. Young was also on five backup space flight crews: backup pilot in Gemini 6, backup command module pilot for the second Apollo mission (before the Apollo Program fire) and Apollo 7, and backup spacecraft commander for Apollo 13 and 17. In preparation for prime and backup crew positions on eleven space flights, Young has put more than 15,000 hours into training so far, mostly in simulators and simulations. He has also logged more than 14,000 hours flying time in props, jets, helicopters, rocket jets, and spacecraft, including 835 hours in six space flights. In January 1973, Young was made Chief of the Space Shuttle Branch of the Astronaut Office, providing operational and engineering astronaut support for the design and development of the Space

Shuttle. In January 1974, he was selected to be Chief of the Astronaut Office, with responsibility for the coordination, scheduling, and control of activities of the astronauts. Young served as Chief of the Astronaut Office until May 1987. During his tenure, astronaut flight crews participated in the Apollo-Soyuz joint American-Russian docking mission, the Space Shuttle Orbiter Approach and Landing Test Program, and 25 Space Shuttle missions. From May 1987 to February 1996, Young served as Special Assistant to the Director of JSC for Engineering, Operations, and Safety. In that position, he had direct access to the Center Director and other senior managers in defining and resolving issues affecting the continued safe operation of the Space Shuttle. Additionally, he assisted the Center Director in providing advice and counsel on engineering, operational, and safety matters related to the Space Station, Shuttle upgrades, and advanced human Space Exploration Programs. In February 1996 Young was assigned as Associate Director (Technical). He is responsible for technical, operational and safety oversight of all Agency Programs and activities assigned to the Johnson Space Center. As an active astronaut, Young remains eligible to command future Shuttle astronaut crews.

NAME: George D. Zamka (Major, USMC)
NASA Astronaut (Pilot Candidate)

PERSONAL DATA: Born June 29, 1962 in Jersey City, New Jersey, but considers Rochester, Michigan to be his hometown. Married to the former Elisa P. Walker of Raymond, Mississippi. They have one child. Recreational interests include weight lifting, running, bicycling, scuba and boating. His mother, Sofia Zamka, resides in Lake Mary, Florida. His father, Conrad Zamka resides in Indianapolis, Indiana.

EDUCATION: Graduated from Rochester Adams High School, Rochester Michigan, in 1980; received a Bachelor of Science degree in Mathematics from the United States Naval Academy in 1984; received a Masters of Science degree in Engineering Management from the Florida Institute of Technology in 1997.

ORGANIZATIONS: United States Naval Academy Alumni Association, Marine Corps Association, and Society of Experimental Test Pilots.

SPECIAL HONORS: Navy Strike Air Medal (6), Navy Commendation Medal with Combat V, and various other military service and campaign awards. Distinguished Graduate, United States Naval Academy. Commodore's list and Academic Achievement Award, Training Air Wing Five.

EXPERIENCE: Zamka was commissioned as a Second Lieutenant in the United States Marine Corps following graduation from the United States Naval Academy in May 1984. He graduated from the Marine Corps Basic School in December 1984. Upon completion of Naval Aviator training he reported to Navy Attack Squadron VA-128 for initial A-6 training in August of 1987. He then reported to Marine All Weather Attack Squadron VMA(AW)-242 in El Toro, California. While assigned to VMA(AW)-242, Zamka made an overseas deployment to Japan, Korea, and the Philippines. He attended the Marine Aviation Warfare and Tactics Instructor Course and was assigned as the Squadron Weapons and Tactics Instructor. In 1990, he was selected for and completed F/A-18 conversion training and was assigned to Marine All Weather Fighter Attack Squadron VMFA(AW)-121, also in El Toro, California. He flew the F/A-18D Night Attack Hornet during overseas deployments to Japan, Korea, Singapore, and Southwest Asia. Zamka flew 66 combat missions over occupied Kuwait and Iraq during Desert Storm. In 1993 he served as a forward air controller with First Battalion, Fifth

Marines in Camp Pendleton, California and the 31st Marine Expeditionary Unit (Special Operations Capable) aboard USS Belleau Wood in the Western Pacific. He was selected to attend the United States Air Force Test Pilot School class 94A and graduated in December 1994. Zamka was then assigned as an F/A-18 test pilot/project officer and the F/A-18 Operations Officer for the Naval Strike Aircraft Test Squadron (NSATS). While assigned to NSATS, Zamka flew a wide variety of tests in the F/A-18 Hornet to include high angle of attack, loads, flutter, and weapon system programs. Major Zamka returned to VMFA(AW)-121 in 1998 and was serving as the Aircraft Maintenance Officer, deployed to Iwakuni, Japan when selected for the astronaut program. He has logged over 2700 flight hours in more than 30 different aircraft.

NASA EXPERIENCE: Selected by NASA in June 1998, he reported for training in August 1998. Astronaut Candidate Training includes orientation briefings and tours, numerous scientific and technical briefings, intensive instruction in Shuttle and International Space Station systems, physiological training and ground school to prepare for T-38 flight training, as well as learning water and wilderness survival techniques. Zamka is currently assigned to the Astronaut Office Shuttle Operations Branch. He will serve in technical assignments until assigned to a space flight.

Chapter Three:

Former

NASA

Astronauts

NAME: James C. Adamson (Colonel, U.S. Army, Ret.)
NASA Astronaut (former)

PERSONAL DATA: Born March 3, 1946, in Warsaw, New York. Since 1969, his permanent residence has been Monarch, Montana. Adamson enjoys many outdoor sports: hunting, fishing, snow skiing, long distance running, and camping. He is an accomplished woodworker and a master machinist and gunsmith.

EDUCATION: Adamson completed his Bachelor of Science in Engineering and was commissioned a Second Lieutenant in the Army at West Point in 1969. In 1977 he completed a Master of Science degree in Aerospace Engineering at Princeton University. Additionally he has completed undergraduate and graduate pilot training, paratrooper training, arctic water and mountain survival training, Nuclear weapons training, basic and advanced officer training, Command and General Staff School, and the U. S. Navy Test Pilot School.

SPECIAL HONORS: He was a two time All American in pistol competition, winner of the Army's Excellency In Competition Award, and recipient of the George S. Patton award. Named an Outstanding College Athlete of America, Adamson captained West Point's pistol team to the national championship in 1969. He was distinguished graduate of his pilot training class as well as distinguished graduate of both his graduate fixed wing and multi-engine pilot training classes. During aerial combat in Southeast Asia he earned 2 Distinguished Flying Crosses, 18 air medals, and 3 Vietnamese Crosses of Gallantry for valor. He also has earned his Nation's Defense Superior Service Medal, Defense Meritorious Service Medal, The Army's Meritorious Service Medal, Two Army Commendation Medals, the Bronze Star, NASA's Exceptional Service Medal, 2 NASA Space Flight Medals, and is a world record holder for space flight lifting the most weight to orbit.

MILITARY EXPERIENCE: As a military test pilot, Adamson has flown research aircraft at Edwards Air Force Base, Princeton University, West Point, Patuxent Naval Air Station, and NASA Houston. He has logged over 3,000 hours of flight time in over 30 types of helicopters, piston props, turbo props, and turbo jet aircraft. During Vietnam, he flew in the IV Corps area and Cambodia with the Air Cavalry as Scout Pilot, Team Lead, and Air Mission Commander. He has also flown with several peacetime flight units at Fort Bliss, Texas, West Point, New York, and Houston, Texas. Following completion of his Masters Degree in Aerospace Engineering at Princeton University, he became Assistant Professor of Aerodynamics at the United States Military Academy at West Point. While at West Point, he developed and taught courses in Fluid Mechanics, Aerodynamics, Aircraft Performance, and Stability and Control. He also developed flight laboratories in aircraft flight testing and completed a text on aircraft performance. In addition to being an Experimental Test Pilot and Master Aviator, Adamson is also a Certified Professional Engineer and licensed Commercial Pilot. In ground assignments with the Army, Adamson has commanded nuclear capable missile units in Europe and in the United States.

NASA EXPERIENCE: Adamson was employed at the Lyndon B. Johnson Space Center from 1981 to 1992. During the Operational Flight Test phase of the Shuttle Program, he served as a research test pilot and aerodynamics officer in Mission Control. Following completion of the operational test flights he became Guidance Navigation and Control Officer for Shuttle Missions 5 through 11. As research test pilot he also conducted airborne remote sensing studies in Biospheric Research. Selected by NASA as an Astronaut in 1984, Adamson became qualified for mission assignment on Space Shuttle flights. In November 1985, he was selected to the crew of a Department of Defense mission, which was subsequently delayed due to the Challenger Accident. During the Shuttle Program reconstruction period Adamson was one of eleven astronauts selected to hold management positions within NASA. He served as Shuttle Program Office Assistant Manager for Engineering Integration. In this position he was responsible for the initial development of a reliability based maintenance program for the Space Shuttle program. He also initiated an enhancements program for Shuttle ground processing. In February 1988 Adamson was assigned to the flight crew of STS-28, the first flight of Columbia following the reconstruction period. Columbia launched from the Kennedy Space Center, Florida, on August 8, 1989. The mission carried a classified Department of Defense payload and a number of secondary payloads. After 80 earth orbits in 121 hours, this five day mission concluded with a dry lakebed landing on runway 17 at Edwards Air Force Base, California, on August 13, 1989. Following STS-28 Adamson once again returned to management. This time he was assigned to the Kennedy Space Center as Director of Shuttle Processing Analysis. He served in this post from September 1989 until October 1990 when he was assigned to the flight crew of STS-43. During this period Adamson developed risk based processing and scheduling programs which resulted in reduction of processing times from 80 days to 50 days. The nine day STS-43 mission aboard Atlantis launched from the Kennedy Space Center on August 2, 1991 setting a new world record for payload weight lifted to orbit. The five member crew deployed a Tracking and Data Relay Satellite (TDRS-E), and conducted 32 physical and life sciences experiments. During this flight Adamson performed the first flight test of the Orbital Digital Autopilot following Shuttle retrofit with new General Purpose Computers and new software. After 142 earth orbits in 213 hours, the STS-43 mission concluded with a landing on runway 15 at the Kennedy Space Center on August 11, 1991. Following Adamson's retirement from government service in June 1992 he continued as a management consultant to NASA and the aerospace industry. Until September of 1994 he served as management consultant and strategic planner for Lockheed Corporation in the area of Human Space Flight Operations. He was also selected by the NASA Administrator to serve on the NASA Advisory Council. In September 1994 Adamson joined Lockheed Corporation as Executive Vice President of Lockheed Engineering and Science company (LESC) where, for several months, he also doubled as Program Manager of the Engineering Test and Analysis Program at the Johnson Space Center. In May 1995 Adamson was appointed President and CEO of LESC. Following completion of the Lockheed-Martin Marietta merger he will assume the role of Group Vice President and General Manager of the newly formed Lockheed Martin Engineering and Sciences product line. LMES is a mid to high tech engineering services business serving primarily NASA and other civil agencies of the U. S. Government. A veteran of two space flight missions, Adamson has logged over 334 hours in space.

PUBLICATIONS:
1. "Synthesis of BIS-2-(1,3-Diphenylimidazolidinylidene)", West Point, 1969
2. "A Helicopter Simulator Study of Control Display Tradeoffs in a Deceleration Approach", Article to the American Helicopter Society Journal, 1976.
3. Fundamentals of Applied Aerodynamics, Text rewrite, West Point, 1978.
4. Principles of Aircraft Performance, Text for USMA Dept. of Mechanics, 1979.
5. T41-B Aircrew Training Manual, West Point, 1979.
6. "The USMA Flight Laboratory Program", Paper to ASEE, 1980.
7. "A Simulator Study of Control and Display Tradeoffs in a Decelerating Approach", Adamson, Born, Dukes, MAE Tech. Rpt. No. 1428, Princeton NJ, 1976.

8."A Helicopter Simulator Study of Control Display Tradeoffs in a Decelerating Approach", Masters Thesis, Princeton NJ, 1976.

9."Dynamic Methods for Performance Flight Testing", Paper to the U.S. Navy Test Pilot School, Patuxent River MD, 1981.

10."An Analysis of The Projected Manpower Requirements for the Shuttle Processing Contract", NASA Report JSC-22662, 1988.

11.NASA Response to the Presidential Commission on the Challenger Accident, contributing author, Houston, 1986.

NAME: Tom Akers (Colonel, USAF, Ret.)
NASA Astronaut (former)

PERSONAL DATA: Born May 20, 1951, in St. Louis, Missouri, but raised and educated in his hometown of Eminence, Missouri. Married to the former Kaye Lynn Parker of Eminence, Missouri. They have two grown children. Tom enjoys hunting, fishing, restoring automobiles, and spending time with his family. His parents, Walter and Arlie Akers, are both deceased.

EDUCATION: Graduated from Eminence High School, Eminence, Missouri, in 1969; received bachelor and master of science degrees in applied mathematics from the University of Missouri-Rolla in 1973 and 1975, respectively.

SPECIAL HONORS: High School Valedictorian. Graduated Summa Cum Laude with a class rank of #1 from University of Missouri-Rolla. Named a Distinguished Graduate of USAF Officer Training School, Squadron Officers School, and Test Pilot School. Recipient of the Department of Defense Superior Service Medal with two oak leaf clusters; Legion of Merit Award; Department of Defense Meritorious Service Medal; USAF Meritorious Service Medal; USAF Commendation Medal; USAF Achievement Medal; NASA Distinguished Service Medal; two NASA Exceptional Service Medals; four NASA Space Flight Medals. Awarded an honorary Doctorate of Engineering from the University of Missouri-Rolla in 1992.

EXPERIENCE: Akers was a National Park Ranger at Alley Springs, Missouri, during the summer seasons from 1972 through 1976. After graduating from the University of Missouri-Rolla in 1975, he spent four years as the high school principal in his hometown of Eminence. Joining the Air Force in 1979, his first assignment after Officer Training School was to Eglin Air Force Base, Florida, as an air-to-air missile data analyst where he also taught night classes in Math and Physics for Troy State University. In 1982 he was selected to attend the Air Force Test Pilot School at Edwards Air Force Base, California. On completing one year of training as a flight test engineer, in 1983 he was reassigned to Eglin Air Force Base, where he worked on a variety of weapons development programs, flying F-4, F-15, and T-38 aircraft until he was selected for the astronaut program. He has logged over 2,500 hours flying time in 25 different types of aircraft.

NASA EXPERIENCE: Akers was selected for the astronaut program in 1987. Positions held since then include: Astronaut Office focal point for Space Shuttle software development; astronaut representative during Shuttle software testing in the Shuttle Avionics Integration Laboratory (SAIL); supported launch activities at the Kennedy Space Center; astronaut representative for EVA activities (space walks); Deputy Director of Mission Operations; Acting Deputy Director of Flight Crew Operations, and Assistant Director (Technical) of Johnson Space Center. Akers left the astronaut program and NASA in August of 1997 to return to the USAF as the commander of the USAFROTC Detachment 442 at the University of Missouri-Rolla. Akers retired from the Air Force in October of 1999 and accepted a position as an instructor in the Math Department at the University of Missouri-Rolla.

SPACE FLIGHT EXPERIENCE: A veteran of four space flights (STS-41 in 1990, STS-49 in 1992, STS-61 in 1993, STS-79 in 1996), Akers has accumulated over 800 hours of space flight including over 29 hours of space walking experience.

On STS-41, October 6-10, 1990, he was responsible for the mission's primary payload, the Ulysses spacecraft. The STS-41 crew successfully deployed the interplanetary probe and started it on its four-year journey via Jupiter to investigate the polar regions of the Sun.

STS-49, May 7-16, 1992, was the maiden flight of the new Space Shuttle Endeavour. The STS-49 crew successfully completed four EVA's (space walks), three rendezvous, and a variety of secondary objectives. Akers was one of a three-member EVA team who successfully captured the stranded INTELSAT (International Telecommunications Satellite). This was the first 3-person EVA and the longest EVA (8.5 hours) in history. Akers also performed a second EVA on this flight to evaluate Space Station Freedom construction techniques.

On STS-61, December 2-13, 1993, Akers again served as an EVA crew member. During the 11-day mission, the crew captured the Hubble Space Telescope and restored it to full capacity through a record five space walks by four astronauts. Akers performed two of these bringing his total EVA time to 29 hours and 40 minutes.

STS-79, September 16-26, 1996, was the fourth Shuttle mission to rendezvous with the Russian Space Station Mir. Akers was the flight engineer and responsible for the transfer of over 3.5 tons of supplies to and from the Mir. This mission also marked the first exchange of U.S. astronauts on Mir leaving John Blaha and returning Shannon Lucid home after her record six month stay in space.

NAME: Buzz Aldrin
      NASA Astronaut (former)

Buzz Aldrin was born in Montclair, New Jersey on January 20, 1930. His mother, Marion Moon, was the daughter of an Army Chaplain. His father, Edwin Eugene Aldrin, was an aviation pioneer, a student of rocket developer Robert Goddard, and an aide to the immortal General Billy Mitchell. Buzz was educated at West Point, graduating with honors in 1951, third in his class. After receiving his wings, he flew Sabre Jets in 66 combat missions in the Korean Conflict, shooting down two MIG-15's. Returning to his education, he earned a Doctorate in Astronautics from the Massachusetts Institute of Technology in Manned Space Rendezvous. The techniques he devised were used on all NASA missions, including the first space docking with the Russian Cosmonauts.

In October 1963, Buzz was selected by NASA as one of the early astronauts. In November 1966, he established a new record for Extra-Vehicular Activity in space on the Gemini XII orbital flight mission. Buzz has logged 4500 hours of flying time, 290 of which were in space, including 8 hours of EVA. As Backup Command Module Pilot for Apollo VIII, man's first flight around the moon, he significantly improved operational techniques for astronautical navigation star display. Then, on July 20, 1969, Buzz and Neil Armstrong made their historic Apollo XI moon walk, thus becoming the first two humans to set foot on another world. This unprecedented heroic endeavor was witnessed by the largest worldwide television audience in history.

Upon returning from the moon, Buzz embarked on an international goodwill tour. He was presented the Presidential Medal of Freedom, the highest honor amongst over 50 other distinguished awards and medals from the United States and numerous other countries.

Since retiring from NASA, the Air Force, and his position as Commander of the Test Pilot School at Edwards Air Force Base, Dr. Aldrin has remained at the forefront of efforts to ensure a continued leading role for America in manned space exploration. To advance his lifelong commitment to venturing outward in space, he has created a master plan of evolving missions for sustained exploration utilizing his concept, "The Cycler", a spacecraft system which makes perpetual orbits between Earth and Mars. In 1993 Dr. Aldrin received a U.S. patent for a permanent space station he designed. More recently he founded his rocket design company, Starcraft Boosters, Inc., and the Share Space Foundation, a nonprofit devoted to opening the doors to space tourism for all people.

Dr. Aldrin has continued to share his vision for the future of space travel by authoring two space novels that dramatically portray man's discovery of the ultimate frontier: The Return (Forge Books, 2000) and Encounter with Tiber (Warner Books, 1996). He has also authored an autobiography, Return to Earth and a historical documentary, Men from Earth, describing his trip to the moon and his unique perspective on America's space program.

On Valentine's Day 1988, Buzz married Lois Driggs Cannon of Phoenix, Arizona. She is a Stanford graduate, an active community leader in Southern California, and personal manager of all of Buzz's endeavors. Their combined family is comprised of six grown children and one grandson. Their leisure time is spent exploring the deep sea world of scuba diving and skiing the mountain tops of Sun Valley, Idaho.

Now Buzz, as Starcraft Enterprises; the name of his private space endeavors ; is lecturing and traveling throughout the world to pursue and discuss his and others' latest concepts and ideas for exploring the universe. He is a leading voice in charting the course of future space efforts from planet Earth.

NAME: Andrew M. Allen (Lieutenant Colonel, USMC)
NASA Astronaut (former)

PERSONAL DATA: Born August 4, 1955, in Philadelphia, Pennsylvania. Two children. Enjoys wood-working, racquetball, weight lifting, and bicycling. His father, Charles A. Allen, resides in Richboro, Pennsylvania. His mother, Loretta T. Allen, is deceased.

EDUCATION: Graduated from Archbishop Wood High School, Warminster, Pennsylvania, in 1973; received a bachelor of science degree in mechanical engineering from Villanova University in 1977.

ORGANIZATIONS: Society of Experimental Test Pilots, Association of Space Explorers.

SPECIAL HONORS: Defense Superior Service Medal; Distinguished Flying Cross; Defense Meritorious Service Medal; Single Mission Air Medal; NASA Outstanding Leadership Medal; NASA Exceptional Service Medal; NASA Space Flight Medal; Honorary Doctorate of Public Service from Bucks County Community College (1993); Honorary Doctorate of Engineering Science from Villanova University (1997).

EXPERIENCE: Allen was a member of the Navy ROTC unit and received his commission in the United States Marine Corps at Villanova University in 1977. Following graduation from flight school, he flew F-4 Phantoms from 1980 to 1983 with VMFA-312 at Marine Corps Air Station (MCAS) Beaufort, South Carolina, and was assigned as the Aircraft Maintenance Officer. He was selected by Headquarters Marine Corps for fleet introduction of the F/A-18 Hornet, and was assigned to VMFA-531 in MCAS El Toro, California, from 1983 to 1986. During his stay in VMFA-531, he was assigned as the squadron Operations Officer, and also attended and graduated from the Marine Weapons & Tactics Instructor Course, and the Naval Fighter Weapons School (Top Gun). A 1987 graduate of the United States Navy Test Pilot School at Patuxent River, Maryland, he was a test pilot under instruction when advised of his selection to the astronaut program. He has logged over 6,000 flight hours in more than 30 different aircraft.

NASA EXPERIENCE: Selected by NASA in June 1987, Allen became an astronaut in August 1988. His technical assignments have included: Astronaut Office representative for all Space Shuttle issues related to landing sites, landing and deceleration hardware, including improvements to nosewheel steering, brakes and tires, and drag chute design; Shuttle Avionics Integration Laboratory (SAIL), which oversees, checks, and verifies all Shuttle flight control software and avionics programs; Technical Assistant to the Flight Crew Operations Director who is responsible for and manages all flight crew operations and support; lead of the Astronaut Support Personnel team which oversee Shuttle test, checkout, and preparation at Kennedy Space Center; Special Assistant to the Director of the Johnson Space Center in Houston, Texas; lead of a Functional Workforce Review at the Kennedy Space Center, Florida, to determine minimal workforce and management structure requirements which allow maximum budget reductions while safely continuing Shuttle Flight Operations; Director of Space Station Requirements at NASA Headquarters, responsible for the International Space Station requirements, policies, external communications and liaison with Congress, international partners, and industry. A veteran of three space flights, Allen has logged over 900 hours in space. He was the pilot on STS-46 in 1992 and STS-62 in 1994, and was mission commander on STS-75 in 1996. Allen retired from the Marine Corps and left NASA in October 1997. He currently serves as President of the FIRST Foundation. The FIRST (For Inspiration and Recognition of Science and Technology) Foundation, based out of Manchester, New Hampshire, promotes youth interest in science and technology.

SPACE FLIGHT EXPERIENCE: STS-46 was an 8-day mission aboard Space Shuttle Atlantis which featured the deployment of the European Retrievable Carrier (EURECA), an ESA-sponsored free-flying science platform, and demonstrated the Tethered Satellite System (TSS), a joint project between NASA and the Italian Space Agency. STS-46 launched July 31, 1992, and landed at the Kennedy Space Center, Florida, on August 8, 1992. The flight completed 126 orbits covering 3.3 million miles in 191.3 hours. STS-62, a 14-day mission aboard Space Shuttle Columbia consisted of 5 crew members who conducted a broad range of science and technology experiments with Earth applications to materials processing, biotechnology, advanced technology, and environmental monitoring. Principal payloads of the mission were the United States Microgravity Payload 2 (USMP-2) and the Office of Aeronautics and Space Technology 2 (OAST-2) package. STS-62 launched March 4, 1994 and landed at the Kennedy Space Center, Florida, on March 18, 1994. The flight completed 224 orbits covering 5.8 million miles in 335.3 hours. STS-75 (February 22 to March 9, 1996), was a 15-day mission with principal payloads being the reflight of the Tethered Satellite System (TSS) and the third flight of the United States Microgravity Payload (USMP-3). The TSS successfully demonstrated the ability of tethers to produce electricity. The TSS experiment produced a wealth of new information on the electrodynamics of tethers and plasma physics before the tether broke at 19.7 km, just shy of the 20.7 km goal. The crew also worked around the clock performing combustion experiments and research related to USMP-3 microgravity investigations used to improve production of medicines, metal alloys, and semiconductors. The mission was completed in 252 orbits covering 6.5 million miles in 377 hours and 40 minutes.

NAME: Joseph P. Allen (Ph.D.)
NASA Astronaut (former)

PERSONAL DATA: Born in Crawfordsville, Indiana, on June 27, 1937. Married to the former Bonnie Jo Darling of Elkhart, Indiana. They have a son and a daughter. Recreational interests include handball, squash, flying, sailing, skiing, music, and photography. His parents, Mr. and Mrs. Joseph P. Allen III, reside in Frankfort, Indiana. Her mother, Mrs. W. C. Darling, resides in Elkhart, Indiana.

EDUCATION: Attended Mills School and is a graduate of Crawfordsville High School in Indiana; received a bachelor of arts degree in math-physics from DePauw University in 1959, and a master of science degree and a doctor of philosophy degree in physics from Yale University in 1961 and 1965, respectively.

ORGANIZATIONS: Member of the American Physical Society, the American Astronautical Society, the American Institute of Aeronautics and Astronautics, the American Association for the Advancement of Science, Phi Beta Kappa, Beta Theta Pi, Sigma Xi, and Phi Eta Sigma.

SPECIAL HONORS: Winner of a Fulbright Scholarship to Germany (1959-1960), the Outstanding Flying Award, Class 69-06, Vance Air Force Base (1969), two NASA Group Achievement Awards (1971 and 1974) in recognition of contributions to the Apollo 15 Lunar Traverse Planning Team and for subsequent work on the Outlook for Space Study Team; presented the 1972 Yale Science and Engineering Association Award for Advancement of Basic and Applied Science, the DePauw University Distinguished Alumnus Award (1972), a NASA Exceptional Scientific Achievement Medal (1973), a NASA exceptional Service Medal (1978), and a NASA Superior Performance Award (1975 and 1981), and honorary doctor of science from DePauw University (1983), and the Komarov Diploma from the Federation Aeronautique Internationale.

EXPERIENCE: Allen was a research associate in the Nuclear Physics Laboratory at the University of Washington prior to his selection as an astronaut. He was a staff physicist at the Nuclear Structure Laboratory at Yale University in 1965 and 1966, and during the period 1963 to 1967, served as a guest research associate at the Brookhaven National Laboratory. He has logged more than 3,000 hours flying time in jet aircraft.

NASA EXPERIENCE: Dr. Allen was selected as a scientist-astronaut by NASA in August 1967. He completed flight training at Vance Air Force Base, Oklahoma. He served as mission scientist while a member of the astronaut support crew for Apollo 15 and served as a staff consultant on science and technology to the President's Council on International Economic Policy. From August 1975 to 1978, Dr. Allen served as NASA Assistant Administrator for Legislative Affairs in Washington, D.C. Returning to the Johnson Space Center in 1978, as a senior scientist astronaut, Dr. Allen was assigned to the Operations Mission Development Group. He served as a support crew member for the first orbital flight test of the Space Transportation System and was the entry CAPCOM for this mission. In addition, in 1980 and 1981, he worked as the technical assistant to the director of flight operations. He was a mission specialist on STS-5 (November 11-16, 1982) and STS-51A (November 8-16,1984) and has logged a total of 314 hours in space. He left NASA in 1985. Dr. Allen is currently Chief Executive Officer of Space Industries International, Inc., 800 Connecticut Avenue, N.W., Suite 1111, Washington, D.C. 20006.

SPACE FLIGHT EXPERIENCE: STS-5 was the first fully operational flight of the Shuttle Transportation System, which launched from Kennedy Space Center, Florida, on November 11, 1982. The crew aboard Columbia included Vance D. Brand (spacecraft commander), Col. Robert F. Overmyer (pilot), and Dr. William B. Lenoir (mission specialist). STS-5, the first mission with a crew of four, clearly demonstrated the Space Shuttle as fully operational by the successful first deployment of two commercial communications satellites from the Orbiter's payload bay. The mission also marked the first use of the Payload Assist Module (PAM-D), and its new ejection system. Numerous flight tests were performed throughout the mission to document Shuttle performance during launch, boost, orbit, atmospheric entry and landing phases. STS-5 was the last flight to carry the Development Flight Instrumentation (DFI) package to support flight testing. A Getaway Special, three Student Involvement Projects, and medical experiments were included on the mission. The crew successfully concluded the 5-day orbital flight of Columbia with the first entry and landing through a cloud deck to a hard-surface runway and demonstrated maximum braking. STS-5 completed 81 orbits of the Earth in 122 hours before landing on a concrete runway at Edwards Air Force Base, California, on November 16, 1982. STS-51A Discovery , which launched from Kennedy Space Center, Florida, on November 8, 1984. The crew aboard Discovery included Captain Frederick (Rick) Hauck (spacecraft commander), Captain David M. Walker (pilot), and fellow mission specialists, Dr. Anna L. Fisher and Commander Dale H. Gardner. This was the second flight of Space Shuttle Discovery. During the mission the crew deployed two satellites, Canada's Anik D-2 (Telsat H) and Hughes' LEASAT-1 (Syncome IV-1), and operated the 3M Company's Diffusive Mixing of Organic Solutions experiment. In the first space salvage attempt in history the crew successfully retrieved for return to Earth the Palapa B-2 and Westar VI communications satellites. STS-51A completed 127 orbits of the Earth in 192 hours before landing at Kennedy Space Center, Florida, on November 16, 1984.

NAME: William A. Anders (Major General, USAF Reserve)
NASA Astronaut (former)

PERSONAL DATA: Born October 17, 1933, in Hong Kong; his parents, Commander (USN Retired) and Mrs. Arthur F. Anders, now reside in La Mesa, California.

PHYSICAL DESCRIPTION: Brown hair; blue eyes; height: 5 feet 8 inches; weight: 155 pounds.

EDUCATION: Received a Bachelor of Science degree from the United States Naval Academy in 1955 and a Master of Science degree in Nuclear Engineering from the Air Force Institute of Technology at Wright-Patterson Air Force Base, Ohio, in 1962. Completed the Harvard Business School Advanced Management Program in 1979.

MARITAL STATUS: Married to the former Valerie E. Hoard of Lemon Grove, California, daughter of Mr. and Mrs. Henry G. Hoard, of Oceanside, California.

CHILDREN: Alan, February 1957; Glen, July 1958; Gayle, December 1960; Gregory, December 1962; Eric, July 1964; Diana, August 1972.

RECREATIONAL INTERESTS: Hobbies are fishing, flying, camping, water and cross-country skiing, and he also enjoys soccer.

ORGANIZATIONS: Member of Tau Beta Pi National Engineering Honor Society, American Nuclear Society, American Institute of Aeronautics and Astronautics, Society of Experimental Test Pilots, and other professional organizations.

SPECIAL HONORS: Distinguished Service Medals from the Air Force, NASA and the Nuclear Regulatory Commission; Air Force Commendation Medal; National Geographic Society's Hubbard Medal for Exploration; Collier, Harmon, Goddard and White Trophies; and the American Astronautical Society's Flight Achievement Award. He has been awarded several honorary doctoral degrees.

EXPERIENCE: Anders was commissioned in the Air Force after graduation from the Naval Academy and served as a fighter pilot in all-weather interception squadrons of the Air Defense Command and later was responsible for technical management of nuclear power reactor shielding and radiation effects programs while at the Air Force Weapons Laboratory in New Mexico.

NASA EXPERIENCE: In 1964, Anders was selected by the National Aeronautics and Space Administration as an astronaut with responsibilities for dosimetry, radiation effects and environmental controls. He was backup pilot for the Gemini XI and Apollo 11 flights, and was "lunar module" pilot for Apollo 8, the first lunar orbit mission in December 1968. He has logged more than 5,000 hours flying time. From June 1969 to 1973 he served as Executive Secretary for the National Aeronautics and Space Council, which was responsible to the President, Vice President and Cabinet-level members of the Council for developing policy options concerning research, development, operations and planning of aeronautical and space systems. On August 6, 1973, Anders was appointed to the five-member Atomic Energy Commission where he was lead commissioner for all nuclear and non-nuclear power Research and Development. He was also named as US Chairman of the joint US/USSR technology exchange program for nuclear fission and fusion power. Following the reorganization of national nuclear regulatory and developmental activities on January19, 1975, Anders was named by President Ford to become the first Chairman of the newly established Nuclear Regulatory Commission (NRC) responsible for nuclear safety and environmental compatibility. At the completion of his term as NRC Chairman, Anders was appointed US Ambassador to Norway and held that position until 1977. Anders left the federal government after 26 years of service and after briefly serving as a Fellow of the American Enterprise Institute he joined the General Electric Company in September 1977 as Vice President and General Manager of the Nuclear Products Division in San Jose, CA. In this position he was responsible for the manufacture of nuclear fuel, reactor internal equipment, and control and instrumentation for GE boilingwater reactors at facilities in San Jose and Wilmington, NC. In addition, he had responsibility for the GE partnership arrangement with Chicago Bridge and Iron for the manufacture of large steel pressure vessels in Memphis, TN. In August 1979, Anders was placed on special assignment to attend the Harvard Business School's Advanced Management Program

CURRENT ASSIGNMENT: On January 1, 1980, Anders was appointed General Manager of the General Electric Aircraft Equipment Division with headquarters in Utica, NY. With more than 8500 employees in five plant locations in the Northeastern US, the Aircraft Equipment Division products include aircraft flight and weapon control systems, cockpit instruments, aircraft electrical generating systems, airborne radars and data processing systems, electronic countermeasures, space command systems, and aircraft/surface multibarrel armament systems. He is also a consultant to the Office of Science and Technology Policy; a member of the Defense Science Board and the NASA Advisory Council; a Major General in the USAF Reserve assigned to the office of the Deputy Chief of Staff for Research and Development in the Pentagon; and a Director of the Congressional Awards Program.

NAME: Jay Apt (Ph.D.)
NASA Astronaut (former)

PERSONAL DATA: Born April 28, 1949, in Springfield, Massachusetts, but considers Pittsburgh, Pennsylvania, to be his hometown. Married to the former Eleanor B. Emmons. They have two daughters. He enjoys flying, scuba diving, camping, photography, model rocketry, and amateur radio.

EDUCATION: Received a bachelor of arts degree in physics (magna cum laude) from Harvard College in 1971, and a doctorate in physics from the Massachusetts Institute of Technology (MIT) in 1976.

ORGANIZATIONS: Member of the American Astronomical Society (Division of Planetary Science), the American Geophysical Union, the American Physical Society, Sigma Xi, and the American Association for the Advancement of Science.

SPECIAL HONORS: Recipient of NASA Distinguished Service Medal, two NASA Exceptional Service Medals, four NASA Space Flight Medals, the Sergei P. Korolev Diploma of the Federation Aeronautique Internationale, two Komarov Diplomas of the FAI, and three NASA Group Achievement Awards. Winner of First and Second Prizes in the 1996 Aviation Week & Space Technology Magazine Space Photography Contest.

PUBLICATIONS: Dr. Apt shared his images and knowledge in the publication Earth in Orbit: NASA Astronauts Photograph the Earth, written in conjunction with NASA scientists Michael Helfert and Justin Wilkinson and published by the National Geographic Society. Results of Dr. Apt;s research in physics and planetary science have been published in over 20 papers in professional journals.

EXPERIENCE: In 1976, Dr. Apt was a post-doctoral fellow in laser spectroscopy at MIT. From 1976 to 1980 he was a staff member of the Center for Earth & Planetary Physics, Harvard University, supporting NASA's Pioneer Venus Mission by making temperature maps of Venus from Mt. Hopkins Observatory. Dr. Apt served as the Assistant Director of Harvard's Division of Applied Sciences from 1978 to 1980.

NASA EXPERIENCE: In 1980 Dr. Apt joined the Earth and Space Sciences Division of NASA's Jet Propulsion Laboratory (JPL), doing planetary research, studying Venus, Mars, and the outer solar system. In 1981 he became Director of JPL's Table Mountain Observatory. From 1982 through 1985, he was a flight controller responsible for Shuttle payload operations at NASA's Johnson Space Center. Dr. Apt is an instrument-rated commercial pilot, and has logged over 4,000 hours flying time in approximately 25 different types of airplanes, seaplanes, sailplanes, and human-powered aircraft. He was selected as an astronaut candidate by NASA in June 1985, and qualified as an astronaut in July 1986. His assignments to date have included Shuttle Orbiter modification support at Kennedy Space Center, developing techniques for servicing the Hubble Space Telescope and the Gamma Ray Observatory, development of EVA (space walk) construction and maintenance techniques for Space Station, as a spacecraft communicator (CAPCOM) for Shuttle flights, the voice link between the flight crew and the Mission Control Center (MCC), and the Astronaut Office EVA point of contact. He has also been the supervisor of Astronaut Training in the Astronaut Office, and has served as Chief of the Astronaut Office Mission Support Branch. Apt flew as a member of the crew of the space Shuttle Atlantis on the STS-37 mission, which launched from Kennedy Space Center, Florida, on April 5, 1991. During the mission, the crew deployed the Gamma Ray Observatory to study the universe by observing the most energetic form of radiation. Apt and crew mate Jerry Ross performed an unscheduled space walk during which they manually deployed the observatory's large radio antenna when remotely controlled motors failed to do so. On the next day, they conducted the first scheduled space walk in 5-1/2 years. They tested concepts for getting around on large space structures, and gathered basic engineering data on the forces a crew member can exert on bolts and equipment. The crew alsoconducted research on biologically important molecules, tested concepts for radiating heat from Space Station, operated an amateur radio station, and took over 4000 photographs of the Earth. After completing 93 orbits of the Earth, the crew landed Atlantis at Edwards Air Force Base, California, on April 11, 1991. Dr. Apt was Endeavour's flight engineer on the crew of STS-47, Spacelab-J. This eight-day cooperative mission between the United States and Japan was launched on September 12, 1992, to perform life science and materials processing experiments in space. Dr. Apt was responsible for operating the Orbiter during one of the two shifts on this dual shift mission. After completing 126 orbits of the Earth, the crew landed Endeavour at Kennedy Space Center, Florida, on September 20, 1992. He flew again aboard Endeavour on STS-59, the first flight of the Space Radar Laboratory, from April 9-20, 1994. As the blue shift commander, he was responsible for operating Endeavour during one of the two shifts on an 11-day mission to observe the land surface and oceans of Earth with three imaging radar systems, and to map air pollution in the lower atmosphere. The crew flew Endeavour through the largest series of maneuvers in Shuttle history to point the radar precisely at hundreds of ecology, geology, and oceanography sites, providing research scientists the equivalent of 26,000 encyclopedia volumes of data. After completing 183 orbits of the Earth, the crew landed Endeavour at

Edwards Air Force Base, California. Most recently, he served aboard Atlantis during mission STS-79, September 16-26, 1996. The crew docked Atlantis with the Russian Mir space station, having ferried supplies, personnel, and scientific equipment to this base 240 miles above the Earth. The crew transferred over 4 tons of scientific experiments and supplies to and from the Mir station and exchanged U.S. astronauts on Mir for the first time; leaving John Blaha and bringing Shannon Lucid home after her record six months stay aboard Mir. This historic mission of international cooperation and scientific research ended at Kennedy Space Center, Florida, after 160 orbits of the Earth. With the completion of his fourth flight, Dr. Apt has logged over 847 hours (35 days) in space, including 10 hours and 49 minutes on two space walks. He has flown around the Earth 562 times.Dr. Apt will leave NASA in late May to become Director of the Carnegie Museum of Natural History in Pittsburgh, Pennsylvania.

NAME: Neil A. Armstrong
NASA Astronaut (former)

PERSONAL DATA: Born August 5, 1930, in Wapakoneta, Ohio Married with 2 sons.

EDUCATION: Bachelor of science degree in aeronautical engineering from Purdue University; master of science degree in aerospace engineering from University of Southern California. He holds an honorary doctorate from a number of universities.

NASA EXPERIENCE: Armstrong joined NACA, (National Advisory Committee for Aeronautics), NASA's predecessor, as a test pilot at Edwards Air Force Base, California. He was a project pilot on many pioneering high speed aircraft, including the 4,000 mph X-15. He has flown over 200 different models of aircraft, including jets, rockets, helicopters, and gliders. In 1962, Armstrong was transferred to astronaut status. He served as command pilot for the Gemini 8 mission, launched March 16, 1966, and performed the first successful docking of two vehicles in space. In 1969, Armstrong was commander of Apollo 11, the first manned lunar landing mission, and gained the distinction of being the first man to land a craft on the Moon and the first man to step on its surface. Armstrong subsequently held the position of Deputy Associate Administrator for Aeronautics, NASA Headquarters Office of Advanced Research and Technology, from 1970 to 1971, when he resigned from NASA.

EXPERIENCE: From 1949 to 1952, he served as a naval aviator; he flew 78 combat missions during the Korean War. During 1971-1979, Armstrong was professor of aerospace engineering at the University of Cincinnati, where he was involved in both teaching and research.

SPECIAL HONORS: He is the recipient of many special honors, including the Presidential Medal for Freedom in 1969; the Robert H. Goddard Memorial Trophy in 1970; the Robert J. Collier Trophy in 1969; and the Congressional Space Medal of Honor, 1978.

NAME: James P. Bagian (M.D., P.E.)
NASA Astronaut (former)

PERSONAL DATA: Born February 22, 1952, in Philadelphia, Pennsylvania. Married to the former Tandi M. Benson of Seattle, Washington. They have four children. He enjoys bicycling, backpacking, climbing, swimming, flying and racquet sports, as well as cabinet-making and automobile rebuilding. His parents, Philip and Rose Bagian, reside in Philadelphia, Pennsylvania. Her parents, Boyd and Barbara Benson, reside in Seattle, Washington.

EDUCATION: Graduated from Central High School in Philadelphia, Pennsylvania, in 1969; received a bachelor of science degree in mechanical engineering from Drexel University in 1973, and a doctorate in medicine from Thomas Jefferson University in 1977.

ORGANIZATIONS: Member of the Aerospace Medicine Association, the College of Emergency Physicians, the American Society of Mechanical Engineers; life member of the Society of NASA Flight Surgeons; and member of Phi Kappa Phi, Phi Eta Sigma, Pi Tau Sigma, Tau Beta Pi, and Alpha Omega Alpha.

SPECIAL HONORS: U.S. Army ROTC Superior Cadet Award (1970); graduated first in class from Drexel University (1973); Orthopedics Prize from Jefferson University (1977); Honor Graduate (first in class) from USAF Flight Surgeons School (1979); Federation Aeronautique Internationale (FAI) Komarov Diploma (1989); Sikorsky Helicopter Rescue Award (1990); NASA Achievement Award for developing treatment of space motion sickness (1991); NASA Space Flight Award (1989 and 1991); NASA Exceptional Service Medal (1992); Society of NASA Flight Surgeons W. Randolf Lovelace Award for "significant contribution to the practice and advancement of aerospace medicine" (1992); American Astronautical Society's Melbourne W. Boynton Award for "outstanding contributions to the biomedical aspects of space flight" (1992).

EXPERIENCE: Bagian worked as a process engineer for the 3M Company in Bristol, Pennsylvania, in 1973, and later as a mechanical +engineer at the U.S. Naval Air Test Center at Patuxent River, Maryland, from 1976 to 1978, and at the same time pursued studies for a doctorate in medicine. Upon graduating from Thomas Jefferson University in 1977, Dr. Bagian completed one year of general surgery residency with the Geisinger Medical Center in Danville, Pennsylvania. He subsequently went to work as a flight surgeon and research medical officer at the Lyndon B. Johnson Space Center in 1978, while concurrently completing studies at the USAF Flight Surgeons School and USAF School of Aerospace Medicine in San Antonio, Texas. He was completing a residency in anesthesiology at the University of Pennsylvania when notified of his selection by NASA for the astronaut candidate program. Dr. Bagian received his Professional Engineers Certification in 1986, and was board-certified in aerospace medicine by the American College of Preventive Medicine in 1987. Since 1981, Dr. Bagian has been active in the mountain rescue community and has served as a member of the Denali Medical Research Project on Mt. McKinley. He has also been a snow-and-ice rescue techniques instructor on Mt. Hood during this period. Dr. Bagian is a colonel in the U.S. Air Force Reserve and is the pararescue flight surgeon for the 939th Air Rescue Wing. He is a USAF-qualified freefall parachutist, holds a private pilot's license and has logged over 1,500 hours flying time in propeller and jet aircraft, helicopters, and gliders.

NASA EXPERIENCE: Bagian became a NASA astronaut in July 1980. He took part in both the planning and provision of emergency medical and rescue support for the first six Shuttle flights. He also served as the Astronaut Office coordinator for Space Shuttle payload software and crew equipment, as well as supporting the development of a variety of payloads and participating in the verification of Space Shuttle flight software. In 1986, Dr. Bagian served as an investigator for the 51-L accident board. He has also been responsible for the development program and implementation of the pressure suit used for crew escape and various other crew survival equipment to be used on future Shuttle missions, and is in charge of Shuttle search and rescue planning and implementation for the Astronaut Office. Dr. Bagian has also been a member of the NASA Headquarters Research Animal Holding Facility Review Board. He has authored numerous scientific papers in the fields of human factors, environmental and aerospace medicine. A veteran of two space flights (STS-29 in 1989 and STS-40 in 1991), Dr. Bagian has logged over 337 hours in space. Dr. Bagian first flew on the crew of STS-29, which launched from Kennedy Space Center, Florida, aboard the Orbiter Discovery, on March 13, 1989. During this highly successful five-day mission, the crew deployed a Tracking and Data Relay Satellite and performed numerous secondary experiments, including a Space Station "heat pipe" radiator experiment, two student experiments, a protein crystal growth experiment, and a chromosome and plant cell division experiment. Also, Dr. Bagian was the principal investigator and performed Detailed Supplementary Objective 470 which described, by the use of transcranial Doppler, the changes of cerebral blood flow and its relationship to Space Adaptation Syndrome (SAS) and Space Motion Sickness (SMS). Dr. Bagian was the first person to treat SMS with the drug Phenergan by intramuscular injection. This represented the first successful treatment regimen for SMS and has now been adopted by NASA as the standard of care for the control of SMS in Shuttle crews and is routinely used. In addition, the crew took over 3,000 photographs of the Earth using several types of cameras, including the IMAX 70 mm movie camera. Mission duration was 80 orbits and concluded with a landing at Edwards Air Force Base, California, on March 18, 1989. With the completion of this mission, he logged over 119 hours in space. More recently, Dr. Bagian served on the crew of STS-40 Spacelab Life Sciences (SLS-1), the first dedicated space and life sciences mission, which launched from the Kennedy Space Center, Florida, on June 5, 1991. SLS-1 was a nine-day mission during which crew members performed experiments which explored how the heart, blood vessels, lungs, kidneys, and hormone-secreting glands respond to microgravity, the causes of space sickness, and changes in muscles, bones, and cells which occur in humans during space flight. Other payloads included experiments designed to investigate materials science, plant biology and cosmic radiation. In addition to the scheduled payload activities on STS-40, Dr. Bagian was successful in personally devising and implementing repair procedures for malfunctioning experiment hardware which allowed all scheduled scientific objectives to be successfully accomplished. Following 146 orbits of the Earth, Columbia and her crew landed at Edwards Air Force Base, California, on June 14, 1991. Completion of this flight logged him an additional 218 hours in space.

Dr. Bagian is taking a leave of absence from NASA. He is currently involved in both the practice of occupational medicine and biomedical research.

Name: Alan Bean
NASA Astronaut (former)

Alan L. Bean walked on the moon during the Apollo 12 mission and commanded the second Skylab flight, spending 59 days aboard the orbiting laboratory.

Personal: He was born March 15, 1932, in Wheeler, Tex. He received a Bachelor of Science degree in aeronautical engineering from the University of Texas in 1955. At Texas he was a Navy ROTC student and was commissioned upon graduation.

Experience: After completing flight training, Bean was assigned to a jet attack squadron at the Naval Air Station in Jacksonville, Fla. After a four-year tour, he attended the Navy Test Pilot School and flew as a test pilot for several types of Navy aircraft.

NASA Experience: Alan Bean was one of 14 selected by NASA in the third group of astronauts in October 1963. He served as backup crewman for the Gemini 10 and Apollo 9 missions before assignment as Lunar Module pilot for Apollo 12. On November 19, 1969, Commander Pete Conrad and Bean landed on the Ocean of Storms and became the third and fourth humans to walk on the moon, while Richard Gordon orbited overhead in the Command Module. During two outside excursions they deployed several surface experiments and installed the first nuclear-powered generator station on the moon to provide the power source. They inspected an unmanned Surveyor spacecraft that landed there two years earlier and collected 60 pounds of rocks and lunar soil for scientists to study back on Earth. On July 28, 1973, Commander Bean, Jack Lousma and Dr. Owen K. Garriott became the second crew to inhabit the Skylab space station. During the 59-day, 24.4-million-mile flight, they accumulated 1,200 pounds of experiment data, including 12,000 photographs and 18 miles of computer tape gathered during surveys of Earth's resources and 76,000 photos of the sun to help scientists better understand how it affects the entire solar system.

Bean retired from the Navy in 1975 but continued with NASA as head of the Astronaut Candidate Operations and Training Group. He retired from NASA in 1981 and since then has devoted his time to creating paintings which serve as an artistic record of Apollo and of humankind's first exploration of other worlds.

NAME: John E. Blaha (Colonel, USAF, Ret.)
NASA Astronaut (former)

PERSONAL DATA: Born August 26, 1942, in San Antonio, Texas. Married to the former Brenda I. Walters of St. Louis, Missouri. They have three grown children and two grandchildren.

EDUCATION: Graduated from Granby High School in Norfolk, Virginia, in 1960; received a bachelor of science in engineering science from the United States Air Force Academy in 1965 and a master of science in astronautical engineering from Purdue University in 1966.

ORGANIZATIONS: Association of Space Explorers; Purdue Alumni Association; Society of Experimental Test Pilots; Air Force Academy Association of Graduates; Chairman, Board of Directors Brooks Aerospace Foundation; Member, Committee on Engineering Challenges to the Long Term Operation of the International Space Station, National Research Council Aeronautics and Space Engineering Board.

SPECIAL HONORS: Russian Order of Friendship Medal, 2 NASA Distinguished Service Medals, NASA Outstanding Leadership Medal, NASA Exceptional Service Medal, 5 NASA Space Flight Medals, Countdown Magazine Outstanding Astronaut of 1991, Defense Superior Service Medal, Legion of Merit, 2 Air Force Distinguished Flying Crosses, Defense Meritorious Service Medal, 3 Meritorious Service Medals, 18 Air Medals, Air Force Commendation Medal, the British Royal Air Force Cross, the Vietnam Cross of Gallantry, Purdue Outstanding Aerospace Engineer Award, and the Purdue Engineering Alumnus Award. Outstanding Pilot, F-4 Combat Crew Training. Outstanding Junior Officer of the Year, 3rd Tactical Fighter Wing. Distinguished Graduate Air Force Test Pilot School. Distinguished Graduate Air Command and Staff College. University Roundtable Annual Best and Brightest Award. Grand Marshall Fiesta Flambeau Parade. Grand Marshall Battle of Flowers Parade. Granby High School Hall of Fame.

AIR FORCE EXPERIENCE: Blaha received his pilot wings at Williams Air Force Base, Arizona, in 1967. He was subsequently assigned as an operational pilot flying F-4, F-102, F-106, and A-37 aircraft (completing 361 combat missions in Vietnam). He attended the USAF Aerospace Research Pilot School at Edwards Air Force Base, California, in 1971, and piloted the NF-104 research aircraft to 104,400 feet. Following graduation, he served as an F-104 instructor pilot at the test pilot school, teaching low lift-to-drag approach, zoom, performance, stability/control, and spin flight test techniques. In 1973, he was assigned as a test pilot working with the Royal Air Force at the Aeroplane and Armament Experimental Establishment, Boscombe Down, United Kingdom. During a 3-year tour, he flew stability/control, performance, spin, and weapons delivery flight tests in the Jaguar, Buccaneer, Hawk, and Jet Provost aircraft. In 1976 he attended the USAF Air Command and Staff College. After graduation, he was assigned to work for the Assistant Chief of Staff, Studies and Analyses, at Headquarters USAF in the Pentagon. During this tour, he presented F-15 and F-16 study results to Department of Defense, State Department, and congressional staffs.

NASA EXPERIENCE: Selected as an astronaut in May 1980, Blaha has logged 161 days in space on 5 space missions. He served as pilot on STS-33 and STS 29, was Spacecraft Commander on STS-58 and STS-43, served on Mir-22 as Board Engineer 2, and was a Mission Specialist on STS-79 and STS-81.Landed at Edwards Air Force Base on March 18, 1989. During this very successful mission the five-man crew aboard Shuttle Discovery deployed the East Tracking and Data Relay Satellite, and performed eight scientific/medical experiments. STS-33 Discovery (November 22-27, 1989). Launched at night, this five-day mission carried Department of Defense payloads and other secondary payloads. After 79 orbits of the Earth, this highly successful mission concluded with a hard surface landing on Runway 4 at Edwards Air Force Base, California. STS-43 Atlantis (August 2-11, 1991) launched from the Kennedy Space Center carrying a five person crew. During the nine-day mission the crew deployed the West Tracking and Data Relay Satellite, and conducted 32 physical, material, and life science experiments that supported the development of the Extended Duration Orbiter and Space Station. After 142 orbits of the Earth, this very significant mission concluded with a landing on Runway 15 at the Kennedy Space Center, Florida. STS-58 Columbia (October 18 to November 1, 1993) launched from the Kennedy Space Center carrying a seven-person crew. This record duration fourteen-day life science research mission has been recognized by NASA management as the most successful and efficient Spacelab flight that NASA has flown. The crew performed neurovestibular, cardiovascular, cardiopulmonary, metabolic, and musculoskeletal medical experiments on themselves and 48 rats, expanding our knowledge of human and animal physiology both on earth and in space flight. In addition, the crew performed 16 engineering tests aboard the Orbiter Columbia and 20 Extended Duration Orbiter Medical Project experiments. Landing was at Edwards Air Force Base on Runway 22. Blaha began Russian language training in August 1994 at the Defense Language Institute in Monterey, California, and commenced an intensive training program at the Cosmonaut Training Center, Star City, Russia in January 1995. He launched on STS-79 on September 16, 1996. After docking he transferred to the Mir Space Station. Assigned as a Board Engineer 2, he spent the following 4 months with the Mir 22 Cosmonaut crew conducting material science, fluid science, and life science research. Blaha returned to earth aboard STS-81 on January 22, 1997.

NAME: Guion S. Bluford, Jr. (Colonel, USAF, Ret.)
NASA Astronaut (former)

PERSONAL DATA: Born in Philadelphia, Pennsylvania, on November 22, 1942. Married to the former Linda Tull of Philadelphia, Pennsylvania. They have two children. Hobbies include reading, swimming, jogging, racquetball, handball, and scuba.

EDUCATION: Graduated from Overbrook Senior High School in Philadelphia, Pennsylvania, in 1960; received a bachelor of science degree in aerospace engineering from the Pennsylvania State University in 1964; a master of science degree with distinction in aerospace engineering from the Air Force Institute of Technology in 1974; a doctor of philosophy in aerospace engineering with a minor in laser physics from the Air Force Institute of Technology in 1978, and a master in business administration from the University of Houston, Clear Lake, in 1987.

ORGANIZATIONS: Associate Fellow, American Institute of Aeronautics and Astronautics; and member of the Air Force Association, Tau Beta Pi, Sigma Iota Epsilon, National Technical Association, and Tuskegee Airmen.

SPECIAL HONORS: Presented the Leadership Award of Phi Delta Kappa (1962); the National Defense Service Medal (1965); Vietnam Campaign Medal (1967); Vietnam Cross of Gallantry with Palm (1967); Vietnam Service Medal (1967); 3 Air Force Outstanding Unit Awards (1967, 1970, 1972); the German Air Force Aviation Badge from the Federal Republic of West Germany (1969); T-38 Instructor Pilot of the Month (1970); Air Training Command Outstanding Flight Safety Award (1970); an Air Force Commendation Medal (1972); the Air Force Institute of Technology's Mervin E. Gross Award (1974); Who's Who Among Black Americans 1975-1977; an Air Force Meritorious Service Award (1978); National Society of Black Engineers Distinguished National Scientist Award (1979); three NASA Group Achievement Awards (1980, 1981 and 1989); the Pennsylvania State University Alumni Association's Distinguished Alumni Award (1983), and Alumni Fellows Award (1986); USAF Command Pilot Astronaut Wings (1983); NASA Space Flight Medal (1983, 1985, 1991 and 1992); Ebony Black Achievement Award (1983); NAACP Image Award (1983); Who's Who in America (1983); Pennsylvania's Distinguished Service Medal (1984); Defense Superior Service Medal; Defense Meritorious Service Medal; the New York City Urban League's Whitney Young Memorial Award; the 1991 Black Engineer of the Year Award; NASA Exceptional Service Medal; National Intelligence Medal of Achievement; Legion of Merit; honorary doctorate degrees from Florida A&M University, Texas Southern University, Virginia State University, Morgan State University, Stevens Institute of Technology, Tuskegee Institute, Bowie State College, Thomas Jefferson University, Chicago State University, Georgian Court College, and Drexel University.

EXPERIENCE: Bluford graduated from Penn State University in 1964 as a distinguished Air Force ROTC graduate.He attended pilot training at Williams Air Force Base, Arizona, and received his pilot wings in January 1966.He then went to F-4C combat crew training in Arizona and Florida and was assigned to the 557th Tactical Fighter Squadron, Cam Ranh Bay, Vietnam. He flew 144 combat missions, 65 of which were over North Vietnam. In July 1967, he was assigned to the 3,630th Flying Training Wing, Sheppard Air Force Base, Texas, as a T-38A instructor pilot. He served as a standardization/evaluation officer and as an assistant flight commander. In early 1971, he attended Squadron Officers School and returned as an executive support officer to the Deputy Commander of Operations and as School Secretary for the Wing. In August 1972, he entered the Air Force Institute of Technology residency school at Wright-Patterson Air Force Base, Ohio. Upon graduating in 1974, he was assigned to the Air Force Flight Dynamics Laboratory at Wright-Patterson Air Force Base, Ohio, as a staff development engineer. He served as deputy for advanced concepts for the Aeromechanics Division and as branch chief of the Aerodynamics and Airframe Branch in the Laboratory. Bluford has written and presented several scientific papers in the area of computational fluid dynamics. He has logged over 5,200 hours jet flight time in the T-33, T-37, T-38, F-4C, F-15, U-2/TR-1, and F-5A/B, including 1,300 hours as a T-38 instructor pilot. He also has an FAA commercial pilot license.

NASA EXPERIENCE: Bluford became a NASA astronaut in August 1979. His technical assignments have included working with Space Station operations, the Remote Manipulator System (RMS), Spacelab systems and experiments, Space Shuttle systems, payload safety issues and verifying flight software in the Shuttle Avionics Integration Laboratory (SAIL) and in the Flight Systems Laboratory (FSL). A veteran of four space flights, Bluford was a mission specialist on STS-8, STS 61-A, STS-39, and STS-53. Bluford's first mission was STS-8, which launched from Kennedy Space Center, Florida, on August 30, 1983. This was the third flight for the Orbiter Challenger and the first mission with a night launch and night landing. During the mission, the STS-8 crew deployed the Indian National Satellite (INSAT-1B); operated the Canadian-built RMS with the Payload Flight Test Article (PFTA); operated the Continuous Flow Electrophoresis System (CFES) with live cell samples; conducted medical measurements to understand biophysiological effects of space flight; and activated four "Getaway Special" canisters. STS-8 completed 98 orbits of the Earth in 145 hours before landing at Edwards Air Force Base, California, on September 5, 1983. Bluford then served on the crew of STS 61-A, the German D-1 Spacelab mission, which launched from Kennedy Space Center, Florida, on October 30, 1985. This mission was the first to carry eight crew members, the largest crew to fly in space and included three European payload specialists. This was the first dedicated Spacelab mission under the direction of the German Aerospace Research Establishment (DFVLR) and the first U.S. mission in which payload control was transferred to a foreign country (German Space Operations Center, Oberpfaffenhofen, Germany). During the mission, the Global Low Orbiting Message Relay Satellite (GLOMR) was deployed from a "Getaway Special" (GAS) container, and 76 experiments were performed in Spacelab in such fields as fluid physics, materials processing, life sciences, and navigation. After completing 111 orbits of the Earth in 169 hours, Challenger landed at Edwards Air Force Base, California, on November 6, 1985. Bluford also served on the crew of STS-39, which launched from the Kennedy Space Center, Florida, on April 28, 1991, aboard the Orbiter Discovery. The crew gathered aurora, Earth-limb, celestial, and Shuttle environment data with the AFP-675 payload. This payload consisted of the Cryogenic Infrared Radiance Instrumentation for Shuttle (CIRRIS-1A) experiment, Far Ultraviolet Camera experiment (FAR UV), the Uniformly Redundant Array (URA), the Quadrupole Ion Neutral Mass Spectrometer (QINMS), and the Horizon Ultraviolet Program (HUP) experiment. The crew also deployed and retrieved the SPAS-II which carried the Infrared Background Signature Survey (IBSS) experiment. The crew also operated the Space Test Payload-1 (STP-1) and deployed a classified payload from the Multi-Purpose Experiment Canister (MPEC). After completing 134 orbits of the Earth and 199 hours in space, Discovery landed at the Kennedy Space Center, Florida, on May 6, 1991. More recently, Bluford served on the crew of

STS-53 which launched from the Kennedy Space Center, Florida, on December 2, 1992. The crew of five deployed the classified Department of Defense payload DOD-1 and then performed several Military-Man-in-Space and NASA experiments. After completing 115 orbits of the Earth in 175 hours, Discoverylanded at Edwards Air Force Base, California, on December 9, 1992. With the completion of his fourth flight, Bluford has logged over 688 hours in space. Bluford left NASA in July 1993 to take the post of Vice President/General Manager, Engineering Services Division, NYMA Inc., Greenbelt, Maryland.

Name: BOBKO, Karol J., Colonel, U.S. Air Force (Retired)

PERSONAL DATA: Born December 23, 1937, in New York, New York.

EDUCATION: Bachelor of science from U.S. Air Force Academy; master of science in aerospace engineering from University of Southern California.

NASA EXPERIENCE: Flew on STS-6, STS 51-D, and STS-51-J. Cumulative hours of space flight are more than 386.

NAME: Charles F. Bolden, Jr. (Brig. General, USMC)
NASA Astronaut (former)

PERSONAL DATA: Born August 19, 1946, in Columbia, South Carolina. Married to the former Alexis (Jackie) Walker of Columbia, South Carolina. They have two children. He enjoys racquetball, running and soccer His mother, Mrs. Ethel M. Bolden, resides in Columbia.

EDUCATION: Graduated from C. A. Johnson High School in Columbia, South Carolina, in 1964; received a bachelor of science degree in electrical science from the United States Naval Academy in 1968, and a master of science in systems management from the University of Southern California in 1977.

ORGANIZATIONS: Member of the Montford Point Marine Association, the United States Naval Institute, and Omega Psi Phi Fraternity. Lifetime member of the Naval Academy Alumni Association, the University of Southern California General Alumni Association.

SPECIAL HONORS: Recipient of the Distinguished Flying Cross, the Defense Superior Service Medal, the Defense Meritorious Service Medal, the Air Medal, the Strike/Flight Medal (8th award), Honorary Doctor of Science Degree from the University of South Carolina (1984), Honorary Doctor of Humane Letters from Winthrop College (1986), the NASA Outstanding Leadership Medal (1992), NASA Exceptional Service Medals (1988, 1989, 1991), the University of Southern California Alumni Award of Merit (1989), and an Honorary Doctor of Humane Letters from Johnson C. Smith University (1990).

EXPERIENCE: Bolden accepted a commission as a second lieutenant in the U.S. Marine Corps following graduation from the United States Naval Academy in 1968. He underwent flight training at Pensacola, Florida, Meridian, Mississippi, and Kingsville, Texas, before being designated a naval aviator in May 1970. He flew more than 100 sorties into North and South Vietnam, Laos, and Cambodia, in the A-6A Intruder while assigned to VMA(AW)-533 at Nam Phong, Thailand, June

1972 to June 1973. Upon returning to the United States, Bolden began a two-year tour as a Marine Corps selection officer and recruiting officer in Los Angeles, California, followed by three years in various assignments at the Marine Corps Air Station El Toro, California. In June 1979, he graduated from the U.S. Naval Test Pilot School at Patuxent River, Maryland, and was assigned to the Naval Air Test Center's Systems Engineering and Strike Aircraft Test Directorates. While there, he served as an ordnance test pilot and flew numerous test projects in the A-6E, EA-6B, and A-7C/E airplanes.

NASA EXPERIENCE: Selected by NASA in May 1980, Bolden became an astronaut in August 1981. His technical assignments included: Astronaut Office Safety Officer; Technical Assistant to the Director of Flight Crew Operations; Special Assistant to the Director of the Johnson Space Center; Astronaut Office Liaison to the Safety, Reliability and Quality Assurance Directorates of the Marshall Space Flight Center and the Kennedy Space Center; Chief of the Safety Division at JSC; Lead Astronaut for Vehicle Test and Checkout at the Kennedy Space Center; and Assistant Deputy Administrator, NASA Headquarters. A veteran of four space flights, he has logged over 680 hours in space. Bolden served as pilot on STS-61C (January 12-18, 1986) and STS-31 (April 24-29, 1990), and was the mission commander on STS-45 (March 24-April 2, 1992), and STS-60 (Feb. 3-11, 1994). Bolden left NASA and returned to active duty in the U.S. Marine Corps as the Deputy Commandant of Midshipmen at the Naval Academy, Annapolis, Maryland, effective June 27, 1994.

Brig. General Bolden is the Assistant Wing Commander, HQ 3rd MAW Miramar, San Diego, California.

SPACE FLIGHT EXPERIENCE: STS-61C Space Shuttle Columbia. During the six-day flight crew members deployed the SATCOM KU satellite and conducted experiments in astrophysics and materials processing. STS-61C launched from the Kennedy Space Center, Florida, on January 12. The mission was accomplished in 96 orbits of Earth, ending with a successful night landing at Edwards Air Force Base, California, on January 18, 1986. STS-31 Space Shuttle Discovery. Launched on April 24, 1990, from the Kennedy Space Center in Florida. During the five-day mission, crew members deployed the Hubble Space Telescope and conducted a variety of middeck experiments. They also used a variety of cameras, including both the IMAX in cabin and cargo bay cameras, for Earth observations from their record-setting altitude over 400 miles. Following 75 orbits of Earth in 121 hours, STS-31 Discovery landed at Edwards Air Force Base, California, on April 29, 1990. On STS-45 Bolden commanded a crew of seven aboard Space Shuttle Atlantis. Launched on March 24 from the Kennedy Space Center in Florida, STS-45 was the first Spacelab mission dedicated to NASA's Mission to Planet Earth. During the nine-day mission, the crew operated the twelve experiments that constituted the ATLAS-1 (Atmospheric Laboratory for Applications and Science) cargo. ATLAS-1 obtained a vast array of detailed measurements of atmospheric chemical and physical properties, which contribute significantly to improving our understanding of our climate and atmosphere. In addition, this was the first time an artificial beam of electrons was used to stimulate a man-made auroral discharge. Following 143 orbits of Earth, STS-45 Atlantis landed at the Kennedy Space Center, Florida, on April 2, 1992. On STS-60 he commanded a crew of six aboard Space Shuttle Discovery. This was the historic first joint U.S./Russian Space Shuttle mission involving the participation of a Russian Cosmonaut as a mission specialist crew member. The flight launched on February 3, 1994, from the Kennedy Space Center, Florida, and carried the Space Habitation Module-2 (Spacehab-2), and the Wake Shield Facility-01 (WSF-1). Additionally, the crew conducted a series of joint U.S./Russian science activities. The mission achieved 130 orbits of the Earth, ending with a landing on February 11, 1994, at the Kennedy Space Center, Florida.

Name: Frank Bormam
NASA Astronaut (former)

Frank Borman commanded Gemini 7, which was part of the first space rendezvous mission, and commanded Apollo 8, the first flight to orbit the moon.

PERSONAL DATA: He was born in Gary, IN, on March 14, 1928.

EDUCATION: He received a Bachelor of Science degree from the U.S. Military Academy, West Point, in 1950 and a Master of Science degree from the California Institute of Technology in 1957. He completed the Harvard Business School's Advanced Management Program in 1970.

EXPERIENCE: Borman was a career Air Force office from 1950 to 1970, when he retired with the rank of colonel. He served as a fighter pilot in the Philippines, as an operational pilot and instructor with various squadrons in the United States, as an assistant professor of thermodynamics and fluid dynamics at West Point and as an experimental test pilot at the USAF Aerospace Pilot School.

NASA EXPERIENCE: NASA selected him as an astronaut in 1962. In December 1965, he and Jim Lovell spent a then-record 14 days in orbit aboard Gemini 7. During the Flight, Gemini 6 astronauts Wally Schirra and Tom Stafford were launched and executed the first space rendezvous, with the two ships maneuvering to within one foot of one another on Dec. 15. Three years later, on Dec 21. 1968, Borman, Lovell and Bill Anders were the first humans launched toward the moon and the first to ride the mammoth Saturn V rocket. While orbiting the moon on Christmas Eve and relaying television pictures of its rugged surface, they captivated millions of viewers by reading from the Bible's Book of Genesis.

In 1969, Borman served Eastern Airlines as a special adviser, and a year later he was named vice president-operations group. He worked his way up in the company and was elected president and chief operating officer in 1975, moving up to chief executive officer later that year. He became chairman of Eastern's board in 1976. Today he is an official of the Patlex Corporation.

NAME: Vance DeVoe Brand
NASA Astronaut (former)

PERSONAL DATA: Born in Longmont, Colorado, May 9, 1931. Married to the former Beverly Ann Whitnel. Two daughters and four sons. Enjoys running to stay in condition, hiking, skiing, and camping.

EDUCATION: Graduated from Longmont High School, Longmont, Colorado; received a bachelor of science degree in Business from the University of Colorado in 1953, a bachelor of science degree in Aeronautical Engineering from the University of Colorado in 1960, and a master's degree in Business Administration from the UCLA in 1964.

ORGANIZATIONS: Fellow, American Institute of Aeronautics and Astronautics, Society of Experimental Test Pilots, and American Astronautical Society. Registered Professional Engineer in Texas. Member, Sigma Nu.

SPECIAL HONORS: JSC Certificate of Commendation (1970); NASA Distinguished Service Medals (1975 & 1992); NASA Exceptional Service Medals (1974 & 1988); Zeta Beta Tau's Richard Gottheil Medal (1975); Wright Brothers International Manned Space Flight Award (1975); VFW National Space Award (1976 & 1984); Sigma Nu Distinguished Alumnus of the Year Award (1976); Federation Aeronautique Internationale (FAI) Yuri Gagarin Gold Medal (1976); University of Colorado Alumnus of the Century (1 of 12) (1976); AIAA Special Presidential Citation (1977); American Astronautical Society's Flight Achievement Award for 1976 (1977); AIAA Haley Astronautics Award (1978); JSC Special Achievement Award (1978); Harmon Trophy (Astronaut) (1993); FAI De La Vaulx Medal (1983); NASA Space Flight Medals (1983, 1984, 1992); Distinguished Visiting Lecturer at University of Colorado (1984); De Molay Hall of Honor (1989); FAI Komarov Awards (1983 & 1991); University of Colorado George Norlin Award (1991); De Molay Legion of Honor (1993). Inductee, International Space Hall of Fame (1996), U.S. Astronaut Hall of Fame (1997). Meritorious Executive, U.S. Senior Executive Service (1997).

EXPERIENCE: Military: Commissioned officer and naval aviator with the U.S. Marine Corps from 1953 to 1957. Military assignments included a 15-month tour in Japan as a jet fighter pilot. Following release from active duty, Brand continued in Marine Corps Reserve and Air National Guard jet fighter squadrons until 1964.

PRE-NASA CIVILIAN: Employed as a civilian by the Lockheed Aircraft Corporation from 1960 to 1966, he worked initially as a flight test engineer on the Navy's P3A aircraft. In 1963, Brand graduated from the U.S. Naval Test Pilot School and was assigned to Palmdale, California as an experimental test pilot on Canadian and German F-104 programs. Prior to selection to the astronaut program, Brand worked at the West German F-104G Flight Test Center at Istres, France as an experimental test pilot and leader of a Lockheed flight test advisory group. Flight Experience: 9,669 flying hours, which includes 8,089 hours in jets, 391 hours in helicopters, 746 hours in spacecraft, and checkout in more than 30 types of military aircraft.

NASA EXPERIENCE: One of the 91 pilot astronauts selected by NASA in April 1966, Brand initially was a crew member in the thermal vacuum chamber testing of the prototype Command Module and support crewman on Apollo 8 and 13. Later he was backup command module pilot for Apollo 15 and backup commander for Skylabs 3 and 4. As an astronaut he held management positions relating to spacecraft development, acquisition, flight safety and mission operations. Brand flew on four space missions; Apollo-Soyuz, STS-5, STS 41-B, and STS-35. He has logged 746 hours in space and has commanded three Shuttle missions. Mr. Brand departed the Astronaut Office in 1992 to become Chief of Plans at the National Aerospace Plane (NASP) Joint Program Office at Wright-Patterson Air Force Base, Dayton, Ohio. In September 1994, he moved to California to become Assistant Chief of Flight Operations at the Dryden Flight Research Center. He later served as Acting Chief Engineer and currently is Deputy Director for Aerospace Projects at Dryden.

SPACE FLIGHT EXPERIENCE: Apollo Soyuz: Brand was launched on his first space flight on July 15, 1975, as Apollo command module pilot on the Apollo-Soyuz Test Project (ASTP) mission. This flight resulted in the historic meeting in space between American astronauts and Soviet cosmonauts. Other crewmen on this 9-day Earth-orbital mission were Thomas Stafford, Apollo commander, Donald Slayton, Apollo docking module pilot; cosmonaut Alexey Leonov, Soyuz commander; and cosmonaut Valeriy Kubasov, Soyuz flight engineer. The Soyuz spacecraft was launched at Baikonur in Central Asia, and the Apollo was launched 7 1/2 hours later at the Kennedy Space Center. Two days later Apollo accomplished a successful rendezvous and docking with Soyuz. The linkup tested a unique, new docking system and demonstrated international cooperation in space. There were 44 hours of docked joint activities which included 4 crew transfers between the Apollo and the Soyuz. Six records for docked and group flight were set on the mission and are recognized by the Federation Aeronautique Internationale. Apollo splashed down in the Pacific Ocean near Hawaii, on July 25, and was promptly recovered by the USS New Orleans, Mission duration was 217 hours.

STS-5: Brand was commander of Columbia for STS-5, the first fully operational flight of the Shuttle Transportation System, which launched on November 11, 1982. His crew comprised Colonel Robert Overmyer, pilot, and two mission specialists, Dr. Joseph Allen and Dr. William Lenoir. STS-5, the first mission with a four man crew, demonstrated the Shuttle as operational by the successful first deployment of two commercial communications satellites from the Orbiter's payload bay. The mission marked the Shuttle's first use of an upper stage rocket, the Payload Assist Module (PAM-D). The satellites were deployed for Satellite Business Systems Corporation of McLean, Virginia, and TELESAT of Ottawa, Canada. Two FAI records for mass to altitude were set on the mission. Numerous flight tests were performed to ascertain Shuttle performance. STS-5 was the last flight to carry the Development Flight Instrumentation package to support extensive flight testing. The STS-5 crew concluded the 5-day orbital flight of Columbia with the landing approach through a cloud deck to Runway 22 at Edwards Air Force Base, California on November 16, 1982. Mission duration as 122 hours.

STS 41-B: Brand commanded Challenger with a crew of five on the tenth flight of the Space Shuttle. The launch was on February 3, 1984. His crew included Commander Robert Gibson, pilot, and 3 mission specialists, Captain Bruce McCandless, II, Dr. Ronald McNair, and Lt. Col. Robert Stewart. The flight accomplished the proper shuttle deployment of two Hughes 376 communications satellites were failed to reach desired geosynchronous orbits due to upper stage rocket failures. This mission marked the first flight checkout of the Manned Maneuvering Unit (MMU) and the Manipulator Foot Restraint (MFR) with McCandless and Stewart performing two spectacular extravehicular activities (EVA's). Shuttle rendezvous sensors and computer programs were flight tested for the first time. The 8-day flight of Challenger ended with the first landing to the runway at the Kennedy Space Center on February 11, 1984. Mission duration was 191 hours.

STS-35: Brand again commanded Columbia on the thirty-eighth flight of the Shuttle, this time with a crew of seven. The spectacular night launch on December 2, 1990 started a 9-day mission devoted to round-the-clock observations of stars and other celestial objects. Crewmen included the pilot, Col. Guy Gardner; three mission specialists, Mike Lounge, Dr. Robert Parker and Dr. Jeffrey Hoffman; and two payload specialists, Dr. Samuel Durrance and Dr. Ronald Parise. The 13-ton payload consisted of the 3 ASTRO-1 Ultraviolet (UV) Telescopes and the Broad Band X-ray Telescope. More than 200 Orbiter maneuvers were required to point the telescopes. This Shuttle flight, the first dedicated to astronomy, provided a rich return of science data to better understand the nature of the universe with emphasis on observation of very active celestial objects. A night landing was made on December 10 to Runway 22 at Edwards Air Force Base. Mission duration was 215 hours.

NAME: Daniel C. Brandenstein (Captain, USN, Ret.)
       NASA Astronaut (former)

PERSONAL DATA: Born January 17, 1943, in Watertown, Wisconsin. Married to the former Jane A. Wade of Balsam Lake, Wisconsin. They have one daughter. Recreational interests include skiing, sailing, basketball, softball, golf, and woodworking. His parents, Mr. and Mrs. Walter Brandenstein, are residents of Watertown, Wisconsin. Her parents, Mr. and Mrs. Albert Wade, reside in Balsam Lake, Wisconsin.

EDUCATION: Graduated from Watertown High School, Watertown, Wisconsin, in 1961; received a bachelor of science degree in mathematics and physics from the University of Wisconsin (River Falls) in 1965.

ORGANIZATIONS: Associate Fellow, American Institute of Aeronautics and Astronautics (AIAA). Member, Society of Experimental Test Pilots (SETP), Association of Space Explorers, United States, Naval Institute, and Association of Naval Aviation.

SPECIAL HONORS: Awarded 2 Defense Superior Service Medals the Legion of Merit, the Distinguished Flying Cross, Defense Meritorious Service Medal, 17 Air Medals, 2 Navy Commendation Medals with Combat V, Meritorious Unit Commendation, 2 NASA Distinguished Service Medals, 2 NASA Outstanding Leadership Medals, 4 NASA Space Flight Medals, National Defense Service Medal, Armed Forces Expeditionary Medal, Vietnam Service Medal, Sea Service Deployment Ribbon, Legion of Honor (France), Medal of King Abdul Aziz (Saudi Arabia), Republic of Vietnam Air Gallantry Cross with Silver Star, Republic of Vietnam Gallantry Cross Unit Citation, and Republic of Vietnam Campaign Medal. Distinguished Alumnus, University of Wisconsin, River Falls. Honorary Doctor of Engineering, Milwaukee School of Engineering, Honorary Doctor of Science, University of Wisconsin - River Falls. Recipient of the SETP Iven C. Kincheloe Award, the AIAA Haley Space Flight Award, the Federation Aeronautique International Yuri Gagarin Gold Medal and American Astronautical Society Flight Achievement Award.

EXPERIENCE: Brandenstein entered active duty with the Navy in September 1965 and was attached to the Naval Air Training Command for flight training. He was designated a naval aviator at Naval Air Station, Beeville, Texas, in May 1967, and then proceeded to VA-128 for A-6 fleet replacement training. From 1968 to 1970, while attached to VA-196 flying A-6 Intruders, he participated in two combat deployments on board the USS Constellation and the USS Ranger to Southeast Asia and flew 192 combat missions. In subsequent assignments, he was attached to VX-5 for the conduct of operational tests of A-6 weapons systems and tactics; and to the Naval Air Test Center where, upon graduation from the U.S. Naval Test Pilot School, Patuxent River, Maryland, he conducted tests of electronic warfare systems in various Navy aircraft. Brandenstein made a nine- month deployment to the Western Pacific and Indian Ocean on board the USS Ranger while attached to VA-145 flying A-6 Intruders during the period March 1975 to September 1977. Prior to reporting to Houston as an astronaut candidate, he was attached to VA-128 as an A-6 flight instructor. He has logged 6,400 hours flying time in 24 different types of aircraft and has 400 carrier landings.

NASA EXPERIENCE: Selected by NASA in January 1978, Brandenstein became an astronaut in August 1979. He was ascent spacecraft communicator (CAPCOM) and a member of the astronaut support crew for STS-1 (the first flight of the Space Shuttle). He was subsequently assigned to the STS-2 astronaut support crew and was the ascent CAPCOM for the second Space Shuttle flight. A veteran of four space flights -- STS-8 (August 30-September 3, 1983), STS-51G (June 17-24, 1985), STS-32 (January 9-20, 1990), and STS-49 (May 7-16, 1992) -- Brandenstein has logged over 789 hoursLin space. Following his second space flight, Brandenstein served as the Deputy Director of Flight Crew Operations. From April 1987 through September 1992 Brandenstein served as Chief of the Astronaut Office. In October 1992 Brandenstein retired from NASA and the U.S. Navy.

SPACE FLIGHT EXPERIENCE: Brandenstein was pilot on STS-8, his first flight, which launched at night from the Kennedy Space Center, Florida, on August 30, 1983. This was the third flight for the Orbiter Challenger and the first mission with a night launch and night landing. During the mission crew members deployed the Indian National Satellite (INSAT-1B); operated the Canadian-built Remote Manipulator System (RMS) with the Payload Flight Test Article (PFTA); operated the Continuous Flow Electrophoresis System (CFES) with live cell samples; conducted medical measurements to understand biophysiological effects on space flight; and activated various earth resources and space science experiments along with four "Getaway Special" canisters. STS-8 completed 98 orbits of the Earth in 145 hours before landing at Edwards Air Force Base, California, on September 3, 1983. On his second mission (June 17-24, 1985). Brandenstein commanded the crew of STS-51G aboard the Orbiter Discovery. During this seven-day mission crew members deployed communications satellites for Mexico (Morelos), the Arab League (Arabsat), and the United States (AT&T Telstar). They used the Remote Manipulator System (RMS) to deploy and later retrieve the SPARTAN satellite which performed 17 hours of x-ray astronomy experiments while separated from the Space Shuttle. In addition, the crew activated the Automated Directional Solidification Furnace (ADSF), six "Getaway Specials", participated in biomedical experiments, and conducted a laser tracking experiment as part of the Strategic Defense Initiative. The mission was accomplished in 112 Earth orbits in approximately 170 hours. Brandenstein then commanded the crew of STS-32 (January 9-20, 1990). In the longest Shuttle mission to date, crew members aboard the Orbiter Columbia successfully deployed the Syncom IV-F5 satellite, and retrieved the 21,400-pound Long Duration Exposure Facility (LDEF) using the RMS. They also operated a variety of middeck experiments including the Microgravity Disturbance Experiment (MDE) using the Fluids Experiment Apparatus (FEA), Protein Crystal Growth (PCG), American Flight Echocardiograph (AFE), Latitude/Longitude Locator (L3), Mesoscale Lightning Experiment (MLE), Characterization of Neurospora Circadian Rhythms (CNCR), and the IMAX camera. Additionally, numerous medical test objectives, including in-flight Lower Body Negative Pressure (LBNP), in-flight aerobic exercise and muscle performance were conducted to evaluate human adaptation to extended duration missions. Following 173 orbits of the Earth in 261 hours, the mission ended with a night landing in California. Brandenstein also commanded the crew of STS-49 (May 7-16, 1992) on the maiden flight of the new Space Shuttle Endeavour. During this mission, the crew conducted the initial test flight of Endeavour, performed a record four EVA's (space walks) to retrieve, repair and deploy the International Telecommunications Satellite (INTELSAT) and to demonstrate and evaluate numerous EVA tasks to be used for the assembly of Space Station Freedom. Additionally, a variety of medical, scientific and operational tests were conducted throughout the mission. STS-49 logged 213 hours inspace and 141 Earth orbits prior to landing at Edwards Air Force Base, California, where the crew conducted the first test of the Endeavour's drag chute.

With the completion of his fourth flight, Brandenstein logged over 789 hours in space.

Name: Roy D. Bridges, Jr.
NASA Astronaut (former)

Current Occupation: Center Director
John F. Kennedy Space Center, Florida

Roy D. Bridges, Jr. became the director of NASA's John F. Kennedy Space Center effective March 2, 1997. As director, Bridges is responsible for managing NASA's only site for processing and launch of the Space Shuttle vehicle; processing the payloads flown on both the Shuttle and expendable launch vehicles; and overseeing expendable vehicle launches carrying NASA payloads. He manages a team of about 2,000 NASA civil servants and about 14,000 contractors.

Bridges is a retired U.S. Air Force Major General who served as the director of requirements, Headquarters Air Force Materiel Command, Wright-Patterson Air Force Base, OH, from June 1993 until his retirement July 1, 1996. In that position he served as the command focal point for product management policy, processes and resources.

Bridges served as a NASA astronaut, piloting the Space Shuttle Challenger on mission STS-51 F (July 29 to August 6, 1985).

Prior to his assignment at Wright-Patterson Air Force Base, Bridges was the commander, Air Force Flight Test Center, Edwards Air Force Base, CA. He has served in several key leadership positions including deputy chief of staff, test and resources, Headquarters Air Force Systems Command, Andrews Air Force Base, MD; commander, Eastern Space and Missile Center, Patrick Air Force Base, FL; commander, 6510th Test Wing, Edwards Air Force Base, CA.

Bridges was born on July 19, 1943, in Atlanta, GA, and graduated from Gainesville High School, GA, in 1961. He is a distinguished graduate of the U.S. Air Force Academy, Colorado Springs, CO, earning a bachelor's degree in engineering science in 1965. He received a master of science degree in astronautics from Purdue University, IN, in 1966.

He is the recipient of several awards and honors including recognition as a distinguished graduate of USAF Pilot Training and a top graduate of the USAF Test Pilot School. He is a recipient of the Distinguished Service Medal; Defense Superior Service Medal with oak leaf cluster; Legion of Merit with oak leaf cluster; Distinguished Flying Cross with two oak leaf clusters; Meritorious Service Medal; Air Medal with 14 oak leaf clusters; Air Force Commendation Medal; NASA Space Flight Medal; and a NASA Certificate of Commendation.

Bridges is married to the former Benita Louise Allbaugh of Tucson, AZ. They have two adult children.

NAME: Mark N. Brown (Colonel, USAF)
NASA Astronaut (former)

PERSONAL DATA: Born November 18, 1951, in Valparaiso, Indiana. Married to the former Lynne A. Anderson of River Grove, Illinois. They have two daughters. Recreational interests include fishing, hiking, jogging, all sports, and chess. His parents, Mr. and Mrs. Richard S. Brown, reside in Valparaiso, Indiana. Her mother, Mrs. Charles E. Anderson, resides in River Grove, Illinois.

EDUCATION: Graduated from Valparaiso High School, Valparaiso, Indiana in 1969; received a bachelor of science degree in aeronautical and astronautical engineering from Purdue University in 1973, and a master of science degree in astronautical engineering from the Air Force Institute of Technology in 1980.

SPECIAL HONORS: NASA Space Flight Medal. Distinguished Graduate from Air Force ROTC, Aerospace Defense Command "We Point With Pride" Award, Air Force Command Pilot, Senior Space Badge, Defense Superior Service Medal, two Air Force Commendation Medals, Air Force Outstanding Unit Award, Combat Readiness Medal, National Defense Medal, and the Small Arms Expert Marksmanship Ribbon.

EXPERIENCE: Brown received his pilot wings at Laughlin Air Force Base, Texas, in 1974. He was then assigned to the 87th Fighter Interceptor Squadron at K.I. Sawyer Air Force Base, Michigan, where he flew both T-33 and F-106 aircraft. In 1979 Brown was transferred to the Air Force Institute of Technology at Wright-Patterson Air Force Base, Ohio, and received his master of science degree in astronautical engineering in 1980.

NASA EXPERIENCE: Brown has been employed at the Lyndon B. Johnson Space Center since 1980. Assigned as an engineer in the Flight Activities Section, he participated in the development of contingency procedures for use aboard the Shuttle and served as an attitude and pointing officer. Brown supported STS flights 2, 3, 4, 6, 8 and 41-C in the Flight Activity Officer/Staff Support Room of the Mission Control Center. Selected by NASA in May 1984, Brown became an astronaut in June 1985, and qualified for assignment as a mission specialist on future Space Shuttle flight crews. In December 1985, he was assigned to the crew of a Department of Defense mission which was subsequently canceled due to the Challenger accident. During 1986 and 1987, he served as an astronaut member of the solid rocket booster redesign team. In February 1988 Brown was assigned to a new flight crew. He flew on STS-28 (August 8-13, 1989), following which he served as astronaut member on the Space Station Freedom Program. He next flew on STS-48 (September 12-18, 1991). With the completion of his second mission, Brown has logged over 249 hours in space. On his first space flight, Brown served as a mission specialist on the crew of STS-28. The Orbiter Columbia launched from Kennedy Space Center, Florida, on August 8, 1989. The mission carried Department of Defense payloads and a number of secondary payloads. After 80 orbits of the Earth, this five-day mission concluded with a dry lakebed landing on Runway17 at Edwards Air Force Base, California on August 13, 1989. Brown next flew on the crew of STS-48 aboard the Orbiter Discovery which launched from Kennedy Space Center, Florida, on September 12, 1991. This was a five-day mission during which the crew deployed the Upper Atmosphere Research Satellite (UARS) which is designed to provide scientists with their first complete data set on the upper atmosphere's chemistry, winds and energy inputs. The crew also conducted numerous secondary experiments ranging from growing protein crystals to studying how fluids and structures react in weightlessness. The mission was accomplished in 81 orbits of the Earth and concluded with a landing at

Edwards Air Force Base, California, on September 18, 1991. Brown left NASA in July 1993 and will retire from the U.S. Air Force to head up the Space Division office of General Research Corporation in Dayton, Ohio.

NAME: James F. Buchli (Colonel, USMC, Ret.)
NASA Astronaut (former)

PERSONAL DATA: Born June 20, 1945, in New Rockford, North Dakota, but also considers Fargo, North Dakota, as his hometown. Married to the former Jean Oliver of Pensacola, Florida. Two grown children. Recreational interests include skiing, scuba diving, hunting, fishing, and racquetball. His parents, Mr. and Mrs. Martin A. Buchli, reside in Fargo, North Dakota. Her parents, Mr. and Mrs. James O. Oliver, reside in Pensacola, Florida.

EDUCATION: Graduated from Fargo Central High School, Fargo, North Dakota, in 1963; received a bachelor of science degree in Aeronautical Engineering from the United States Naval Academy in 1967 and a master of science degree in Aeronautical Engineering Systems from the University of West Florida in 1975.

ORGANIZATIONS: Associate member of Naval Academy Alumni, American Legion, Association of Space Explorers, and American Geophysical Union.

SPECIAL HONORS: Recipient of the Defense Service Medal, Legion of Merit, Defense Meritorious Service Medal, four NASA Space Flight Medals, NASA Exceptional Service Medal, NASA Distinguished Service Medal, Air Medal, Navy Commendation Medal, Purple Heart, Combat Action Ribbon, Presidential Unit Citation, Navy Unit Citation, a Meritorious Unit Citation, and a Vietnamese Cross of Gallantry with the Silver Star.

EXPERIENCE: Buchli received his commission in the United States Marine Corps following graduation from the United States Naval Academy at Annapolis in 1967. He graduated from U.S. Marine Corps Basic Infantry Course and was subsequently sent to the Republic of Vietnam for a 1-year tour of duty, where he served as Platoon Commander, 9th Marine Regiment, and then as Company Commander and Executive Officer, "B" Company, 3rd Company, 3rd Reconnaissance Battalion. He returned to the United States in 1969 for naval flight officer training at Pensacola, Florida, and spent the next 2 years assigned to Marine Fighter/Attack Squadron 122, at Kaneohe Bay, Hawaii, and Iwakuni, Japan; and in 1973, he proceeded to duty with Marine Fighter/Attack Squadron 115 at Namphong, Thailand, and Iwakuni, Japan. Upon completing this tour of duty, he again returned to the United States and participated in the Marine Advanced Degree Program at the University of West Florida. He was assigned subsequently to Marine Fighter/Attack Squadron 312 at the Marine Corps Air Station, Beaufort, South Carolina, and in 1977, to the U.S. Test Pilot School, Patuxent River, Maryland. He has logged over 4,200 hours flying time -- 4,000 hours in jet aircraft.

NASA EXPERIENCE: Buchli became a NASA astronaut in August 1979. He was a member of the support crew for STS-1 and STS-2, and On-Orbit CAPCOM for STS-2. A veteran of four space flights, Buchli has orbited the earth 319 times, traveling 7.74 million miles in 20 days, 10 hours, 25 minutes, 32 seconds. He served as a mission specialist on STS-51C (January 24-27, 1995), STS-61A (October 30 to November 6, 1985), STS-29 (March 13-18, 1989), and STS-48 (Sep 12-18, 1991). From March 1989 till May 1992 he also served as Deputy Chief of the Astronaut Office. On 1 September 1992 Buchli retired from the U.S. Marine Corps and the NASA Astronaut Office to accept a position as Manager, Space Station Systems Operations and Requirements with Boeing Defense and Space Group, Huntsville, Alabama. In April 1993, he was reassigned as Boeing Deputy for Payload Operations, Space Station Freedom Program. Buchli currently serves as Operations & Utilization Manager for Space Station, Boeing Defense and Space Group, Houston, Texas.

SPACE FLIGHT EXPERIENCE: STS 51-C Discovery, was the first dedicated Department of Defense mission. Launched January 24, 1985, from Kennedy Space Center, Florida, STS-51C performed its DOD mission which included deployment of a modified Inertial Upper Stage (IUS) vehicle from the Space Shuttle. Landing occurred on January 27, 1985, after slightly more than three days on orbit. Mission duration was 73 hours, 33 minutes, 27 seconds. STS-61A Challenger (October 30 to November 6, 1985) was a West German D-1 Spacelab mission, the first to carry eight crew members, the largest crew to fly in space, and the first in which payload activities were controlled from outside
the United States. More than 75 scientific experiments were completed in the areas of physiological sciences, materials processing, biology, and navigation. Mission duration was 168 hours, 44 minutes, 51 seconds. STS-29 Discovery (March 13-18, 1989) was a highly successful five day mission during which the crew deployed a Tracking and Data Relay Satellite, and performed numerous secondary experiments, including a space station "heat pipe" radiator experiment, two student experiments, a protein crystal growth experiment, and a chromosome and plant cell division experiment. In addition, the crew took over 3,000 photographs of the earth using several types of cameras, including the IMAX 70 mm movie camera. Mission duration was 119 hours, 39 minutes, 40 seconds. STS-48 Discovery (September 12-18, 1991) was a five day mission during which the crew deployed the Upper Atmosphere Research Satellite (UARS) designed to provide scientists with their first complete data set on the upper atmosphere's chemistry, winds and energy inputs. The crew also conducted numerous secondary experiments ranging from growing protein crystals, to studying how fluids and structures react in weightlessness. Mission duration was 128 hours, 27 minutes; 34 seconds.

Name: John S. Bull, Civilian

Personal Data: Born September 25, 1934, in Memphis, Tennessee.

Education: Bachelor of science in mechanical engineering from Rice University; master of science and doctorate of philosophy in aeronautical engineering from Stanford University.

NAME: Kenneth D. Cameron (Colonel, USMC)
NASA Astronaut(former)

PERSONAL DATA: Born November 29, 1949, in Cleveland, Ohio. Married Michele Renee Fulford of Pensacola, Florida, in November 1973. They have two sons. He enjoys flying (CFI-SEL), athletics, camping, fishing, woodworking, reading, amateur radio, and volunteering as a youth soccer coach and Boy Scout leader. Former board member for church day school, and for community association.

EDUCATION: Graduated from Rocky River High School, Rocky River, Ohio, in 1967, and entered Massachusetts Institute of Technology. Received a Bachelor of Science degree in aeronautics and astronautics from MIT in 1978, and a Master of Science degree in aeronautics and astronautics from MIT in 1979. Graduated from U.S. Navy Test Pilot School in 1983. Completed numerous courses in Russian language and Russian space systems at MIT, JSC, and at Gagarin Cosmonaut Training Center, Moscow, Russia. Presently enrolled, evenings, at University of Houston, Clear Lake, in the Master of Business Administration degree program.

SPECIAL HONORS: Defense Superior Service Medal, Distinguished Flying Cross, Navy Commendation Medal with Combat "V", NASA Leadership Medals (2), NASA Exceptional Achievement Medals (2), NASA Space Flight Medals (3), Combat Action Ribbon, Vietnamese Meritorious Unit Citation, the Admiral Louis de Flores Award (MIT), C.S. Draper Laboratory Fellowship, Marine Corps Association Leadership Sword.

EXPERIENCE: Cameron was commissioned in the U.S. Marine Corps in 1970 at Officer's Candidate School in Quantico, Virginia. After graduating from the Officer's Basic Infantry Course and Vietnamese Language School, he was assigned to the Republic of Vietnam for a one-year tour of duty as an infantry platoon commander with the 1st Battalion, 5th Marine Regiment and, later, with the Marine Security Guards at the U.S. Embassy, Saigon. Upon his return to the United States he served as Executive Officer, "I" Company, 3rd Battalion, 2nd Marine Regiment, at Camp Lejeune, North Carolina. He reported to Pensacola, Florida, in 1972 for flight training, receiving his naval aviator wings in 1973. He was then assigned to Marine Corps Air Station, Yuma, Arizona, as pilot, flying A-4M Skyhawks, and aircraft maintenance officer, in charge of 200 Marines and 16 aircraft. In 1976, Cameron was reassigned to the Massachusetts Institute of Technology, where he participated in the Marine College Degree and Advanced Degree Programs. Upon graduation, he was assigned to flying duty for one year with Marine Aircraft Group 12 in Iwakuni, Japan. He was subsequently assigned to the Pacific Missile Test Center in 1980, and, in 1982, to the U.S. Navy Test Pilot School, Patuxent River, Maryland. Following graduation in 1983, he was assigned as project officer and test pilot in the F/A-18, A-4, and OV-10 airplanes with the Systems Engineering Test Directorate at the Naval Air Test Center. He has logged over 4,000 hours flying time in 48 different types of aircraft.

NASA EXPERIENCE: Selected by NASA in May 1984, Cameron became an astronaut in June 1985. His technical assignments have included work on Tethered Satellite Payload, flight software testing in the Shuttle Avionics Integration Laboratory (SAIL), launch support activities at Kennedy Space Center, and spacecraft communicator (CAPCOM) in Mission Control for STS-28, 29,30, 33 & 34. Management assignments include: Section Chief, for astronaut software testing in SAIL, and astronaut launch support activities; and Operations Assistant to the Hubble Repair Mission Director. Cameron served as the first NASA Director of Operations in Star City, Moscow, where he worked with the Cosmonaut Training Center staff to set up a support system for astronaut operations and training in Star City, and received Russian training in Soyuz and Mir spacecraft systems, and flight training in Russian L-39 aircraft. A veteran of three space flights, Cameron has logged over 561 hours in space. He served as pilot on STS-37 (April 5-11, 1991), and was the spacecraft commander on STS-56 (April 9-17, 1993) and STS-74 (November 12-20, 1995). Cameron flew his first mission as pilot on STS-37. This mission was launched on April 5,

1991, and featured the deployment of the Gamma Ray Observatory for the purpose of exploring gamma ray sources throughout the universe. Atlantis landed on April 11, 1991. On his second mission he was spacecraft commander on STS-56, carrying ATLAS-2. During this nine-day mission the crew of Discovery conducted atmospheric and solar studies in order to better understand the effect of solar activity on the Earth's climate and environment, and deployed and retrieved the autonomous observatory Spartan. STS-56 launched on April 8, 1993, and landed at Kennedy Space Center on April 17, 1993. Most recently, Cameron commanded STS-74, NASA's second Space Shuttle mission to rendezvous and dock with the Russian Space Station Mir, and the first mission to use the Shuttle to assemble a module and attach it to a Space Station. STS-74 launched on November 12, 1995, and landed at Kennedy Space Center on November 20, 1995.

Cameron left NASA on August 5, 1996 to join Hughes Training, Inc., as Executive Director, Houston Operations.

Name: Scott Carpenter
NASA Astronaut (former)

Scott Carpenter, a dynamic pioneer of modern exploration, has the unique distinction of being the only human ever to penetrate both inner and outer space, thereby acquiring the dual title, Astronaut/Aquanaut.

PERSONAL DATA: He was born in Boulder, Colorado, on May 1, 1925, the son of research chemist Dr. M. Scott Carpenter and Florence Kelso Noxon Carpenter. He attended the University of Colorado from 1945 to 1949 and received a bachelor of science degree in Aeronautical Engineering.

EXPERIENCE: Carpenter was commissioned in the U.S. Navy in 1949. He was given flight training at Pensacola, Florida and Corpus Christi, Texas and designated a Naval Aviator in April, 1951. During the Korean War he served with patrol Squadron SIX, flying anti-submarine, ship surveillance, and aerial mining missions in the Yellow Sea, South China Sea, and the Formosa Straits. He attended the Navy Test Pilot School at Patuxent River, Maryland, in 1954 and subsequently was assigned to the Electronics Test Division of the Naval Air Test Center. In the assignment he flew tests in every type of naval aircraft including multi and single-engine jet and propeller-driven fighters, attack planes, patrol bombers, transports, and seaplanes. From 1957 to 1959 he attended the Navy General Line School and the Navy Air Intelligence School and was then assigned as Air Intelligence Officer to the Aircraft Carrier, USS Hornet.

NASA EXPERIENCE: Carpenter was selected as one of the original seven Mercury Astronauts on April 9, 1959. He underwent intensive training with the National Aeronautics and Space Administration (NASA), specializing in the fields of communication and navigation. He served as backup pilot for John Glenn during the preparation for America's first manned orbital space flight. Carpenter flew the second American manned orbital flight on May 24, 1962. He piloted his Aurora 7 spacecraft through three revolutions of the earth, reaching a maximum altitude of 164 miles. The spacecraft landed in the Atlantic Ocean about 1000 miles southeast of Cape Canaveral after 4 hours and 54 minutes of flight time.

NAVY EXPERIENCE: On leave of absence from NASA, Carpenter participated in the Navy's Man-in the-Sea Project as an Aquanaut in the SEALAB II program off the coast of La Jolla, California, in the summer of 1965. During the 45-day experiment, Carpenter spent 30 days living and working on the ocean floor. He was team leader for two of the three ten-man teams of Navy and civilian divers who conducted deep sea diving activities based in a sea floor habitat at a depth of 205 feet.He eturned to duties with NASA as Executive Assistant to the Director of the Manned Spaceflight Center and was active in the design of the Apollo Lunar Landing Module and in underwater extra-vehicular activity (EVA) crew training. In 1967, he returned to the Navy's Deep Submergence Systems Project (DSSP) as Director of Aquanaut Operations during the SEALAB III experiment. (The DSSP office was responsible for directing the Navy's Saturation Diving Program, which included development of deep-ocean search, rescue, salvage, ocean engineering, and Man-in-the-Sea capabilities.)

CIVILIAN LIFE: Upon retirement from the Navy in 1969, Carpenter founded and was chief executive officer of Sear Sciences, Inc., a venture capital corporation active in developing programs aimed at enhanced utilization of ocean resources and improved health of the planet. In pursuit of these and other objectives, he worked closely with the French oceanographer J.Y. Cousteau and members of his Calypso team. He has dived in most of the world's oceans, including the Artic under ice.

As a consultant to sport and professional diving equipment manufacturers, he has contributed to design improvements in diving instruments, underwater breathing equipment, swimmer propulsion units, small submersibles, and other underwater devices.

Additional projects brought to fruition by his innovative guidance have involved biological pest control and the production of energy from agricultural and industrial waste. He has also been instrumental in the design and improvement of several types of waste handling and transfer equipment.

Carpenter continues to apply his knowledge of aerospace and ocean engineering as a consultant to industry and the private sector. He lectures frequently in the U.S. and abroad on the history and future of ocean and space technology, the impact of scientific and technological advance on human affairs, space-age perspectives, the health of planet Earth and man's continuing search for excellence. An avid skier, he spends much of his free time on the slopes in his home of Vail, Colorado.

He recently completed his first novel entitled "The Steel Albatross." It has been dubbed an "Underwater Techno-thriller" and deals with the impact of advanced diving and medical technology on deep sea and submarine combat.

AWARDS: Carpenter's awards include the Navy's Legion of Merit, the Distinguished Flying Cross, NASA Distinguished Service Medal, U.S. Navy Astronaut Wings. University of Colorado Recognition Medal, the Collier Trophy, New York City Gold Medal of Honor, The Elisha Kent Kane Medal, The Ustica Gold Trident and the Boy Scouts of America Silver Buffalo.

Name: Gerald P. Carr, Colonel, U.S. Marine Corps (Retired)

PERSONAL DATA: Born August 22, 1932, in Denver, Colorado.

EDUCATION: Bachelor of science in mechanical engineering from University of Southern California; bachelor of science in aeronautical engineering from U.S. Naval Postgraduate School; master of science in aeronautical engineering from Princeton University; honorary doctor of science in aeronautical engineering from Parks College, St. Louis University. Flew on Skylab 4. Cumulative hours of space flight are more than 2,017. Cumulative EVA time is more than 15 hours.

NAME: John H. Casper (Colonel, USAF (ret.))
NASA Astronaut (former)

PERSONAL DATA: Born July 9, 1943, in Greenville, South Carolina, but considers Gainesville, Georgia, to be his hometown. Married to Beth Taylor Casper. Four children. He enjoys flying general aviation aircraft, running, and listening to classical music. His father, Colonel (Ret.) John Casper Jr., resides in Gainesville, Georgia.

EDUCATION: Graduated from Chamblee High School, Chamblee, Georgia, in 1961; received a bachelor of science degree in engineering science from the U.S. Air Force Academy in 1966, and a master of science degree in astronautics from Purdue University in 1967. He is a 1986 graduate of the Air Force Air War College.

ORGANIZATIONS: Member of the Society of Experimental Test Pilots, the Association of Space Explorers, the American Institute of Aeronautics and Astronautics, the Aircraft Owners and Pilots Association, and the USAF Academy Association of Graduates.

SPECIAL HONORS: Awarded two Defense Meritorious Service Medals, the Defense Superior Service Medal, two Legion of Merit Awards, two Distinguished Flying Crosses, 11 Air Medals, 6 Air Force Commendation Medals, the Vietnamese Cross of Gallantry, the NASA Distinguished Service Medal, the NASA Exceptional Service Award, the NASA Medal for Outstanding Leadership, four NASA Space Flight Medals, and the National Intelligence Medal of Achievement.

EXPERIENCE: Casper received his pilot wings at Reese Air Force Base, Texas, in 1968. After F-100 training at Luke Air Force Base, Arizona, he flew 229 combat missions with the 35th Tactical Fighter Wing at Phan Rang Air Base, Vietnam. From 1970 to 1974, Casper was assigned to the 48th Tactical Fighter Wing, RAF Lakenheath, United Kingdom, and flew the F-100 and F-4 aircraft. In 1974, Casper graduated from the USAF Test Pilot School and became a test pilot at Edwards Air Force Base, California, flying weapons delivery and avionics testing for F-4 and A-7 aircraft. As chief of the F-4 Test Team, he flew initial performance and weapons separation tests for the F-4G Wild Weasel aircraft. From 1976 to 1980, Casper was operations officer and later commander of the 6513th Test Squadron, conducting flight test programs to evaluate and develop tactical aircraft weapons systems. Casper was assigned to Headquarters USAF in the Pentagon in 1980 and was Deputy Chief of the Special Projects Office, where he developed USAF positions on requirements, operational concepts, policy and force structure for tactical and strategic programs. Casper has logged over 7,000 flying hours in 51 different aircraft.

NASA EXPERIENCE: A veteran of four space flights, Casper has logged over 825 hours in space. He was the pilot on STS-36 (1990), and was the spacecraft commander on STS-54 (1993), STS-62 (1994) and STS-77 (1996). Selected by NASA in May 1984, Casper became an astronaut in June 1985. His technical assignments to date include: lead astronaut in improving Shuttle computer software and hardware; Astronaut Office lead for improvements to the nosewheel steering, brakes, tires, and development of a landing drag chute; astronaut team leader for the Shuttle Avionics

Integration Laboratory (SAIL) where final testing of the flight software and hardware is conducted; ascent/entry spacecraft communicator (CAPCOM) in the Mission Control Center; and Chief of the Operations Development Branch in the Astronaut Office. STS-36 launched from the Kennedy Space Center, Florida, on February 28, 1990, aboard Space Shuttle Atlantis. This mission carried classified Department of Defense payloads and was unique in flying at 62 degrees inclination, the highest inclination flown to date by the U.S. manned space program. After 72 orbits of the Earth, the STS-36 mission concluded with a lakebed landing at Edwards Air Force Base, California, on March 4, 1990, after traveling 1.87 million miles. Mission duration was 106 hours, 19 minutes, 43 seconds.

STS-54 launched from the Kennedy Space Center, Florida, on January 13, 1993, aboard Space Shuttle Endeavour. A crew of five successfully accomplished the primary objectives of this six-day mission. A $200 million NASA Tracking and Data Relay Satellite (TDRS-F) satellite was deployed, joining four others to complete a national communications network supporting Space Shuttle and other low-Earth orbit scientific satellites. A Diffuse X-Ray Spectrometer (DXS), carried in the payload bay, collected over 80,000 seconds of quality X-ray data to enable investigators to answer questions about the origin of X-rays in the Milky Way galaxy. A highly successful extravehicular activity (EVA) resulted in many lessons learned that will benefit the International Space Station assembly. The flight was also the first to shut down and restart a fuel cell in flight, successfully demonstrating another Space Station application. Casper landed Endeavour at the Kennedy Space Center on January 19, 1993, after 96 Earth orbits covering over 2.5 million miles. Mission duration was 143 hours and 38 minutes.

STS-62 (March 4-18, 1994) was a two-week microgravity research mission aboard Space Shuttle Columbia. Primary payloads were the United States Microgravity Payload (USMP-2) and the Office of Aeronautics and Space Technology (OAST-2) payloads. These payloads included experiments to understand the process of semiconductor crystal growth, investigating the process of metal alloys as they solidify, studying materials at their critical point (where they exist as both a liquid and gas), and testing new technology for use on future spacecraft, such as advanced solar arrays, radiators, heat sinks, and radiation shielding. The flight also tested new technology for aligning the Remote Manipulator System arm and for grasping payloads with a new magnetic end effector. Columbia flew at a record low altitude of 195 km (105 nautical miles) to gather data on spacecraft glow and erosion caused by atomic oxygen and nitrogen molecules. Casper landed Columbia at the Kennedy Space Center after 224 Earth orbits and 5.82 million miles.

STS-77 (May 19-29, 1996) was a ten-day mission aboard Space Shuttle Endeavour. The crew performed a record number of rendezvous sequences (one with a SPARTAN satellite and three with a deployed Satellite Test Unit) and approximately 21 hours of formation flying in close proximity of the satellites. During the flight the crew also conducted 12 materials processing, fluid physics and biotechnology experiments in a Spacehab Module. STS-77 deployed and retrieved a SPARTAN satellite, which carried the Inflatable Antenna Experiment designed to test the concept of large, inflatable space structures. A small Satellite Test Unit was also deployed to test the concept of self-stabilization by using aerodynamic forces and magnetic damping. Casper brought Endeavour back to Earth at the Kennedy Space Center after 160 Earth orbits and 4.1 million miles. Mission duration was 240 hours and 39 minutes.

Casper presently serves as the Director of Safety, Reliability, and Quality Assurance for the Johnson Space Center.

NAME: Eugene A. Cernan (Captain, USN, Retired)
NASA Astronaut (former)

PERSONAL DATA: Born in Chicago, Illinois, on March 14, 1934. His mother, Mrs. Andrew G. Cernan, resides in Bremerton, Washington.

PHYSICAL DESCRIPTION: Gray hair; blue eyes; height: 6 feet; weight: 190 pounds.

EDUCATION: Graduated from Proviso Township High School in Maywood, Illinois; received a bachelor of science degree in Electrical Engineering from Purdue University in 1956 and a master of science degree in Aeronautical Engineering from the U. S. Naval Postgraduate School, Monterey, California; recipient of an Honorary Doctorate of Law degree from Western State University College of Law in 1969, an Honorary Doctorate of Engineering from Purdue University in 1970, and Drexel University in 1977. Petroleum Economics and Management Seminar, Northwestern University, 1978.

MARITAL STATUS: Single

CHILDREN: Teresa Dawn, Born March 4, 1963.

RECREATIONAL INTERESTS: His hobbies include love for horses, all competitive sports activities, including hunting, fishing and flying.

ORGANIZATIONS: Fellow, American Astronautical Society; member, Society of Experimental Test Pilots; member, Tau Beta Pi (National Engineering Society), Sigma Xi (National Science Research Society), Phi Gamma Delta (National Social Fraternity), and the Explorer's Club.

SPECIAL HONORS: Awarded two NASA Distinguished Service Medals, the NASA Exceptional Service Medal, the JSC Superior Achievement Award, two Navy Distinguished Service Medals, the Navy Astronaut Wings, the Navy Distinguished Flying Cross, the National Academy of Television Arts and Sciences Special Trustees Award (1969), the Federation Aeronautique Internationale Gold Space Medal for 1972, the Cities of Houston, Chicago, Los Angeles, and New York Gold Medals, the VFW National Space Medal in 1973.

EXPERIENCE: Cernan, a retired United States Navy Captain, received his commission through the Navy ROTC Program at Purdue. He entered flight training upon graduation and was assigned to Attack Squadrons 26 and 113 at the Miramar, California, Naval Air Station, and subsequently attended the Naval Postgraduate School. He has logged more than 5,000 hours flying time with more than 4,800 hours in jet aircraft and over 200 jet aircraft landings.

NASA EXPERIENCE: Captain Cernan was one of fourteen astronauts selected by NASA in October 1963. He occupied the pilot seat alongside of command pilot Tom Stafford on the Gemini IX mission. During this three-day flight, which began on June 3, 1966, the spacecraft achieved a circular orbit of 161 statute miles; the crew used three different techniques to effect rendezvous with the previously launched Augmented Target Docking Adapter; and Cernan, the second American to walk in space, logged two hours and ten minutes outside the spacecraft in extravehicular activities. The flight ended after 72 hours and 20 minutes with a perfect reentry and recovery as Gemini IX landed within 1-1/2 miles of the prime recovery ship USS WASP and 3/8 of a mile from the predetermined target. Cernan subsequently served as backup pilot for Gemini 12 and as backup lunar module pilot for Apollo 7. On his second space flight, he was lunar module pilot of Apollo 10, May 18-26, 1969, the first comprehensive lunar orbital qualification and verification flight test of an Apollo lunar module. He was accompanied on the 248,000 nautical sojourn to the moon by Thomas P. Stafford (spacecraft commander) and John W. Young (command module pilot). In accomplishing all of the assigned objectives of this mission, Apollo 10 confirmed the operations performance, stability, and reliability of the command/service module and lunar module configuration during translunar coast, lunar orbit insertion, and lunar module separation and descent to within eight nautical miles of the lunar surface. The latter maneuver involved employing all but the final minutes of the technique prescribed for use in an actual lunar landing, and allowed critical evaluations of the lunar module propulsions sytems and rendezvous and landing radar devices in subsequent rendezvous and redocking maneuvers. In addition to demonstrating that man could navigate safely and accurately in the moon's gravitational fields, Apollo 10 photographed and mapped tentative landing sites for future missions.

Cernan's next assignment was backup spacecraft commander for Apollo 14.

He made his third space flight as spacecraft commander of Apollo 17,the last scheduled manned mission to the moon for the United States, which commenced at 11:33 P.M. (CST), December 6, 1972, with the first manned night time launch, and concluded on December 19, 1972. With him on the voyage of the command module America and the lunar module Challenger were Ronald Evans (command module pilot) and Harrison H. "Jack" Schmitt (lunar module pilot). In maneuvering Challenger to a landing at Taurus-Littrow, located on the southeast edge of Mare Serenitatis, Cernan and Schmitt activated a base of operations from which they completed three highly successful excursions to the nearby craters and the Taurus mountains, making the Moon their home for over three days. This last mission to the moon established several new records for manned space flight that include: longest manned lunar landing flight (301 hours 51minutes); longest lunar surface extravehicular activities (22 hours 6 minutes); largest lunar sample return (an estimated 115 kg, or 249 lbs.); and longest time in lunar orbit (147 hours 48 minutes). While Cernan and Schmitt conducted activities on the lunar surface, Evans remained in lunar orbit aboard the America, completing assigned work tasks requiring geological observations, handheld photography of specific targets, and the control of cameras and other highly sophisticated scientific equipment carried in the command module SIM-bay. Evans also completed a one-hour, six-minute extravehicular activity on the transearth coast phase of the return flight, successfully retrieving three camera cassetes and completing a personal inspection of the equipment bay area. Apollo 17 ended with a splashdown in the Pacific Ocean approximately 0.4 miles from the target point and 4.3 miles from the prime recovery ship USS TICONDEROGA. Captain Cernan has logged 566 hours and 15 minutes in space, of which more than 73 hours were spent on the surface of the moon, and was the last man of Apollo to leave his footprints on the surface of the moon. In September 1973, Cernan assumed additional duties as Special Assistant to the Program Manager of the Apollo Spacecraft Program at the Johnson Space Center. In this capacity, he assisted in the planning, development, and evaluation of the joint United States/Soviet Union Apollo-Soyuz mission, and he acted for the program manager as thesenior United States negotiator in direct discussions with the USSR on the Apollo-Soyuz Test Project. On July 1, 1976, Captain Cernan retired after over 20 years with the U. S. Navy. He concurrently terminated his formal association with NASA. Cernan joined Coral Petroleum, Inc., of Houston, Texas, as Executive Vice President-International. His responsibilities were to enhance Coral's energy related programs on a worldwide basis. In September 1981, Captain Cernan started his own company, The Cernan Corporation, to pursue management and consultant interests in the energy, aerospace, and other related industries. Additionally, he has been actively involved as a co-anchorman on ABC-TV's presentations of the flight of the shuttle. Captain Cernan was the second American to have walked in space, having spanned the circumference of the world twice in a little more than two and one half hours. He was one of the two men to have flown to the moon on two occasions, and as commander of the last mission to the moon, Apollo 17, had the privilege and distinction of being the last man to have left his footprints on the surface of the moon.

NAME: Philip Kenyon Chapman (ScD)
NASA Astronaut (former)

PERSONAL DATA: Born March 5, 1935, in Melbourne, Australia; his parents, Mr. and Mrs. Colin R. Chapman, reside now in Sydney, N.S.W., Australia.

PHYSICAL DESCRIPTION: Blond hair; blue eyes; height: 5 feet 11 inches; weight: 175 pounds.

EDUCATION: Graduated from Parramatta High School in Parramatta, N.S.W., Australia; received a bachelor of science degree in Physics and Mathematics from Sydney University in 1956; and, from the Massachusetts Institute of Technology, received a master of science degree in Aeronautics and Astronautics in 1964 and a Doctorate of Science in Instrumentation in 1967.

MARITAL STATUS: Married to the former Pamela Gatenby, daughter of Mr. and Mrs. Charles Gatenby of Ipswich, Queensland, Australia.

CHILDREN: Peter Hume, Born November 20, 1960; Kristen de Querilleau, Born October 31, 1968.

RECREATIONAL INTERESTS: Enjoys oil painting, skiing, swimming, sailing, and playing squash.

ORGANIZATIONS: Senior member of the American Astronautical Society; and member of the Australian National Antarctic Research Expedition (ANARE) Club, the American Association for the Advancement of Science, the American Physical Society, and the American Institute of Aeronautics and Astronautics.

SPECIAL HONORS: Recipient of the British Polar Medal.

EXPERIENCE: Chapman served with the Royal Australian Air Force Reserve from 1953 to 1955. From 1956 to 1957, he worked for Philips Electronics Industries Proprietary Limited in Sydney, Australia. He then joned the Australian National Antarctic Research Expedition (IGY) serving for two years as an auroral/radio physicist. From 1960 to 1961, he was an electro-optics staff engineer in flight simulators for Canadian Aviation Electronics Limited in Dorval, Quebec. His next assignment was as a staff physicist at the Massachusetts Institute of Technology where he worked in electro-optics, inertial systems, and gravitational theory until the summer of 1967. He has logged 1,000 hours flying time in jet aircraft.

NASA EXPERIENCE: Dr. Chapman was selected as a scientist-astronaut by NASA in August 1967. After initial academic training and a 53-week course in flight training at Randolph Air Force Base, Texas, he was involved in preparations for lunar missions, serving in particular as mission scientist for the Apollo 14 mission. Because of the lack of space flight opportunities for scientist-astronauts in the 1967 intake, Dr. Chapman left NASA in July 1972. He is now with Arthur D. Little Company, Inc., Cambridge, Massachusetts.

NAME: Maurizio Cheli
       ESA Astronaut (former)

PERSONAL DATA: Born May 4, 1959, in Modena, Italy. Married to the former Marianne Merchez. Her parents, Marcel and Annie Merchez, reside in Brussels, Belgium. He enjoys soccer, cycling, tennis and traveling. His parents, Araldo and Eulalia Cheli, reside in Zocca (Modena), Italy.

EDUCATION: Graduated from Liceo Classico "M. Minghetti" in Bologna in 1978, from the Italian Air Force Academy in 1982, from the Italian Air Force War College in 1987 and from the Empire Test Pilot School in 1988. He studied geophysics at the University of Rome in 1989 received a Master of Science in Aerospace Engineering from the University of Houston.

SPECIAL HONORS: Distinguished graduate, Fighter lead-in training (1983). Top graduate, Italian Air Force War College (1987). Top graduate, Empire Test Pilot's School (1988).

AWARDS: Italian Air Force Long Service Medal (1988). McKenna Trophy, Sir Alan Cobham Trophy and Hawker Hunter Trophy, Empire Test Pilot's School (1988).

EXPERIENCE: After graduation from the Italian Air Force Academy, Cheli underwent pilot training at Vance Air Force Base, Oklahoma, in 1982-1983. Following fighter lead-in training at Holloman Air Force Base, New Mexico and initial training in the F-104G in Italy, he joined the 28th Squadron, 3rd Recce Wing in 1984. In 1987, he attended the Italian Air Force War College and in 1988 he graduated from the Empire Test Pilot's School, Boscombe Down, United Kingdom. While assigned to the Italian Air Force Flight Test Center in Pratica di Mare, Rome, he served as a Tornado and B-707 Tanker project pilot on a variety of test programs and as display pilot. His flight experience includes more than 3000 flying hours in over 50 different types of fixed wing aircraft and helicopters. In June 1992, he was selected by the European Space Agency as a member of the second group of European astronauts. Cheli holds a commission as a Lieutenant Colonel in the Italian Air Force.

NASA EXPERIENCE: Cheli reported to the Johnson Space Center in August 1992 and completed one year of training in August 1993. He is qualified for assignment as a mission specialist on future Space Shuttle flight crews. His technical assignments to date include: flight software verification in the Shuttle Avionics Integration Laboratory (SAIL); remote manipulator system/robotics; crew equipment. He flew on STS-75 in 1996 and has logged over 377 hours in space. Most recently, Cheli was a mission specialist on the crew of STS-75. The principal payloads on STS-75 were the reflight of Tethered Satellite System (TSS) and the third flight of the United States Microgravity Payload (USMP-3). The TSS successfully demonstrated the ability of tethers to produce electricity. The TSS experiment produced a wealth of new information on the electrodynamics of tethers and plasma physics before the tether broke at 19.7 km, just shy of the 20.7 km goal. The crew also worked around the clock performing combustion experiments and research related to USMP-3 microgravity investigations used to improve production of medicines, metal alloys, and semiconductors. STS-75 launched February 22, 1996 and landed back at the Kennedy Space Center on March 9, 1996. The mission was completed in 252 orbits covering 6.5 million miles in 377 hours and 40 minutes.

NAME: Kevin P. Chilton (Brigadier General, USAF)
   NASA Astronaut (former)

PERSONAL DATA: Born November 3, 1954, in Los Angeles, California. Married; four children. He enjoys reading and all sports, including running, snow skiing, sailing, and softball. He also plays the guitar in a rock and roll band.

EDUCATION: Graduated from St. Bernard High School, Playa del Rey, California, in 1972; received a bachelor of science degree in engineering sciences from the USAF Academy in 1976, and a master of science degree in mechanical engineering from Columbia University on a Guggenheim Fellowship in 1977.

ORGANIZATIONS: Member, Order of Daedalians, USAF Academy Association of Graduates, American Legion.

SPECIAL HONORS: Distinguished Graduate USAF Academy, and Guggenheim Fellowship recipient (1976). Commanders Trophy winner as top graduate from Air Force Undergraduate Pilot Training (1978). Secretary of the Air Force Leadership Award recipient as top graduate of Air Force Squadron Officer School for 1982. Recipient of the Liethen-Tittle Award as the outstanding test pilot of the USAF Test Pilot School Class 84A (1984). NASA "Top Fox" Flight Safety Award Winner (1991). Awarded the Defense Superior Service Medal, the Distinguished Flying Cross, the Defense Meritorious Service Medal, two USAF Meritorious Service Medals and the Air Force Commendation Medal.

EXPERIENCE: Chilton received his Air Force commission from the USAF Academy in 1976, and then completed a masters degree in mechanical engineering on a Guggenheim Fellowship at Columbia University in 1977. In 1978, after receiving his wings at Williams Air Force Base, Arizona, he qualified in the RF-4 Phantom II and was assigned to the 15th Tactical Reconnaissance Squadron at Kadena Air Base, Japan. From 1978 until 1980, he served as a combat-ready pilot and instructor pilot in the RF-4 in Korea, Japan, and the Philippines. In 1981, he converted to the F-15 Eagle and was assigned to the 67th Tactical Fighter Squadron at Kadena Air Base in Japan as a squadron pilot. In 1982, Chilton attended the USAF Squadron Officer School at Maxwell Air Force Base, Alabama, and finished as the number one graduate for the year, receiving the Secretary of the Air Force Leadership Award. Subsequently assigned to the 9th and 7th Tactical Fighter Squadrons at Holloman Air Force Base, New Mexico, Chilton served as an F-15 squadron weapons officer, instructor pilot, and flight commander until 1984, when he was selected for the USAF Test Pilot School. Graduating number one in his class in 1984, Chilton was assigned to Eglin Air Force Base, Florida, where he conducted weapons and systems tests in all models of the F-15 and F-4. While a member of the 3247th Test Squadron, Chilton served as squadron safety officer, as chief of test and evaluation, and as squadron operations officer. In August 1987 he was assigned to NASA as an astronaut candidate.

NASA EXPERIENCE: Selected by NASA in June 1987, Chilton became an astronaut in August 1988, qualified for assignment as a pilot on future Space Shuttle flight crews. Since then he has held a variety of technical assignments. He served in the Mission Development Branch of the Astronaut Office in support of the Infrared Background Signature Survey (IBSS) satellite, and the Orbital Maneuvering Vehicle (OMV) programs. He also served as the Astronaut Office T-38 safety officer, was leader of the Astronaut Support Personnel team at the Kennedy Space Center, and lead spacecraft communicator (CAPCOM) for several Shuttle flights. Most recently, he served as Deputy Program

Manager for the International Space Station Program. A veteran of three space flights, Chilton has logged over 704 hours in space. He was the pilot on STS-49 in 1992 and STS-59 in 1994, and commanded STS-76 in 1996. Chilton left NASA in 1998. Currently he serves as Deputy to the Director of Operations, USAF Space Command, Peterson Air Force Base, Colorado.

SPACE FLIGHT EXPERIENCE: STS-49, May 7-16, 1992, was the maiden voyage of Space Shuttle Endeavour. During the mission, the crew conducted the initial test flight of Endeavour, performed a record four EVA's (space walks) to retrieve, repair and deploy the International Telecommunications Satellite (INTELSAT), and to demonstrate and evaluate numerous EVA tasks to be used for the assembly of Space Station Freedom. Additionally, a variety of medical, scientific and operational tests were conducted throughout the mission. STS-49 logged 213 hours in space and 141 Earth orbits prior to landing at Edwards Air Force Base, California, where the crew conducted the first test of the Endeavour's drag chute. STS-59, the Space Radar Laboratory (SRL) mission, April 9-20, 1994, was launched aboard Space Shuttle Endeavour. SRL consisted of three large radars, SIR-C/X-SAR (Shuttle Imaging Radar C/X-Band Synthetic Aperture Radar), and a carbon monoxide sensor that were used to enhance studies of the Earth's surface and atmosphere. The imaging radars operated in three frequencies and four polarizations. This multispectral capability of the radars provided information about the Earth's surface over a wide range of scales not discernible with previous single-frequency experiments. The carbon monoxide sensor (MAPS) used gas filter radiometry to measure the global distribution of CO in the troposphere. Real-time crew observations of surface phenomena and climatic conditions augmented with over 14,000 photographs aided investigators in interpretation and calibration of the data. The mission concluded with a landing at Edwards AFB after orbiting the Earth 183 times in 269 hours. Col. Chilton commanded STS-76, the third docking mission to the Russian space station Mir, which launched on March 22, 1996 with a crew of six aboard Atlantis. Following rendezvous and docking with Mir, transfer of a NASA astronaut to Mir for a 5-month stay was accomplished to begin a continuous presence of U.S. astronauts aboard Mir for the next two-year period. The crew also transferred 4800 pounds of science and mission hardware, food, water and air to Mir and returned over 1100 pounds of U.S. and ESA science and Russian hardware. The first spacewalk from the Shuttle while docked to Mir was conducted. Experiment packages were transferred from the Shuttle and mounted on the Mir docking module to detect and assess debris and contamination in a space station environment. The Spacehab module carried in the Shuttle payload bay was utilized extensively for transfer and return stowage of logistics and science and also carried Biorack, a small multipurpose laboratory used during this mission for research of plant and animal cellular function. This mission was also the first flight of Kidsat, an electronic camera controlled by classroom students via a Ku-band link between JSC Mission Control and the Shuttle, which uses digitized photography from the Shuttle for science and education. Following 145 orbits of the Earth, Atlantis landed with a crew of five at Edwards Air Force Base in California on March 31, 1996, 221 hours after liftoff.

NAME: Mary L. Cleave (Ph.D., P.E.)
NASA Astronaut (former)

PERSONAL DATA: Born February 5, 1947, in Southampton, New York. Her father, Dr. Howard E. Cleave, resides in Williamstown, Massachusetts. Her mother is deceased.

EDUCATION: Graduated from Great Neck North High School, Great Neck, New York, in 1965; received a bachelor of science degree in Biological Sciences from Colorado State University in 1969 and master of science in Microbial Ecology and a doctorate in Civil and Environmental Engineering from Utah State University in 1975 and 1979, respectively.

ORGANIZATIONS: Member of the Texas Society of Professional Engineers, the Water Pollution Control Federation, Tri-Beta, Sigma XI, and Tau Beta Pi; association member of the American Society of Civil Engineers.

EXPERIENCE: Dr. Cleave held graduate research, research phycologist, and research engineer assignments in the Ecology Center and the Utah Water Research Laboratory at Utah State University from September 1971 to June 1980. Her work included research on the productivity of the algal component of cold desert soil crusts in the Great Basin Desert south of Snowville, Utah; algal removal with intermittent sand filtration and prediction of minimum river flow necessary to maintain certain game fish; the effects of increased salinity and oil shale leachates on freshwater phytoplankton productivity; development of the Surface Impoundment Assessment document and computer program (FORTRAN) for current and future processing of data from surface impoundments in Utah; and design and implementation of an algal bioassay center and a workshop for bioassay techniques for the Intermountain West. In conjunction with her research efforts, she has published numerous scientific papers.

NASA EXPERIENCE: Dr. Cleave was selected as an astronaut in May 1980. Her technical assignments have included: flight software verification in the Shuttle Avionics Integration Laboratory (SAIL); CAPCOM on five Space Shuttle flights; Malfunctions Procedures Book; Crew Equipment Design. A veteran of two space flights, Dr. Cleave has logged a total of 10 days, 22 hours, 02 minutes, 24 seconds in space, orbited the earth 172 times and traveled 3.94 million miles. She wasa mission specialist on STS 61-B (November 26 to December 3, 1985) and STS-30 (May 4-8, 1989). Dr. Cleave left JSC in May 1991 to join NASA's Goddard Space Flight Center in Greenbelt, Maryland. She is working in the Laboratory for Hydrospheric Processes. She is the Deputy Project Manager for SeaWiFS (Sea-viewing, Wide-Field-of-view-Sensor), an ocean color sensor for monitoring global marine chlorophyll concentration. SeaWiFS is scheduled to launch July 1991.

SPACE FLIGHT EXPERIENCE: STS-61B Atlantis (Nov. 26 to Dec. 3, 1985) launched at night from the Kennedy Space Center, Florida, and returned to land on Runway 22 at Edwards Air Force Base, California. During the mission, the crew deployed the MORELOS-B, AUSSAT II, and SATCOM K-2 communications satellites, conducted 2 six-hour spacewalks to demonstrate space station construction techniques with the EASE/ACCESS experiments, operated the Continuous Flow Electrophoresis (CFES) experiment for McDonnell Douglas and a Getaway Special (GAS) container for Telesat, Canada, conducted several Mexican Payload Specialist Experiments for the Mexican Government, and tested the Orbiter Experiments Digital Autopilot (OEX DAP). This was the heaviest payload weight carried to orbit by the Space Shuttle to date. Mission duration was 165 hours, 4 minutes, 49 seconds. STS-30 Atlantis (May 4-8, 1989) was a four day mission during which the crew successfully deployed the MagellanVenus-exploration spacecraft, the first U.S. planetary science mission launched since 1978, and the first planetary probe to be deployed from the Shuttle. Magellan arrived at Venus in August 1990 and mapped over 95% of the surface of Venus. Magellan has been one of NASA's most successful scientific missions providing valuable information about the Venetian atmosphere and magnetic field. In addition, the crew also worked on secondary payloads involving Indium crystal growth, electrical storm, and earth observation studies. Mission duration was 96 hours, 57 minutes, 35 seconds.

NAME: Michael Richard "Rich" Clifford (Lieutenant Colonel, USA)
NASA Astronaut (former)

PERSONAL DATA: Born October 13, 1952 in San Bernadino, California, but considers Ogden, Utah, to be his hometown. Married to the former Nancy Elizabeth Brunson of Darlington, South Carolina. They have two sons. He enjoys flying, golf, tennis, water and snow skiing, baseball, and coaching youth sports. His parents, Gordon and Lenore Clifford, reside in Ogden. Her parents, R. Ben and Mary Lee Brunson, reside in Darlington..

EDUCATION: Graduated from Ben Lomond High School, Ogden, Utah in 1970; received a bachelor of science degree from the United States Military Academy, West Point, New York, in 1974, and a master of science degree in aerospace engineering from the Georgia Institute of Technology in 1982.

MARITAL STATUS: Married to the former Nancy Elizabeth Brunson of Darlington, South Carolina. Her parents, R. Ben and Mary Lee Brunson, reside in Darlington.

CHILDREN: Richard Benjamin, March 14, 1980; Brandon Brunson, May 19, 1983.

RECREATIONAL INTERESTS: Enjoys flying, golf, tennis, water and snow skiing, baseball, and coaching youth sports.

ORGANIZATIONS: Member of the Association of Space Explorers, American Helicopter Society, Army Aviation Association, and the Aircraft Owners and Pilots Association.

SPECIAL HONORS: Recipient of the Defense Superior Service Medal, the Legion of Merit, the Defense Meritorious Service Medal, the National Intelligence Medal of Achievement, NASA Space Flight Medal and the Army Commendation Medal.

EXPERIENCE: Clifford graduated from West Point in June 1974 and was commissioned as a Second Lieutenant in the U.S. Army. He served a tour with the 10th Cavalry in Fort Carson, Colorado. He then entered the U.S. Army Aviation School in 1976. He was the top graduate of his flight class and was designated an Army Aviator in October 1976. He was subsequently assigned for three years as a service platoon commander with the Attack Troop, 2nd Armored Cavalry Regiment in Nuremberg, West Germany. After completing a master of science degree at Georgia Tech in 1982, he was assigned to the Department of Mechanics at West Point as an instructor and assistant professor. In December 1986 he graduated from the U.S. Naval Test Pilot School and was designated an Experimental Test Pilot. A Master Army Aviator, he has logged 3,400 flying hours in a wide variety of fixed and rotary winged aircraft. In December 1995 Lieutenant Colonel Clifford retired from the United States Army.

NASA EXPERIENCE: As a military officer, Clifford was assigned to the Johnson Space Center in July of 1987. As a Space Shuttle Vehicle Integration engineer, his duties involved engineering liaison for launch and landing operations of the Space Shuttle Program. He was involved in design certification and integration of the Shuttle Crew Escape System, and was an executive board member of the Solid Rocket Booster Postflight Assessment Team. Selected as an astronaut by NASA in July 1990, Clifford has served in a variety of technical assignments. From April to August 1991, Clifford was assigned to the Astronaut Office Mission Development Branch where he participated in the design, development, and evaluation of Space Shuttle payloads and crew equipment having extra-vehicular activity (EVA) interfaces. From May 1994 to September 1995 he served as lead for space station vehicle/assembly issues. A veteran of three space flights, Clifford flew as a mission specialist on STS-53 in 1992, STS-59 in 1994, and STS-76 in 1996. He has logged 665 hours in space, including a 6-hour spacewalk.

Clifford first flew on the crew of STS-53 which launched from the Kennedy Space Center, Florida, on December 2, 1992, aboard the Space Shuttle Discovery. The mission carried a Department of Defense payload and a variety of secondary payloads. Clifford was responsible for operating a number of experiments which included the Fluid Acquisition and Resupply Experiment (FARE) and the Battlefield Laser Acquisition Sensor Test (BLAST). FARE was a microgravity fluid transfer experiment designed to evaluate improved spacecraft propellant tanks. BLAST was a hand-held laser energy detector designed to detect and interpret a data message in a low-power Earth-based laser.

After completing 115 orbits of the Earth, STS-53 landed at Edwards Air Force Base, California, on December 9, 1992. He next served aboard Endeavour on the STS-59 Space Radar Laboratory (SRL) mission which launched April 9, 1994. SRL consisted of three large radars, SIR-C/X-SAR (Shuttle Imaging Radar C/X-Band Synthetic Aperture Radar), and a carbon monoxide sensor that were used to enhance studies of the Earth's surface and atmosphere. The imaging radars operated in three frequencies and four polarizations. This multispectral capability of the radars provided information about the Earth's surface over a wide range of scales not discernible with previous single-frequency experiments. The carbon monoxide sensor (MAPS) used gas filter radiometry to measure the global distribution of CO in the troposphere. Real time crew observations of surface phenomena and climatic conditions augmented with over 14,000 photographs aided investigators in interpretation and calibration of the data. The mission concluded on April 20, 1994, with a landing at Edwards Air Force Base after orbiting the Earth 183 times in 269 hours.

Clifford next served on STS-76, the third docking mission to the Russian space station Mir, which launched on March 22, 1996 with a crew of six aboard Atlantis. Following rendezvous and docking with Mir, transfer of a NASA Astronaut to Mir for a five month stay was accomplished to begin a continuous presence of U.S. astronauts aboard Mir for the next two year period. The crew also transferred 4800 pounds of science and mission hardware, food, water and air to Mir and returned over 1100 pounds of U.S. and ESA science and Russian hardware. Clifford performed a 6-hour spacewalk, the first while docked to an orbiting space station, to mount experiment packages on the Mir docking module to detect and assess debris and contamination in a space station environment. The experiments will be retrieved by a future shuttle mission. This mission was also the first flight of Kidsat, an electronic camera controlled by classroom students via a Ku-bank link between JSC Mission Control and the Shuttle, which uses digitized photography from the Shuttle for science and education. Following 145 orbits of the Earth, Atlantis landed with a crew of five at Edwards Air Force Base in California on March 31, 1996.

Rich Clifford left NASA in January 1997 to accept the position of Space Station Flight Operations Manager for Boeing Defense and Space Group.

NAME: Michael L. Coats (Captain, USN)
NASA Astronaut (former)

PERSONAL DATA: Born January 16, 1946, in Sacramento, California, but considers Riverside, California, as his hometown. His father, Col. Loyd A. Coats (USAF Ret.), resides in Dunbar, Wisconsin. His mother, Mrs. Jan Coats, resides in Ft. Collins, Colorado.

PHYSICAL DESCRIPTION: Brown hair; blue eyes; height: 6 feet; weight: 190 pounds.

EDUCATION: Graduated from Ramona High School, Riverside, California, in 1964; received a bachelor of science degree from the United States Naval Academy in 1968, a master of science in Administration of Science and Technology from George Washington University in 1977, and master of science in Aeronautical Engineering from the U.S. Naval Postgraduate School in 1979.

MARITAL STATUS: Married to the former Diane Eileen Carson of Oklahoma City, Oklahoma. Her parents, Dr. and Mrs. James W. Carson, reside in O'Fallon, Illinois.

CHILDREN: Laura M., August 29, 1973; Paul M., November 2, 1978.

RECREATIONAL INTERESTS: He enjoys reading, racquetball, and jogging.

ORGANIZATIONS: Member, Society of Experimental Test Pilots; Associate Fellow, American Institute of Aeronautics and Astronautics.

SPECIAL HONORS: Awarded the Defense Superior Service Medal, 2 Navy Distinguished Flying Crosses, 32 Strike Flight Air Medals, 3 Individual Action Air Medals, 9 Navy Commendation Medals with Combat V, and the NASA Space Flight Medal.

EXPERIENCE: Coats graduated from Annapolis in 1968 and was designated a naval aviator in September 1969. After training as an A-7E pilot, he was assigned to Attack Squadron 192 (VA-192) from August 1970 to September 1972 aboard the USS KITTYHAWK and, during this time, flew 315 combat missions in Southeast Asia. He served as a flight instructor with the A-7E Readiness Training Squadron (VA-122) at Naval Air Station, Lemoore, California, from September 1972 to December 1973 and was then selected to attend the U.S. Naval Test Pilot School, Patuxent River, Maryland. Following test pilot training in 1974, he was project officer and test pilot for the A-7 and A-4 aircraft at the Strike Aircraft Test Directorate. He served as a flight instructor at the U.S. Naval Test Pilot School from April 1976 until May 1977. He then attended the U.S. Naval Postgraduate School at Monterey, California, from June 1977 until his selection for the astronaut candidate program. He has logged over 5,000 hours flying time in 28 different types of aircraft, and 400 carrier landings.

NASA EXPERIENCE: Selected as an astronaut candidate in 1978, Coats became a NASA Astronaut in August 1979. He was a member of the STS-4 astronaut support crew, and was a capsule communicator for STS-4 and STS-5. A veteran of three space flights, Coats flew on STS-41D in 1984, STS-29 in 1989, and STS-39 in 1991. From May1989 to March 1990, he served as Acting Chief of the Astronaut Office. On his first mission, Coats was pilot on the crew of STS-41D, which launched fromKennedy Space Center, Florida, on August 30, 1984. This was the maiden flight of theOrbiter Discovery. During this 6-day mission the crew successfully activated the OAST-1 solar cell wing experiment, deployed three satellites (SBS-D, SYNCOM IV-2, and TELSTAR 3-C), operated the CFES-III experiment, the student crystal growth experiment, and photography experiments using the IMAX motion picture camera. The crew earned the name "Icebusters" in successfully removing hazardous ice particles from the orbiter using the Remote Manipulator System. STS-41D completed 96 orbits of the earth before landing at Edwards Air Force Base, California, on September 5, 1984. In February 1985, Coats was selected as spacecraft commander of STS-61H, which was subsequently canceled after the Challenger accident. As spacecraft commander of STS-29, Coats and his crew launched from Kennedy Space Center, Florida, aboard the Orbiter Discovery, on March 13, 1989. During this highly successful five day mission, the crew deployed a Tracking and Data Relay Satellite, and performed numerous secondary experiments, including a Space Station "heat pipe" radiator experiment, two student experiments, a protein crystal growth experiment, and a chromosome and plant cell division experiment. In addition, the crew took over 3,000 photographs of the earth using several types of cameras, including the IMAX 70 mm movie camera. Mission duration was 80 orbits and concluded with a landing at Edwards Air Force Base, California, on March 18, 1989. With the completion of his second mission, Coats has logged a total of 264 hours in space. More recently, Coats commanded a seven man crew on STS-39. This unclassified eight day Department of Defense mission launched from the Kennedy Space Center, Florida on April 28, 1991. Crew members worked around-the-clock in two-shift operations during which they deployed, operated and retrieved the SPAS-II spacecraft, in addition to conducting various science experiments including research of both natural and induced phenomena in the Earth's atmosphere. After completing 134 orbits of the Earth, Discovery and her crew landed at the Kennedy Space Center, Florida on May 6, 1991.

With the completion of his third mission, Coats has logged over 463 hours in space.

NAME: Michael Collins (Major General, USAF, Retired) Aerospace Consultant and Author, Washington D.C. NASA Astronaut (former)

PERSONAL DATA: Born October 31, 1930, in Rome, Italy.

EDUCATION: Graduated from Saint Albans School in Washington, D.C.; received a Bachelor of Science degree from the United States Military Academy at West Point, N.Y., in 1952. He also attended the Harvard Business School in the advanced management program. He has honorary degrees from six colleges and universities.

MARITAL STATUS: Married to the former Patricia Finnegan of Boston.

CHILDREN: Kathleen, Born May 6, 1959; Ann S., Born October 31, 1961; Michael L., Born February 23, 1963.

SPECIAL HONORS: Collins has received numerous decorations and awards, including the Presidential Medal for Freedom in 1969, the Robert J. Collier Trophy, the Robert H. Goddard Memorial Trophy, and the Harmon International Trophy.

EXPERIENCE: Prior to joining NASA, Collins served as a fighter pilot and an experimental test pilot at the Air Force Flight Test Center, Edwards Air Force Base, California, from 1959 to 1963. He logged more than 4,200 hours flying time.

NASA EXPERIENCE: Collins was one of the third group of astronauts named by NASA in October 1963. He served as pilot on the 3-day Gemini 10 mission, launched July 18, 1966, during which he set a world altitude record and became the nation's third spacewalker, completing two extravehicular activities (EVAs).

His second flight was as command module pilot of the historic Apollo 11 mission in July 1969. He remained in lunar orbit while Neil Armstrong and Buzz Aldrin became the first men to walk on the Moon.

Collins has completed two space flights, logging 266 hours in space, of which 1 hour and 27 minutes were spent in EVA.

CURRENT EXPERIENCE: Upon leaving NASA in January 1970, Collins became Assistant Secretary of State for Public Affairs. In April 1971, Collins joined the Smithsonian Institution as Director of the National Air and Space Museum, where he remained for 7 years. He was responsible for planning and construction of the new museum building, which opened to the public in July 1976, a few days ahead of schedule and below its budgeted cost. In April 1978, Collins became Undersecretary of the Smithsonian Institution. In 1980, Collins became Vice President of the LTV Aerospace and Defense Company, resigning in 1985 to start his own firm. He is author of CARRYING THE FIRE (1974), which describes his experience in the space program. He followed it with FLYING TO THE MOON AND OTHER STRANGE PLACES (1976), a book about space for younger readers. In 1988 he wrote LIFTOFF: THE STORY OF AMERICA'S ADVENTURE IN SPACE.

NAME: Leroy Gordon Cooper, Jr.
NASA Astronaut (former)

PERSONAL DATA: Shawnee, Oklahoma, March 6, 1927. His father, Leroy Gordon Cooper, Sr., is deceased and his mother, Hattie Cooper, resides in Carbondale, Colorado.

PHYSICAL DESCRIPTION: Brown hair; blue eyes; height: 5 ft. 8 in.; weight: 155 lbs.

EDUCATION: Attended primary and secondary school in Shawnee, Oklahoma and Murray, Kentucky, respectively.

COLLEGES: University of Hawaii , University of Maryland - European Extension U.S. Air Force Institute of Technology. Advanced Level: Eleven years graduate level training in Space Technology, Space Mechanics, Lunar Geology, Spacecraft Design, Spacecraft Check Out and Flight Testing with NASA. Degrees: B.S.A.E. - Air Force Institute of Technology, Dr. of Science - Oklahoma City University. Other Schools: Graduate of U.S.A.F. Jet Pilot School,Graduate of U.S. Navy Underwater Demolition Team School,Graduate of U.S.N. Helicopter School

RECREATIONAL INTERESTS: Enjoys treasure hunting, archeology, racing, flying, skiing, boating, hunting, and fishing.

ORGANIZATIONS: The Society of Experimental Test Pilots, The American Institute of Aeronautics and Astronautics, The American Astronautical Society, The Blue Lodge Masons, The York Rite Masons, Scottish Rite Masons, Royal Order Sojourners, Rotary Club, Daedalians, Confederate Air Force Boy Scouts of America, Girl Scouts of America.

SPECIAL HONORS: Air Force Legion of Merit, Air Force Distinguished Flying Cross, Air Force Distinguished Flying Cross Cluster, NASA Exceptional Service Medal, NASA Distinguished Service Medal, USAF Command Astronaut Wings, The Collier Trophy, The Harmon Trophy, The Scottish Rite 33¡, The York Rite Knight of the Purple Cross, The DeMolay Legion of Honor, The John F. Kennedy Trophy, The Ivan E. Kincheloe Trophy, The Air Force Association Trophy, The Primus Trophy, The John Montgomery Trophy, The General Thomas E. White Trophy, The Association of Aviation Writers Award, The University of Hawaii Regents Medal, The Columbus Medal, The Silver Antelope, The Sport Fishing Society of Spain Award.

RECORDS AND FIRSTS: 1963 - Flew 22 orbits (solo) in Mercury 9 (Faith 7), 1963 - Gave one of the opening addresses to the first meeting of the League of African Nations (from Space), 1963 - Used the first television camera in Space, 1963 - First pilot-controlled reentry from Space, 1963-1965 - First Military man to address the Joint Sessions of Congress twice, 1965 - Flew l22 orbits as command pilot of Gemini 5, 1965 - First man to fly two orbital flights, 1965 - First man to fly a fuel cell in space, 1965 - First man to fly a radar set in space, 1965 - First man to track a typhoon from Space, 1965 - Established the World Record of most hours in Space for the United States National Aeronautic Association, Record Distance in Earth orbit 1965 - National Aeronautic Association Record Duration in Earth orbit.

FLYING EXPERIENCE: 7000 hours total time, 4000 hours jet time; flies all types of commercial and general aviation airplane and helicopters

MILITARY EXPERIENCE: 1945-1946 - United States Marine Corps. 1946-1949 - Attended the University of Hawaii - obtained commission. 1949 - Called to active duty USAF (for pilot training) 1950 - 1954 - Fighter pilot with 86th Fighter-Bomber group in Germany. 1954 - 1956 - Attended the Air Force Institute of Technology Attended the USAF Experimental Flight Test School. 1956 - 1957 - Served as Experimental Flight Test Engineer and Flight Test Pilot at the Air Force Flight Test Center at Edwards AFB, California. 1957 - 1959 - Selected in First Group of Seven Astronauts for the NASA Mercury Program. May 15-16, l963 - Command Pilot on MA9 - "Faith 7" August 21-28, 1965 - Command Pilot on Gemini 5. October 1965 - October 1966 - Served as Back-up Command Pilot on Gemini 12. April 1968 - April 1969 - Served as Back-up Command Pilot on Apollo 10. July 31, 1970 - Retired from the Air Force and the Space Program.

MILITARY TECHNICAL AND MANAGEMENT EXPERIENCE: 1956-1959 - Experimental Flight Engineer and Test Pilot at the Air Force Flight Test Center. Served as Project Manager on several flight development projects. Helped to develop new new techniques of flight testing and new aircraftstability parameters. 1950-1970 - In addition to training for Space Flight, has had extensive experience in test project management from thedrawing board to the flight test phase of check out and qualification for various major systems of the Space Program.

BUSINESS TECHNICAL AND MANAGEMENT EXPERIENCE: 1962-1967 - Performance Unlimited, Inc., President - Manufactured race engines, fiberglass boats, distributed marineengines and products, raced high performance boats. 1963-1967 - GCR, Inc., President - Designed, tested and raced championship cars at Indianapolis and other USAC tracks, conducted tire tests for Firestone Tire and Rubber Company, pioneered turbine engine installation. 1965-1970 - Teletest, Inc., President - Designed, installed and tested various systems using advanced Telemetry. 1966-1969 - Doubloon, Inc. - Participated with Doubloon Inc. on design, construction, and utilization of new types of Treasure Hunting equipment. 1968-1969 - Cosmos, Inc. - Participated with Cosmos, Inc. on

Archeology exploration projects. 1968-1970 · Profile Race Team · Part owner and race project manager, designed constructed and raced high performance boats. 1968-1970 · Republic Corp. Technical Consultant · Technical consultant for corporate acquisitions and public relations. 1967-1969 · Thompson Industries Technical Consultant · Technical Consultant for design and construction of various automotive production items for General Motors, Ford, and Chrysler Motor Companies. 1970-1972 · Canaveral International, Inc. · Member of Board of Directors and Technical Consultant for developing technical products, public relations in land development projects. 1970 · Present · Gordon Cooper and Associates, Inc. · President for consultant firm specializing in technical projects from airline and aerospace fields to land and hotel development projects. 1970-1974 · APECO · Board of Director for corporation which produces and markets modular homes, computer systems, office systems, copy machines and boats and marine equipment. July 1972-June 1973 · Campco · Member of Board of Directors and Technical consultant for corporation which builds campers and mobile homes. August 1972-December 1973 · LowCom Systems, Inc. · Board of Directors and Technical Consultant for design and production of various advanced electronic systems. 1972-1973 · Aerofoil Systems, Inc. · Board of Directors and Technical Consultant for design and construction of lifting, inflatable, steerable foils which could land cargo and/or personnel at a precise spot. July 1973-January 1974 · Craftech Construction, Inc., Vice President and member of the Board of Directors · Design and construction of economical homes, garages, storage buildings, and hangars of Craftboard and fiberglass. January 1973-Present · Constant Energy Systems, Inc. · Development of a large energy system to use for metropolitan power and ship engines without use of petrochemicals. Development and sales of improvements to automotive engines to increase their efficiency. 1975 · Vice President for Research and Development for Walter E. Disney Enterprises, Inc., the research and development subsidiary of Walt Disney Productions located in Glendale, California.

NAME: Richard O. Covey (Colonel, USAF)
NASA Astronaut (former)

PERSONAL DATA: Born August 1, 1946, in Fayetteville, Arkansas, but considers Fort Walton Beach, Florida, to be his hometown. His parents, Lt. Col. and Mrs. Charles D. Covey, USAF (Ret.), are deceased.

PHYSICAL DESCRIPTION: Brown hair; gray eyes; height: 5 feet 11-1/2 inches; weight: 155 pounds.

EDUCATION: Graduated from Choctawhatchee High School, Shalimar, Florida, in 1964; received a Bachelor of Science in Engineering Sciences with a major in Astronautical Engineering from the United States Air Force Academy in 1968, and a Master of Science in Aeronautics and Astronautics from Purdue University in 1969.

MARITAL STATUS: Married to the former Kathleen Allbaugh of Emmettsburg, Iowa. Her parents, Mr. and Mrs. Eugene B. Allbaugh, are residents of San Jose, California.

CHILDREN: Sarah Suzanne, Born February 5, 1974; Amy Kathleen, Born May 18, 1976.

RECREATIONAL INTERESTS: He enjoys golf, water sports, photography, skiing, and volleyball.

ORGANIZATIONS:Member of the Air Force Association, the Order of Daedalians, the USAF Academy Association of Graduates, the Society of Experimental Test Pilots, and the Association of Space Explorers.

SPECIAL HONORS: Awarded the Department of Defense Distinguished Service Medal, the Department of Defense Superior Service Medal, 4 Air Force Distinguished Flying Crosses, 16 Air Medals, the Air Force Meritorious Service Medal, the Air Force Commendation Medal, the NASA Exceptional Service Medal, 3 NASA Space Flight Medals, the Johnson Space Center Certificate of Commendation, the American Institute of Aeronautics and Astronautics Haley Space Flight Award for 1988, and the American Astronautical Society Flight Achievement Award for 1988. He is a Distinguished Graduate of the U.S. Air Force Academy, received the Liethen-Tittle Award as the Outstanding Graduate of USAF Test Pilot School Class 74B, and is a Distinguished Astronaut Engineering Alumnus of Purdue University.

EXPERIENCE: Between 1970 and 1974, Covey was an operational fighter pilot,flying the F-100, A-37, and A-7D. He flew 339 combat missions during two tours in Southeast Asia. At Eglin Air Force Base, Florida, between 1975 and 1978, he was an F-4 and A-7D weapons system test pilot and Joint Test Force Director for electronic warfare testing of the F-15 "Eagle." He has flown over 5,000 hours in more than 30 different types of aircraft.

NASA EXPERIENCE: Selected as an astronaut candidate by NASA in January 1978, Covey became an Astronaut in August 1979. He has flown three space flights - STS 51-I in 1985, STS-26 in 1988, and STS-38 in 1990. Prior to the first flight of the Space Shuttle, he provided astronaut support in Orbiter engineering development and testing. He was a T-38 chase pilot for the second and third Shuttle flights and support crewman for the first operational Shuttle flight, STS-5. Covey also served as Mission Control spacecraft communicator (CAPCOM) for Shuttle missions STS-5, 6, 61-B, 61-C, and 51-L. During 1989, he was Chairman of NASA's Space Flight Safety Panel . On his first mission, Covey was the pilot on the five man crew of STS 51-1, which launched from Kennedy Space Center, Florida, on August 27, 1985. During this seven day mission, crewmembers deployed three communications satellites, the Navy SYNCOM IV-4, the Australian AUSSAT, and American Satellite Company's ASC-1. The crew also performed the successful on-orbit rendezvous and repair of the ailing 15,000 pound SYNCOM IV-3 satellite. This repair activity involved the first manual grapple and manual deployment of a satellite by a crew member. The Mission duration was 170 hours. Space Shuttle Discovery completed 112 orbits of the Earth before landing at Edwards Air Force Base, California, on September 3,1985. He then served as pilot on ST5-26, the first flight to be flown after the Challenger accident. The five man crew launched from the Kennedy Space Center, Florida, on September 29, 1988, aboard the Space Shuttle Discovery. Mission duration was 97 hours, during which crewmembers successfully deployed the TDRS-C satellite and operated eleven secondary payloads which included two student experiments. Discovery completed 64 orbits of the earth before landing at Edwards Air Force Base, California, on October 3, 1988. More recently, Covey was the spacecraft commander on STS-38. The five man crew launched at night from the Kennedy Space Center, Florida, on November 15, 1990. During the five day mission crewmembers conducted Department of Defense operations. After 80 orbits of the earth, Covey piloted the Space Shuttle Atlantis to a landing on the runway at the Kennedy Space Center on November 20, 1990. This was the first Shuttle recovery in Florida since 1985.

With the completion of his third space flight, Colonel Covey has logged over 385 hours in space.

NAME: John O. Creighton (Captain, USN, Ret.)
NASA Astronaut (former)

PERSONAL DATA: Born April 28, 1943, in Orange, Texas, but considers Seattle, Washington, to be his hometown. Married to the former Terry Stanford of Little Rock, Arkansas. Recreational interests include skiing, tennis and boating. His mother, Mrs. C. Alberta Creighton, resides in Seattle, Washington. Terry's parents, Helen and Jim Stanford, reside in Stone Mountain, Arkansas.

EDUCATION: Graduated from Ballard High School, Seattle, Washington, in 1961; received a bachelor of science degree from the United States Naval Academy in 1966 and a master of science in Administration of Science and Technology from George Washington University in 1978.

ORGANIZATIONS: Member of the Society of Experimental Test Pilots and the Association of Space Explorers.

SPECIAL HONORS: Awarded the Defense Superior Service Medal, Legion of Merit, Distinguished Flying Cross, 10 air Medals, the Armed Forces Expeditionary Medal, the Vietnam Cross of Gallantry, the NASA Distinguished Service & Leadership Medal, 3 United States Space Flight Medals, the French Legion of Honor and the Saudi Arabia King Fahd Medal.

EXPERIENCE: Creighton started flight training following graduation from Annapolis and received his wings in October, 1967. He was with VF-154 from July 1968 to May 1970, flying F-4J's and made two combat deployments to Vietnam aboard the USS RANGER (CVA-61). From June 1970 to February 1971, he attended the U.S. Naval Test Pilot School at Patuxent River, Maryland, and upon graduation was assigned as a project test pilot with the Service Test Division at the Naval Air Station Patuxent River. During this two year tour of duty, he served as the F-14 engine development project officer. In July 1973, Creighton commenced a four year assignment with VF-2 and became a member of the first F-14 operational squadron, completing two deployments aboard the USS ENTERPRISE (CVN-65) to the Western Pacific. He returned to the United States in July 1977 and was assigned to the Naval Air Test Center's Strike Directorate as operations officer and F-14 program manager. He has logged over 6,000 hours flying time, the majority of it in jet fighters, and has completed 500 carrier landings and 175 combat missions.

NASA EXPERIENCE: Selected as an astronaut candidate by NASA in January 1978, Creighton became an astronaut in August 1979. During the following four years he held a variety of technical assignments in support of the Space Shuttle Program. Following his first flight, Creighton became the astronaut representative to the Shuttle Program Manager. During the ensuing two years, Creighton participated in all the key decisions following the Challenger disaster helping to shape the plan for resuming safe manned space flight. Starting with STS-26, Creighton served as Lead "CAPCOM" for the first four Space Shuttle flights. In March 1989 he was assigned to command STS-36 but continued to serve as Head of the Mission Support Branch in the Astronaut Office until commencing full time training for his upcoming flight. Following his second flight, Creighton headed up the Operations Development Branch within the Astronaut Office for one year prior to resuming full-time training for his next command. Creighton served as pilot on STS-51G (June 17-24, 1985), was spacecraft commander on STS-36 (February 28 to March 4, 1990) and STS-48 (September 12-18, 1991), and has logged over 403 hours in space. Captain Creighton left NASA and retired from the Navy in July 1992. He is currently a Test Pilot with Boeing Airplane Company.

SPACE FLIGHT EXPERIENCE: STS-51G Discovery (June 17-24, 1985) was a 7-day mission during which the crew deployed communications satellites for Mexico (Morelos), the Arab League (Arabsat), and the United States (AT&T Telstar). They used the Remote Manipulator System (RMS) to deploy and later retrieve the SPARTAN satellite which performed 17 hours of x-ray astronomy experiments while separated from the Space Shuttle. In addition, the crew activated the Automated Directional Solidification Furnace (ADSF), six Getaway Specials, participated in biomedical experiments, and conducted a laser tracking experiment as part of the Strategic Defense Initiative. Mission duration was 112 earth orbits in 169 hours and 39 minutes. STS-36 Atlantis (February 28 to March 4, 1990) carried Department of Defense payloads and a number of secondary payloads. Mission duration was 72 earth orbits in 106 hours, 19 minutes, 43 seconds. STS-48 Discovery (September 12-18, 1991) was a 5-day mission during which the crew deployed the Upper Atmosphere Research Satellite (UARS) which is designed to provide scientists with their first complete data set on the upper atmosphere's chemistry, winds and energy inputs. The crew also conducted numerous secondary experiments ranging from growing protein crystals, to studying how fluids and structures react in weightlessness. Mission duration was 81 earth orbits in 128 hours, 27 minutes, 34 seconds.

NAME: Robert L. Crippen (Captain, USN, Ret.)
NASA Astronaut (former)

PERSONAL DATA: Born in Beaumont, Texas, on September 11, 1937. Married to the former Pandora Lee Puckett of Miami, Florida. Three grown daughters.

EDUCATION: Graduated from New Caney High School in Caney, Texas; received a bachelor of science degree in Aerospace Engineering from the University of Texas in 1960.

ORGANIZATIONS: Fellow, American Institute of Aeronautics and Astronautics; American Astronautical Society; and Society of Experimental Test Pilots.

SPECIAL HONORS: NASA Outstanding Leadership Medal (1988); Distinguished Service Medals (1985, 1988, 1993); U.S. Navy Distinguished Flying Cross (1984); Defense Meritorious Service Medal (1984); Federal Aviation Administration's Award for Distinguished Service (1982), Goddard Memorial Trophy (1982), Harmon Trophy (1982); NASA Space Flight Medals (1981, 1983, and 2 in 1984); NASA Distinguished Service Medal (1981), Department of Defense Distinguished Service Award (1981); American Astronautical Society Flight Achievement Award (1981); National Geographic Society's Gardiner Greene Hubbard Medal (1981); Aviation Hall of Fame 1981 Al J. Engel Ward; American Legion's Distinguished Service Medal (1981), Society of Experimental Test Pilots Ivan C. Kincheloe Award (1981); NASA Exceptional Service Medal (1972).

EXPERIENCE: Crippen received his commission through the Navy's Aviation Officer Program at Pensacola, Florida, which he entered after graduation from the University of Texas. He continued his flight training at Whiting Field, Florida, and went from there to Chase Field in Beeville, Texas, where he received his wings. From June 1962 to November 1964, he was assigned to Fleet Squadron VA-72--completing 2 1/2 years of duty as an attack pilot aboard the aircraft carrier USS INDEPENDENCE. He later attended the USAF Aerospace Research Pilot School at Edwards Air Force Base, California, and upon graduation, remained there as an instructor until his selection in October 1966 to the USAF Manned Orbiting Laboratory Program. Crippen was among the second group of aerospace research pilots to be assigned to the MOL program. He has logged more than 6,500 hour flying time, which includes more than 5,500 hours in jet aircraft.

NASA EXPERIENCE: Crippen became a NASA astronaut in September 1969. He was a member of the astronaut support crew for the Skylab 2, 3, and 4 missions, and served in this same capacity for the Apollo-Soyuz Test Project (ASTP) mission, which was completed successfully in July 1975. He served as pilot on STS-1 (April 12-14, 1981), and was the spacecraft commander on STS-7 (June 18-24, 1983), STS-41C (April 6-13, 1984) and STS-41G (October 5-13, 1984). A four flight veteran, Crippen has logged over 565 hours in space, orbited the earth 374 times and traveled over 9.4 million miles. From 1986-1989, he was assigned as deputy director, Shuttle Operations, for NASA Headquarters at Kennedy Space Center, Florida, responsible for final Shuttle preparation, mission execution, and return of the orbiter to KSC after landing at Edwards Air Force Base, California. He also served as director, Space Shuttle, at NASA Headquarters in Washington, D.C. from 1990 until he was named KSC director in 1992. In his headquarters post, Crippen presided over the overall Shuttle program requirements and performance, and total program control including budget, schedule, and program content. At KSC, he managed the processing, launch, and recovery of Space Shuttle missions. He next served as vice president of Training Simulation Systems at Lockheed Martin Information Systems. Effective December 1996, Crippen was named President of the Thiokol Propulsion Group, Brigham City, Utah. This newly established Group is composed of three divisions: Space Operations, Defense and Launch Vehicles, and Science and Engineering.

SPACE FLIGHT EXPERIENCE: STS-1 (April 12-14, 1981) was the first orbital test flight of the Shuttle Columbia, the first true manned spaceship. It was also the first manned vehicle to be flown into orbit without benefit of previous unmanned "orbital" testing; the first to launch with wings using solid rocket boosters. It was also the first winged reentry vehicle to return to a conventional runway landing, weighing more than 99-tons as it was braked to a stop on the dry lakebed at Edwards Air Force Base, California. Mission duration was 54 hours, 20 minutes, 53 1 seconds. STS-7 (June 18-24, 1983) was the second flight for the Orbiter Challenger. This was also the first mission with a 5-person crew. During the 6-day flight the crew deployed satellites for Canada (ANIK C-2) and Indonesia (PALAPA B-1); operated the Canadian-built Remote Manipulator System (RMS) to perform the first deployment and retrieval exercise with the Shuttle Pallet Satellite (SPAS-01); conducted the first formation flying of the orbiter with a free-flying satellite (SPAS-02); carried and operated the first U.S./German cooperative materials science payload (OSTA-2); and operated the Continuous Flow Electrophoresis System (CFES) and the Monodisperse Latex Reactor (MLR) experiments, in addition to activating seven Getaway Specials. Mission duration was 146 hours, 23 minutes, 59 seconds. STS-41C (April 6-13, 1984) was a 7-day mission during which the crew successfully deployed the Long Duration Exposure Facility (LDEF); retrieved the ailing Solar Maximum Satellite, repaired it on-board the orbiting Challenger, and replaced it in orbit using the robot arm called the Remote Manipulator System (RMS); flight tested the Manned Maneuvering Units (MMU's) in two extravehicular activities (EVA's); as well as operating the Cinema 360 and IMAX Camera Systems, and a Bee Hive Honeycomb Structures student experiment. Mission duration was 167 hours, 40 minutes, 07 seconds. STS-41G (October 5-13, 1984) was the first mission with a 7-person crew. During the 8-day flight the crew deployed the Earth Radiation Budget Satellite, conducted scientific observations of the earth with the OSTA-3 pallet and Large Format Camera, as well as demonstrating potential satellite refueling with an EVA and associated hydrazine transfer. Mission duration was 197 hours, 23 minutes, 37 seconds and concluded with a landing at Kennedy Space Center, Florida.

NAME: R. Walter Cunningham
NASA Astronaut (former)

PERSONAL DATA: Born March 16, 1932, in Creston, Iowa. His parents, Mr. and Mrs. Walter W. Cunningham, reside in Venice, California.

PHYSICAL DESCRIPTION: Blond hair; hazel eyes; height: 5 feet 10 inches; weight: 165 pounds.

EDUCATION: Graduated from Venice High School, Venice, California; received a Bachelor of Arts degree with honors in Physics in 1960 and a Master of Arts degree in Physics in 1961 from the University of California at Los Angeles; has completed work at UCLA on doctorate in Physics with exception of thesis. Advanced Management Program, Harvard Graduate School of Business, 1974.

MARITAL STATUS: Married

CHILDREN: Brian, Born September 12, 1960; Kimberly, Born February 12, 1963.

RECREATIONAL INTERESTS: He is an avid sports enthusiast and is particularly interested in hunting, tennis, and sports.

ORGANIZATIONS: Associate Fellow of the American Institute of Aeronautics and Astronautics; Fellow of the American Astronautical Society; member of the Society of Experimental Test Pilots; the American Geophysical Union; Explorers Club; Sigma Pi Sigma, and Sigma Xi. Chairman of UCLA Alumni Fund Drive, 1969 and 1970; member of Steering Committee of the Aviation Subcommittee of the Houston Chamber of Commerce, and a Member of Houston American Revolution Bicentennial Commission. Director of University Savings Association, Houston, Texas. Director of Nitron Inc., Cupertino, California.

SPECIAL HONORS: Awarded the NASA Exceptional Service Medal and Navy Astronaut Wings; corecipient of the AIAA 1969 Haley Astronautics Award; and presented the UCLA Alumni Professional Achievement Award for 1969 and the National Academy of Television Arts and Sciences Special Trustee Award (1969); the American Legion Medal of Valor, and Outstanding American Award of the American Conservative Union, 1975.

EXPERIENCE: Cunningham joined the Navy in 1951 and began his flight training in 1952. In 1953 he joined a Marine squadron and served on active duty with the United States Marine Corps until August 1956 and in the Marine Corps Reserve program until 1975. His present rank is Colonel USMCR (Retired). He worked as a scientist for the RAND Corporation prior to joining NASA. While with RAND, he worked on classified defense studies and problems of the earth's magnetosphere. He has accumulated more than 4,500 hours of flying time, including more than 3,400 in jet aircraft and 260 hours in space.

NASA EXPERIENCE: Mr. Cunningham was one of the third group of astronauts selected by NASA in October 1963.On October 11, 1968, he occupied the lunar module pilot seat for the eleven-day flight of Apollo 7, the first manned flight test of the third generation United States spacecraft. With Walter M. Schirra, Jr., and Donn F. Eisele, Cunningham participated in and executed maneuvers enabling the crew to perform exercises in transposition and docking, and lunar orbit rendezvous with the S-IVB stage of their Saturn IB launch vehicle; completed eight successful test and maneuvering ignitions of the service module propulsion engine; measured the accuracy of performance of all spacecraft systems; and provided the first effective television transmissions of on-board crew activities. The 260-hour, 4 1/2 million mile shakedown flight was successfully concluded on October 22, 1968, with splashdown occurring in the Atlantic, some eight miles from the carrier ESSEX (only 3/10 of a mile from the originally predicted aiming point). Mr. Cunningham's last assignment at the Johnson Space Center was Chief of the Skylab Branch of the Flight Crew Directorate. In this capacity he was responsible for the operational inputs for five separate major pieces of manned space hardware and two different boosters that comprised the Skylab program. The Skylab program utilized the first manned systems employing arrays for electrical power, molecular sieves for environmental control systems, and inertia storage devices for attitude control systems.

Mr. Cunningham is presently the sole principal in the Capital Group, a private investment banking firm headquartered in Houston, Texas.

NAME: Charles Moss Duke, Jr. (Brigadier General, USAF, Ret.)
NASA Astronaut (former)

PERSONAL DATA: Born in Charlotte, North Carolina, on October 3, 1935. Married to the former Dorothy Meade Clairborne of Atlanta, Georgia. They have two grown sons. Recreational interests include hunting, fishing, reading, and playing golf.

EDUCATION: Attended Lancaster High School in Lancaster, South Carolina, and was graduated valedictorian from the Admiral Farragut Academy in St. Petersburg, Florida; received a bachelor of science degree in Naval Sciences from the U.S. Naval Academy in 1957 and a master of science degree in Aeronautics from the Massachusetts Institute of Technology in 1964; presented an honorary doctorate of philosophy from the University of South Carolina in 1973, and an honorary doctorate of Humanities from Francis Marion College in 1990.

ORGANIZATIONS: Member of the Air Force Association, the Society of Experimental Test Pilots, Reserve Officer Association, Full Gospel Businessmen's Fellowship, Christian Businessmen's Committee; National Space Society.

SPECIAL HONORS: Awarded the NASA Distinguished Service Medal, the JSC Certificate of Commendation (1970), the Air Force Distinguished Service Medal with Oak Leaf Cluster and AF Legion of Merit, and Air Force Command Pilot Astronaut Wings, the SETP Iven C. Kincheloe Award of 1972, the AAS Flight Achievement Award for 1972, the AIAA Haley Astronautics Award for 1973, and the Federation Aeronautique Internationale V.M. Komarov Diploma in 1973; named South Carolina Man of the Year in 1973 and inducted into the South Carolina Hall of Fame in 1973; and presented the Boy Scouts of America Distinguished Eagle Scout Award in 1975.

EXPERIENCE: When notified of his selection as an astronaut, Duke was at the Air Force Aerospace Research Pilot School as an instructor teaching control systems and flying in the F-101, F-104, and T-33 aircraft. He graduated from the Aerospace Research Pilot School in September 1965 and stayed on there as an instructor. He is a retired Air Force Reserve Brigadier General and was commissioned in 1957 upon graduation from the Naval Academy. Upon entering the Air Force, he went to Spence Air Base, Georgia, for primary flight training and then to Webb Air Force Base, Texas, for basic flying training, where in 1958 he became a distinguished graduate. He was again a distinguished graduate at Moody Air Force Base, Georgia, where he completed advanced training in F-86L aircraft. Upon completion of this training, he served three years as a fighter interceptor pilot with the 526th Fighter Interceptor Squadron at Ramstein Air Base, Germanypilot with the 526th Fighter Interceptor Squadron at Ramstein Air Base, Germany. He has logged 4,147 hours flying time, which includes 3,632 hours in jet aircraft. Duke was one of the 19 astronauts selected by NASA in April 1966. He served as member of the astronaut support crew for the Apollo 10 flight. He was CAPCOM for Apollo 11, the first landing on the Moon and he served as backup lunar module pilot on Apollo 13.

Duke served as lunar module pilot of Apollo 16, April 16-27, 1972. He was accompanied on the fifth manned lunar landing mission by John W. Young (spacecraft commander) and Thomas K. Mattingly II (command module pilot). Apollo 16 was the first scientific expedition to inspect, survey, and sample materials and surface features in the Descartes region of the rugged lunar highlands. Duke and Young commenced their record setting lunar surface stay of 71 hours and 14 minutes by maneuvering the lunar module "Orion" to a landing on the rough Cayley Plains. In three subsequent excursions onto the lunar surface, they each logged 20 hours and 15 minutes in extravehicular activities involving the emplacement and activation of scientific equipment and experiments, the collection of nearly 213 pounds of rock and soil samples, and the evaluation and use of Rover-2 over the roughest and blockiest surface yet encountered on the moon.

Other Apollo 16 achievements included the largest payload placed in lunar orbit (76,109 pounds); first cosmic ray detector deployed on lunar surface; first lunar observatory with the far UV camera; and longest in-flight EVA from a command module during transearth coast (1 hour and 13 minutes). The latter feat was accomplished by Mattingly when he ventured out to "Casper's" SIM-bay for the retrieval of vital film cassettes from the panoramic and mapping cameras. Apollo 16 concluded with a Pacific Ocean splashdown and subsequent recovery by the USS TICONDEROGA. With the completion of his first space flight, Duke has logged 265 hours in space and over 21 hours of extra vehicular activity. Duke also served as backup lunar module pilot for Apollo 17.

In December 1975, Duke retired from the Astronaut program to enter private business. He is owner of Duke Investments, and is President of Charlie Duke Enterprises. He is an active speaker and Christian lay witness and President of Duke Ministry For Christ.

NAME: Joe Frank Edwards, Jr., (Commander, USN)
NASA Astronaut (former)

PERSONAL DATA: Born February 3, 1958, in Richmond, Virginia. Considers Lineville, Alabama, and Roanoke, Alabama, to be his hometowns. Married to the former Janet Leigh Ragan of Leonardtown, Maryland. He enjoys basketball, running, football and softball. His parents, Joe Frank and Jane McMurray Edwards, reside in Roanoke, Alabama.

EDUCATION: Graduated from Lineville High School, Lineville, Alabama, in 1976. Bachelor of Science degree in Aerospace Engineering from the United States Naval Academy, 1980. Master of Science degree in Aviation Systems from University of Tennessee, Knoxville, 1994.

ORGANIZATIONS: Society of Experimental Test Pilots, Association of Naval Aviation, U.S. Naval Institute.

SPECIAL HONORS: Distinguished Flying Cross, Defense Superior Service Medal, Air Medal, Defense Meritorious Service Medal, Navy Commendation Medal, Navy Achievement Medal. Daedalian

Superior Airmanship Award 1992, Fighter Squadron 143 Fighter Pilot of the Year, 1984, 1985, Fighter Squadron 142 Fighter Pilot of the Year, 1990, 1991, 1992. Carrier Airwing Seven Pilot of the Year, 1985, 1990, 1991.

EXPERIENCE: Designated a Naval Aviator in February 1982. Assigned to Fighter Squadron 143 in 1983 after completion of F-14 Tomcat training. Flew fighter escort and reconnaissance combat missions over Lebanon in 1983 and graduated from U.S. Navy Fighter Weapons School in 1984. Graduated from U.S. Naval Test Pilot School in 1986 and subsequently worked as project flight test officer and pilot for F-14A(PLUS) and F-14D Full Scale Development. Flew the first Navy flight of the F-14D and a high angle of attack/departure from controlled flight test program for the F-14 airframe/F110 engine integration. Served as Operations and Maintenance Officer in Fighter Squadron 142 1989-1992. Worked as Operations Officer in the Operations Directorate of the Joint Chiefs of Staff, Washington D.C. from 1992-1994. He has flown 4000 hours in over 25 different aircraft and logged over 650 carrier arrested landings.

NASA EXPERIENCE: Selected as an astronaut by NASA in December 1994, Edwards reported to the Johnson Space Center in March 1995. He has worked technical issues for the Space Shuttle and Space Station in the Safety Department of the Astronaut Office, and served as Technical Assistant to the Director, Flight Crew Operations Directorate. Most recently, Edwards served as pilot on STS-89. In completing his first space flight, Edwards logged over 211 hours in space. He recently completed an assignment as the NASA Director of Operations (DOR), Russia and is currently the Astronaut CAPCOM representative in Mission Control for Shuttle ascent and entry.

SPACE FLIGHT EXPERIENCE: STS-89 (January 22-31, 1998), was the eighth Shuttle-Mir docking mission during which the crew transferred more than 9,000 pounds of scientific equipment, logistical hardware and water from Space Shuttle Endeavour to Mir. In the fifth and last exchange of a U.S. astronaut, STS-89 delivered Andy Thomas to Mir and returned with David Wolf. Mission duration was 8 days, 19 hours and 47 seconds, traveling 3.6 million miles in 138 orbits of the Earth.

NAME: Joe Henry Engle (Colonel, USAF)
NASA Astronaut (former)

PERSONAL DATA: Born August 26, 1932, Dickinson County, Kansas; home, Chapman, Kansas.

PHYSICAL DESCRIPTION: Blond hair; hazel eyes; height: 6 feet; weight: 165 pounds.

EDUCATION: Attended primary and secondary schools in Chapman, Kansas, and is a graduate of Dickinson County High School; received a bachelor of science degree in aeronautical engineering from the University of Kansas in 1955.

MARITAL STATUS: Married to the former Mary Catherine Lawrence of Mission Hills, Kansas.

CHILDREN: Laurie J., Born April 25, 1959; and Jon L., Born May 9, 1962.

RECREATIONAL INTERESTS: His hobbies include flying (including World War II fighter aircraft), big game hunting, backpacking, and athletics.

ORGANIZATIONS: Member of the Society of Experimental Test Pilots (SETP).

SPECIAL HONORS: Member of the Society of Experimental Test Pilots (SETP). For flight testing of the NASA-USAF X-15 research rocket airplane, he received the: USAF Astronaut Wings (1964), USAF Distinguished Flying Cross (1964), AFA Outstanding Young USAF Officer of 1964, U.S. Junior Chamber of Commerce -- Ten Outstanding, Young Men in America (1964), AIAA Lawrence Sperry Award for Flight Research (1966), and AIAA Pioneer of Flight Award (1965). For flight testing of the Space Shuttle Enterprise during the Approach and Landing Test program in 1977, he received the: USAF Distinguished Flying Cross (1978), SETP Iven C. Kincheloe Award for Flight Test (1977) NASA Exceptional Service Medal, NASA Special Achievement Award, AFA David C. Schilling Award for Flight, AIAA Haley Space Flight Award for 1980, AAS Flight Achievement Award, and Soaring Society of America - Certificate of Achievement. For the orbital test flight of the Space Shuttle Columbia during STS-2 in November 1981, he received the: Department of Defense Distinguished Service Medal; NASA Distinguished Service Medal; Robert H. Goddard Memorial Trophy; Thomas D. White Space Trophy; Robert J. Collier Trophy; Clifford B. Harmon International Trophy; Kansan of the Year, 1981; Distinguished Service Award, University of Kansas, 1982; Distinguished Engineering Service Award, University of Kansas, 1982; and DAR Medal of Honor, 1981.

EXPERIENCE: Engle was a test pilot in the X-15 research program at Edwards AirForce Base, California, from June 1963 until his assignment to the Lyndon B. Johnson Space Center. Three of his 16 flights in the X-15 exceeded an altitude of 50 miles (the altitude that qualifies a pilot for astronaut rating). Prior to that time, he was a test pilot in the Fighter Test Group at Edwards. He received his commission in the Air Force through the AFROTC Program at the University of Kansas and entered flying school in 1957. He served with the 474th Fighter Day Squadron and the 309th Tactical Fighter Squadron at George Air Force Base, California. He is a graduate of the USAF Experimental Test Pilot School and the Air Force Aerospace Research Pilot School. He has flown over 140 different types of aircraft during his career (25 different fighters), logging more than 11,600 hours flight time -- 8,060 in jet aircraft.

NASA EXPERIENCE: Engle is one of the 19 astronauts selected by NASA in April 1966. He was back-up lunar module pilot for the Apollo 14 mission. He was commander of one of the two crews that flew the Space Shuttle approach and landing test flights from June through October 1977. The Space Shuttle "Enterprise" was carried to 25,000 feet on top of the Boeing 747 carrier aircraft, and then released for its two minute glide flight to landing. In this series of flight tests, he evaluated the Orbiter handling qualities and landing characteristics, and obtained the stability and control, and performance data in the subsonic flight envelope for the Space Shuttle. Engle and Richard Truly flew the first flight of the Space Shuttle in the orbital configuration. Engle was the back-up commander for STS-1, the first Shuttle orbital test flight of the Shuttle Columbia. Engle was commander of the second orbital test flight of the Space Shuttle Columbia, which launched from Kennedy Space Center, Florida, on November, 12, 1981. His pilot for this flight, STS-2, was Richard H. Truly. Despite a mission shortened from 5 days to 2 days because of a failed fuel cell, the crew accomplished more than 90% of the objectives set for STS-2 before returning to a landing on the dry lake bed at Edwards Air Force Base, California, November 14, 1981. Major test objectives included the first tests in space of the 50-foot remote manipulator arm. Also, twenty-nine flight test maneuvers were performed during the entry profile at speeds from Mach 24 (18,500 mph) to subsonic. These maneuvers were designed to extract aerodynamic and aerothermodynamic data during hypersonic entry into the Earth's atmosphere. Engle served as Deputy Associate Administrator for Manned Space Flight at NASA Headquarters from March 1982 to December 1982. He retained his flight astronaut status and returned to the Johnson Space Center in January 1983.

On his next mission, Engle was commander of STS 51-I which launched from Kennedy Space Center, Florida, on August 27, 1985. His crew was Richard O. Covey (pilot), and three mission specialists, William F. Fisher, John M. Lounge, and James D. van Hoften. The mission was acknowledged as the most successful Space Shuttle mission yet flown. The crew deployed three communications satellites, the Navy SYNCOM IV-4, the Australian AUSSAT, and American Satellite Company's ASC-1. The crew also performed the successful on-orbit rendezvous and repair of the ailing 15,000 lbSYNCOM IV-3 satellite. This repair activity saw the first manual grapple and manual deployment of a satellite by a crew member. STS 51-I completed 112 orbits of the Earth before landing at Edwards Air Force Base, California, on September 3, 1985. With the completion of this flight Engle has logged over 224 hours in space. Currently Air National Guard Assistant to CINC, U.S. Space Command; maintains Currency in F-16 ANG aircraft; also aerospace and sporting goods consultant.

NAME: John M. Fabian (Colonel, USAF, Ret.)
NASA Astronaut (former)

PERSONAL DATA: Born January 28, 1939, in Goosecreek, Texas, but considers Pullman, Washington, to be his hometown. Married to the former, Donna Kay Buboltz of Spokane, Washington. They have two grown children. Recreational interests include skiing, stamp collecting, and jogging.

EDUCATION: Graduated from Pullman High School, Pullman, Washington, in 1957; received a bachelor of science degree in Mechanical Engineering from Washington State University in 1962; a master of science in Aerospace Engineering from the Air Force Institute of Technology in 1964; and a doctorate in Aeronautics and Astronautics from the University of Washington in 1974.

ORGANIZATIONS: Associate Fellow, American Institute of Aeronautics and Astronautics; Fellow, American Astronautical Society; President, Association of Space Explorers; Corresponding Member, International Academy of Astronautics.

SPECIAL HONORS: Air Force Astronaut Wings; NASA Space Flight Medal with one Oak Leaf Cluster; Federation Aeronautique Internationale - Komarov Diploma; Air Force Meritorious Service Medal; Defense Superior Service Medal Legion of Merit, Defense Meritorious Service Medal, French Legion of Honor, Saudi Arabian King Abdul Aziz Medal; Air Medal with 2 Oak Leaf Clusters; Air Force Commendation Medal; Washington State University Sloan Engineering Award (1961); Air Training Command Academic Training Award (1966); Squadron Officer School Commandant's Trophy (1968); Squadron Officer School Chief of Staff Award (1968); Washington State University Distinguished Alumnus Award (1983); Washington State Service to Humanity Award (1983); Distinguished Alumnus Award (1985); Medallion of Merit (1987); Phi Sigma Kappa.

EXPERIENCE: Fabian, an Air Force ROTC student at Washington State University, was commissioned upon graduation in 1962. After an assignment at the Air Force Institute of Technology at Wright-Patterson Air Force Base, Ohio, he was assigned as an aeronautics engineer in the service engineering division, San Antonio Air Material Area, Kelly Air Force Base, Texas. He then attended flight training at Williams Air Force Base, Arizona, and subsequently spent 5 years as a KC-135 pilot at Wurtsmith Air Force Base, Michigan. He saw action in Southeast Asia, flying 90 combat missions. Following additional graduate work at the University of Washington, he served 4 years on the faculty of the Aeronautics Department at the USAF Academy in Colorado. He has logged 4,000 hours flying time, including 3,400 hours in jet aircraft.

NASA EXPERIENCE: Selected as an astronaut candidate by NASA in January 1978, and became an astronaut in August 1979. During the following years, he worked extensively on satellite deployment and retrieval activities, including development of the Canadian Remote Manipulator System. A veteran of two space flights, he has logged over 316 hours in space. He served as a mission specialist on STS-7 (June 18-24, 1983) and STS-51G (June 17-24, 1985). He was scheduled to fly next in May 1986 on STS-61G. This flight was one of several deferred by NASA in the wake of the Challenger accident . Fabian left NASA on January 1, 1986 to become Director of Space, Deputy Chief of Staff, Plans and Operations, Headquarters USAF. Colonel Fabian retired from the USAF in June 1987 and joined Analytic Services Inc (ANSER), a non-profit aerospace professional services firm in Arlington, Virginia, where he is now President and Chief Executive Officer.

SPACE FLIGHT EXPERIENCE: Fabian first flew as a mission specialist on STS-7, which launched from Kennedy Space Center, Florida, on June 18, 1983. This was the second flight for the Orbiter Challenger and for the first mission with a 5-person crew. During the mission, the crew deployed satellites for Canada (ANIK C-2) and Indonesia (PALAPA B-1); operated the Canadian-built Remote Manipulator System (RMS) to perform the first deployment and retrieval exercise with the Shuttle Pallet Satellite (SPAS-01); conducted the first formation flying of the Orbiter with a free-flying satellite (SPAS-01); carried and operated the first U.S./German cooperative materials science payload (OSTA-2): and operated the Continuous Flow Electrophoresis System (CFES) and the Monodisperse Latex Reactor (MLR) experiments, in addition to activating seven Getaway Specials, Mission duration was 147 hours before landing at Edwards Air Force Base, California, on June 24, 1983. On his second mission, Fabian flew on STS 51-G which launched from the Kennedy Space Center, Florida, on June 17, 1985, and landed at Edwards Air Force Base, California, on June 24, 1985, after completing approximately 170 hours of space flight. This international crew deployed communications satellites for Mexico (Morelos), the Arab League (Arabsat), and the United Stated (AT&T Telstar). They used the Remote Manipulator System (RMS) to deploy and later retrieve the SPARTAN satellite which performed 17 hours of x-ray astronomy experiments while separated from the Space Shuttle. In addition, the crew activated the Automated Directional Solidification Furnace (ADSF), six Getaway Specials, participated in biomedical experiments, and conducted a laser tracking experiment as part of the Strategic Defense Initiative.

NAME: William F. Fisher (M.D.)
NASA Astronaut (former)

PERSONAL DATA: Born April 1, 1946, in Dallas, Texas. Married to the former Anna L. Tingle of St. Albans, New York. They have two daughters.

EDUCATION: Graduated from North Syracuse Central High School, North Syracuse, New York, in 1964; received a bachelor of arts from Stanford University in 1968, and a doctorate in Medicine from the University of Florida in 1975. He did graduate work in biology at the University of Florida from 1969 to 1971, and did graduate work in Engineering at the University of Houston from 1978 to 1980.

ORGANIZATIONS: Diplomate of the American Board of Emergency Medicine and a member of the American College of Emergency Physicians.

SPECIAL HONORS: American Astronautical Society Victor A. Prather Award for Outstanding Achievement in the field of Extravehicular Activity (1985), the FAI Komarov Diploma (1985), the NASA

Space Flight Medal (1985), and the NASA Exceptional Service Medal (1988). Dr. Fisher has also received Group Achievement Awards for EMU and MMU Development (1983), and for Payload Assist Module (PAM) Software Development and Vehicle Integration (1983). In 1986 he was named an ad hoc member of the U.S. Air Force Scientific Advisory Board, and was appointed a member of the NASA Medicine Policy Board in 1987.

EXPERIENCE: After medical school, Dr. Fisher completed a surgical residency from 1975 to 1977 at UCLA's Harbor General Hospital in Torrance, California. He entered private practice in emergency medicine from 1977 to 1980, while serving as an instructor in medicine at the University of South Florida.

He has logged over 2,000 hours in prop, rotary-wing, jet aircraft and spacecraft.

NASA EXPERIENCE: Selected by NASA in May 1980, Dr. Fisher became an astronaut in August 1981. His technical assignments to date include: scientific equipment operator for high altitude research on the WB57-F aircraft (1980-1981); astronaut medical support for the first four Shuttle missions (1980-1982); astronaut office representative for Extravehicular Mobility Unit (spacesuit) and Extravehicular Activity (EVA) procedures and development, including thermal vacuum testing of the suit (1981-1984); astronaut office representative for the Payload Assist Module (PAM-D) procedures and development (1982-1983); astronaut office representative for Shuttle Mission Simulator (SMS) development (1983); support crewman for STS-8; CAPCOM for STS-8 and STS-9; Remote Manipulator System (RMS) hardware and software development team (1983); Manned Maneuvering Unit (MMU) development team (1983); Deputy Director of NASA Government-furnished and Contractor-furnished Equipment (1982-1983); Chief of Astronaut Public Appearances (1985-1987); Head, Astronaut Office Space Station Manned Systems Division, and Health Maintenance Facility (1987-1989); Astronaut Office representative on space crew selection and retention standards for Space Station (1989-1991). Dr. Fisher also practiced emergency medicine at a hospital in the greater Houston area in conjunction with his astronaut duties. Dr. Fisher was a mission specialist on STS-51I, which launched from Kennedy Space Center, Florida, on August 27, 1985. STS-51I was acknowledged as the most successful Space Shuttle mission yet flown. The crew aboard Space Shuttle Discovery deployed three communications satellites, the Navy SYNCOM IV-4, the Australian AUSSAT, and American Satellite Company's ASC-1. They also performed a successful on-orbit rendezvous with the ailing 15,400 pound SYNCOM IV-3 satellite, and two EVA's (space walks) by Dr. Fisher and Dr. van Hoften to repair it, including the longest space walk in history. Discovery completed 112 orbits of the Earth before landing at Edwards Air Force Base, California, on September 3, 1985. In completing this flight, Dr. Fisher has logged over 170 hours in space, including 11 hours and 52 minutes of EVA.

Dr. Fisher left NASA in 1991 and is currently practicing full-time medicine at Humana Hospital in Webster, Texas.

Name: C. Gordon Fullerton
NASA Astronaut (former)

C. Gordon Fullerton is a research pilot at NASA's Dryden Flight Research Facility, Edwards, California. His assignments include a variety of flight research and support activities piloting NASA's B-52 launch aircraft, the 747 Shuttle Carrier Aircraft (SCA), and other multi-engine and high performance aircraft. Fullerton, who logged more than 380 hours in space flight, was a NASA astronaut from September 1969 until November 1986 when he joined the research pilot office at Dryden. In July 1988, he completed a 30-year career with the U.S. Air Force and retired as a Colonel. He continues in his position of research pilot as a civilian. As project pilot on the B-52 launch aircraft, Fullerton is involved in tests to develop a new F-111 crew module recovery system, and air launching the commercially developed Pegasus space vehicle. Fullerton also serves as project pilot on the NASA/Convair 990 aircraft which has been modified as a Landing Systems Research Aircraft to test space shuttle landing gear components.

Additionally, Fullerton is also project pilot on F-18 Systems Research Aircraft, a testbed to develop new flight control actuators, fiber optic control systems, and other advanced aircraft technology. As the project pilot on the Propulsion Controlled Aircraft program, he successfully landed an F-15 with all control surfaces fixed, using only engine thrust modulation for control. The project continues with the goal of flight testing a similar system in an MD-11 transport. In addition to these current activities, Fulleton has been project pilot on a number of other research programs at Dryden. Among them were the C-140 Jetstar Laminar Flow Control, F-111 Mission Adaptive Wing, F-14 Variable Sweep Flow Transition, space shuttle orbiter drag chute and F-111 crew module parachute tests with the B-52, and X-29 vortex flow control. With over 13,000 hours of flying time, Fullerton has piloted 114 different types of aircraft, including full qualification in the T-33, T-34, T-37, T-39, F-86, F-101, F-106, F-111, F-14, X-29, KC-135, C-140, B-47. Since joining Dryden as a research pilot, Fullerton has piloted nearly all the research and support aircraft flown at the facility and currently flies the T-38, F-18, F-15, B-52, the NASA/Conair 990, 747 Shuttle Carrier Aircraft, and the DC-8.

Born October 11, 1936, in Rochester, NY, Fullerton graduated from U.S. Grant High School, Portland, OR. He received Bachelor of Science and Master of Science degrees in Mechanical Engineering from the California Institute of Technology, Pasadena, CA, in 1957 and 1958, respectively.

Fullerton entered the U.S. Air Force in July 1958 after working as a mechanical design engineer for Hughes Aircraft Co., Culver City, CA. After primary and basic flight school he was trained as an F-86 interceptor pilot, and later became a B-47 bomber pilot at Davis-Monthan AFB, AZ. In 1964 he was chosen to attend the Air Force Aerospace Research Pilot School (now the Air Force Test Pilot School), Edwards AFB, CA. Upon graduation he was assigned as a test pilot with the Bomber Operations Division at Wright-Patterson AFB, OH. In 1966, Fullerton was selected for and served as a flight crew member for the Air Force Manned Orbiting Laboratory program until its termination in 1969. After assignment to the NASA Johnson Space Center, as an astronaut Fullerton served on the support crews for the Apollo 14, 15, 16 and 17 lunar missions. In 1977, Fullerton was assigned to one of the two two-man flight crews which piloted the Space Shuttle prototype Enterprise during the Approach and Landing Test Program at Dryden that same year.

Fullerton was the pilot on the eight-day STS-3 Space Shuttle orbital flight test mission March 22-30, 1982. Launched from the Kennedy Space Center, FL., the mission exposed the orbiter Columbia to extremes in thermal stress and tested the 50-foot Remote Manipulator System used to grapple and maneuver payloads to orbit. STS-3 landed at Northrup Strip, White Sands, NM, because Rogers Dry Lake at Edwards AFB was wet due to heavy seasonal rains. Fullerton was commander of the STS-51F Spacelab 2 mission, launched from the Kennedy Space Center, FL, on July 29, 1985. This mission, with the orbiter Challenger was the first pallet-only Spacelab mission and the first to operate the Spacelab Instrument Pointing System (IPS). It carried 13 major experiments in the fields of astronomy, solar physics, ionospheric science, life science, and a super fluid helium experiment. The mission ended August 6, 1985, with a landing at Dryden.

Among the special awards and honors Fullerton has received are the Iven C. Kincheloe Award from the Society of Experimental Test Pilots in 1978; Department of Defense Distinguished Service and Superior Service Medals; Air Force Distinguished Flying Cross; NASA Distinguished and Exceptional Service Medals; NASA Space Flight Medals in 1983 and 1985; General Thomas D. White Space Trophy; Haley Space Flight Award from the American Institute of Aeronautics and Astronautics; and the Certificate of Achievement Award from the Soaring Society of America, and the Ray E. Tenhoff Award from the Society of Experimental Test Pilots in 1992 and 1993.

Fullerton, inducted into the International Space Hall of Fame in 1982, is a Fellow of the Society of Experimental Test Pilots; member, Tau Beta Pi; honorary member of the National World War II Glider Pilot Association; and a Fellow of the American Astronautical Society.

Fullerton and his wife and their two children live in Lancaster, California.

NAME: Dale A. Gardner
NASA Astronaut (former)

PERSONAL DATA: Born November 8, 1948 in Fairmont, Minnesota. Grew up in Sherburn, Minnesota and Savanna, Illinois. Considers his hometown to be Clinton, Iowa, where his mother, Mrs. Alice Gardner, resides. Now lives in Colorado Springs, Colorado. Divorced. Two children. An avid sports enthusiast, he enjoys snow skiing, golfing, tennis, and jogging. Other interests include woodworking and photography.

EDUCATION: Graduated as Valedictorian of his class from Savanna Community High School, Savanna, Illinois, in 1966. Received bachelor of science degree in Engineering Physics from the University of Illinois (Urbana-Champaign) in 1970.

ORGANIZATIONS: Member, Phi Eta Sigma, Sigma Tau, and Tau Beta Pi. Fellow, American Astronautical Society.

SPECIAL HONORS: Defense Superior Service Medal (1984, 1989, 1990); Distinguished Flying Cross (1989); Meritorious Unit Commendation (1976); Humanitarian Service Medal (1979); Sea Service Deployment Ribbon (1984). Other honors include the NASA Space Flight Medal (1983 and 1984); Master Space Badge (1989); Lloyd's of London Meritorious Service Medal (1984).

EXPERIENCE: Upon graduation from the University of Illinois in 1970, Gardner entered into active duty with the U.S. Navy and was assigned to the Aviation Officer Candidate School at Pensacola, Florida. He was commissioned an Ensign and was selected as the most promising naval officer from his class. In October 1970 he began Basic Naval Flight Officer training with the VT-10 squadron at Pensacola, graduating with the highest academic average ever achieved in the history of the squadron. He proceeded to the Naval Technical Training Center at Glynco, Georgia, for Advanced Flight Officer training and was selected a Distinguished Naval Graduate and awarded his Naval Flight Officer wings on May 5, 1971. At the Naval Air Test Center Patuxent River, Maryland, from May 1971 to July 1973, he was assigned to the Weapons Systems Test Division and involved in initial F-14 TOMCAT developmental test and evaluation as Project Officer for Inertial Navigation and Avionics Systems. Gardner's next assignment was with the first operational F-14 squadron (VF-1) at NAS Miramar, San Diego, California, from where he flew the TOMCAT and participated in two Western Pacific and Indian Ocean cruises while deployed aboard the aircraft carrier USS ENTER-PRISE. From December 1976 until July 1978, he was assigned to Air Test and Evaluation Squadron 4(VX-4) at NAS Pt. Mugu, California, involved in the operational test and evaluation of Navy fighter aircraft.

NASA EXPERIENCE: Gardner was selected as an Astronaut Candidate by NASA in January 1978, reporting to the Johnson Space Center in July 1978. In August 1979 he completed a 1-year training and evaluation period, making him eligible for assignment as a Mission Specialist Astronaut. He subsequently served as the Astronaut Project Manager for the flight software in the Shuttle onboard computers leading up to the first flight in April 1981. He then served as a Support Crew Astronaut for the fourth flight (STS-4). He flew as a mission specialist on STS-8 (August 30 to September 5, 1983) and STS-51A (November 8-16, 1984). Gardner logged a total of 337 hours in space and 225 orbits of the Earth on these two flights. He has logged more than 2300 hours flying time in over 20 different types of aircraft and spacecraft. Prior to the Challenger accident, Gardner was chosen to be a member of the first Shuttle mission to launch from Vandenberg Air Force Base, California, into a polar orbit. That flight and the Vandenberg launch capability itself were canceled after the accident. In October 1986, following 8-1/2 years with NASA, Gardner returned to his Navy duties and was assigned to the U.S. Space Command, Colorado Springs, Colorado. He served over two years as the Deputy Chief, Space Control Operations Division in Cheyenne Mountain Air Force Base and, after promotion to the rank of Captain in June 1989, became the command's Deputy Director for Space Control at Peterson Air Force Base. His space control responsibilities included the surveillance and tracking of all man-made objects in Earth orbit and the protection of U.S. and friendly space systems. Gardner retired from the U.S. Navy in October 1990 and accepted a position with TRW Inc. in Colorado Springs, Colorado. He is a program manager in the Colorado Springs Engineering Operations of TRW's Space and Defense Sector. In that capacity, he is involved in the development of both civilian space and military space and defense high technology programs.

SPACE FLIGHT EXPERIENCE: STS-8 launched from the Kennedy Space Center, Florida on August 30, 1983. The crew aboard Space Shuttle Challenger included Richard Truly (Spacecraft Commander), Daniel Brandenstein (Pilot), and fellow Mission Specialists Guion Bluford and William Thornton. This was the third flight of the Orbiter Challenger and the first night launch and landing mission of the Shuttle program. During the flight, the crew of STS-8 deployed the Indian National Satellite (INSAT-1B), operated and tested the Canadian-build Remote Manipulator System (RMS) robot arm, and performed numerous earth resources and space science experiments. STS-8 completed 98 Earth orbits in 145 hours before landing at Edwards Air Force Base, California on September 5, 1983. STS-51A, the fourteenth flight of the Shuttle program, launched on November 8, 1984 (his birthday). The crew aboard Space Shuttle Discovery included Frederick Hauck (Spacecraft Commander), David Walker (Pilot), and fellow Mission Specialists Joseph Allen and Anna Fisher. This was the second flight of Discovery. During this mission the crew deployed two satellites, Canada's ANIK D-2 (TELESAT-H) and the Hughes' LEASAT-1 (SYNCOM IV-1), now in service with the U.S. Navy.

In a dramatic salvage effort, they also rendezvoused with and returned from space two satellites previously launched into improper orbits, the Indonesian PALAPA B-2 and the Western Union WESTAR VI communication satellites. Gardner and Allen completed two space walks totaling 12 hours and flew the Manned Maneuvering Unit (MMU) backpack during the salvage operation. STS-51A completed 127 orbits of the Earth before landing at the Kennedy Space Center on November 16, 1984.

NAME: Guy S. Gardner (Colonel, USAF, retired)
NASA Astronaut former)

PERSONAL DATA: Born January 6, 1948, in Alta Vista, Virginia, and grew up in Alexandria, Virginia.

EDUCATION: Was graduated from George Washington High School in Alexandria, Virginia in 1965; received a bachelor of science degree with majors in astronautics, mathematics, and engineering sciences from the United States Air Force Academy in 1969; received a master of science degree in aeronautics and astronautics from Purdue University in 1970.

MARITAL STATUS: Married to the former Linda A. McCabe of Guilderland, New York. They have three wonderful children: Jennifer, Sarah, and Jason.

SPECIAL HONORS: Air Force Legion of Merit, 2 Defense Superior Service Medals, Defense Distinguished Service Medal, 3 Air Force Distinguished Flying Crosses, 14 Air Medals, National Intelligence Medal of Achievement, Distinguished Graduate of the USAF Academy, Top Graduate in Pilot Training, Top Graduate from the USAF Test Pilot School, Test Pilot School Outstanding Academic Instructor, Test Pilot School Outstanding Flying Instructor, and Distinguished Astronaut Engineering Alumnus of Purdue University.

EXPERIENCE: Gardner completed U.S. Air Force pilot training at Craig Air Force Base, Alabama, and F-4 upgrade training at MacDill Air Force Base, Florida in 1971. In 1972, he flew 177 combat missions in Southeast Asia while stationed in Udorn, Thailand. In 1973-74, he was an F-4 instructor and operational pilot at Seymour Johnson Air Force Base, North Carolina. He attended the USAF Test Pilot School at Edwards Air Force Base, California, in 1975, and then served as a test pilot with the 6512th Test Squadron located at Edwards in 1976. In 1977-78, he was an instructor test pilot at the USAF Test Pilot School. In 1979-80, he was operations officer of the 1st Test Squadron at Clark Air Base, Philippines.

NASA EXPERIENCE: Gardner was selected as a pilot astronaut by NASA in May 1980. During his 11 years as an astronaut, he worked in many areas of Space Shuttle and Space Station development and support. Gardner first flew in space as pilot on the crew of STS-27, aboard the Orbiter Atlantis, on December 2-6, 1988. The mission carried a Department of Defense payload. Gardner next flew as pilot on the crew of STS-35, aboard the Orbiter Columbia, on December 2-10 1990. The mission carried the ASTRO-1 astronomy laboratory consisting of three ultraviolet telescopes and one x-ray telescope.

Gardner left NASA in June 1991, returning to the Air Force as Commandant of the USAF Test Pilot School at Edwards Air Force Base, California.

In August 1992, Gardner retired from the Air Force to go to NASA Headquarters as Program Director of the joint U.S. and Russian Shuttle-Mir Program. He attended the Defense Systems' Management College in 1994, and then became the Director of the Quality Assurance Division, Office of Safety and Mission Assurance at NASA Headquarters.

In September 1995, Gardner joined the Federal Aviation Administration as Director of the FAA Technical Center in New Jersey.

NAME: Owen K. Garriott (Ph.D.)
NASA Astronaut (former)

PERSONAL DATA: Born November 22, 1930, in Enid, Oklahoma. Married to Evelyn (Eve) L. Garriott from Huntsville, Alabama. He has four children from a previous marriage: Randall, Robert, Richard, and Linda. Recreational interests include skiing, sailing, scuba diving, and amateur radio.

EDUCATION: Graduated from Enid High School; received a bachelor of science degree in electrical engineering from the University of Oklahoma in 1953, a master of science degree and a doctor of philosophy degree in electrical engineering from Stanford University in 1957 and 1960, respectively; and presented an honorary doctor of philosophy degree in science from Phillips University (Enid, Oklahoma) in 1973.

ORGANIZATIONS: Fellow of the American Astronautical Society; Associate Fellow of the American Institute of Aeronautics and Astronautics; and member of the American Geophysical Union, the Institute of Electrical and Electronic Engineers, Tau Beta Pi, Sigma XI, the International Scientific Radio Union (URSI), and the American Association for the Advancement of Science.

SPECIAL HONORS: National Science Foundation Fellowship at Cambridge University and at the Radio Research Station at Slough, England, 1960-1961; the NASA Distinguished Service Medal in 1973; the City of Chicago Gold Medal in 1974, the Robert J. Collier Trophy for 1973 in 1974; the Federation Aeronautique Internationale's V. M. Komarov Diploma for 1973 in 1974; the Dr. Robert H. Goddard Memorial trophy for 1975; Education for Public Management Fellowship at Stanford University, 1975-1976; and elected to the International Academy of Astronautics in 1975. Recipient of NASA Space Flight Medal (1983).

EXPERIENCE: Garriott served as an electronics officer while on active duty with the United States Navy from 1953 to 1956, and was stationed aboard several U.S. destroyers at sea. From 1961 until 1965, he taught electronics, electromagnetic theory, and ionospheric physics as an associate professor in the Department of Electrical Engineering at Stanford University. He has performed research in ionospheric physics since obtaining his doctorate and has authored or co-authored more than 40 scientific papers and one book on this subject.

NASA EXPERIENCE: Dr. Garriott was selected as a scientist-astronaut by NASA in June 1965. He then completed a 53-week course in flight training at Williams Air Force Base, Arizona. He has since logged over 5,000 hours flying time; including over 2,900 hours in jet aircraft and the remainder in spacecraft, light aircraft and helicopters. In addition to NASA ratings, he holds FAA commercial pilot and flight instructor certification for instrument and multi-engine aircraft. Dr. Garriott was science-pilot for Skylab-3 (SL-3), the second manned Skylab mission, and was in orbit from July 28 to September 25, 1973. With him on this 59-1/2-day flight were Alan L. Bean (spacecraft commander) and Jack R. Lousma (pilot). SL-3 accomplished 150% of many mission goals while completing 858 revolutions of the Earth and traveling some 24,400,000 miles. The crew installed six replacement rate gyros used for attitude control of the spacecraft and a twin pole sunshade used for thermal control, and repaired nine major experiment or operational equipment items. They devoted 305 manhours to extensive solar observations and completed 333 medical experiment performances to obtain valuable data on the effects of extended weightlessness on man. Skylab-3 ended with a Pacific Ocean splashdown and recovery by the USS New ORLEANS. The crew of Skylab-3 logged 1,427 hours and 9 minutes each in space, setting a new world record for a single mission, and Garriott also spent 13 hours and 43 minutes in three separate extravehicular activities outside the orbital workshop.

Following his Skylab flight, Dr. Garriott served as Deputy and then Director of Science and Applications, and as the Assistant Director for Space and Life Science at the Lyndon B. Johnson Space Center. He later served (1984-1986) as the Space Station Project Scientist.

Dr. Garriott was a mission specialist on STS-9/Spacelab-1 which launched from Kennedy Space Center, Florida, on November 28, 1983. He was accompanied by spacecraft commander, Mr. John W. Young; pilot, Lt. Col. Brewster H. Shaw, Jr.; fellow mission specialist, Dr. Robert A. Parker; and payload specialists, Dr. Byron Lichtenberg and Dr. Ulf Merbold. This six-man crew was the largest yet to fly aboard a single spacecraft, the first international shuttle crew, and the first to carry payload specialists.

During this maiden flight of the European Space Agency (ESA) - developed laboratory, the crew conducted more than 70 multi-disciplinary scientific and technical investigations in the fields of life sciences, atmospheric physics and Earth observations, astronomy and solar physics, space plasma physics, and materials processing. In off duty hours, the first manned amateur radio operations in space were conducted, using Garriott's station call, W5LFL. After 10-days of Spacelab hardware verification and around-the-clock scientific operations, Columbia and its laboratory cargo landed on the dry lakebed at Edwards Air Force Base, California, on December 8, 1983.

Dr. Garriott resigned from the NASA in 1986 and later served as Vice President, Space Programs for Teledyne Brown Engineering in Huntsville, AL (1988-1993). He is currently a co-founder and President of Immutherapeutics, Inc. in Huntsville.

NAME: Charles D. (nickname Sam) Gemar (Lieutenant Colonel, USA)
NASA Astronaut (former)

PERSONAL DATA: Born August 4, 1955 in Yankton, South Dakota, but home is Scotland, South Dakota, where his parents, Mr. & Mrs. Leighton A. Gemar, reside. Married to the former Charlene Stringer of Savannah, Georgia. They have two children. He enjoys water sports, jogging, woodworking, and travel.

EDUCATION: Graduated from Scotland Public High School, Scotland, South Dakota, in 1973; received a bachelor of science degree in engineering from the U. S. Military Academy in 1979.

ORGANIZATIONS: United States Military Academy Association of Graduates; Army Aviation Association of America; Association of Space Explorers-USA; Mount Rushmore National Monument Preservation Society; Nassau Bay Volunteer Fire Department.

SPECIAL HONORS: Gemar was Distinguished Graduate of his class in undergraduate pilot training, and Distinguished Graduate of his class in graduate fixed-wing and multi-engine pilot training. Recipient of the Defense Superior Service Medal, Defense Meritorious Service Medal, Army Commendation Medal, Army Achievement Medal, Good Conduct Medal, two National Defense Service Medals, National Intelligence Medal of Achievement, NASA Achievement Medal, and three NASA Space Flight Medals. Honorary Doctor of Engineering from the South Dakota School of Mines and Technology. Honorary Chair for Membership of the South Dakota Congress of Parents and Teachers. Member of South Dakota Aviation Hall of Fame. Recipient of South Dakota Newspaper Association 1993 Distinguished Service Award.

EXPERIENCE: Gemar enlisted in the Army in January 1973 and reported for duty on June 11, 1973. In November 1973, he was assigned to the 18th Airborne Corps at Ft. Bragg, North Carolina, where he received an appointment to the U.S. Military Academy Preparatory School at Ft. Belvoir, Virginia, and later a Department of the Army appointment to join the U.S. Military Academy Class of 1979. After graduation he attended the Infantry Officers Basic Course at Ft. Benning, Georgia, the Initial Entry Rotary Wing Aviation Course and the Fixed Wing Multi-Engine Aviators Course, both at Ft. Rucker, Alabama. In October 1980, he transferred to the 24th Infantry Division, Ft. Stewart, Georgia, where he remained until January 1, 1985. While at Ft. Stewart/Hunter Army Airfield he served as an Assistant Flight Operations Officer and Flight Platoon Leader for the 24th Combat Aviation Battalion, Wright Army Airfield Commander, and Chief, Operations Branch, Hunter Army Airfield. Other military schools completed include the Army Parachutist Course, Ranger School, and the Aviation Officers Advanced Course.

NASA EXPERIENCE: Selected by NASA in June 1985, Gemar completed a one-year training and evaluation program and became an astronaut in July 1986. He is qualified for assignment as a mission specialist on future Space Shuttle flight crews. Since then he has held a variety of technical assignments in support of the Space Shuttle Program including: flight software testing in the Shuttle Avionics Integration Laboratory (SAIL); launch support activities at the Kennedy Space Center; spacecraft communicator (CAPCOM) in mission control during Space Shuttle missions; Chief of Astronaut Appearances. Gemar has flown three times and has logged over 580 hours in space. He flew on STS-38 (November 15-20, 1990), STS-48 (September 12-18, 1991), and STS-62 (March 4-18, 1994). On his first mission, Gemar served on the five-man crew of STS-38 which launched at night from the Kennedy Space Center, Florida, on November 15, 1990. During the five-day mission crew members conducted Department of Defense operations. After 80 orbits of the Earth in 117 hours, in the first Shuttle recovery in Florida since 1985, Space Shuttle Atlantis and her crew landed back at the Kennedy Space Center on November 20, 1990. Gemar then served on the five-man crew of STS-48 aboard the Space Shuttle Discovery, which launched from the Kennedy Space Center, Florida, on September 12, 1991. During 81 orbits of the Earth, the crew successfully deployed the Upper Atmosphere Research Satellite (UARS), designed to study the Earth's upper atmosphere on a global scale thus providing scientists with their first complete data set on the upper atmosphere's chemistry, winds and energy inputs, in addition to conducting numerous secondary experiments ranging from growing protein crystals, to studying how fluids and structures react in weightlessness. This five-day mission concluded with a landing at Edwards Air Force Base, California, on September 18, 1991. Mission duration was 128 hours. Gemar's most recent mission was STS-62 aboard the Space Shuttle Columbia, which launched from the Kennedy Space Center, Florida, on March 4, 1994. This microgravity science and technology demonstration mission carried the United States Microgravity Payload (USMP-2) and the Office of Aeronautics and Space Technology (OAST-2) payloads. Sixty experiments or investigations were conducted in many scientific and engineering disciplines including materials science, human physiology, biotechnology, protein crystal growth, robotics, structural dynamics, atmospheric ozone monitoring and spacecraft glow. During the spacecraft glow investigation, Columbia's orbital altitude was lowered to 105 nautical miles, the lowest ever flown by a Space Shuttle. STS-62, the second longest Space Shuttle mission to date, concluded after 13 days, 23 hours, and 16 minutes, following 224 orbits of the Earth with a landing at the Kennedy Space Center on March 18, 1994, after traveling 5.8 million miles.

NAME: Edward G. Gibson (Ph.D.)
NASA Astronaut (former)

PERSONAL DATA: Born November 8, 1936, in Buffalo, New York. His parents, Mr. and Mrs. Calder A. Gibson, reside in Naples, Florida.

PHYSICAL DESCRIPTION: Brown hair; brown eyes; height: 5 feet 9 inches; weight: 160 pounds.

EDUCATION: Graduated from Kenmore Senior High School, Kenmore, New York; received a bachelor of science degree in Engineering from the University of Rochester, New York, in June 1959; a master of science degree in Engineering (Jet Propulsion Option) from the California Institute of Technology in June 1960; a doctorate in Engineering with a minor in Physics from the California Institute of Technology in June 1964; an honorary doctorate of science from University of Rochester (NY) in 1974; and an honorary doctorate of science from Wagner College, Staten Island, NY, in 1974.

MARITAL STATUS: Married to the former Julie Anne Volk of Township of Tonawanda, New York.

CHILDREN: Jannet Lynn, Born November 9, 1960; John Edward, Born May 2, 1964; Julie Ann, Born October 12, 1968; Joseph Michael, Born July 11, 1971.

RECREATIONAL INTERESTS: His hobbies include distance running, swimming, photography, flying, and motorcycling.

ORGANIZATIONS: Elected a Fellow of the American Astronautical Society; member of the American Institute of Aeronautics and Astronautics, Tau Beta Pi, Sigma Xi, and Theta Chi. He is a member of the Seniors Track Club.

SPECIAL HONORS: Awarded a National Science Foundation Fellowship and an R. C. Baker Fellowship at the California Institute of Technology, and listed in several Who's Who Publications. He received the JSC Certificate of Commendation (1970), the NASA Distinguished Service Medal (presented by President Richard M. Nixon in 1974), the City of New York Gold Medal (1974), the Robert J. Collier Trophy for 1973 (1974), the Dr. Robert H. Goddard Memorial Trophy for 1975 (1975), the Federation Aeronautique Internationale's De La Vaulx Medal and V. M. Romarov Diploma for 1974 (1975), the American Astronautical Society's 1975 Flight Achievement Award (1976), the AIAA Haley Astronautics Award for 1975 (1976), a Senior U.S. Scientist Award from the Alexander von Humboldt Foundation (1976), and a JSC Special Achievement Award (1978).

EXPERIENCE: While studying at Cal. Tech., Gibson was a research assistant in the fields of jet propulsion and classical physics. His technical publications are in the fields of plasma physics and solar physics. He was senior research scientist with the Applied Research Laboratories of Philco

Corporation at Newport Beach, California, from June 1964 until coming to NASA. While at Philco, he did research on lasers and the optical breakdown of gases. Subsequent to joining NASA in 1965, he wrote a textbook in solar physics entitled THE QUIET SUN.

Gibson's training and data acquisition as science-pilot on the last Skylab mission were in the areas of solar physics, comet observations, stellar observations, earth resources studies, space medicine and physiology, and flight surgeon activities.

He has logged more than 4,300 hours flying time, including 2,270 hours in jet aircraft.

NASA EXPERIENCE: Dr. Gibson was selected as a scientist-astronaut by NASA in June 1965. He completed a 53-week course in flight training at Williams Air Force Base, and earned his Air Force wings. Since then, he has flown helicopters and the T-38.

He served as a member of the astronaut support crew and as a capcom for the Apollo 12 lunar landing. He has also participated in the design and testing of many elements of the Skylab space station.

Dr. Gibson was the science-pilot of Skylab 4 (third and final manned visit to the Skylabspace station), launched November 16, 1973, and concluded February 8, 1974. Thiswas the longest manned flight (84 days 1 hour 15 minutes) in the history of manned space exploration to date. Dr. Gibson was accompanied on the record-setting 34.5 million mile flight by Gerald P. Carr (commander) and William R. Pogue (pilot). They successfully completed 56 experiments, 26 science demonstrations, 15 subsystem detailed objectives, and 13 student investigations during their 1,214 revolutions of the earth. They also acquired a wide variety of earth resources observations data using Skylab's earth resources experiment package camera and sensor array. Dr. Gibson was the crewman primarily responsible for the 338 hours of Apollo Telescope Mount operation which made extensive observations of solar processes.

Until March 1978, Dr. Gibson and his Skylab-4 teammates held the world record for individual time in space: 2,017 hours 15 minutes 32 seconds; 15 hours and 17 minutes of which Dr. Gibson logged in three EVAs outside the orbital workshop.

Gibson resigned from NASA in December 1974 to do research on Skylab solar physics data as a senior staff scientist with the Aerospace Corporation of Los Angeles, California. Beginning in March 1976, he served for one year as a consultant to ERNO Raumfahrttechnik GmbH in West Germany on Spacelab design under the sponsorship of a U. S. Senior Scientist Award from the Alexander von Humboldt Foundation. In March 1977, Dr. Gibson returned to the Astronaut Office astronaut candidate selection and training as chief of the scientist-astronaut candidates.

CURRENT POSITION: In November 1980, Dr. Gibson joined TRW, Inc., as an Advanced Systems Manager in projects which employ high technology for the efficient extraction of energy from abundant resources.

NAME: Robert L. Gibson (Captain, USN)
NASA Astronaut (former)

PERSONAL DATA: Born October 30, 1946, in Cooperstown, New York, but considers Lakewood, California, to be his hometown. Married to Dr. M. Rhea Seddon of Murfreesboro, Tennessee. Four children. He enjoys home built aircraft, formula one air racing, running and surfing during his free time. His mother, Mrs. Paul A. Gibson, resides in Seal Beach, California. His father is deceased. Her father, Mr. Edward C. Seddon, resides in Murfreesboro; her mother is deceased.

EDUCATION: Graduated from Huntington High School, Huntington, New York, in 1964; received an associate degree in engineering science from Suffolk County Community College in 1966, and a bachelor of science degree in aeronautical engineering from California Polytechnic State University in 1969.

SPECIAL HONORS: Awarded the Federation Aeronautique Internationale (FAI) "Louis Bleriot Medal" (1992), and the Experimental Aircraft Association (EAA) "Freedom of Flight" Award (1989). Established world records for "Altitude in Horizontal Flight," Airplane Class C1A in 1991, and "Time to Climb to 9000 Meters" in 1994. Military awards include: the Defense Superior Service Medal; the Distinguished Flying Cross; 3 Air Medals; the Navy Commendation Medal with Combat "V"; a Navy Unit Commendation; Meritorious Unit Commendation; Armed Forces Expeditionary Medal; Humanitarian Service Medal; and Vietnam Campaign Medal.

EXPERIENCE: Gibson entered active duty with the Navy in 1969. He received primary and basic flight training at Naval Air Stations Saufley Field and Pensacola, Florida, and Meridian, Mississippi, and completed advanced flight training at the Naval Air Station at Kingsville, Texas. While assigned to Fighter Squadrons 111 and 1, during the period April 1972 to September 1975, he saw duty aboard the USS Coral Sea (CVA-43) and the USS Enterprise (CVAN-65) -- flying combat missions in Southeast Asia. He is a graduate of the Naval Fighter Weapons School, "Topgun." Gibson returned to the United States and an assignment as an F-14A instructor pilot with Fighter Squadron 124. He graduated from the U.S. Naval Test Pilot School, Patuxent River, Maryland, in June 1977, and later became involved in the test and evaluation of F-14A aircraft while assigned to the Naval Air Test Center's Strike Aircraft Test Directorate. His flight experience includes over 6,000 hours in over 50 types of civil and military aircraft. He holds airline transport pilot, multi-engine, and instrument ratings, and has held a private pilot rating since age 17. Gibson has also completed over 300 carrier landings.

NASA EXPERIENCE: Selected by NASA in January 1978, Gibson became an astronaut in August 1979. Gibson has flown five missions: STS 41-B in 1984, STS 61-C in 1986, STS-27 in 1988, STS-47 in 1992, and STS-71 in 1995. Gibson served as Chief of the Astronaut Office (December 1992 to September 1994) and as Deputy Director, Flight Crew Operations (March-November 1996). On his first space flight Gibson was the pilot on the crew of STS 41-B which launched from the Kennedy Space Center, Florida, on February 3, 1984. The flight accomplished the proper Shuttle deployment of two Hughes 376 communications satellites which failed to reach desired geosynchronous orbits due to upper stage rocket failures. Rendezvous sensors and computer programs were flight tested for the first time. The STS 41-B mission marked the first checkout of the Manned Maneuvering Unit (MMU),and Manipulator Foot Restraint (MFR), with Bruce McCandless and Bob Stewart performing two spectacular EVA's (space walks). The German Shuttle Pallet Satellite (SPAS), Remote Manipulator System (RMS), six "Getaway Specials," and materials processing experiments were included on the mission. The eight-day orbital flight of Challenger culminated in the first landing on the runway at the Kennedy Space Center on February 11, 1984, and Gibson logged 191 hours in space. Gibson was the spacecraft commander of the STS 61-C mission. The seven-man crew on board the Orbiter Columbia launched from the Kennedy Space Center, Florida, on January 12, 1986. During the six-day flight the crew deployed the SATCOM KU satellite and conducted experiments in astrophysics and materials processing. The mission concluded with a successful night landing at Edwards Air Force Base, California, on January 18, 1986, and logged him an additional 146 hours in space.Gibson subsequently participated in the investigation of the Space Shuttle Challenger accident, and also participated inthe redesign and recertification of the solid rocket boosters. As the spacecraft commander of STS-27, Gibson and his five-man crew launched from the Kennedy Space Center, Florida, on December 2, 1988, aboard the Orbiter Atlantis. The mission carried a Department of Defense payload, and a number of secondary payloads. After 68 orbits of the Earth the mission concluded with a dry lakebed landing on Runway 17 at Edwards Air Force Base, California, on December 6, 1988. Mission duration was 105 hours.On Gibson's fourth space flight, the 50th Space Shuttle mission, he served as spacecraft commander of STS-47, Spacelab-J, which launched on September 12, 1992 aboard the Orbiter Endeavour. The mission was a cooperative venture between the United States and Japan, and included the first Japanese astronaut as a member of the seven-person crew. During the eight-day flight, the crew focused on life science and materials processing experiments in over forty investigations in the Spacelab laboratory, as well as scientific and engineering tests performed aboard the Orbiter Endeavour. The mission ended with a successful landing on the runway at the Kennedy Space Center in Floridaafter 126 orbits of the Earth on September 20, 1992. Most recently, (June 27 to July 7, 1995), Captain Gibson commanded a crew of seven-members (up) and eight-members (down) on Space Shuttle mission STS-71. This was the first Space Shuttle mission to dock with the Russian Space Station Mir, and involved an exchange of crews. The Atlantis Space Shuttle was modified to carry a docking system compatible with the Russian Mir Space Station. It also carried a Spacelab module in the payload bay in which the crew performed various life sciences experiments and data collections. Mission duration was 235 hours, 23 minutes.In five space flights, Gibson has completed a total of 36-1/2 days in space.

Gibson left NASA in mid-November to pursue private business interests.

NAME: John Herschel Glenn, Jr. (Colonel, USMC, Ret.)
NASA Astronaut (former)

PERSONAL DATA: Born July 18, 1921 in Cambridge, Ohio. Married to the former Anna Margaret Castor of New Concord, Ohio. They have two grown children and two grandchildren.

EDUCATION: Glenn attended primary and secondary schools in New Concord, Ohio. He attended Muskingum College in New Concord and received a Bachelor of Science degree in Engineering. Muskingum College also awarded him an honorary Doctor of Science degree in engineering. He has received honorary doctoral degrees from nine colleges or universities.

SPECIAL HONORS: Glenn has been awarded the Distinguished Flying Cross on six occasions, and holds the Air Medal with 18 Clusters for his service during World War II and Korea. Glenn also holds the Navy Unit Commendation for service in Korea, the Asiatic-Pacific Campaign Medal, the American Campaign Medal, the World War II Victory Medal, the China Service Medal, the National Defense Service Medal, the Korean Service Medal, the United Nations Service Medal, the Korean Presidential Unit Citation, the Navy's Astronaut Wings, the Marine Corps' Astronaut Medal, the NASA Distinguished Service Medal, and the Congressional Space Medal of Honor.

EXPERIENCE: He entered the Naval Aviation Cadet Program in March 1942 and was graduated from this program and commissioned in the Marine Corps in 1943. After advanced training, he joined Marine Fighter Squadron 155 and spent a year flying F-4U fighters in the Marshall Islands. During his World War II service, he flew 59 combat missions. After the war, he was a member of Marine Fighter Squadron 218 on the North China patrol and served on Guam. From June 1948 to December 1950 Glenn was an instructor in advanced flight training at Corpus Christi, Texas. He then attended Amphibious Warfare Training at Quantico, Virginia. In Korea he flew 63 missions with Marine Fighter Squadron 311. As an exchange pilot with the Air Force Glenn flew 27 missions in theF-86 Sabrejet. In the last nine days of fighting in Korea Glenn downed three MIG's in combat along the Yalu River.

After Korea, Glenn attended Test Pilot School at the Naval Air Test Center, Patuxent River, Maryland. After graduation, he was project officer on a number of aircraft. He was assigned to the Fighter Design Branch of the Navy Bureau of Aeronautics (now Bureau of Naval Weapons) in Washington from November 1956 to April 1959, during which time he also attended the University of Maryland. In July 1957, while project officer of the F8U Crusader, he set a transcontinental speed record from Los Angeles to New York, spanning the country in 3 hours and 23 minutes. This was the first transcontinental flight to average supersonic speed. Glenn has nearly 9,000 hours of flying time, with approximately 3,000 hours in jet aircraft.

NASA EXPERIENCE: Glenn was assigned to the NASA Space Task Group at Langley Research Center, Hampton, Virginia, in April 1959 after his selection as a Project Mercury Astronaut. The Space Task Group was moved to Houston and became part of the NASA Manned Spacecraft Center in 1962. Glenn flew on Mercury-6 (February 20, 1962) and STS-95 (October 29 to November 7, 1998), and has logged over 218 hours in space. Prior to his first flight, Glenn had served as backup pilot for Astronauts Shepard and Grissom. When astronauts were given special assignments to ensure pilot input into the design and development of spacecraft, Glenn specialized in cockpit layout and control functioning, including some of the early designs for the Apollo Project. Glenn resigned from the Manned Spacecraft Center on January 16, 1964. He was promoted to the rank of Colonel in October 1964 and retired from the Marine Corps on January 1, 1965. He was a business executive from 1965 until his election to the United States Senate in November 1974 where he now serves.

SPACE FLIGHT EXPERIENCE: On February 20, 1962, Glenn piloted the Mercury-Atlas 6 "Friendship 7" spacecraft on the first manned orbital mission of the United States. Launched from Kennedy Space Center, Florida, he completed a successful three-orbit mission around the earth, reaching a maximum altitude (apogee) of approximately 162 statute miles and an orbital velocity of approximately 17,500 miles per hour. Glenn's "Friendship 7" Mercury spacecraft landed approximately 800 miles southeast of KSC in the vicinity of Grand Turk Island. Mission duration from launch to impact was 4 hours, 55 minutes, and 23 seconds. STS-95 Discovery (October 29 to November 7, 1998) was a 9-day mission during which the crew supported a variety of research payloads including deployment of the Spartan solar-observing spacecraft, the Hubble Space Telescope Orbital Systems Test Platform, and investigations on space flight and the aging process. The mission was accomplished in 134 Earth orbits, traveling 3.6 million miles in 213 hours and 44 minutes.

NAME: Richard F. Gordon, Jr., (Captain, USN, Ret.)
    NASA Astronaut (former)

PERSONAL DATA: Born October 5, 1929, in Seattle, Washington.

EDUCATION: Graduated from North Kitsap High School, Poulsbo, Washington; received a bachelor of science degree in Chemistry, University of Washington, 1951; a SCD (honorary), Niagara University, 1972; Operations Analysis, USN Post Graduate School, Monterey, California, 1963; and graduated USN Test Pilots School, 1957.

MARITAL STATUS: Married to the former Linda A. Saundera of Miami, Florida.

CHILDREN: Carleen, July 8, 1954; Richard, October 6, 1955; Lawrence, December 18, 1957; Thomas, March 25, 1959; James, April 26, 1960 (deceased); and Diane, April 23, 1961.

COMMUNITY INTERESTS: Gordon has served as chairman and cochairman of the Louisiana Heart Fund, chairman of the March of Dimes (Mother's March), honorary chairman for Muscular Dystrophy, and board of directors for the Boy Scouts of America and Boys' Club of Greater New Orleans.

ORGANIZATIONS: Fellow, American Astronautical Society; Associate Fellow, Society of Experimental Test Pilots; and Navy League.

SPECIAL HONORS: Awarded the NASA Distinguished Service Medal; NASA Exceptional Service Medal; two Navy Distinguished Flying Crosses; Navy Astronaut Wings; Navy Distinguished Service Medal; Institute of Navigation Award for 1969; Godfrey L. Cabot Award, 1970; the Rear Admiral William S. Parsons Award for Scientific and Technical Progress,1970; Phi Sigma Kappa Merit Award,1966; NASA MSC Superior Achievement Award; NASA Group Achievment Award; FAI Record, 1961 (Transcontinental Speed Record); and FAI World Record (Altitutde Record, Gemini XI).

EXPERIENCE: Gordon, a retired Navy Captain, received his wings as a naval aviator in 1953. He then attended All-Weather Flight School and jet transitional training and was subsequently assigned to an all-weather fighter squadron at the Naval Air Station at Jacksonville, Florida. In 1957, he attended the Navy's Test Pilot School at Patuxent River, Maryland, and served as a flight test pilot until 1960. During this tour of duty, he did flight test work on the F8U Crusader, F11F Tigercat, FJ Fury, and A4D Skyhawk, and was the first project test pilot for the F4H Phantom II. He served with Fighter Squadron 121 at the Miramar, California, Naval Air Station as a flight instructor in the F4H and participated in the introduction of that aircraft to the Atlantic and Pacific fleets. He was also flight safety officer, assistant operations officer, and ground training officer for Fighter Squadron 96 at Miramar. Winner of the Bendix Trophy Race from Los Angeles to New York in May 1961, he established a new speed record of 869.74 miles per hour and a transcontinental speed record of 2 hours and 47 minutes. He was also a student at the U.S. Naval Postgraduate School at Monterey, California. He has logged more than 4,500 hours flying time, including 3,500 hours in set aircraft.

NASA EXPERIENCE: Gordon was one of the third group of astronauts named by NASA in October 1963. He served as backup pilot for the Gemini VIII flight. On September 12, 1966, he served as pilot for the 3-day Gemini XI mission, which acheived rendezvous with an Agena in less than one orbit. He executed docking maneuvers with the previously launched Agena and performed two periods of extravehicular activity, which included attaching a tether to the Agena and retrieving a nuclear emulsion experiment package. Other highlights accomplished by Gordon and command pilot Charles Conrad on this flight included the successful completion of the first tethered station-keeping exercise, establishment of a new altitude record of 850 miles, and completion of the first fully automatic controlled reentry. The flight was concluded on September 15, 1966, with the spacecraft landing in the Atlantic, 2 and 1/2 miles from the prime recovery ship USS GUAM. Gordon was subsequently assigned as backup command module pilot for Apollo 9. He occupied the command module pilot seat on Apollo 12, November 14-24, 1969. Other crewmen on man's second lunar landing mission were Charles Conrad, spacecraft commander, and Alan L. Bean, lunar module pilot. Throughout the 31 hour lunar surface stay by Conrad and Bean, Gordon remained in lunar orbit aboard the command module, "Yankee Clipper," obtaining desired mapping photographs of tentative landing sites for future missions. He also performed the final redocking maneuvers following the successful lunar orbit rendezvous which was initiated by Conrad and Bean from within "Intrepid" after their ascent from the Moon's surface. All of the mission's objectives were accomplished, and Apollo 12 achievements include: the precision lunar landing with "Intrepid's" touchdown in the Moon's Ocean of Storms; and the first lunar traverse by Conrad and Bean as they deployed the Apollo Lunar Surface Experiment Package (ALSEP), installed a nuclear power generator station to provide the power source for these long-term scientific experiments, gathered samples of the lunar surface for return to Earth, and completed a close-up inspection of the Surveyor III spacecraft. The Apollo 12 mission lasted 244 hours and 36 minutes and was concluded with a Pacific splashdown and subsequent recovery operations by the USS HORNET. Gordon completed two space flights, logging a total of 315 hours and 53 minutes in space, of which 2 hours and 44 minutes were spent in EVA. He served as backup spacecraft commander for Apollo 15. At the completion of the Apollo 15 flight in 1971, Gordon was given new responsibilities as Chief, Advanced Programs of the Astronaut Office, and worked on the design and testing of the Shuttle and Development Equipment.

In January, 1972, Gordon retired from NASA and the U.S. Navy after 22 years of military service and accepted a position with John W. Mecom, Jr., as Executive Vice President of the New Orleans Saints Professional Football Club in the National Football League. As the Executive Vice President, he was responsible to the President of the New Orleans Saints for the administrative, contractual, and other fiscal operations of the entire Saints' organization.

In April 1977, Gordon returned to Houston at the request of Mecom to act as the General Manager of Energy Developers, Limited (EDL), a Texas Partnership involved in a joint venture with Rocket Research Corporation for the development of a liquid chemical explosive for use in the oil and gas industry. In addition, Gordon was engaged in the utilization of space technology for application to our Earth resources as it applied to the discovery and development of oil and gas resources.

In May 1978, Gordon became President of Resolution Engineering and Development Company (REDCO). REDCO provides design and operational requirements for wild oil well control and fire fighting equipment on board a large semisubmersible utility vessel designed by REDCO and the Southeast Drilling Co. (SEDCO) for operation in the North Sea. Two vessels are presently operating in the North Sea for Phillips Petroleum and Occidental of Britain. Gordon also participated in North Sea production platform safety inspections under the auspices of Red Adair Company for Shell/Esso in the Brent and Cormorant field and for Mobil in the Statford Fields. He was also responsible for the preparation and presentation of the technical report submitted to the respective management personnel for the above companies in London, England; Aberdeen, Scotland; and Stavanger,

Norway. In January 1980, after the merger of REDCO with Amarco Resources, Gordon assumed the additional duties of Vice President for Marketing, Westdale, an oil well servicing subsidiary of AMARCO operating in North Central Texas and Oklahoma. Responsibilities included eatablishment and maintenance of customer files, direct contact with the customer at the management level, analysis of new areas of operation and acquisition possibilities for expansion purposes, and the introduction of allied equipment for the well servicing business of the company. In August 1980, additional responsibilities of Vice President for Operations, Texas Division were assumed. This included the operation of 17 well servicing rigs and 8 pump/transport trucks in Jacksboro and Rule, Texas, as well as the supervision of 92 operational personnel and support staff. From September 1981 to February 1983, Gordon accepted the position of Director: Scott Science and Technology, Inc., Los Angeles Division. He was responsible for all systems management activities of the company in the Los Angeles area. Scott Science and Technology, Inc., is an international corporation dedicated to the commercial application of advanced technology. Based on the expertise residing within the firms, as well as the accessibility of advanced technology in the aerospace community, the company conducts research and development, project management, and product improvement activities to enhance the products, processes, and services of business and industry. In March 1982, Mr. Gordon became President of Astro Sciences Corporation, which was incorporated as Astro Systems and Engineering, Inc., Los Angeles, California. He is responsible as the CEO of Astro Sciences Corporation (a subsidary of Transworld Services, Inc., of which he is a Corporate Vice President) for all activities of the company. The company provides a versatile range of services including engineering, project management, project field support teams, and product support activities. Software and hardware system design for control room applications has also become a recent product. In the Summer of 1984, Gordon was a Technical Advisor for and played the part of "Capcom" in the CBS miniseries SPACE, by James A. Michener.

NAME: Ronald J. Grabe (Colonel, USAF)
NASA Astronaut (former)

PERSONAL DATA: Born June 13, 1945, in New York, New York. His mother, Mrs. Martha Grabe, resides in Lakewood, New Jersey.

PHYSICAL DESCRIPTION: Brown hair; hazel eyes; 6 feet; 185 pounds.

EDUCATION: Graduated from Stuyvesant High School, New York, New York, in 1962; received a bachelor of science degree in Engineering Science from the United States Air Force Academy in 1966; studied aeronautics as a Fulbright Scholar at the Technische Hochschule, Darmstadt, West Germany, in 1967.

MARITAL STATUS: Married to the former Marijo A. Landon. Her parents, Mr. and Mrs. Jack N. Landon, reside in Clovis, New Mexico.

CHILDREN: Hilary, December 25, 1974; and Alison, March 9, 1979.

RECREATIONAL INTERESTS: He enjoys skiing, wind surfing, and racquet sports.

SPECIAL HONORS: The Air Force Distinguished Flying Cross, the Air Medal with 7 Oak Leaf Clusters, the Air Force Meritorious Service Medal, the Liethen-Tittle Award (for Outstanding Student at the USAF Test Pilot School), the Royal Air Force Cross, the NASA Exceptional Service Medal, and NASA Space Flight Medals.

NASA EXPERIENCE: Grabe became a NASA astronaut in August 1981. He served as chief verification pilot for STS-3 and STS-4 entry guidance, navigation and control simulation testing, as the Deputy Manager for Operations Integration, Space Shuttle Program Office, and subsequently as the Chief of Training within the Astronaut Office. Grabe was pilot for STS 51-J, the second Space Shuttle Department of Defense mission, which launched from Kennedy Space Center, Florida, on October 3, 1985. This was the maiden voyage of the Atlantis, the final Orbiter in the Shuttle fleet. After 98 hours of orbital operations, Atlantis landed on Edwards Air Force Base, California, on October 7, 1985. On his second mission, Grabe was pilot for STS-30, which launched from Kennedy Space Center, Florida, on May 4, 1989. On board the Orbiter Atlantis during this four day mission, crew members successfully deployed the Magellan Venus-exploration spacecraft, the first U.S. planetary science mission launched since 1978, and the first planetary probe to be deployed from the Shuttle. Magellan arrived at Venus in mid-1990, and using specialized radar instruments mapped the surface of Venus. In addition, crew members also worked on secondary payloads involving fluid research in general, chemistry and electrical storm studies. Following 64 orbits of the earth, the STS-30 mission concluded a landing at Edwards Air Force Base, California on May 8, 1989. More recently, Grabe was commander of the seven person STS-42 crew, aboard the Shuttle Discovery, which lifted off from the Kennedy Space Center, Florida, on January 22, 1992. Fifty five major experiments conducted in the International Microgravity Laboratory-1 module were provided by investigators from eleven countries, and represented a broad spectrum of scientific disciplines. During 128 orbits of the Earth, the STS-42 crew accomplished the mission's primary objective of investigating the effects of microgravity on materials processing and life sciences. In this unique laboratory in space, crew members worked around-the-clock in two shifts. Experiments investigated the microgravity effects on the growth of protein and semiconductor crystals. Biological experiments on the effects of zero gravity on plants, tissues, bacteria, insects and human vestibular response were also conducted. This eight-day mission culminated in a landing at Edwards Air Force Base, California, on January 30, 1992. With the completion of his third mission, he has logged over of 387 hours in space.

NAME: Duane Edgar Graveline (M.D.)
NASA Astronaut (former)

PERSONAL DATA: Born March 2, 1931, Newport, Vermont.

EDUCATION: Received bachelor of science degree from the University of Vermont (1952), doctor of medicine degree from the University of Vermont Medical School (1955), master of science in public health from Johns Hopkins University (1958).

MARITAL STATUS: Married.

CHILDREN: Five.

EXPERIENCE: Served in the U.S. Air Force, and was chosen with the fourth group of astronauts in 1965. Dr. Graveline resigned from NASA in August 1965 for personal reasons and took a position with the State of Vermont Department of Health. He later resigned that position and set up his own practice, the Health Maintenance Center, in Colchester, Vermont.

NAME: Frederick D. Gregory (Colonel, USAF)
NASA Astronaut (former)

PERSONAL DATA: Born January 7, 1941, in Washington, D.C. His mother, Mrs. Nora D. Gregory, is a resident of Washington, D.C.

PHYSICAL DESCRIPTION: Brown hair; brown eyes; 5 feet 11 inches; 190 pounds.

EDUCATION: Graduated from Anacostia High School, Washington, D.C., in 1958; received a bachelor of science degree from the United States Air Force Academy in 1964, and a master's degree in Information Systems from George Washington University in 1977.

MARITAL STATUS: Married to the former Barbara Archer of Washington, D.C. Her father, Mr. Aaron E. Archer, resides in Forest Heights, Maryland.

CHILDREN: Frederick D., Jr., a Captain in the Air Force, and a graduate of Stanford University. Heather Lynn, a social worker and graduate of Sweet Briar College.

RECREATIONAL INTERESTS: During his free time, he enjoys water skiing, fishing, hunting, specialty cars, and stereo equipment.

ORGANIZATIONS: Member, Society of Experimental Test Pilots, Order of Daedalians, American Helicopter Society, Air Force Academy Association of Graduates, the Air Force Association, Sigma Pi Phi Fraternity, the National Technical Association, and the Tuskegee Airmen. He is also on the Board of Directors for the Young Astronaut Council, the Challenger Center for Space Science Education, and the Virginia Air and Space Center-Hampton Roads History Center.

SPECIAL HONORS: Awarded the Defense Superior Service Medal, 2 Distinguished Flying Crosses, the Defense Meritorious Service Medal, the Meritorious Service Medal, 16 Air Medals, the Air Force Commendation Medal, and 3 NASA Space Flight Medals. Recipient of the NASA Outstanding Leadership Award; the National Society of Black Engineers Distinguished National Scientist Award (1979); an honorary doctor of science degree from the University of the District of Columbia (1986); and the George Washington University Distinguished Alumni Award. Designated an "Ira Eaker Fellow" by the Air Force Association. Recipient of numerous NASA group and individual achievement awards as well as civic and community awards.

EXPERIENCE: After graduating from the United States Air Force Academy in 1964, Gregory entered pilot training and attended undergraduate helicopter training at Stead AFB, Nevada. He received his wings in 1965 and was assigned as an H-43 helicopter rescue pilot at Vance AFB, Oklahoma, from October 1965 until May 1966. In June 1966, he was assigned as an H-43 combat rescue pilot at Danang AB, Vietnam. When he returned to the United States in July 1967, he was assigned as a missile support helicopter pilot flying the UH-1F at Whiteman AFB, Missouri. In January 1968, Gregory was retrained as a fixed-wing pilot flying the T-38 at Randolph AFB, Texas. He was then assigned to the F-4 Phantom Combat Crew Training Wing at Davis-Monthan AFB, Arizona. Gregory attended the United States Naval Test Pilot School at Patuxent River Naval Air Station, Maryland, from September 1970 to June 1971. Following completion of this training, he was assigned to the 4950th Test Wing, Wright Patterson AFB, Ohio, as an operational test pilot flying fighters and helicopters. In June 1974, Gregory was detailed to the NASA Langley Research Center, Hampton,

Virginia. He served as a research test pilot at Langley until selected for the Astronaut Program in January 1978. Gregory has logged more than 6,500 hours flying time in over 50 types of aircraft - - including 550 combat missions in Vietnam. He holds an FAA commercial and instrument certificate for single- and multi-engine airplanes and helicopters. He has authored or co-authored several papers in the areas of aircraft handling qualities and cockpit design.

NASA EXPERIENCE: Gregory was selected as an astronaut in January 1978. His technical assignments have included Astronaut Office Representative at the Kennedy Space Center during initial Orbiter checkout and launch support for STS-1 and STS-2, Flight Data File Manager, lead Capsule Communicator (CAPCOM), Chief, Operational Safety, NASA Headquarters, Washington, D.C., Chief, Astronaut Training, and a member of the Orbiter Configuration Control Board. A veteran of three Shuttle missions, he served as pilot on STS-51B (April 29 - May 6, 1985), and was the spacecraft commander on STS-33 (November 22-27, 1989), and STS-44 (November 24 - December 1, 1991). On his first mission, Gregory was pilot on STS-51B/Spacelab-3 which launched from Kennedy Space Center, Florida, on April 29, 1985. The crew on board the Orbiter Challenger included spacecraft commander, Robert Overmyer; mission specialists, Norman Thagard, William Thornton, and Don Lind; and payload specialists, Taylor Wang and Lodewijk Vandenberg. On this second flight of the European Space Agency (ESA) developed laboratory, the crew members conducted a broad range of scientific experiments ranging from space physics to the suitability of animal holding facilities. The crew also deployed the Northern Utah Satellite (NUSAT). After seven days of around-the-clock scientific operations, Challenger and its laboratory cargo landed on the dry lakebed at Edwards AFB, California, on May 6, 1985. He was the spacecraft commander on STS-33 which launched, at night, from Kennedy Space Center, Florida, on November 22, 1989. On board the Orbiter Discovery, his crew included the pilot, John Blaha, and three mission specialists, Manley (Sonny) Carter, Story Musgrave, and Kathryn Thornton. The mission carried Department of Defense payloads and other secondary payloads. After 79 orbits of the earth, this five day mission concluded on November 27, 1989, with a hard surface landing on Runway 04 at Edwards AFB, California.

More recently, Colonel Gregory commanded a crew of six aboard the Orbiter Atlantis. STS-44 launched at night on November 24, 1991 from the Kennedy Space Center, Florida. During 110 orbits of the Earth the crew successfully deployed their prime payload, the Department of Defense Support Program (DSP) satellite in addition to working on a variety of secondary payloads ranging from the Military Man in Space experiment designed to evaluate the ability of a spaceborne observer to gathering information about ground troops, equipment and facilities, to participating in extensive studies evaluating medical countermeasures to long duration space flight. His crew included the pilot Tom Henricks, three mission specialists, Story Musgrave, Jim Voss and Mario Runco Jr., and payload specialist Tom Hennen. The mission concluded on December 1, 1991 with a landing at Edwards Air Force Base in California. With the completion of his third mission, Gregory has logged over 455 hours in space.

NAME: William G. Gregory (Lieutenant Colonel, USAF, Ret.)
NASA Astronaut (former)

PERSONAL DATA: Born May 14, 1957, in Lockport, New York. Married. He enjoys distance running, biking, triathlon, water and snowskiing.

EDUCATION: Graduated from Lockport Senior High School, Lockport, New York, in 1975; received a bachelor of science degree in engineering sciences from the United States Air Force Academy in

1979, a master of science degree in engineering mechanics from Columbia University in 1980, and a master of science degree in Management from Troy State in 1984.

ORGANIZATIONS: Member of the USAF Academy Association of Graduates.

SPECIAL HONORS: Awarded the Defense Superior Service Medal, the Air Force Meritorious Service Medal, the Air Force Commendation Medal with Oak Leaf Cluster, the NASA Space Flight Medal, and the National Defense Service Medal. He is a Distinguished Graduate of the United States Air Force Academy, a Guggenheim Fellowship recipient, and is a Professional Engineer registered in the State of Colorado. Recipient of the 1996 Ellis Island Medal of Honor.

EXPERIENCE: Between 1981 and 1986, Gregory served as an operational fighter pilot flying the D and F models of the F-111. In this capacity, he served as an instructor pilot at RAF Lakenheath, U.K., and Cannon Air Force Base (AFB), New Mexico. He attended the USAF Test Pilot School in 1987. Between 1988 and 1990 Gregory served as a test pilot at Edwards AFB flying the F-4, A-7D, and all five models of the F-15. Having flown in excess of 40 types of aircraft, Gregory has accumulated over 5,000 hours of flight time. Selected by NASA in January 1990, Gregory became an astronaut in July 1991. Gregory's technical assignments included: Shuttle Avionics Integration Laboratory (SAIL); astronaut office representative for Landing/Rollout, T-38 Flying Safety; Kennedy Space Center Astronaut Support Personnel (ASP); spacecraft communicator (CAPCOM) in mission control; astronaut office representative for rendezvous and proximity operations; and Spacecraft Operations Branch Chief. He flew on STS-67 (1995) and has logged 400 hours in space. Gregory retired from the Air Force and left NASA in the Summer of 1999. He currently serves as Manager of Business Development, Honeywell, Phoenix, Arizona.

SPACE FLIGHT EXPERIENCE: Gregory served as the STS-67 pilot on the seven-person astronomical research mission aboard the Space Shuttle Endeavour. Launching from the Kennedy Space Center on March 2, 1995, and landing at Edwards AFB on March 18, 1995, the crew established a new mission duration record of 16 days, 15 hours, 8 minutes and 46 seconds, while completing 262 orbits and traveling nearly seven million miles. This second flight of the ASTRO telescope primary payload also included numerous secondary payloads.

NAME: Sidney M. Gutierrez
NASA Astronaut (former)

PERSONAL DATA: Born June 27, 1951, in Albuquerque, New Mexico. Father, Mr. Robert A. Gutierrez, resides in Albuquerque, New Mexico. Mother, Mrs. Sarah E. Gutierrez, deceased.

EDUCATION: Graduated from Valley High School, Albuquerque, New Mexico, in 1969; received a bachelor of science degree in aeronautical engineering from the U.S. Air Force Academy in 1973, and a master of arts degree in management from Webster College in 1977.

MARITAL STATUS: Married to the former Marianne Sue Cremer of Jefferson City, Missouri. Her parents, Mr. and Mrs. Lee G. Cremer, reside in Brackettville, Texas.

CHILDREN: Jennifer Anne, August 30, 1980; David McNeill, March 31, 1984; Katherine Elizabeth, January 29, 1988.

RECREATIONAL INTERESTS: Enjoys camping, woodworking, and racquetball.

ORGANIZATIONS: Member of the Society of Experimental Test Pilots, the Air Force Association, the U.S. Air Force Academy Association of Graduates, and the Society of Space Explorers.

SPECIAL HONORS: NASA Outstanding Leadership Medal, NASA Exceptional Achievement Medal, Two NASA Space Flight Medals, 1990 Congressional Hispanic Caucus Award, Awarded Aviation Week and Space Technology Aerospace Laureate in Space and Missiles for 1991, Hispanic Engineer magazine 1992 Hispanic Engineer of the Year National Achievement Award, Aviation Week and Space Technology Citation for Aerospace Laureate in Space and Missiles for 1994, 1994 selected by Hispanic Business magazine as one or the 100 most Influential Hispanics, selected by Hispanic Magazine for the 1995 Hispanic Achievement Award in Science, 1995 inductee into the International Space Hall of Fame, Distinguished Graduate of the USAF Academy; awarded the Distinguished Flying Cross, Legion of Merit, Defense Superior Service Medal, Air Force Meritorious Service Medal, Air Force Commendation Medal with 1 Oak Leaf Cluster, National Defense Service Medal, and Air Training Command Master Instructor.

EXPERIENCE: Gutierrez was a member of the National Collegiate Championship Air Force Academy Parachute Team with over 550 jumps, and a Master Parachutist rating. After graduation from the Academy he completed undergraduate pilot training at Laughlin Air Force Base in Del Rio, Texas. He remained there as a T-38 instructor pilot from 1975 through 1977. In 1978 Gutierrez was assigned to the 7th Tactical Fighter Squadron at Holloman Air Force Base, Alamogordo, New Mexico, where he flew the F-15 Eagle. He attended the USAF Test Pilot School in 1981 and was assigned to the F-16 Falcon Combined Test Force after graduation. While there, Gutierrez served as primary test pilot for airframe and propulsion testing on the F-16 aircraft. Test projects included the F-100 Digital Electronic Engine Control, F-16C & D Model Structural and Performance Testing, F-16 Maximum Performance Braking Tests, and F-16 Mobile Arrestment Qualification. He has logged over 4,500 hours flying time in approximately 30 different types of airplanes, sailplanes, balloons, and rockets.

NASA EXPERIENCE: Selected by NASA in May 1984, Gutierrez became an astronaut in June 1985. In his first technical assignment he served as commander for the Shuttle Avionics Integration Laboratory (SAIL), flying simulated missions to verify Shuttle flight software. Following the Shuttle Challenger accident he served as an action officer for the Associate Administrator for Space Flight at NASA Headquarters. His duties includedcoordinating requests from the Presidential Commission and the U.S. Congress during the investigation. In 1986 and 1987, he participated in the recertification of the Space Shuttle Main Engines, Main Propulsion System, and External Tank. In 1988, he became the Astronaut Office lead for Shuttle software development, verification, and future requirements definition. In 1989 he supported launches of STS-28, 30, 32, 33 and 34 at the Kennedy Space Center in Florida. On his first mission Gutierrez served as pilot on the crew of STS-40 Spacelab Life Sciences (SLS-I), a dedicated space and life sciences mission, which launched from the Kennedy Space Center, Florida, on June 5, 1991. SLS-I was a nine-day mission during which crew members performed experiments which explored how humans, animals, and cells respond to microgravity and re-adapt to Earth's gravity on return. Other payloads included experiments designed to investigate materials science, plant biology and cosmic radiation. Following 146 orbits of the Earth and 218 hours in space, Columbia and her crew returned to land at Edwards Air Force Base, California, on June 14, 1991. After his first flight, Gutierrez served as spacecraft communicator (CAPCOM) - the voice link between the flight crew and mission control - for STS-42, 45, 46, 49 and 52. In 1992 he became the Astronaut Office Branch Chief for Operations Development, overseeing ascent, entry, abort, software, rendezvous, Shuttle systems, main engines, solid rocket boosters, external tank, and landing and rollout issues. On his second mission, Col. Gutierrez served as Commander of STS-59 Space Radar Laboratory (SRL-I). SRL-I, part of Mission to Planet Earth, was an II-day flight dedicated to the study of the Earth and the atmosphere around it. The two primary payloads were the Space-borne Imaging Radar-C/X-Band Synthetic Aperture Radar (SIR-C/X-SAR), and Measurement of Air Pollution from Space (MAPS). The crew completed over 400 precise maneuvers (a Shuttle record) to properly point the radar, imaged over 400 selected sites with approximately 14,000 photographs (a Shuttle record) and recorded enough data to fill 26,000 encyclopedias. Areas of investigation included ecology, oceanography, geology, and hydrology. Launching on April 9, 1994, from the Kennedy Space Center in Florida, the Endeavour and her crew of six completed 183 orbits of the Earth and 270 hours in space before landing at Edwards AFB, California, on April 20, 1994.

SANDIA EXPERIENCE: In September of 1994 Gutierrez retired at the rank of Colonel from the U.S. Air Force and NASA, returned to his native home of Albuquerque, New Mexico, and joined Sandia National Laboratories. From then until March of 1995 he served as Manager for their Strategic Initiatives Department. In March he became Manager of the Airborne Sensors and Integration Department in the Exploratory Systems Development Center. He also served as Chairman of the Governor's Technical Excellence Committee Spaceport Task Force.

BOARDS AND DIRECTORS: Gutierrez serves on the Boards of Directors of the Texas-New Mexico Power Company and Goodwill Industries of New Mexico and is vice-chairman of the New Mexico Space Center's Governor's Commission.

NAME: Fred Wallace Haise, Jr.
NASA Astronaut (former)

PERSONAL DATA: Born in Biloxi, Mississippi, on November 14, 1933; his mother, Mrs. Fred W. Haise, Sr., resides in Biloxi.

PHYSICAL DESCRIPTION: Brown hair; brown eyes; height: 5 feet 9-1/2 inches; weight: 155 pounds.

EDUCATION: Graduated from Biloxi High School, Biloxi, Mississippi; attended Perkinston Junior College (Association of Arts); received a Bachelor of Science degree with honors in Aeronautical Engineering from the University of Oklahoma in 1959, and an honorary Doctorate of Science from Western Michigan University in 1970.

MARITAL STATUS:Married to the former F. Patt Price of Rogers, Texas.

CHILDREN: Mary M., January 25, 1956; Frederick T., May 13, 1958; Stephen W., June 30, 1961; Thomas J., July 6, 1970.

ORGANIZATIONS:Fellow of the American Astronautical Society and the Society of Experimental Test Pilots (SETP); member, Tau Beta Pi, Sigma Gamma Tau, and Phi Theta Kappa; and honorary member, National WWII Glider Pilots Association.

SPECIAL HONORS: Awarded the Presidential Medal for Freedom (1970); the NASA Distinguished Service Medal; the AIAA Haley Astronautics Award for 1971; the American Astronautical Society Flight Achievement Awards for 1970 and 1977; the City of New York Gold Medal in 1970; the City of Houston Medal for Valor in 1970; the Jeff Davis Award (1970); the Mississippi Distinguished Civilian Service Medal (1970); the American Defense Ribbon; the SETP's Ray E. Tenhoff Award for 1966; the A. B. Honts Trophy as the outstanding graduate of Class 64A from the Aerospace Research Pilot School in 1964; the NASA Exceptional Service Medal (1978); the JSC Special Achievement Award (1978); the Soaring Society of America's Certificate of Achievement Award (1978); the General Thomas D. White Space Trophy for 1977 (1978); the SETP's Iven C. Kincheloe Award (1978); and the Air Force Association's David C. Schilling Award (1978).

EXPERIENCE: Haise was a research pilot at the NASA Flight Research Center at Edwards, California, before coming to Houston and the Lyndon B. Johnson Space Center; and from September 1959 to March 1963, he was a research pilot at the NASA Lewis Research Center in Cleveland, Ohio. During this time, he had several papers published. He was the Aerospace Research Pilot School's outstanding graduate of Class 64A and served with the U. S. Air Force from October 1961 to August 1962 as a tactical fighter pilot and as chief of the 164th Standardization Evaluation Flight of the 164th Tactical Fighter Squadron at Mansfield, Ohio. From March 1957 to September 1959, Haise was a fighter interceptor pilot with the 185th Fighter Interceptor Squadron in theOklahoma Air National Guard. He also served as a tactics and all weather flight instructor in the U. S. Navy Advanced Training Command at NAAS Kingsville, Texas, and was assigned as a U. S. Marine Corps fighter pilot to VMF-533 and 114 at MCAS Cherry Point, North Carolina, from March 1954 to September 1956. His military career began in October 1952 as a Naval Aviation Cadet at the Naval Air Station in Pensacola, Florida. Haise has accumulated 8,700 hours flying time, including 5,700 hours in jets.

NASA EXPERIENCE: Was one of the 19 astronauts selected by NASA in April 1966. He served as backup lunar module pilot for the Apollo 8 and 11 missions. Haise was lunar module pilot for Apollo 13, April 11-17, 1970. Apollo 13 was programmed for ten days and was committed to our first landing in the hilly, upland Fra Mauro region of the moon; however, the original flight plan was modified in route to the moon due to a failure of the service module cryogenic oxygen system which occurred approximately 55 hours into the flight. Haise and fellow crewmen, James A. Lovell (spacecraft commander) and John L. Swigert (command module pilot), working closely with Houston ground controllers, converted their lunar module Aquarius into an effective lifeboat. Their emergency activation and operation of lunar module systems conserved both electrical power and water in sufficient supply to assure their safety and survival while in space and for the return to earth. In completing his first space flight, Mr. Haise logged a total of 142 hours and 54 minutesin space. He served as backup spacecraft commander for the Apollo 16 mission. From April 1973 to January 1976, he was technical assistant to the Manager of the Space Shuttle Orbiter Project. Haise was commander of one of the two 2-man crews who piloted space shuttle approach and landing test (ALT) flights during the period June through October 1977. This series of critical orbiter flight tests initially involved Boeing 747/orbiter captive-active flights, followed by air-launched, unpowered glide, approach, and landing tests (free flights). There were three captive mated tests with the orbiter Enterprise carried atop the Boeing 747 carrier aircraft, allowing in-flight low altitude and low-speed test, and checkout of flight control systems and orbiter controls, and five free flights which permitted extensive evaluations of the orbiter's subsonic flying qualities and performance characteristics during separation, up and away flight, flare, landing, and rollout, which provided valuable real-time data duplicating the last few minutes of an operational shuttle mission.

CURRENT ASSIGNMENT: Haise resigned from NASA June 1979 and became Vice-President, Space Programs at Grumman Aerospace Corporation.

NAME: L. Blaine Hammond, Jr. (Colonel, USAF)
NASA Astronaut (Former)

PERSONAL DATA: Born January 16, 1952, in Savannah, Georgia, but considers St. Louis, Missouri, as his hometown. Son, Michael Blaine. He enjoys tennis, golf, racquetball, squash, snow skiing, sailing, and scuba diving. His parents, Mr. and Mrs. Lloyd B. Hammond, Sr., reside in Stuart, Florida.

EDUCATION: Graduated from Kirkwood High School, Kirkwood, Missouri, in 1969; received a bachelor of science degree in engineering science and mechanics from the U.S. Air Force Academy in 1973, and a master of science degree in engineering science and mechanics from Georgia Institute of Technology in 1974.

ORGANIZATIONS: Member of the Air Force Academy Association of Graduates, Air Force Association, and the Order of Daedalians.

SPECIAL HONORS: Distinguished Graduate USAF Academy, Commander's Trophy, and Flying Training Award in Undergraduate Pilot Training. Defense Superior Service Medal, NASA Space Flight Medal, Air Force Commendation Medal (2).

EXPERIENCE: Hammond received his pilot wings at Reese Air Force Base, Texas, in 1975. He was assigned to the 50th Tactical Fighter Wing 496th Tactical Fighter Squadron, Hahn Air Base, Germany, flying the F-4E from 1976 to 1979. In 1979-1980, he was an Instructor Pilot in the F-5B/E/F at Williams Air Force Base, Arizona, training a variety of foreign national students. He attended the Empire Test Pilot School (ETPS) at A&AEE Boscombe Down, United Kingdom, in 1981. Hammond returned to Edwards Air Force Base, California, in 1982, where he managed several projects in the 6512 Test Squadron until being assigned as an instructor at the USAF Test Pilot School. As a test pilot school instructor, he flew the F-4/A-7/A-37, and was the High Angle of Attack program monitor, teaching stall/spin theory and flight training. He has logged over 4,500 hours in 15 American and 10 RAF aircraft.

NASA EXPERIENCE: Selected by NASA in May 1984, Hammond became an astronaut in June 1985, and is qualified for assignment as a pilot/commander on future Space Shuttle flight crews. His technical assignments include having served in Mission Control as an ascent/entry spacecraft communicator (CAPCOM). In that capacity he was directly involved in the decision-making process for flight rules, procedures, techniques, and launch commit criteria. He was also assigned as an Astronaut Support Person (ASP), or "Cape Crusader," responsible for monitoring Orbiter status as it undergoes testing and maintenance at KSC during preparations for the next flight. Hammond also served as the lead astronaut supporting the Shuttle Avionics Integration Laboratory (SAIL) which tests and verifies the flight software for each Shuttle mission. Hammond was the lead astronaut supporting Orbiter software development and changes, including the Global Positioning Satellite (GPS) avionics upgrade. He also worked on designing new cockpit flight instruments/systems displays for the Multifunctional Electronic Display System (MEDS), a major cockpit upgrade to electronic display systems. A veteran of two space flights, Hammond has logged over 462 hours in space. He flew on STS-39 in 1991, and STS-64 in 1994. Colonel Hammond flew as pilot of Discovery on STS-39, the first unclassified Department of Defense mission (April 28 to May 6, 1991). He logged 199 hours and 23 minutes of space flight. The seven-man crew performed numerous scientific experiments to collect data on atmospheric infrared and ultraviolet phenomena including a deploy and rendezvous in support of the Strategic Defense Initiative Office (SDIO). Recently, he was the pilot on STS-64 aboard the Space Shuttle Discovery. Mission highlights included: first use of lasers for environmental research; deployment and retrieval of a solar science satellite; robotic processing of semiconductors; use of RMS boom for jet thruster research; first untethered spacewalk in 10 years to test a self-rescue jetpack. Mission duration was 10 days, 22 hours, 51 minutes. Following STS-64, Hammond completed 5 months of intensive Russian language training as preparation for assignment as the Deputy for Operations, Russia. That assignment was subsequently changed to NASA Liaison to USAF HQ/AFSPC, Colorado Springs, where he worked several issues to strengthen ties between NASA, AFSPC, and USAF Astronauts. Hammond was also assigned as Lead Ascent/Entry CAPCOM for missions STS-73 through STS-78. During the same period, Hammond served as the Branch Chief of the Flight Support Branch, supervising CAPCOM and ASP activities. Hammond is currently assigned as the Branch Chief of the Astronaut Office Safety Branch where he monitors all T-38, Shuttle, and Space Station safety issues.

NAME: Bernard A. Harris, Jr., (M.D.)
NASA Astronaut (former)

PERSONAL DATA: Born June 26, 1956, in Temple, Texas. Married to the former Sandra Fay Lewis of Sunnyvale, California. They have one child. He enjoys flying, sailing, skiing, running, scuba diving, art and music. Bernard's mother, Mrs. Gussie H. Burgess, and his stepfather, Mr. Joe Roye Burgess, reside in San Antonio, Texas. His father, Mr. Bernard A. Harris, Sr., resides in Philadelphia, Pennsylvania. Sandra's parents, Mr. & Mrs. Joe Reed, reside in Sunnyvale.

EDUCATION: Graduated from Sam Houston High School, San Antonio, Texas, in 1974; received a bachelor of science degree in biology from University of Houston in 1978, a doctorate in medicine from Texas Tech University School of Medicine in 1982. Dr. Harris completed a residency in internal medicine at the Mayo Clinic in 1985. In addition, he completed a National Research Council Fellowship at NASA Ames Research Center in 1987, and trained as a flight surgeon at the Aerospace School of Medicine, Brooks Air Force Base, San Antonio, Texas, in 1988. Dr. Harris also received a master's degree in biomedical science from the University of Texas Medical Branch at Galveston in 1996.

ORGANIZATIONS: Member of the American College of Physicians, American Society for Bone and Mineral Research, Aerospace Medical Association, National Medical Association, American Medical Association, Minnesota Medical Association, Texas Medical Association, Harris County Medical Society, Phi Kappa Phi Honor Society, Kappa Alpha Psi Fraternity, Texas Tech University Alumni Association, and Mayo Clinic Alumni Association. Aircraft Owners and Pilot Association. Association of Space Explorers. American Astronautical Society. Member, Board of Directors, Boys and Girls Club of Houston. Committee Member, Greater Houston Area Council on Physical Fitness and Sports. Member, Board of Directors, Manned Space Flight Education Foundation Inc.

SPECIAL HONORS: 1996 Honorary Doctorate of Science, Morehouse School of Medicine. Medal of Excellence, Golden State Minority Foundation 1996. NASA Award of Merit 1996. NASA Equal Opportunity Medal 1996. NASA Outstanding Leadership Medal 1996. The Challenger Award, The Ronald E. McNair Foundation 1996. Award of Achievement, The Association of Black Cardiologists 1996. Space Act Tech Brief Award 1995. Alpha Omega Alpha Medical Honor Society, Zeta of Texas

Chapter 1995. Election of Fellowship in the American College of Physicians 1994. Distinguished Alumnus, The University of Houston Alumni Organization 1994. Distinguished Scientist of the Year, ARCS Foundation, Inc., 1994. Life Membership, Kappa Alpha Psi Fraternity.NASA Space Flight Medals 1993, 1995. NASA Outstanding Performance Rating 1993. JSC Group Achievement Award 1993. Physician of the Year, National Technical Association, 1993. Achiever of the Year, National Technical Association, 1993. American Astronautical Society Melbourne W. Boynton Award for Outstanding Contribution to Space Medicine 1993. Achievement Award, Kappa Alpha Psi Fraternity 1993. Who's Who Among Rising Young Americans Citation 1992. Certificate of Merit, Governor of Texas 1990. City of San Antonio Citation for Achievement 1990. NASA Sustained Superior Performance Award 1989. NASA Outstanding Performance Rating 1988. NASA Sustained Superior Performance Award 1988, 1989. National Research Council Fellowship 1986, 1987. Phi Kappa Phi Honor Society 1985. Outstanding Young Men of America 1984. University of Houston Achievement Award 1978. Achievement Award 1978.

EXPERIENCE: After completing his residency training in 1985 at the Mayo Clinic, Dr. Harris then completed a National Research Council Fellowship at NASA Ames Research Center, Moffett Field, California. While at Ames he conducted research in the field of musculoskeletal physiology, and disuse osteoporosis, completing his fellowship in 1987. He then joined NASA Johnson Space Center as a clinical scientist and flight surgeon. His duties included clinical investigations of space adaptation and the development of countermeasures for extended duration space flight. Assigned to the Medical Science Division, he held the title of Project Manager, Exercise Countermeasure Project. Dr. Harris holds several faculty appointments. He is an associate professor in internal medicine at the University of Texas Medical Branch; an assistant professor at the Baylor College of Medicine; a clinical professor at the University of Texas School of Medicine; and is an adjunct professor at the University of Texas School of Public Health. He is a member, Board of Regents for the Texas Tech University Health Science Center in Lubbock, Texas. Fellow, American College of Physicians. He is the author and co-author of numerous scientific publications. In addition, Dr. Harris has been in group medical practice in internal medicine with both the South Texas Primary Care in San Antonio, Texas, and with the San Jose Medical Group in San Jose, California. Dr. Harris is also a licensed private pilot.

NASA EXPERIENCE: Selected by NASA in January 1990, Dr. Harris became an astronaut in July 1991. He is qualified for assignment as a mission specialist on future Space Shuttle flight crews. He served as the crew representative for Shuttle Software in the Astronaut Office Operations Development Branch. A veteran of two space flights, Dr. Harris has logged more than 438 hours in space. He was a mission specialist on STS-55 (April 26 to May 6, 1993), and was the Payload Commander on STS-63 (February 2-11, 1995). Dr. Harris was assigned as a mission specialist on STS-55, Spacelab D-2, in August 1991, and later flew on board Columbia for ten days, (April 26 to May 6, 1993), marking the Shuttle's one year of total flight time. Dr. Harris was part of the payload crew of Spacelab D-2, conducting a variety of research in physical and life sciences. During this flight, Dr. Harris logged over 239 hours and 4,164,183 miles in space. Most recently, Dr. Harris was the Payload Commander on STS-63 (February 2-11, 1995), the first flight of the new joint Russian-American Space Program. Mission highlights included the rendezvous with the Russian Space Station, Mir, operation of a variety of investigations in the Spacehab module, and the deployment and retrieval of Spartan 204. During the flight, Dr. Harris became the first African-American to walk in space. He logged 198 hours, 29 minutes in space, completed 129 orbits, and traveled over 2.9 million miles. Dr. Harris left NASA in April 1996. He is Chief Scientist and Vice-President of Science and Health Services.

NAME: Terry J. Hart
NASA Astronaut (former)

PERSONAL DATA: Born October 27, 1946, in Pittsburgh, Pennsylvania. Married to the former Wendy Marie Eberhardt of Warren, Pennsylvania. They have two children. Recreational interests include golf and woodworking.

EDUCATION: Graduated from Mt. Lebanon High School, Pittsburgh, Pennsylvania, in 1964; received a bachelor of science degree in mechanical engineering from Lehigh University in 1968, a master of science in mechanical engineering from the Massachusetts Institute of Technology in 1969, a master of science in electrical engineering from Rutgers University in 1978, and an honorary doctorate of engineering from Lehigh University in 1988.

ORGANIZATIONS: Member of the Institute of Electrical and Electronic Engineers, Tau Beta Pi, Sigma Xi, and Delta Upsilon.

SPECIAL HONORS: Awarded the National Defense Medal, NASA Space Flight Medal and named Outstanding Officer of Undergraduate Pilot Training Class in 1970. Rutgers Distinguished Alumnus Award.

EXPERIENCE: Hart entered on active duty with the Air Force reserve in June 1969. He completed undergraduate pilot training at Moody Air Force Base, Georgia, in December 1970, and from then until 1973, flew F-106 interceptors for the Air Defense Command at Tyndall Air Force Base, Florida, at Loring Air Force Base, Maine, and at Dover Air ForceBase, Delaware. In 1973, he joined the New Jersey Air National Guard and continued flying with the Guard until 1985, retiring in 1990. He has logged 3,000 hours flying time -- 2,400 hours in jets. From 1968 to 1978, Hart was employed as a member of the Technical Staff of Bell Telephone Laboratories. His principle duties included electrical and mechanical design responsibilities for a variety of electronic power equipment used in the Bell System. He has received 2 patents.

NASA EXPERIENCE: Mr. Hart was selected as an astronaut candidate by NASA in January 1978. In August 1979, he completed a 1-year training and evaluation period, making him eligible for flight assignment on future Space Shuttle crews. Mr. Hart was a member of the support crews for STS-1, STS-2, STS-3, and STS-7. He was Ascent and Orbit CAPCOM with the Mission Control Team for those flights. Mr. Hart flew as a mission specialist on STS-41C (April 6-13, 1984) and has logged a total of 168 hours in space.

He is currently the Director of Engineering and Operations for AT&T's satellite network.

SPACE FLIGHT EXPERIENCE: STS 41-C Challenger launched from Kennedy Space Center, Florida, on April 6, 1984. The crew included Captain Robert L. Crippen (spacecraft commander), Mr. F. R. (Dick) Scobee (pilot), and fellow mission specialist, Dr. G. D. (Pinky) Nelson and Dr. Jr. D. A. (Ox) van Hoften. During this mission the crew successfully deployed the Long Duration Exposure Facility (LDEF); retrieved the ailing Solar Maximum Satellite, repaired it on board Challenger, and replaced it in orbit using the robot arm called the Remote Manipulator System (RMS). The mission also included flight testing of Manned Maneuvering Units (MMU's) in two extravehicular activities (EVA's); operation of the Cinema 360 and IMAX Camera Systems, as well as a Bee Hive Honeycomb Structures student experiment. Mission duration was 7-days before landing at Edwards Air Force Base, California, on April 13, 1984.

NAME: Henry W. Hartsfield, Jr. (Mr.)
NASA Astronaut (former)

PERSONAL DATA: Born in Birmingham, Alabama, on November 21, 1933. Married to the former Judy Frances Massey of Princeton, North Carolina. They have two grown daughters.

EDUCATION: Graduated from West End High School, Birmingham, Alabama; received a bachelor of science degree in physics at Auburn University in 1954; performed graduate work in physics at Duke University and in astronautics at the Air Force Institute of Technology; and awarded a master of science degree in engineering science from the University of Tennessee in 1971.

SPECIAL HONORS: Awarded the Air Force Meritorious Service Medal; the General Thomas D. White Space Trophy for 1973 (1974). Inducted into Alabama Aviation Hall of Fame (1983). Distinguished Civilian Service Award (DOD) (1982). NASA Distinguished Service Medals (1982, 1988). NASA Space Flight Medals (1982, 1984, 1985). NASA Exceptional Service Medal (1988). Honorary Doctor of Science degree from Auburn University (1986). Presidential Rank of Meritorious Executive in the Senior Executive Service (1996).

EXPERIENCE: Hartsfield received his commission through the Reserve Officer Training Program (ROTC) at Auburn University. He entered the Air Force in 1955, and his assignments have included a tour with the 53rd Tactical Fighter Squadron in Bitburg, Germany. He is also a graduate of the USAF Test Pilot School at Edwards Air Force Base, California, and was an instructor there prior to his assignment in 1966 to the USAF Manned Orbiting Laboratory (MOL) Program as an astronaut. After cancellation of the MOL Program in June 1969, he was reassigned to NASA. He has logged over 7,400 hours flying time -- of which over 6,150 hours are in the following jet aircraft: F-86, F-100, F-104, F-105, F-106, T-33, and T-38.

NASA EXPERIENCE: Hartsfield became a NASA astronaut in September 1969. He was a member of the astronaut support crew for Apollo 16 and served as a member of the astronaut support crew for the Skylab 2, 3, and 4 missions. Hartsfield retired in August 1977 from the United States Air Force with more than 22 years of active service but continues his assignment as a NASA astronaut in a civilian capacity. He was a member of the orbital flight test missions group of the astronaut office and was responsible for supporting the development of the Space Shuttle entry flight control system and its associated interfaces. Hartsfield served as backup pilot for STS-2 and STS-3, Columbia's second and third orbital flight tests. A veteran of three space flights, Hartsfield has logged 483 hours in space. He served as the pilot on STS-4 (June 27 to July 4, 1982), and was the spacecraft commander on STS-41D (August 30 to September 5, 1984) and STS-61A (October 30 to November 6 1985). From 1986 to 1987 Mr. Hartsfield served as the Deputy Chief of the Astronaut Office. In 1987, he became the Deputy Director for Flight Crew Operations, supervising the activities of the Astronaut Office and the Aircraft Operations Division at the Johnson Space Center. In 1989, he accepted a temporary assignment in the Office of Space Flight, NASA Headquarters, Washington, D.C. There he served as Director of the Technical Integration and Analysis Division reporting directly to the Associate Administrator for Space Flight. In this assignment he was responsible for facilitating the integration of the Space Station and its unique requirements into the Space Shuttle systems. His office also served as a technical forum for resolving technical and programmatic issues.In 1990, Mr. Hartsfield accepted another temporary assignment as the Deputy Manager for Operations, Space Station Projects Office, at the Marshall Space Flight Center, Alabama. In that capacity he was responsible for the planning and management of Space Station Operations and

Utilization Capability Development and operations activities including budget preparation. Later in that assignment he also acted as the Deputy Manager for the Space Station Projects Office.In 1991, Mr. Hartsfield accepted the position of the Man-Tended Capability (MTC) Phase Manager, Space Station Freedom Program and Operations (SSFPO), with a duty station at the Johnson Space Center. Reporting directly to the Deputy Director, SSFPO, he represented the Deputy Director in providing appropriate program guidance and direction to the Space Shuttle Program, and across the Space Station Freedom Program for all MTC phase mission unique activities to assure appropriate resolution of issues. In December 1993, Mr. Hartsfield accepted the position of Manager, International Space Station Independent Assessment. In this capacity he reports directly to the Associate Administrator for Safety and Mission Assurance and manages and focuses the oversight activities and assessment of the International Space Station Alpha Program. In September 1996, the scope of Mr. Hartsfield's work was expanded to include independent assessment of the programs and projects of the Human Exploration and Development of Space (HEDS) Enterprise and he was named Director, HEDS Independent Assurance.

SPACE FLIGHT EXPERIENCE: STS-4, the fourth and final orbital test flight of the Shuttle Columbia, launched from Kennedy Space Center, Florida, on 27 June 1982. He accompanied Thomas K. Mattingly (spacecraft commander) on this seven-day mission designed to: further verify ascent and entry phases of Shuttle missions; perform continued studies of the effects of long-term thermal extremes on the Orbiter subsystems; and conduct a survey of Orbiter-induced contamination on the Orbiter payload bay. Additionally, the crew operated several scientific experiments located in the Orbiter's cabin as well as in the payload bay. These experiments included the Continuous Flow Electrophoresis System (CFES), designed to investigate the separation of biological materials in a fluid according to their surface electrical charge. The crew was credited with effecting an in-flight repair which enabled them to activate the first operational "Getaway Special" which was comprised of nine experiments that ranged from algae and duckweed growth in space, to fruit fly and brine shrimp genetic studies. STS-4 completed 112 orbits of the Earth before landing on a concrete runway at Edwards Air Force Base, California, on July 4, 1982. Mission duration was 169 hours 11 minutes, 11 seconds. STS-41D launched from Kennedy Space Center, Florida, on August 30, 1984. The crew included Mike Coats (pilot), Judy Resnik, Steve Hawley, and Mike Mullane (mission specialists), and Charlie Walker (payload specialist). This was the maiden flight of the Orbiter Discovery. During the six-day mission the crew successfully activated the OAST-1 solar cell wing experiment, deployed three satellites, SBS-D, SYNCOM IV-2, and TELSTAR 3-C, operated the CFES-III experiment, the student crystal growth experiment, and photography experiments using the IMAX motion picture camera. The crew earned the name "Icebusters" when Hartsfield successfully removed a hazardous ice-buildup from the Orbiter using the Remote Manipulator System. STS-41D completed 96 orbits of the Earth before landing at Edwards Air Force Base, California, on September 5, 1984. Mission duration was 144 hours, 56 minutes, 4 seconds. STS-61A, the West German D-1 Spacelab mission, launched from Kennedy Space Center, Florida, on October 30, 1985. The crew included Steve Nagel (pilot), Jim Buchli, Guy Bluford and Bonnie Dunbar (mission specialists), and Reinhard Furrer, Ernst Messerschmid, and Wubbo Ockels (payload specialists). The seven-day mission was the first with eight crew members, and the first Spacelab science mission planned and controlled by a foreign customer. More than 75 scientific experiments were completed in the areas of physiological sciences, materials processing, biology, and navigation. After completing 111 orbits of the Earth, STS-61A landed at Edwards Air Force Base, California, on November 6, 1985. Mission duration was 168 hours, 44 minutes, 51 seconds.

NAME: Frederick H. Hauck (Captain, USN, Ret.)
NASA Astronaut (former)

PERSONAL DATA: Born April 11, 1941, in Long Beach, California, but considers Winchester, Massachusetts, and Washington, D.C., to be his hometowns. Married to Susan Cameron Bruce. He has two grown children. Recreational interests include skiing, sailing, squash, golf, tennis and working on his 1958 Corvette.

EDUCATION: Graduated from St. Albans School in Washington D.C. in 1958; received a bachelor of science degree in Physics from Tufts University in 1962 and a master of science degree in Nuclear Engineering from the Massachusetts Institute of Technology in 1966; graduate, U.S. Naval Test Pilot School, 1971.

ORGANIZATIONS: Fellow, Society of Experimental Test Pilots; Associate Fellow, American Institute of Aeronautics and Astronautics; Board of Trustees, Tufts University; Board of Governors, St. Albans School; Vice President, Association of Space Explorers; Member, Commercial Space Transportation Advisory Committee (COMSTAC), Department of Transportation; Chair, COMSTAC Task Group on Russian Entry into Commercial Space Markets (1992); Member, NASA Commercial Programs Advisory Committee; Member, Department of Commerce U.S. - Russian Space Commerce Mission to Russia (1992); Member, NASA Mission Review Task Group (Space Salvage) 1992).

SPECIAL HONORS: Two Defense Distinguished Service Medals; the NASA Distinguished Service Medal; the NASA Medal for Outstanding Leadership; the Defense Superior Service Medal; the Legion of Merit; the Distinguished Flying Cross; the Air Medal (9); the Navy Commendation Medal with Gold Star and Combat V; the NASA Space Flight Medal (3); the Presidential Cost Saving Commendation; the AIAA Haley Space Flight Award; Lloyd's of London Silver Medal for Meritorious Service; the American Astronautical Society Flight Achievement Award; the Federation Aeronautique Internationale (FAI) Yuri Gagarin Gold Medal; the FAI Komarov Diploma (2); the Tufts University Presidential Medal; the Delta Upsilon Distinguished Alumnus Award; and the Navy's Outstanding Test Pilot (1972).

EXPERIENCE: Hauck, a Navy ROTC student at Tufts University, was commissioned upon graduation in 1962 and reported to the USS Warrington (DD-843) where he served 20 months as communications officer and CIC officer. In 1964, he attended the U.S. Naval Postgraduate School, Monterey, California, for studies in math and physics and, for a brief time in 1965, studied Russian at the Defense Language Institute in Monterey. Selected for the Navy's Advanced Science Program, he received his master's degree in Nuclear Engineering from MIT the next year. He commenced flight training at the Naval Air Station, Pensacola, Florida, in 1966, and upon receiving his wings in 1968, he reported to the Naval Air Station at Oceana, Virginia, for replacement pilot training in the A-6. As a pilot with VA-35 he deployed to the Western Pacific with Air Wing 15 aboard USS CORAL SEA (CVA-43), flying 114 combat and combat support mission. In August 1970, Hauck returned to the east coast A-6 replacement training squadron, VA-42, as a visual weapons delivery instructor. Selected for test pilot training, he reported to the U.S. Naval Test Pilot School at Patuxent River, Maryland, in 1971. A 3-year tour in the Naval Air Test Center's Carrier Suitability Branch of the Flight Test Division followed. During this period, Hauck served as a project test pilot for automatic carrier landing systems in the A-6, A-7, F-4, and F-14 aircraft and was team leader for the Navy Board of Inspection and Survey aircraft carrier trials of the F-14. In 1974 he reported as operations office to Commander Carrier Air Wing 14 aboard USS ENTERPRISE (CV(N)-65). On two cruises he flew the A-6, A-7, and F-14 during both day and night carrier operations. He reported to Attack Squadron 145 as executive officer in February 1977.

NASA EXPERIENCE: Selected by NASA in January 1978. In August 1979, he completed a 1-year training and evaluation period qualifying him for future assignment as a pilot. Subsequent assignments included: support crew for STS-1; reentry capsule communicator (CAPCOM) for STS-2; project test pilot for development of flight techniques and landing aids in preparation for the first Shuttle night landing; astronaut office project officer for Shuttle integration of the liquid-fueled Centaur upper stage rocket. In May 1985 he was named to command the Centaur-boosted Ulysses solar probe mission (sponsored by the European Space Agency). After the Challenger accident this mission was postponed, and the Shuttle Centaur project was terminated. From August 1986 to February 1987, he served as NASA Associate Administrator for External Relations (the policy advisor to the NASA Administrator for congressional, public, international, intergovernmental, and educational affairs). A veteran of three spaceflights, Hauck has logged over 5500 flight hours, 436 in space. He served as pilot on STS-7 (June 18-24, 1983), and was the spacecraft commander on STS-51A (November 8-16, 1984) and STS-26, the first flight to be flown after the Challenger accident, (September 29 to October 3, 1988). In May 1989 he returned to Navy duty to become Director, Navy Space Systems Division, in the Office of the Chief of Naval Operations. In this capacity he held budgeting responsibility for the Navy's space programs. Captain Hauck left military active duty on June 1, 1990. In October 1990 he joined International Technology Underwriters (INTEC) as President and Chief Operating Officer and on January 1, 1993 assumed responsibilities as Chief Executive Officer. INTEC is a world leader in providing property and casualty insurance for the risk of launching and operating satellites.

SPACE FLIGHT EXPERIENCE: STS-7 Challenger launched from Kennedy Space Center, Florida, on June 18, 1983. The crew included Bob Crippen (spacecraft commander), and three mission specialists, John Fabian, Sally Ride, and Norm Thagard. This was Challenger's second flight and the first mission with a 5-person crew. During the mission, the crew deployed satellites for Canada (ANIK C-2) and Indonesia (PALAPA B-1); operated the Canadian-built Remote Manipulator System (RMS) to perform the first deployment and retrieval exercise (with the Shuttle Pallet Satellite (SPAS-01); conducted the first formation flying of the orbiter with a free-flying satellite (SPAS-01); carried and operated the first U.S./German cooperative materials science payload (OSTA-2); operated the Continuous Flow Electrophoresis System (CFES) and the Monodisperse Latex Reactor (MLR) experiments; and activated seven Getaway Specials. Mission duration was 147 hours before landing on a lakebed runway at Edwards Air Force Base, California, on June 24, 1983. STS-51A Discovery launched from Kennedy Space Center, Florida, on November 8, 1984. The flight crew included Dave Walker (pilot), and three mission specialists, Joe Allen, Anna Fisher, and Dale Gardner. This was Discovery's second flight. During the mission the crew deployed two satellites, Telesat Canada's Anik D-2, and Hughes' LEASAT-1 (Syncom IV-1), and operated the 3M Company's Diffusive Mixing of Organic Solutions (DMOS) experiment. In the first space salvage mission in history the crew also retrieved for return to earth the Palapa B-2 and Westar VI satellites. STS-51A completed 127 orbits of the Earth before landing at Kennedy Space Center, Florida, on November 16, 1984. STS-26 Discovery launched from the Kennedy Space Center, Florida, on September 29, 1988. STS-26 was the first flight to be flown after the Challenger accident. The flight crew included the pilot, Dick Covey, and three mission specialists, Dave Hilmers, Mike Lounge, and George (Pinky) Nelson. During the four day mission, the crew successfully deployed the Tracking and Data Relay Satellite (TDRS-C), which was subsequently carried to geosynchronous orbit by the Inertial Upper Stage (IUS) rocket. They also operated eleven mid-deck experiments. Discovery completed 64 orbits of the earth before landing at Edwards Air Force Base, California, on October 3, 1988. Mission duration as 97 hours.

NAME: Terence T. "Tom" Henricks (Colonel, USAF, Retired)
      NASA Astronaut (former)

PERSONAL DATA: Born July 5, 1952, in Bryan, Ohio, but considers Woodville, Ohio, to be his hometown. Married to the former Rebecca Grantham of Marshall, Texas. Three children.

EDUCATION: Graduated from Woodmore High School in 1970; received a bachelor of science degree in civil engineering from the United States Air Force (USAF) Academy in 1974, and a masters degree in public administration from Golden Gate University in 1982.

SPECIAL HONORS: The Distinguished Flying Cross, the NASA Outstanding Leadership Medal, the Defense Superior Service Medal, the Defense Meritorious Service Medal, two Air Force Meritorious Service Medals, two Air Force Commendation Medals, four NASA Space Flight Medals, Honorary Doctor of Science degree from the Defiance College (1993), F-4 Fighter Weapons School Outstanding Flying Award. Named Pilot Training Distinguished Graduate and F-16 Conversion Course Top Gun. Inducted into the Ohio Veterans Hall of Fame.

EXPERIENCE: Henricks completed pilot training at Craig Air Force Base (AFB) in Selma, Alabama, and F-4 conversion training at Homestead AFB in Miami, Florida. He then flew the F-4 in fighter squadrons in England and Iceland. In 1980, he was reassigned to Nellis AFB, Las Vegas, Nevada. After attending the USAF Test Pilot School in 1983, he remained at Edwards AFB, California, as an F-16C test pilot and Chief of the 57th Fighter Weapons Wing Operating Location until his NASA selection. He has 749 parachute jumps and a Master Parachutist rating. He has flown 30 different types of aircraft, has logged over 6,000 hours flying time, and holds an FAA commercial pilot rating.

NASA EXPERIENCE: Selected by NASA in June 1985, Henricks became an astronaut in July 1986. His technical assignments to date include: re-evaluating Shuttle landing sites world wide; Assistant Manager for Engineering Integration in the Shuttle Program Office; Lead Astronaut of the Shuttle Avionics Integration Laboratory at Johnson Space Center, and of Vehicle Test and Checkout at the Kennedy Space Center; Chief of the Astronaut Office Operations Development Branch. He also served as the Assistant for Shuttle to the Chief of the Astronaut Office, directing crew involvement in the development and operation of the Shuttle. A commander of two Space Shuttle missions and pilot of two others, Henricks became the first person to log over 1,000 hours as a Space Shuttle pilot/commander. Tom Henricks left government service in November 1997 to pursue a career in business.

SPACE FLIGHT EXPERIENCE: STS-44 Atlantis launched the night of November 24, 1991. The primary mission objective was the deployment of a Defense Support Program (DSP) satellite with an Inertial Upper Stage (IUS) rocket booster. The mission was concluded after 110 orbits of the Earth returning to a landing on the lakebed at Edwards Air Force Base, California, on December 1, 1991. STS-55, the German D-2 Spacelab mission, was launched on April 26, 1993, aboard Columbia, and landed 10-days later on May 6, 1993, at Edwards AFB California. During the ambitious mission 89 experiments were performed in many disciplines such as materials processing, life sciences, robotics, technology, astronomy, and Earth mapping. STS-70 launched from the Kennedy Space Center, Florida, on July 13, 1995, and returned there July 22, 1995. During 142 orbits of the Earth, the crew performed a variety of experiments in addition to deploying the sixth and final NASA Tracking and Data Relay Satellite. STS-70, with an "all-Ohio" crew, was the first mission controlled from the new combined control center. STS-78 launched June 20, 1996 and landed July 7, 1996 becoming the longest Space Shuttle mission to date. The 16-day mission included studies sponsored by ten nations and five space agencies, and was the first mission to combine both a full microgravity studies agenda and a comprehensive life science investigation. The Life and Microgravity Spacelab mission served as a model for future studies on board the International Space Station.

NAME: Richard J. Hieb (Mr.)
NASA Astronaut (former)

PERSONAL DATA: Born September 21, 1955, in Jamestown, North Dakota. Married to the former Jeannie Hendricks of Norfolk, Virginia. They have two children. He enjoys sports and family outings. His parents, Mr. & Mrs. Fred Hieb, reside in Jamestown, North Dakota. Her parents, Mr. & Mrs. John R. Hendricks, reside in Norfolk, Virginia.

EDUCATION: Graduated from Jamestown High School, Jamestown, North Dakota, in 1973; received a bachelor of arts degree in math and physics from Northwest Nazarene College in 1977, and a master of science degree in aerospace engineering from the University of Colorado in 1979.

NASA EXPERIENCE: After graduating from the University of Colorado in 1979, Mr. Hieb came directly to NASA to work in crew procedures development and crew activity planning. He worked in the Mission Control Center on the ascent team for STS-1, and during rendezvous phases on numerous subsequent flights. He has an extensive background in on-orbit procedures development, particularly in rendezvous and proximity operations. Selected by NASA in June 1985, Mr. Hieb became an astronaut in July 1986, qualified for assignment as a mission specialist on future Space Shuttle flight crews. Since then he has held a variety of technical assignments including launch support activities at Kennedy Space Center, and has served in both the Mission Development Branch and in the Operations Development Branch of the Astronaut Office. He supported the STS-26 mission as a part of the close-out crew prior to launch and as a part of the change-out crew just after landing. A veteran of three space flights, Mr. Hieb flew on STS-39 in 1991, STS-49 in 1992, and STS-65 in 1994. He has logged over 750 hours in space, including over 17 hours of EVA (space walk). Mr. Hieb first flew on the crew of STS-39, an unclassified Department of Defense mission which launched on April 28, 1991 from the Kennedy Space Center in Florida. During the mission, he was responsible for operating the Infrared Background Signature Satellite (IBSS) from within the payload bay, on the Remote Manipulator System (RMS) and as a free-flying satellite. He also operated the RMS to release the IBSS, and then to retrieve the IBSS a day and a half later. After 134 orbits of the Earth which covered 3.5 million miles and lasted just over 199 hours, the crew landed at California, on May 6, 1991. Mr. Hieb was also a mission specialist on the crew of STS-49, the maiden voyage of the new Space Shuttle Endeavour, which launched from the Kennedy Space Center on May 7, 1992. During that mission, Hieb along with astronaut Pierre Thuot, performed three space walks which resulted in the capture and repair of the stranded Intelsat VI F3 communications satellite. The third space walk, which also included astronaut Tom Akers, was the first ever three-person space walk. This 8 hour and 29 minute space walk, the longest in history, broke a twenty year old record that was held by Apollo 17 astronauts. The mission concluded on May 16, 1992 with a landing at Edwards Air Force Base after orbiting the Earth 141 times in 213 hours and traveling 3.7 million miles. Mr. Hieb was the payload commander on the second flight of the International Microgravity Laboratory (IML-2) on Space Shuttle Mission STS-65. The mission launched from Kennedy Space Center in Florida on July 8, 1994, and returned there on July 23, 1994, setting a new flight duration record for the Space Shuttle program. During the 15-day flight the crew conducted more than 80 experiments focusing on materials and life sciences research in microgravity. The mission was accomplished in 236 orbits of the Earth, traveling 6.1 million miles.

NAME: David C. Hilmers (Colonel, USMC, Ret.)
NASA Astronaut (former)

PERSONAL DATA: Born January 28, 1950, in Clinton, Iowa, but considers DeWitt, Iowa, to be his hometown. Married to the former Lynn Beneke of Vinton, Iowa. Two grown sons. Recreational interests include playing playing the piano, gardening, electronics, spending time with his family, and all types of sports. His father, Paul C. Hilmers, lives in Clinton, Iowa, and his mother, Matilda Hilmers, lives in DeWitt, Iowa. Her parents, Mr. and Mrs. Leland Beneke, reside in Vinton, Iowa.

EDUCATION: Graduated from Central Community High School in DeWitt, Iowa, in 1968; received a bachelor of arts degree in mathematics (Summa Cum Laude) from Cornell College in 1972, a master of science degree in electrical engineering (with distinction) in 1977, and the degree of electrical engineer from the U.S. Naval Postgraduate School in 1978.

ORGANIZATIONS: Phi Beta Kappa, and Eta Kappa Nu.

SPECIAL HONORS: Named Outstanding Scholar-Athlete, Midwest Conference (1971); graduated Summa Cum Laude from Cornell College (1972); awarded an NCAA Post-Graduate Fellowship (1972); named to Phi Beta Kappa and named Outstanding Athlete, Cornell College (1972). Recipient of three NASA Exceptional Service Medals, three NASA Space Flight Medals, the American Institute of Aeronautics and Astronautics Haley Space Flight Award for 1988, and the American Astronautical Society Flight Achievement Award for 1988. Awarded the Department of Defense Distinguished Service Medal, the Defense Superior Service Medal, and the Meritorious Service Medal.

EXPERIENCE: Hilmers entered active duty with the United States Marine Corps in July 1972. On completing Marine Corps Basic School and Naval Flight Officer School, he was assigned to VMA(AW)-121 at Marine Corps Air Station Cherry Point, North Carolina, flying the A-6 Intruder as a bombardier-navigator. In 1975, he became an air liaison officer with the 1st Battalion, 2d Marines, stationed with the 6th Fleet in the Mediterranean. He graduated from the U.S. Naval Postgraduate School in 1978 and was later assigned to the 1st Marine Aircraft Wing in Iwakuni, Japan. He was stationed with the 3d Marine Aircraft Wing in El Toro, California, at the time of his selection by NASA.

NASA EXPERIENCE: Hilmers was selected a NASA astronaut in July 1980, and completed the initial training period in August 1981. In 1983 he was selected as a member of the launch ready standby crew. His early NASA assignments have included work on upper stages such as PAM, IUS, and Centaur, as well as Shuttle software verification at the Shuttle Avionics Integration Laboratory (SAIL). In addition, he was the Astronaut Office training coordinator, worked on various Department of Defense payloads, served as a spacecraft communicator (CAPCOM) at Mission Control for STS-41D, STS-41G, STS-51A, STS-51C and STS-51D, worked Space Station issues for the Astronaut Office, and served as head of the Mission Development Branch within the Astronaut Office. In May 1985 he was named to the crew of STS-61F which was to deploy the Ulysses spacecraft on an interplanetary trajectory using a Centaur upper stage. This mission was to have flown in May 1986, but the Shuttle Centaur project was terminated in July 1986, and Hilmers then worked in the areas of ascent abort development, payload safety, and shuttle on-board software. During 1987 he was involved in training for STS-26 and in flight software development. A veteran of four space flights, he has logged over 493 hours in space. He served as a mission specialist on STS-51J (October 3-7, 1985), STS-26 (September 29 to October 3, 1988), STS-36 (February 28 to March 4, 1990), and STS-42 (January 22-30, 1992). Hilmers retired from NASA in October 1992, and is currently enrolled as a medical student at the Baylor College of Medicine in Houston, Texas.

SPACE FLIGHT EXPERIENCE: STS 51-J Atlantis, a classified Department of Defense mission, launched from Kennedy Space Center, Florida, on October 3, 1985. This was the maiden voyage of the Orbiter Atlantis. Hilmers had prime responsibility for a number of on-orbit activities during the mission. After 98 hours of orbital operations, Atlantis landed at Edwards Air Force Base, California, on October 7, 1985. STS-26 Discovery, the first flight to be flown after the Challenger accident, was launched from the Kennedy Space Center, Florida, on September 29, 1988. During the four-day mission, the crew successfully deployed the Tracking and Data Relay Satellite (TDRS-C), which was subsequently carried to orbit by the Inertial Upper Stage (IUS) rocket. They also operated eleven mid-deck experiments. Discovery completed 64 orbits of the Earth before landing at Edwards Air Force Base, California, on October 3, 1988. STS-36 Atlantis launched from the Kennedy Space Center, Florida, on February 28, 1990. This mission carried Department of Defense payloads and a number of secondary payloads. After 72 orbits of the Earth, the STS-36 mission concluded with a lakebed landing at Edwards Air Force Base, California, on March 4, 1990, after traveling 1.87 million miles. STS-42 Discovery launched from the Kennedy Space Center, Florida, on January 22, 1992. Fifty five major experiments conducted in the International Microgravity Laboratory-1 module were provided by investigators from eleven countries, and represented a broad spectrum of scientific disciplines. During 128 orbits of the Earth, the STS-42 crew accomplished the mission's primary objective of investigating the effects of microgravity on materials processing and life sciences. In this unique laboratory in space, crew members worked around-the-clock in two shifts. Experiments investigated the microgravity effects on the growth of protein and semiconductor crystals. Biological experiments on the effects of zero gravity on plants, tissues, bacteria, insects and human vestibular response were also conducted. This eight-day mission culminated in a landing at Edwards Air Force Base, California, on January 30, 1992.

NAME: Jeffrey A. Hoffman (Ph.D.)
NASA Astronaut (former)

PERSONAL DATA: Born November 2, 1944, in Brooklyn, New York, but considers Scarsdale, New York, to be his hometown. Married to the former Barbara Catherine Attridge of Greenwich, London, England. They have two sons, Sam and Orin. Dr. Hoffman enjoys skiing, mountaineering, hiking, bicycling, swimming, sailing, and music. His parents, Dr. and Mrs. Burton P. Hoffman, are residents of White Plains, New York.

EDUCATION: Graduated from Scarsdale High School, Scarsdale, New York, in 1962; received a bachelor of arts degree in astronomy (graduated summa cum laude) from Amherst College in 1966, a doctor of philosophy in astrophysics from Harvard University in 1971, and a masters degree in materials science from Rice University in 1988.

ORGANIZATIONS: Member of the International Astronomical Union; the American Astronomical Society; Phi Beta Kappa; and Sigma Xi.

SPECIAL HONORS: Awarded the Amherst College 1963 Porter Prize in Astronomy, 1964 Second Walker Prize in Mathematics, 1965 John Summer Runnells Scholarship Prize, and 1966 Stanley V. and Charles B. Travis Prize and Woods Prize for Scholarship. Elected to Phi Beta Kappa in 1965 and Sigma Xi in 1966. Also received a Woodrow Wilson Foundation Pre-Doctoral Fellowship, 1966-67; a National Science Foundation Pre-Doctoral Fellowship, 1966-71; a National Academy of Sciences Post-Doctoral Visiting Fellowship, 1971-72; a Harvard University Sheldon International Fellowship, 1972-73; and a NATO Post-Doctoral Fellowship, 1973-74. Dr. Hoffman was awarded NASA Space

Flight Medals in 1985, 1991, 1992, 1994 and 1996, NASA Exceptional Service Medals in 1988 and 1992, and the NASA Distinguished Service Medal in 1994.

SCIENTIFIC EXPERIENCE: Dr. Hoffman's original research interests were in high-energy astrophysics, specifically cosmic gamma ray and x-rayastronomy. His doctoral work at Harvard was the design, construction, testing, and flight of a balloon-borne, low-energy, gamma ray telescope. From 1972 to 1975, during post-doctoral work at Leicester University, he worked on several x-ray astronomy rocket payloads. He also designed and supervised the construction and testing of the test equipment for use in an x-ray beam facility which he used to measure the scattering and reflectivity properties of x-ray concentrating mirrors. During his last year at Leicester, he was project scientist for the medium-energy x-ray experiment on the European Space Agency's EXOSAT satellite and played a leading role in the proposal and design studies for this project. He worked in the Center for Space Research at the Massachusetts Institute of Technology (MIT) from 1975 to 1978 as project scientist in charge of the orbiting HEAO-1 A4 hard x-ray and gamma ray experiment, launched in August 1977. His involvement included pre-launch design of the data analysis system, supervising its operation post-launch, and directing the MIT team undertaking the scientific analysis of flight data being returned. He was also involved extensively in analysis of x-ray data from the SAS-3 satellite being operated by MIT. His principal research was the study of x-ray bursts, about which he authored or co-authored more than 20 papers.

NASA EXPERIENCE: Selected by NASA in January 1978, Dr. Hoffman became an astronaut in August 1979. During preparations for the Shuttle Orbital Flight Tests, Dr. Hoffman worked in the Flight Simulation Laboratory at Downey, California, testing guidance, navigation and flight control systems. He has worked with the orbital maneuvering and reaction control systems, with Shuttle navigation, with crew training, and with the development of satellite deployment procedures. Dr. Hoffman served as a support crew member for STS-5 and as a CAPCOM (spacecraft communicator) for the STS-8 and STS-82 missions. Dr. Hoffman has been the Astronaut Office Payload Safety Representative. He has also worked on EVA, including the development of a high-pressure spacesuit, and preparations for the assembly of the Space Station. Dr. Hoffman helped set up the Astronaut Office Science Support Group. During 1996 he led the Payload and Habitability Branch of the Astronaut Office. Dr. Hoffman left the astronaut program in July 1997 to become NASA's European Representative in Paris.

SPACE FLIGHT EXPERIENCE: Dr. Hoffman made his first space flight as a mission specialist on STS 51-D, April 12-19, 1985, on the Shuttle Discovery. On this mission, he made the first STS contingency space walk, in an attempted rescue of a malfunctioning satellite. Dr. Hoffman made his second space flight as a mission specialist on STS-35, December 2-10, 1990, on the Shuttle Columbia. This Spacelab mission featured the ASTRO-1 ultraviolet astronomy laboratory, a project on which Dr. Hoffman had worked since 1982. Dr. Hoffman made his third space flight as payload commander and mission specialist on STS-46, July 31-August 8, 1992, on the Shuttle Atlantis. On this mission, the crew deployed the European Retrievable Carrier (EURECA), an ESA-sponsored free-flying science platform, and carried out the first test flight of the Tethered Satellite System (TSS), a joint project between NASA and the Italian Space Agency. Dr. Hoffman had worked on the Tethered Satellite project since 1987. Dr. Hoffman made his fourth flight as an EVA crew member on STS-61, December 2-13, 1993, on the Shuttle Endeavour. During this flight, the Hubble Space Telescope (HST) was captured, serviced, and restored to full capacity through a record five space walks by four astronauts. Dr. Hoffman last flew on STS-75 (February 22 to March 9, 1996) on the Shuttle Columbia. This was a 16-day mission whose principal payloads were the reflight of the Tethered

Satellite System (TSS) and the third flight of the United States Microgravity Payload (USMP-3). The TSS successfully demonstrated the ability of tethers to produce electricity. The TSS experiment produced a wealth of new information on the electrodynamics of tethers and plasma physics before the tether broke at 19.7 km, just shy of the 20.7 km goal. The crew also worked around the clock performing combustion experiments and research related to USMP-3 microgravity investigations. The mission was completed in 252 orbits covering 6.5 million miles in 377 hours and 40 minutes. With the completion of his fifth space flight, Dr. Hoffman has logged more than 1,211 hours and 21.5 million miles in space.

NAME: Donald Lee Holmquest (MD, PhD)
NASA Astronaut (former)

PERSONAL DATA: Born in Dallas, Texas, on April 7, 1939; his mother, Mrs. Sidney B. Holmquest, resides in Dallas.

PHYSICAL DESCRIPTION: Brown hair; blue eyes; height: 5 feet 10 inches; weight: 135 pounds.

EDUCATION: Attended Roger Q. Mills Elementary School and is a 1957 graduate of W. H. Anderson High School in Dallas, Texas; received a Bachelor of Science degree in Electrical Engineering from Southern Methodist University in 1962 and Doctorates in Medicine and Physiology from Baylor University in 1967 and 1968, respectively. Has completed specialty training in Nuclear Medicine and is a Diplomate of the American Board of Nuclear Science.

MARITAL STATUS: Married to Dr. Ann Nixon James, formerly from Floyd, Virginia.

CHILDREN: Hilary Catherine, August 24, 1970.

RECREATIONAL INTERESTS: He enjoys skiing and handball.

ORGANIZATIONS: Member of the Society of Nuclear Medicine, American College of Nuclear Physicians, the Association for the Advancement of Medical Instrumentatlon. Dr. Holmquest holds a faculty appointment as Visiting Professor of Physiology at Baylor College of Medicine, and works in the private practice of Nuclear Medicine.

EXPERIENCE: When selected for the astronaut program, Dr. Holmquest was serving an internship at Methodist Hospital in Houston, Texas. For four years he was a Research Associate at the Massachusetts Institute of Technology. He logged 750 hours flying time in jet aircraft prior to resigning from NASA.

NASA EXPERIENCE: Dr. Holmquest was selected as a scientist-astronaut by NASA in August 1967. After completing initial academic training and a 53-week course in flight training at Williams Air Force Base, Arizona, he worked on Skylab habitability systems and medical experiments for a period of 1 1/2 years. After an academic leave of absence for the purpose of pursuing medical research and further training in nuclear medicine and after a year at the Eisenhower Medical Center, he assumed the position as Associate Dean for Academic Affairs in the new College of Medicine at Texas A&M University in College Station, Texas. He now practices medicine on a full-time basis.

NAME: Mae C. Jemison (M.D.)
        NASA Astronaut (former)

PERSONAL DATA: Born October 17, 1956, in Decatur, Alabama, but considers Chicago, Illinois, to be her home-town. Her parents, Charlie & Dorothy Jemison, reside in Chicago.

PHYSICAL DESCRIPTION: Black hair; brown eyes; 5 feet 9 inches; 140 pounds.

EDUCATION: Graduated from Morgan Park High School, Chicago, Illinois, in 1973; received a bachelor of science degree in chemical engineering from Stanford University in 1977 (also fulfilled the requirements for a B.A. in African and Afro-American Studies), and a doctorate in medicine degree from Cornell University in 1981.

RECREATIONAL INTERESTS: She enjoys traveling, graphic arts, photography, sewing, skiing, collecting African Art, languages (Russian, Swahili, Japanese), weight training, has an extensive dance and exercise background, and is an avid reader.

ORGANIZATIONS: Member, American Medical Association and American Chemical Society. Honorary member, Alpha Kappa Alpha Sorority; Member, Association for the Advancement of Science; Board Member, World Sickle Cell Foundation; Honorary Board Member, Center for the Prevention of Childhood Malnutrition.

SPECIAL HONORS: National Achievement Scholarship (1973-1977); Stanford representative to Carifesta '76 in Jamaica; 1979 CIBA Award for Student Involvement; American Medical Student Association (AMSA) study group to Cuba; Grant from International Travelers Institute for health studies in rural Kenya (1979); organized New York city-wide health and law fair for National Student Medical Association (1979); worked refugee camp in Thailand (1980). Recipient of Essence Award (1988), and Gamma Sigma Gamma Woman of the Year (1989).

EXPERIENCE: Dr. Jemison has a background in both engineering and medical research. She has worked in the areas of computer programming, printed wiring board materials, nuclear magnetic resonance spectroscopy, computer magnetic disc production and evaluation of trophic factors for rat epididymides. Dr. Jemison com-pleted her internship at Los Angeles County/USC Medical Center in July 1982 and worked as a General Practi-tioner with INA/Ross Loos Medical Group in Los Angeles until December 1982. From January 1983 thru June 1985, Dr. Jemison was the Area Peace Corps Medical Officer for Sierra Leone and Liberia in West Africa. Her task of managing the health care delivery system for U.S. Peace Corps and U.S. Embassy personnel included provi-sion of medical care, supervision of the pharmacy and laboratory, medical administrative issues, and supervi-sion of medical staff. She developed curriculum for and taught volunteer personal health training, wrote manu-als for self care, developed and implemented guidelines for public health/safety issues for volunteer job place-ment and training sites. Dr. Jemison developed and participated in research projects on Hepatitis B vaccine, schistosomaisis and rabies in conjunction with the National Institute of Health and the Center for Disease Control. On return to the United States, Dr. Jemison joined CIGNA Health Plans of California in October 1985 and was working as a General Practitioner and attending graduate engineering classes in Los Angeles when selected to the astronaut program.

NASA EXPERIENCE: Selected as an astronaut candidate by NASA in June 1987, Dr. Jemison completed a one-year training and evaluation program in August 1988. She is qualified for assignment as a mission specialist on Space Shuttle flight crews. Her technical assignments to date have included: astronaut office representative to the Kennedy Space Center, Cape Canaveral, Florida, which involved participation in the processing of the Space Shuttle for launch, especially its payloads and thermal protection system (tiles), and launch countdown; work in the Shuttle Avionics Integration Laboratory (SAIL) performing verification of Shuttle computer software. Dr. Jemison was assigned as a mission specialist on STS-47, Spacelab-J. This cooperative mission between the United States and Japan, to conduct experiments in life sciences and materials processing, which was launched in September 1992.

POST NASA EXPERIENCE:

Dr. Jemison is currently the president of the Jemison Group, a consulting company that has worked on the design and installation of solar electricity generating systems for developing countries and the use of satellite communications to assist in health-care delivery in west Africa. She also runs Earth We Share, an international science camp for teenagers. One of the missions of Jemison is to promote science literacy and speaks on a lecture circuit about her experiences in science and in the space program. Dr. Jemison has also written a book for young people entitled, "Find Where the Wind Goes: Moments From My Life."

NAME: Joseph P. Kerwin (Captain, MC, USN) NASA Astronaut
NASA Astronaut (Former)

PERSONAL DATA: Born February 19,1932, in Oak Park, Illinois. His mother, Mrs. Edward M. Kerwin, resides in Milwaukee, Wisconsin.

PHYSICAL DESCRIPTION: Brown hair; blue eyes; height: 6 feet; weight: 177 pounds.

EDUCATION: Graduated from Fenwick High School, Oak Park, Illinois, in 1949; received a bachelor of arts degree in Philosophy from College of the Holy Cross, Worcester, Massachusetts, in 1953; a doctor of medicine degree from Northwestern University Medical School, Chicago, Illinois, in 1957; completed internship at the District of Columbia General Hospital in Washington, D.C.; and attended the U.S. Navy School of Aviation Medicine at Pensacola, Florida, and was designated a naval flight surgeon in December 1958.

MARITAL STATUS: Married to the former Shirley Ann Good of Danville, Pennsylvania.

CHILDREN: Sharon, September 14, 1963; Joanna, January 5, 1966; Kristina, May 4, 1968.

RECREATIONAL INTERESTS: His hobbies are reading and classical music.

ORGANIZATIONS: Fellow of the Aerospace Medical Association; member of the Aircraft Owners and Pilots Association.

EXPERIENCE: Kerwin, a Captain, has been in the Navy Medical Corps since July 1958. He earned his wings at Beeville, Texas, in 1962. He has logged 4,500 hours flying time.

NASA EXPERIENCE: Captain Kerwin was selected as a scientist-astronaut by NASA in June 1965. Kerwin served as science-pilot for the Skylab 2 (SL-2) mission which launched on May 25 and terminated on June 22, 1973. With him for the initial activation and 28-day night qualification operations of the Skylab orbital workshop were Charles Conrad, Jr., (spacecraft commander) and Paul J. Weitz (pilot). Kerwin was subsequently in charge of the on-orbit branch of the Astronaut Office. In this capacity, he coordinated astronaut activity involving rendezvous, satellite deployment and retrieval, and other Shuttle payload operations. From April 1982 until December 1983, Kerwin served as the National Aeronautics and Space Administration's senior science representative in Australia. In this capacity, he served as liaison between NASA's Office of Space Tracking and

Data Systems and Australia's Department of Science and Technology.

CURRENT ASSIGNMENT: Dr. Kerwin is currently Director, Space and Life Sciences, Johnson Space Center. In this capacity, he is responsible for direction and coordination of medical support to operational manned spacecraft programs, including health care and maintenance of the astronauts and their families; for direction of life services, supporting research and light experiment project; and manages JSC earth sciences and scientific efforts in lunar and planetary research.

NAME: William B. Lenoir (Ph.D.)
NASA Astronaut (former)

PERSONAL DATA: Born on March 14, 1939, in Miami, Florida. Divorced. Two grown children. Recreational interests include sailing, wood-working, and outdoor activities.

EDUCATION: Attended primary and secondary schools in Coral Gables, Florida; is a graduate of the Massachusetts Institute of Technology where he received a bachelor of science degree in electrical engineering in 1961, a master of science degree in 1962, and a doctor of philosophy degree in 1965.

ORGANIZATIONS: Senior member of the Institute of Electrical and Electronics Engineers; and member of American Institute of Aeronautics and Astronautics, Eta Kappa Nu, and the Society of Sigma Xi.

SPECIAL HONORS: Sloan Scholar at the Massachusetts Institute of Technology and winner of the Carleton E. Tucker Award for Teaching Excellence at MIT; awarded the NASA Exceptional Service Medal (1974), and NASA Space Flight Medal (1982).

EXPERIENCE: From 1964 to 1965, Lenoir was an instructor at MIT; and in 1965, he was named assistant professor of electrical engineering. His work at MIT included teaching electromagnetic theory and systems theory as well as performing research in remote sensing. He was an investigator in several satellite experiments and continued research in this area while fulfilling his astronaut assignments. Lenoir is a registered professional engineer in Texas. He has logged over 3,000 hours of flying time in jet aircraft.

NASA EXPERIENCE: Dr. Lenoir was selected as a scientist-astronaut by NASA in August 1967. He completed the initial academic training and a 53-week course in flight training at Laughlin Air Force Base, Texas. Lenoir was backup science-pilot for Skylab 3 and Skylab 4, the second and third manned missions in the Skylab Program. During Skylab 4, he was co-leader of the visual observations project and coordinator between the flight crew and the principal investigators for the solar science experiments. From September 1974 to July 1976, Lenoir spent approximately one-half of his time as leader of the NASA Satellite Power Team. This team was formed to investigate the potential of large-scale satellite power systems for terrestrial utility consumption and to make program recommendations to NASA Headquarters. Lenoir supported the Space Shuttle program in the areas of orbit operations, training, extravehicular activity, and payload deployment and retrieval. Dr. Lenoir flew as a mission specialist on the STS-5 (November 11-16, 1982, the first flight to deploy commercial satellites, and has logged over 122 hours in space. Following STS-5, Dr. Lenoir was responsible for the direction and management of mission development within the Astronaut Office. Dr. Lenoir resigned from NASA in September 1984, to assume a position with the management and technology consulting firm of Booz, Allen & Hamilton, Inc. in Arlington, Virginia. He returned to NASA in June 1989 as the Associate Administrator for Space Flight, responsible for the development, operating and implementation of the necessary policy for the Space Shuttle and all U.S. government civil launch activities. Dr. Lenoir resigned from NASA in April 1992, to assume the position of Vice President of the Applied Systems Division at Booz, Allen & Hamilton, Inc. in Bethesda, Maryland.

SPACE FLIGHT EXPERIENCE: STS-5 Columbia launched from Kennedy Space Center, Florida, on November 11, 1982. This was the first operational flight of the Spaceship Columbia and became known as the "We Deliver" mission. Two commercial communications satellites with Payload Assist Module upper stages (PAM-D) were successfully deployed from the Orbiter's cargo bay, a new first. This activity was shared with the world when the onboard television tape was played to the control center later that evening. In addition to collecting precise data to document the Shuttle's performance during launch, boost, orbit, atmospheric entry and landing phases, STS-5 carried a Getaway Special experiment, three Student Involvement Project experiments, and medical experiments. STS-5 was the last flight to carry the Development Flight Instrumentation (DFI) package to support flight testing. The STS-5 crew successfully concluded the 5-day orbital flight of Columbia with the first entry and landing through a cloud deck to a hard-surface runway, demonstrating maximum braking. STS-5 completed 81 orbits of the Earth before landing at Edwards Air Force Base, California, on November 16, 1982.

NAME: Don (not "Donald") Leslie Lind (Ph.D.)
NASA Astronaut (former)

PERSONAL DATA: Born in Midvale, Utah, on May 18, 1930. Married to the former Kathleen Maughan of Logan, Utah. They have seven grown children. Recreational interests include amateur theatricals, play writing, and painting; and he is a swimmer and skier.

EDUCATION: Attended Midvale Elementary School and is a graduate of Jordan High School, Sandy, Utah; received a bachelor of science degree with high honors in Physics from the University of Utah in 1953 and a doctor of Philosophy degree in High Energy Nuclear Physics in 1964 from the University of California, Berkeley; performed post-doctoral study at the Geophysical Institute, University of Alaska, in 1975-1976.

ORGANIZATIONS: Member of the American Geophysical Union, American Association for Advancement of Science, and Phi Kappa Phi.

SPECIAL HONORS: Awarded the NASA Exceptional Service Medal (1974).

EXPERIENCE: Before his selection as an astronaut, he worked at the NASA Goddard Space Flight Center as a space physicist. He had been with Goddard since 1964 and was involved in experiments to determine the nature and properties of low-energy particles within the Earth's magnetosphere and interplanetary space. Previous to this, he worked at the Lawrence Radiation Laboratory, Berkeley, California, doing research in pion-nucleon scattering, a type of basic high energy particle interaction. Lind holds the rank of Commander in the U.S. Naval Reserve. He served four years on active duty with the Navy at San Diego and later aboard the carrier USS HANCOCK. He received his wings in 1957. He has logged more than 4,500 hours flying time -- 4,000 hours in jet aircraft.

NASA EXPERIENCE: Dr. Lind was selected as an astronaut in April 1966. He served as backup science-pilot for Skylab 3 and Skylab 4 (the second and third manned Skylab missions) and as a member of the rescue crew for the Skylab missions. Dr. Lind was a member of the astronaut office's operations missions development group, responsible for developing payloads for the early Space Shuttle orbital flight test (OFT) missions. Dr. Lind was a mission specialist on STS-51B (April 29 to May 6, 1985) and has logged over 168 hours in space. Dr. Lind left NASA in 1986.

SPACE FLIGHT EXPERIENCE: STS-51B, the Spacelab-3 science mission, launched from Kennedy Space Center, Florida, on April 29, 1985. This was the first operational Spacelab mission. The seven man crew conducted investigations in crystal growth, drop dynamics leading to containerless material processing, atmospheric trace gas spectroscopy, solar and planetary atmospheric simulation, cosmic rays, laboratory animals and human medical monitoring. Dr. Lind developed and conducted an experiment to make unique 3-dimensional video recordings of the earth's aurora. After completing 110 orbits of the earth, the Orbiter Challenger landed at Edwards Air Force Base, California, on May 6, 1985.

NAME: J. M. Linenger, M.D., M.S.S.M., M.P.H., Ph.D. (Captain, Medical Corps, USN)
NASA Astronaut (former)

PERSONAL DATA: Born January 16, 1955, and raised in Eastpointe, Michigan. Married to the former Kathryn M. Bartmann of Arlington Heights, Illinois. They have two sons. He enjoys competitive triathalons, ocean swim racing, marathons, downhill and cross-country skiing, scuba diving, backpacking, camping. Siblings include Kenneth Linenger, Susan Barry, Karen Brandenburg, and Barbara Vallone, all residing in Michigan. His mother, Frances J. Linenger, resides in Eastpointe, Michigan. His father, Donald W. Linenger, is deceased.

EDUCATION: Graduated from East Detroit High School, Eastpointe, Michigan, in 1973; received a bachelor of science degree in bioscience from the U.S. Naval Academy in 1977; a doctorate in medicine from Wayne State University in 1981; a master of science degree in systems management from University of Southern California in 1988; a master of public health degree in health policy from the University of North Carolina in 1989; a doctor of philosophy degree in epidemiology from the University of North Carolina in 1989.

ORGANIZATIONS: The U.S. Naval Academy, University of Southern California, Wayne State University School of Medicine, and University of North Carolina Alumni Associations; the Association of Naval Aviation; the U. S. Navy Flight Surgeons Association; the Aerospace Medicine Association; the American Medical Association; the American College of Preventive Medicine; the Society of U.S. Navy Preventive Medicine Officers; and the American College of Sports Medicine. Linenger is board certified in preventive medicine.

SPECIAL HONORS: Awarded the Meritorious Unit Commendation; Navy Unit Commendation; National Defense Service Medal; Navy Battle Efficiency Award; Navy Commendation Medal with gold star; and 2 NASA Space Flight Medals. Top graduate, Naval Flight Surgeon Training and Naval Safety Officer's School. Elected to Phi Kappa Phi and Alpha Omega Alpha academic honor societies. Distinguished Alumni Award, Wayne State University School of Medicine. Gihon Award, Society of Naval Preventive Medicine Officers.

EXPERIENCE: Linenger graduated from the U.S. Naval Academy and proceeded directly to medical school. After completing surgical internship training at Balboa Naval Hospital, San Diego, California, and aerospace medicine training at the Naval Aerospace Medical Institute, Pensacola, Florida, he served as a naval flight surgeon at Cubi Point, Republic of the Philippines. He was then assigned as medical advisor to the Commander, Naval Air Forces, U.S. Pacific Fleet, San Diego. After completing doctorate-level training in epidemiology, Linenger returned to San Diego as a research principal investigator at the Naval Health Research Center. He concurrently served as a faculty member at the University of California-San Diego School of Medicine in the Division of Sports Medicine.

NASA EXPERIENCE: Linenger joined astronaut selection Group XIV at the Johnson Space Center in August 1992. He flew on STS-64 (September 9-20, 1994) aboard the Space Shuttle Discovery. Mission highlights included: first use of lasers for environmental research; deployment and retrieval of a solar science satellite; robotic processing of semiconductors; use of an RMS-attached boom for jet thruster research; first untethered spacewalk in 10 years to test a self-rescue jetpack. In completing his first mission, Linenger logged 10 days, 22 hours, 51 minutes in space, completed 177 orbits, and traveled over 4.5 million miles. Following his first mission, he began training at the Cosmonaut Training Center in Star City, Russia, in preparation for a long-duration stay aboard the Russian Space Station Mir. All training was conducted using the Russian language, and consisted of learning all Mir space station systems (life support/electrical/communication/attitude control/computer systems), simulator training, Soyuz launch/return vehicle operations, and spacewalk water tank training. He also trained as chief scientist to conduct the entire US science program, consisting of over one-hundred planned experiments in various disciplines. A sampling includes: medicine (humoral immunity, sleep monitoring, radiation dosimetry), physiology (spatial orientation/performance changes during long duration flight), epidemiology (microbial surface sampling), metallurgy (determination of metal diffusion coefficients), oceanography/geology/limnology/physical science (photographic survey (over 10,000 photos) of the planet), space science (flame propagation), microgravity science (behavior of fluids, critical angle determination). Linenger launched aboard U.S. Space Shuttle Atlantis (STS-81) on January 12, 1997, remained onboard the space station with two Russian cosmonauts upon undocking of the Shuttle, and eventually returned upon a different mission of Atlantis (STS-84) on May 24, 1997-spending a total of 132 days, 4 hours, 1 minute in space-the longest duration flight of an American male to date. During his stay aboard space station Mir, Linenger became the first American to conduct a spacewalk from a foreign space station and in a non-American made spacesuit. During the five hour walk, he and his Russian colleague tested for the first time ever the newly designed Orlan-M Russian-built spacesuit, installed the Optical Properties Monitor (OPM) and Benton dosimeter on the outer surface of the station, and retrieved for analysis on Earth numerous externally-mounted material-exposure panels. The three crewmembers also performed a "flyaround" in the Soyuz spacecraft-undocking from one docking port of the station, manually flying to and redocking the capsule at a different location-thus making Linenger the first American to undock from a space station aboard two different spacecraft (U.S. Space Shuttle and Russian Soyuz). While living aboard the space station , Linenger and his two Russian crewmembers faced numerous difficulties-the most severe fire ever aboard an orbiting spacecraft, failures of onboard systems (oxygen generator, carbon dioxide scrubbing, cooling line loop leaks, communication antenna tracking ability, urine collection and processing facility), a near collision with a resupply cargo ship during a manual docking system test, loss of station electrical power, and loss of attitude control resulting in a slow, uncontrolled "tumble" through space. In spite of these challenges and added demands on their time (in order to carry out the repair work), they still accomplished all mission goals-spacewalk, flyaround, and one-hundred percent of the planned U.S. science experiments. In completing the nearly five month mission,

Linenger logged approximately 50 million miles (the equivalent of over 110 roundtrips to the Moon and back), more than 2000 orbits around the Earth, and traveled at an average speed of 18,000 miles per hour. Because of the flawless launch, docking, undocking, and landing of the Space Shuttle Atlantis (STS-84) crew-exchange mission, he made it back to the planet just in time to be reunited with Kathryn and to witness the birth of their second son.

NAME: John Anthony Llewellyn (Ph.D.)
NASA Astronaut (former)

PERSONAL DATA: Born April 22, 1933 in Cardiff, Wales; became U.S. citizen February 17, 1966; married, three children.

EDUCATION: Received bachelor of science from University College, Cardiff, Wales (1955), and a doctorate in chemistry from University College (1958).

NASA EXPERIENCE:
Dr. Llewellyn was chosen with the sixth group of astronauts in 1967. He withdrew from the program on September 6, 1968, for personal reasons.

CURRENT ASSIGNMENT: Dr. Llewellyn is presently a professor in the Department of Energy Conversion and Mechanical Design, College of Engineering, University of South Florida.

NAME: John M. "Mike" Lounge
NASA Astronaut (former)

PERSONAL DATA: Born June 28, 1946, in Denver, Colorado, but considers Burlington, Colorado, to be his hometown. Married. Three children. Recreational interests include jogging, chess, squash, tennis, flying, golfing, and blue grass guitar.

EDUCATION: Graduated from Burlington High School, Burlington, Colorado, in 1964; received a bachelor of science Academy in 1969 and a master of science degree in Astrogeophysics from the University of Colorado in 1970.

ORGANIZATIONS: Associate fellow of the American Institute of Aeronautics and Astronautics.

SPECIAL HONORS: 6 Navy Air Medals, 3 Navy Commendation Medals (with Combat "V"), the JSC Superior Achievement Award (for service as a member of the Skylab Reentry Team), three NASA Exceptional Service Medals and 3 NASA Space Flight Medals.

EXPERIENCE: Lounge entered on active duty with the United States Navy following graduation from the U.S. Naval Academy and spent the next nine years in a variety of assignments. He completed Naval flight officer training at Pensacola, Florida, went on to advanced training as a radar intercept officer in the F-4J Phantom, and subsequently reported to Fighter Squadron 142 based at Naval Air Station Miramar, California. While with VF-142, he completed a 9-month Southeast Asia cruise aboard the USS ENTERPRISE (participating in 99 combat missions) and a 7-month Mediterranean cruise aboard the USS AMERICA. In 1974, he returned to the U.S. Naval Academy as an instructor in the Physics Department. Lounge transferred to the Navy Space Project Office in Washington, D.C., in 1976, for a two year tour as a staff project office. He resigned his regular United States Navy commission in 1978.

NASA EXPERIENCE: Mr. Lounge has been employed at the Lyndon B. Johnson Space Center since July 1978. During this time, he worked as lead engineer for Space Shuttle launched satellites, and also served as a member of the Skylab Reentry Flight Control Team. He completed these assignments while with the Payloads Operations Division. Selected as an astronaut candidate by NASA in 1980, he completed a one year training and evaluation period, and became an astronaut in August 1981. He served as a member of the launch support team at Kennedy Space Center for the STS-1, STS-2, and STS-3 missions. Following his first flight, he was assigned to the first mission to carry the Centaur (cryogenically fueled) upper stage (STS-61F). After the mission was canceled, he participated in Space Station design development. From 1989 thru 1991, Mr. Lounge served as Chief of the Space Station Support Office, representing astronaut interests in Space Station design and operation planning. A veteran of three space flights, Mike Lounge has logged over 482 hours in space. He was a mission specialist on STS-51I (August 27 to September 3, 1985) and STS-26 (September 29 to October 3, 1988) and was the flight engineer on STS-35 (December 2-10, 1990). Mr. Lounge resigned from NASA in June 1991. He is currently Director of Houston Operations for SPACEHAB, INC.

SPACE FLIGHT EXPERIENCE: STS-51I Discovery, launched from Kennedy Space Center, Florida, on August 27, 1985. During that mission Mike's duties included deployment of the Australian AUSSAT communications satellite and operation of the Remote Manipulator System (RMS). The crew deployed two other communications satellites, the Navy's SYNCOM IV-4, and American Satellite Company's ASC-1, and also performed a successful on-orbit rendezvous and repair of the ailing 15,400 lb. SYNCOM IV-3 satellite. STS-51I completed 112 orbits of the Earth before landing at Edwards Air Force Base, California, on September 3, 1985. Mission duration was 171 hours, 17 minutes, 42 seconds. STS-26 Discovery, the first flight to be flown after the Challenger accident, launched from the Kennedy Space Center, Florida, on September 29, 1988. During the four day mission, the crew successfully deployed the Tracking and Data Relay Satellite (TDRS-C), which was subsequently carried to orbit by the Inertial Upper Stage (IUS) rocket. They also operated eleven mid- deck experiments. Discovery completed 64 orbits of the Earth before landing at Edwards Air Force Base, California, on October 3, 1988. Mission duration was 97 hours, 57 seconds. STS-35 Columbia, launched from the Kennedy Space Center, Florida on December 2, 1990. Mike served as flight engineer on this 9-day flight which was dedicated to astronomy. Very exciting observations of the Universe were collected by the ASTRO-1 ultraviolet telescope and by the Broad Band X-Ray Telescope. Columbia completed 142 orbits of the Earth before landing at Edwards Air Force Base, California, on December 10, 1990. Mission duration was 215 hours, 5 minutes, 8 seconds.

NAME: Jack Robert Lousma (Colonel, USMC, Ret.)
NASA Astronaut (former)

PERSONAL DATA: Born February 29, 1936, in Grand Rapids, Michigan. Lousma and his wife, Gratia Kay, have been married since 1956. They have four children and six grandchildren. He is a golfing enthusiast and enjoys hunting, fishing, and aviation.

EDUCATION: Graduated from Ann Arbor High School in Ann Arbor, Michigan; received a bachelor of science degree in Aeronautical Engineering from the University of Michigan in 1959, and a master of science degree in Aeronautical Engineering from the U. S. Naval Postgraduate School in 1965; presented an honorary doctorate of Astronautical Science from the University of Michigan in 1973, an honorary Doctor of Science from Hope College in 1982, and an honorary Doctor of Science in Business Administration from Cleary College in 1986.

ORGANIZATIONS: Fellow of the American Astronautical Society; member of the Society of the Sigma Xi, the University of Michigan "M" Club, the Officer's Christian Fellowship, and the Association of Space Explorers.

SPECIAL HONORS: Awarded the Johnson Space Center Certificate of Commendation (1970) and the NASA Distinguished Service Medal (1973); presented the Navy Distinguished Service Medal and the Navy Astronaut Wings (1974), the City of Chicago Gold Medal (1974), the Robert J. Collier Trophy for 1973 (1974), the Marine Corps Aviation Association's Exceptional Achievement Award (1974), the Federation Aeronautique Internationale's V. M. Komarov Diploma for 1973 (1974), the Dr. Robert H. Goddard Memorial Trophy for 1975 (1975), the AIAA Octave Chanute Award for 1975 (1975), the AAS Flight Achievement Award for 1974 (1975); inducted into the International Space Hall of Fame (1982). NASA Distinguished Service Medal (1982), Department of Defense Distinguished Service Medal (1982), NCAA Silver Anniversary Award (1983). Inducted into the Michigan Aviation Hall of Fame (1988).

EXPERIENCE: Lousma was a reconnaissance pilot with VMCJ-2, 2nd Marine Air Wing, at Cherry Point, North Carolina, before being assigned to Houston and the Lyndon B. Johnson Space Center. He became a Marine Corps officer in 1959 and received his wings in 1960 after completing training at the U.S. Naval Air Training Command. He was then assigned to VMA-224, 2nd Marine Air Wing, as an attack pilot and later served with VMA-224, 1st Marine Air Wing, at Iwakuni, Japan. He has logged 7000 hours of flight time--including 700 hours in general aviation aircraft and 1619 hours in space, 4,500 hours in jet aircraft, 240 hours in helicopters, and 700 hours in general aviation aircraft.

NASA EXPERIENCE: Lousma is one of the 19 astronauts selected by NASA in April 1966. He served as a member of the astronaut support crews for the Apollo 9, 10, and 13 missions. He was the pilot for Skylab-3 (July 28 to September 25, 1973) and was spacecraft commander on STS-3 (March 22-30, 1982), logging a total of over 1,619 hours in space. Lousma also spent 11 hours on two spacewalks outside the Skylab space station. He also served as backup docking module pilot of the United States flight crew for the Apollo-Soyuz Test Project (ASTP) mission which was completed successfully in July 1975. Jack Lousma left NASA in 1983.

SPACE FLIGHT EXPERIENCE: Skylab-3 (SL-3) (July 28 to September 25, 1973). The crew on this 59-1/2 day flight included Alan L. Bean (spacecraft commander), Jack Lousma (pilot), and Owen K. Garriott (science-pilot). SL-3 accomplished 150% of mission goals while completing 858 revolutions of the earth and traveling some 24,400,000 miles in earth orbit. The crew installed six replacement rate gyros used for attitude control of the spacecraft and a twin-pole sun-shade used for thermal control, and they repaired nine major experiment or operational equipment items. They devoted 305 man hours to extensive solar observations from above the earth's atmosphere, which included viewing two major solar flares and numerous smaller flares and coronal transients. Also acquired and returned to earth were 16,000 photographs and 18 miles of magnetic tape documenting earth resources observations. The crew completed 333 medical experiment performances and obtained valuable data on the effects of extended weightlessness on humans. Skylab-3 ended with a Pacific Ocean splashdown and recovery by the USS NEW ORLEANS. STS-3, the third orbital test flight of space shuttle Columbia, launched from the Kennedy Space Center, Florida, on March 22, 1982, into a 180-mile circular orbit above the earth. Jack Lousma was the spacecraft commander and C. Gordon Fullerton was the pilot on this 8-day mission. Major flight test objectives included exposing the Columbia to extremes in thermal stress and the first use of the 50-foot remote manipulator system (RMS) to grapple and maneuver a payload in space. The crew also operated several scientific experiments in the orbiter's cabin and on the OSS-1 pallet in the payload bay. Space Shuttle Columbia responded favorably to the thermal tests and was found to be better than expected as a scientific platform. The crew accomplished almost 100% of the objectives assigned to STS-3, and after a 1-day delay dueto bad weather, landed on the lakebed at White Sands, New Mexico, on March 30,1982, having traveled 3.4 million miles during 129.9 orbits of the earth. Mission duration was 192 hours, 4 minutes, 49 seconds.

NAME: James A. Lovell (Captain, USN Retired)
NASA Astronaut (Former)

PERSONAL DATA: Born March 25, 1928, Cleveland, Ohio.

EDUCATION: University of Wisconsin; United States Naval Academy, bachelor of science, 1952; Test Pilot School, NATC, Patuxent River, Maryland, 1958; Aviation Safety School, University of Southern California, 1961; Advanced Management Program, Harvard Business School, 1971; and honorary doctorates from Rockhurst College, Illinois Wesleyan University, Western Michigan University, and Mary Hardin Baylor College.

BUSINESS AFFILIATION: Group Vice President, Centel Corporation (Business Communications Group)

MARITAL STATUS: Married to the former Marilyn Gerlach, Milwaukee, Wisconsin.

CHILDREN: Barbara L., October 13, 1953; James A., February 15, 1955; Susan K., July 14, 1958; Jeffrey C., January 14, 1966.

PREVIOUS ASSIGNMENT: During his Naval career he has had numerous aviator assignments, including a four-year tour as a test pilot at the Naval Air Test Center, Patuxent River, Maryland. While there he served as Program Manager for the F4H "Phantom" Fighter. A graduate of the Aviation Safety School of the University of Southern California, he also served as Safety Engineer with the Fighter Squadron 101 at the Naval Air Station, Oceana, Virginia. He has logged more than 5,000 hours flying time, including more than 3,500 hours in jet aircraft. Captain Lovell was selected as an Astronaut by NASA in September 1962. He has since served as backup pilot for the Gemini 4 flight and backup Commander for the Gemini 9 flight, as well as backup Commander to Neil Armstrong for the Apollo 11lunar landing mission. On December 4, 1965, he and Frank Borman were launched into space on the history making Gemini 7 mission. The flight lasted 330 hours and 35 minutes and included the first rendezvous of two manned maneuverable spacecraft. The Gemini 12 mission, commanded by Lovell with Pilot Edwin Aldrin, began on November 11, 1966. This four-day, 59 revolution flight brought the Gemini program to a successful close. Lovell served as Command Module Pilot and Navigator on the epic six-day journey of Apollo 8, man's maiden voyage to the moon, December 21-Z7, 1968. Apollo 8 was the first manned spacecraft to be lifted into near-earth orbit by a 7-1/2 million pound thrust Saturn V launch vehicle; and Lovell and fellow crewmen, Frank Borman and William A. Anders, became the first humans to leave the Earth's gravitational influence. He completed his fourth mission as Spacecraft Commander of the Apollo 13 flight, April 11-17, 1970, and became the first man to journey twice to the moon. Apollo 13 was programmed for ten days; however, the original flight plan was modified en route to the moon due to a failure of the Apollo 13 Service Module cryogenic oxygen system. Lovell and fellow crewmen, John L. Swigert and Fred W. Haise, working closely with Houston ground controllers, converted their lunar module

Aquarius into an effective lifeboat. Their emergency activation and operation of lunar module systems conserved both electrical power and water in sufficient supply to assure their safety and survival while in space and for the return to earth. Captain Lovell held the record for time in space with a total of 715 hours and 5 minutes until surpassed by the Skylab flights. On March 1, 1973, Captain Lovell retired from the Navy and from the Space Program to join Bay-Houston Towing Company in Houston, Texas. Bay-Houston Towing Company is a diversified company involved in harbor and coastwise towing, mining, and marketing of peat products for the lawn and garden industry, and ranching. He waspromoted to the position of President and Chief Executive Officer on March 1, 1975.

BUSINESS BACKGROUND: On January 1, 1977, Captain Lovell became president of Fisk Telephone Systems, Inc., in Houston, Texas (marketing business communications equipment) in the southwestern United States. On January 1, 1981, he was appointed Group Vice President, Business Communications Systems, a Centel Corporation.

SPECIAL ASSIGNMENT: President Lyndon B. Johnson appointed Captain Lovell as his consultant for Physical Fitness and Sports in June, 1967. When the Physical Fitness Council was revised under President Nixon in 1970, Captain Lovell was assigned the additional duty of Chairman of the Council. After eleven years of performing his dual role with the Council, he relinquished these positions in 1978. However, he is still a Consultant to the Council and is presently assisting the Council in achieving its objective of making all citizens aware of the importance of being physically fit. The office of the President's Council on Physical Fitness and Sports is located in Washington, D.C.

DIRECTORSHIPS: First City Bank-Almeda Genoa, Houston.

AFFILIATIONS: Board of Directors of the North American Telephone Association; Trustee of the National Space Institute; Associate Fellow of the Society of Experimental Test Pilots; member Explorers Club; Fellow American Astronautical Society; Advisory Board, Health and Tennis Corporation of America; Board, Houstonian Fitness Center in Houston; Association of Physical Fitness Centers, Washington, D.C.; Executive Board, Sam Houston Area Boy Scouts of America.

SPECIAL HONORS: Eagle Scout; Sam Houston Area Council 1976 Distinguished Eagle Scout Award; Presidential Medal for Freedom, 1970; NASA Distinguished Service Medal; two NASA Exceptional Service Medals; the Navy Astronauts Wings; the Navy Distinguished Service Medal; two Navy Distinguished Flying Crosses; 1967 FAI De Laval and Gold Space Medals (Athens, Greece); the American Academy of Achievement Golden Plate Award; City of New York Gold Medal in 1969; City of Houston Medal for Valor in 1969; the National Academy of Television Arts and Sciences Special Trustees Award, 1969; the Institute of Navigation Award, 1969; the University of Wisconsin's Distinguished Alumni Service Award, 1970; corecipient of the American Astronautical Society Flight Achievement Awards, 1966 and 1968; the Harmon International Trophy, 1966, 1967 and 1969; the Robert H. Goddard Memorial Trophy, 1969; the H. H. Arnold Trophy, 1969; General Thomas D. White USAF Space Trophy, 1969; Robert J. Collier Trophy, 1968; Henry G. Bennett Distinguished Service Award; and the AIAA Haley Astronautics Award, 1970.

NAME: G. David Low
NASA Astronaut (former)

PERSONAL DATA: Born February 19, 1956, in Cleveland, Ohio. Married to the former JoAnn Andochick of Weirton, West Virginia. They have one child. He enjoys tennis, squash, scuba diving, and running. His mother, Mrs. Mary Ruth Low, resides in Potomac, Maryland. His father, Mr. George M. Low, is deceased.

EDUCATION: Graduated from Langley High School, McLean, Virginia, in 1974; received a bachelor of science degree in physics-engineering from Washington & Lee University in 1978, a bachelor of science degree in mechanical engineering from Cornell University in 1980, and a master of science degree in aeronautics & astronautics from Stanford Universityin 1983.

ORGANIZATIONS: Associate Fellow of the American Institute of Aeronautics and Astronautics; member of Omicron Delta Kappa.

SPECIAL HONORS: Recipient of three NASA Space Flight Medals, the NASA Exceptional Service Medal, the NASA Outstanding Leadership Medal, and an honorary doctor of engineering degree from Rensselaer Polytechnic Institute.

EXPERIENCE: Low worked in the Spacecraft Systems Engineering Section of the Jet Propulsion Laboratory, California Institute of Technology, from March 1980 until June 1984. During that time he was involved in the preliminary planning of several planetary missions, an Autonomous Spacecraft Maintenance study, and the systems engineering design of the Galileo spacecraft. Following a one-year leave to pursue graduate studies, Low returned to JPL where he was the principal spacecraft systems engineer for the Mars Geoscience/Climatology Observer Project.

NASA EXPERIENCE: Selected by NASA in May 1984, Low became an astronaut in June 1985. He has held a variety of technical assignments including work on the Remote Manipulator System (RMS), on Extravehicular Activity (EVA), and Orbiter test and checkout tasks at the Kennedy Space Center. Low served as a spacecraft communicator (CAPCOM) in the Mission Control Center during STS Missions 26, 27, 29 and 30. He also served as the lead astronaut in the Man-Systems Group and Station Operations Group of the Space Station Support Office. In 1993 Low was a member of the Russian Integration Team which worked for several months in Crystal City, Virginia to define the changes from the old Space Station Freedom to the new International Space Station. In 1994 he served as the Manager of the EVA Integration and Operations Office, and in 1995 he served as an assistant in the NASA Legislative Affairs Office where he worked with Members of Congress and their staffs to keep them informed about NASA's aeronautics and space programs. A veteran of three space flights, Low has logged over 714 hours in space, including nearly 6 hours on a spacewalk. He was a mission specialist on STS-32 (January 9-20, 1990) and STS-43 (August 2-11, 1991), and was the payload commander on STS-57 (June 21 to July 1, 1993). On his first mission, Low was a crew member on STS-32 which launched from the Kennedy Space Center, Florida, on January 9, 1990. On board the Orbiter Columbia the crew successfully deployed the Syncom IV-F5 communications satellite, and retrieved the 21,400-pound Long Duration Exposure Facility (LDEF) using the RMS. They also operated a variety of middeck materials and life sciences experiments, as well as the IMAX camera. Following 173 orbits of the Earth in 261 hours, Columbia returned to a night landing at Edwards Air Force Base, California, on January 20, 1990. Low next served as the flight engineer aboard the Orbiter Atlantis on STS-43. The nine-day mission launched from the Kennedy

Space Center, Florida, on August 2, 1991. During the flight, crew members deployed the fifth Tracking and Data Relay Satellite (TDRS-E), in addition to conducting 32 physical, material, and life science experiments, mostly relating to the Extended Duration Orbiter and Space Station Freedom. After 142 orbits of the Earth in 213 hours, the mission concluded with a landing on Runway 15 at the Kennedy Space Center on August 11, 1991. On STS-57, Low served as payload commander aboard the Orbiter Endeavour, which launched from the Kennedy Space Center, Florida, on June 21, 1993. The primary objective of this flight was the retrieval of the European Retrievable Carrier satellite (EURECA) using the RMS. Additionally, this mission featured the first flight of Spacehab, a commercially-provided middeck augmentation module for the conduct of microgravity experiments. Spacehab carried 22 individual flight experiments in materials and life sciences research. During the mission Low, along with crew mate Jeff Wisoff, conducted a 5-hour, 50-minute spacewalk during which the EURECA communications antennas were manually positioned for latching, and various extravehicular activity (EVA) tools and techniques were evaluated for use on future missions. Endeavour landed at the Kennedy Space Center on July 1, 1993, after 155 orbits of the Earth in 239 hours. David Low left NASA in February 1996 to pursue an aerospace career with Orbital Sciences Corporation's Launch Systems Group in Dulles, VA.

NAME: Thomas K. Mattingly II (Rear Admiral, USN, Ret.)
NASA Astronaut (former)

PERSONAL DATA: Born in Chicago, Illinois, March 17, 1936. One grown son.

EDUCATION: Attended Florida elementary and secondary schools and is a graduate of Miami Edison High School, Miami, Florida; received a bachelor of science degree in Aeronautical Engineering from Auburn University in 1958.

ORGANIZATIONS: Associate Fellow, American Institute of Aeronautics and Astronautics; Fellow, American Astronautical Society; and Member, Society of Experimental Test Pilots, and the U.S. Naval Institute.

SPECIAL HONORS: Department of Defense Distinguished Service Medal (1982); NASA Distinguished Service Medals (2); JSC Certificate of Commendation (1970); JSC Group Achievement Award (1972); Navy Distinguished Service Medal; Navy Astronaut Wings; SETP Ivan C. Kincheloe Award (1972); Delta Tau Delta Achievement Award (1972); Auburn Alumni Engineers Council Outstanding Achievement Award (1972); AAS Flight Achievement Award for 1972, AIAA Haley Astronautics Award for 1973; Federation Aeronautique Internationale's V. M. Komarov Diploma in 1973.

EXPERIENCE: Prior to reporting for duty at the Lyndon B. Johnson Space Center, he was a student at the Air Force Aerospace Research Pilot School. Mattingly began his Naval career as an Ensign in 1958 and received his wings in 1960. He was then assigned to VA-35 and flew A1H aircraft aboard the USS SARATOGA from 1960 to 1963. In July 1963, he served in VAH-11 deployed aboard the USS FRANKLIN D. ROOSEVELT where he flew the A3B aircraft for two years.

NASA EXPERIENCE: Mattingly is one of the 19 astronauts selected by NASA in April 1966. He served as a member of the astronaut support crews for the Apollo 8 and 11 missions and was the astronaut representative in development and testing of the Apollo spacesuit and backpack (EMU). He was designated command module pilot for the Apollo 13 flight but was removed from flight status 72 hours prior to the scheduled launch due to exposure to the German measles.

He has logged 7,200 hours of flight time ·· 5,000 hours in jet aircraft. From January 1973 to March 1978, Mattingly worked as head of astronaut office support to the STS (Shuttle Transportation System) program. He was next assigned as technical assistant for flight test to the Manager of the Orbital Flight Test Program. From December 1979 to April 1981, he headed the astronaut office ascent/entry group. He subsequently served as backup commander for STS-2 and STS-3, Columbia's second and third orbital test flights. From June 1983 through May 1984, Mattingly served as Head of the Astronaut Office DOD Support Group. A veteran of three space flights, Mattingly has logged 504 hours in space, including 1 hour and 13 minutes of EVA (extravehicular activity) during his Apollo 16 flight. He was the command module pilot on Apollo 16 (April 16-27, 1972), was the spacecraft commander on STS-4 (June 26 to July 4, 1982) and STS 51-C (January 24-27, 1985). Captain Mattingly resigned from NASA in 1985.

SPACE FLIGHT EXPERIENCE: Apollo 16 (April 16-27, 1972) was the fifth manned lunar landing mission. The crew included John W. Young (spacecraft commander), Ken Mattingly (command module pilot), and Charles M. Duke, Jr. (lunar module pilot). The mission assigned to Apollo 16 was to collect samples from the lunar highlands at a location near the crater Descartes. While in lunar orbit the scientific instruments aboard the command and service module "Casper" extended the photographic and geochemical mapping of a belt around the lunar equator. Twenty-six separate scientific experiments were conducted both in lunar orbit and during cislunar coast. Major emphasis was placed on using man as an orbital observer capitalizing on the human eye's unique capabilities and man's inherent curiosity. Although the mission of Apollo 16 was terminated one day early, due to concern over several spacecraft malfunctions, all major objectives were accomplished through the ceaseless efforts of the mission support team and were made possible by the most rigorous preflight planning yet associated with an Apollo mission. STS-4, the fourth and final orbital test flight of the Shuttle Columbia, launched from Kennedy Space Center, Florida, on June 27,1982. Mattingly was the spacecraft commander and Henry W. Hartsfield, Jr., was the pilot. This 7-day mission was designed to: further verify ascent and entry phases of shuttle missions; perform continued studies of the effects of long-term thermal extremes on the Orbiter subsystems; and conduct a survey of Orbiter-induced contamination on the Orbiter payload bay. Additionally, the crew operated several scientific experiments located in the Orbiter's cabin and in the payload bay. These experiments included the Continuous Flow Electrophoresis System experiment designed to investigate the separation of biological materials in a fluid according to their surface electrical charge. This experiment was a pathfinder for the first commercial venture to capitalize on the unique characteristics of space. The crew is also credited with effecting an in-flight repair which enabled them to activate the first operational "Getaway Special" (composed of nine experiments that ranged from algae and duckweed growth in space to fruit fly and brine shrimp genetic studies). STS-4 completed 112 orbits of the Earth before landing on a concrete runway at Edwards Air Force Base, California, on July 4, 1982. STS-51C Discovery, the first Space Shuttle Department of Defense mission, launched from Kennedy Space Center, Florida on January 24, 1985. The crew included Ken Mattingly (spacecraft commander), Loren Shriver (pilot), Jim Buchli and Ellison Onizuka (mission specialists), and Gary Payton (DOD payload specialist). STS-51C performed its DOD mission which included deployment of a modified Inertial Upper Stage (IUS) vehicle from the Space Shuttle Discovery. Landing occurred on January 27, 1985.

NAME: Jon A. McBride (Captain, USN)
NASA Astronaut (Former)

PERSONAL DATA: Born August 14, 1943, in Charleston, West Virginia, but considers Beckley, West Virginia, to be his hometown. His mother, Mrs. W. L. McBride, resides in Charleston, West Virginia.

PHYSICAL DESCRIPTION: Red hair; blue eyes; height: 6 feet 2 inches; weight: 205 pounds.

EDUCATION: Graduated from Woodrow Wilson High School, Beckley, West Virginia, in 1960; received a bachelor of science degree in Aeronautical Engineering from the U.S. Naval Postgraduate School in 1971. Graduate work in Human Resources Management at Pepperdine University.

MARITAL STATUS: Married to the former Sharon Lynne White of Nacogdoches, Texas.

CHILDREN: Lt. Richard M. (USN), March 3, 1962; Melissa L., December 12, 1966; and Jon A., October 21, 1970; Stephen Michael, August 4, 1971.

RECREATIONAL INTERESTS: He enjoys flying, basketball, golf, softball, racquetball, gourmet cooking, numismatics, gardening, and carpentry.

ORGANIZATIONS: Member of Association of Naval Aviation, the Tailhook Association, Veterans of Foreign Wars, and the American Legion; associate member, Society of Experimental Test Pilots; and life member of Phi Delta Theta and the National Honor Society.

SPECIAL HONORS: Awarded the Defense Superior Service Medal (DSSM), 3 Air Medals, the Navy Commendation Medal with Combat V, a Navy Unit Commendation, the National Defense Medal, the Vietnamese Service Medal, and the NASA Space Flight Medal; recipient of West Virginia Secretary of State's "State Medallion" and appointed "West Virginia Ambassador of Good Will Among All Men" (1980). Received Honorary Doctorate in Aerospace Engineering from Salem College (1984); Honorary Doctorate of Science from West Virginia University (1985); Honorary Doctorate of Science from University of Charleston (1987); Honorary Doctorate of Science from West Virginia Institute of Technology (1987).

EXPERIENCE: McBride's naval service began in 1965 with flight training at Pensacola, Florida. After winning his wings as a naval aviator, he was assigned to Fighter Squadron 101 based at Naval Air Station Oceana, Virginia, for training in the F-4 "Phantom II" aircraft. He was subsequently assigned to Fighter Squadron 41 where he served 3 years as a fighter pilot and division officer. He has also served tours with Fighter Squadrons 11 and 103. While deployed to Southeast Asia, McBride flew 64 combat missions. He attended the U.S. Air Force Test Pilot School at Edwards Air Force Base prior to reporting to Air Test and Development Squadron Four at Point Mugu, California, where he served as maintenance officer and Sidewinder project officer. He has flown over 40 different types of military and civilian aircraft and piloted the Navy "Spirit of '76" bicentennial-painted F-4J "Phantom" in various air shows during 1976, 1977, and 1978. He holds current FAA ratings which include commercial pilot (multi-engine), instrument, and glider; and he previously served as a certified flight instructor (CFI).

He has logged more than 5,200 hours flying time -- including 4,700 hours in jet aircraft.

NASA EXPERIENCE: Selected as an astronaut candidate by NASA in January 1978, McBride became an astronaut in August 1979. His NASA assignments have included lead chase pilot for the maiden voyage of "Columbia"; software verification in the Shuttle Avionics Integration Laboratory (SAIL); and capsule communicator (CAPCOM) for STS-5, STS-6, and STS-7. McBride was pilot of STS 41-G, which launched from Kennedy Space Center, Florida, on October 5, 1984,aboard the Orbiter Challenger. This was the first crew of seven. During their eight day mission, crew members deployed the Earth Radiation Budget Satellite, conducted scientific observations of the earth with the OSTA-3 pallet and Large Format Camera, and demonstrated potential satellite refueling with an EVA and associated hydrazine transfer. Mission duration was 197 hours and concluded with a landing at Kennedy Space Center, Florida, on October 13, 1984. McBride was scheduled to fly next in March 1986, as the commander of STS 61-E crew. This flight was one of several deferred by NASA in the wake of the Challenger accident in January 1986. On July 30, 1987, Captain McBride was assigned to NASA Headquarters to serve as Acting Assistant Administrator for Congressional Relations, with responsibility for NASA's relationship with Congress, and for providing coordination and direction to all Headquarters and Field Center communications with Congressional support organizations. He held this post from September 1987 thru March 1989. Last year McBride was named to command the crew of the STS-35 (ASTRO-1) mission, scheduled for launch in March 1990. In May 1989, Captain McBride retired from NASA and the Navy, in order to pursue a business career. He is currently President and Chief Executive Officer, Flying Eagle Corp., Lewisburg, West Virginia.

NAME: Bruce McCandless II (Captain, USN, Ret.)
NASA Astronaut (former)

PERSONAL DATA: Born June 8, 1937, in Boston, Massachusetts. Married to the former Bernice Doyle of Rahway, New Jersey. They have two grown children. Recreational interests include electronics, photography, scuba diving, and flying. He also enjoys cross country skiing.

EDUCATION: Graduate of Woodrow Wilson Senior High School, Long Beach, California; received a bachelor of science degree from the United States Naval Academy in 1958, a master of science degree in Electrical Engineering from Stanford University in 1965, and a masters degree in Business Administration from the University of Houston at Clear Lake in 1987.

ORGANIZATIONS: Member of the U.S. Naval Academy Alumni Association (Class of 1958), the U.S. Naval Institute, the Institute of Electrical & Electronic Engineers, the American Institute for Aeronautics and Astronautics, the Association for Computing Machinery, and the National Audubon Society; fellow of the American Astronautical Society, and former president of the Houston Audubon Society.

SPECIAL HONORS: Legion of Merit (1988); Department of Defense Distinguished Service Medal (1985); National Defense Service Medal; American Expeditionary Service Medal; NASA Exceptional Service Medal (1974); American Astronautical Society Victor A. Prather Award (1975 & 1985); NASA Space Flight Medal (1984); NASA Exceptional Engineering Achievement Medal (1985); National Aeronautic Association Collier Trophy (1985); Smithsonian Institution National Air and Space Museum Trophy (1985). Awarded one patent for the design of a tool tethering system that is currently used during Shuttle "spacewalks."

EXPERIENCE: McCandless was graduated second in a class of 899 from Annapolis and subsequently received flight training from the Naval Aviation Training Command at bases in Pensacola, Florida, and Kingsville, Texas. He was designated a naval aviator in March of 1960 and proceeded to Key West, Florida, for weapons system and carrier landing training in the F-6A Skyray. He was assigned to Fighter Squadron 102 (VF-102) from December 1960 to February 1964, flying the Skyray and the F-4B Phantom II, and he saw duty aboard the USS FORRESTAL (CVA-59) and the USS ENTERPRISE (CVA(N)-65), including the latter's participation in the Cuban blockade. For three months in early 1964, he was an instrument flight instructor in Attack Squadron 43 (VA-43) at the Naval Air Station, Apollo Soucek Field, Oceana, Virginia, and then reported to the Naval Reserve Officer's Training Corps Unit at Stanford University for graduate studies in electrical engineering. He has gained flying proficiency in the T-33B Shootingstar, T-38A Talon, F-4B Phantom II, F-6A Skyray, F-11 Tiger, TF-9J Cougar, T-1 Seastar, and T-34B Mentor airplane, and the Bell 47G helicopter. He has logged more than 5,200 hours flying time -- 5,000 hours in jet aircraft.

NASA EXPERIENCE: McCandless is one of the 19 astronauts selected by NASA in April 1966. He was a member of the astronaut support crew for the Apollo 14 mission and was backup pilot for the first manned Skylab mission (SL-1/SL-2). He was a co-investigator on the M-509 astronaut maneuvering unit experiment which was flown in the Skylab Program, and collaborated on the development of the Manned Maneuvering Unit (MMU) used during Shuttle EVAs. He has been responsible for crew inputs to the development of hardware and procedures for the Inertial Upper Stage (IUS), Space Telescope, the Solar Maximum Repair Mission, and the Space Station Program. A veteran of two space flights, McCandless has logged over 312 hours in space, including 4 hours of MMU flight time. He flew as a mission specialist on STS-41B (February 3-11, 1984) and STS-31 (April 24-29, 1990).

SPACE FLIGHT EXPERIENCE: STS-41B Challenger, launched from the Kennedy Space Center, Florida, on February 3, 1984. The crew on this tenth Space Shuttle Mission included Mr. Vance Brand (spacecraft commander), Commander Robert L. Gibson, USN, (pilot), and fellow mission specialists, Dr. Ronald E. McNair, and Lt. Col. Robert L. Stewart, USA. The flight accomplished the proper shuttle deployment of two Hughes 376-series communications satellites. Rendezvous sensors and computer programs were flight tested for the first time. This mission marked the first checkout of the Manned Maneuvering Unit (MMU), and Manipulator Foot Restraint (MFR). McCandless made the first, untethered, free flight on each of the two MMU's carried on board and alternated with Stewart in the activities constituting two spectacular extravehicular activities (EVAS). The German Shuttle Pallet Satellite (SPAS), Remote Manipulator System (RMS), six Getaway Specials, and materials processing experiments were included on the mission. The 8 day orbital flight of Challenger (OV-099) culminated in the first landing on the runway at the Kennedy Space Center on February 11, 1984. With the completion of this flight McCandless logged 191 hours in space (including 4 hours of MMU flight time). STS-31 Discovery, launched on April 24, 1990, from the Kennedy Space Center in Florida. The crew aboard Space Shuttle Discovery included Col. Loren J. Shriver, USAF, (spacecraft commander), Col. Charles F. Bolden, USMC, (pilot), and Dr's. Steven A Hawley, and Dr. Kathryn D. Sullivan (mission specialists). During this 5 day mission, the crew deployed the Hubble Space Telescope, and conducted a variety of middeck experiments involving the study of protein crystal growth, polymer membrane processing, and the effects of weightlessness and magnetic fields on an ion arc. They also operated a variety of cameras, including both the IMAX in cabin and cargo bay cameras, for earth observations from their record setting altitude of 380 miles. Following 76 orbits of the earth in 121 hours, STS-31 Discovery landed at Edwards Air Force Base, California, on April 29, 1990.

NAME: Michael J. McCulley (Captain, USN, Ret.)
NASA Astronaut (former)

PERSONAL DATA: Born August 4, 1943, in San Diego, California, but considers Livingston, Tennessee to be his hometown. Married to the former Jane Emalie Thygeson of Melbourne, Florida. Six children. Recreational interests include skiing, reading, camping, and jogging.

EDUCATION: Graduated from Livingston Academy Livingston, Tennessee, in 1961; received a bachelor of science degree and a master of science degree in Metallurgical Engineering from Purdue University.

ORGANIZATIONS: Member of the Society of Experimental Test Pilots, the Association of Space Explorations, the Boy Scouts of America (Eagle Scout), and Tau Beta Pi.

SPECIAL HONORS: Awarded the Legion of Merit, Defense Superior Service Medal, NASA Space Flight Medal, Navy Commendation medal, Armed Forces Expeditionary Medal, Meritorious Unit Commendation, Navy Good Conduct Medal, Sea Service Ribbon, National Defense Medal, Small Arms Expert Ribbon, and the Battle "E" Ribbon.

EXPERIENCE: After graduation from high school, McCulley enlisted in the U.S. Navy and subsequently served on one diesel-powered and two nuclear-powered submarines. In 1965 he entered Purdue University, and in January 1970, received his Naval Officers commission and both degrees. Following flight training, he served tours of duty in A-4 and A-6 aircraft, and was selected to attend the Empire Test Pilots School in Great Britain. He served in a variety of test pilots billets at the Naval Air Test Center, Patuxent River, Maryland, before returning to sea duty on USS SARATOGA and USS NIMITZ. He has flown over 50 aircraft types, logging over 5,00 flying hours, and has nearly 400 carrier landings from six aircraftcarriers.

NASA EXPERIENCE: Selected by NASA in May 1984, McCulley completed a one-year training and evaluation program in June 1985, qualifying him for assignment as a pilot on future Space Shuttle flight crews. His technical assignments include: Astronaut Office weather coordinator; flight crew representative to the Shuttle Requirements Control Board; Technical Assistant to the Director of Flight Crew Operations; lead of the Astronaut Support Team at the Kennedy Space Center. He flew on STS-34 in 1989 and has logged a total of 119 hours and 41 minutes in space. In October 1990, McCulley retired from NASA and the Navy to join the Lockheed Space Operations Company as the Deputy Director of the Kennedy Space Center Launch Site with responsibility for over 6000 people who are involved in the processing of space shuttles from wheels-stop on the runway through T-0 on the Launch pad. Currently, McCulley is Vice President and Deputy Program Manager for the Space Flight Operation Contract and United Space Alliance. He is responsible for over 9000 people involved in virtually all aspects of Space Shuttle operation including flight controllers, astronaut training, and both launch and mission control facilities and operations in Texas and Florida.

SPACE FLIGHT EXPERIENCE: McCulley was the pilot on STS-34. The crew aboard Shuttle Orbiter Atlantis launched from Kennedy Space Center, Florida on October 18, 1989, and landed at Edwards Air Force Base, California, on October 23, 1989. During the mission crew members successfully deployed the Galileo spacecraft on its journey to explore Jupiter, operated the Shuttle Solar Backscatter Ultraviolet Instrument (SSBUV) to map atmospheric ozone, and performed numerous secondary experiments involving radiation measurements, polymer morphology, lightning research, microgravity effects on plants, and a student experiment on ice crystal growth in space. Mission duration was 4 days, 23 hours, 41 minutes.

NAME: James A. McDivitt (Brig. General, USAF, Retired)
NASA Astronaut (former)

PERSONAL DATA: Born June 10, 1929, in Chicago, Illinois. His parents, Mr. and Mrs. James McDivitt, reside in Jackson, Michigan.

PHYSICAL DESCRIPTION: Grey hair; blue eyes; height: 5 feet 11 inches; weight: 165 pounds.

EDUCATION: Graduated from Kalamazoo Central High School, Kalamazoo, Michigan; received a Bachelor of Science degree in Aeronautical Engineering from the University of Michigan (graduated first in class) in 1959 and an Honorary Doctorate in Astronautical Science from the University of Michigan in 1965; Honorary Doctor of Science, Seton Hall University, 1969; Honorary Doctor of Science, Miami University (Ohio), 1970; Honorary Doctor of Laws, Eastern Michigan University, 1975.

MARITAL STATUS: Single

CHILDREN: Michael A., April 14, 1957; Ann L., July 21, 1958; Patrick W., August 30, 1960; Kathleen M., June 16, 1966.

RECREATIONAL INTERESTS: His hobbies include hunting, golf, swimming, tennis, and racquet ball.

ORGANIZATIONS: Member of the Society of Experimental Test Pilots, the American Institute of Aeronautics and Astronautics, Tau Beta Pi, and Phi Kappa Phi.

SPECIAL HONORS: Awarded two NASA Distinguished Service Medals; NASA Exceptional Service Medal; two Air Force Distinguished Service Medals; four Distinguished Flying Crosses; five Air Medals; the Chong Moo Medal from South Korea; the USAF Air Force Systems Command Aerospace Primus Award; the Arnold Air Society JFK Trophy; the Sword of Loyola; the Michigan Wolverine Frontiersman Award; and USAF Astronaut Wings.

EXPERIENCE: McDivitt joined the Air Force in 1951 and retired in the rank of Brig. General. He flew 145 combat missions during the Korean War in F-80s and F-86s. He is a graduate of the USAF Experimental Test Pilot School and the USAF Aerospace Research Pilot course and served as an experimental test pilot at Edwards Air Force Base, California. He has logged over 5,000 flying hours.

NASA EXPERIENCE: General McDivitt was selected as an astronaut by NASA in September 1962. He was command pilot for Gemini 4, a 66-orbit four-day mission that began on June 3 and ended June 7, 1965. Highlights of the mission included a controlled extravehicular activity period and a number of experiments. He was commander of Apollo 9, a ten-day earth orbital flight launched on March 3, 1969. This was the first flight of the complete set of Apollo hardware and was the first flight of the Lunar Module. He became Manager of Lunar Landing Operation in May 1969, and led a team that planned the lunar exploration program and redesigned the spacecraft to accomplish this task. In August 1969, he became Manager of the Apollo Spacecraft Program and was the program manager for Apollo 12, 13, 14, 15, and 16. He retired from the USAF and left NASA in June 1972, to take the position of Executive Vice President, Corporate Affairs for Consumers Power Company. In March 1975, he joined Pullman, Inc. as a Vice President and in October 1975 he became President of the Pullman Standard Division of Pullman, Inc. Pullman Standard is the largest builder of railroad cars in the United States. In January 1981 he joined Rockwell International Corporation where he is Senior Vice President, Strategic Management.

Name: Donald R. McMonagle
Manager, Launch Integration
Space Shuttle Program
John F. Kennedy Space Center, Florida
NASA Astronaut (former)

Donald R. McMonagle (Retired Colonel, USAF) became the Manager, Launch Integration,at the Kennedy Space Center, Florida, effective August 15, 1997. In this capacity he is responsible for final Shuttle preparation, launch execution, and return of the orbiter to KSC following landings at any location other than KSC. He is chair of the Mission Management Team, and is the final authority for launch decision.

McMonagle was born on May 14, 1952, in Flint, Michigan, and graduated from Hamady High School, Flint, Michigan, in 1970. McMonagle received a Bachelor of Science degree in Astronautical Engineering from the United States Air Force Academy in 1974 and a Master of Science degree in Mechanical Engineering from California State University-Fresno in 1985.

McMonagle completed pilot training at Columbus Air Force Base (AFB), Mississippi, in 1975. After F-4 training at Homestead AFB, Florida, he went on a 1-year tour of duty as an F-4 pilot at Kunsan Air Base, South Korea. He returned from overseas to Holloman AFB, New Mexico, in 1977. In 1979, McMonagle was assigned to Luke AFB, Arizona, as an F-15 instructor pilot. In 1981, he entered the USAF Test Pilot School at Edwards AFB, California, and was the outstanding graduate in his class. From 1982 to 1985, McMonagle was the operations officer and a project test pilot for the Advanced Fighter Technology Integration F-16 aircraft. After attending the Air Command and Staff College at Maxwell AFB, Alabama, from 1985 to 1986, he was assigned as the operations officer of the 6513th Test Squadron at Edwards AFB. McMonagle has over 5,000 hours of flying experience in a variety of aircraft, primarily the T-38, F- 4, F-15, and F-16.

McMonagle was selected as an astronaut by NASA in June 1987. A veteran of three space flights, McMonagle has logged over 605 hours in space. McMonagle flew as a mission specialist aboard the Space Shuttle Discovery on Department of Defense mission STS-39 in April 1991. During this highly successful 8-day mission, the seven-man crew deployed, operated, and retrieved a remotely-controlled spacecraft and conducted several science experiments to include research of both natural and induced phenomena in the Earth's atmosphere. In January 1993, McMonagle served as pilot on STS-54 aboard the Space Shuttle Endeavour. The 6-day mission featured the deployment of a Tracking and Data Relay Satellite (TDRS), and the collection of information about celestial x-rays using a Diffuse X-Ray Spectrometer. McMonagle commanded a crew of six aboard Space Shuttle Atlantis on the STS-66 Atmospheric Laboratory for Applications and Science-3 (ATLAS-3) 11-day mission in November 1994. In January 1996 McMonagle was assigned the task to establish a new Extra-Vehicular Activity (EVA) Project Office responsible for managing all NASA resources associated with space suits and tools used to conduct space walks in support of Space Shuttle and the

International Space Station. This role included responsibility for developing and implementing a plan for research and development of next generation space suits to support future human space exploration.

McMonagle's accomplishments have earned him many notable awards. He has received the Air Medal, Meritorious Service Medal, three Air Force Commendation Medals, the Defense Meritorious Service Medal, the Distinguished Flying Cross, the Liethen-Tittle Award (Top Graduate from USAF Test Pilot School), three NASA Space Flight Medals, the NASA Exceptional Service Medal, and the NASA Outstanding Leadership Medal.

McMonagle is a member of the Society of Experimental Test Pilots; Association of Graduates, U. S. Air Force Academy; and Association of Space Explorers.

McMonagle is married to the former Janyce Morton of Phoenix, Arizona. They have two children and reside in Merritt Island, Florida.

NAME: Carl J. Meade (Colonel, USAF)
NASA Astronaut (former)

PERSONAL DATA: Born November 16, 1950, at Chanute Air Force Base, Illinois. Single. One son. He enjoys woodworking, home-built aircraft construction, racquetball, jogging, and snow skiing. His father, Mr. John Meade, resides in Universal City, Texas. His mother, Mrs. Esther J. Meade, is deceased.

EDUCATION: Graduated from Randolph High School, Randolph Air Force Base, Texas, in 1968; received a bachelor of science degree (with honors) in electronics engineering from the University of Texas in 1973, and a master of science degree in electronics engineering from California Institute of Technology in 1975.

ORGANIZATIONS: Member of the Society of Experimental Test Pilots (SETP), Tau Beta Pi, Eta Kappa Nu, Phi Kappa Phi, the Experimental Aircraft Association, and is a registered professional engineer.

SPECIAL HONORS: Hughes Fellow, California Institute of Technology. Distinguished graduate of both USAF Undergraduate Pilot Training and USAF Test Pilot School. Recipient of the Liethen-Tittle Award as the Outstanding Test Pilot of USAF Test Pilot School Class 80B. Awarded the Distinguished Flying Cross, Intelligence Medal. National Defense Service Medal, Air Force Commendation Medal, Defense Superior Service Medal, 2 Air Force Outstanding Unit Awards, NASA Group Achievement Award, NASA Space Flight Medal, and NASA Exceptional Service Medal.

EXPERIENCE: Prior to entering active duty in the United States Air Force, Meade was a Hughes Fellow at the California Institute of Technology and an electronics design engineer at Hughes Aircraft Company in Culver City, California. He entered the U.S. Air Force at Laughlin Air Force Base, Texas, where he was a distinguished graduate of undergraduate pilot training. In 1977, Meade was assigned to the 363rd Tactical Reconnaissance Wing at Shaw Air Force Base, South Carolina, where he flew the RF-4C. He was then selected as a member of the USAF Test Pilot School Class 80B. Upon graduation he received the Liethen-Tittle Award as the Outstanding Test Pilot and was assigned to the 6510th Test Wing at Edwards Air Force Base, California. While there, Meade was involved with research development test and evaluation of the F-5E, RF-5E and F-20 aircraft and the ground-launched and air-launched cruise missiles. He also performed high speed taxi, braking, tailhook, takeoff, landing, flying qualities, performance and weapon systems tests in the F-4E aircraft. Meade was then assigned to the F-16 Combined Test Force where he flew performance, loads and flutter, flying qualities, and weapon systems tests in both the F-16A and F-16C aircraft. In 1985, he was reassigned to the USAF Test Pilot School as a test pilot instructor in the F-4, A-7, A-37, and various gliders, teaching performance, stability/control, departure/spins, and radar flight test techniques. He was also the departure/spin lead instructor and avionics systems test training aircraft program manager. He has logged over 4,800 hours of jet time in 27 different aircraft.

NAME: Bruce E. Melnick (Commander, USCG, Ret.)
NASA Astronaut (former)

PERSONAL DATA: Born December 5, 1949, in New York, New York, but considers Clearwater, Florida to be his hometown. Married to the former Kaye Aughtman of Andalusia, Alabama. They have two grown children. Recreational interests include fishing, hunting, running, tennis, golf.

EDUCATION: Graduated from Clearwater High School, Clearwater, Florida, in 1967; attended Georgia Tech 1967-1968; received a bachelor of science degree in engineering (with honors) from the U.S. Coast Guard Academy in 1972, and a master of science degree in aeronautical systems from the University of West Florida in 1975.

ORGANIZATIONS: Member, USCG Academy Alumni Association; USCG Pterodactyl Society; North American Hunters Club; Benevolent and Protective Order of Elks; Early and Pioneer Naval Aviators; Naval Aviation Museum Foundation, National Management Association; Boy Scout First Class.

SPECIAL HONORS: NCAA Academic All American, Football (1971); Navy Helicopter Association Search and Rescue Aircrew Award (1983); Secretary of Transporatation Heroism Award (1983); Department of Defense Superior Service Medal; Distinguished Flying Cross (2); Coast Guard Commendation Medal; Coast Guard Achievement Medal; National Defense Medal; Humanitarian Service Medal; four USCG Unit Commendations (4); Sea Service Ribbon; Expert Rifle Medal; Expert Pistol Medal; NASA Space Flight Medals (2); Vladimir M. Komarov Diploma (1990); NASA Group Achievement Award 1990; NASA Exceptional Service Medal; U.S. Coast Guard Academy Distinguished Alumni Award (1992); Air Force Association David C. Schilling Award (1992); American Astronautical Society Flight Achievement Award (1993).

EXPERIENCE: Upon graduation from the Coast Guard Academy, Melnick was assigned as a deck watch officer aboard the USCG Cutter STEADFAST, home ported in St. Petersburg, Florida. After 16 months sea duty, he was sent to Navy flight training in Pensacola and participated in the CNTRA's Masters Program. After earning his wings in 1974, and his degree in 1975, he served two 3-1/2 year tours as a Coast Guard Rescue Pilot at CGAS Cape Cod, Massachusetts, and at Sitka, Alaska. He was then assigned to the Aircraft Program Office in Grand Prairie, Texas, where he conducted many of the developmental and acceptance tests on the Coast Guard's HH-65A "Dolphin" helicopter. In 1986, he was transferred to CGAS Traverse City, Michigan, where he served as the Operations Officer until his selection to theastronaut program.

He has logged over 5,000 hours flying time, predominantly in the H-3, H-52, H-65, and T-38 aircraft.

NASA EXPERIENCE: Selected by NASA in June 1987, Melnick became an astronaut in August 1988, qualified for flight assignment as a mission specialist. Subsequent technical assignments include: serving on the Astronaut Support Personnel (ASP) team at the Kennedy Space Center assigned to prepare Shuttle Orbiter cockpits and middecks prior to each flight; representing the Astronaut Office in the assembly and checkout of the new Space Shuttle Orbiter "Endeavour" (OV-105) at the contractor facilities in California; serving as the head of the flight software verification team in the Shuttle Avionics Integration Laboratory (SAIL). A veteran of two space flights, Melnick has logged over 300 hours in space. He.was a mission specialist on STS-41 (October 6-10, 1990) and was the flight engineer on STS-49 (May 7-16, 1992). Commander Melnick retired from the U.S. Coast Guard and left NASA in July 1992. He is now Vice President and Director of Shuttle Engineering with Lockheed Space Operations Company (LSOC) at Kennedy Space Center, Florida.

NASA EXPERIENCE: STS-41 Discovery, launched from the Kennedy Space Center, Florida, on October 6, 1990 and returned to land at Edwards Air Force Base, California, on October 10, 1990. STS-41 carried a five man crew. During 66 orbits of the Earth the crew successfully deployed the Ulysses spacecraft, starting this inter-planetary probe on its four year journey, via Jupiter, to investigate the polar regions of the Sun; operated the Shuttle Solar Backscatter Ultraviolet instrument (SSBUV) to map atmospheric ozone levels; activated a controlled "fire in space" experiment (the Solid Surface Combustion Experiment); and conducted numerous other middeck experiments involving radiation measurements, polymer membrane production and micro gravity effects on plants. Mission duration was 98 hours 10 minutes 04 seconds. STS-49 (May 7-16, 1992) was the maiden flight of the new Space Shuttle Endeavour. During 141 orbits of the Earth, the crew rendezvoused with, captured, attached a new rocket motor to, and deployed the Intelsat VI communications satellite, and conducted the Assembly of Station by EVA (Extra vehicular activity) methods (ASEM) evaluation. The mission included the most space walks (4) during a Shuttle flight, the first ever 3 person space walk, and the longest space walk in Shuttle history. Melnick performed the duties of Flight Engineer (MS-2) and was the principal Remote Manipulator System (RMS) operator throughout the mission.

NAME: F. Curtis Michel, Ph.D.
NASA Astronaut (former)

PERSONAL DATA: Born June 5, 1934, in LaCrosse, Wisconsin. His mother, Mrs. Viola Bloom, resides in Sacramento, California.

PHYSICAL DESCRIPTION: Brown hair; brown eyes; height: 5 feet 11 inches; weight: 165 pounds.

EDUCATION: Graduated from C. K. McClatchey High School, Sacramento, California; received a bachelor of science degree with honors in Physics in 1955 and a doctorate in physics in 1962, both from the California Institute of Technology.

MARITAL STATUS: Married to the former Beverly Muriel Kaminsky of Sacramento, California.

CHILDREN: Jeffrey B., August 19, 1963; Alice E., July 30, 1966.

RECREATIONAL INTERESTS: His hobbies are photography, tennis, handball, and baseball.

ORGANIZATIONS: Member of the American Physical Society, the American Geophysical Union, and the American Astronomical Society.

SPECIAL HONORS: He was named a Guggenheim Fellow to the University of Paris, France, 1979-1980, and has been awarded an Alexander von Humboldt Senior U.S. Scientist Award to study in Heidelberg, 1982-1983.

EXPERIENCE: Michel was a junior engineer with the Firestone Tire and Rubber Company's Guided Missile Division before joining the Air Force in 1955. As an AFROTC graduate, he received flight training at Marana Air Force Base, Arizona, and at Laredo and Perrin Air Force Bases in Texas. During his three years of military service, he flew F-86D interceptors in the United States and in Europe. Following his tour of active duty in the Air Force, he was a research fellow at the California Institute of Technology, doing experimental and theoretical work in nuclear physics. He came to Houston in July 1963 and became a member of the faculty at Rice University. His efforts there were directed to researching and teaching space sciences, such as the interaction of solar winds and the lunar atmosphere. He has accumulated 1,000 hours flying time, including 900 hours in jet aircraft.

NASA EXPERIENCE: Dr. Michel was selected in June 1965 as a sientist-astronaut by NASA He resigned in September 1969 to return to teaching and research, and was department chairman of the Space Physics and Astronomy Department at the Rice University in Houston, Texas, 1974-1979. He has been the Andrew Hays Buchanan Professor of Astrophysics since 1974. He was named a Guggenheim Fellow to the University of Paris, France, 1979-1980, and has been awarded an Alexander von Humboldt Senior U.S. Scientist Award to study in Heidelberg, 1982-1983.

NAME: Edgar Dean Mitchell (Captain, USN, Ret.)
NASA Astronaut (former)

PERSONAL DATA: Born in Hereford, Texas, on September 17, 1930, but considers Artesia, New Mexico, his hometown.

PHYSICAL DESCRIPTION: Brown hair; green eyes; height: 5 feet, 11 inches; weight: 180 pounds.

EDUCATION: Attended primary schools in Roswell, New Mexico, and is a graduate of Artesia High School in Artesia, New Mexico; received a bachelor of science degree in Industrial Management from the Carnegie Institute of Technology in 1952, a bachelor of science degree in Aeronautical Engineering from the U.S. Naval Postgraduate School in 1961, and a doctorate of science degree in Aeronautics/Astronautics from the Massachusetts Institute of Technology in 1964; presented an honorary doctorate of science from New Mexico State University in 1971, and an honorary doctorate of engineering from Carnegie-Mellon University in 1971.

MARITAL STATUS: Married to the former Anita Orr Rettig of Medina, Ohio. Mr. and Mrs. William Orr now reside in Winterpark, Florida.

CHILDREN: Karlyn L., August 12, 1953; Elizabeth R., March 24, 1959; Kimberley, October 7, 1961; Paul, March 21, 1963; and Mary Beth, March 19, 1964.

RECREATIONAL INTERESTS: He enjoys handball, tennis, and swimming, and his hobbies are scuba diving and soaring.

ORGANIZATIONS: Member of the American Institute of Aeronautics and Astronautics; the Society of Experimental Test Pilots; Sigma Xi; and Sigma Gamma Tau, New York Academy of Sciences.

SPECIAL HONORS: Presented the Presidential Medal of Freedom (1970), the NASA Distinguished Service Medal, the MSC Superior Achievement Award (1970), the Navy Astronaut Wings, the Navy Distinguished Service Medal, the City of New York Gold Medal (1971), and the Arnold Air Society's John F. Kennedy Award (1971).

EXPERIENCE: Captain Mitchell's experience includes Navy operational flight, test flight, engineering, engineering management, and experience as a college instructor. Mitchell came to the Manned Spacecraft Center after graduating first in his class from the Air Force Aerospace Research Pilot School where he was both student and instructor. He entered the Navy in 1952 and completed his basic training at the San Diego Recruit Depot. In May 1953, after completing instruction at the Officers' Candidate School at Newport, Rhode Island, he was commissioned as an Ensign. He completed flight training in July 1954 at Hutchinson, Kansas, and subsequently was assigned to Patrol Squadron 29 deployed to Okinawa. From 1957 to 1958, he flew A3 aircraft while assigned to Heavy Attack Squadron Two deployed aboard the USS BON HOMME RICHARD and USS TICONDEROGA; and he was a research project pilot with Air Development Squadron Five until 1959. His assignment from 1964 to 1965 was as Chief, Project Management Division of the Navy Field Office for Manned Orbiting Laboratory. He has accumulated 5,000 hours flight time--2,000 hours in jets.

NASA EXPERIENCE: Captain Mitchell was in the group selected for astronaut training in April 1966. He served as a member of the astronaut support crew for Apollo 9 and as backup lunar module pilot for Apollo 10. He completed his first space flight as lunar module Pilot on Apollo 14, January 31 - February 9, 1971. With him on man's third lunar landing mission were Alan B. Shepard, spacecraft commander, and Stuart A. Roosa, command module pilot. Maneuvering their lunar module, "Antares," to a landing in the hilly upland Fra Mauro region of the moon, Shepard and Mitchell subsequently deployed and activated various scientific equipment and experiments and collected almost 100 pounds of lunar samples for return to Earth. Other Apollo 14 achievements include: first use of Mobile Equipment Transporter (MET); largest payload placed in lunar orbit; longest distance traversed on the lunar surface; largest payload returned from the lunar surface; longest lunar surface stay time (33 hours); longest lunar surface EVA (9 hours and 17 minutes); first use of shortened lunar orbit rendezvous techniques; first use of color TV with new vidicon tube on lunar surface; and first extensive orbital science period conducted during CSM solo operations. In completing his first space flight, Mitchell logged a total of 216 hours and 42 minutes. He was subsequently designated to serve as backup lunar module pilot for Apollo 16. He is currently Chairman of the Board, Forecast Systems Inc., Provo, Utah, and West Palm Beach, Florida.

NAME: Richard M. Mullane (Colonel, USAF, Ret.)
NASA Astronaut (former)

PERSONAL DATA: Born September 10, 1945, in Wichita Falls, Texas, but considers Albuquerque, New Mexico, to be his hometown. Married to the former Donna Marie Sei of Albuquerque, New Mexico. They have three grown children. Recreational interests include backpacking, skiing, and running.

EDUCATION: Graduated from St. Pius X Catholic High School, Albuquerque, New Mexico, in 1963; received a bachelo of science degree in Military Engineering from the United States Military Acad emy in 1967; and awarded a master of science degree in Aeronautical Engineering from the Air Force Institute of Technology in 1975.

SPECIAL HONORS: Awarded 6 Air Medals, the Air Force Distinguished Flying Cross, Meritorious Service Medal, Vietnam Campaign Medal, National Defense Service Medal, Vietnam Service Medal, and Air Force Commendation Medal, and NASA Space Flight Medal; named a Distinguished Graduate of the USAF Navigator Training School (and recipient of its Commander's Trophy), the USAF Institute of Technology; and the USAF Test Pilot School.

EXPERIENCE: Mullane, an Air Force Colonel, was graduated from West Point in 1967. He completed 150 combat missions as an RF-4C weapon system operator while stationed at Tan Son Nhut Air Base, Vietnam, from January to November 1969. He subsequently served a 4-year tour of duty in England. In July 1976, upon completing the USAF Flight Test Engineering Course at Edwards Air Force Base, California, he was assigned as a flight test weapon system operator to the 3246th Test Wing at Eglin Air Force Base, Florida.

NASA EXPERIENCE: Selected by NASA in January 1978, Mullane became an astronaut in August 1979. A veteran of three space flights, he has logged a total of 356 hours in space. He was a mission specialist on the crew of STS-41D (August 30 to September 5, 1984), STS-27 (December 2-6, 1988), and STS-36 in (February 28 to March 4, 1990). Colonel Mullane retired from NASA and the USAF in September 1990. He is self-employed as a professional speaker & writer and resides in Albuquerque, NM. His first novel, Red Sky, A Novel of Love, Space, & War was published in June 1993 by Northwest Publishing, Inc. of Salt Lake City, UT.

SPACE FLIGHT EXPERIENCE: STS-41D Discovery, launched from Kennedy Space Center, Florida, on August 30, 1984. This was the maiden flight of the Orbiter Discovery. During this 7-day mission the crew successfully activated the OAST-1 solar cell wing experiment, deployed three satellites, operated the CFES-III experiment, the student crystal growth experiment, and photography experiments using the IMAX motion picture camera. STS-41D completed 96 orbits of the earth in 145 hours before landing at Edwards Air Force Base, California, on September 5, 1984. STS-27 Atlantis, launched from Kennedy Space Center, Florida, on December 2, 1988. The mission carried a DOD payload, as well as a number of secondary payloads. After 68 orbits of the earth, the mission concluded with a dry lakebed landing on Runway 17 at Edwards Air Force Base, California, on December 6, 1988. Mission duration was 105 hours. STS-36 Atlantis, launched from the Kennedy Space Center, Florida, on February 28, 1990. This mission carried Department of Defense payloads together with a number of secondary payloads. After 72 orbits of the earth, the STS-36 mission concluded with a lakebed landing at Edwards Air Force Base, California, on March 4, 1990.

NAME: Story Musgrave (M.D.)
       NASA Astronaut (Former)

PERSONAL DATA: Born August 19, 1935, in Boston, Massachusetts, but considers Lexington, Kentucky, to be his hometown. Single. Six children (one deceased). His hobbies are chess, flying, gardening, literary criticism, microcomputers, parachuting, photography, reading, running, scuba diving, and soaring.

EDUCATION: Graduated from St. Mark's School, Southborough, Massachusetts, in 1953; received a bachelor of science degree in mathematics and statistics from Syracuse University in 1958, a master of business administration degree in operations analysis and computer programming from the University of California at Los Angeles in 1959, a bachelor of arts degree in chemistry from Marietta College in 1960, a doctorate in medicine from Columbia University in 1964, a master of science in physiology and biophysics from the University of Kentucky in 1966, and a master of arts in literature from the University of Houston in 1987.

ORGANIZATIONS: Member of Alpha Kappa Psi, the American Association for the Advancement of Science, Beta Gamma Sigma, the Civil Aviation Medical Association, the Flying Physicians Association, the International Academy of Astronautics, the Marine Corps Aviation Association, the National Aeronautic Association, the National Aerospace Education Council, the National Geographic Society, the Navy League, the New York Academy of Sciences, Omicron Delta Kappa, Phi Delta Theta, the Soaring Club of Houston, the Soaring Society of America, and the United States Parachute Association.

SPECIAL HONORS: National Defense Service Medal and an Outstanding Unit Citation as a member of the United States Marine Corps Squadron VMA-212 (1954); United States Air Force Post-doctoral Fellowship (1965-1966); National Heart Institute Post-doctoral Fellowship (1966-1967); Reese Air Force Base Commander's Trophy (1969); American College of Surgeons I.S. Ravdin Lecture (1973); NASA Exceptional Service Medals (1974 & 1986); Flying Physicians Association Airman of the Year Award (1974 & 1983); NASA Space Flight Medals (1983, 1985, 1989, 1991, 1993, 1996); NASA Distinguished Service Medal (1992).

EXPERIENCE: Musgrave entered the United States Marine Corps in 1953, served as an aviation electrician and instrument technician, and as an aircraft crew chief while completing duty assignments in Korea, Japan, Hawaii, and aboard the carrier USS WASP in the Far East. He has flown 17,700 hours in 160 different types of civilian and military aircraft, including 7,500 hours in jet aircraft. He has earned FAA ratings for instructor, instrument instructor, glider instructor, and airline transport pilot, and U.S. Air Force Wings. An accomplished parachutist, he has made more than 500 free falls -- including over 100 experimental free-fall descents involved with the study of human aerodynamics. Dr. Musgrave was employed as a mathematician and operations analyst by the Eastman Kodak Company, Rochester, New York, during 1958. He served a surgical internship at the University of Kentucky Medical Center in Lexington from 1964 to 1965, and continued there as a U. S. Air Force post-doctoral fellow (1965-1966), working in aerospace medicine and physiology, and as a National Heart Institute post-doctoral fellow (1966-1967), teaching and doing research in cardiovascular and exercise physiology. From 1967 to 1989, he continued clinical and scientific training as a part-time surgeon at the Denver General Hospital and as a part-time professor of physiology and biophysics at the University of Kentucky Medical Center. He has written 25 scientific papers in the areas of aerospace medicine and physiology, temperature regulation, exercise physiology, and clinical surgery.

NASA EXPERIENCE: Dr. Musgrave was selected as a scientist-astronaut by NASA in August 1967. He completed astronaut academic training and then worked on the design and development of the Skylab Program. He was the backup science-pilot for the first Skylab mission, and was a CAPCOM for the second and third Skylab missions. Dr. Musgrave participated in the design and development of all Space Shuttle extravehicular activity equipment including spacesuits, life support systems, airlocks, and manned maneuvering units. From 1979 to 1982, and 1983 to 1984, he was assigned as a test and verification pilot in the Shuttle Avionics Integration Laboratory at JSC. He served as a spacecraft communicator (CAPCOM) for STS-31, STS-35, STS-36, STS-38 and STS-41, and lead CAPCOM for a number of subsequent flights. He was a mission specialist on STS-6 in 1983, STS-5F/Spacelab-2 in 1985, STS-33 in 1989 and STS-44 in 1991, was the payload commander on STS-61 in 1993, and a mission specialist on STS-80 in 1996. A veteran of six space flights, Dr. Musgrave has spent a total of 1,281 hours 59 minutes, 22 seconds in space. Dr. Musgrave left NASA in August 1997 to pursue private interests.

SPACE FLIGHT EXPERIENCE: Dr. Musgrave first flew on STS-6, which launched from the Kennedy Space Center, Florida, on April 4, 1983, and landed at Edwards Air Force Base, California, on April 9, 1983. During this maiden voyage of Space Shuttle Challenger, the crew performed the first Shuttle deployment of an IUS/TDRS satellite, and Musgrave and Don Peterson conducted the first Space Shuttle extravehicular activity (EVA) to test the new space suits and construction and repair devices and procedures. Mission duration was 5 days, 23 minutes, 42 seconds. On STS-51F/Spacelab-2, the crew aboard Challenger launched from the Kennedy Space Center, Florida, on July 29, 1985, and landed at Edwards Air Force Base, California, on August 6, 1985. This flight was the first pallet-only Spacelab mission, and the first mission to operate the Spacelab Instrument Pointing System (IPS). It carried 13 major experiments in astronomy, astrophysics, and life sciences. During this mission, Dr. Musgrave served as the systems engineer during launch and entry, and as a pilot during the orbital operations. Mission duration was 7 days, 22 hours, 45 minutes, 26 seconds. On STS-33, he served aboard the Space Shuttle Discovery, which launched at night from the Kennedy Space Center, Florida, on November 22, 1989. This classified mission operated payloads for the Department of Defense. Following 79 orbits, the mission concluded on November 27, 1989, with a landing at sunset on Runway 04 at Edwards Air Force Base, California. Mission duration was 5 days, 7 minutes, 32 seconds. STS-44 also launched at night on November 24, 1991. The primary mission objective was accomplished with the successful deployment of a Defense Support Program (DSP) satellite with an Inertial Upper Stage (IUS) rocket booster. In addition the crew also conducted two Military Man in Space Experiments, three radiation monitoring experiments, and numerous medical tests to support longer duration Shuttle flights. The mission was concluded in 110 orbits of the Earth with Atlantis returning to a landing on the lakebed at Edwards Air Force Base, California, on December 1, 1991. Mission duration was 6 days, 22 hours, 50 minutes, 42 seconds. STS-61 was the first Hubble Space Telescope (HST) servicing and repair mission. Following a night launch from Kennedy Space Center on December 2, 1993, the Endeavour rendezvoused with and captured the HST. During this 11-day flight, the HST was restored to its full capabilities through the work of two pairs of astronauts during a record 5 spacewalks. Dr. Musgrave performed 3 of these spacewalks. After having travelled 4,433,772 miles in 163 orbits of the Earth, Endeavour returned to a night landing in Florida on December 13, 1993. Mission duration was 10 days, 19 hours, 59 minutes. On STS-80 (November 19 to December 7, 1996), the crew aboard Space Shuttle Columbia deployed and retrieved the Wake Shield Facility (WSF) and the Orbiting Retrievable Far and Extreme Ultraviolet Spectrometer (ORFEUS) satellites. The free-flying WSF created a super vacuum in its wake in which to grow thin film wafers for use in semiconductors and the electronics industry. The ORFEUS instruments, mounted on the reusable Shuttle Pallet Satellite, studied the origin and makeup of stars. In completing this mission he logged a record 278 earth orbits, traveled over 7 million miles in 17 days, 15 hours, 53 minutes.

NAME: Steven R. Nagel (Colonel, USAF, Ret.)
NASA Astronaut (former)

PERSONAL DATA: Born October 27, 1946, in Canton, Illinois. Married Linda M. Godwin of Houston, Texas. Two daughters. His hobbies include sport flying and music. His parents, Mr. and Mrs. Ivan R. Nagel, reside in Canton, Illinois. Her father, Mr. James M. Godwin, resides in Oak Ridge, Missouri.

EDUCATION: Graduated from Canton Senior High School, Canton, Illinois, in 1964; received a bachelor of science degree in aeronautical and astronautical engineering (high honors) from the University of Illinois in 1969, and a master of science degree in mechanical engineering from California State University, Fresno, California, in 1978.

ORGANIZATIONS: Life member of the Order of Daedalians and Alpha Delta Phi; and honorary member of Phi Eta Sigma, Sigma Tau, Tau Beta Pi, and Sigma Gamma Tau.

SPECIAL HONORS: Awarded the Air Force Distinguished Flying Cross and the Air Medal with 7 Oak Leaf Clusters; and for undergraduate pilot training, recipient of the Commander's Trophy, the Flying Trophy, the Academic Trophy, and the Orville Wright Achievement Award (Order of Daedalians); also presented the Air Force Meritorious Service Medal (1978). Recipient of 4 NASA Space Flight Medals, (1985, 1991, 1993), Exceptional Service Medals (1988, 1989), Outstanding Leadership Medal (1992), AAS Flight Achievement Award, STS-37 Crew (1992), Outstanding Alumni Award, University of Illinois (1992), Distinguished Service Medal (1994), Distinguished Alumni Award, California State University, Fresno (1994), Lincoln Laureate, State of Illinois (1994).

EXPERIENCE: Nagel received his commission in 1969 through the Air Force Reserve Officer Training Corps (AFROTC) program at the University of Illinois. He completed undergraduate pilot training at Laredo Air Force Base, Texas, in February 1970, and subsequently reported to Luke Air Force Base, Arizona, for F-100 training. From October 1970 to July 1971, Nagel was an F-100 pilot with the 68th Tactical Fighter Squadron at England Air Force Base, Louisiana. He served a 1-year tour of duty as a T-28 instructor for the Laotian Air Force at Udorn RTAFB, Udorn, Thailand, prior to returning to the United States in October 1972 to assume A-7D instructor pilot and flight examiner duties at England Air Force Base, Louisiana. Nagel attended the USAF Test Pilot School at Edwards Air Force Base, California, from February to December 1975; and in January 1976, he was assigned to the 6,512th Test Squadron located at Edwards. As a test pilot, he has worked on various projects which have included flying the F-4 and A-7D. He has logged 9,400 hours flying time--6,650 hours in jet aircraft.

NASA EXPERIENCE: Nagel became a NASA astronaut in August 1979. His technical assignments have included: backup T-38 chase pilot for STS-1; support crew and backup entry spacecraft communicator (CAPCOM) for STS-2; support crew and primary entry CAPCOM for STS-3; software verification at the Shuttle Avionics Integration Laboratory (SAIL), and the Flight Simulation Laboratory (FSL); representing the Astronaut Office in the development of a crew escape system for the Space Shuttle; Acting Chief of the Astronaut Office. Nagel is a veteran of four space flights (STS-51G and STS-61 in 1985, STS-37 in 1991, and STS-55 in 1993) as described below: Nagel first flew as a mission specialist on the crew of STS-51G which launched from the Kennedy Space Center, Florida, on June 17, 1985. The crew on board the Orbiter Discovery deployed communications satellites for Mexico (Morelos), the Arab League (Arabsat), and the United States (AT&T Telstar). They used the Remote Manipulator System (RMS) to deploy and later retrieve the SPARTAN satellite which performed 17 hours of x-ray astronomy experiments while separated from the Space Shuttle. In addition, the crew activated the Automated Directional Solidification Furnace (ADSF), six "Getaway Specials," participated in biomedical experiments, and conducted a laser tracking experiment as part of the Strategic Defense Initiative. After completing approximately 170 hours of space flight, Discovery landed at Edwards Air Force Base, California, on June 24, 1985. Nagel then flew as pilot on the crew of STS-61A, the West German D-1 Spacelab mission, which launched from Kennedy Space Center, Florida, on October 30, 1985. This mission was the first in which payload activities were controlled from outside the United States. More than 75 scientific experiments were completed in the areas of physiological sciences, materials processing, biology, and navigation. After completing 111 orbits of the Earth, the Orbiter Challenger landed at Edwards Air Force Base, California, on November 6, 1985. On his third flight, Nagel was commander of the STS-37 crew on board the Shuttle Atlantis, which launched into orbit on April 5, 1991, from Kennedy Space Center, Florida, and landed on April 11, 1991, at Edwards Air Force Base, California. During this mission the crew deployed the Gamma Ray Observatory (GRO) for the purpose of exploring gamma ray sources throughout the universe, and conducted the first scheduled space walk in more than five and one-half years. Also, the crew performed the first successful unscheduled space walk to free a stuck antenna on GRO. Nagel also served as commander of STS-55, the German D-2 Spacelab mission. After launching on April 26, 1993, on the Shuttle Columbia, the crew landed 10-days later on May 6, 1993, at Edwards Air Force Base, California. During the ambitious mission 89 experiments were performed in many disciplines such as materials processing, life sciences, robotics, technology, astronomy and earth mapping. With the completion of his fourth flight Nagel has logged a total of 723 hours in space.

Nagel retired from the Air Force, effective February 28, 1995. He retired from the Astronaut Office, effective March 1, 1995, to assume the full-time position of Deputy Director for Operations Development, Safety, Reliability, and Quality Assurance Office, Johnson Space Center, Houston, Texas. In September 1996, Nagel transferred to Aircraft Operations Division where he performs duties as a Research Pilot.

NAME: George D. (nickname Pinky) Nelson (Ph.D.)
NASA Astronaut (former)

PERSONAL DATA: Born July 13, 1950, in Charles City, Iowa. Considers Willmar, Minnesota, to be his hometown. His wife Susie is from Alhambra, California. They have two daughters. Pinky enjoys playing golf, reading, swimming, running, and music.

EDUCATION: Graduated from Willmar Senior High School, Willmar, Minnesota, in 1968; received a bachelor of science degree in Physics from Harvey Mudd College in 1972 and a master of science and a doctorate in Astronomy from the University of Washington in 1974 and 1978, respectively.

SPECIAL HONORS: NASA Exceptional Engineering Achievement Medal, NASA Exceptional Service Medal, 3 NASA Space Flight Medals, AIAA Haley Space Flight Award, Federation Aeronautique Internationale's V. M. Komarov Diploma.

EXPERIENCE: Dr. Nelson performed astronomical research at the Sacramento Peak Solar Observatory, Sunspot, New Mexico; the Astronomical Institute at Utrecht, Utrecht, the Netherlands, and the University of Gottingen Observatory, Gottingen, West Germany, and at the Joint Institute for Laboratory Astrophysics in Boulder, Colorado.

NASA EXPERIENCE: Dr. Nelson was selected as an astronaut candidate by NASA in January 1978. He flew as a scientific equipment operator in the WB 57-F earth resources aircraft; served as the Astronaut Office representative in the Space Shuttle Extravehicular Mobility Unit (space suit) development effort. During STS-1 he was the photographer in the prime chase plane. He also served as support crewman and CAPCOM for the last two OFT flights, STS-3 and STS-4, and as head of the Astronaut Office Mission Development Group. A verteran of three space flights, Dr. Nelson served aboard STS-41C in 1984, STS-61C in 1986 and STS-26 in 1988. He has logged a total of 411 hours in space, including 10 hours of EVA flight time.

SPACE FLIGHT EXPERIENCE: STS-41C Challenger (April 6-13, 1984) was a seven day mission during which the crew successfully deployed the Long Duration Exposure Facility (LDEF); retrieved the ailing Solar Maximum Satellite, repaired it on-board the Orbiter, and replaced it in orbit. The mission also included flight testing of Manned Maneuvering Units (MMUs) in two extravehicular activities (EVAs), and operation of the Cinema 360 and IMAX Camera Systems. STS-61C Columbia (January 12-18, 1986) launched from the Kennedy Space Center, Florida, and returned to a night landing at Edwards Air Force Base, California. During the six day flight the crew deployed the SATCOM KU satellite, and conducted experiments in astrophysics and materials processing. STS-26 Discovery (September 29 to October 3, 1988) was the first mission flown after the Challenger accident. During the four day flight, the crew successfully deployed the Tracking and Data Relay Satellite (TDRS-C), and operated eleven mid-deck science experiments.

NAME: Wubbo J. Ockels
NASA Payload Specialist (Former)

PERSONAL DATA: He was born March 28, 1946, in Almelo, the Netherlands.

EDUCATION: He received a doctor of philosophy in physics and mathematics from the University of Groningen and completed a thesis on experimental work at the Nuclear Physic Accelerator Institute in Groningen.

EXPERIENCE: Ockels performed experimental investigations at the Nuclear Physics Accelerator Institute in Groningen.

NASA EXPERIENCE: He was selected by the European Space Agency (ESA) as one of three European payload specialists. He flew on the Spacelab Shuttle Mission STS-61-A TO CARRY D-1 -- THE FIRST GERMAN SPACELAB.

NAME: Bryan D. O'Connor (Colonel, USMC, Ret.)
NASA Astronaut (former)

PERSONAL DATA: Born September 6, 1946, in Orange, California, but considers Twentynine Palms, California to be his hometown. Bryan and his wife Susie have two sons, Thomas, and Kevin. The O'Connor family enjoys hiking, scuba diving, music, and travel.

EDUCATION: Graduated from Twentynine Palms High School, Twentynine Palms, California, in 1964; received a Bachelor of Science degree in Engineering (minor in Aeronautical Engineering) from the United States Naval Academy in 1968 and a Master of Science degree in Aeronautical Systems from the University of West Florida in 1970. He graduated from the Naval Safety School at the Naval

Postgraduate School, Monterey, California in 1972 and from the Naval Test Pilot School, Naval Air Test Center, Patuxent River, Maryland in 1976.

SPECIAL HONORS: Naval Safety School Top Graduate; Naval Test Pilot School Distinguished Graduate Award; Defense Superior Service Medal (2); Distinguished Flying Cross; Navy Meritorious Service Medal; NASA Distinguished Service Medal; NASA Outstanding Leadership Medal (2); NASA Exceptional Service Medal (2); NASA Exceptional Achievement Medal; NASA Silver Snoopy Award; AIAA System Effectiveness and Safety Award; AIAA Barry M.Goldwater Education Award; Aviation Week and Space Technology Laureate (Space and Missiles).

EXPERIENCE: O'Connor began active duty with the United States Marine Corps in June 1968 following graduation from the U.S. Naval Academy at Annapolis. He received his Naval Aviator's wings in June 1970, and served as an attack pilot flying the A-4 Skyhawk and the AV-8A Harrier on land and sea assignments in the United States, Europe and the Western Pacific. O'Connor attended the U.S. Naval Test Pilot School in 1975 and served as a test pilot with the Naval Air Test Center's Strike Test Directorate at Patuxent River, Maryland. During this 3-½ year assignment, he participated in evaluations of various conventional and VSTOL aircraft, including the A-4, OV-10, AV-8, and X-22 VSTOL research aircraft. From June 1977 to June 1979 he was the Naval Air Test Center project officer in charge of all Harrier flight testing, including the planning and execution of the First Navy Preliminary Evaluation of the YAV-8B advanced Harrier prototype. When informed of his selection to NASA's Astronaut Program in 1980, he was serving as the Deputy Program Manager (Acquisition) for the AV-8 program at the Naval Air Systems Command in Washington, D.C.

NASA EXPERIENCE: O'Connor was selected as an astronaut in May 1980. After a one-year initial training program at NASA's Johnson Space Center in Houston, Texas, O'Connor served in a variety of functions in support of the first test flights of the Space Shuttle, including simulator test pilot for STS-1and 2, safety/photo chase pilot for STS-3, and support crew for STS-4. He was CAPCOM (spacecraft communicator) for STS-5 through STS-9. He also served as Aviation Safety Officer for the Astronaut Corps. When the Challenger and its crew were lost in January, 1986 O'Connor was given a number of safety and management assignments over the next three years as the Space Agency recovered from the disaster. In the first days after the accident, he organized the initial wreckage reassemby activities at Cape Canaveral. Then he established and managed the operation of the NASA Headquarters Action Center, the link between NASA and the Presidential Blue Ribbon Accident Investigation Panel (The Rogers Commission). In March 1986 he was assigned duties as Assistant (Operations) to the Space Shuttle Program Manager, as well as first Chairman of NASA's new Space Flight Safety Panel; jobs he held until February 1988 and 1989 respectively. He subsequently served as Deputy Director of Flight Crew Operations from February 1988 until August 1991. As of this writing, O'Connor has flown over 5000 hours in over 40 types of aircraft. A veteran of two space flights, he has over 386 hours in space, covering five and three quarter million miles in 253 orbits of the earth. O'Connor was pilot on STS-61B in 1985 and was crew commander on STS-40 in 1991. O'Connor left NASA in August 1991 to become commanding officer of the Marine Aviation Detachment, Naval Air Test Center, Patuxent River. During this 10 month assignment, he led 110 marine test pilots and technicians, participated as an AV-8B project test pilot, instructed students at the Test Pilot School, directed the Naval Air Test Center Museum, and became the first marine to serve as Deputy Director and Chief of Staff of the Flight Test and Engineering Group. O'Connor returned to NASA Headquarters in Washington, retiring from the Marine Corps to become the Deputy Associate Administrator for Space Flight. He was immediately assigned the task of developing a comprehensive flight safety improvement plan for the Space Shuttle, working closely with Congress and the Administration for funding of the major upgrade program. Then in late summer 1992, he was assigned as leader of the negotiating team that traveled to Moscow to establish the framework for what subsequently became the ambitious and complex joint manned space program known as Shuttle/MIR. In March 1993 O'Connor was assigned as Director, Space Station Redesign. He and his 50 person team of engineers, managers, and International Partners developed, then recommended substantial vehicle and program restructure strategies which amounted to $300 million in savings per year, thus helping to save the program from cancellation by Congress. In September, he was named Acting Space Station Program Director. He held that position throughout the transition from the Freedom Program to the new International Space Station Program and the announcement of a permanent Program Director in January 1994. In April 1994, O'Connor was reassigned as Director, Space Shuttle Program. As such, he was responsible for all aspects of the $3.5 billion per year program, leading over 27,000 government and contractor personnel. By the time he left NASA in March 1996, he had directed NASA's largest and most visible program through twelve safe, successful missions, including the first three flights to the Russian Space Station, MIR. He planned and led an extensive program restructure designed to save the taxpayers approximately $1 billion over the five-year budget horizon. Of equal importance he oversaw the introduction of several major safety improvements developed to prevent another "Challenger". O'Connor left NASA in February 1996 to become an aerospace consultant. He also served on the Advisory Board of Airship Resources Corporation, a startup company planning to introduce high technology night sign display systems to the next generation large airships then under development in the United Kingdom. He currently serves as Director of Engineering for Futron Corporation, a Washington DC based company providing risk management and aerospace safety and dependability services to government and commercial organizations including the FAA, DOD, NASA, DOE, Westinghouse, Allied Signal and others.

SPACE FLIGHT EXPERIENCE: STS-61B Atlantis (November 26 to December 3, 1985). STS-61B was the 22nd Shuttle flight and was the second-ever night shuttle launch from the Kennedy Space Center, Florida. It was the heaviest payload weight carried to orbit by the Space Shuttle to date, and the first flight to deploy 4 satellites. After completing 108 orbits of the earth in 165 hours, Atlantis returned to land at Edwards Air Force Base, California. STS-40 Columbia (June 5-14, 1991). STS-40/SLS-1 was the first Space Shuttle mission dedicated to life science studies. During the 9-day mission the crew performed an extensive series of biomedical experiments. After 145 orbits of the Earth travelling 3.29 million miles in 218 hours, O'Connor piloted Columbia to a landing at Edwards Air Force Base, California, his crew having safely and successfully completed over 100% of their mission objectives.

NAME: Brian Todd O'Leary (PhD)
NASA Astronaut (former)

PERSONAL DATA: Born January 27, 1940, in Boston, Massachusetts.

EDUCATION: Received bachelor of arts degree in physics from Williams College (1961); master of arts in astronomy from Georgetown University (1964); and doctorate in astronomy from the University of California at Berkeley (1967). His Master's thesis was on the Martian atmosphere, and his doctoral thesis dealt with the optical properties of Mars.

ORGANIZATIONS: Co-founder, International Association for New Science.

SPECIAL HONORS: NASA Outstanding Group Achievement Award as Deputy Team Leader of the Mariner 10 Venus-Mercury Television Science Team. For The Making of an ex-Astronaut, Houghton Mifflin, 1970 Dr. O'Leary received the ALA Best Young Adult book award.

EXPERIENCE: He was an assistant professor at Hampshire College, and later became a special consultant on nuclear energy matters from the Committee on the Interior, U.S. House of Representatives. He was on the research faculty in the Department of Physics at Princeton University. He was (1985) a senior scientist at Science Applications International Corp., and Chairman of the National Space Council under the Aerospace Eudcation Association. Faculty member at UC Berkeley, Cornell University, California Institute of Technology, and Princeton University.

NASA EXPERIENCE: Was chosen with the sixth group of astronauts in 1967. He resigned from NASA in 1968 for personal reasons and took a position on the Cornell University staff. Served at he only planetary scientist in the NASA astronaut corps during the Apollo program. Deputy team leader, NASA Mariner 10 Venus-Mercury television science team.

ADDITIONAL INFORMATION: Faculty member at UC Berkeley, Cornell University, California Institute of Technology, and Princeton University. Author of over 100 peer-reviewed articles in the field of planetary science and astronautics. Currently a writer and lecturer on the future opportunities in space exploration and the transformation of science. Dr. O'Leary's books include Mars 1999, Exploring Inner and Outer Space, and The Second Coming of Science.

NAME: Stephen S. Oswald (Mr.)
NASA Astronaut (former)

PERSONAL DATA: Born June 30, 1951, in Seattle, Washington, but considers Bellingham, Washington, to be his hometown. Married to the former Diane K. Kalklosch of Fullerton, California. They have three children, Monique, Janna, and Scott.

EDUCATION: Graduated from Bellingham High School, Bellingham, Washington, in 1969; received a bachelor of science degree in aerospace engineering from the U.S. Naval Academy in 1973.

ORGANIZATIONS: Member of the Society of Experimental Test Pilots, the Association of Space Explorers, the Naval Reserve Association, the Distinguished Eagle Scout Association, and the American Institute of Aeronautics and Astronautics.

AWARDS: Recipient of the Legion of Merit, the Distinguished Flying Cross, the Meritorious Service Medal, the Navy Commendation Medal (2), the NASA Outstanding Leadership Medal, the NASA Exceptional Service Medal (2), the NASA Space Flight Medal (3), and various service awards.

EXPERIENCE: Oswald graduated from the U.S. Naval Academy in 1973, and was designated a naval aviator in September 1974. Following training in the A-7 aircraft, he flew aboard the USS Midway from 1975 through 1977. In 1978, Oswald attended the U.S. Naval Test Pilot School at Patuxent River, Maryland. Upon graduation, he remained at the Naval Air Test Center conducting flying qualities, performance, and propulsion flight tests on the A-7 and F/A-18 aircraft through 1981. Following tours as an F/A-18 flight instructor and as a catapult officer aboard the USS Coral Sea, Oswald resigned from active Navy duty and joined Westinghouse Electric Corporation as a civilian test pilot. Oswald is a captain in the Naval Reserve, currently assigned to the Office of Naval Research. He has logged 7,000+ flight hours in over 40 different aircraft.

NASA EXPERIENCE: Oswald joined NASA in November 1984 as an aerospace engineer and instructor pilot and was selected as an astronaut candidate in June 1985. His technical assignments within the Astronaut Office have included: flight crew representative to Kennedy Space Center; flight software testing with the Shuttle Avionics Integration Laboratory; crew representative to the Marshall Space Flight Center on solid rocket booster redesign; and spacecraft communicator (CAPCOM) in the Mission Control Center during Space Shuttle missions. He was also the Chief of the Operations Development Branch within the Astronaut Office and served as Assistant Director of Engineering at Johnson Space Center. Oswald has piloted two missions aboard the Space Shuttle Discovery: STS-42, the International Microgravity Laboratory-1 mission, flown in January 1992, and STS-56, the second Atmospheric Laboratory for Applications and Science (ATLAS-2) mission, flown in April 1993. Oswald commanded STS-67, the second flight of the Astro observatory (Astro II), which flew on the Space Shuttle Endeavour in March, 1995. This mission established a mission duration record for Space Shuttle at 17 days. With the completion of his third space flight, Oswald has logged over 33 days in space. After STS-67, Oswald was assigned to NASA Headquarters in Washington, DC as Deputy Associate Administrator for Space Operations. In this capacity, he was responsible for Space Shuttle, Expendable Launch Vehicles, and Space Communications for the Agency. After nearly two and a half years in Washington, Oswald returned to the Astronaut Office in July 1998.

NAME: Robert Allan Ridley Parker (Ph.D.)
NASA Astronaut (former)

PERSONAL DATA: Born in New York City on December 14, 1936, but grew up in Shrewsbury, Massachusetts. Married to the former Judy Woodruff of San Marino, California. Five Children and seven grandchildren.

EDUCATION: Attended primary and secondary schools in Shrewsbury, Massachusetts; received a bachelor of arts degree in Astronomy and Physics from Amherst College in 1958, and a doctorate in Astronomy from the California Institute of Technology in 1962.

ORGANIZATIONS: Member of the American Astronomical Society, and the International Astronomical Union.

SPECIAL HONORS: Awarded the NASA Exceptional Scientific Achievement Medal (1973), and the NASA Outstanding Leadership Medal (1974).

EXPERIENCE: Prior to his selection for astronaut training, Dr. Parker was an associate professor of astronomy at the University of Wisconsin. He has logged over 3,500 hours flying time in jet aircraft, and 463 hours in space.

NASA EXPERIENCE: Dr. Parker was selected as a scientist-astronaut by NASA in August 1967. He was a member of the astronaut support crews for the Apollo 15 and 17 missions and served as Program Scientist for the Skylab Program Director's Office during the three manned Skylab flights. From March 1988 to March 1989 Dr. Parker was stationed at NASA Headquarters in Washington D.C. where he served as Director of the Space Flight/Space Station Integration Office. A veteran of two Spacelab missions, Dr. Parker was a mission specialist on STS-9/Spacelab-1 (Nov 28 to Dec 8,

1983) and on STS-35 (Dec 2-10, 1990) which featured the ASTRO-1 ultraviolet astronomy laboratory. Dr. Parker was the Director of the Division of Policy and Plans for the Office of Space Flight at NASA Headquarters in Washington, D.C. from January 1991 to December 1991. From January 1992 to November 1993 he was Director of the Spacelab and Operations Program. From December 1993 to August 1997 he was Manager of the Space Operations Utilization Program. In August 1997 he was named Director of the NASA Management Office at the Jet Propulsion Laboratory, Pasadena, California.

NAME: Donald H. Peterson (Colonel, USAF, ret.)
NASA Astronaut (former)

PERSONAL DATA: Born in Winona, Mississippi, on October 22, 1933. Married. Three children and four grandchildren.

EDUCATION: Graduated from Winona City High School, Winona, Mississippi; received a bachelor of science degree from the United States Military Academy at West Point, New York, in 1955, and a master's degree in Nuclear Engineering from the Air Force Institute of Technology, Wright-Patterson Air Force Base, Ohio, in 1962.

SPECIAL HONORS: Awarded the Air Force Commendation Medal, the Meritorious Service Medal, and the JSC Group Achievement Award (1972).

EXPERIENCE: Peterson graduated from West Point in 1955. His assignments included four years as a flight instructor and military training officer with the Air Training Command, three years as a nuclear systems analyst with the Air Force Systems Command, and one year as a fighter pilot with Tactical Air Command, including 3 months combat weapons training. He is a graduate of the Aerospace Research Pilot School. Edwards Air Force Base, California, and was one of the third group of astronauts assigned to the USAF Manned Orbiting Laboratory Program. He has logged over 5,300 hours flying time--including more than 5,000 hours in jet aircraft.

NASA EXPERIENCE: Peterson became a NASA astronaut in September 1969. He served on the astronaut support crew for Apollo 16. Peterson retired from the United States Air Force with the rank of colonel after having completed more than 24 years of active service, but continued his assignment as a NASA astronaut in a civilian capacity. His areas of responsibility have included engineering support, man/machine interface, and safety assessment. Peterson was a mission specialist on STS-6, which launched from Kennedy Space Center, Florida, on April 4, 1983. He was accompanied by Mr. Paul J. Weitz (spacecraft commander), Col. Karol J. Bobko (pilot), and Dr. F. Story Musgrave (mission specialist). During this maiden voyage of the spacecraft Challenger, the STS-6 crew conducted numerous experiments in materials processing, recorded lightning activities, deployed the first Tracking and Data Relay Satellite (TDRS-A), and activated three Getaway Specials. Peterson and Musgrave conducted an extravehicular activity (EVA), commonly called a "spacewalk," to test the new suit, the Shuttle airlock, and new tools and techniques for construction and repair outside a spacecraft. After 120 hours of orbital operations STS-6 landed on the concrete runway at Edwards Air Force Base, California, on April 9, 1983. With the completion of this flight Don Peterson has logged 4 hours 15 minutes in extravehicular activity, and a total of 120 hours in space.

POST-NASA EXPERIENCE: Peterson resigned from the Astronaut Office in November 1984, and since that time has worked as a consultant in the area of manned aerospace operations.

NAME: William Reid Pogue (Colonel, USAF, Retired)
NASA Astronaut (former)

PERSONAL DATA: Born January 23, 1930, in Okemah, Oklahoma, and is the son of Mr. and Mrs. Alex W. Pogue who live in Sand Springs, Oklahoma.

PHYSICAL DESCRIPTION: Brown hair; blue eyes; height: 5 feet 9 inches; weight: 160 pounds.

EDUCATION: Attended primary and secondary schools in Oklahoma; received a Bachelor of Science degree in Education from Oklahoma Baptist University in 1951 and a Master of Science degree in Mathematics from Oklahoma State University in 1960; awarded an Honorary Doctorate of Science degree from Oklahoma Baptist University in 1974.

MARITAL STATUS: Married to the former Jean A. Baird of Fayetteville, Arkansas.

CHILDREN: William R., September 5, 1953; Layna S., June 9, 1955; Thomas R., September I2, 1957.

RECREATIONAL INTERESTS: Enjoys running, playing paddle ball and handball, and his hobbies are gardening and the study of Biblical history.

ORGANIZATIONS: Member of the Air Force Association, Explorers Club, and American Astronautical Society.

SPECIAL HONORS: Awarded the NASA Distinguished Service Medal (1974) and JSC Superior Achievement Award (1970); winner of the Air Medal, Air Force Commendation Medal, the National Defense Service Medal, and an Outstanding Unit Citation (while a member of the USAF Thunderbirds); the Air Force Distinguished Service Medal and Command Pilot Astronaut Wings (1974); presented the City of Chicago Gold Medal (1974); the Robert J. Collier Trophy for 1973 (1974); the City of New York Gold Medal (1974); the Dr. Robert H. Goddard Memorial Trophy for 1975 (1975); the Federation Aeronautique Internationale's De La Vaulx Medal and V.M. Komarov Diploma for 1974 (1975); the General Thomas D. White USAF Space Trophy for 1974 (1975); Fellow of the Academy of Arts and Sciences of Oklahoma State University (1975); AIAA Haley Astronautics Award for 1974 (1975); and the American Astronautical Society's 1975 Flight Achievement Award (1976). Inductee 5 Civilized Tribes Hall of Fame (1975).

EXPERIENCE: He enlisted in the Air Force in 1951 and received his commission in 1952. While serving with the Fifth Air Force during the Korean conflict, from 1953 to 1954, he completed a combat tour in fighter bombers. From 1955 to 1957, he was a member of the USAF Thunderbirds. He has gained proficiency in more than 50 types and models of American and British aircraft and is qualified as a civilian flight instructor. Pogue served in the mathematics department as an assistant professor at the USAF Academy in Colorado Springs, Colorado, from 1960 to 1963. In September 1965, he completed a two-year tour as test pilot with the British Ministry of Aviation under the USAF/RAF Exchange Program, after graduating from the Empire Test Pilots' School in Farnborough, England.

NASA EXPERIENCE: Pogue, a retired Air Force Colonel, came to the Lyndon B. Johnson Space Center from an assignment at Edwards Air Force Base, California, where he had been an instructor at the Air Force Aerospace Research Pilot School since October 1965.

He has logged 7,200 hours flight time, including 4,200 hours in jet aircraft and 2,017 hours in space flight. Colonel Pogue is one of the 19 Astronauts selected by NASA in April 1966. He served as a member of the astronaut support crews for the Apollo 7, 11, and 14 missions. Pogue was pilot of Skylab 4 (third and final manned visit to the Skylab orbital workshop), launched November 16, 1973, and concluded February 8, 1974. This was the longest manned flight (84 days, 1 hour and 15 minutes) in the history of manned space exploration to date. Pogue was accompanied on the record setting 34.5 million mile flight by Gerald P. Carr (commander) and Dr. Edward G. Gibson (science-pilot). They success-fully completed 56 experiments, 26 science demonstrations, 15 sub-system detailed objectives, and 13 student investigations during their 1,214 revolutions of the earth. They also acquired extensive earth resources observations data using Skylab's earth re-sources experiment package camera and sensor array, and logged 338 hours of operations of the Apollo Telescope Mount which made extensive observations of the sun's solar processes. He also logged 13 hours and 31 minutes in two EVA's outside the orbital workshop. Pogue retired from the United States Air Force on September 1, 1975, and he is now retired from NASA.

CURRENT EMPLOYMENT: Self-employed as a consultant to aerospace and energy firms.

NAME: Kenneth S. Reightler, Jr. (Captain, USN)
   NASA Astronaut (former)

PERSONAL DATA: Born March 24, 1951, in Patuxent River, Maryland, but considers Virginia Beach, Virginia, to be his hometown. Married to the former Maureen Ellen McHenry of Virginia Beach, Virginia. They have two daughters. He enjoys sailing, wind surfing, camping. His parents, Mr. & Mrs. Kenneth S. Reightler, Sr., reside in Virginia Beach. Her mother, Mrs. Jean W. McHenry, resides in Virginia Beach. Her father, Cdr. William H. McHenry, USN, is deceased.

EDUCATION: Graduated from Bayside High School, Virginia Beach, Virginia, in 1969; received a bachelor of science degree in aerospace engineering from United States Naval Academy in 1973, and master of science degrees, in 1984, in aeronautical engineering from the United States Naval Postgraduate School and in systems management from University of Southern California.

ORGANIZATIONS: Member, Society of Experimental Test Pilots (SETP); U.S. Naval Academy Alumni Association; Association of Space Explorers; National Aeronautic Association.

SPECIAL HONORS: Defense Superior Service Medal; Defense Meritorious Service Medal; Navy Com-mendation Medal; Navy Unit Commendation; Meritorious Unit Commendation; Armed Forces Expe-ditionary Medal; National Defense Service Medal; NASA Exceptional Service Medal; two NASA Space Flight Medals; Johnson Space Center Certificate of Commendation; NASA Group Achievement Award; INTELSAT EVA Recovery Team Award. Distinguished graduate, U.S. Naval Academy and U.S. Naval Test Pilot School. Absolute world altitude record for Class P aero-spacecraft. Mac Short Award in Aviation from U.S. Naval Academy (1973).

EXPERIENCE: Reightler graduated from the United States Naval Academy in 1973, and was desig-nated a naval aviator in August 1974 at Corpus Christi, Texas. After replacement pilot training in the P-3C airplane, he reported to Patrol Squadron Sixteen in Jacksonville, Florida, serving as both a mission commander and patrol plane commander. He made deployments to Keflavik, Iceland, and to Sigonella, Sicily. Following jet transition training, Reightler attended the United States Naval Test Pilot School at Patuxent River, Maryland. Upon graduation in 1978, he remained at the Naval Air Test Center (NATC) where he served as test pilot and project officer for a variety of flight test programs involving the P-3, S-3, and T-39 airplanes. He later returned to the Test Pilot School, serving as a flight test instructor and safety officer flying the P-3, T-2, OV-1, T-39, and TA-7 airplanes. In June 1981 Reightler was assigned to the USS Dwight D. Eisenhower (CVN-69) as communications officer and carrier on-board delivery pilot, making two deployments to the Mediterranean Sea. Selected for postgraduate education, he attended the Naval Postgraduate School in Monterey, California. Redesignated an aerospace engineering duty officer (AEDO) he was sent to transition training for the F/A-18 airplane with Strike Fighter Squadron 125 (VFA-125) at Naval Air Station Lemoore, California. He then reported for duty at the United States Naval Test Pilot School in March 1985, serving as the chief flight instructor until his selection for the astronaut program. He has logged over 4,700 hours flying time in over 60 different types of aircraft.

NASA EXPERIENCE: Selected by NASA in June 1987, Reightler became an astronaut in August 1988. From September 12-18, 1991, he was the pilot on the crew of STS-48. This was the first Space Shuttle flight in support of "Mission to Planet Earth." During the five-day mission, the crew aboard the Space Shuttle Discovery successfully deployed the Upper Atmosphere Research Satellite (UARS), designed to provide scientists with their first complete data set on the upper atmosphere's chemistry, winds and energy inputs. The crew also conducted numerous secondary experiments ranging from growing protein crystals, to studying how fluids and structures react in weightlessness. After 81 orbits of the Earth, STS-48/Discovery landed at Edwards Air Force Base, California. More recently, Reightler served as pilot on STS-60, the first joint U.S./Russian Space Shuttle Mission. Launching from the Kennedy Space Center on February 3, 1994, STS-60 was the first flight of the Wake Shield Facility (WSF-1) and the second flight of the Space Habitation Module (Spacehab-2). During the eight-day flight, the crew of Discovery, including Russian cosmonaut Sergei Krikalev, conducted a wide variety of biological, materials science, earth observation, and life science experiments. Following 130 orbits of the Earth, STS-60 landed at Kennedy Space Center, Florida, on February 11, 1994. With the completion of his second mission, Reightler has logged over 327 hours in space. His technical assignments to date have included: Chief of the Astronaut Office Space Station Branch; Chief of the Astronaut Office Mission Support Branch; Lead Spacecraft Communicator (CAPCOM); Lead Astronaut for flight software development and computer systems; Flight Crew Operations Directorate representative to the Program Requirements Control Board; weather coordinator for Space Shuttle launches and landings; Astronaut Office representative in the areas of ascent, entry, and aborts.

NAME: Richard (Dick) N. Richards (Captain, USN)
NASA Astronaut (former)

PERSONAL DATA: Born August 24, 1946, in Key West, Florida, but considers St. Louis, Missouri, to be his hometown. Married to the former Lois Hollabaugh of Amarillo, Texas. He enjoys skiing, running, and racquetball. His mother, Mrs. Marjorie Richards, resides in St. Louis.

EDUCATION: Graduated from Riverview Gardens High School in St Louis, Missouri, in 1964; received a bachelor of science degree in chemical engineering from the University of Missouri in 1969, and a master of science in aeronautical systems from the University of West Florida in 1970.

ORGANIZATIONS: Member of the Society of Experimental Test Pilots; Tau Beta Pi, Engineering

Honorary; and Lambda Chi Alpha, Social Fraternity.

SPECIAL HONORS: Defense Superior Service Medal, Distinguished Flying Cross, Defense Meritorious Service Medal, NASA Distinguished Service Medal, NASA Space Flight Medals (4), NASA Exceptional Service Medal, National Defense Service Medals (2), Vietnam Service Medal. Distinguished Graduate of U.S. Naval Test Pilot School, and Naval Air Test Center Test Pilot of the Year for 1980.

EXPERIENCE: Richards was commissioned an ensign in the United States Navy upon graduating from the University of Missouri in 1969 and was designated a naval aviator in August of the following year. From 1970 to 1973, he flew support missions in the A-4 Skyhawk and F-4 Phantom airplanes while assigned to Tactical Electronic Warfare Squadron Thirty-Three at Norfolk Naval Air Station, Virginia. He subsequently reported to Fighter Squadron 103 and deployed to the North Atlantic and Mediterranean aboard the USS America (CV-66) and USS Saratoga (CV-61), flying F-4 airplanes. Selected for test pilot training, he reported to the United States Naval Test Pilot School at Patuxent River, Maryland, in 1976. A tour in the Naval Air Test Center's Carrier Systems Branch and F/A-18A Program Office of the Strike Aircraft Test Directorate followed Test Pilot School graduation. Over the next 3-1/2 years, Richards served as a project test pilot for automatic carrier landing systems development work in F-4 and A-7 aircraft and also conducted approach/landing/catapult flying qualities and catapult minimum end speed performance testing of a prototype "slatted" F-4S airplane. As carrier suitability project officer for the F/A-18A Hornet airplane, he made the first shipboard catapults and arrested landings during Initial Sea Trials of the F/A-18A on board the USS AMERICA in 1979. He was reassigned to Fighter Squadron 33 in May 1980 and was en route to that assignment when notified of his selection as an astronaut candidate. Flight experience has included over 5,300 hours in 16 different types of airplanes. He has also completed more than 400 landings on board various aircraft carriers.

NASA EXPERIENCE: Selected as an astronaut candidate by NASA in May 1980, Richards became an astronaut in August 1981. Richards has flown four times--STS-28 (August 8-13, 1989), STS-41 (October 6-10, 1990), STS-50 (June 25-July 9, 1992), and STS-64 (September 9-20, 1994)--and has logged a total of 33 days, 21 hours, 32 minutes, 15 seconds in space. On his first space flight, Richards was pilot on the crew of STS-28 which launched from Kennedy Space Center, Florida, on August 8, 1989. The mission carried Department of Defense payloads and a number of secondary payloads. After 80 orbits of the Earth, this five-day mission concluded with a dry lakebed landing on Runway 17 at Edwards Air Force Base, California, on August 13, 1989. Mission duration was 121 hours 9 seconds. Slightly more than one year later, Richards commanded the crew of STS-41. The five-man crew launched aboard the Space Shuttle Discovery on October 6 from the Kennedy Space Center, Florida, and landed at Edwards Air Force Base, California, on October 10, 1990. During 66 orbits of the Earth, the STS-41 crew successfully deployed the Ulysses spacecraft, starting this interplanetary probe on its four-year journey, via Jupiter, to investigate the polar regions of the Sun. In June 1992, Richards commanded the crew of STS-50 aboard the Space Shuttle Columbia. STS-50 was the first flight of the United States Microgravity Laboratory and the first extended duration Orbiter flight. Over a two-week period, the STS-50 flight crew conducted a wide variety of experiments relating to materials processing and fluid physics in a microgravity environment. At that time this was the longest Space Shuttle flight in history. In September 1994, Richards commanded the STS-64 crew aboard the Space Shuttle Discovery. Mission highlights included: the first use of a space based laser for environmental research; deployment and retrieval of a spacecraft in support of solar wind and corona studies; robotic processing of semiconductors; maneuvered the robotic arm in close proximity to over 100 Shuttle reaction control system jet firings to measure forces imparted to a plume detection instrument in support of future Space Station/Shuttle rendezvous flights; first untethered spacewalk in 10 years to test a self-rescue jetpack. Mission duration was 10 days, 22 hours, 51 minutes. In April 1995, Captain Richards left the Astronaut Office and is now assigned to the Space Shuttle Program Office at the Johnson Space Center. He has been designated as the Mission Director/Manager for the second Hubble Space Telescope Servicing Space Shuttle Mission (STS-82), and Mission Manager for the second Tethered Satellite System Space Shuttle mission (STS-75).

NAME: Sally K. Ride (Ph.D.)
  NASA Astronaut (former)

PERSONAL DATA: Born May 26, 1951, in Los Angeles, California. Her parents, Dr. and Mrs. Dale B. Ride, reside in Encino, California. She enjoys tennis (having been an instructor and having achieved national ranking as a junior), running, volleyball, softball & stamp collecting.

EDUCATION: Graduated from Westlake High School, Los Angeles, California, in 1968; received from Stanford University a bachelor of science in Physics and a bachelor of arts in English in 1973, and master of science and doctorate degrees in Physics in 1975 and 1978, respectively.

EXPERIENCE: Dr. Ride was selected as an astronaut candidate by NASA in January 1978. In August 1979, she completed a 1-year training and evaluation period, making her eligible for assignment as a mission specialist on future Space Shuttle flight crews. She subsequently performed as an on-orbit capsule communicator (CAPCOM) on the STS-2 and STS-3 missions. Dr. Ride was a mission specialist on STS-7, which launched from Kennedy Space Center, Florida, on June 18, 1983. She was accompanied by Captain Robert L. Crippen (spacecraft commander), Captain Frederick H. Hauck (pilot), and fellow mission specialists Colonel John M. Fabian and Dr. Norman E. Thagard. This was the second flight for the Orbiter Challenger and the first mission with a 5-person crew. During the mission, the STS-7 crew deployed satellites for Canada (ANIK C-2) and Indonesia (PALAPA B-1); operated the Canadian-built Remote Manipulator System (RMS) to perform the first deployment and retrieval exercise with the Shuttle Pallet Satellite (SPAS-01); conducted the first formation flying of the orbiter with a free-flying satellite (SPAS-01); carried and operated the first U.S./German cooperative materials science payload (OSTA-2); and operated the Continuous Flow Electrophoresis System (CFES) and the Monodisperse Latex Reactor (MLR) experiments, in addition to activating seven Getaway Specials. Mission duration was 147 hours before landing on a lakebed runway at Edwards Air Force Base, California, on June 24, 1983. Dr. Ride served as a mission specialist on STS 41-G, which launched from Kennedy Space Center, Florida, on October 5, 1984. This was the largest crew to fly to date and included Captain Robert L. Crippen (spacecraft commander), Captain Jon A. McBride (pilot), fellow mission specialists, Dr. Kathryn D. Sullivan and Commander David C. Leestma, as well as two payloads specialists, Commander Marc Garneau and Mr. Paul Scully-Power. Their 8-day mission deployed the Earth Radiation Budget Satellite, conducted scientific observations of the earth with the OSTS-3 pallet and Large Format Camera, as well as demonstrating potential satellite refueling with an EVA and associated hydrazine transfer. Mission duration was 197 hours and concluded with a landing at Kennedy Space Center, Florida, on October 13, 1984. In June 1985 Dr. Ride was assigned to serve as a mission specialist on STS 61-M. She terminated mission training in January 1986 in order to serve as a member of the Presidential Commission on the Space Shuttle Challenger Accident. Upon completion of the investigation she was assigned to NASA Headquarters as Special Assistant to the Administrator for long range and strategic planning.

Dr. Ride has written a children's book, To Space and Back, describing her experiences in space, has received the Jefferson Award for Public Service, and has twice been awarded the National Space-flight Medal. Two of her latest books, Voyager: An Adventure to the Edge of the Solar System and The Third Planet: Exploring the Earth from Space are currently in bookstores. Dr. Ride is a physicist, and in 1989 joined the faculty at the University of California, San Diego, as a physics professor. She is also Director of the California Space Institute, a research institute of the University of California.

NAME: Walter M. Schirra (Captain, USN, Ret.)
NASA Astronaut (former)

PERSONAL DATA: Born: Born March 12, 1923, in Hackensack, New Jersey.

PHYSICAL DESCRIPTION: Brown hair; brown eyes; height: 5 feet 10 inches; weight: 185 pounds.

EDUCATION: Schirra graduated from the U.S. Naval Academy in 1945 and Naval Flight Training, Pensacola, Florida in 1947. Honorary Doctorate in Astronautical Engineering, Lafayette College; Honorary Doctorate in Astronautics, Newark College of Engineering; Honorary Doctorate in Science, University of Southern California. (NASA Astronaut Training, beginning April 1959 - ending July 1969).

MARITAL STATUS: Married to the former Josephine Fraser of Seattle, Washington.

CHILDREN: Walter M., III, June 23, 1950; Suzanne, September 29, 1957.

RECREATIONAL ACTIVITIES: His hobbies include skiing, hunting, sailing, and fishing.

OTHER ACTIVITIES: Director, Rocky Mountain Airways; U.S. Department of Interior Advisory Board on National Parks, Historical Sites and Monuments; Honorary Belgian Consul, Colorado; Director, Electromedics, Colorado and Director Watt Count, Nashville, Tennessee.

ORGANIZATIONS: 33 Mason; Fellow, Society of Engineering Test Pilots; Fellow, American Astronautical Society.

SPECIAL HONORS: U.S. Distinguished Service Medal; three DFCs; two Air Medals; two NASA DSMs; two NASA Exceptional Service Medals; Navy Astronaut Wings; Collier Trophy; Kitty Hawk Award; Great American Award; Golden Key Award; Haley Astronautic Award; Aerospace Hall of Fame.

EXPERIENCE: 1948-1959: Pilot, Officer, United States Navy, Carrier Based Fighter Pilot, Operations Officer and Test Pilot. Flew with the U.S. Air Force as an exchange (Jet Fighter) Pilot during the Korean conflict.

1959-1969: One of the original seven astronauts and the only astronaut to have flown on all three spacecraft - Mercury, Gemini, and Apollo. As Command Pilot, he flew the initial flight of the Apollo series (Apollo 7) and was deeply involved in the quality assurance and quality control aspects of the "total vehicle system."

1969-1970: Following retirement from the U.S. Navy and NASA, Schirra accepted the Presidency of

Regency Investors, Inc., a major financial complex and world-wide leasing company based in Denver, Colorado. Regency specialized in leasing oil completion equipment, jet transport aircraft and major facilities.

1970-1972: Chairman and Chief Executive Officer of the ECOO Corp., an environmental control company. As head of ECCO Corp., Schirra was instrumental in forming a new concept in environmental management. ECOO was designed to provide quick reaction to the environmental problems of government, industry and private business and the application of systems management techniques to their solution. January 1973: Elected Vice Chairman of the Board, SERNCO, Inc. July 1973: Elected Chairman of the Board, SERNCO, Inc. January 1975: Director of Technology Purchase, Johns-Manville Corporation. October 1976: Director, Power Plant and Aerospace Systems, Johns-Manville. January 1978: Vice President, Development, Goodwin Company, Inc. January 1979: President, Schirra Enterprises.

NAME: Harrison H. Schmitt (Ph.D.)
NASA Astronaut (former)

PERSONAL DATA: Born July 3, 1935, in Santa Rita, New Mexico. His mother, Mrs. Harrison A. Schmitt, resides Silver City, New Mexico.

PHYSICAL DESCRIPTION: Black hair; brown eyes; height: 5 feet 9 inches; weight: 165 pounds.

EDUCATION: Graduated from Western High School, Silver City, New Mexico; received a bachelor of science degree in science from the California Institute of Technology in 1957; studied at the University of Oslo in Norway during 1957 and 1958; and received a doctorate in geology from Harvard University in 1964.

MARITAL STATUS: Single.

RECREATIONAL INTERESTS: His hobbies include skiing, fishing, carpentry, hiking, handball, squash, and running.

ORGANIZATIONS: Member of the Geological Society of America, the American Geophysical Union, the American Association for the Advancement of Science, the American Association of Petroleum Geologists, the American Institute of Aeronautics and Astronautics, Sigma Xi, the Geological Association of Canada, and Navy League.

SPECIAL HONORS: Winner of a Fulbright Fellowship (1957-58); a Kennecott Fellowship in Geology (1958-59); a Harvard Fellowship (1959-60); a Harvard Traveling Fellowship (1960); a Parker Traveling Fellowship (1961-62); a National Science Foundation Post-Doctoral Fellowship, Department of Geological Sciences, Harvard University (1963-64); awarded the Johnson Space Center Superior Achievement Award (1970) and the NASA Distinguished Service Medal (1973); presented the City of New York Gold Medal (1973), the Nassau County New York Distinguished Service Medal (1973), the American Institute of Mining, Metallurgical, Petroleum Engineer's Ceremonial Medallion and Certificate of Honorary Membership (1973); Honorary Fellow of the Geological Society of America (1973); the Arthur S. Fleming Award in 1973; an honorary doctorate of engineering from the Colorado School of Mines in 1973; Philadelphia's Academy of Natural Sciences' Richard Hopper Day Medal (1973); the Republic of Senegal's National Order of the Lion (1973); Honorary Life Membership in the New Mexico Geological Society (1973); Honorary Member of the Norwegian Geographical Society (1973); and an honorary doctorate of geology from Franklin and Marshall College in 1977.

EXPERIENCE: Schmitt was a teaching fellow at Harvard in 1961 where he assisted in teaching a course in ore deposits. Prior to his teaching assignment, he did geological work for the Norwegian Geological Survey on the west coast of Norway, and for the U.S. Geological Survey in New Mexico and Montana. He also worked for two summers as a geologist in southeastern Alaska. Before joining NASA, he was with the U.S. Geological Survey's Astrogeology Center at Flagstaff, Arizona. He was project chief for lunar field geological methods and participated in photo and telescopic mapping of the moon, and was among USGS astrogeologists instructing NASA astronauts during their geological field trips. He has logged more than 2,100 hours flying time, including 1,600 hours in jet aircraft.

NASA EXPERIENCE: Dr. Schmitt was selected as a scientist-astronaut by NASA in June 1965. He later completed a 53-week course in flight training at Williams Air Force Base, Arizona. In addition to training for future manned space flights, he was instrumental in providing Apollo flight crews with detailed instruction in lunar navigation, geology, and feature recognition. Schmitt also assisted in the integration of scientific activities into the Apollo lunar missions and participated in research activities requiring geologic, petrographic, and stratigraphic analyses of samples returned from the moon by Apollo missions. He was backup lunar module pilot for Apollo 15. On his first journey into space, Dr. Schmitt occupied the lunar module pilot seat for Apollo 17, the last scheduled manned Apollo mission to the moon for the United States, which commenced at 11:33 p.m. (CST), December 6, 1972, and concluded on December 19, 1972. He was accompanied on the voyage of the command module America and the lunar module Challenger by Eugene Cernan (spacecraft commander) and Ronald Evans (command module pilot). In maneuvering Challenger to a landing at Taurus-Littrow, which is located on the southeast edge of Mare Serenitatis, Schmitt and Cernan activated a base of operations facilitating their completion of three Mountains. This last Apollo mission to the moon for the United States broke several records set by previous flights and include: longest manned lunar landing flight (301 hours, 51 minutes); longest lunar surface extravehicular activities (22 hours, 4 minutes); largest lunar sample return (an estimated 115 Kg (249 lbs); and longest time in lunar orbit (147 hours, 48 minutes). Apollo 17 ended with a splashdown in the Pacific Ocean approximately 0.4 mile from the target point and 4.3 miles from the prime recovery ship, USS TICONDEROGA. Dr. Schmitt logged 301 hours and 51 minutes in space, of which 22 hours and 4 minutes were spent in extravehicular activity on the lunar surface.

In July of 1973, Dr. Schmitt was appointed as one of the first Sherman Fairchild Distinguished Scholars at the California Institute of Technology. His appointment was extended to run through July 1975. This appointment ran concurrently with his other activities in NASA.

In February 1974, Schmitt assumed additional duties as Chief of Scientist-Astronauts.

CURRENT ASSIGNMENT: Dr. Schmitt was appointed NASA Assistant Administrator for Energy Programs in May 1974. This office has the responsibility for coordinating NASA support to other Federal Agencies conducting energy research and development and for managing NASA programs applying aeronautics and space technology to the generation, transmission, storage, conservation, utilization and management of energy for terrestrial applications. In August of 1975, Dr. Schmitt resigned his post with NASA to run for the United States Senate in his home state of New

Mexico. He was elected on November 2, 1976, with 57% of the votes cast. In January 1977, Schmitt began a six-year term as one of New Mexico's Senators in Washington, D.C. His major committee assignments are on the Commerce, Science and Transportation Committee; the Banking, Housing and Urban Affairs Committee and the Select Committee on Ethics. He is the ranking Republican member of the Ethics Committee; of the Science, Technology and Space Subcommittee of Commerce; and the Consumer Subcommittee of Banking.

Currently, Mr. Schmitt teaches advance level geology courses at the University of Wisconsin at Madison. He is also an author and lecturer of space travel and an advocate of using the moon's resources to better mankind.

NAME: Russell L. "Rusty" Schweickart
NASA Astronaut (former)

PERSONAL DATA: Born: Born October 25, 1935 in Neptune, New Jersey. His parents, Mr. and Mrs. George Schweickart, reside in spring Hill, Florida.

EDUCATION: Graduated from Manasquan High School, New Jersey; received a bachelor of science degree in Aeronautical Engineering and a master of science degree in Aeronautics and Astronautics from MIT.

MARITAL STATUS: Married to the former Clare G. Whitfield of Atlanta, Georgia.

CHILDREN: Vicki, Randolph, Russell, Elin and Diana.

RECREATIONAL INTERESTS: His hobbies are bicycling, backpacking, hunting and fishing.

ORGANIZATIONS: Fellow of the America Astronautical Society; Associate Fellow of the American Institute of Aeronautics and Astronautics; and a member of the Society of Experimental Test Pilots, the Exploreers Club, and Sigma Xi.

SPECIAL HONORS: Awarded the NASA Distinguished Services Medal (1969), the NASA Exceptional Service Medal (1973), the Federation Aeronuatique Internationale De La Vaux Medal (1970), and the National Academy of Television Arts and Sciences Special Trustees Award (1969).

EXPERIENCE: Schweickart was named Chairman of the California Energy Commission by Governor Edmund G. Brown, Jr., on August 24, 1979. The Energy Commission consists of five commissioners and staff responsible for power plant siting, energy supply and demand forecasts, conservation, and development of alternative energy sources. Schweickart was appointed to the Commission in July 1979. Prior to his present assignment, Schweickart served on Governor Brown's staff as Assistant to the Governor for Science and Technology. In that capacity, he fostered the use of new technologies by state agencies. He also served as liaison with California's important aerospace and electronics industry as well as federal research and development agencies. Schweickart was responsible for overseeing the state's emergency services and National Guard programs. Following the incident at the Three Mile Island nuclear plant, he headed a Task Force which made recommendations on emergency preparedness for nuclear plant accidents. During his tenure at the Governor's Office, Schweickart was on leave from the National Aeronautics and Space Administration. He resigned from that Agency in July 1979 to accept his current appointment.

NASA EXPERIENCE: Schweickart came to NASA as one of the 14 astronauts named in October 1963. He served as lunar module pilot for Apollo 9, March 3-13, 1969, logging 241 hours in space. This was the third manned flight in the Apollo series, the second to be launched by a Saturn V and the first manned flight of the lunar module. With him on the flight into Earth orbit were James A. McDivitt, spacecraft commander, and David R. Scott, command module pilot. During a 46-minute EVA, Schweickart tested the portable life support backpack subsequently used on the lunar surface explorations. Schweickart served as backup commander for the first Skylab mission which flew in the Spring of 1973. Following the loss of the thermal shield during the launch of the Skylab vehicle, he assumed responsibility for the development of hardware and procedures associated with erecting the emergency solar shade and deploying the jammed solar array wing. After the Skylab program, Schweickart went to NASA Headquarters in Washington, D.C. as Director of User Affairs in the Office of Applications. In this position he was responsible for transferring NASA technology to the outside world and working with technology users to bring an understanding of their needs into NASA's program. Schweickart also worked on policies for space shuttle payload operations. Prior to joining NASA, Schweickart was a research scientist at the Experimental Astronomy Laboratory at the Massachusetts Institute of Technology, and his work there involved research upper atmospheric physics, star tracking and stabilization of stellar images. His thesis for a master's degree at MIT concerned stratospheric radiance. Schweickart served as pilot in the United States Air Force and Air National Guard from 1956 to 1963. He has logged 4,200 hours flight time, including 3,500 in jet aircraft.

NAME: David R. Scott (Col., USAF, Ret.)
NASA Astronaut (former)

PERSONAL DATA: Born June 6, 1932, San Antonio, Texas. His father, Brigadier General (USAF, Ret.), and his mother, Mrs. Tom W. Scott reside in La Jolla, California.

EDUCATION: Received a BS from the US Military Academy in 1954, standing fifth in a class of 633; received a MS and an Engineering degree in Aeronautics and Astronautics from MIT in 1962; was awarded an Honorary Doctorate of Astronautical Science from the University of Michigan in 1971; and has graduated from the Air Force Experimental Test Pilot School and Aerospace Research Pilot School.

MARITAL STATUS: Married to the former Ann Lurton Ott of San Antonio, Texas and the couple and their two children reside in Lancaster, California.

CHILDREN: Two

ORGANIZATIONS: Fellow of the American Institute of Aeronautics and Astronautics, a Fellow of the American Astronautical society, an Associate Fellow in the Society of Experimental Test Pilots, and a member of the Royal Aeronautical society, the Society of Experimental Test Pilots, and Tau Beta Pi, Sigma Xi and Sigma Gamma Tau. He is also a member of the Board of Governors of the Flight Safety Foundation, Inc.

SPECIAL HONORS: Three NASA Distinguished Service Medals, the NASA Exceptional Service Medal, two Air Force Distinguished Service Medals, the Air Force Distinguished Flying Cross, and the Air Force Association's David C. Schilling Trophy (1971), the Robert J. Collier Trophy, the Federation Aeronautique Internationale Gold Medal (1971), and the United Nations Peace Medal (1971).

EXPERIENCE: Scott is President of Scott Science and Technology, Inc., an advanced technology company specializing in research and development and project management. These activities include the application of concepts, technology and scientific and engineering expertise to products, operations and management in business and industry. Dr. Scott was formally the director of the National Aeronautics and Space Administration's Hugh L. Dryden Flight Research Center at Edwards, California. In this capacity, he was responsible for all operational and institutional activities at NASA's premiere aeronautical flight research facility.

NASA EXPERIENCE: As a NASA astronaut, Scott flew on Gemini 8, Apollo 9 and was Spacecraft Commander on Apollo 15. He has logged 546 hours and 54 minutes in space, of which 20 hours and 46 minutes were in extravehicular activity. In 1972 Scott was named as Technical Assistant to the Apollo Program Manager at Johnson Space Center. Prior to coming to the Dryden Flight Research Center, he was Special Assistant for Mission Operations for the Apollo-Soyuz Test Project. He retired from the U.S. Air Force in March 1975 with the rank of Colonel and over 5600 hours of flying time. On the Gemini VIII mission in 1966, Scott and Command Pilot Neil Armstrong performed the first successful docking of two vehicles in space. As Command Module Pilot for Apollo 9 in 1969, Scott was instrumental in completing the first comprehensive Earth orbital qualification and verification test of a fully configured Apollo spacecraft. In 1971 Scott commanded Apollo 15 which was the first extended scientific exploration of the Moon, doubling the lunar stay time of previous flights and utilizing the first Lunar Roving Vehicle to explore the Hadley Rille and the Apennine Mountains.

NAME: Winston E. Scott (Captain, USN, Ret.)
NASA Astronaut (former)

PERSONAL DATA: Born August 6, 1950, in Miami, Florida. Married to the former Marilyn K. Robinson. They have two children. He enjoys martial arts and holds a 2nd degree black belt in Shotokan karate. He also enjoys music, and plays trumpet with a Houston-based Big Band. In addition to flying general aviation aircraft, he is an electronics hobbyist. Winston's father, Alston Scott, resides in Miami, Florida. His mother, Rubye Scott, is deceased. Marilyn's parents, Albert and Josephine Robinson, reside in Chipley, Florida.

EDUCATION: Graduated from Coral Gables High School, Coral Gables, Florida, in 1968; received a bachelor of arts degree in music from Florida State University in 1972; a master of science degree in aeronautical engineering from the U.S. Naval Postgraduate School in 1980.

ORGANIZATIONS: American Institute of Aeronautics & Astronautics; National Naval Officers Association; Naval Helicopter Association; Alpha Phi Alpha Fraternity; Phi Mu Alpha Sinfonia Fraternity; Skotokan Karate Association; Association of International Tohgi Karate-Do; Bronze Eagles Association of Texas.

EXPERIENCE: Scott entered Naval Aviation Officer Candidate School after graduation from Florida State University in December 1972. He completed flight training in fixed-wing and rotary-wing aircraft and was designated a Naval Aviator in August 1974. He then served a 4-year tour of duty with Helicopter Anti-Submarine Squadron Light Thirty Three (HSL-33) at the Naval Air Station (NAS) North Island, California, flying the SH-2F Light Airborne Multi-Purpose System (LAMPS) helicopter. In 1978 Scott was selected to attend the Naval Postgraduate School at Monterey, California, where he earned his master of science degree in aeronautical engineering with avionics. After completing jet training in the TA-4J Skyhawk, Scott served a tour of duty with Fighter Squadron Eighty Four (VF-84) at NAS Oceana, Virginia, flying the F-14 Tomcat. In June 1986 Scott was designated an Aerospace Engineering Duty Officer. He served as a production test pilot at the Naval Aviation Depot, NAS Jacksonville, Florida, flying the F/A-18 Hornet and the A-7 Corsair aircraft. He was also assigned as Director of the Product Support (engineering) Department. He was next assigned as the Deputy Director of the Tactical Aircraft Systems Department at the Naval Air Development Center at Warminster, Pennsylvania. As a research and development project pilot, he flew the F-14, F/A-18 and A-7 aircraft. Scott has accumulated more than 4,000 hours of flight time in 20 different military and civilian aircraft, and more than 200 shipboard landings. Additionally, Scott was an associate instructor of electrical engineering at Florida A&M University and Florida Community College at Jacksonville, Florida.

NASA SPACE FLIGHT EXPERIENCE: Scott was selected by NASA in March 1992, and reported to the Johnson Space Center in August 1992. He served as a mission specialist on STS-72 in 1996 and STS-87 in 1997, and has logged a total of 24 days, 14 hours and 34 minutes in space, including 3 spacewalks totaling 19 hours and 26 minutes. STS-72 Endeavour (January 11-20, 1996) was a 9-day flight during which the crew retrieved the Space Flyer Unit satellite (launched from Japan 10-months earlier), deployed and retrieved the OAST-Flyer satellite, and conducted two spacewalks to demonstrate and evaluate techniques to be used in the assembly of the International Space Station. The mission was accomplished in 142 orbits of the Earth, traveling 3.7 million miles, and logged him a total of 214 hours and 41 seconds in space, including his first EVA of 6 hours and 53 minutes. STS-87 (November 19 to December 5, 1997) was the fourth U.S Microgravity Payload flight, and focused on experiments designed to study how the weightless environment of space affects various physical processes, and on observations of the Sun's outer atmospheric layers. Scott performed two spacewalks. The first, a 7 hour 43 minute EVA featured the manual capture of a Spartan satellite, in addition to testing EVA tools and procedures for future Space Station assembly.. The second spacewalk lasted 5 hours and also featured space station assembly tests. The mission was accomplished in 252 Earth orbits, traveling 6.5 million miles in 376 hours and 34 minutes. Winston Scott retired from NASA and the U.S. Navy at the end of July 1999 to accept a position at his alma mater, Florida State University, as Vice President for Student Affairs.

NAME: Richard A. Searfoss (Colonel, USAF, Ret.)
NASA Astronaut (former)

PERSONAL DATA: Born June 5, 1956, in Mount Clemens, Michigan, but considers Portsmouth, New Hampshire, to be his hometown. Married; three children. He enjoys running, soccer, radio-controlled model aircraft, Scouting, backpacking, and classical music.

EDUCATION: Graduated from Portsmouth Senior High School, Portsmouth, New Hampshire in 1974; received a bachelor of science degree in aeronautical engineering from the USAF Academy in 1978, and a master of science degree in aeronautics from the California Institute of Technology on a National Science Foundation Fellowship in 1979. USAF Squadron Officer School, Air Command and Staff College, and Air War College.

ORGANIZATIONS: Association of Space Explorers, National Eagle Scout Association, Air Force Association, Academy of Model Aeronautics.

SPECIAL HONORS: Awarded the Harmon, Fairchild, Price and Tober Awards (top overall, academic, engineering, and aeronautical engineering graduate), United States Air Force Academy Class of 1978. Air Force Aero Propulsion Laboratory Excellence in Turbine Engine Design award. USAF Squadron Officer's School Commandant's Trophy as top graduate. Distinguished graduate, USAF Fighter Weapons School. Named the Tactical Air Command F-111 Instructor Pilot of the Year, 1985. Selected for Outstanding Young Men of America, 1987. Recipient of the Air Force Commendation Medal, Air Force Meritorious Service Medal, Defense Meritorious Service Medal, Defense Superior Service Medal, NASA Outstanding Leadership Medal, and Air Force Distinguished Flying Cross.

EXPERIENCE: Searfoss graduated in 1980 from Undergraduate Pilot Training at Williams Air Force Base, Arizona. From 1981-1984, he flew the F-111F operationally at RAF Lakenheath, England, followed by a tour at Mountain Home AFB, Idaho, where he was an F-111A instructor pilot and weapons officer until 1987. In 1988 he attended the U.S. Naval Test Pilot School, Patuxent River, Maryland, as a USAF exchange officer. He was a flight instructor at the U.S. Air Force Test Pilot School at Edwards AFB, California, when selected for the astronaut program. He has logged over 5,000 hours flying time in 56 different types of aircraft and over 939 hours in space. He also holds FAA Airline Transport Pilot, glider, and flight instructor ratings.

NASA EXPERIENCE: Selected by NASA in January 1990, Searfoss became an astronaut in July 1991. Initially assigned to the Astronaut Office Mission Support Branch, Searfoss was part of a team responsible for crew ingress/strap-in prior to launch and crew egress after landing. He was subsequently assigned to flight software verification in the Shuttle Avionics Integration Laboratory (SAIL). Additionally, he served as the Astronaut Office representative for both flight crew procedures and Shuttle computer software development. He also served as the Astronaut Office Vehicle System and Operations Branch Chief, leading a team of several astronauts and support engineers working on Shuttle and International Space Station systems development, rendezvous and landing/rollout operations, and advanced projects initiatives. A veteran of three space flights, Searfoss has logged over 39 days in space. He served as pilot on STS-58 (October 18 to November 1, 1993) and STS-76 (March 22-31, 1996), and was the mission commander on STS-90 (April 17, to May 3, 1998). Searfoss retired from the Air Force and left NASA in 1998.

SPACE FLIGHT EXPERIENCE: Searfoss served as STS-58 pilot on the seven-person life science research mission aboard the Space Shuttle Columbia, launching from the Kennedy Space Center on October 18, 1993, and landing at Edwards Air Force Base on November 1, 1993. The crew performed neurovestibular, cardiovascular, cardiopulmonary, metabolic, and musculoskeletal medical experiments on themselves and 48 rats, expanding our knowledge of human and animal physiology both on earth and in space flight. In addition, the crew performed 16 engineering tests aboard the Orbiter Columbia and 20 Extended Duration Orbiter Medical Project experiments. The mission was accomplished in 225 orbits of the Earth. Launching March 22, 1996, Searfoss flew his second mission as pilot of STS-76 aboard the Space Shuttle Atlantis. During this 9-day mission the STS-76 crew performed the third docking of an American spacecraft with the Russian space station Mir. In support of a joint U.S./Russian program, the crew transported to Mir nearly two tons of water, food, supplies, and scientific equipment, as well as U.S. Astronaut Shannon Lucid to begin her six-month stay in space. STS-76 included the first ever spacewalk on a combined Space Shuttle-Space Station complex. The flight crew also conducted scientific investigations, including European Space Agency sponsored biology experiments, the Kidsat earth observations project, and several engineering flight tests. Completed in 145 orbits, STS-76 landed at Edwards Air Force Base, California, on March 31, 1996. Searfoss commanded a seven person crew on the STS-90 Neurolab mission which launched on April 17, 1998. During the 16-day Spacelab flight the crew served as both experiment subjects and operators for 26 individual life science experiments focusing on the effects of microgravity on the brain and nervous system. STS-90 was the last and most complex of the twenty-five Spacelab missions NASA has flown. Neurolab's scientific results will have broad applicability both in preparing for future long duration human space missions and in clinical applications on Earth. Completed in 256 orbits, STS-90 landed at Kennedy Space Center, Florida, on May 3, 1998.

NAME: Margaret Rhea Seddon (M.D.)
NASA Astronaut (former)

PERSONAL DATA: Born November 8, 1947, in Murfreesboro, Tennessee. Married to Former Astronaut Robert L. Gibson of Cooperstown, New York. Three children. Her father, Mr. Edward C. Seddon, resides in Murfreesboro. Her mother, Mrs. Clayton Dann Seddon, is deceased. His mother, Mrs. Paul A. Gibson, resides in Seal Beach, California.

EDUCATION: Graduated from Central High School in Murfreesboro, Tennessee, in 1965; received a bachelor of arts degree in physiology from the University of California, Berkeley, in 1970, and a doctorate of medicine from the University of Tennessee College of Medicine in 1973.

EXPERIENCE: After medical school, Dr. Seddon completed a surgical internship and 3 years of a general surgery residency in Memphis with a particular interest in nutrition in surgery patients. Between the period of her internship and residency, she served as an Emergency Department physician at a number of hospitals in Mississippi and Tennessee, and served in this capacity in the Houston area in her spare time. Dr. Seddon has also performed clinical research into the effects of radiation therapy on nutrition in cancer patients.

NASA EXPERIENCE: Selected as an astronaut candidate by NASA in January 1978, Dr. Seddon became an astronaut in August 1979. Her work at NASA has been in a variety of areas, including Orbiter and payload software, Shuttle Avionics Integration Laboratory, Flight Data File, Shuttle medical kit and checklist, launch and landing rescue helicopter physician, support crew member for STS-6, crew equipment, membership on NASA's Aerospace Medical Advisory Committee, Technical Assistant to the Director of Flight Crew Operations, and crew communicator (CAPCOM) in the Mission Control Center. She was Assistant to the Director of Flight Crew Operations for Shuttle/Mir Payloads. A three-flight veteran with over 722 hours in space, Dr. Seddon was a mission specialist on STS-51D (1985) and STS-40 (1991), and was the payload commander on STS-58 (1993). In September 1996, she was detailed by NASA to Vanderbuilt University Medical School in Nashville, Tennessee. She assisted in the preparation of cardiovascular experiments which flew aboard Space Shuttle Columbia on the Neurolab Spacelab flight in April 1998. Dr. Seddon retired from NASA in November 1997. She is now the assistant Chief Medical Officer of the Vanderbuilt Medical Group in Nashville, Tennessee.

SPACE FLIGHT EXPERIENCE: STS-51D (Discovery), April 12-19, 1985, was launched from and returned to land at the Kennedy Space Center, Florida. The crew deployed ANIK-C for Telesat of Canada, and Syncom IV-3 for the U.S. Navy. A malfunction in the Syncom spacecraft resulted in the first unscheduled EVA (spacewalk), rendezvous and proximity operations for the Space Shuttle in an attempt to activate the satellite using the Remote Manipulator System. The crew conducted several medical experiments, activated two "Getaway Specials," and filmed experiments with toys in space. In completing her first space flight Dr. Seddon logged 168 hours in space in 109 Earth orbits.

STS-40 (Columbia) Spacelab Life Sciences (SLS-1), June 5-14, 1991, a dedicated space and life sciences mission was launched from the Kennedy Space Center, Florida, and returned to land at Edwards Air Force Base, California. During the nine-day mission the crew performed experiments which explored how humans, animals and cells respond to microgravity and re-adapt to Earth's gravity on return. Other payloads included experiments designed to investigate materials science, plant biology and cosmic radiation, and tests of hardware proposed for the Space Station Freedom Health Maintenance Facility. Mission completed in 146 orbits of the Earth, and logged her an additional 218 hours in space. STS-58 (Columbia), Spacelab Life Sciences-2, flew October 18 to November 1, 1993. Dr. Seddon was the Payload Commander on this life science research mission which received NASA management recognition as the most successful and efficient Spacelab flown to date. During the fourteen day flight the seven-person crew performed neurovestibular, cardiovascular, cardiopulmonary, metabolic, and musculoskeletal medical experiments on themselves and 48 rats, expanding our knowledge of human and animal physiology both on earth and in space flight. In addition, the crew performed 10 engineering tests aboard the Orbiter Columbia and 9 Extended Duration Orbiter Medical Project experiments. The mission was accomplished in 225 orbits of the Earth in over 336 hours.

NAME: Ronald M. Sega (Ph.D.)
NASA Astronaut (former)

PERSONAL DATA: Born December 4, 1952, in Cleveland, Ohio.

EDUCATION: Graduated from Nordonia High School, Macedonia, Ohio, in 1970; received a bachelor of science degree in Mathematics and Physics from the U.S. Air Force Academy in 1974, a master of science degree in Physics from Ohio State in 1975, and a doctorate in Electrical Engineering from University of Colorado in 1982.

ORGANIZATIONS: American Institute of Aeronautics and Astronautics (AIAA) - Associate Fellow (1992), Institute of Electrical and Electronics Engineers (IEEE), American Physical Society (APS), Institute for the Advancement of Engineering - Fellow (1992), Society for Photo-Optical Instrumentation Engineers (SPIE), Air Force Reserve Officer Association, Association of Space Explorers, and Eta Kappa Nu.

SPECIAL HONORS: Distinguished Graduate of the U.S. Air Force Academy, 1974. Top Graduate of the Pilot Instructor Training Course, 1976. Officer of the Year in the Department of Physics, U.S. Air Force Academy, 1980. Recipient of Air Force Meritorious Service Medal, Commendation Medal, and Reserve Achievement Medal. Air Force Research Fellow - Air Force Office of Scientific Research, 1985. Received the Outstanding Faculty Award - Department of Electrical Engineering at the University of Colorado, 1985. Selected to the Academic Hall of Fame of his high school in Macedonia, Ohio, 1988. Reserve Officer of the Year (IMA), Air Force Space Command, 1988; Reserve Officer of the Year (IMA), U.S. Air Force, 1988. Received an honorary doctorate from Clarkson University, 1993. Recipient of the NASA Space Flight Medal, 1994 and 1996. Superior Achievement Award (NASA Director of Operations, Russia), 1995.

EXPERIENCE: Dr. Sega graduated from the U.S. Air Force Academy in 1974, and was commissioned a Second Lieutenant in the U.S. Air Force. He earned a masters degree in Physics at Ohio State University in 1975. Completing pilot training in 1976 he served as an Instructor Pilot at Williams AFB, Arizona, until 1979. From 1979 to 1982 he was on the faculty of the U.S. Air Force Academy in the Department of Physics where he designed and constructed a laboratory facility to investigate microwave fields using infrared techniques while pursuing a doctorate in Electrical Engineering. In 1982 he joined the faculty of the University of Colorado at Colorado Springs as Assistant Professor in the Department of Electrical and Computer Engineering. He was promoted to Associate Professor in 1985, granted tenure in 1988, promoted to Professor in 1990, and is currently on an extended leave of absence. From 1987 to 1988 he served as Technical Director, Lasers and Aerospace Mechanics Directorate, of the Frank J. Seiler Research Laboratory at the U.S. Air Force Academy. From 1989 to 1990, while on leave from the University of Colorado, he served as Research Associate Professor of Physics at the University of Houston, affiliated with the Space Vacuum Epitaxy Center, and currently is Adjunct Professor of Physics. Dr. Sega is a Co-Principal Investigator of the Wake Shield Facility (WSF) which has flown on Space Shuttle mission STS-60 in February 1994 and STS-69 in 1995, also serving as mission director for WSF. He has authored or co-authored over 100 technical publications. An Air Force Reserve Officer, he holds an aeronautical rating of Command Pilot and the rank of Colonel. He serves as a reserve augmentee to the Director, Plans, Air Force Space Command. As a pilot, Dr. Sega has logged over 4,000 hours in the Air Force, Air Force Reserves, and NASA.

Selected by NASA in January 1990, Dr. Sega became an astronaut in July 1991, qualified for assignment as a mission specialist on Space Shuttle flight crews. His technical assignments have included: working Remote Manipulator System (RMS) issues for the Astronaut Office Mission Development Branch; supporting Orbiter software verification in the Shuttle Avionics Integration Laboratory (SAIL); Chief of Astronaut Appearances; Science Support Group Lead; Space Station integration team; Astronaut Representative to the Space Station Science and Utilization Advisory Board (primarily an external board for NASA).

Dr. Sega was a mission specialist on STS-60, the first joint U.S./Russian Space Shuttle Mission. Launched on February 3, 1994, STS-60 was the second flight of the Space Habitation Module-2 (Spacehab-2), and the first flight of the Wake Shield Facility (WSF-1). During the 8-day flight, the crew of Discovery conducted a wide variety of biological materials science, earth observation, and life science experiments. He was the "flight engineer" for ascent and entry on this mission, performed several experiments on orbit, and operated the robotic arm, berthing the Wake Shield onto its payload bay carrier on four separate occasions. Following 130 orbits of the Earth in 3,439,705 miles, STS-60 landed at Kennedy Space Center, Florida, on February 11, 1994. With the completion of his first space flight, Dr. Sega has logged 199 hours in space.

From November 1994 to March 1995, Dr. Sega was the NASA Director of Operations, Star City, Russia (The Gagarin Cosmonaut Training Center) responsible for managing NASA activities at Star City. These activities involved building an organization and infrastructure to support Astronaut and Cosmonaut mission and science training for flight on the Russian Space Station Mir. He also participated in training on Russian Space Systems and was the first American to train in the Russian EVA suit (Orlan) in their underwater facility (Hydrolaboratory).

Dr. Sega was a mission specialist on STS-76, the third docking mission to the Russian space station Mir, launched on March 22, 1996 with a crew of six aboard Atlantis. Following rendezvous and docking with Mir, a NASA Astronaut transferred to Mir for a five month stay to begin a continuous presence of U.S. astronauts aboard Mir for the next two year period. Dr. Sega was the Payload Commander for this mission and lead on Biorack, a small multipurpose laboratory located in the Spacehab module carried in the Shuttle payload bay. Biorack was used to technology development, fundamental biology (research into plant and animal cellular function), and environment characterization. He was responsible for planning and on-orbit operations, including extensive transfer of logistics and science, including 4800 pounds of science and mission hardware, food, water and air to Mir, and returning over 1100 pounds of U.S. and ESA science and Russian hardware. Following 144 orbits of the Earth, Atlantis landed with a crew of five at Edwards Air Force Base in California on March 31, 1996. Dr. Sega left NASA on July 1, 1996 to become Dean of the College of Engineering and Applied Science, University of Colorado at Colorado Springs.

NAME: Brewster H. Shaw, Jr. (Colonel, USAF, Ret.)
NASA Astronaut (former)

PERSONAL DATA: Born May 16, 1945, in Cass City, Michigan. He is married and has grown children.

EDUCATION: Graduated from Cass City High School, Cass City, Michigan in 1963; received Bachelor and master of science degrees in engineering mechanics from the University of Wisconsin (Madison) in 1968 and 1969; respectively.

SPECIAL HONORS: Awarded the Defense Superior Service Medal, Air Force Distinguished Flying Cross with 7 Oak Leaf Cluster, Defense Meritorious Service Medal, Air Medal with 20 Oak Leaf Clusters, Air Force Commendation Medal with 1 Oak Leaf Cluster, Air Force Outstanding Unit Award, Combat Readiness Medal, National Defense Service Medal, Vietnam Service Medal, Air Force Longevity Service Awards, Small Arms Expert Marksmanship Ribbon, Republic of Vietnam Campaign Medal, Republic of Vietnam Gallantry Cross. Named a Distinguished Graduate from Officer Training School and the United States Test Pilot School. Recipient of undergraduate pilot training Commanders Trophy, Outstanding Flying Trophy, Outstanding Academic Trophy, Best T-38 Pilot Award, and Top Formation Pilot Award, F-100 Barry Goldwater Top Gun Award. Recipient of Group Achievement Award 1981 Launch and Landing Operations Team, NASA Space Flight Medals (1983, 1985, 1989), American Astronautical Society 1983 Flight Achievement Awards STS-9 (Spacelab 1), Veterans of Foreign Wars 1984 National Space Award STS-9, NASA Group Achievement Award 61-B EASE/ACCESS (1986), NASA JSC Aviation Safety Award (1987, NASA Special Achievement Award (1988), NASA Outstanding Leadership Medal (1988).

EXPERIENCE: Shaw entered the Air Force in 1969 after completing Officer Training School, and attended undergraduate pilot training at Craig Air Force Base, Alabama. He received his wings in 1970 and was then assigned to the F-100 Replacement Training Unit at Luke Air Force Base, Arizona. In March 1971, he was assigned as an F-100 combat fighter pilot to the 352nd Tactical Fighter Squadron at Phan Rang Air Base, Republic of Vietnam. He returned to the United States in August 1971 for assignment to the F-4 Replacement Training Unit at George Air Force Base, California. He was subsequently sent to the 25th Tactical Fighter Squadron at Ubon RTAFB, Thailand, where he flew combat missions as an F-4 fighter pilot. In April 1973, he reported to the 20th Tactical Fighter Training Squadron, George Air Force Base, California, for F-4 instructor duties. Shaw attended the USAF Test Pilot School at Edwards Air Force Base, California, from July 1975 to 1976.

Following completion of this training, he remained at Edwards as an operational test pilot with the 6512th Test Squadron (Test Operations). He served as an instructor at the USAF Test Pilot School from August 1977 to July 1978. He has logged more than 5,000 hours flying time in over 30 types of aircraft -- including 644 hours of combat in F- 100 and F-4 aircraft.

NASA EXPERIENCE: Shaw was selected as an astronaut in January 1978. His technical assignments have included support crew and Entry CAPCOM for STS-3 and STS-4, staff member of the Roger's Presidential Commission investigating the STS 51-L Challenger accident, head of the Orbiter return to flight team responsible for implementing safety modifications to the Orbiter fleet, and Astronaut Office Liaison with the Department of Defense for classified payloads. A veteran of three space flights, STS-9, STS-61B, and STS-28, Shaw has logged a total of 534 hours in space.

Col. Shaw left the Johnson Space Center in October 1989 to assume the NASA Headquarters Senior Executive position of Deputy Director, Space Shuttle Operations, located at the Kennedy Space Center. In this capacity, as the Operations Manager, Shaw was responsible for all operational aspects of the Space Shuttle Program and has Level II authority over the Space Shuttle elements from the time the Orbiters leave the Orbiter Processing Facility, are mated to the external tank and solid rocket boosters, transported to the launch pad, launched and recovered, and returned to the Orbiter Processing Facility. He was the final authority for the launch decision, and chaired the Mission Management Team.

In September 1992, Col. Shaw began serving as the Deputy Program Manager, Space Shuttle, as a NASA Headquarters employee located at the Kennedy Space Center. In addition to the duties he previously held as Deputy Director, Space Shuttle Operations, he also shared with the Program Manager, Space Shuttle, full authority and responsibility for the conduct of the Space Shuttle Program. As Director, Space Shuttle Operations, Col. Shaw is currently responsible for the development of all Space Shuttle elements, including the Orbiter, external tank, solid rocket boosters, Space Shuttle main engines, and the facilities required to support mission operations, and in the planning necessary to efficiently conduct Space Shuttle operations.

SPACE FLIGHT EXPERIENCE: STS-9/Spacelab-1 Columbia (November 28 to December 8, 1983) was launched from Kennedy Space Center, Florida. The crew included: spacecraft commander John Young; pilot Brewster Shaw; mission specialists Owen Garriott and Robert Parker; and payload specialists, Byron Lichtenbert and Ulf Merbold. It was the largest crew to fly aboard a single spacecraft, the first international Shuttle crew, and the first to carry payload specialists. During this maiden flight of the European Space Agency (ESA)-developed laboratory, the crew conducted more than seventy multi-disciplinary scientific and technical investigations in the fields of life sciences, atmospheric physics and earth observations, astronomy and solar physics, space plasma physics, and materials processing. After ten days of spacelab hardware verification and around-the-clock scientific operations, Columbia and its laboratory cargo (the heaviest payload to be returned to earth in the Shuttle Orbiter's cargo bay) returned to land on the dry lakebed at Edwards Air Force Base, California.

STS-61B Atlantis (November 26 to December 3, 1985) was launched at night from Kennedy Space Center, Florida. The crew included: spacecraft commander Brewster Shaw; pilot, Bryan O'Connor; mission specialists, Mary Cleave, Jerry Ross, and Woody Springs; as well as payload specialists Rodolfo Neri Vela (Mexico), and Charles Walker (McDonnell Douglas).

During the mission the crew deployed the MORELOS-B, AUSSATT II, and SATCOM K-2 communications satellites, conducted 2 six hour spacewalks to demonstrate Space Station construction techniques with the EASE/ACCESS experiments, operated the Continuous Flow Electrophoresis (CRFES) experiment for McDonell Douglas and a Getaway Special (GAS) container for Telesat, Canada, conducted several Mexican Payload Specialists Experiments for the Mexican Government, and tested the Orbiter Experiments Digital Autopilot (OEX DAP). This was the heaviest payload weight carried to orbit by the Space Shuttle to date. After completing 108 orbits of the Earth in 165 hours, Shaw landed Atlantis on Runway 22 at Edwards Air Force Base, California.

STS-28 Columbia (August 8-13, 1989) was also commanded by Brewster Shaw and included pilot Dick Richards, and three mission specialist, Jim Adamson, Dave Leestma, and Mark Brown. The STS-28 mission carried Department of Defense payloads and a number of secondary payloads. After 80 orbits of the earth, this five day mission concluded with a dry lakebed landing on Runway 17 at Edwards Air Force Base, California.

Name: Loren J. Shriver
Deputy Director For Launch and Payload Processing
John F. Kennedy Space Center, Florida
NASA Astronaut (former)

Loren J. Shriver (Colonel, USAF, retired) became the Deputy Director of NASA's Kennedy Space Center for Launch and Payload Processing, effective Aug. 17, 1997.

Shriver provides executive leadership, strategic planning, and direction for Kennedy's Agency-assigned responsibilities as the Center of Excellence for Launch and Payload Processing Sys tems. This includes payload carriers, Space Shuttle processing and launch, and processing of payloads including International Space Station elements, and responsibilities assigned to the Center for expendable launch vehicles.

Shriver has served as the Space Shuttle Program Manager, Launch Integration, since May 14, 1993. In this capacity he was responsible for final Shuttle preparation, mission execution, and return of the orbiter to KSC following landings at Edwards Air Force Base, California.

Born September 23, 1944, in Jefferson, Iowa, Shriver received a Bachelor of Science degree in Aeronautical Engineering from the United States Air Force Academy in 1967, and a Master of Science degree in Astronautical Engineering from Purdue University in 1968. He was commissioned in 1967 upon graduation from the United States Air Force Academy in Colorado Springs, Colorado. From 1969 to 1973, he served as a T-38 academic instructor pilot at Vance Air Force Base, Oklahoma. He completed F-4 combat crew training at Homestead Air Force Base, Florida, in 1973, and was then assigned to an overseas tour in Thailand until October 1974. In 1975, he attended the United States Air Force Test Pilot School at Edwards Air Force Base, California, and upon completion of this training was assigned to the 6512th Test Squadron at Edwards Air Force Base, and participated in the Air Force development test and evaluation of the T-38 lead-in fighter. In 1976, Shriver began serving as a test pilot for the F-15 Joint Test Force at Edwards Air Force Base. He has flown in 30 different types of single and multiengine civilian and military fixed-wing and helicopter aircraft, has logged over 6,200 hours in jet aircraft, and holds commercial pilot and private glider ratings.

Shriver was selected as an astronaut by NASA in January 1978. In September of 1982, he was selected as pilot for the first Department of Defense (DoD) mission, STS-10. That mission was later canceled. A veteran of three space flights, Shriver flew on STS-51C in 1985, STS-31 in 1990, and STS-46 in 1992, and has logged over 386 hours in space. In October 1992, he was assigned as Deputy Chief of the Astronaut Office.

Shriver was pilot of STS-51C which launched from Kennedy Space Center, Florida, on January 24, 1985. STS-51C performed its DoD mission which included deployment of a modified Inertial Upper Stage (IUS) vehicle from the Space Shuttle's payload bay. Landing occurred on January 27, 1985, after slightly more than 3 days on orbit. Mission duration was 73 hours 33 minutes 27 seconds.

On his second mission, Shriver commanded a crew of five. STS-31 launched on April 24, 1990, from the Kennedy Space Center, Florida. During the 5-day mission, crew members deployed the Hubble Space Telescope (HST) and conducted a variety of middeck experiments involving the study of protein crystal growth, polymer membrane processing, and the effects of weightlessness and magnetic fields on an ion arc. They also operated a variety of cameras, including both the IMAX in-cabin and cargo bay cameras for Earth observations from their then record-setting altitude of 333 nautical miles. Mission duration was 121 hours 16 minutes 6 seconds. Following 76 orbits of the Earth, STS-31 Discovery landed at Edwards Air Force Base, California, on April 29, 1990.

As spacecraft commander of STS-46, Shriver and his crew launched from the Kennedy Space Center, Florida, on July 31, 1992. STS-46 was an 8-day mission, during which crew members deployed the European Retrievable Carrier (EURECA) satellite (an ESA-sponsored free-flying science platform), and conducted the first Tethered Satellite System (TSS) test flight (a joint project between NASA and the Italian Space Agency). Mission duration was 191 hours 16 minutes 7 seconds. After completing 126 orbits of the Earth, Space Shuttle Atlantis landed at the Kennedy Space Center, Florida, on August 8, 1992, having traveled 3.35 million miles.

Shriver's accomplishments have earned him many notable awards. He has received the United States Air Force Distinguished Flying Cross, the Defense Superior Service Medal, the Defense Meritorious Service Medal, the Air Force Meritorious Service Medal, the Air Force Commendation Medal, the NASA Distinguished Service Medal, the NASA Outstanding Leadership Medal, the NASA Space Flight Medal (three times), the American Astronautical Society 1990 Flight Achievement Award, and the American Institute of Aeronautics and Astronautics Haley Space Flight Award for 1990.

Shriver is married to the former Susan Diane Hane of Paton, Iowa. He has three daughters: Camilla, Melinda, and Rebecca, and one son; Jered. The Shrivers reside in Titusville, Florida.

NAME: Sherwood C. (Woody) Spring (Colonel, USA, Ret.)
NASA Astronaut (former)

PERSONAL DATA: Born September 3, 1944, in Hartford, Connecticut, but considers Harmony, Rhode Island, to be his hometown. Married, two children. He enjoys flying, scuba diving, river running, skiing, and carpentry.

EDUCATION: Graduated from Ponaganset high School, Chepachet, Rhode Island, in 1963; received a bachelor of science degree in General Engineering from the United States Military Academy in 1967 and a master of science degree in Aerospace Engineering from the University of Arizona in 1974. Graduated from the U.S. Navy Test Pilot School in 1976.

ORGANIZATIONS: Member of the Society of Experimental Test Pilots and the United States Army Association; and lifetime member of the Association of Graduates of the United States Military Academy.

SPECIAL HONORS: Defense Distinguished Service Medal, Distinguished Flying Cross, 2 Army Bronze Stars, 1 Army Meritorious Service Medal, 3 Army Commendations, 9 Army Air Medals, a Vietnam Cross of Gallantry with Palm, National Defense Service Medal, Vietnam Service Medals, and NASA Space Flight Medal. Recipient, in 1986, of two honorary doctorate degrees; Doctor of Science, and Doctor of Human Letters.

EXPERIENCE: After graduation from West Point in 1967, Spring served two tours of duty in Vietnam. The first was from 1968 to 1969 with the 101st Airborne Division. The second tour, 1970-1971, came immediately after flight school and was served as a helicopter pilot with the 1st Cavalry Division. Upon return, he received fixed wing training enroute to a master's degree program with the University of Arizona in 1974. After a short tour at Edwards Air Force Base, California, as a flight test engineer, he attended the Navy Test Pilot School at Patuxent River, Maryland. He then returned to the Army's Flight Test Facility at Edwards AFB to complete 4 years as an experimental test pilot. He has military and civilian experience in 25 types of airplanes and helicopters and has logged more than 3,500 hours flying time--including over 1,500 hours in jet aircraft.

NASA EXPERIENCE: Spring was selected as an astronaut in May 1980. His technical assignments have included software verification at the Shuttle Avionics Integration Laboratory and Flight Simulation Laboratory; vehicle and satellite integration at the Kennedy Space Center, Florida, for STS-5, 6, 7, 8, and 9; Astronaut Office EVA (Extra Vehicular Activity) expert; and Space Station construction, EVA maintenance, and design. Spring served as a mission specialist on STS-61B which flew November 26 thru December 3, 1985. During that mission he was responsible for launching three communications satellites and performed two EVA's. The EVA's, which totaled more than 12 hours, investigated Space Station construction techniques, large structure manipulation while on the end of the remote arm, and a time and motion study for comparison between Earth training and Space performance. With the completion of STS-61B he has logged a total of 165 hours in space, including over 12 hours of EVA.

Following his retirement form NASA in August 1988, Colonel Spring spent the next five years directing the Army Space Program Office in Washington, D.C. He retired from the Army in July, 1994, and is now an Aerospace Consultant with TASC (The Application Science Corporation), Inc. of Reston Virginia.

NAME: Robert C. Springer (Colonel, USMC)
NASA Astronaut (former)

PERSONAL DATA: Born May 21,1942, in St Louis, Missouri, but considers Ashland, Ohio, to be his hometown. His parents, Mr. and Mrs. Walter Springer, reside in Ashland.

PHYSICAL DESCRIPTION: Brown hair; blue eyes; height: 6 feet 1/2 inch; weight: 170 pounds.

EDUCATION: Graduated from Ashland High School, Ashland, Ohio, in 1960; received a bachelor of science degree in Naval Science from the United States Naval Academy in 1964 and a master of science in Operations Research and Systems Analysis from the U.S. Naval Postgraduate School in 1971.

MARITAL STATUS: Married to the former "Molly" (Mary) M. McCoy of Parma, Ohio. Her father, Mr. James McCoy, resides in Seabrook, Texas; her mother is deceased.

CHILDREN: Chad, August 12, 1970; Kira, February 12, 1972; and Derek, December 1, 1976.

RECREATIONAL INTERESTS: He enjoys long-distance running, tennis, golf, and windsurfing.

ORGANIZATIONS: Member of the Society of Experimental Test Pilots, the Marine Corps Aviation Association, and the United States Naval Academy Alumni Association; past member of the Operations Research Society and the Military Operations Research Society; named one of the Jaycee's Outstanding Young Men in America in 1977.

SPECIAL HONORS: Navy Distinguished Flying Cross, Bronze Star, Air Medal (21st award), Navy Commendation Medal (2nd award), Navy Achievement Medal, NASA Space Flight Medal, Combat Action Ribbon, Presidential Unit Citation, Navy Unit Citation, and various Vietnam Campaign ribbons and service awards.

EXPERIENCE: Springer received a commission in the United States Marine Corps following graduation from Annapolis in 1964. He attended the Marine Corps Basic School at Quantico, Virginia, before reporting to the Navy Air Training Command for flight training at Pensacola, Florida, and Beeville, Texas. Upon receiving his aviator wings in August 1966, he was assigned to VMFA-513 at the Marine Corps Air Station, Cherry Point, North Carolina, where he flew F-4 aircraft. He was subsequently assigned to VMFA-115 at Chu Lai in the Republic of Vietnam, where he flew F-4s and completed 300 combat missions. In June 1968, he served as an advisor to the Republic of Korea Marine Corps in Vietnam and flew 250 combat missions in O1 "Bird Dogs" and UH1 "Huey" helicopters. Springer returned to the United States later that year to attend the U. S. Naval Postgraduate School in Monterey, California, and in March 1971, he reported to the 3rd Marine Aircraft Wing at El Toro, California, for an assignment as wing operations analysis officer. He flew UH1 E "Huey's" in 1972 while with HML-267 at Camp Pendleton, California, and then went to Okinawa to fly " Huey's" with HML-367, 1st Marine Aircraft Wing. Springer flew F-4 "Phantoms" as an aircraft maintenance officer with VMFA-451 in Beaufort, South Carolina, and also attended Navy Fighter Weapons School (Top Gun). A 1975 graduate of the U. S. Navy Test Pilot School at Patuxent River, Maryland, he served as Head of the Ordnance Systems Branch and as a test pilot for more than 20 different types of fixed and rotary-winged aircraft. In this capacity he performed the first flights in the AHIT helicopter.

He graduated from the Armed Forces Staff College in Norfolk, Virginia, in 1978, and, assigned to Headquarters Fleet Marine Force, Atlantic, assumed responsibility for joint operational planning for Marine Forces in NATO and the Mid-East. He was serving as aide-de-camp for the Commanding General, Fleet Marine Force, Atlantic, when advised of his selection by NASA.

He has logged more than 4,500 hours flying time, including 3,500 hours in jet aircraft.

NASA EXPERIENCE: Selected as an astronaut candidate by NASA in May 1980, Springer became an astronaut in August 1981. His technical assignments have included support crew for STS-3, concept development studies for the Space Operations Center, and the coordination of various aspects of the final development of the Remote Manipulator System for operational use. He worked in the Mission Control Center as Orbit CAPCOM for 7 flights in 1984 and 1985.

Springer was responsible for astronaut office coordination of Design Requirements Reviews (DRR) and Design Certification Reviews (DCR). These review efforts encompassed the total recertification and reverification of the NSTS prior to STS-26 return to flight status.

Springer was a mission specialist on the crew of STS-29, which launched from Kennedy Space Center, Florida, aboard the Orbiter Discovery, on March 13, 1989. During 80 orbits of the earth on this highly successful five- day mission, the crew deployed a Tracking and Data Relay Satellite and performed numerous secondary experiments, including a Space Station "heat pipe" radiator experiment, two student experiments, a protein crystal growth experiment, and a chromosome and plant cell division experiment. In addition, the crew took over 4,000 photographs of the earth using several types of cameras, including the IMAX 70 mm movie camera. Mission duration was 119 hours and concluded with a landing at Edwards Air Force Base, California, on March 18, 1989.

More recently Springer served as a mission specialist on STS-38. The five-man crew launched at night from the Kennedy Space Center, Florida, on November 15, 1990. During the five day mission crewmembers conducted Department of Defense operations. After 80 orbits of the earth, in the first Shuttle recovery in Florida since 1985, Space Shuttle Atlantis and her crew landed back at the Kennedy Space Center on November 20, 1990. With the completion of his second mission, Springer has logged over 237 hours in space.

NAME: Thomas P. Stafford (Lieutenant General, USAF, Retired)
NASA Astronaut (former)

PERSONAL DATA: Born September 17, 1930, in Weatherford, Oklahoma. His mother, Mrs. Mary Ellen Stafford, is a resident of Weatherford.

PHYSICAL DESCRIPTION: Black hair, blue eyes; height: 6 feet; weight: 175 pounds.

EDUCATION: Graduated from Weatherford High School, Weatherford, Oklahoma; received a Bachelor of Science degree from the United States Naval Academy in 1952. In addition, General Stafford is the recipient of several honorary degrees. These include a doctorate of science from Oklahoma City University; a doctorate of laws, Western State University, Los Angeles, California; doctorate of communications, Emerson College, Boston, Massachuaetts; a doctorate of aeronautical engineering, Embry-Riddle Aeronautical University, Daytona Beach, Florida; and a doctorate of humanities, Oklahoma Christian College, Edmond, Oklahoma.

MARITAL STATUS: Married to the former Faye L. Shoemaker of Weatherford, Oklahoma. They have two daughters, Dionne Kay and Garin Elaine.

RECREATIONAL INTERESTS: Hobbies include hunting, soaring, weight lifting, and swimming.

ORGANIZATIONS: Fellow of the American Astronautical Society, American Institute of Aeronautics and Astronautics, the Society of Experimental Test Pilots, and a member of the Explorers Club.

SPECIAL HONORS: Awarded two NASA Distinguished Service Medals, two NASA Exceptional Service Medals, the JSC Certificate of Commendation (1970), the Air Force Distinguished Service Medal with 3 Oak Leaf Clusters, the Air Force Command Pilot Astronaut Wings, and the Air Force Distinguished Flying Cross. Other awards presented to General Stafford include the American Institute of Aeronautics and Astronautics (AIAA) Chanute Flight Award, the Veterans of Foreign Wars National Space Award, National Geographic Society's General Thomas D. White USAF Space Trophy, and the Federation Aeronautique Internationale Gold Space Medal. In 1966, he was corecipient of the AIAA Award. He was honored with the Harmon International Aviation Trophy in 1966. His military decorations and awards include the Distinguished Service Medal (Air Force design), Distinguished Flying Cross with one Oak Leaf Cluster, Air Force Commendation Medal, Air Force Outstanding Unit Award with one Oak Leaf Cluster, the NASA Distinguished Service Medal, and the NASA Exceptional Service Medal (twice).

He has logged 507 hours and 43 minutes in space flight and wears the Air Force Command Pilot Astronaut Wings. He has flown over 110 different types of aircraft and has over 7,100 flying hours.

General Stafford assumed command of the Air Force Flight Test Center November 4, 1975. He was promoted to the grade of Major General August 9, 1975, with date of rank of June 1, 1973. Promoted to grade of Lieutenant General on March 15, 1978 and on May 1, 1978, assumed duties as Deputy Chief of Staff, Research Development and Acquisition, Headquarters USAF, Washington, D.C.; retired from the Air Force November 1, 1979.

EXPERIENCE: Stafford graduated with honors in 1952 from the U.S. Naval Academy, Annapolis, Maryland, and was commissioned a second lieutenant in the United States Air Force. General Stafford received his pilot wings at Connally AFB, Waco, Texas, in September 1953. He completed advanced interceptor training and was assigned to the 54th Fighter Interceptor Squadron, Ellsworth AFB, Rapid City, South Dakota. In December 1955 he was assigned to the 496th Fighter Interceptor Squadron, Hahn Air Base, Germany, where he performed the duties of pilot, flight leader, and flight test maintenance officer, flying F-86Ds.

Upon returning to the United States in August 1958 he attended the Air Force Experimental Flight Test Pilot School at Edwards AFB, graduated in April 1959, and received the A. B. Honts award as the outstanding graduate. He remained with the school as an instructor and later was chief of the Performance Branch. In this capacity, he was instructor in flight test training and specialized academic subjects, establishing basic textbooks and directing the writing of flight test manuals for use by the staff and students. He is coauthor of the Pilot's Handbook for Performance Flight Testing and the Aerodynamics Handbook for Performance Flight Testing.

NASA EXPERIENCE: General Stafford was selected among the second group of astronauts in September 1962 by the National Aeronautics and Space Administration (NASA) to participate in Projects Gemini and Apollo.

In December 1965, he was the pilot of Gemini VI, which was the first rendezvous in space, and helped in the development of techniques to prove the basic theory and practicality of space rendezvous.

In June 1966, he was commander of Gemini IX and performed three different types of rendezvous, including a demonstration of an early rendezvous that would be used in Apollo; the first optical rendezvous; and a lunar or abort rendezvous. From August 1966 to October 1968, he headed the mission planning analysis and software development responsibilities for the astronaut group for Project Apollo.

General Stafford was the lead member of the group which helped formulate the sequence of missions leading to the first lunar landing mission. He demonstrated and implemented the theory of a pilot manually flying the Saturn booster into orbit and the translunar injection maneuver. In May 1969, General Stafford was commander of Apollo 10, the first flight of the lunar module to the moon, He performed the first rendezvous around the Moon and the entire lunar landing mission except the actual landing.

He also made reconnaissance and tracking on future Apollo landing sites. Stafford was cited in the Guiness Book of World Records for highest speed ever attained by man; these occurred during Apollo 10 reentry when the spacecraft attained 28,547 statute miles per hour. This set the world's all-time speed record.

He was assigned as head of the astronaut group in June 1969 and, as such, was responsible for the selection of flight crews for Projects Apollo and Skylab. He reviewed and monitored flight crew training status reports, and was responsible for coordination, scheduling, and control of all activities involving NASA astronauts.

In June 1971, General Stafford was assigned as Deputy Director of Flight Crew Operations at the NASA Manned Spacecraft Center. In this role he was responsible for assisting the director in planning and implementation of programs for the astronaut group, the Aircraft Operations, Flight Crew Integration, Flight Crew Procedures, and Crew Simulation and Training Divisions.

He logged his fourth space flight as Apollo commander of the Apollo-Soyuz Test Project (ASTP) mission, July 15-24, 1975, a joint space flight culminating in the historic first meeting in space between American Astronauts and Soviet Cosmonauts.

The event signaled a major advance in efforts for the conduct of joint experiments and the exchange of mutual assistance in future international space explorations.

CURRENT ASSIGNMENT: General Stafford is currently Vice-President of Gibraltar Exploration, Ltd., Oklahoma City, OK; Chairman of The Board of Omega Watch Company of America, New York City, NY; and a member of the board of Bendix Corporation, Southfield, MI; and Gulfstream American, Savannah, GA. He is also a member of the board of several financial institutions.

NAME: Robert L. Stewart (Brigadier General, USA, Ret.)
NASA Astronaut (former)

PERSONAL DATA: Born August 13, 1942, in Washington D.C. Married. Two children. His interests include woodworking, photography and skiing.

EDUCATION: Graduated from Hattiesburg High School, Hattiesburg, Mississippi, in 1960; received a bachelor of science degree in Mathematics from the University of Southern Mississippi in 1964, and a master of science in Aerospace Engineering from the University of Texas at Arlington, in 1972.

ORGANIZATIONS: Member of the Society of Experimental Test Pilots, Association of Space Explorers past member of Phi Eta Sigma, and the Scabbard and Blade (military honor society).

SPECIAL HONORS: Awarded Army Distinguished Service Medal, Defense Superior Service Medal, 2 Legion of Merit, 4 Distinguished Flying Crossed, a Bronze Star, a Meritorious Service Medal, 33 Air Medals, the Army Commendation Medal with Oak Leaf Cluster and "V" Device, 2 Purple Hearts, the National Defense Service Medal, the Armed Forces Expeditionary Medal, the U.S. and Vietnamese Vietnam Service Medals, and the Vietnamese Cross of Gallantry; also Army Aviation of the Year, 1984, AHS Feinberg Memorial Award, AIAA Oberth Award. Recipient of NASA Space Flight Medal (1984 & 1985).

EXPERIENCE: Stewart entered on active duty with the United States Army in May 1964 and was assigned as an air defense artillery director at the 32nd NORAD Region Headquarters (SAGE), Gunter Air Force Base, Alabama. In July 1966, after completing rotary wing training at Ft. Wolters, Texas, and Ft. Rucker, Alabama, he was designated an Army aviator. He flew 1,035 hours combat time from August 1966 to 1967, primarily as a fire team leader in the armed helicopter platoon of "A" Company, 101st Aviation Battalion (redesignated 336th Assault Helicopter Company). He was an instructor pilot at the U.S. Army Primary Helicopter School -- serving 1 year in the pre- solo/ primary-1 phase of instruction and about 6 months as commander of methods of instruction flight III, training rated aviators to become instructor pilots. He is a graduate of the U.S. Army's Air Defense School's Air Defense Officers Advanced Course and Guided Missile Systems Officers Course. Stewart served in Seoul, Korea, from 1972 to 1973, with the 309th Aviation Battalion (Combat) as a battalion operations officer and battalion executive officer. He next attended the U.S. Naval Test Pilot School at Patuxent River, Maryland, completing the Rotary Wing Test Pilot Course in 1974, and was then assigned as an experimental test pilot to the U.S. Army Aviation Engineering Flight Activity at Edwards Air Force Base, California. His duties there included being chief of the integrated systems test division, as well as participating in engineering flight tests of UH-1 and AH-1 helicopters and U-21 and OV-1 fixed wing aircraft, serving as project officer and senior test pilot on the Hughes YAH-64 advanced attack helicopter during government competitive testing; and participation with Sikorsky Aircraft test pilots in developing an electronic automatic flight control system for the new Army transport helicopter -- the UH-60A Black Hawk.

He has military and civilian experience in 38 types of airplanes and helicopters and logged approximately 6,000 hours total flight time.

NASA EXPERIENCE: Stewart became a NASA Astronaut in August 1979. His technical duties in the astronaut office have included testing and evaluation of the entry flight control systems for STS-1 (the first Space Shuttle orbital mission), ascent abort procedures development, and payload coordination. He also served as support crewman for STS-4, and Ascent/Orbit CAPCOM for STS-5. He served as a mission specialist on STS-41B in 1984 and STS-51J in 1985, and has logged a total of 289 hours in space, including approximately 12 hours of EVA operations.

In 1986, while in training for his scheduled third flight to be know as 61-K, Col Stewart was selected by the Army for promotion to Brigadier General. Upon accepting this promotion General Stewart was reassigned from NASA to be the Deputy Commanding General, US Army Strategic Defense Command, in Huntsville, Alabama. In this capacity General Stewart managed research efforts in developing ballistic missile defense technology. In 1989, he was reassigned as the Director of Plans, US Space Command, Colorado Springs, CO. General Stewart retired from the Army in 1992 and currently makes his home in Woodland Park, Co. He is presently employed as Director, Advanced Programs, Nichols Research Corporation, Colorado Springs, CO.

SPACE FLIGHT EXPERIENCE: STS-41B Challenger (February 3-11, 1984) was launched from Kennedy Space Center, Florida, and returned to land there 8-days later. During the mission, Stewart and McCandless participated in two extravehicular activities (EVA's) to conduct first flight evaluations of the Manned Maneuvering Units (MMU's). These EVA's represented man's first untethered operations from a spacecraft in flight.

STS-51J Atlantis (October 3-7, 1985) was launched from Kennedy Space Center, Florida, and after 98 hours of orbital operations returned to land at Edwards Air Force Base, California. It was the second Space Shuttle Department of Defense mission, and the maiden voyage of Atlantis, the final Orbiter in the Shuttle fleet. During the mission he was responsible for a number of on-orbit activities.

NAME: Kathryn D. Sullivan (Ph.D.)
NASA Astronaut (former)

PERSONAL DATA: Born October 3, 1951, in Paterson, New Jersey, but considers Woodland Hills, California, to be her hometown. She enjoys flying, squash, bicycling, backpacking, and reading in her spare time. Her father, Donald P. Sullivan, resides in Cupertino, California; her mother, Barbara K. Sullivan, is deceased.

EDUCATION: Graduated from Taft High School, Woodland Hills, California, in 1969; received a bachelor of science degree in Earth sciences from the University of California, Santa Cruz, in 1973, and a doctorate in geology from Dalhousie University (Halifax, Nova Scotia) in 1978. Awarded honorary degrees by Dalhousie in 1985 and the State University of New York in 1991.

ORGANIZATIONS: Appointed to the Chief of Naval Operations Executive Panel in 1988. In March 1985, Dr. Sullivan was appointed by President Reagan to the National Commission on Space. The Commission's report, entitled "Pioneering the Space Frontier," laid out goals for U.S. civilian space activities over the next 25 years. She is also a member of the Geological Society of America, the American Geophysical Union, the American Institute of Aeronautics and Astronautics, the Explorers Club, the Society of Woman Geographers, and the Sierra Club.

SPECIAL HONORS: NASA Exceptional Service Medal (1988 & 1991); Ten Outstanding Young People of the World Award, Jaycees International (1987); Ten Outstanding Young Americans Award, U.S. Jaycees (1987); National Air and Space Museum Trophy, Smithsonian Institution (1985); NASA Space Flight Medal (1984 & 1990); AIAA Haley Space Flight Award (1991); AAS Space Flight Achievement Award (1991).

EXPERIENCE: Most of Dr. Sullivan's efforts prior to joining NASA were concentrated in academic study and research. She was an earth sciences major at the University of California, Santa Cruz, and spent 1971-1972 as an exchange student at the University of Bergen, Norway. Her bachelor's degree (with honors) was awarded in 1973. Her doctoral studies at Dalhousie University included participation in a variety of oceanographic expeditions, under the auspices of the U.S. Geological Survey, Wood's Hole Oceanographic Institute, and the Bedford Institute. Her research included the Mid-Atlantic Ridge, the Newfoundland Basin, and fault zones off the Southern California Coast.

Dr. Sullivan is an oceanography officer in the U.S. Naval Reserve, currently holding the rank of lieutenant commander. She is a private pilot, rated in powered and glider aircraft. In 1985, Dr. Sullivan became Adjunct Professor of Geology at Rice University, Houston, Texas.

NASA EXPERIENCE: Selected by NASA in January 1978, Dr. Sullivan became an astronaut in August 1979. Her Shuttle support assignments since then include: software development; launch and landing lead chase photographer; Orbiter and cargo test, checkout and launch support at Kennedy Space Center, Florida; extravehicular activity (EVA) and spacesuit support crew for several flights; and capsule communicator (CAPCOM) in Mission Control for numerous Shuttle missions. A veteran of three space flights, Dr. Sullivan was a mission specialist on STS-41G (October 5-13, 1984), STS-31 (April 24-29, 1990), and STS-45 (March 24-April 2, 1992).

Since joining NASA, Dr. Sullivan's research interests have focused on remote sensing. She qualified as a systems engineer operator in NASA's WB-57F high-altitude research aircraft in 1978 and has participated in several remote sensing projects in Alaska. She was a co-investigator on the Shuttle Imaging Radar-B (SIR-B) experiment which she flew on Mission STS-41G.

Her first mission, STS-41G, launched from Kennedy Space Center, Florida, on October 5, 1984, with a crew of seven. During their eight-day mission, the crew deployed the Earth Radiation Budget Satellite, conducted scientific observations of the Earth with the OSTA-3 pallet (including the SIR-B radar, FILE, and MAPS experiments) and large format camera (LFC), conducted a satellite refueling demonstration using hydrazine fuel with the Orbital Refueling System (ORS), and conducted numerous in-cabin experiments as well as activating eight "Getaway Special" canisters. Dr. Sullivan and Commander Leestma also successfully conducted a 3-1/2 hour Extravehicular Activity (EVA) to demonstrate the feasibility of actual satellite refueling, making her the first U.S. woman to perform an EVA. STS-41G completed 132 orbits of the Earth in 197.5 hours, before landing at Kennedy Space Center, Florida, on October 13, 1984.

In April 1990, Dr. Sullivan served on the crew of STS-31, which launched from Kennedy Space Center, Florida, on April 24, 1990. During this five-day mission, crew members aboard the Space Shuttle Discovery deployed the Hubble Space Telescope, and conducted a variety of middeck experiments involving the study of protein crystal growth, polymer membrane processing, and the effects of weightlessness and magnetic fields on an ion arc.

They also operated a variety of cameras, including both the IMAX in-cabin and cargo bay cameras, for Earth observations from their record setting altitude of 380 miles. Following 76 orbits of the Earth in 121 hours, STS-31 Discovery landed at Edwards Air Force Base, California, on April 29, 1990.

More recently, Dr. Sullivan served as Payload Commander on STS-45, the first Spacelab mission dedicated to NASA's Mission to Planet Earth. During this nine-day mission, the crew operated the twelve experiments that constituted the ATLAS-1 (Atmospheric Laboratory for Applications and Science) cargo. ATLAS-1 obtained a vast array of detailed measurements of atmospheric chemical and physical properties, which will contribute significantly to improving our understanding of our climate and atmosphere. In addition, this was the first time an artificial beam of electrons was used to stimulate a man-made auroral discharge. With the completion of her third mission, Dr. Sullivan has logged over 532 hours in space.

Dr. Sullivan left NASA in August 1992 to assume the position of Chief Scientist, National Oceanic and Atmospheric Administration (NOAA). She currently serves as President and CEO, Center of Science & Industry, Columbus, Ohio.

NAME: Norman E. Thagard (M.D.)
NASA Astronaut (former)

PERSONAL DATA: Born July 3, 1943, in Marianna, Florida, but considers Jacksonville, Florida, to be his hometown. Married to the former Rex Kirby Johnson of South Ponte Vedra Beach, Florida. They have three sons. During his free time, he enjoys classical music, and electronic design. Dr. Thagard has published articles on digital and analog electronic design. His father, Mr. James E. Thagard, is deceased; his mother, Mrs. Mary F. Nicholson, is a resident of St. Peterburg, Florida. Her mother, Mrs. Rex Johnson, resides in Tallahassee, Florida.

EDUCATION: Graduated from Paxon Senior High School, Jacksonville, Florida, in 1961; attended Florida State University where he received bachelor and master of science degrees in engineering science in 1965 and 1966, respectively, and subsequently performed pre-med course work; received a doctor of medicine degree from the University of Texas Southwestern Medical School in 1977.

ORGANIZATIONS: Member, American Institute of Aeronautics and Astronautics, Aerospace Medical Association, and Phi Kappa Phi.

SPECIAL HONORS: Awarded 11 Air Medals, the Navy Commendation Medal with Combat "V", the Marine Corps "E" Award, the Vietnam Service Medal, and the Vietnamese Cross of Gallantry with Palm.

EXPERIENCE: Dr. Thagard held a number of research and teaching posts while completing the academic requirements for various earned degrees.

In September 1966, he entered active duty with the United States Marine Corps Reserve. He achieved the rank of Captain in 1967, was designated a naval aviator in 1968, and was subsequently assigned to duty flying F-4s with VMFA-333 at Marine Corps Air Station, Beaufort, South Carolina. He flew 163 combat missions in Vietnam while assigned to VMFA-115 from January 1969 to 1970.

He returned to the United States and an assignment as aviation weapons division officer with VMFA-251 at the Marine Corps Air Station, Beaufort, South Carolina.

Thagard resumed his academic studies in 1971, pursuing additional studies in electrical engineering, and a degree in medicine; prior to coming to NASA, he was interning in the Department of Internal Medicine at the Medical University of South Carolina. He is a licensed physician.

He is a pilot and has logged over 2,200 hours flying time--the majority in jet aircraft.

NASA EXPERIENCE: Dr. Thagard was selected as an astronaut candidate by NASA in January 1978. In August 1979, he completed a one-year training and evaluation period, making him eligible for assignment as a mission specialist on future Space Shuttle flights. A veteran of five space flights, he has logged over 140 days in space. He was a mission specialist on on STS-7 in 1983, STS 51-B in 1985, STS-30 in 1989, was the payload commander on STS-42 in 1992, and was the cosmonaut/researcher on the Russian Mir 18 mission in 1995.

Dr. Thagard first flew on the crew of STS-7, which launched from Kennedy Space Center, Florida, on June 8, 1983. This was the second flight for the Orbiter Challenger and the first mission with a crew of five persons. During the mission, the STS-7 crew deployed satellites for Canada (ANIK C-2) and Indonesia (PALAPA B-1); operated the Canadian-built Remote Manipulator System (RMS) to perform the first deployment and retrieval exercise with the Shuttle Pallet Satellite (SPAS-01); conducted the first formation flying of the Orbiter with a free-flying satellite (SPAS-01); carried and operated the first U.S./German cooperative materials science payload (OSTA-2); and operated the Continuous Flow Electrophoresis System (CFES) and the Monodisperse Latex Reactor (MLR) experiments, in addition to activating seven "Getaway Specials." During the flight Dr. Thagard conducted various medical tests and collected data on physiological changes associated with astronaut adaptation to space. He also retrieved the rotating SPAS-01 using the RMS. Mission duration was 147 hours before landing at Edwards Air Force Base, California, on June 24, 1983.

Dr. Thagard then flew on STS 51-B, the Spacelab-3 science mission, which launched from Kennedy Space Center, Florida, on April 29, 1985, aboard the Challenger. He assisted the commander and pilot on ascent and entry. Mission duration was 168 hours. Duties on orbit included satellite deployment operation with the NUSAT satellite as well as animal care for the 24 rats and two squirrel monkeys contained in the Research Animal Holding Facility (RAHF). Other duties were operation of the Geophysical Fluid Flow Cell (GFFC), Urinary Monitoring System (UMS), and the Ionization States of Solar and Galactic Cosmic Ray Heavy Nuclei (IONS) experiment. After 110 orbits of the Earth, Challenger landed at Edwards Air Force Base, California, on May 6, 1985.

He next served on the crew of STS-30, which launched from Kennedy Space Center, Florida, on May 4, 1989, aboard the Orbiter Atlantis. During this four-day mission, crew members successfully deployed the Magellan Venus-exploration spacecraft, the first U.S. planetary science mission launched since 1978, and the first planetary probe to be deployed from the Shuttle. Magellan is scheduled to arrive at Venus in mid-1990 and will map the entire surface of Venus for the first time, using specialized radar instruments. In addition, crew members also worked on secondary payloads involving fluid research in general, chemistry and electrical storm studies. Mission duration was 97 hours. Following 64 orbits of the Earth, the STS-30 mission concluded with a landing at Edwards Air Force Base, California, on May 8, 1989.

Dr. Thagard served as payload commander on STS-42, aboard the Shuttle Discovery, which lifted off from the Kennedy Space Center, Florida, on January 22, 1992. Fifty five major experiments conducted in the International Microgravity Laboratory-1 module were provided by investigators from eleven countries, and represented a broad spectrum of scientific disciplines. During 128 orbits of the Earth, the STS-42 crew accomplished the mission's primary objective of investigating the effects of microgravity on materials processing and life sciences. In this unique laboratory in space, crew members worked around-the-clock in two shifts. Experiments investigated the microgravity effects on the growth of protein and semiconductor crystals. Biological experiments on the effects of zero gravity on plants, tissues, bacteria, insects and human vestibular response were also conducted. This eight-day mission culminated in a landing at Edwards Air Force Base, California, on January 30, 1992.

Most recently, Dr. Thagard was the cosmonaut/researcher for the Russian Mir 18 mission. Twenty eight experiments were conducted in the course of the 115 day flight. Liftoff was from the Baikonur Cosmodrome in Kazakstan on March 14, 1995. The mission culminated in a landing at the Kennedy Space Center in the Space Shuttle Atlantis on July 7, 1995.

With the completion of his fifth mission, Dr. Thagard has logged over 140 days in space.

NAME: Kathryn C. Thornton (Ph.D.)
NASA Astronaut (former)

PERSONAL DATA: Born August 17, 1952, in Montgomery, Alabama. Married to Stephen T. Thornton, Ph.D., of Oak Ridge, Tennessee. She has two stepsons and three daughters. She enjoys scuba diving and skiing. Her parents, Mr. William C. Cordell and Mrs. Elsie Cordell, are deceased. His mother, Mrs. Helen Lee Gardner, and his father, Mr. Barton Brown Thornton, are deceased.

EDUCATION: Graduated from Sidney Lanier High School, Montgomery, Alabama, in 1970; received a bachelor of science degree in physics from Auburn University in 1974, a master of science degree in physics from the University of Virginia in 1977, and a doctorate of philosophy in physics from the University of Virginia in 1979.

ORGANIZATIONS: Member of the American Physical Society, American Association for the Advancement of Science, Sigma Xi, Phi Kappa Phi, and Sigma Pi Sigma.

EXPERIENCE: After Dr. Thornton earned her Ph.D. at the University of Virginia in 1979, she was awarded a NATO Postdoctoral Fellowship to continue her research at the Max Planck Institute for Nuclear Physics in Heidelberg, West Germany. In 1980, she returned to Charlottesville, Virginia, where she was employed as a physicist at the U.S. Army Foreign Science and Technology Center.

NASA EXPERIENCE: Selected by NASA in May 1984, Dr. Thornton became an astronaut in July 1985. Her technical assignments have included flight software verification in the Shuttle Avionics Integration Laboratory (SAIL), serving as a team member of the Vehicle Integration Test Team (VITT) at KSC, and as a spacecraft communicator (CAPCOM). A veteran of three space flights, Dr. Thornton flew on STS-33 in 1989, STS-49 in 1992, and STS-61 in 1993. She has logged over 975 hours in space, including more than 21 hours of extravehicular activity (EVA).

Dr. Thornton was a mission specialist on the crew of STS-33 which launched at night from Kennedy Space Center, Florida, on November 22, 1989, aboard the Space Shuttle Discovery. The mission carried Department of Defense payloads and other secondary payloads. After 79 orbits of the Earth, this five-day mission concluded on November 27, 1989, at Edwards Air Force Base, California.

On her second flight, Dr. Thornton served on the crew of STS-49, May 7-16, 1992, on board the maiden flight of the new Space Shuttle Endeavour. During the mission the crew conducted the initial test flight of Endeavour, performed a record four EVA's (space walks) to retrieve, repair and deploy the International Telecommunications Satellite (INTELSAT), and to demonstrate and evaluate numerous EVA tasks to be used for the assembly of Space Station Freedom. Dr. Thornton was one of two EVA crew members who evaluated Space Station assembly techniques on the fourth EVA. STS-49 logged 213 hours in space and 141 Earth orbits prior to landing at Edwards Air Force Base, California.

On her third flight, Dr. Thornton was a mission specialist EVA crew member aboard the Space Shuttle Endeavour on the STS-61 Hubble Space Telescope (HST) servicing and repair mission. STS-61 launched at night from the Kennedy Space Center, Florida, on December 2, 1993. During the 11-day flight, the HST was captured and restored to full capacity through a record five space walks by four astronauts. After having travelled 4,433,772 miles in 163 orbits of the Earth, the crew of Endeavour returned to a night landing at the Kennedy Space Center on December 13, 1993.

From October 20 to November 5, 1995, Dr. Thornton served aboard Space Shuttle Columbia on STS-73, as the payload commander of the second United States Microgravity Laboratory mission. The mission focused on materials science, biotechnology, combustion science, the physics of fluids, and numerous scientific experiments housed in the pressurized Spacelab module. In completing her fourth space flight, Dr. Thornton orbited the Earth 256 times, traveled over 6 million miles, and logged a total of 15 days, 21 hours, 52 minutes and 21 seconds in space. Dr. Thornton has announced she will leave NASA on August 1, 1996, to join the faculty of the University of Virginia.

NAME: William Edgar Thornton (M.D.)
NASA Astronaut (former)

PERSONAL DATA: Born in Faison, North Carolina, on April 14, 1929. Married to the former Elizabeth Jennifer Fowler of Hertfordshire, England. They have two sons.

EDUCATION: Attended primary and secondary schools in Faison, North Carolina; received a bachelor of science degree in physics and a doctorate in medicine from the University of North Carolina in 1952 and 1963, respectively.

SPECIAL HONORS: Recipient of the Air Force Legion of Merit (1956); the NASA Exceptional Service Medal (1972); the NASA Exceptional Scientific Achievement Medal (1974); the American Astronautical Society's Melbourne W. Boynton Award for 1975 (1977); two NASA Space Flight Medals (1983, 1985); the University of North Carolina Distinguished Alumni Award (1983); the Aerospace Medical Association Randy Lovelace Award (1984); the AIAA Jeffries Medical Research Award (1985); the Association of Military Surgeons of the United States Kern Award (1986); the NASA Exceptional Engineering Achievement Award (1988).

EXPERIENCE: Following graduation from the University of North Carolina and having completed Air Force ROTC training, Thornton served as officer-in-charge of the Instrumentation Lab at the Flight Test Air Proving Ground. He later became a consultant to Air Proving Ground Command.

As chief engineer of the electronics division of the Del Mar Engineering Labs at Los Angeles from 1956 to 1959, he also organized and directed its Avionics Division. He returned to the University of North Carolina Medical School in 1959, graduated in 1963, and completed internship training in 1964 at the Wilford Hall USAF Hospital at Lackland Air Force Base, San Antonio, Texas.

Dr. Thornton returned to active duty with the United States Air Force and was then assigned to the USAF Aerospace Medical Division, Brooks Air Force Base, San Antonio, where he completed the Primary Flight Surgeon's training in 1964. It was during his two-year tour of duty there that he became involved in space medicine research and subsequently applied and was selected for astronaut training. Dr. Thornton developed and designed the first mass measuring devices for space, which remain in use today.

Dr. Thornton has logged over 2,500 hours pilot flying time in jet aircraft, is currently a Clinical Assistant Professor in the Department of Medicine, University of Texas Medical Branch, Galveston, Texas, and is an adjunct Professor at University of Houston, Clear Lake.

NASA EXPERIENCE: Dr. Thornton was selected as a scientist-astronaut by NASA in August 1967. He completed the required flight training at Reese Air Force Base, Texas. Dr. Thornton was physician crew member on the highly successful Skylab Medical Experiments Altitude Test (SMEAT) -- a 56-day simulation of a Skylab mission enabling crewmen to collect medical experiments baseline data and evaluate equipment, operations, and procedures. Dr. Thornton was also the mission specialist on SMD III, a simulation of a Spacelab life sciences mission.

Dr. Thornton was a member of the astronaut support crew for the Skylab 2, 3, and 4 missions, and principal investigator for Skylab experiments on mass measurement, anthropometric measurements, hemodynamics, and human fluid shifts and physical conditioning. He first documented the shift and loss of fluid changes in body posture size and shape, including increase in height and the rapid loss of muscle strength and mass in space flight.

As a member of the Astronaut Office Operations Missions Development group, Dr. Thornton was responsible for developing crew procedures and techniques for deployable payloads, and for maintenance of crew conditions in flight. He developed advanced techniques for, and made studies in, kinesiology and kinesimetry related to space operations.

During Space Shuttle operations he continued physiological investigations in the cardiovascular and musculoskeletal and neurological areas. He developed the Shuttle treadmill for in-flight exercise and several other on-board devices. His work concentrated on the space adaptation syndrome, with relevant investigations on STS-4, STS-5, STS-6, STS-7, and STS-8.

Dr. Thornton holds more than 35 issued patents that range from military weapons systems through the first real-time EKG computer analysis. Space-related items include the first in-flight mass measurement devices, shock and vibration isolation systems, an improved waste collection system, an improved lower body negative pressure (LBNP) apparatus, and others.

A veteran of two space flights, Dr. Thornton has logged over 313 hours in space. He served as a mission specialist on STS-8 in 1983, and STS-51B in 1985.

Dr. Thornton continued his work in space medicine while awaiting his next flight opportunity. He worked on problems relative to extending mission durations in the Space Shuttle, in Space Station, and in space exploration, and has designed the necessary exercise and other hardware to support such missions. He continued analysis and publication of results from studies of neurological adaptation, and the study of neuromuscular inhibition following flight, osteoporosis in space and on Earth, and postflight orthostasis. He has completed designs for exercise and other countermeasure equipment for the Extended Duration Orbiter (EDO), and for Space Station Freedom, including improved treadmills, rowing machines, isotonic exercise devices, and a bicycle. Much of this is currently scheduled for flight.

Dr. Thornton retired from NASA effective May 31, 1994.

SPACE FLIGHT EXPERIENCE: STS-8 Challenger (August 30 to September 5, 1983). This was the third flight for the Orbiter Challenger and the first mission with a night launch from Kennedy Space Center, Florida, and a night landing at Edwards Air Force Base, California. During the flight Dr. Thornton made almost continuous measurements and investigations of adaptation of the human body to weightlessness, especially of the nervous system and of the space adaptation syndrome. This was a continuation of his previous work in these areas. Much of the equipment used was designed and developed by Dr. Thornton. The mission was accomplished in 98 orbits of the Earth, traveling 2.2 million miles in 145 hours, 8 minutes, 4 seconds.

STS-51B/Spacelab-3 Challenger (April 29 to May 6, 1985). The Spacelab-3 science mission was launched from Kennedy Space Center, Florida, and returned to land at Edwards Air Force Base, California. During the 7-day flight, Dr. Thornton was responsible for the first animal payload in manned flight and other medical investigations. The mission was accomplished in 110 orbits of the Earth, traveling 2.9 million miles in 169 hours and 39 minutes.

NAME: Pierre J. Thuot (pronounced THOO-it) (Commander, USN)
NASA Astronaut (former)

PERSONAL DATA: Born May 19, 1955, in Groton, Connecticut, but considers Fairfax, Virginia, and New Bedford, Massachusetts, to be his hometowns. Married to the former Cheryl Ann Mattingly of Leonardtown, Maryland. They have two children. He enjoys golf, running, music, and family activities. His parents, Capt. & Mrs. Clifford G. Thuot, Sr., (USNR, Ret.), reside in Fairfax, Virginia. Her parents, Mr. & Mrs. Robert L. Mattingly, reside in Leonardtown, Maryland.

EDUCATION: Graduated from Fairfax High School, Fairfax, Virginia, in 1973; received a bachelor of science degree in physics from the U.S. Naval Academy in 1977, and a master of science degree in systems management from the University of Southern California in 1985.

ORGANIZATIONS: Member of the U.S. Naval Academy Alumni Association, the Association of Naval Aviation, the University of Southern California Alumni Association, the Association of Space Explorers-USA, the American Astronautical Society, and an Associate Fellow of the American Institute of Aeronautics and Astronautics.

SPECIAL HONORS: Two Defense Superior Service Medals, three NASA Space Flight Medals, two NASA Exceptional Service Medals the National Intelligence Medal of Achievement, the American Astronautical Society Flight Achievement and Victor A. Prather Awards for 1993, the National Defense Service Medal, two Navy Meritorious Unit Commendations, two Navy Battle Efficiency Awards, the Sea Service Deployment Ribbon, and seven NASA Group Achievement Awards.

EXPERIENCE: Thuot graduated 30th in his class from the U.S. Naval Academy in 1977 and commenced Naval Flight Officer training in July 1977. He received his wings in August 1978 and then reported to Fighter Squadron 101 at NAS Oceana, Virginia Beach, Virginia, for initial F-14 Tomcat training as a Radar Intercept Officer (RIO). Upon completion of this training he was assigned to Fighter Squadron 14 and made overseas deployments to the Mediterranean and Caribbean Seas aboard the USS John F. Kennedy and USS Independence. While assigned to Fighter Squadron 14 he attended the Navy Fighter Weapons School (TOPGUN). He was then selected to attend the U.S. Naval Test Pilot School in May 1982. Upon graduation in June 1983 he worked as a project test flight officer at the Naval Air Test Center flying the F-14A Tomcat, A-6E Intruder and the F-4J Phantom II until June 1984 when he returned to the U.S. Naval Test Pilot School as a flight instructor.

He has over 3,500 flight hours in more than 40 different aircraft, and has over 270 carrier landings.

NASA EXPERIENCE: Selected as an astronaut by NASA in June 1985, Thuot has served in a variety of technical assignments. As the Remote Manipulator System (robot arm), crew equipment, and Extravehicular Activity (EVA) representative for the Astronaut Office, he participated in the design, development, and evaluation of Space Shuttle payloads, crew equipment, and crew procedures. He performed Space Shuttle flight software verification in the Shuttle Avionics Integration Laboratory and served as a CAPCOM in the Mission Control Center, responsible for communications with the crew for numerous Space Shuttle missions. He served as the lead astronaut for Space Station integrated assembly and maintenance operations within the Astronaut Office. He served as Chief of the Astronaut Office Mission Support Branch, as well as supervising Astronaut Candidate training for the Class of 1995. A veteran of three space flights, STS-36 in 1990, STS-49 in 1992, and STS-62 in 1994, Thuot has logged over 654 hours in space, including 17.7 hours on three space walks.

On his first flight, Thuot was a mission specialist on the crew of STS-36 which launched from the Kennedy Space Center, Florida, on February 28, 1990, aboard the Space Shuttle Atlantis. This mission carried Department of Defense payloads and a number of secondary payloads. Following 72 orbits of the Earth in 106 hours, the STS-36 mission concluded with a lakebed landing at Edwards Air Force Base, California, on March 4, 1990, after traveling 1.87 million miles.

Thuot was a mission specialist on the crew of STS-49, the maiden voyage of the Space Shuttle Endeavour, which launched from the Kennedy Space Center on May 7, 1992. During that mission, Thuot, along with astronaut Rick Hieb, performed three space walks which resulted in the capture and repair of the stranded Intelsat VI F3 communications satellite. The third space walk, which also included astronaut Tom Akers, was the first ever three-person space walk. This 8 hour and 29 minute space walk, the longest in history, broke a twenty year old record that was held by Apollo 17 astronauts. The mission concluded on May 16, 1992 with a landing at Edwards Air Force Base after orbiting the Earth 141 times in 213 hours and traveling 3.7 million miles.

On March 4, 1994, Thuot launched aboard Columbia on STS-62, a microgravity science and technology demonstration mission which carried the United States Microgravity Payload (USMP-2) and the Office of Aeronautics and Space Technology (OAST-2) payloads. More than sixty experiments or investigations were conducted in many scientific and engineering disciplines including materials science, human physiology, biotechnology, protein crystal growth, robotics, structural dynamics, atmospheric ozone monitoring, and spacecraft glow. During the spacecraft glow investigation, Columbia's orbital altitude was lowered to 105 nautical miles, the lowest ever flown by a Space Shuttle. STS-62, one of the longest Space Shuttle missions, concluded on March 18, 1994 with a landing at the Kennedy Space Center after orbiting the Earth 224 times in 13 days, 23 hours, and 16 minutes and traveling 5.8 million miles.

With the completion of his third mission, Thuot has logged over 654 hours in space, including over 17.7 hours on three space walks.

Thuot left NASA in June 1995, and returned to the Navy. He is an Associate Chairman in the Aerospace Engineering Department, United States Naval Academy, Annapolis, Maryland.

NAME: Richard Harrison Truly (Admiral, USN)
NASA Astronaut (former)

PERSONAL DATA: Born November 12, 1937, in Fayette, Mississippi.

EDUCATION: Received bachelor of aeronautical engineering degree from the Georgia Institute of Technology (1959).

MARITAL STATUS: Married.

CHILDREN: Three.

NASA EXPERIENCE: Was selected for the MOL program in 1965, and transferred to the NASA astronaut group in 1969. He was a member of the astronaut support crew for Skylab 2, 3, and 4; and the Apollo-Soyuz Test Project; and was assigned to space shuttle development. He was a member of one of the two shuttle approach and landing test crews and was the pilot on the STS-2 flight, and commander for STS-8. Admiral Truly was commander of Naval Space Command before becoming the current Administrator of NASA (1991).

NAME: James D. A. (nickname "Ox") van Hoften (Ph.D.)
NASA Astronaut (former)

PERSONAL DATA: Born June 11, 1944, in Fresno, California, but considers Burlingame, California, to be his hometown. Married. Three children. He enjoys skiing, playing handball and racquetball, and jogging.

EDUCATION: Graduated from Mills High School, Millbrae, California, in 1962; received a bachelor of science degree in Civil Engineering from the University of California, Berkeley, in 1966; and a master of science degree in Hydraulic Engineering and a doctor of philosophy in Hydraulic Engineering from Colorado State University in 1968 and 1976, respectively.

ORGANIZATIONS: Member of the American Institute of Aeronautics and Astronautics (AIAA), Sigma Xi, Chi Epsilon, and Pi Kappa Alpha.

SPECIAL HONORS: Meritorious Service Medal, 2 Navy Air Medals, National Defense Service Medal, Vietnam Service Medal, and 2 NASA Space Flight Medals.

EXPERIENCE: From 1969 to 1974, van Hoften was a pilot in the United States Navy. He received flight training at Pensacola, Florida, and completed jet pilot training at Beeville, Texas, in November 1970. He was then assigned to the Naval Air Station, Miramar, California, to fly F-4 Phantoms, and subsequently to VF-121 Replacement Air Group. As a pilot with VF-154 assigned to the carrier USS RANGER in 1972, van Hoften participated in two cruises to Southeast Asia where he flew approximately 60 combat missions. He resumed his academic studies in 1974 and completed a dissertation on the interaction of waves and turbulent channel flow for his doctorate. In September 1976, he accepted an assistant professorship of Civil Engineering at the University of Houston, and until his selection as an astronaut candidate, taught fluid mechanics and conducted research on biomedical fluid flows concerning flows in artificial internal organs and valves. Dr. van Hoften has published a number of papers on turbulence, waves, and cardiovascular flows. From 1977 until 1980 he flew F4N's with Naval Reserve Fighter Squadron 201 at NAS Dallas and then three years as a member of the Texas Air National Guard with the 147th Fighter Interceptor Group as a pilot in the F4C.

He has logged 3,300 hours flying time, the majority in jet aircraft.

NASA EXPERIENCE: Dr. van Hoften was selected as an astronaut candidate by NASA in January 1978. He completed a 1-year training and evaluation period in August 1979.

From 1979 through the first flight, STS-1, van Hoften supported the Shuttle entry and on-orbit guidance, navigation and flight control testing at the Flight Systems Laboratory at Downey, California. Subsequently he was lead of the Astronaut Support Team at Kennedy Space Center, Florida, responsible for the Space Shuttle turn-around testing and flight preparations. He served as a mission specialist on STS-41C in 1984, and STS-51I in 1985. Dr. Van Hoften has logged a total 338 hours in space, including 22 hours of EVA flight time.

POST-NASA: Dr. van Hoften joined the Bechtel Corporation in 1986 and for 6 years managed Bechtel's engineering and construction business for the defense and space markets. He is currently Senior Vice President and a partner in Bechtel and is presently located in Hong Kong as project manager for the New Hong Kong Airport and Related Infrastructure program.

SPACE FLIGHT EXPERIENCE: STS-41C Challenger (April 6-13, 1984) was launched from the Kennedy Space Center, Florida, and returned to land at Edwards Air Force Base, California. During the 7-day mission the crew successfully deployed the Long Duration Exposure Facility (LDEF); retrieved the ailing Solar Maximum Satellite, repaired it on-board the orbiting Challenger and replaced it in orbit, using the robot arm called the Remote Manipulator System (RMS). The mission also included flight testing of Manned Maneuvering Units (MMU's) in two extravehicular activities (EVA's); operation of the Cinema 360 and IMAX Camera Systems, as well as a Bee Hive Honeycomb Structures student experiment. Mission accomplished in 107 Earth orbits in 167 hours, 40 minutes, 7 seconds.

STS-51I Discovery (August 27 to September 3, 1985) launched from the Kennedy Space Center, Florida, and returned to land at Edwards Air Force Base, California. During this mission the crew successfully deployed three communications satellites, the Navy's Syncom IV-4, Australian Aussat, and American Satellite Company's ASC-1. The crew also performed the successful salvage of the ailing Navy Syncom IV-3 satellite. These tasks included two Extravehicular Activities (EVA's) in which Dr. van Hoften attached to the Remote Manipulator System (RMS) performed the first manual grapple and manual deployment of a satellite in orbit. The mission also included the Physical Vapor Transport of Organic Solids (PVTOS), the second material processing experiment to be flown aboard a Shuttle for 3M. Mission accomplished in 112 orbits of the Earth in 171 hours, 17 minutes, 42 seconds.

NAME: David M. Walker (Captain, USN, Ret.)
NASA Astronaut (former)

PERSONAL DATA: Born May 20, 1944, in Columbus, Georgia. He is married to the former Paige Lucas and has two sons from a previous marriage.

EDUCATION: Graduated from Eustis High School, Eustis, Florida, in 1962; received a bachelor of science degree from the United States Naval Academy in 1966.

SPECIAL HONORS: Awarded the Defense Superior Service Medal, the Distinguished Flying Cross, the National Intelligence Medal of Achievement, the Legion of Merit, two Defense Meritorious Service Medals, six Navy Air Medals, the Battle Efficiency Ribbon, the Armed Forces Expeditionary Medal, the National Defense Service Medal, two NASA Distinguished Service Medals, the NASA Outstanding Leadership Medal, four NASA Space Flight Medals, the Vietnamese Cross of Gallantry, the Vietnam Service Medal, and the Republic of Vietnam Campaign Medal.

ORGANIZATIONS: Associate Fellow of the Society of Experimental Test Pilots. Senior Member of the American Institute of Aeronautics and Astronautics. Member of the Naval Academy Alumni Association, and the Eagle Scout Association.

EXPERIENCE: Walker was graduated from Annapolis and subsequently received flight training from the Naval Aviation Training Command at bases in Florida, Mississippi, and Texas. He was designated a naval aviator in December 1967 and proceeded to Naval Air Station Miramar, California, for assignment to F-4 Phantoms aboard the carriers USS Enterprise and USS America. From December 1970 to 1971, he attended the USAF Aerospace Research Pilot School at Edwards Air Force Base, California, and was subsequently assigned in January 1972 as an experimental and engineering test pilot in the flight test division at the Naval Air Test Center, Patuxent River, Maryland. While there, he participated in the Navy's preliminary evaluation and Board of Inspection and Survey trials of the F-14 Tomcat and tested a leading edge slat modification to the F-4 Phantom. He then attended the U.S. Navy Safety Officer School at Monterey, California, and completed replacement pilot training in the F-14 Tomcat at Naval Air Station Miramar, California. In 1975, Walker was assigned to Fighter Squadron 142, stationed at Naval Air Station Oceana, Virginia, as a fighter pilot and was deployed to the Mediterranean Sea twice aboard the USS America.

He has logged more than 7500 hours flying time--over 6500 hours in jet aircraft.

NASA EXPERIENCE: Selected by NASA in January 1978, Walker became an astronaut in August 1979. Among his technical assignments he served as Astronaut Office Safety Officer; Deputy Chief of Aircraft Operations; STS-1 chase pilot; software verification at the Shuttle Avionics Integration Laboratory (SAIL); mission support group leader for STS-5 and STS-6; Assistant to the Director, Flight Crew Operations; leader of the astronaut support crew at Kennedy Space Center; Branch Chief, Space Station Design and Development; and Special Manager for Assembly, Space Station Project Office. From July 1993 to June 1994, Walker was Chief of the Station/Exploration Support Office, Flight Crew Operations Directorate, after which he chaired the JSC Safety Review Board.

A veteran of four space flights, Walker has logged over 724 hours in space. He was the pilot on STS 51-A in 1984, and was the mission commander on STS-30 in 1989, STS-53 in 1992 and STS-69 in 1995.

Walker left NASA in April 1996 to become Vice President, Sales & Marketing, for NDC Voice Corporation in Southern California.

SPACE FLIGHT EXPERIENCE: STS 51-A Discovery (November 8-16, 1984) was launched from and returned to land at Kennedy Space Center, Florida.. During the mission the crew deployed two satellites, Canada's Anik D-2 (Telesat H), and Hughes' LEASAT-1 (Syncom IV-1). In the first space salvage mission in history the crew also retrieved for return to Earth the Palapa B-2 and Westar VI satellites. Mission duration was 127 Earth orbits in 7 days, 23 hours, 44 minutes, 56 seconds.

STS-30 Atlantis (May 4-8, 1989) was launched from Kennedy Space Center, Florida. During the 4-day mission the crew successfully deployed the Magellan Venus-exploration spacecraft, the first U.S. planetary science mission launched since 1978, and the first planetary probe to be deployed from the Shuttle. Magellan arrived at Venus in August 1990, and mapped over 95% of the surface of Venus. In addition, the crew also worked on secondary payloads involving fluid research in general, chemistry, and electrical storm studies. Following 64 orbits of the Earth, the STS-30 mission concluded with the first cross-wind landing test of the Shuttle Orbiter at Edwards Air Force Base, California.

STS-53 Discovery (December 2-9, 1992) was launched from the Kennedy Space Center, Florida, and also returned to land at Edwards Air Force Base, California. During 115 Earth orbits the five-man crew deployed a classified Department of Defense payload DOD-1 and then performed several Military-Man-in-Space and NASA experiments. Mission duration was 175 hours, 19 minutes, 17 seconds.

STS-69 Endeavour (September 7-18, 1995) was launched from and returned to land at Kennedy Space Center, Florida. During the mission the crew successfully deployed and retrieved a SPARTAN satellite and the Wake Shield Facility. Also on board was the International Extreme Ultraviolet Hitchhiker payload, and numerous secondary payloads and medical experiments. Mission duration was 10-days, 20 hours, 28 minutes.

NAME: Paul J. Weitz (pronounced WHITES) (Mr.)
NASA Astronaut (former)

PERSONAL DATA: Born in Erie, Pennsylvania, on July 25, 1932. Married to the former Suzanne M. Berry of Harborcreek, Pennsylvania. Two children: Matthew and Cynthia. Hunting and fishing are among his hobbies. His mother, Mrs. Violet Futrell, now resides in Norfolk, Virginia.

EDUCATION: Graduated from Harborcreek High School in Harborcreek, Pennsylvania; received a bachelor of science degree in aeronautical engineering from Pennsylvania State University in 1954 and a master's degree in aeronautical engineering from the U.S. Naval Postgraduate School in Monterey, California, in 1964.

ORGANIZATIONS: Fellow, American Astronautical Association.

SPECIAL HONORS: Awarded the NASA Distinguished Service Medal, the Navy Distinguished Service Medal, Astronaut Wings, Air Medal (5 awards), and Commendation Medal (for combat flights in Vietnam), the Los Angeles Chamber of Commerce Kitty Hawk Award (1973), the Robert J. Collier Trophy for 1973 (1974), the Pennsylvania State University Alumni Association's Distinguished Alumni Award, named a Pennsylvania State University Alumni Fellow (1974), the AIAA Haley Astronautics Award for 1974, the Federation Aeronautique Internationale's V. M. Komarov Diploma for 1973 (1974), the Dr. Robert H. Goddard Memorial Trophy for 1975, the 1974 Harmon International Aviation Trophy for Astronaut (1975), NASA Space Flight Medal (1983), the 1984 Harmon International Award (1989).

EXPERIENCE: Weitz received his commission as an ensign through the NROTC program at Pennsylvania State University. He served for one year at sea aboard a destroyer before going to flight training and was awarded his wings in September 1956. He served in various naval squadrons until he was selected as an astronaut in 1966. He has logged more than 7,700 hours flying time--6,400 hours in jet aircraft.

NASA EXPERIENCE: Mr. Weitz is one of the 19 astronauts selected by NASA in April 1966. He served as pilot on the crew of Skylab-2 (SL-2), which launched on May 25 and ended on June 22, 1973. SL-2 was the first manned Skylab mission, and activated a 28-day flight. In logging 672 hours and 49 minutes aboard the orbital workshop, the crew established what was then a new world record for a single mission. Mr. Weitz also logged 2 hours and 11 minutes in extravehicular activities.

Mr. Weitz was spacecraft commander on the crew of STS-6, which launched from Kennedy Space Center, Florida, on April 4, 1983. This was the maiden voyage of the Orbiter Challenger. During the mission, the crew conducted numerous experiments in materials processing, recorded lightning activities, deployed IUS/TDRS-A, conducted spectacular extravehicular activity while testing a variety of support systems and equipment in preparation for future space walks, and also carried three "Getaway Specials." Mission duration was 120 hours before landing Challenger on a concrete runway at Edwards Air Force Base, California, on April 9, 1983. With the completion of this flight, Paul Weitz logged a total of 793 hours in space.

Mr. Weitz was Deputy Director of the Johnson Space Center when he retired from NASA service in May 1994.

NAME: Donald E. Williams (Captain, USN, Ret.)
   NASA Astronaut (former)

PERSONAL DATA: Born February 13, 1942, in Lafayette, Indiana. Married. Two children. He enjoys all sports activities and his interests also include running and photography.

EDUCATION: Graduated from Otterbein High School, Otterbein, Indiana, in 1960; received a bachelor of science degree in Mechanical Engineering from Purdue University in 1964.

ORGANIZATIONS: Society of Experimental Test Pilots, the Association of Space Explorers, and the National Aeronautic Association.

SPECIAL HONORS: Awarded the Legion of Merit, Distinguished Flying Cross, Defense Superior Service Medal, 2 Navy Commendation Medals with Combat V, 2 Navy Unit Commendations, a Meritorious Unit Commendation, the National Defense Medal, an Armed Forces Expeditionary Medal, the NASA Outstanding Leadership Medal, the NASA Space Flight Medal, the NASA Exceptional Service Medal, the Vietnam Service Medal (with 4 stars), a Vietnamese Gallantry Cross (with gold star), and the Vietnam Campaign Medal.

EXPERIENCE: Williams received his commission through the NROTC program at Purdue University. He completed flight training at Pensacola, Florida; Meridian, Mississippi; and Kingsville, Texas, receiving his wings in May 1966. After A-4 training, he made two Vietnam deployments aboard the USS ENTERPRISE with Attack Squadron 113. He served as a flight instructor in Attack Squadron 125 at Naval Air Station Lemoore, California, for 2 years and transitioned to A-7 aircraft. He made two additional Vietnam deployments aboard the USS ENTERPRISE with CVW-14 staff and Attack Squadron 97. Williams completed a total of 330 combat missions.

In 1973, Williams attended the Armed Forces Staff college. He graduated from the U.S. Naval Test Pilot School at Patuxent River, Maryland, in June 1974, and was assigned to the Naval Air Test Center's Carrier Suitability Branch of Flight Test Division. From August 1976 to June 1977, following reorganization of the Naval Air Test Center, he was head of the Carrier Systems Branch, Strike Aircraft Test Directorate. He reported next for A-7 refresher training and was assigned to Attack Squadron 94 when selected by NASA. He has logged more than 6,000 hours flying time, which includes 5,700 hours in jets and 745 carrier landings.

NASA EXPERIENCE: Selected by NASA in January 1978, Williams became an astronaut in August 1979, qualified for assignment as a pilot on future Space Shuttle flight crews. Since then he has had various support assignments, including working at the Shuttle Avionics Integration Laboratory as a test pilot, and at the Kennedy Space Center participating in Orbiter test, checkout, launch and landing operations.

From September 1982 through July 1983, he was assigned as the Deputy Manager, Operations Integration, National Space Transportation System Program Office at the Johnson Space Center. From July 1985 through August 1986, Williams was the Deputy Chief of the Aircraft Operations Division at the Johnson Space Center, and from September 1986 through December 1988, he served as Chief of the Mission Support Branch within the Astronaut Office. Twice flown, Williams served as pilot on STS-51D in 1985, and was the spacecraft commander on STS-34 in 1989. He has logged a total of 287 hours and 35 minutes in space.

In March 1990, Williams retired from the U.S. Navy and left NASA. He is currently a Division Manager with Science Applications International Corporation, working on several projects in the Houston area, nationally, and internationally.

SPACE FLIGHT EXPERIENCE: STS-51D Discovery (April 12-19, 1985) was launched from and returned to land at the Kennedy Space Center, Florida. During the mission, the crew deployed ANIK-C for Telesat of Canada, and Syncom IV-3 for the U.S. Navy. A malfunction in the Syncom spacecraft resulted in the first unscheduled EVA, rendezvous and proximity operations for the Space Shuttle in an attempt to activate the satellite. Additional, the crew also conducted several medical experiments, two student experiments, activated two Getaway Specials, and filmed experiments with toys in space. The mission was accomplished in 109 orbits of the Earth in 167 hours, 54 minutes.

STS-34 Atlantis (October 18-23, 1989) was launched from Kennedy Space Center, Florida and returned to land at Edwards Air Force Base, California. During the mission the crew successfully deployed the Galileo spacecraft, starting its journey to explore Jupiter, operated the Shuttle Solar Backscatter Ultraviolet Instrument (SSBUV) to map atmospheric ozone, and performed numerous secondary experiments involving radiation measurements, polymer morphology, lightning research, microgravity effects on plants, and a student experiment on ice crystal growth in space. The mission was accomplished in 79 orbits of the Earth in 119 hours, 41 minutes.

NAME: Alfred Merrill Worden (Colonel, USAF, Retired)
NASA Astronaut (former)

PERSONAL DATA: The son of Merrill and Helen Worden, he was born in Jackson, Michigan, on February 7, 1932. His mother resides in West Palm Beach, Florida.

PHYSICAL DESCRIPTION: Brown hair; blue eyes; height: 5 feet 10-1/2 inches; weight: 160 pounds.

EDUCATION: Attended Dibble, Griswold, Bloomfield, and East Jackson grade schools and completed his secondary education at Jackson High School; received a bachelor of military science degree from the United States Military Academy in 1955 and master of science degrees in Astronautical/Aeronautical Engineering and Instrumentation Engineering from the University of Michigan in 1963.

MARITAL STATUS: Single.

CHILDREN: Merrill E., January 16, 1958; Allison P., April 6, 1960.

RECREATIONAL INTERESTS: Enjoys bowling, water skiing, swimming, and handball.

SPECIAL HONORS: Recipient of the Air Force Command Pilot Astronaut Wings.

EXPERIENCE: Worden, an Air Force Lt. Colonel, graduated from the U. S. Military Academy in June 1955 and, after being commissioned in the Air Force, received flight training at Moore Air Base, Texas; Laredo Air Force Base, Texas; and Tyndall Air Force Base, Florida. Prior to his arrival for duty at the Johnson Space Center (formerly the Manned Spacecraft Center), he served as an instructor at the Aerospace Research Pilots School, from which he graduated in September 1965. He is also a graduate of the Empire Test Pilots School in Farnborough, England, having completed training there in February 1965.

He attended Randolph Air Force Base Instrument Pilots Instructor School in 1963 and served as a pilot and armament officer from March 1957 to May 1961 with the 95th Fighter Interceptor Squadron at Andrews Air Force Base, Maryland.

He has logged more than 3,840 hours flying time, including 2,500 hours in jets.

Worden was one of the 19 astronauts selected by NASA in April 1966. He served as a member of the astronaut support crew for the Apollo 9 flight and as backup command module pilot for the Apollo 12 flight.

Worden served as command module pilot for Apollo 15, July 26 - August 7, 1971. His companions on the flight were David R. Scott, spacecraft commander, and James B. Irwin, lunar module commander. Apollo 15 was the fourth manned lunar landing mission and the first to visit and explore the moon's Hadley Rille and Apennene Mountains which are located on the southeast edge of the Mare Imbrium (Sea of Rains). Apollo 15 achievements include the largest payloads placed in earth and lunar orbits; first scientific instrument module bay flown and operated on an Apollo spacecraft; longest lunar surface stay time (the lunar module Falcon remained on ground for 66 hours and 54 minutes); longest lunar surface EVA (Scott and Irwin logged 18 hours and 35 minutes each during three excursions onto the lunar surface); longest distance traversed on lunar surface; first use of lunar roving vehicle; first use of a lunar surface navigation device (mounted on Rover-I); first subsatellite launched in lunar orbit; and first EVA from a command module during transearth coast.

Scott and Irwin collected approximately 171 pounds of lunar surface materials on their three expeditions onto the lunar surface; and Worden logged 38 minutes in extravehicular activity outside the command module Endeavour. In completing his three excursions to Endeavour's scientific instrument module bay, Worden retrieved film cassettes from the panoramic and mapping cameras and reported his personal observations of the general condition of equipment housed there.

Apollo 15 concluded with a Pacific splashdown and subsequent recovery by the USS OKINAWA. In completing his first space flight, Worden logged 295 hours and 11 minutes in space.

He was designated backup command module pilot for the Apollo 17 mission.

During 1972-1973, Worden was Senior Aerospace Scientist at the NASA Ames Research Center, and from 1973 to 1975, he was chief of Systems Studies Division at Ames.

Worden is currently president, Alfred M. Worden, Inc., an energy management services company, subsidiary of Bowmar Instrument Corporation, Palm Beach, Florida; director, Energy Management Programs, Northwood Institute, Midland, Michigan, and vice president, High Flight Foundation, Colorado Springs, Colorado.

Chapter Four:

NASA

Astronaut

Candidates

NAME: Dominic A. Antonelli (Lieutenant Commander, USN)
NASA Astronaut Candidate (Pilot)

PERSONAL DATA: Born in Detroit, Michigan. Raised in Indiana and North Carolina. Married to the former Janeen Rose Steves of Puyallup, Washington. Expecting their first child in May 2001. NASCAR enthusiast whose recreational interests include swimming, hiking, snow boarding, kayaking, and boat building.

EDUCATION: Graduated from Douglas Byrd High School, Fayetteville, NC, 1985. B.S., Aeronautics & Astronautics, Massachusetts Institute of Technology, 1989. M.S., Aeronautics & Astronautics, University of Washington, 2000 (expected).

ORGANIZATIONS: Graduated from Douglas Byrd High School, Fayetteville, North Carolina, 1985. Bachelor of science degree in Aeronautical & Astronautical Engineering from Massachusetts Institute of Technology, 1989.

SPECIAL HONORS: Navy Achievement Medals (2), Unit Battle Efficiency Awards (2), CVW-9 Landing Signal Officer of the Year (1996), and various service awards.

EXPERIENCE: Antonelli has accumulated over 1900 hours in 39 different kinds of aircraft and has completed 273 carrier arrested landings. He is a Distinguished Graduate of the U.S. Air Force Test Pilot School (Navy Exchange Pilot, Class 97B).

Antonelli earned the designation of Naval Aviator in May 1991. During his tenure as a fleet Navy pilot, Antonelli served aboard the aircraft carrier USS Nimitz with the Blue Diamonds, Strike Fighter Squadron 146, flying F/A-18C Hornets in support of Operation Southern Watch (1996). He earned a Wing Qualification as a Landing Signal Officer (LSO) and served as the Global Positioning System (GPS) Subject Matter Expert for Carrier Air Wing Nine during his tour.

As a Navy test pilot, Antonelli participated in the development and flight testing of Weapons System Integration Software for the F/A-18 for the Advanced Weapons Lab (China Lake, California). He has flown test flights for various projects including radar systems, air-to-air weapons and targeting systems, and air-to-ground targeting systems of the Hornet.

At the time of his selection to the astronaut program, Antonelli was completing final preparations for his return to fleet operations with Strike Fighter Squadron 195 in Atsugi, Japan.

NASA EXPERIENCE: Selected by NASA in July 2000, Antonelli reported for training in August 2000. Astronaut Candidate Training includes orientation briefings and tours, numerous scientific and technical briefings, intensive instruction in Shuttle and International Space Station systems, physiological training and ground school to prepare for T-38 flight training, as well as learning water and wilderness survival techniques. Following initial training, he will serve in technical assignments until assigned to a space flight.

NAME: Michael Reed Barratt (M.D.)
NASA Astronaut Candidate (Mission Specialist)

PERSONAL DATA: Born on April 16, 1959 in Vancouver, Washington. Considers Camas, Washington, to be his home town. Married to the former Michelle Lynne Sasynuik. They have four children. His father and mother, Joseph and Donna Barratt, reside in Camas, Washington. Personal and recreational interests include family and church activities, writing, sailing, boat restoration and maintenance, aikido, and international space activities. Certified open water diver and private pilot.

EDUCATION: Graduated from Camas High School, Camas, WA, 1977. B.S., Zoology, University of Washington, 1981. M.D., Northwestern University, 1985. Completed three year residency in Internal Medicine at Northwestern University 1988, completed Chief Residency year at Veterans Administration Lakeside Hospital in Chicago, 1989; Completed residency and Master's program in Aerospace Medicine, Wright State University, 1991. Board certified in Internal and Aerospace Medicine.

ORGANIZATIONS: Aerospace Medical Association; American College of Physicians; American Institute for Aeronautics and Astronautics; Alpha Omega Alpha Medical Honor Society; American Institute for the Advancement of Science; Aikido Association of America; Aircraft Owners and Pilot's Association.

SPECIAL HONORS: JSC Certificate of Commendation (1998); W. Randolph Lovelace Award (1998), Society of NASA Flight Surgeons; Rotary National Award for Space Achievement Foundation Nominee (1998); Melbourne W. Boynton Award (1995), American Astronautical Society; USAF Flight Surgeons Julian Ward Award (1992); Aerospace Medical Association Young Investigator Certificate of Merit (1992); Undersea and Hyperbaric Medical Society Edgar End Award (1992); Wright State University Outstanding Graduate Student, Aerospace Medicine (1991); Alpha Omega Alpha Medical Honor Society, Northwestern University Medical School, Chicago, IL (1988); Phi Beta Kappa, University of Washington, Seattle, WA (1981); Excellence in Experimental Biology Award, University of Washington, Seattle, WA (1981); Mortar Board National Collegiate Honor Society, University of Washington, Seattle, WA (1980); Mark Reed Academic Scholarship, University of Washington, Seattle, WA; Valedictorian, Camas High School, Camas, Washington (1977).

EXPERIENCE: Dr. Barratt came to NASA JSC in May 1991 employed as aerospace project physician with KRUG Life Sciences. From May 91 to July 92, he served on the Health Maintenance Facility Project as manager of the Hyperbaric and Respiratory Subsystems for Space Station Freedom. He was involved in development of on-orbit treatment capability for space decompression disorders and advanced life support protocols for the microgravity environment. In July 92 he was assigned as NASA Flight Surgeon working in Space Shuttle Medical Operations. In January 94 he was assigned to the joint US/Russian Space Program. He spent over 12 months onsite working and training in the Cosmonaut Training Center, Star City, Russia in support of the Mir-18 / STS-71 mission. From July 95 through July 98, he served as Medical Operations Lead for the International Space Station (ISS). Activities included drafting ISS Medical Operations requirements, revising and coordinating ISS medical standards among international partner participants, medical hardware development and evaluation for ISS. A frequent traveler to Russia, he worked with counterparts at the Gagarin Cosmonaut Training Center and Institute of Biomedical Problems, as well as other International Partner centers. Dr. Barratt served as lead crew surgeon for first expedition crew to ISS from July 98 until selected as an astronaut candidate.

NASA EXPERIENCE: Selected by NASA in July 2000, Dr. Barratt reported for training in August 2000. Astronaut Candidate Training includes orientation briefings and tours, numerous scientific and technical briefings, intensive instruction in Shuttle and International Space Station systems, physiological training and ground school to prepare for T-38 flight training, as well as learning water and wilderness survival techniques. Following initial training, he will serve in technical assignments until assigned to a space flight.

NAME: Robert L. Behnken (Ph.D., Captain, USAF)
NASA Astronaut Candidate (Mission Specialist)

PERSONAL DATA: Born on July 28, 1970 in Creve Coeur Missouri, but considers St. Ann, Missouri his hometown. Recreational Interests include mountain biking, skiing, and backpacking. He has a younger sister who resides in Hazelwood Missouri with her husband and two children. His father resides in St. Ann Missouri.

EDUCATION: Pattonville High School, Maryland Heights, Missouri, 1988. B.S. Mechanical Engineering, Washington University, 1992. B.S. Physics, Washington University, 1992. M.S. Mechanical Engineering, California Institute of Technology, 1993. Ph.D. Mechanical Engineering, California Institute of Technology, 1997.

SPECIAL HONORS: Outstanding Mechanical Engineering Senior, Washington University (1992); National Science Foundation Graduate Research Fellow (1993-1996); Air Force Research Laboratory Munitions Directorate, Eglin AFB Florida Company Grade Officer of the Year (1997); United States Air Force Achievement Medal (1997); United States Air Force Commendation Medal (1998); Distinguished graduate from the United States Air Force Test Pilot School Program. Recipient of the United States Air Force Test Pilot School Colonel Ray Jones Award as the top Flight Test Engineer/ Flight Test Navigator in class 98B.

EXPERIENCE: Graduate Research in Nonlinear control. Dr. Behnken's thesis research was in the area of nonlinear control applied to stabilizing rotating stall and surge in axial flow compressors. The project used phased air injection to eliminate rotating stall and a bleed valve actuator to stabilize the surge phenomenon. The research included nonlinear analysis, real-time software implementation development, and extensive hardware construction. During his first two years of graduate study, Dr. Behnken developed and implemented real-time control algorithms and hardware for flexible robotic manipulators.

Prior to entering graduate school, Behnken was an Air Force ROTC scholarship student at Washington University in St. Louis, and after graduate school was assigned to enter Air Force active duty at Eglin Air Force Base, Florida, as a developmental engineer in the Air Force Research Laboratory. While at Eglin, he worked both as a technical manager for the development of new munitions guidance algorithms and a flight test manager leading an effort to collect standardized data with a set of new munitions sensor systems. He was also a technical advisor for micro-electro-mechanical-systems development.

Behnken was next assigned to attend the Air Force Test Pilot School Flight Test Engineer's course at Edwards Air Force Base, California. After graduating, he was assigned to the F-22 Combined Test Force (CTF) and remained at Edwards. While assigned to the F-22 program, Behnken was the lead flight test engineer for Raptor 4004 and a special projects test director. Raptor 4004 is the first production representative F-22 avionics test aircraft, and Behnken was responsible for ensuring that the CTF at Edwards would be prepared to flight test that aircraft after it's arrival from Lockheed in Marietta, Georgia. These responsibilities included flight test sortie planning, control room configuration development, and test conduct. Behnken also flew in both the F-15 and F-16 aircraft in support of the F-22 flight test program. Captain Behnken has nearly 200 flight hours in more than 25 different aircraft types.

NASA EXPERIENCE: Selected by NASA in July 2000, Captain Behnken reported for training in August 2000. Astronaut Candidate Training includes orientation briefings and tours, numerous scientific and technical briefings, intensive instruction in Shuttle and International Space Station systems, physiological training and ground school to prepare for T-38 flight training, as well as learning water and wilderness survival techniques. Following initial training, he will serve in technical assignments until assigned to a space flight.

NAME: Eric A. Boe (Major, USAF)
NASA Astronaut Candidate (Pilot)

PERSONAL DATA: Born October 1, 1964, in Miami, Florida. He grew up in Atlanta, Georgia. Married to the former Kristen Newman of Thousand Oaks, California. They have two children. He enjoys outdoor sports, reading, scuba diving, and skiing.

EDUCATION: Graduated from Henderson High School, Chamblee, Georgia, 1983. Bachelor of Science in Astronautical Engineering, United States Air Force Academy, 1987. Master of Science in Electrical Engineering, Georgia Institute of Technology, 1997.

ORGANIZATIONS: Member of the Society of Experimental Test Pilots, and Civil Air Patrol.

SPECIAL HONORS: Distinguished Graduate from the United States Air Force Academy, 1987. Awarded the Fannie and John Hertz Foundation Fellowship for graduate studies, 1987. Military decorations include the Meritorious Service Medal, Air Medal (2), Aerial Achievement Medal (3), the Commendation Medal (3), Achievement Medal, Outstanding Unit Award (3), Combat Readiness Medal, and various other service awards.

EXPERIENCE: Boe was commissioned from the Air Force Academy in 1987. He completed Euro-NATO Joint Jet Pilot Training at Sheppard Air Force Base (AFB), Texas, in 1988. He was then assigned to the 3rd Tactical Fighter Squadron, Clark Air Base, Philippines as a combat ready pilot in the F-4E. In 1991, he served as a T-38 instructor pilot in the 50th Flying Training Squadron, and as an AT-38B instructor pilot in the 49th Fighter Squadron at Columbus AFB, Mississippi. In 1994, he was assigned to the 60th Fighter Squadron, Eglin AFB, Florida serving as an F-15C flight commander. In 1997, he attended the USAF Test Pilot School at Edwards AFB, California. After graduation, he was assigned as the Director of Test, Air-to-Air Missile Test Division, 46th Test Wing, Eglin AFB, Florida where he served as a test pilot flying the F-15A-E and the UH-1N. He has logged over 3,000 flight hours in more than 40 different aircraft.

NASA EXPERIENCE: Selected by NASA in July 2000, Boe reported to the Johnson Space Center in August 2000. Astronaut Candidate Training includes orientation briefings and tours, numerous scientific and technical briefings, intensive instruction in Shuttle and International Space Station systems and operations, physiological training, and flight training in T-38N and Gulfstream II aircraft. Following initial training, he will serve in technical assignments until assigned to a space flight.

NAME: Stephen G. Bowen, Lieutenant Commander, USN, Mission Specialist

BIRTHDATE/PLACE: Februrary 13, 1964 - Cohasset, MA

RESIDENCE: Yorktown, VA

EDUCATION: Cohasset High School, Cohasset, MA, 1982. B.S., Electrical Engineering, U.S. Naval Academy, 1986. Degree of Ocean Engineer, Massachusetts Institute of Technology, 1993

CURRENT POSITION: Executive Officer, USS Virginia, Groton, CT

NAME: Benjamin Alvin Drew (Lieutenant Colonel, USAF)
NASA Astronaut Candidate (Mission Specialist)

PERSONAL DATA: Born November 5, 1962 in Washington, DC. Single. Enjoys literature, sketching, running, biking and jazz. His parents, Muriel and Benjamin Drew, Sr., reside in Fort Washington, Maryland.

EDUCATION: 1980 High School Diploma from Gonzaga College High School in Washington, DC. 1984 Bachelor of Science in Astronautical Engineering from the United States Air Force Academy. 1984 Bachelor of Science in Physics from the United States Air Force Academy. 1995 Master of Science in Aerospace Science from Embry Riddle University.

ORGANIZATIONS: Society of Experimental Test Pilots, American Helicopter Society.

SPECIAL HONORS: Meritorious Service Medal with 1 Oak Leaf Cluster; Air Medal; Aerial Achievement Medal with 5 Oak Leaf Clusters; Air Force Commendation Medal with 2 Oak Leaf Clusters; Air Force Achievement Medal; Air Force Outstanding Unit Medal with 3 Oak Leaf Clusters; Combat Readiness Medal with 5 Oak Leaf Clusters; National Defense Service Medal; Armed Forces Expeditionary Medal; Southwest Asia Service Medal with 3 Oak Leaf Clusters.

EXPERIENCE: Drew received his commission as a Second Lieutenant from the United States Air Force Academy in May 1984. He completed Undergraduate Pilot Training - Helicopter at Fort Rucker, Alabama and earned his wings in March 1985. His initial assignment was to the HH-3E flying combat rescue. He transitioned to the MH-60G and was assigned to the Air Force Special Operations Command. There, he flew combat missions in operations JUST CAUSE, DESERT SHIELD/DESERT STORM and PROVIDE COMFORT. He completed USAF Fixed-Wing Qualification in April 1993, and the United States Naval Test Pilot School in June 1994. He has commanded two flight test units and served on Air Combat Command Staff. He is a Command Pilot with 3000 hours flying time in over 30 types of aircraft.

NASA EXPERIENCE: Selected by NASA in July 2000, Lieutenant Colonel Drew reported for training in August 2000. Astronaut Candidate Training includes orientation briefings and tours, numerous scientific and technical briefings, intensive instruction in Shuttle and International Space Station systems, physiological training and ground school to prepare for T-38 flight training, as well as learning water and wilderness survival techniques. Following initial training, he will serve in technical assignments until assigned to a space flight.

NAME: Andrew J. Feustel, Ph.D., Mission Specialist

BIRTHDATE/PLACE: August 25, 1965 - Lancaster, PA

RESIDENCE: The Woodlands, TX

EDUCATION: Lake Orion High School, Lake Orion, MI, 1983. B.S., Solid Earth Sciences, Purdue University, 1989. M.S., Geophysics, Purdue University, 1991. Ph.D., Seismology, Queen's University-Canada, 1995.

CURRENT POSITION: Senior Petroleum Geophysicist, Exxon Exploration Company, Houston, TX

NAME: Kevin A. Ford (Lieutenant Colonel, USAF)
NASA Astronaut Candidate (Pilot)

PERSONAL DATA: Born July 7, 1960 in Portland, Indiana. Montpelier, Indiana is his hometown. Married to the former Kelly Ann Bennett of Hartford City, Indiana. They have two children, Anthony and Heidi. His parents, Clayton and Barbara Ford, and Kelly's parents, Arlan and Nancy Bennett, reside in Hartford City, Indiana. He enjoys golf, running, reading, and music.

EDUCATION: Graduated from Blackford High School, Hartford City, Indiana in 1978. He received his Bachelor of Science Degree in Aerospace Engineering from the University of Notre Dame in 1982, a Master of Science in International Relations from Troy State University in 1989, a Master of Science in Aerospace Engineering from the University of Florida in 1994, and a Ph.D. in Astronautical Engineering from the Air Force Institute of Technology in 1997. Graduate of Squadron Officer School and the Air Command and Staff College Associate Program.

ORGANIZATIONS: Senior Member of the American Institute of Aeronautics and Astronautics. Member of the Society of Experimental Test Pilots, the Air Force Association, and the Experimental Aircraft Association.

SPECIAL HONORS: Distinguished Graduate of Detachment 225, Reserve Officer Training Corps, 1982. Distinguished Graduate of Undergraduate Pilot Training, Columbus AFB, Mississippi, 1984. Distinguished Graduate of the United States Air Force Test Pilot School, 1990. Recipient of the Air Force Meritorious Service Medal, the Air Force Commendation Medal, the Aerial Achievement Medal, and the Armed Forces Expeditionary Medal. Recipient of the Air Force Test Pilot School David B. Barnes Outstanding Flight Instructor Award, 1998.

EXPERIENCE: Ford was commissioned through the Reserve Officer Training Corps program in 1982 and completed primary Air Force jet training at Columbus Air Force Base, Mississippi in 1984. He trained in the F-15 Eagle and was assigned to the 22nd Tactical Fighter Squadron, Bitburg Air Base, Germany, from 1984-1987, and then to the 57th Fighter Interceptor Squadron at Keflavik Naval Air Station, Iceland until 1989, intercepting and escorting 18 Soviet combat aircraft over the North Atlantic. After spending 1990 as a student at the United States Air Force Test Pilot School, Edwards Air Force Base, California, Kevin flew flight test missions in the F-16 Fighting Falcon with the 3247th Test Squadron at Eglin Air Force Base, Florida from 1991-1994. Test experience there included multiple F-16 flutter missions, development of the ALE-47 Countermeasures Dispenser System, multiple safe separation, ballistics, and fuse tests, and air-to-air missile development testing, including the first AMRAAM shot from the F-16 Air Defense Fighter variant. Following a three-year assignment to pursue full-time studies as a doctoral candidate at Wright-Patterson Air Force Base, Ohio, he was assigned to the Air Force Test Pilot School where he served as as the Director of Plans and Programs, taught academics, and instructed students on flight test techniques in the F-15, F-16, and gliders. Kevin is an FAA certificated flight instructor in airplanes and gliders.

NASA EXPERIENCE: Selected by NASA in July 2000, Lieutenant Colonel Ford reported for training in August 2000. Astronaut Candidate Training includes orientation briefings and tours, numerous scientific and technical briefings, intensive instruction in Shuttle and International Space Station systems, physiological training and ground school to prepare for T-38 flight training, as well as learning water and wilderness survival techniques. Following initial training, he will serve in technical assignments until assigned to a space flight.

NAME: Ronald J. Garan, Jr. (Lieutenant Colonel, USAF)
NASA Astronaut Candidate (Pilot)

PERSONAL DATA: Born on October 30, 1961 in Yonkers, New York. Married to the former Carmel Courtney of Brooklyn, New York, and Scranton, Pennsylvania. They have three sons. Recreational interests include running, football, coaching Little League baseball and soccer and teaching Sunday School classes to children. His father, Ronald Garan Sr., resides in Yonkers, New York. His mother, Linda Lichtblau, resides in Port St. Lucie, Florida. Carmel's parents, Joseph and Bridget Courtney, reside in Scranton, Pennsylvania.

EDUCATION: Graduated from Roosevelt High School, Yonkers, New York in 1979. Earned a Bachelor of Science degree in Business Economics from the SUNY College at Oneonta, 1982. Earned a Masters of Aeronautical Science degree from Embry-Riddle Aeronautical University, 1994. Earned a Master of Science degree in Aerospace Engineering from the University of Florida, 1996.

ORGANIZATIONS: Society of Experimental Test Pilots.

AWARDS: Military decorations include the Distinguished Flying Cross, Meritorious Service Medal, Air Medal, Aerial Achievement Medal, Air Force Outstanding Unit Award with Valor, National Defense Service Medal, Air Force Expeditionary Medal, SouthWest Asia Service Medal, Humanitarian Service Award, Kuwait Liberation Medal, Kuwait Service Medal, and various other service awards.

SPECIAL HONORS: Distinguished Graduate and Top Academic Award USAF Fighter Weapons School; Twice selected as Top Academic Instructor Pilot, USAF Weapons School; USAF Weapons School and USAF Weapons and Tactics Center Lt. Gen. Claire Lee Chennault Award; Distinguished Graduate Squadron Officers School, Top Academic Award F-16 Replacement Training Unit (RTU).

EXPERIENCE: Garan received his commission as a Second Lieutenant in the United States Air Force from the Air Force Officer Training School at Lackland Air Force Base (AFB), Texas, in March 1984. Upon completion, he attended Undergraduate Pilot Training (UPT) at Vance AFB, Oklahoma and earned his wings in March of 1985. Upon completion he attended Fighter Lead-In training at Holloman AFB, New Mexico and F-16 Training at Luke AFB, Arizona. He then reported to Hahn Air Base in former West Germany were he served as a combat ready F-16 pilot in the 496th Tactical Fighter Squadron, from February 1986 until February 1988. In March 1988 he was reassigned to the 17th Tactical Fighter Squadron, Shaw AFB, South Carolina, were he served as an instructor pilot, evaluator pilot, and combat ready F-16 pilot. While stationed at Shaw he attended the USAF Fighter Weapons School, graduating in 1989, and then returned to the 17th Tactical Fighter Squadron to assume the position of Squadron Weapons Officer. From August 1990 through March 1991, he deployed to SouthWest Asia in support of Operations Desert Shield/Desert Storm and flew 32 combat missions in the F-16 during the Gulf War.

In June 1991, Garan was reassigned to the USAF Weapons School where he served as a Weapons School Instructor Pilot, Flight Commander and Assistant Operations Officer. In October 1994, he was reassigned to the 39th Flight Test Squadron, Eglin AFB FL were he served as a developmental test pilot and chief F-16 pilot. Garan attended the US Naval Test Pilot School at the Patuxent River Naval Air Station from January 1997 through December 1997 after which he was reassigned to the 39th Flight Test Squadron, Eglin AFB, Florida, were he served as the Director of the Joint Air to Surface Standoff Missile Combined Test Force. Garan was the Operations Officer of the 40th Flight Test Squadron when he was selected for the astronaut program. He has logged over 3000 hours in more than 30 different aircraft.

NASA EXPERIENCE: Selected by NASA in July 2000, Lieutenant Colonel Garan reported for training in August 2000. Astronaut Candidate Training includes orientation briefings and tours, numerous scientific and technical briefings, intensive instruction in Shuttle and International Space Station systems, physiological training and ground school to prepare for T-38 flight training, as well as learning water and wilderness survival techniques. Following initial training, he will serve in technical assignments until assigned to a space flight.

NAME: Michael T. Good (Lieutenant Colonel, USAF)
NASA Astronaut Candidate (Mission Specialist)

PERSONAL DATA: Born on October 13, 1962 in Parma, Ohio. Married to the former Joan M. Dickinson of Broadview Heights, Ohio. They have three children: Bryan, Jason and Shannon. Recreational interests include running, golfing and family activities. Mike's father and mother, Robert and Carol Good, reside in Broadview Heights, Ohio. Joan's mother, Marj Dickinson, also resides in Broadview Heights, Ohio. Her father, David Dickinson, is deceased.

EDUCATION: Brecksville-Broadview Heights High School, Broadview Heights, Ohio, 1980. B.S., Aerospace Engineering, University of Notre Dame, 1984. M.S., Aerospace Engineering, University of Notre Dame, 1986.

ORGANIZATIONS: Sigma Gamma Tau, National Honor Society for Aerospace Engineering; Air Force Association.

SPECIAL HONORS/AWARDS: Distinguished Graduate from the University of Notre Dame, Reserve Officer Training Corps, 1984; Lead-in Fighter Training, 1989; Squadron Officer School, 1993. Top Academic Graduate of Specialized Undergraduate Navigator Training, 1989; F-111 Replacement Training Unit, 1989; USAF Test Pilot School, 1994. Aircrew of the Year, 77th Fighter Squadron, 1991. Military decorations include the Meritorious Service Medal (3), Aerial Achievement Medal (2), Air Force Commendation Medal, Air Force Achievement Medal, Combat Readiness Medal and various other service awards.

EXPERIENCE: Good graduated from the University of Notre Dame in 1984 and was commissioned a second lieutenant. After completing a graduate degree he was assigned to the Tactical Air Warfare Center, Eglin Air Force Base, Florida. While at Eglin, he served as a flight test engineer for the Ground Launched Cruise Missile program. He was selected to attend Undergraduate Navigator Training at Mather Air Force Base, California, receiving his wings in January 1989. After Lead-in Fighter Training at Holloman Air Force Base, New Mexico, and transition training in the F-111 at Mt. Home Air Force Base, Idaho, Good was assigned to the 20th Fighter Wing, RAF Upper Heyford, England. He served as an F-111 instructor weapon systems officer. In 1993, he was selected for Air Force Test Pilot School at Edwards Air Force Base, California, graduating in 1994. After graduation, he was assigned to the 420th Flight Test Squadron at Edwards where he flew and tested the B-2 Stealth Bomber. In 1997, he was assigned to Maxwell Air Force Base, Alabama, to attend Air Command and Staff College. After graduation he was assigned to the 46th Operations Support Squadron, Eglin Air Force Base, Florida. He served as operations officer and F-15 test weapon systems officer. He has logged over 1,700 hours in more than 30 different aircraft.

NASA EXPERIENCE: Selected by NASA in July 2000, Lieutenant Colonel Good reported for training in August 2000. Astronaut Candidate Training includes orientation briefings and tours, numerous scientific and technical briefings, intensive instruction in Shuttle and International Space Station systems, physiological training and ground school to prepare for T-38 flight training, as well as learning water and wilderness survival techniques. Following initial training, he will serve in technical assignments until assigned to a space flight.

NAME: Douglas G. Hurley (Major, USMC)
NASA Astronaut Candidate (Pilot)

PERSONAL DATA: Born on October 21, 1966, in Endicott, New York, but considers Apalachin, New York his hometown. Married to the former Amelia Bellamy of Dallas, Texas. Recreational interests include hunting, mountain climbing, backcountry camping, and NASCAR racing. Doug's parents, Harvey and Sherry, reside in Apalachin, New York. Amelia's mother Charlotte resides in St. Petersburg Beach, Florida, and her father Lee lives in New Smyrna Beach, Florida.

EDUCATION: Graduated from Owego Free Academy, in Owego, New York, 1984. B.S.E., Civil Engineering, Tulane University, Louisiana, 1988.

SPECIAL HONORS: Magna Cum Laude with Honors, Tulane University, Distinguished Graduate, Tulane University NROTC, Distinguished Graduate, Navy Flight School. Stephen A. Hazelrigg Memorial Award for best Test Pilot/Engineer Team, Naval Strike Aircraft Test Squadron. Awarded the Navy and Marine Corps Commendation Medal and various other service awards.

EXPERIENCE: Hurley received his commission as a Second Lieutenant in the United States Marine Corps from the Naval Reserve Officer Training Corps at Tulane University, New Orleans, Louisiana, in 1988. After graduation, he attended The Basic School (TBS) in Quantico, Virginia, and later the Infantry Officers Course. Following Aviatin Indoctrination in Pensacola, Florida, he entered flight training in Texas in 1989 and was designated a Naval Aviator in August 1991. He then reported to Marine Fighter/Attack Training Squadron 101 at Marine Corps Air Station El Toro, California, for initial F/A-18 training. Upon completion of training, he was assigned to Marine All Weather Fighter/Attack Squadron 225 at El Toro, California, where he made three overseas deployments to the Western Pacific. While assigned to VMFA(AW)-225, he attended the United States Marine Weapons and Tactics Instructor Course (WTI), the Marine Division Tactics Course (MDTC), and the Aviation Safety Officers Course, and served as the Aviation Safety Officer and the Pilot Training Officer. Hurley was selected for the United States Naval Test Pilot School at Naval Air Station Patuxent River, Maryland, and began the course in January of 1997. After graduation in December 1997, he was assigned to the Naval Strike Aircraft Test Squadron as an F/A-18 Project Officer and Test Pilot. At Strike, he participated in a variety of flight testing including flying qualities, ordnance separation, and systems testing and became the first ever Marine pilot to fly the F/A-18 E/F Super Hornet. He was serving as the Operations Officer at Strike when selected for the astronaut program. Hurley has logged over 2200 hours in more than 20 aircrafts.

NASA EXPERIENCE: Selected by NASA in July 2000, Major Hurley reported for training in August 2000. Astronaut Candidate Training includes orientation briefings and tours, numerous scientific and technical briefings, intensive instruction in Shuttle and International Space Station systems, physiological training and ground school to prepare for T-38 flight training, as well as learning water and wilderness survival techniques. Following initial training, he will serve in technical assignments until assigned to a space flight.

NAME: Timothy L. Kopra (Major, USA)
       NASA Astronaut Candidate (Mission Specialist)

PERSONAL DATA: Born on April 9, 1963, in Austin, Texas. Married to the former Dawn Kaye Lehman of Lewisburg, Kentucky. They have two children. He enjoys running, swimming, and biking. His mother, Martha A. Kopra, resides in Austin, Texas. His father, Dr. Lennart L. Kopra, is deceased. Dawn's parents, Charles B. and Betty H. Lehman, reside in Lewisberg, Kentucky.

EDUCATION: McCallum High School, Austin, Texas, 1981. Bachelor of Science, United States Military Academy, West Point, New York, 1985. Master of Science in Aerospace Engineering, Georgia Institute of Technology, 1995.

ORGANIZATIONS: Society of Experimental Test Pilots; Army Aviation Association of America; American Helicopter Society; United States Military Academy Association of Graduates; West Point Society of Greater Houston; Phi Kappa Phi.

SPECIAL HONORS: Empire Test Pilot School Award for the best Developmental Test thesis, Class 110, U.S. Naval Test Pilot School (1996); Bronze Order of Saint Michael, Army Aviation Award (1999). Awarded the Bronze Star Medal, two Meritorious Service Medals, Air Medal, Army Commendation Medal, Army Achievement Medal, and various other service awards.

EXPERIENCE: Kopra received his commission as a second lieutenant from the U.S. Military Academy in May 1985 and was designated as an Army aviator in August 1986. He then completed a three-year assignment at Fort Campbell, Kentucky, where he served as an aeroscout platoon leader, troop executive officer, and squadron adjutant in the 101st Airborne Division's air cavalry squadron. In 1990, he was assigned to the 3rd Armored Division in Hanau, Germany, and was deployed to Southwest Asia where he served in Operations Desert Shield and Desert Storm. He completed his tour in Germany as an attack helicopter company commander and an operations officer. After returning to the United States and completing graduate studies at Georgia Tech, he was selected in 1995 to attend the U.S. Naval Test Pilot School. Upon graduation, he was assigned to the U.S. Army Aviation Technical Test Center, where he worked as an experimental test pilot on various projects and served as the developmental test director for the Comanche helicopter program. Other military schools include the Army Parachutist Course, Pathfinder Course, Air Assault Course, the Combined Services Staff School, and the Command and General Staff College.

NASA EXPERIENCE: Kopra was assigned to NASA at the Johnson Space Center in September 1998 as a vehicle integration test engineer. In this position, he primarily served as an engineering liaison for Space Shuttle launch operations and International Space Station hardware testing. He was actively involved in the contractor tests of the Extravehicular Activity (EVA) interfaces for each of the space station truss segments.

Selected by NASA in July 2000, Kopra reported for Astronaut Candidate Training the following month. This training includes scientific and technical briefings, instruction in Space Shuttle and International Space Station systems, and T-38 flight training. Following initial training, he will serve in technical assignments until assigned to a space flight.

NAME: K. Megan McArthur
  NASA Astronaut Candidate (Mission Specialist)

PERSONAL DATA: Born on August 30, 1971 in Honolulu, Hawaii. Considers San Jose, California, to be her hometown, where her parents, Don & Kit McArthur, reside. Her brother Sean McArthur, and sisters Shannon McArthur Silva and Erin Dahlby, also reside in California. Megan enjoys camping, backpacking, and SCUBA diving.

EDUCATION: Graduated from St. Francis High School, Mountain View, California, 1989. B.S. Aerospace Engineering, University of California-Los Angeles, 1993. Ph.D., Oceanography, University of California-San Diego, 2000 (expected).

EXPERIENCE: At Scripps Institution of Oceanography she Megan McArthur conducted graduate research in nearshore underwater acoustic propagation and digital signal processing. She obtained funding for, planned and conducted sea-floor sediment survey aboard the 170 ft. research vessel New Horizon. She analyzed echosounding data, sediment core data, and information from coastal geology literature to determine geologic features relevant to acoustic propagation in nearshore region. She served as Chief Scientist during six at-sea data collection operations. She planned and led diving operations during three sea-floor instrument deployment-recoveries and during one sediment-sample collection trip. She is experienced at in-water instrument testing, deployment, maintenance, and recovery, and collection of plants, animals, and sediment. She provided training for six students during at-sea research operations. She also provided public outreach and science education via classroom visits and one-on-one mentoring.

Concurrent volunteer work at the Birch Aquarium involved educational demonstrations for the public from inside 70,000 gallon exhibit tank using SCUBA and underwater communications mask, including in-water tank maintenance, animal feeding and observation. She facilitated educational lectures aboard grey whale-watching cruises. She also served as Science Judge for the 1998 and 1999 National Ocean Sciences Bowl, Southern California Section.

NASA EXPERIENCE: Selected by NASA in July 2000, Megan McArthur reported for training in August 2000. Astronaut Candidate Training includes orientation briefings and tours, numerous scientific and technical briefings, intensive instruction in Shuttle and International Space Station systems, physiological training, five weeks of T-34 training in Pensacola, Florida, and ground school to prepare for T-38 flight training, as well as learning water and wilderness survival techniques. Following initial training, she will serve in technical assignments until assigned to a space flight.

NAME: Karen L. Nyberg (Ph.D.)
NASA Astronaut Candidate (Mission Specialist)

PERSONAL DATA: Born on October 7, 1969 in Parkers Prairie, Minnesota. Her hometown is Vining, Minnesota. Recreational interests include art, running, volleyball, sewing, backpacking, piano, and spending time with her three dogs. Married to Mark Landeck. Karen's parents, Kenneth & Phyllis Nyberg reside in Vining, Minnesota. Mark's parents, Walter & Virginia Landeck, reside in Livingston, Texas.

EDUCATION: Graduated from Henning Public High School, Henning, Minnesota, 1988. B.S., Mechanical Engineering, University of North Dakota, 1994. M.S., Mechanical Engineering, University of Texas at Austin, 1996. Ph.D., Mechanical Engineering, University of Texas at Austin, 1998.

ORGANIZATIONS: Tau Beta Pi (National Engineering Honor Society); American Society of Mechanical Engineers; Aerospace Medical Association.

SPECIAL HONORS/AWARDS: Space Act Award (1993); NASA JSC Patent Application Award (1993); NASA Tech Briefs Award (1993); NASA JSC Cooperative Education Special Achievement Award (1994); UND Summa Cum Laude graduate (1994); Joyce Medalen Society of Women Engineers Award (1993-94); D.J. Robertson Award of Academic Achievement (1992); University of North Dakota School of Engineering & Mines Meritorious Service Award (1991-1992). Recipient of numerous scholarships and other awards.

EXPERIENCE: Graduate research was completed at The University of Texas at Austin BioHeat Transfer Laboratory where she developed expertise in the area of human thermoregulation and experimental metabolic testing and control, specifically related to the control of thermal neutrality in space suits.

NASA EXPERIENCE: Co-op at Johnson Space Center from 1991-1995, working in a variety of areas. She received a patent for work done in 1991 on Robot Friendly Probe and Socket Assembly. In 1998, on completing her doctorate, she accepted a position with the Crew and Thermal Systems Division, working as an Environmental Control Systems Engineer. Her prime responsibility involved using expertise in human thermal physiology and engineering control for improvements in the space suit thermal control system and evaluation of firefighter suit cooling technologies. Other responsibilities included providing computational fluid dynamic analysis for the TransHab module air distribution system, coordinating and monitoring analysis tasks performed by a team of contractor personnel for the X-38 environmental control and life support system, providing conceptual designs of the thermal control system for the Advanced Mars and Lunar Lander Mission studies, and environmental control system analysis for a collapsible hyperbaric chamber.

Selected by NASA in July 2000, Dr. Nyberg reported for training in August 2000. Astronaut Candidate Training includes orientation briefings and tours, numerous scientific and technical briefings, intensive instruction in Shuttle and International Space Station systems, physiological training and ground school to prepare for T-38 flight training, as well as learning water and wilderness survival techniques. Following initial training, she will serve in technical assignments until assigned to a space flight.

NAME: Nicole Passonno Stott
NASA Astronaut Candidate (Mission Specialist)

PERSONAL DATA: Born November 19, 1962 in Albany, New York. Her hometown is Clearwater, Florida. She is married to Christopher Stott of the Isle of Man, British Isles. She enjoys flying, snow skiing, scuba diving, woodworking, painting, and gardening. Her parents are Joan Passonno of Palm Harbor, Florida, and the late Fredrick Passonno. Her two younger sisters, Michele and Noelle, live with their husbands in Tarpon Springs, Florida. Christopher's parents are Bryan and Liz Stott of the Isle of Man, British Isles.

EDUCATION: Clearwater High School, Clearwater, Florida, 1980. B.S., Aeronautical Engineering, Embry-Riddle Aeronautical University, 1987. M.S., Engineering Management, University of Central Florida, 1992.

ORGANIZATIONS: Aircraft Owners and Pilot's Association (AOPA); The Mars Society

SPECIAL HONORS: Aircraft Operations Division, Newt Myers Team Spirit Award (2000); KSC Public Affairs Certificate of Appreciation for Service (1998); NASA Exceptional Achievement Medal (1997); NASA Certificates of Commendation (1993, 1995, 1998); NASA Performance Awards (1990, 1992, 1993, 1995, 1996, 1997, 1998, 1999, 2000); NASA On-the-Spot Award (1995); Lockheed Certificate of Appreciation (1989).

EXPERIENCE: Ms. Stott began her career in 1987 as a structural design engineer with Pratt and Whitney Government Engines in West Palm Beach, FL. She spent a year with the Advanced Engines Group performing structural analyses of advanced jet engine component designs. Nicole Stott is an instrument rated private pilot.

NASA EXPERIENCE: In 1988, Ms. Stott joined NASA at the Kennedy Space Center (KSC), Florida as an Operations Engineer in the Orbiter Processing Facility (OPF). After 6 months, she was detailed to the Director of Shuttle Processing as part of a two-person team tasked with assessing the overall efficiency of Shuttle processing flows, identifying and implementing process improvements, and implementing tools for measuring the effectiveness of improvements. She was the NASA KSC Lead for a joint Ames/KSC software project to develop intelligent scheduling tools. The Ground Processing Scheduling System (GPSS) was developed as the technology demonstrator for this project. GPSS was a success at KSC and is still in use today for OPF scheduling, and also a commercial success that is part of the PeopleSoft suite of software products. During her time at KSC, Ms. Stott also held a variety of positions within NASA Shuttle Processing, including Vehicle Operations Engineer; NASA Convoy Commander; Shuttle Flow Director for Endeavour; and Orbiter Project Engineer for Columbia. During her last two years at KSC, she was a member of the Space Station Hardware Integration Office and relocated to Huntington Beach, CA where she served as the NASA Project Lead for the ISS truss elements under construction at the Boeing Space Station facility. In 1998, she joined the Johnson Space Center (JSC) team in Houston, TX as a member of the NASA Aircraft Operations Division., where she served as a Flight Simulation Engineer (FSE) on the Shuttle Training Aircraft (STA).

Selected as an astronaut candidate by NASA in July 2000, Nicole Stott reported for training in August 2000. Astronaut Candidate Training includes orientation briefings and tours, numerous scientific and technical briefings, intensive instruction in Shuttle and International Space Station systems, physiological training and ground school to prepare for T-38 flight training, as well as learning water and wilderness survival techniques. Following initial training, she will serve in technical assignments until assigned to a space flight.

NAME: Terry W. Virts, Jr., (Major, USAF)
NASA Astronaut Candidate (Pilot)

PERSONAL DATA: Born on December 1, 1967 in Baltimore, Maryland, but considers Columbia, Maryland, to be his hometown. Married to the former Stacy Hill of Columbia, Maryland. They have one son. Terry enjoys running, biking, swimming, golf, cross-country skiing, SCUBA diving, church activities, and reading. His mother and step father, Evelyn and Jack Coulson, reside in Maryland. His father, Terry Virts Sr., also resides in Maryland.

EDUCATION: Oakland Mills High School, Columbia, Maryland, 1985. B.S., Mathematics (French minor), U.S. Air Force Academy, 1989. M.A.S., Aeronautics, Embry-Riddle Aeronautical University, 1997.

ORGANIZATIONS: Officers' Christian Fellowship, Association of Graduates (U.S. Air Force Academy).

SPECIAL HONORS/AWARDS: Graduated with Academic Distinction from the United States Air Force Academy and Embry-Riddle Aeronautical University; Distinguished Graduate of Undergraduate Pilot Training at Williams Air Force Base, Arizona; Distinguished Graduate of F-16 initial training at Macdill Air Force Base, Florida. Military decorations include the Meritorious Service Medal, Air Medal, Aerial Achievement Medal, Air Force Commendation Medal, et al.

EXPERIENCE: Virts attended the Ecole de l'Air (French Air Force Academy) in 1988 on an exchange program from the United States Air Force Academy. He received his commission as a Second Lieutenant upon graduation from the United States Air Force Academy in 1989. He earned his pilot wings from Williams Air Force Base, Arizona, in 1990. From there he completed basic fighter and F-16 training and was assigned to Homestead Air Force Base, Florida, as an operational F-16 pilot in the 307th Tactical Fighter Squadron. After Hurricane Andrew struck Homestead in 1992, his squadron was moved to Moody Air Force Base, Georgia. From 1993 to 1994 he was assigned to the 36th Fighter Squadron at Osan Air Base, Republic of Korea, where he flew low altitude night attack missions in the F-16. Following his tour in Korea, he was reassigned to the 22nd Fighter Squadron at Spangdahlem Air Base, Germany, from 1995 to 1998. There he flew suppression of enemy air defenses missions in the F-16. During this assignment he flew 45 combat missions over Iraq in support of Operations Provide Comfort and Northern Watch. Virts was selected for Test Pilot School in 1997 and was a member of the USAF Test Pilot School class 98B at Edwards Air Force Base, California. Following graduation, he was an F-16 Experimental Test Pilot at the Combined Test Force at Edwards from 1999 until his selection as a member of the 18th group of astronaut candidates in 2000. He has logged over 2,400 flight hours in more than 40 different aircraft.

NASA EXPERIENCE: Selected by NASA in July 2000, Major Virts reported for training in August 2000. Astronaut Candidate Training includes orientation briefings and tours, numerous scientific and technical briefings, intensive instruction in Shuttle and International Space Station systems, physiological training and ground school to prepare for T-38 flight training, as well as learning water and wilderness survival techniques. Following initial training, he will serve in technical assignments until assigned to a space flight.

NAME: Barry E. "Butch" Wilmore (Lieutenant Commander, USN)
NASA Astronaut Candidate (Pilot)

PERSONAL DATA: Born on December 29, 1962 in Murfreesboro, Tennessee, but considers Mt. Juliet, Tennesse his hometown. He is married to the former Miss Deanna Newport of Helenwood, Tennessee. His parents, Eugene and Faye Wilmore, reside in the home in which he grew up in Mt. Juliet. His brother Jack resides in Franklin, Tennessee.

EDUCATION: Graduated from Mt. Juliet High School, Mt. Juliet, TN, 1981. B.S., Electrical Engineering, Tennessee Technological University, 1985. M.S., Electrical Engineering, Tennessee Technological University, 1994. M.S., Aviation Systems, University of Tennessee-Knoxville, 1994.

SPECIAL HONORS: Air Medal (5), 3 with the Combat 'V' designation, Navy Commendation Medal (6), 3 of which also hold the Combat 'V' designation, Navy Achievement Medal (2) and numerous Unit decorations. U. S. Atlantic Fleet "Strike Fighter Aviator of the Year" 1999.

EXPERIENCE: Wilmore has accumulated over 3800 flight hours and 660 carrier landings in tactical jet aircraft. He is a 1992 graduate of the United States Naval Test Pilot School (USNTPS).

During his 14 year tenure as a Naval officer and pilot, Wilmore completed 4 operational deployments, flying the A-7E and FA-18 aircraft from the decks of the USS Forrestal, USS Kennedy, USS Enterprise and the USS Eisenhower aircraft carriers. He has flown missions in support of Operations Desert Shield, Desert Storm and Southern Watch over the skies of Iraq, as well as missions over Bosnia in support of U. S. and NATO interests. Wilmore successfully completed 21 combat missions during Operation Desert Storm while operating from the flight deck of the USS Kennedy. His most recent operational deployment was aboard the USS Eisenhower with the "Blue Blasters" of Strike Fighter Squadron 34 (VFA-34), an F/A-18 squadron based at Naval Air Station Oceana, Virginia.

As a Navy Test Pilot Wilmore participated in all aspects of the initial development of the T-45 jet trainer to include carrier landing certification and high angle of attack flight tests. His test tour also included a stint at USNTPS as a systems and fixed wing flight test instructor. Prior to his selection to NASA Wilmore was on exchange to the Air Force as a flight test instructor at the United States Air Force Test Pilot School at Edwards Air Force Base, California.

NASA EXPERIENCE: Selected by NASA in July 2000, Lieutenant Commander Wilmore reported for training in August 2000. Astronaut Candidate Training includes orientation briefings and tours, numerous scientific and technical briefings, intensive instruction in Shuttle and International Space Station systems, physiological training and ground school to prepare for T-38 flight training, as well as learning water and wilderness survival techniques. Following initial training, he will serve in technical assignments until assigned to a space flight.

Chapter Five:

Deceased

NASA

Astronauts

NAME: Charles A. Bassett, II (Captain, USAF)
     NASA Astronaut (Deceased)

PERSONAL DATA: Born in Dayton, Ohio, on December 30, 1931. Died February 28, 1966, in St. Louis, Missouri, in the crash of a T-38 jet. He is survived by his wife, Jean, and two children.

EDUCATION: He attended Ohio State University from 1950 to 1952, and Texas Technological College from 1958 to 1960. He received a Bachelor of Science Degree in Electrical Engineering with honors from Texas Tech; He had done graduate work at University of Southern California.

ORGANIZATIONS: Member of the American Institute of Aeronautics and Astronautics, Phi Kappa Tau, Eta Kappa Nu, Tau Beta Pi and the Daedalians

EXPERIENCE: Bassett was an Air Force Captain. He graduated from the Aerospace Research Pilot School and the Air Force Experimental Pilot School. He served as an experimental test pilot and engineering test pilot in the Fighter Projects Office at Edwards Air Force Base, California.

He logged over 3,600 hours-flying time, including over 2,900 hours in a jet aircraft.

NASA EXPERIENCE: Bassett was one of the third group of astronauts named by NASA in October 1963. In addition to participating in the overall astronaut-training program, he had specific responsibilities pertaining to training and simulators. On November 8, 1965, he was selected as pilot of the upcoming Gemini 9 mission. He died on February 28, 1966, in the crash of a T-38 jet.

NAME: Manley Lanier "Sonny" Carter, Jr. (Captain, USN)
     NASA Astronaut (Deceased)

PERSONAL DATA: Born August 15, 1947, in Macon, Georgia, but considered Warner Robins, Georgia, to be his hometown. Died April 5, 1991. He is survived by his wife, Dana, and two daughters. He enjoyed wrestling, golf, tennis, L.A. Dodger baseball, and old movies. Carter was a professional soccer player from 1970-73 for the Atlanta Chiefs of the NASL.

EDUCATION: Graduated from Lanier High School, Macon, Georgia , in 1965; received a bachelor of arts degree in chemistry from Emory University in 1969, and a doctor of medicine degree from Emory University in 1973.

ORGANIZATIONS: Member of Sigma Delta Psi, Alpha Tau Omega, the Marine Corps Aviation Association, and SETP.

SPECIAL HONORS: Recipient of the Air Medal, Meritorious Service Medal, Navy Achievement Medal, Meritorious Unit Citation, Marine Corps Aviation Association Special Category Award 1982, NASA Meritorious Service Medal 1988, and NASA Space Flight Medal 1989. Carter was the Guest of Honor at the 215th Marine Corps Birthday Ball.

EXPERIENCE: Carter graduated from medical school in June 1973 and completed a straight internal medicine internship at Grady Memorial Hospital in Atlanta, Georgia. In July 1974 he entered the U.S. Navy and completed flight surgeon school in Pensacola, Florida.

After serving tours as a flight surgeon with the 1st and 3rd Marine Air Wings he returned to flight training in Beeville, Texas, and was designated a Naval Aviator in April 1978. He was assigned as the senior medical officer of USS Forrestal, and in March 1979 completed F-4 training at VMFAT-101 Marine Corps Air Station, Yuma, Arizona. He was subsequently reassigned as a fighter pilot to duty flying F-4 phantoms with Marine Fighter Attack Squadron 333 at MCAS Beaufort, South Carolina. In 1981 he completed a 9-month Mediterranean cruise aboard USS Forrestal with VMFA-115. In September 1982 he attended U.S. Navy Fighter Weapons School (TOPGUN) and then served as 2nd Marine Air Wing standardization officer and F-4 combat readiness evaluator at MCAS Cherry Point, North Carolina. He then attended the U.S. Naval Test Pilot School, graduating in June 1984. He has logged 3,000 flying hours and 160 carrier landings.

NASA EXPERIENCE: Selected by NASA in May 1984, Carter became an astronaut in June 1985, qualified for assignment as a mission specialist on future Space Shuttle flight crews. Carter was assigned as Extravehicular Activity (EVA) Representative for the Mission Development Branch of the Astronaut Office when selected to the crew of STS-33. The STS-33 crew launched, at night, from Kennedy Space Center, Florida, on November 22, 1989, aboard the Space Shuttle Discovery. The mission carried Department of Defense payloads and other secondary payloads. After 79 orbits of the earth, this five-day mission concluded on November 27, 1989 with a hard surface landing on Runway 04 at Edwards Air Force Base, California. With the completion of his first mission, Carter logged 120 hours in space. At the time of his death, Captain Carter was assigned as a mission specialist on the crew of STS-42, the first International Microgravity Laboratory (IML-1). He died April 5, 1991, near New Brunswick, Georgia, in the crash of a commercial airplane while on NASA business travel.

NAME: Roger B. Chaffee (Lieutenant Commander, USN)
NASA Astronaut (Deceased)

PERSONAL DATA: Born February 15, 1935 in Grand Rapids, Michigan. Died January 27, 1967, at NASA Kennedy Space Center, Florida, in the Apollo spacecraft fire. He is survived by his wife Martha and two children.

EDUCATION: Chaffee graduated from Central High School, Grand Rapids, Michigan. He received a Bachelor of Science degree in Aeronautical Engineering, Purdue University in 1957.

ORGANIZATIONS: Member, Tau Beta Pi, National Engineering Society, Sigma Gamma Tau, and Phi Kappa Sigma

SPECIAL HONORS: Awarded the United States Navy Air Medal.

EXPERIENCE: Chaffee, a United States Navy Lieutenant Commander, entered the Navy in 1957. He served as safety officer and quality control officer for Heavy Photographic Squadron 62 at the Naval Air Station in Jacksonville, Florida.

In January 1963, he entered the Air Force Institute of Technology at Wright-Patterson Air Force Base, Ohio, to work on a Master of Science Degree in Reliability Engineering.

He logged more than 2,300 hours flying time, including more than 2,000 hours in jet aircraft.

NASA EXPERIENCE: Chaffee was one of the third group of astronauts selected by NASA in October 1963. In addition to participating in the overall training program, he was also tasked with working on flight control communications systems, instrumentation systems, and attitude and translation control systems in the Apollo Branch of the Astronaut office. On March 21, 1966, he was selected as one of the pilots for the AS-204 mission, the first 3-man Apollo flight.

Lieutenant Commander Chaffee died on January 27, 1967, in the Apollo spacecraft flash fire during a launch pad test at Kennedy Space Center, Florida.

NAME: Charles Conrad, Jr., (Captain, USN, Ret.)
NASA Astronaut (Deceased)

PERSONAL DATA: Born June 2, 1930, in Philadelphia, Pennsylvania. Died July 8, 1999, from injuries sustained in a motorcycle accident in Ojai, California. Conrad, who divorced his first wife, is survived by his wife Nancy, three sons and seven grandchildren. A son preceded him in death.

EDUCATION: Attended primary and secondary schools at Haverford School in Haverford, Pennsylvania, and the Darrow School, New Lebanon, New York; received a bachelor of science degree in Aeronautical Engineering from Princeton University in 1953; an honorary master of arts degree from Princeton in 1966; an honorary doctorate of laws degree from Lincoln-Weslyan University in 1970, and an honorary doctorate of science degree from Kings college, Wilkes-Barre, Pennsylvania in 1971.

ORGANIZATIONS: Fellow, American Astronautical Society; New York Academy of Science; American Institute of Aeronautics and Astronautics, and a Fellow of the Society of Experimental Test Pilots.

SPECIAL HONORS: Awarded Congressional Space Medal of Honor (October 1978); awarded two NASA Distinguished Service Medals, two NASA Exceptional Service Medals, the Navy Astronaut Wings, two Navy Distinguished Service Medals, and two Distinguished Flying Crosses; recipient of Princeton's Distinguished Alumnus Award for 1965; the U.S. Jaycee's 10 Outstanding Young Men Award in 1965; American Astronautical Society Flight Achievement Award for 1966; Pennsylvania's Award for Excellence in Science and Technology in 1967 and 1969; the Rear Admiral William S. Parsons Award for Scientific and Technical Progress in 1970; Godfrey L. Cabot Award in 1970; Silver Medal of the Union League of Philadelphia in 1970; the FAI Yur Gagarin Gold Space Medal and the De La Vaulx Medal in 1970 for Apollo 12; National Academy of Television Arts and Sciences Special Trustees Award in 1970; Federal Aviation Agency's Space Mechanic Technician Award in 1973; the Collier Trophy in 1973; FAI gold Medal and the De La Vaulx Medal in 1974 for Skylab I, and the AIAA Haley Astronautics Award in 1974 for Skylab I; the Harmon Trophy in 1974; enshrined in the Aviation Hall of Fame in 1980.

AEROSPACE AND PROFESSIONAL EXPERIENCE: Following graduation from Princeton University in 1953, Mr. Conrad entered the Navy and became a naval aviator. He then attended the Navy Test Pilot School at Patuxent River, Maryland, where he was assigned as a Project Test Pilot. Mr. Conrad also served as a flight instructor and performance engineer at the Test Pilot School. After completing his tour of duty at Patuxent River, he served as instructor pilot in F4H Phantoms on VF-121 and was then assigned duty in VF-96 on board USS Ranger.

In September of 1962, Mr. Conrad was selected as an astronaut by NASA. His first flight was Gemini V, which established the space endurance record and placed the United States in the lead for man-hours in space. As commander of Gemini XI, Mr. Conrad helped to set a world's altitude record. He then served as commander of Apollo XII, the second lunar landing. On Mr. Conrad's final mission, he served as commander of Skylab I, the first United States Space Station.

After serving 20 years (11 of which were as an astronaut in the space program), Mr. Conrad retired from the U.S. Navy to accept a position as Vice President - Operations and Chief Operating Office of American Television and Communications Corporation (ATC). At ATC, he was responsible for both the operation of existing systems and the national development of new cable television systems. In 1976, he resigned from ATC to accept the position of Vice President and consultant to McDonnell Douglas Corporation. In 1978, he became Vice President of marketing and was responsible for all commercial and military sales for Douglas Aircraft Company. Mr. Conrad then became Senior Vice President-Marketing in 1980. He was appointed as Senior Vice President Marketing and Product Support in 1982 and 1984, was named Staff Vice President of International Business Development for McDonnell Douglas Corporation.

In 1990, Mr. Conrad became Staff Vice President - New Business for McDonell Douglas Space Company, where he participated in research and development for the Space Exploration Initiative. Included for research and development in the Space Exploration Initiative are the construction of Space Station Freedom, the return to and colonization of the Moon, and the exploration of Mars. Mr. Conrad contributed his expertise on SSTO, the Single-Stage-To-Orbit and return space transportation system called the Delta Clipper. In 1993, Mr. Conrad became Vice President-Project Development.

Mr. Conrad died July 8, 1999 from injuries sustained in a motorcycle accident in Ojai, California.

NAME: Donn F. Eisele
NASA Astronaut (Deceased)

PERSONAL DATA: Born: June 23, 1930 in Columbus, Ohio. Deceased December 1, 1987 of a heart attack.

EXPERIENCE: A lifelong interest in flying prompted him to choose an Air Force career after he graduated from the Naval Academy. He flew jet fighters, became a test pilot, and in 1964 joined NASA as an astronaut. In 1968, Eisele flew aboard Apollo 7, the pioneer voyage of the Apollo moon landing program. He also served on the back-up crews for the ill-fated Apollo 1 and for Apollo 10, the prelude to the first moon landing. In 1972, Colonel Eisele retired from the Air Force and left the space program to become Director of the U. S. Peace Corps in Thailand. Upon returning from Thailand, Eisele became Sales Manager for Marion Power Shovel Company, a division o Dresser Industries. Presently, he handles private and corporate accounts for the investment firm of Oppenheimer and Company.

Eisele holds a master of science degree in Astronautics. He has flown several thousand hours in a variety of flying machines ranging from hand gliders to rocket ships. His awards include the Distinguished Flying Cross, the NASA Exceptional Service Medal, and a television "Emmy" for his performance in the first live telecast from outer space, on board Apollo Seven.

Eisele resided in Ft. Lauderdale with his wife Susan, daughter Kristin and son Andrew. Eisele's interests include investments, energy, travel and writing. His published works include personal story articles, technical notes and speeches.

NAME: Ronald E. Evans (Captain, USN, Retired)
NASA Astronaut (Deceased)

PERSONAL DATA: Born November 10, 1933, in St. Francis, Kansas. His father, Mr. Clarence E. Evans, and his mother, Mrs. Marie A. Evans, reside in Iola, Kansas.

PHYSICAL DESCRIPTION: Brown hair; brown eyes; height: 5 feet 11 inches; Weight: 170 pounds.

EDUCATION: Graduated from Highland Park High School in Topeka, Kansas; received a Bachelor of Science degree in Electrical Engineering from the University of Kansas in 1956 and a Master of Science degree in Aeronautical Engineering from the U.S. Naval Postgraduate School in 1964.

MARITAL STATUS: Married to the former Jan Pollom of Topeka, Kansas.

CHILDREN: Jaime D., August 21, 1959; Jon P., October 9, 1961.

SPECIAL HONORS: Presented the NASA Distinguished Service Medal (1973); the Johnson Space Center Superior Achievement Award (1970); the Navy Distinguished Service Medal (1973); Navy Astronaut Wings; eight Air Medals; the Vietnam Service Medal; and the Navy Commendation Medal with combat distinguishing device (1966); the University of Kansas Distinguished Service Citation (1973); and Kansan of the Year (1972) .

EXPERIENCE: When notified of his selection to the astronaut program, Evans was on sea duty in the Pacific,assigned to VF-51 and flying F8 aircraft from the carrier USS TICONDEROGA during a period of seven months in Vietnam combat operations. He was a combat flight instructor (F8 aircraft) with VF124 from January 1961 to June 1962 and, prior to this assignment, participated in two WESTPAC aircraft carrier cruises while a pilot with VF-142. In June 1957, he completed flight training after receiving his commission as an Ensign through the Navy ROTC Program at the University of Kansas. Total flight time accrued during his career is 5,500 hours, 5,000 hours of which is in jet aircraft.

NASA EXPERIENCE: Captain Evans was one of the 19 astronauts selected by NASA in April 1966. He served as a member of the astronaut support crews for the Apollo 7 and 11 flights and as a backup command module pilot for Apollo. On his first journey into space, Captain Evans occupied the command module pilot seat for Apollo 17, the last scheduled manned mission to the moon for the United States, which commenced at 11:33 p.m. (CST) December 6, 1972, and concluded on December 19, 1972. He was accompanied on this voyage of the command module America and the lunar module Challenger by Eugene Cernan (spacecraft commander) and Harrison H. (Jack) Schmitt (lunar module pilot). While Cernan and Schmitt completed their explorations of the Taurus-Littrow landing area down on the lunar surface, Evans maintained a solo vigil in lunar orbit aboard the American, completing assigned work tasks which required visual geological observations, hand-held photography of specific targets, and the control of cameras and other highly sophisticated scientific equipment carried in the command module SIM-bay.

Evans later completed a one hour and six minute extravehicular activity during the trans-earth coast of the return flight, successfully retrieving three camera cassettes and completing a personal inspection of the equipment bay area. This last mission to the moon for the United States broke several set by previous flights which include: longest manned lunar landing flight (301 hours, 51 minutes); longest lunar surface extravehicular activities (22 hours and 4 minutes); largest lunar sample return (an estimated 115 kg (249 lbs)); and longest time in lunar orbit (147 hours, 48 minutes). Apollo 17 ended with a splashdown in the Pacific Ocean approximately 0.4 mile from the target point and 4.3 miles from the prime recovery ship, the USS TICONDEROGA.

Completing his first space flight, Captain Evans logged 301 hours and 51 minutes in space, I hour and 6 minutes of which were spent in extravehicular activity. He holds the record of more time in lunar orbit than anyone else in the world.

Evans was backup command module pilot for the Apollo-Soyuz Test Project (ASTP) mission. This joint United States - Soviet Union earth-orbital mission, launched successfully in July 1975, was designed to test equipment and techniques that would establish an international crew rescue capability in space, as well as permit future cooperative scientific missions.

Evans retired from the United States Navy on April 30, 1976, with 21 years of service, and remained active as a NASA astronaut involved in the development of NASA's Space Shuttle Program until March 1977.

NAME: Theodore C. Freeman (Captain, USAF)
NASA Astronaut (Deceased)

PERSONAL DATA: Born February 18, 1930, in Haverford, Pennsylvania. Died October 31, 1964, at Ellington Air Force Base, Houston, Texas, in the crash of a T-38 jet. Survived by his wife Faith and one daughter.

EDUCATION: Freeman completed his secondary education in 1948. He attended the University of Delaware at Newark for one year, then entered the United States Naval Academy and graduated in 1953 with a Bachelor of Science degree. In 1960, he received a Master of Science degree in Aeronautical Engineering from the University of Michigan.

ORGANIZATIONS: Member of the American Institute of Aeronautics and Astronautics, and the Society of Experimental Test Pilots.

EXPERIENCE: Freeman graduated from both the Air Force's Experimental Test Pilot and Aerospace Research Pilot Courses. He elected to serve with the Air Force. His last Air Force assignment was as a flight test aeronautical engineer and experimental flight test instructor at the Aerospace Research Pilot School at Edwards Air Force Base, California. He served primarily in performance flight testing and stability testing areas.

He logged more than 3,300 hours flying time, including more than 2,400 hours in jet aircraft.

NASA EXPERIENCE: Freeman was one of the third group of astronauts selected by NASA in October 1963.

NAME: Edward G. Givens (Major, USAF)
NASA Astronaut (Deceased)

PERSONAL DATA: Born January 5, 1930, in Quanah, Texas. Died June 6, 1967, near Houston, Texas, in an automobile accident. He is survived by his wife Ada and two children.

EDUCATION: Graduated from Quanah High School, Quanah, Texas; received a Bachelor of Science degree in Naval Sciences from the U. S. Naval Academy in 1952.

SPECIAL HONORS: Awarded the "Outstanding Graduate Certificate" from the U. S. Naval Academy in 1952.

EXPERIENCE: Givens, an Air Force Major, was commissioned in the Air Force upon graduating from Annapolis in 1952 and received his flight training as a student pilot at the United States Air Force Air Training Command. In 1954, he was a flight commander and fighter pilot with the 35th Fighter Interceptor Group on duty in Japan. He served as an instructor at the Air Force Interceptor Weapons School from January 1956 to March 1958 and subsequently attended the United States Air Force Experimental Flight Test Pilot School at Edwards Air Force Base, California. Upon graduation he became an instructor in the Stability and Control Section. His next assignment took him to the Naval Air Station, Point Mugu, California, where he was a project pilot with Air Development Squadron 4. While there, he not only conducted operational evaluations but also was responsible for compiling and developing the operation procedures and tactics for fleet operation of the F8U-2N.

He served as Assistant to the Commandant at the USAF Experimental Flight Test Pilot School from November 1961 to September 1962 and then attended the USAF Aerospace Research Pilot School, from which he graduated in 1963. When informed of his selection for astronaut training, he was assigned as Project Officer with USAF SSD Detachment 2 at the Manned Spacecraft Center. He logged more than 3,500 hours flight time; 2,800 hours in jet craft.

NASA EXPERIENCE: Major Givens was one of the 19 astronauts selected by NASA in April 1966.

NAME: S. David Griggs (Mr.)
NASA Astronaut (Deceased)

PERSONAL DATA: Born September 7, 1939, in Portland, Oregon. Died June 17, 1989. He is survived by his wife, Karen, and two daughters. He enjoyed flying, auto restoration, running, and skiing.

EDUCATION: Graduated from Lincoln High School, Portland, Oregon, in 1957; received a bachelor of science degree from the United States Naval Academy in 1962 and a master of science in administration from George Washington University in 1970.

ORGANIZATIONS: Member, Society of Experimental Test Pilots, National Air Racing Group, Naval Reserve Association, Naval Academy Alumni Association, Association of Naval Aviators, Naval Institute, Naval Aviation Museum Foundation, Naval Order of the United States, Tailhook Association.

SPECIAL HONORS: Awarded the Navy Distinguished Flying Cross, Meritorious Service Medal, 15 Air Medals, 3 Navy Commendation Medals, Navy Unit Commendation, Meritorious Unit Citation, Defense Distinguished Service Medal, National Defense Service Medal, Republic of Vietnam Campaign Medal, Vietnamese Cross of Gallantry, NASA Space Flight Medal, NASA Achievement Award, and NASA Sustained Superior Performance Award.

EXPERIENCE: Mr. Griggs graduated from Annapolis in 1962 and entered pilot training shortly thereafter. In 1964, he received his Navy wings and was attached to Attack Squadron-72 flying A-4 aircraft. He completed one Mediterranean cruise and two Southeast Asia combat cruises aboard the aircraft carriers USS Independence and USS Roosevelt. Mr. Griggs entered the U.S. Naval Test Pilot School at Patuxent River, Maryland, in 1967, and upon completion of test pilot training, was assigned to the Flying Qualities and Performance Branch, Flight Test Division, where he flew various test projects on fighter and attack-type aircraft. In 1970, he resigned his regular United States Navy commission and affiliated with the Naval Air Reserve in which he currently holds the rank of Rear Admiral.

As a Naval Reservist, Rear Admiral Griggs has been assigned to several fighter and attack squadrons flying A-4, A-7 and F-8 aircraft based at Naval Air Station New Orleans, LA, and Miramar, CA. His most recent assignments have been as Commanding Officer, Attack Squadron 2082, Executive Officer, Carrier Group 0282, mobilizing to Battle Force Sixth Fleet, Commanding Officer, Naval Reserve Naval Space Command 0166 stationed at the Naval Space Command Headquarters, Dahlgren, Virginia, and Commanding Officer, Office of Naval Research/Naval Research Laboratory 410, Houston, Texas. Rear Admiral Grigg's current mobilization assignment is as Chief of Staff Commander Naval Air Force, United States Pacific Fleet, San Diego, California.

He has logged 9,500 hours flying time -- 7,800 hours in jet aircraft -- and has flown over 45 different types of aircraft including single and multi engine prop, turbo prop and jet aircraft, helicopters, gliders, hot air balloons and the Space Shuttle. He has made over 300 carrier landings, and holds an airline transport pilot license and is a certified flight instructor.

NASA EXPERIENCE: In July 1970, Mr. Griggs was employed at the Lyndon B. Johnson Space Center as a research pilot, working on various flight test and research projects in support of NASA programs. In 1974, he was assigned duties as the project pilot for the shuttle trainer aircraft and participated in the design, development, and testing of those aircraft pending their operational deployment in 1976. He was appointed Chief of the Shuttle Training Aircraft Operations Office in January 1976 with responsibility for the operational use of the shuttle trainer, and held that position until being selected as an astronaut candidate by NASA in January 1978. In August 1979, he completed a 1-year training and evaluation period and became eligible for Space Shuttle flight crew assignment.

From 1979 to 1983 Mr. Griggs was involved in several Space Shuttle engineering capacities including the development and testing of the Head-Up Display (HUD) approach and landing avionics system, development of the Manned Maneuvering Unit (MMU), and the requirements definition and verification of on-orbit rendezvous and entry flight phase software and procedures. In September 1983 he began crew training as a mission specialist for flight STS 51-D, which flew April 12-19, 1985. During the flight, Mr. Griggs conducted the first unscheduled extravehicular activity (space walk) of the space program. The space walk lasted for over three hours during which preparations for a satellite rescue attempt were completed.

At the time of his death, Mr. Griggs was in flight crew training as pilot for STS-33, a dedicated Department of Defense mission, scheduled for launch in August 1989. He died on June 17, 1989, near Earle, Arkansas, in the crash of a vintage World War II airplane.

NAME: Virgil I. Grissom (Lieutenant Colonel, USAF)
NASA Astronaut (Deceased)

PERSONAL DATA: Born April 3, 1926, in Mitchell, Indiana. Died January 27, 1967, at NASA Kennedy Space Center, Florida, in the Apollo spacecraft fire. He is survived by his wife Betty and their two children.

EDUCATION: Graduated from Mitchell High School; received a Bachelor of Science degree in Mechanical Engineering from Purdue University.

ORGANIZATIONS: Member of the Society of Experimental Test Pilots.

SPECIAL HONORS: Distinguished Flying Cross and the Air Medal with cluster for his Korean service, two NASA Distinguished Service medals and the NASA Exceptional Service Medal; the Air Force Command Astronaut Wings.

EXPERIENCE: Grissom, an Air Force Lieutenant Colonel, received his wings in March 1951. He flew 100 combat missions in Korea in F-86s with the 334th Fighter Interceptor Squadron and, upon returning to the United States in 1952, became a jet instructor at Bryan, Texas. In August 1955, he entered the Air Force Institute of Technology at Wright-Patterson Air Force Base, Ohio, to study Aeronautical Engineering. He attended the Test Pilot School at Edwards Air Force Base, California, in October 1956 and returned to Wright-Patterson in May 1957 as a test pilot assigned to the fighter branch. He has logged 4,600 hours flying time-3,500 hours in jet aircraft.

NASA EXPERIENCE: Grissom was one of the seven Mercury astronauts selected by NASA in April 1959. He piloted the Liberty Bell 7 spacecraft ; the second and final suborbital Mercury test flight on July 21, 1961. This flight lasted 15 minutes and 37seconds, attained an altitude of 118 statute miles, and traveled 302 miles downrange from the launch pad at Cape Kennedy.

On March 23, 1965, he served as command pilot on the first manned Gemini flight, A 3-orbit mission during which the crew accomplished the first orbital trajectory modifications and the first lifting reentry of a manned spacecraft. Subsequent to this assignment, he served as backup command pilot for Gemini 6.Grissom was named to serve as command pilot for the AS-204 mission, the first 3-man Apollo flight

Lieutenant Colonel Grissom died on January 27, 1967, in the Apollo spacecraft flash fire during a launch pad test at Kennedy Space Center, Florida.

NAME:S. Karl G. Henize (Ph.D.)
NASA Astronaut (Deceased)

PERSONAL DATA: Born on October 17, 1926, in Cincinnati, Ohio. Died October 5, 1993. He is survived by his wife, Caroline, and four children. His hobbies included home computers, stamp collecting, and astronomy; and he also enjoyed racquet ball, baseball, skin diving, and mountain climbing.

EDUCATION: Attended primary and secondary schools in Plainville and Mariemont, Ohio; received a bachelor of arts degree in Mathematics in 1947 and a master of arts degree in Astronomy in 1948 from the University of Virginia; and awarded a doctor of philosophy in Astronomy in 1954 by the University of Michigan.

ORGANIZATIONS: Member of the American Astronomical Society; the Royal Astonomical Society; the Astronomical Society of the Pacific; the International Astronomical Union; and Phi Beta Kappa.

SPECIAL HONORS: Presented the Robert Gordon Memorial Award for 1968; recipient of NASA Group Achievement Awards (1971, 1974, 1975, 1978); awarded the NASA Exceptional Scientific Achievement Medal (1974).

EXPERIENCE: Henize was an observer for the University of Michigan Observatory from 1948 to 1951, stationed at the Lamont-Hussey Observatory in Bloemfontein, Union of South Africa. While there he conducted an objective-prism spectroscopic survey of the southern sky for stars and nebulae showing emission lines of hydrogen. In 1954 he became a Carnegie post-doctoral fellow at the Mount Wilson Observatory in Pasadena, California, and conducted spectroscopic and photometric studies of emission-line stars and nebulae. From 1956 to 1959 he served as a senior astronomer at the Smithsonian Astrophysical Observatory. He was in charge of photographic satellite tracking stations for the satellite tracking program and responsible for the establishment and operation of a global network of 12 stations for photographic tracking of artificial earth satellites. Dr. Henize was appointed associate professor in Northwestern University's Department of Astronomy in 1959 and was awarded a professorship in 1964. In addition to teaching, he conducted research on planetary nebulae, peculiar emission-line stars, S-stars, and T-associations. During 1961 and 1962, he was a guest observer at Mt. Stromlo Observatory in Canberra, Australia, where he used instruments ranging from the Uppsala 20/26-inch schmidt to the 74-inch parabolic reflector. Henize also engaged in studies of ultraviolet optical systems and astronomical programs suited to the manned space flight program. He became principal investigator of experiment S-013 which obtained ultraviolet stellar spectra during the Gemini 10, 11, and 12 flights. He also became principal investigator of experiment S-019 in which a 6-inch aperture objective-prism spectrograph was used on Skylab to obtain ultraviolet spectra of faint stars. From 1974 to 1978 Dr. Henize chaired the NASA Facility Definition Team for STARLAB, a proposed 1-meter UV telescope for Spacelab. From 1978 to 1980 he chaired the NASA Working Group for the Spacelab Wide-Angle Telescope. Since 1979 he has been the chairman of the International Astronomical Union Working Group for Space Schmidt Surveys and continues to be one of the leaders in proposing the use of a 1-meter all-reflecting Schmidt telescope to carry out a deep full-sky survey in far-ultraviolet wavelengths. He authored and/or co-authored 70 scientific publications dealing with astronomy research.

NASA EXPERIENCE: Dr. Henize was selected as a scientist-astronaut by NASA in August 1967. He completed the initial academic training and the 53-week jet pilot training program at Vance Air

Force Base, Oklahoma. He was a member of the astronaut support crew for the Apollo 15 mission and for the Skylab 2, 3, and 4 missions. He was mission specialist for the ASSESS-2 spacelab simulation mission in 1977. He has logged 2,300 hours flying time in jet aircraft. Dr. Henize was a mission specialist on the Spacelab-2 mission (STS 51-F) which launched from Kennedy Space Center, Florida, on July 29, 1985. He was accompanied by Col. Charles G. Fullerton (spacecraft commander), Col. Roy D. Bridges (pilot), fellow mission specialists, Dr's. Anthony W. England, and F. Story Musgrave, as well as two payload specialists, Dr's. Loren Acton, and John-David Bartoe. This mission was the first pallet-only Spacelab mission and the first mission to operate the Spacelab Instrument Pointing System (IPS). It carried 13 major experiments of which 7 were in the field of astronomy and solar physics, 3 were for studies of the Earth's ionosphere, 2 were life science experiments, and 1 studied the properties of superfluid helium. Dr. Henize's responsibilities included testing and operating the IPS, operating the Remote Manipulator System (RMS), maintaining the Spacelab systems, and operating several of the experiments. After 126 orbits of the earth, STS 51-F Challenger landed at Edwards Air Force Base, California, on August 6, 1985. With the completion of this flight Henize logged 188 hours in space. In 1986 he accepted a position as senior scientist in the Space Sciences Branch. Dr. Henize died October 5, 1993 of respiratory and heart failure during a climb of Mount Everest.

NAME: James Benson Irwin (Colonel, USAF, Retired)
NASA Astronaut (Deceased)

PERSONAL DATA: Born March 17, 1930 in Pittsburgh, Pennsylvania.

EDUCATION: Received bachelor of science from the U.S. Naval Academy (1951), master of science in aeronautical and instrumentation engineering from the University of Michigan (1957).

CHILDREN: Four.

NASA EXPERIENCE: Was chosen with the fifth group of a astronauts in 1966. He was backup lunar module pilot for Apollo 12 and lunar module pilot for Apollo 15 (eighth man to walk on the Moon). Colonel Irwin resigned from NASA and the Air Force in July 1972 to form a Christian organization, "High Flight Foundation," in Colorado Springs, Colorado, of which he is Chairman of the Board. His book, TO RULE THE NIGHT, describes his early life, selection into the astronaut program, conversion to Christ, and experiences on Apollo 15. Prior to his death in 1991, Colonel Irwin was an active lay witness for Christ. Additionally, he participated in trips to Asia (Turkey) in search for Noah's Ark.

NAME: Ronald E. McNair (Ph.D.)
NASA Astronaut (Deceased)

PERSONAL DATA: Born October 21, 1950, in Lake City, South Carolina. Died January 28, 1986. He is survived by his wife Cheryl, and two children. He was a 5th degree black belt Karate instructor and a performing jazz saxophonist. He also enjoyed running, boxing, football, playing cards, and cooking.

EDUCATION:Graduated from Carver High School, Lake City, South Carolina, in 1967; received a bachelor of science degree in Physics from North Carolina A&T State University in 1971 and a doctor of philosophy in Physics from Massachusetts Institute of Technology in 1976; presented an honorary doctorate of Laws from North Carolina A&T State University in 1978, an honorary doctorate of Science from Morris College in 1980, and an honorary doctorate of science from the University of SouthCarolina in 1984.

ORGANIZATIONS: Member of the American Association for the Advancement of Science, the American Optical Society, the American Physical Society (APS), the APS Committee on Minorities in Physics, the North Carolina School of Science and Mathematics Board of Trustees, the MIT Corporation Visiting Committee, Omega Psi Phi, and a visiting lecturer in Physics at Texas Southern University.

SPECIAL HONORS: Graduated magna cum laude from North Carolina A&T (1971); named a Presidential Scholar (1967-1971), a Ford Foundation Fellow (1971-1974), a National Fellowship Fund Fellow (1974-1975), a NATO Fellow (1975); winner of Omega Psi Phi Scholar of the Year Award (1975), Los Angeles Public School System's Service Commendation (1979), Distinguished Alumni Award (1979), National Society of Black Professional Engineers Distinguished National Scientist Award (1979), Friend of Freedom Award (1981), Who's Who Among Black Americans (1980), an AAU Karate Gold Medal (1976), five Regional Blackbelt Karate Championships, and numerous proclamations and achievement awards.

EXPERIENCE: While at Massachusetts Institute of Technology, Dr. McNair performed some of the earliest development of chemical HF/DF and high-pressure CO lasers. His later experiments and theoretical analysis on the interaction of intense CO_2 laser radiation with molecular gases provided new understandings and applications for highly excited polyatomic molecules. In 1975, he studied laser physics with many authorities in the field at E'cole D'ete Theorique de Physique, Les Houches, France. He published several papers in the areas of lasers and molecular spectroscopy and gave many presentations in the United States and abroad. Following graduation from MIT in 1976, he became a staff physicist with Hughes Research Laboratories in Malibu, California. His assignments included the development of lasers for isotope separation and photochemistry utilizing non-linear interactions in low-temperature liquids and optical pumping techniques. He also conducted research on electro-optic laser modulation for satellite-to-satellite space communications, the construction of ultra-fast infrared detectors, ultraviolet atmospheric remote sensing, and the scientific foundations of the martial arts.

NASA EXPERIENCE: Selected as an astronaut candidate by NASA in January 1978, he completed a 1-year training and evaluation period in August 1979, qualifying him for assignment as a mission specialist astronaut on Space Shuttle flight crews. He first flew as a mission specialist on STS 41-B which launched from Kennedy Space Center, Florida, on February 3, 1984. The crew included spacecraft commander, Mr. Vance Brand, the pilot, Commander Robert L. Gibson, and fellow mission specialists, Captain Bruce McCandless II, and Lt. Col. Robert L. Stewart. The flight accomplished the proper shuttle deployment of two Hughes 376 communications satellites, as well as the flight testing of rendezvous sensors and computer programs. This mission marked the first flight of the Manned Maneuvering Unit and the first use of the Canadian arm (operated by McNair) to position EVA crewman around Challenger's payload bay. Included were the German SPAS-01 Satellite, acoustic levitation and chemical separation experiments, the Cinema 360 motion picture filming, five Getaway Specials, and numerous mid-deck experiments -- all of which Dr. McNair assumed primary responsibility. Challenger culminated in the first landing on the runway at Kennedy Space Center on February 11, 1984. With the completion of this flight, he logged a total of 191 hours in space. Dr. McNair was assigned as a mission specialist on STS 51-L. Dr. McNair died on January 28, 1986 when the Space Shuttle Challenger exploded after launch from the Kennedy

Space Center, Florida, also taking the lives of the spacecraft commander, Mr. F.R. Scobee, the pilot, Commander M.J. Smith (USN), mission specialists, Lieutenant Colonel E.S. Onizuka (USAF), and Dr. J.A. Resnik, and two civilian payload specialists, Mr. G.B. Jarvis and Mrs. S. C. McAuliffe.

NAME: Ellison S. Onizuka (Lieutenant Colonel, USAF)
NASA Astronaut (Deceased)

PERSONAL DATA: Born June 24, 1946, in Kealakekua, Kona, Hawaii. Died January 28, 1986. He is survived by his wife, Lorna, and two daughters. He enjoyed running, hunting, fishing, and indoor/outdoor sports.

EDUCATION: Graduated from Konawaena High School, Kealakekua, Hawaii, in 1964; received bachelor and master of science degrees in Aerospace Engineering in June and December 1969, respectively, from the University of Colorado.

ORGANIZATIONS: Member of the Society of Flight Test Engineers, the Air Force Association, the American Institute of Aeronautics and Astronautics, Tau Beta Pi, Sigma Tau, and the Triangle Fraternity.

SPECIAL HONORS: Presented the Air Force Commendation Medal, Air Force Meritorious Service Medal, Air Force Outstanding Unit Award, Air Force Organizational Excellence Award, and National Defense Service Medal.

EXPERIENCE: Onizuka entered on active duty with the United States Air Force in January 1970 after receiving his commission at the University of Colorado through the 4-year ROTC program as a distinguished military graduate. As an aerospace flight test engineer with the Sacramento Air Logistics Center at McClellan Air Force Base, California, he participated in flight test programs and systems safety engineering for the F-84, F-100, F-105, F-111, EC-121T, T-33, T-39, T-28, and A-1 aircraft. He attended the USAF Test Pilot School from August 1974 to July 1975, receiving formal academic and flying instruction in performance, stability and control, and systems flight testing of aircraft. In July 1975, he was assigned to the Air Force Flight Test Center at Edwards Air Force Base, California, serving on the USAF Test Pilot School staff initially as squadron flight test engineer and later as chief of the engineering support section in the training resources branch. His duties involved instruction of USAF Test Pilot School curriculum courses and management of all flight test modifications to general support fleet aircraft (A-7, A-37, T-38, F-4, T-33, and NKC-135) used by the test pilot school and the flight test center. He has logged more than 1,700 hours flying time.

NASA EXPERIENCE: Selected as an astronaut candidate by NASA in January 1978, he completed a 1-year training and evaluation period in August 1979. He subsequently worked on orbiter test and checkout teams and launch support crews at the Kennedy Space Center for STS-1 and STS-2. He worked on software test and checkout crew at the Shuttle Avionics and Integration Laboratory (SAIL), and has supported numerous other technical assignments ranging from astronaut crew equipment/orbiter crew compartment coordinator to systems and payload development. He first flew as a mission specialist on STS 51-C, the first Space Shuttle Department of Defense mission, which launched from Kennedy Space Center, Florida on January 24, 1985. He was accompanied by Captain Thomas K. Mattingly (spacecraft commander), Colonel Loren J. Shriver (pilot), fellow mission specialist, Colonel James F. Buchli, and Lieutenant Colonel Gary E. Payton (DOD payload specialist). During the mission Onizuka was responsible for the primary payload specialist). During the mission Onizuka was responsible for the primary payload activities, which included the deployment of a modified Inertial Upper Stage (IUS). STS 51-C Discovery completed 48 orbits of the Earth before landing at Kennedy Space Center, Florida, on January 27, 1985. With the completion of this flight he logged a total of 74 hours in space. Lieutenant Colonel Onizuka was a mission specialist on STS 51-L which was launched from the Kennedy Space Center, Florida, at 11:38:00 EST on January 28, 1986. The crew on board the Orbiter Challenger included the spacecraft commander, Mr. F.R. Scobee, the pilot, Commander M.J. Smith (USN), fellow mission specialists, Dr. R.E. McNair, and Dr. J.A. Resnik, as well as two civilian payload specialists, Mr. G.B. Jarvis and Mrs. S. C. McAuliffe. The STS 51-L crew died on January 28, 1986 when Challenger exploded 1 min. 13 sec. after launch.

NAME: Robert F. Overmyer (Colonel, USMC, Ret.)
NASA Astronaut (Deceased)

PERSONAL DATA: Born July 14, 1936, in Lorain, Ohio, but considered Westlake, Ohio, his hometown. Died March 22, 1996. He is survived by his wife, Katherine, and three children. Hobbies included skiing, water skiing, boating, acrobatic flying in open cockpit biplanes, coaching baseball, and running.

EDUCATION: Attended and graduated from Westlake High School, Westlake, Ohio, in 1954. Received a bachelor of science degree in Physics from Baldwin Wallace College in 1958. Received a master of science degree in Aeronautics with a major in Aeronautical Engineering from the U. S. Naval Postgraduate School in 1964.

ORGANIZATIONS: Member of the Society of Experimental Test Pilots, Experimental Aircraft Association, and Aircraft Owners and Pilots Association.

SPECIAL HONORS: Awarded the USAF Meritorious Service Medal in 1969 for duties with the USAF Manned Orbiting Laboratory Program; awarded the USMC Meritorious Service Medal in 1978 for duties as the Chief Chase Pilot and support crewman for the Shuttle Approach and Landing Test Program; received an Honorary Doctor of Philosophy degree from Baldwin Wallace College, December 1982; awarded the U.S. Naval Postgraduate School Distinguished Engineers Award, January 1983; the USMC Distinguished Flying Cross (1983); and the NASA Space Flight Medal (1983).

EXPERIENCE: Colonel Overmyer entered active duty with the Marine Corps in January 1958. After completing Navy flight training in Kingsville, Texas, he was assigned to Marine Attack Squadron 214 in November 1959. Colonel Overmyer was assigned to the Naval Postgraduate School in 1962 to study aeronautical engineering. Upon completion of his graduate studies, he served 1 year with Marine Maintenance Squadron 17 in Iwakuni, Japan. He was then assigned to the Air Force Test Pilots School at Edwards Air Force Base, California. Colonel Overmyer was chosen as an astronaut for the USAF Manned Orbiting Laboratory Program in 1966. The program was canceled in 1969. Colonel Overmyer has over 7,500 flight hours with over 6,000 in jet aircraft.

NASA EXPERIENCE: He was selected as a NASA astronaut in 1969 after the MOL Program was canceled. His first assignment with NASA was engineering development duties on the Skylab Program from 1969 until November 1971. From November 1971 until December 1972, he was a support crew member for Apollo 17 and was the launch capsule communicator. From January 1973 until July 1975, he was a support crew member for the Apollo-Soyuz Test Project and was the NASA capsule communicator in the mission control center in Moscow, USSR. In 1976, he was assigned duties on the Space Shuttle Approach and Landing Test (ALT) Program and was the prime T-38 chase pilot for Orbiter Free-Flights 1 and 3. In 1979 Colonel Overmyer was assigned as the Deputy Vehicle Manager of OV-102 (Columbia) in charge of finishing the manufacturing and tiling of Columbia at the Kennedy Space Center preparing it for its first flight. This assignment lasted until Columbia was transported to the launch pad in 1980. Colonel Overmyer was the pilot for STS-5, the first fully operational flight of the Shuttle Transportation System, which launched from Kennedy Space Center, Florida, on November 11, 1982. He was accompanied by spacecraft commander, Vance D. Brand, and two mission specialists, Dr. Joseph P. Allen and Dr. William B. Lenoir. STS-5, the first mission with a four-man crew, clearly demonstrated the Space Shuttle as fully operational by the successful first deployment of two commercial communications satellites from the Orbiter's payload bay. The mission marked the first use of the Payload Assist Module (PAM-D), and its new ejection system. Numerous flight tests were performed throughout the mission to document Shuttle performance during launch, boost, orbit, atmospheric entry and landing phases. STS-5 was the last flight to carry the Development Flight Instrumentation (DFI) package to support flight testing. A Getaway Special, three Student Involvement Projects and medical experiments were included on the mission. The STS-5 crew successfully concluded the 5-day orbital flight of Columbia with the first entry and landing through a cloud deck to a hard-surface runway and demonstrated maximum braking. Mission duration was 122 hours before landing on a concrete runway at Edwards Air Force Base, California, on November 16, 1982. Colonel Overmyer was the commander of STS 51-B, the Spacelab-3 (SL-3) mission. He commanded a crew of 4 astronauts and 2 payload specialists conducting a broad range of scientific experiments from space physics to the suitability of animal holding facilities. Mission 51-B was also the first Shuttle flight to launch a small payload from the -Getaway Special" canisters. Mission 51-B launched at 12:02 p.m. EDT on April 29, 1985 from Kennedy Space Center, Florida, and landed at Edwards Air Force Base, California, at 9:07 a.m. PDT on May 6, 1985. Mission 51-B completed 110 orbits of the earth at an altitude of 190 n.m. Colonel Overmyer retired from NASA and the Marine Corps in May 1986. Colonel Overmyer died on March 22, 1996, in the crash of a light aircraft he was testing.

NAME: Judith A. Resnik (Ph.D.)
NASA Astronaut (Deceased)

PERSONAL DATA: Born April 5, 1949, in Akron, Ohio. Died January 28, 1986. Unmarried. She was a classical pianist and also enjoyed bicycling, running, and flying during her free time.

EDUCATION: Graduated from Firestone High School, Akron, Ohio, in 1966; received a bachelor of science degree in Electrical Engineering from Carnegie-Mellon University in 1970, and a doctorate in Electrical Engineering from the University of Maryland in 1977.

ORGANIZATIONS: Member of the Institute of Electrical and Electronic Engineers; American Association for the Advancement of Science; IEEE Committee on Professional Opportunities for Women; American Association of University Women; American Institute of Aeronautics and Astronautics; Tau Beta Pi; Eta Kappa Nu; Mortarboard; Senior Member of the Society of Women Engineers.

SPECIAL HONORS: Graduate Study Program Award, RCA, 1971; American Association of University Women Fellow, 1975-1976. NASA Space Flight Medal, 1984.

EXPERIENCE: Upon graduating from Carnegie-Mellon University in 1970, she was employed by RCA located in Moorestown, New Jersey; and in 1971, she transferred to RCA in Springfield, Virginia.

Her projects while with RCA as a design engineer included circuit design and development of custom integrated circuitry for phased-array radar control systems; specification, project management, and performance evaluation of control system equipment; and engineering support for NASA sounding rocket and telemetry systems programs. She authored a paper concerning design procedures for special-purpose integrated circuitry. Dr. Resnik was a biomedical engineer and staff fellow in the Laboratory of Neurophysiology at the National Institutes of Health in Bethesda, Maryland, from 1974 to 1977, where she performed biological research experiments concerning the physiology of visual systems. Immediately preceding her selection by NASA in 1978, she was a senior systems engineer in product development with Xerox Corporation at El Segundo, California.

NASA EXPERIENCE: Selected as an astronaut candidate by NASA in January 1978, she completed a 1-year training and evaluation period in August 1979. Dr. Resnik worked on a number of projects in support of Orbiter development, including experiment software, the Remote Manipulator System (RMS), and training techniques. Dr. Resnik first flew as a mission specialist on STS 41-D which launched from the Kennedy Space Center, Florida, on August 30, 1984. She was accompanied by spacecraft commander Hank Hartsfield, pilot Mike Coats, fellow mission specialists, Steve Hawley and Mike Mullane, and payload specialist Charlie Walker. This was the maiden flight of the orbiter Discovery. During this 7-day mission the crew successfully activated the OAST-1 solar cell wing experiment, deployed three satellites, SBS-D, SYNCOM IV-2, and TELSTAR 3-C, operated the CFES-III experiment, the student crystal growth experiment, and photography experiments using the IMAX motion picture camera. The crew earned the name "Icebusters" in successfully removing hazardous ice particles from the orbiter using the Remote Manipulator System. STS 41-D completed 96 orbits of the earth before landing at Edwards Air Force Base, California, on September 5, 1984. With the completion of this flight she logged 144 hours and 57 minutes in space. Dr. Resnik was a mission specialist on STS 51-L which was launched from the Kennedy Space Center, Florida, at 11:38:00 EST on January 28, 1986. The crew on board the Orbiter Challenger included the spacecraft commander, Mr. F.R. Scobee, the pilot, Commander M.J. Smith (USN), fellow mission specialists, Dr. R.E. McNair, and Lieutenant Colonel E.S. Onizuka (USAF), as well as two civilian payload specialists, Mr. G.B. Jarvis and Mrs. S. C. McAuliffe. The STS 51-L crew died on January 28, 1986 when Challenger exploded after launch.

NAME: Stuart Allen Roosa (Colonel, USAF, Retired)
NASA Astronaut (Deceased)

PERSONAL DATA: Born August 15, 1933, Durango, Colorado.

EDUCATION: Received bachelor of science in aeronautical engineering from the University of Colorado (1960).

CHILDREN: Four

NASA EXPERIENCE: Was chosen with the fifth group of astronauts in 1966. He was the command module pilot of Apollo 14, and backup command module pilot for Apollo 16 and Apollo 17. Colonel Roosa resigned from NASA on February 1, 1976 to become Vice-President for International Affairs, U.S. Industries Middle East Development Company, based in Athens, Greece. In 1977 he returned to the United States to become President of Jet Industries in Austin, Texas. He was later in private business in Austin.

NAME: Francis R. (Dick) Scobee (Mr.)
NASA Astronaut (Deceased)

PERSONAL DATA: Born May 19, 1939, in Cle Elum, Washington. Died January 28, 1986. He is survived by his wife, June, and two children. He enjoyed flying, oil painting, woodworking, motorcycling, racquetball, jogging, and most outdoor sports.

EDUCATION: Graduated from Auburn Senior High School, Auburn, Washington, in 1957; received a bachelor of science degree in Aerospace Engineering from the University of Arizona in 1965.

ORGANIZATIONS: Member of the Society of Experimental Test Pilots, the Tau Beta Pi, the Experimental Aircraft Association, and the Air Force Association.

SPECIAL HONORS: Awarded the Air Force Distinguished Flying Cross, the Air Medal, and two NASA Exceptional Service Medals.

EXPERIENCE: Scobee enlisted in the United States Air Force in 1957, trained as a reciprocating engine mechanic, and was subsequently stationed at Kelly Air Force Base, Texas. While there, he attended night school and acquired 2 years of college credit which led to his selection for the Airman's Education and Commissioning Program. He graduated from the University of Arizona with a bachelor of science degree in Aerospace Engineering. He received his commission in 1965 and, after receiving his wings in 1966, completed a number of assignments including a combat tour in Vietnam. He returned to the United States and attended the USAF Aerospace Research Pilot School at Edwards Air Force Base, California. Since graduating in 1972, he has participated in test programs for which he has flown such varied aircraft as the Boeing 747, the X-24B, the transonic aircraft technology (TACT) F-111, and the C-5. He has logged more than 6,500 hours flying time in 45 types of aircraft.

NASA EXPERIENCE: Scobee was selected as an astronaut candidate by NASA in January 1978. In August 1979, he completed a 1-year training and evaluation period, making him eligible for assignment as a pilot on future Space Shuttle flightcrews. In addition to astronaut duties, Mr. Scobee was an Instructor Pilot on the NASA/Boeing 747 shuttle carrier airplane. He first flew as pilot of STS 41-C which launched from Kennedy Space Center, Florida, on April 6, 1984. Crew members included spacecraft commander Captain Robert L. Crippen, and three mission specialists, Mr. Terry J. Hart, Dr. G.D. (Pinky) Nelson, and Dr. J.D.A. (Ox) van Hoften. During this mission the crew successfully deployed the Long Duration Exposure Facility (LDEF); retrieved the ailing Solar Maximum Satellite, repaired it on-board the orbiting Challenger, and replaced it in orbit using the robot arm called the Remote Manipulator System (RMS). The mission also included flight testing of Manned Maneuvering Units (MMU's) in two extravehicular activities (EVA's); operation of the Cinema 360 and IMAX Camera Systems, as well as a Bee Hive Honeycomb Structures student experiment. Mission duration was 7-days before landing at Edwards Air Force Base, California, on April 13, 1984. With the completion of this flight he logged a total of 168-hours in space. Mr. Scobee was spacecraft commander on STS 51-L which was launched from Kennedy Space Center, Florida, at 11:38:00 EST on January 28, 1986. The crew on board the Orbiter Challenger included the pilot, Commander M.J. Smith (USN) pilot), three mission specialists, Dr. R.E. McNair, Lieutenant Colonel E.S. Onizuka (USAF), and Dr. J.A. Resnik, as well as two civilian payload specialists, Mr. G.B. Jarvis and Mrs. S. C. McAuliffe. The STS 51-L crew died on January 28, 1986 when Challenger exploded after launch.

NAME: Elliott M. See, Jr.
NASA Astronaut (Deceased)

PERSONAL DATA: Born in Dallas, Texas, on July 23, 1927. Died February 28, 1966, in St. Louis Missouri in the crash of a T-38 jet. He is survived by his wife Marilyn and their three children.

EDUCATION: Bachelor of Science degree, U.S. Merchant Marine Academy; Master of Science degree in engineering, University of California at Los Angeles.

ORGANIZATIONS: Member of the Society of Experimental Test Pilots; Associate Fellow of the American Institute of Aeronautics and Astronautics.

EXPERIENCE: Naval Aviator from 1953 to 1956. General Electric Company from 1949 to 1953 and 1956 to 1962 as a flight test engineer, group leader, and experimental test pilot. Served as project pilot on J79-8 engine development program in connection with F4H aircraft. Conducted powerplant flight tests on the J-47, J-73, J-79, CJ805 and CJ805 aft-fan engines. This work involved flying in F-86, XF4D, F-104, F11F-1F, RB-66, F4H, and T-38 aircraft. See logged over 3,700 hours flying time, including 3,200 hours in jet aircraft.

NASA EXPERIENCE: See was one of nine pilot astronauts selected in September 1962. He participated in all phases of the astronaut training program and was subsequently given responsibility for monitoring the design and development of guidance and navigation systems. He also aided in the coordination for mission planning. He was selected as pilot of the back-up crew for the Gemini 5 mission, and the command pilot for the Gemini 9 flight. Mr. See died on February 28, 1966, in St. Louis, Missouri, in the crash of a T-38 aircraft.

NAME: Alan B. Shepard, Jr. (Rear Admiral, USN, Ret.)
NASA Astronaut (Deceased)

PERSONAL DATA: Born November 18, 1923, in East Derry, New Hampshire. Died on July 21, 1998. He is survived by wife, Louise; daughters Julie, Laura and Alice, and six grandchildren.

EDUCATION: Attended primary and secondary schools in East Derry and Derry, New Hampshire; received a Bachelor of Science degree from the United States Naval Academy in 1944, an Honorary Master of Arts degree from Dartmouth College in 1962, and Honorary Doctorate of Science from Miami University (Oxford, Ohio) in 1971, and an Honorary Doctorate of Humanities from Franklin Pierce College in 1972. Graduated Naval Test Pilot School in 1951; Naval War College, Newport, Rhode Island in 1957.

ORGANIZATIONS: Fellow of the American Astronautical Society and the Society of Experimental Test Pilots; member of the Rotary, the Kiwanis, the Mayflower Society, the Order of the Cincinnati, and the American Fighter Aces; honorary member, Board of Directors for the Houston School for Deaf Children, Director, National Space Institute, and Director, Los Angeles Ear Research Institute.

SPECIAL HONORS: Congressional Medal of Honor (Space); Awarded two NASA Distinguished Service Medals, the NASA Exceptional Service Medal, the Nave Astronaut Wings, the Navy Distinguished Service Medal, and the Navy Distinguished Flying Cross; recipient of the Langley Medal (highest award of the Smithsonian Institution) on May recipient of the Langley Medal (highest award of the Smithsonian Institution) on May 5, 1964, the Lambert Trophy, the Kinchloe Trophy, the Cabot Award, the Collier Trophy, the City of New York Gold Medal (1971), Achievement Award for 1971. Shepard was appointed by the President in July 1971 as a delegate to the 26th United Nations General Assembly and served through the entire assembly which lasted from September to December 1971.

EXPERIENCE: Shepard began his naval career, after graduation from Annapolis, on the destroyer Cogswell, deployed in the pacific during World War II. He subsequently entered flight training at Corpus Christi, Texas, and Pensacola, Florida, and received his wings in 1947. His next assignment was with Fighter Squadron 42 at Norfolk, Virginia, and Jacksonville, Florida. He served several tours aboard aircraft carriers in the Mediterranean while with this squadron. In 1950, he attended the United States Navy Test Pilot School at Patuxent River, Maryland. After graduation, he participated in flight test work which included high-altitude tests to obtain data on light at different altitudes and on a variety of air masses over the American continent; and test and development experiments of the Navy's in-flight refueling system, carrier suitability trails of the F2H3 Banshee, and Navy trials of the first angled carrier deck. He was subsequently assigned to Fighter Squadron 193 at Moffett Field, California, a night fighter unit flying Banshee jets. As operations officer of this squadron, he made two tours to the Western pacific onboard the carrier Oriskany. He returned to Patuxent for a second tour of duty and engaged in flight testing the F3H Demon, F8U Crusader, F4D Skyray, and F11F Tigercat. He was also project test pilot on the F5D Skylancer, and his last five months at Patuxent were spent as an instructor in the Test Pilot School. He later attended the Naval War College at Newport, Rhode Island, and upon graduating in 1957 was subsequently assigned to the staff of the Commander-in-Chief, Atlantic Fleet, as aircraft readiness officer. He has logged more than 8,000 hours flying time--3,700 hours in jet aircraft.

NASA EXPERIENCE: Rear Admiral Shepard was one of the Mercury astronauts named by NASA in April 1959, and he holds the distinction of being the first American to journey into space. On May 5, 1961, in the Freedom 7 spacecraft, he was launched by a Redstone vehicle on a ballistic trajectory suborbital flight--a flight which carried him to an altitude of 116 statute miles and to a landing point 302 statute miles down the Atlantic Missile Range. In 1963, he was designated Chief of the Astronaut Office with responsibility for monitoring the coordination, scheduling, and control of all activities involving NASA astronauts. This included monitoring the development and implementation of effective training programs to assure the flight readiness of available pilot/non-pilot personnel for assignment to crew positions on manned space flights; furnishing pilot evaluations applicable to the design, construction, and operations of spacecraft systems and related equipment; and providing qualitative scientific and engineering observations to facilitate overall mission planning, formulation of feasible operational procedures, and selection and conduct of specific experiments for each flight. He was restored to full flight status in May 1969, following corrective surgery for an inner ear disorder. Shepard made his second space flight as spacecraft commander on Apollo 14, January 31 - February 9, 1971. He was accompanied on man's third lunar landing mission by Stuart A. Roosa, command module pilot, and Edgar D. Mitchell, lunar module pilot. Maneuvering their lunar module, Antares, to a landing in the hilly upland Fra Mauro region of the moon, Shepard and Mitchell subsequently deployed and activated various scientific equipment and experiments and collected almost 100 pounds of lunar samples for return to earth. Other Apollo 14 achievements included: first use of Mobile Equipment Transporter (MET); largest payload placed in lunar orbit; longest distance traversed on the lunar surface; largest payload returned from the lunar surface; longest lunar surface stay time (33 hours); longest lunar surface EVA (9 hours and 17 minutes); first use of shortened lunar orbit rendezvous techniques; first use of colored TV with new vidicon tube on lunar surface; and first extensive orbital science period conducted during CSM solo operations. Rear Admiral Shepard has logged a total of 216 hours and 57 minutes in space, of which 9 hours and 17 minutes were spent in lunar surface EVA. He resumed his duties as Chief of the Astronaut Office in June 1971 and served in this capacity until he retired from NASA and the Navy on August 1, 1974. Shepard was in private business in Houston, Texas. He served as the President of the Mercury Seven Foundation, a non-profit organization which provides college science scholarships for deserving students.

NAME: Donald (Deke) Slayton
NASA Astronaut (Deceased)

PERSONAL DATA: Born March 1, 1924, in Sparta, Wisconsin. Died June 13, 1993. He is survived by wife, Bobbie, and son, Kent.

EDUCATION: Graduated from Sparta High School; received a bachelor of science degree in Aeronautical Engineering from the University of Minnesota, Minneapolis, Minnesota, in 1949.

ORGANIZATIONS: Fellow of the Society of Experimental Test Pilots and the American Astronautical Society; associate fellow of the American Institute of Aeronautics and Astronautics; member of the Experimental Aircraft Association, the Space Pioneers, and the Confederate Air Force; life member of the Order of Daedalians, the National Rifle Association of America, the Veterans of Foreign Wars, and the Fraternal Order of Eagles; honorary member of the American Fighter Aces Association, and the National WWII Glider Pilots Association.

SPECIAL HONORS: NASA Distinguished Service Medal (3); NASA Exceptional Service Medal; the Collier Trophy; the SETP Iven C. Kincheloe Award; the Gen. Billy Mitchell Award; the SEPT J.H. Doolittle Award (1972); the National Institute of Social Sciences Gold Medal (1975); the Zeta Beta Tau's Richard Gottheil Medal (1975); the Wright Brothers International Manned Space Flight Award (1975); the Veterans of Foreign Wars National Space Award (1976); the American Heart Association's Heart of the Year Award (1976); the District 35-R Lions International American of the Year Award (1976); the AIAA Special Presidential Citation (1977); the University of Minnesota's Outstanding Achievement Award (1977); the Houston Area Federal Business Association's Civil Servant of the Year Award (1977); the AAS Flight Achievement Award for 1976 (1977); the AIAA Haley Astronautics Award for 1978; the NASA Outstanding Leadership Medal (1978); honorary doctorate in Science from Carthage College, Carthage, Illinois, in 1961; honorary doctorate in Engineering from Michigan Technological University in Houghton, Michigan, in 1965.

EXPERIENCE: Slayton entered the Air Force as an aviation cadet and received his wings in April 1943 after completing flight training at Vernon and Waco, Texas. As a B-25 pilot with the 340th Bombardment Group, he flew 56 combat missions in Europe. He returned to the United States in mid-1944 as a B-25 instructor pilot at Columbia, South Carolina, and later served with a unit responsible for checking pilot proficiency in the A-26. In April 1945, he was sent to Okinawa with the 319th Bombardment Group and flew seven combat missions over Japan. He served as a B-25 instructor for one year following the end of the war and subsequently left the Air Force to enter the University of Minnesota. He became an aeronautical engineer after graduation and worked for two years with the Boeing Aircraft Corporation at Seattle, Washington, before being recalled to active duty in 1951 with the Minnesota Air National Guard. Upon reporting for duty, he was assigned as maintenance flight test officer of an F-51 squadron located in Minneapolis, followed by 18-months as a technical inspector at Headquarters Twelfth Air Force, and a similar tour as fighter pilot and maintenance office with the 36th Fighter Day Wing at Bitburg, Germany. Returning to the United States in June 1955, he attended the USAF Test Pilot School at Edwards Air Force Base, California. He was a test pilot there from January 1956 until April 1959 and participated in the testing of fighter aircraft built for the United States Air Force and some foreign countries. He has logged more than 6,600 hours flying time, including 5,100 hours in jet aircraft.

NASA EXPERIENCE: Mr. Slayton was named as one of the Mercury astronauts in April 1959. He was originally scheduled to pilot the Mercury-Atlas 7 mission but was relieved of this assignment due to a heart condition discovered in August 1959. Slayton became Coordinator of Astronaut Activities in September 1962 and was responsible for the operation of the astronaut office. In November 1963, he resigned his commission as an Air Force Major to assume the role of Director of Flight Crew Operations. In this capacity, he was responsible for directing the activities of the astronaut office, the aircraft operations office, the flight crew integration division, the crew training and simulation division, and the crew procedures division. Slayton was restored to full flight status and certified eligible for manned space flights in March 1972, following a comprehensive review of his medical status by NASA's Director of Life Sciences and the Federal Aviation Agency. Mr. Slayton made his first space flight as Apollo docking module pilot of the Apollo-Soyuz Test Project (ASTP) mission, July 15-24, 1975—a joint space flight culminating in the first historical meeting in space between American astronauts and Soviet cosmonauts. Completing the United States flight crew for this 9-day earth-orbital mission were Thomas P. Stafford (Apollo commander) and Vance D. Brand (Apollo command module Pilot). In the Soviet spacecraft were cosmonauts Alexey Leonov (Soyuz commander) and Valeriy Kubasov (Soyuz flight engineer). The crewmen of both nations participated in a rendezvous and subsequent docking, with Apollo the active spacecraft. The event marked the successful testing of a universal docking system and signaled a major advance in efforts to pave the way for the conduct of joint experiments and/or the exchange of mutual assistance in future international space explorations. There were 44 hours of docked joint activities during ASTP, highlighted by four crew transfers and the completion of a number of joint scientific experiments and engineering investigations. All major ASTP objectives were accomplished and included: testing a compatible rendezvous system in orbit; testing of androgynous docking assemblies; verifying techniques for crew transfers; and gaining experience in the conduct of joint international flights. Apollo splashed down in the Pacific Ocean near Hawaii and was quickly recovered by the USS New Orleans. Slayton logged 217 hours and 28 minutes in his first space flight. From December 1975 through November 1977, Slayton served as Manager for Approach and Landing Test Project. He directed the Space Shuttle approach and landing test project through a series of critical orbiter flight tests that allowed in-flight test and checkout of flight controls and orbiter subsystems and permitted extensive evaluations of the orbiter's subsonic flying qualities and performance characteristics. He next served as Manager for Orbital Flight Test, directing orbital flight mission preparations and conducting mission operations. He was responsible for OFT operations scheduling, mission configuration control, preflight stack configuration control, as well as conducting planning reviews, mission readiness reviews, and postflight mission evaluations. He was also responsible for the 747/orbiter ferry program.

Slayton retired from NASA in 1982. He was president of Space Services Inc., of Houston, a company he founded to develop rockets for small commercial payloads.

NAME: Michael J. Smith (Captain, USN)
NASA Astronaut (Deceased)

PERSONAL DATA: Born April 30, 1945, in Beaufort, North Carolina. Died January 28, 1986. He is survived by his wife, Jane, and three children. Michael enjoyed woodworking, running, tennis, and squash.

EDUCATION: Graduated from Beaufort High School, Beaufort, North Carolina, in 1963; received a bachelor of science degree in Naval Science from the United States Naval Academy in 1967 and a master of science degree in Aeronautical Engineering from the U.S. Naval Postgraduate School in 1968.

SPECIAL HONORS: The Defense Distinguished Service Medal (posthumous), Navy Distinguished Flying Cross, 3 Air Medals, 13 Strike Flight Air Medals, the Navy Commendation Medal with "V", the Navy Unit Citation, and the Vietnamese Cross of Gallantry with Silver Star.

EXPERIENCE: Graduated from the United States Naval Academy in 1967 and subsequently attended the U.S. Naval Postgraduate School at Monterey, California. He completed Navy aviation jet training at Kingsville, Texas, receiving his aviator wings in May 1969. He was then assigned to the Advanced Jet Training Command (VT-21) where he served as an instructor from May 1969 to March 1971. During the 2-year period that followed, he flew A-6 Intruders and completed a Vietnam cruise while assigned to Attack Squadron 52 aboard the USS Kitty Hawk (CV-63). In 1974, he completed U.S. Navy Test Pilot School and was assigned to the Strike Aircraft Test Directorate at Patuxent River, Maryland, to work on the A-6E TRAM and CRUISE missile guidance systems. He returned to the U.S. Navy Test Pilot School in 1976 and completed an 18-month tour as an instructor. From Patuxent River, he was assigned to Attack Squadron 75 where he served as maintenance and operations officer while completing two Mediterranean deployments aboard the USS Saratoga. He flew 28 different types of civilian and military aircraft, logging 4,867.7 hours of flying time.

NASA EXPERIENCE: Selected as an astronaut candidate by NASA in May 1980, he completed a 1-year training and evaluation period in August 1981, qualifying him for assignment as a pilot on future Space Shuttle flight crews. He served as a commander in the Shuttle Avionics Integration Laboratory, Deputy Chief of Aircraft Operations Division, Technical Assistant to the Director, Flight Operations Directorate, and was also assigned to the Astronaut Office Development and Test Group.

Captain Smith was assigned as pilot on STS 51-L. He was also assigned as pilot for Space Shuttle Mission 61-N scheduled for launch in the Fall of 1986. Captain Smith died on January 28, 1986 when the Space Shuttle Challenger exploded after launch from the Kennedy Space Center, also taking the lives of spacecraft commander, Mr. F.R. Scobee, three mission specialists, Dr. R.E. McNair, Lieutenant Colonel E.S. Onizuka (USAF), and Dr. J.A. Resnik, and two civilian payload specialists, Mr. G.B. Jarvis and Mrs. S. C. McAuliffe.

NAME: John Leonard "Jack" Swigert, Jr.
       NASA Astronaut (Deceased)

PERSONAL DATA: Denver, Colorado, August 30, 1931. Son of Mrs. J. Leonard Swigert, who resides in Denver, and the late Dr. J. Leonard Swigert.

PHYSICAL DESCRIPTION: Blond hair, blue eyes; height: 5 feet 11-1/2 inches; weight: 180 pounds.

EDUCATION: Attended Regis and East High Schools in Denver; received bachelor of science degree in Mechanical Engineering from University of Colorado, 1953; master of science in Aerospace Science from Rensselear Polytechnic Institute, 1965; master of business Administration from the University of Hartford, 1967; and was presented Honorary Doctorate of Science by American International College, 1970, Honorary Doctorate of Laws by Western State College, 1970; Honorary Doctorate of Science by Western Michigan University, 1970.

ORGANIZATIONS: Fellow of the American Astronautical Society; Associate Fellow of the Society of Experimental Test Pilots and the American Institute of Aeronautics and Astronautics; and member of the Quiet Birdmen, Phi Gamma Delta, Pi Tau Sigma and Sigma Tau.

SPECIAL HONORS: Presented the Presidential Medal for Freedom, 1970, and the NASA Distinguished Service Medal; corecipient of the American Astronautical Society Flight Achievement Award for 1970, the AIAA Octave Chanute Award for 1966 (for his participation in demonstrating the Rogallo Wing as a feasible land landing system for returning space vehicles and astronauts); and recipient of University of Colorado Distinguished Alumnus Award, 1970; City of New York Gold Medal, 1970; City of Houston Medal for Valor, 1970; City of Chicago Gold Medal, 1970; Antonian Gold Medal, 1972; and the Sons of the American Revolution Gold Citizenship Medal, 1979.

EXPERIENCE: Swigert served with the Air Force from 1953 to 1956, including a tour of duty as a fighter pilot in Japan and Korea. He also served as a jet fighter pilot with the Massachusetts Air National Guard (1957 to 1960) and the Connecticut Air National Guard (1960 to 1965). He has logged over 8,000 hours of flight time, of which more than 6,430 hours are in jet aircraft.

NASA EXPERIENCE: Swigert was one of 19 Astronauts selected by NASA in 1966. He served as a member of the astronaut support crews for the Apollo 7 and Apollo 11 missions. He was next assigned to the Apollo 13 backup crew and subsequently replaced prime crewman, Thomas K. Mattingly as Command Module Pilot 24 hours prior to flight, following Mattingly's exposure to German measles. Apollo 13, April 11-17, 1970, was programmed for a ten day flight as America's third lunar landing. However, at 55 hours into the flight and 200,000 miles from Earth, an explosion in the Service Module oxygen system required modification of the flight plan and the emergency conversion of the Lunar Module into a lifeboat for survival and safety in space and the return to earth. In completing his first space flight, Swigert logged a total of 142 hours and 54 minutes.

POST NASA EXPERIENCE: From April 1973, to September 1977, Swigert served as Executive Director of the Committee on Science and Technology in the U.S. House of Representatives in Washington, D.C. In that capacity, he was responsible for assuring the accomplishment of the legislative and oversight functions of the staff of the Committee, the jurisdiction of which included all Federal research and development in the areas of energy, environment, space, science, and civil aviation. His responsibilities included personnel acquisition, planning, organizing, budgeting, directing and controlling the staff of the Committee (some 80 people). In 1978, Swigert ran for the United States Senate from Colorado and was unsuccessful in his first attempt at elective office. In 1979, Swigert joined the BDM Corporation, a broad-based professional services company as Vice President for Technology Development and directed the Company's Denver operations. He was responsible for the formulation of programs with emphasis on energy, space, environment and transportation. In 1981, Swigert left BDM to join International Gold and Minerals Limited as Vice President for Financial and Corporate Affairs In February 1982, Swigert left International Gold and Minerals Limited to initiate his compaign for the U.S. Congress. On November 2, 1982, Swigert won the new seat for Colorado's Sixth Congressional District receiving 64% of the popular vote. Swigert died of complications from cancer in Washington December 27, 1982, a week before he would have taken the congressional seat he won in the November 2 election.

NAME: Stephen D. Thorne (Lieutenant Commander, USN)
NASA Astronaut (Deceased)

BIRTHPLACE AND DATE: Born February 11, 1953, in Frankfurt-on-Main, West Germany. Died May 24, 1986. He is survived by his wife, Sue. He enjoyed baseball, running, reading, and general aviation.

EDUCATION: Graduated from T.L. Hanna High School, Anderson, South Carolina, in 1971; received a bachelor of science degree in systems engineering from the U.S. Naval Academy in 1975.

ORGANIZATIONS: Member of the Society of Experimental Test Pilots. Life member of the Naval Academy Alumni Association.

SPECIAL HONORS: Received Navy Commendation Medal in January 1986.

EXPERIENCE: Upon graduation from the Naval Academy, Thorne entered flight training and received his wings in December 1976. Following training in the F-4 Phantom, he joined Fighter Squadron 21 (VF-21) and deployed to the Western Pacific aboard the USS Ranger. After training at the U.S. Naval Test Pilot School in 1981, Thorne spent the next two years at Strike Aircraft Test at the Naval Air Test Center, Patuxent River, Maryland, flying mostly ordnance and weapons systems tests in the F-4 and A-7 Corsair II. He completed F-18 Hornet transition training in October 1984 and joined Strike Fighter Squadron 132 (VFA-132) aboard USS Coral Sea until departing for NASA. He accumulated over 2,500 hours and 200 carrier landings in approximately 30 different types of aircraft.

NASA EXPERIENCE: Thorne was selected as an astronaut by NASA in June 1985 and, in August, commenced a one-year training and evaluation program to qualify him for subsequent assignment as a pilot on future Space Shuttle flightcrews.

Lieutenant Commander Thorne was killed in an aircraft accident, in which he was a passenger, on May 24, 1986.

NAME: Charles Lacy Veach (Mr.)
       NASA Astronaut (Deceased)

PERSONAL DATA: Born September 18, 1944, in Chicago, Illinois, but considered Honolulu, Hawaii, to be his hometown. mMarried to the former Alice Meigs Scott of Waycross, Georgia. Two children. He enjoyed surfing, bicycling, reading, and activities with his family. His parents, Mr. and Mrs. Marshall E. Veach, reside in Honolulu, Hawaii. Her mother, Mrs. Myrtle Lee Scott, resides in Augusta, Georgia. Her father, Commander Frank V. Scott, Jr., is deceased.

EDUCATION: Graduated from Punahou School, Honolulu, Hawaii, in 1962; received a bachelor of science degree in engineering management from the U.S. Air Force Academy in 1966.

SPECIAL HONORS: Distinguished Flying Cross with 2 Oak Leaf Clusters, Air Medal with 13 Oak Leaf Clusters, Air Force Commendation Medal with 1 Oak Leaf Cluster, and Purple Heart.

EXPERIENCE: Veach was commissioned in the United States Air Force upon graduation from the Air Force Academy. He received his pilot wings at Moody Air Force Base, Georgia, in 1967, and then attended fighter gunnery school at Luke Air Force Base, Arizona. Over the next 14 years, he served as a USAF fighter pilot, flying the F-100 Super Sabre, the F-111, and the F-105 Thunderchief, on assignments in the United States, Europe, and the Far East, including a 275-mission combat tour in the Republic of Vietnam. In 1976 and 1977, he was a member of the USAF Air Demonstration Squadron, the Thunderbirds. Veach left active duty in 1981, but continued to fly fighters as an F-16 pilot with the Texas Air National Guard. He had logged over 5,000 flying hours.

NASA EXPERIENCE: Veach came to work for NASA in January 1982 as an engineer and research pilot at the Johnson Space Center in Houston. His primary duty was as an instructor pilot in the Shuttle Training Aircraft, the highly modified Gulfstream II used to train astronaut pilots to land the Space Shuttle. Veach was selected as an astronaut candidate in May 1984, and became an astronaut in June 1985. He held a variety of technical assignments, and had flown as a mission specialist on two Space Shuttle missions, STS-39 in 1991 and STS-52 in 1992. He had logged 436.3 hours in space. Most recently, Lacy had worked as the lead astronaut for the development and operation of robotics for the International Space Station. On STS-39, Veach was responsible for operating a group of instruments which included an ultraviolet astronomical camera, an x-ray telescope, and a liquid helium-cooled infrared telescope which performed landmark observations of the Earth's atmosphere and the Aurora Australis (the Southern Lights). The 8-day unclassified Department of Defense mission aboard the Orbiter Discovery launched from the Kennedy Space Center in Florida on April 28, 1991, and landed at Kennedy on May 6, 1991. STS-52 was a 10-day mission aboard the Orbiter Columbia during which the crew successfully deployed the Laser Geodynamic Satellite (LAGEOS), a joint Italian-American project. They also operated the first U.S. Microgravity Payload (USMP) with French and American experiments. Veach was the primary Remote Manipulator System (RMS) operator on the mission, supporting the initial flight tests of the Canadian-built Space Vision System (SVS). STS-52 launched from the Kennedy Space Center in Florida on October 22, 1992, and landed at Kennedy on November 1, 1992.

Lacy Veach died in Houston, Texas, on October 3, 1995, of cancer.

NAME: Edward H. White, II (Lieutenant Colonel)
NASA Astronaut (Deceased)

PERSONAL DATA: Born in San Antonio, Texas, on November 14, 1930. Died January 27, 1967, at NASA Kennedy Space Center, Florida, in the Apollo spacecraft fire. He is survived by his wife Patricia and their two children.

EDUCATION: Bachelor of Science degree from United States Military Academy; Master of Science degree in Aeronautical Engineering, University of Michigan.

ORGANIZATIONS: Associate member of Institute of Aerospace Sciences; Member of Sigma Delta Psi, athletic honorary; and Member of Tau Delta Pi, engineering honorary.

SPECIAL HONORS: Golden Plate Award; Honorary Doctorate degree in Astronautics, University of Michigan; NASA Exceptional Service Medal and Senior Astronaut Wings; Medalha Bandeirantes va Cosmonautica; Firefly Club Award; Ten Outstanding Young Men of the Nation for 1965; Five Out-standing Young Texans for 1965; The John Fitzgerald Kennedy Trophy; Aerospace Primus Club; 1966 Achievement Award, National Aviation Club; General Thomas White Award.

EXPERIENCE: White, an Air Force Lieutenant Colonel, received flight training in Florida and Texas, following his graduation from West Point. He then spent 3-1/2 years in Germany with a fighter squadron, flying F-86's and F-100's. He attended the Air Force Test Pilot School at Edwards Air Force Base, California, in 1959. White was later assigned to Wright-Patterson Air Force Base, Ohio, as an experimental test pilot with the Aeronautical Systems Division. In this assignment he made flight tests for research and weapons systems development, wrote technical engineering reports, and made recommendations for improvement in aircraft design and construction. He logged more than 3,000 hours flying time, including more than 2,200 hours in jet aircraft.

NASA EXPERIENCE: White was named as a member of the astronaut team selected by NASA in September 1962. He was pilot for Gemini 4, which was a 66-revolution, 4-day mission that began on June 3, and ended on June 7, 1965. During the third revolution, he carried out the first extra vehicular activity in the United States manned space flight program. He was outside Gemini 4 for 21 minutes, and became the first man to control himself in space during EVA with a maneuvering unit. Other highlights of the mission included cabin depressurization, opening of cabin doors, and 12 scientific and medical experiments. He received the NASA Exceptional Service Medal and the U.S. Air Force Senior Astronaut Wings for this Flight. On March 21, 1966, he was named as one of the pilots of the AS-204 mission, the first 3-man Apollo flight.

Lieutenant Colonel White died on January 26, 1967, in the Apollo spacecraft flash fire during a launch pad test at Kennedy Space Center, Florida.

NAME: Clifton C. Williams, Jr. (Major, USMC)
NASA Astronaut (Deceased)

PERSONAL DATA: Born September 26, 1932, in Mobile, Alabama. Died on October 5, 1967, near Tallahassee, Florida, in the crash of a T-38 jet. He is survived by his wife Jane and a daughter.

EDUCATION: Graduated from Murphy High School, Mobile, Alabama; received a Bachelor of Science degree in Mechanical Engineering from Auburn University, Auburn, Alabama.

ORGANIZATIONS: Associate member of the Society of Experimental Test Pilots and member of Pi Tau Sigma (national mechanical honorary, and Tau Beta Pi (national engineering society).

EXPERIENCE: Williams, a Marine Corps Major, graduated from the Navy Test Pilot School at Patuxent River, Maryland. He was test pilot for three years in the Carrier Suitability Branch of the Flight Test Division at Patuxent River. His work there included land based and shipboard tests of the F8E, TF8A, F8E (attack), and A4E and automatic carrier landingsystem.

Of the 2,500 hours flying time accumulated, he has more than 2,100 hours in jet aircraft.

NASA EXPERIENCE: Williams was one of the third group of astronauts named by NASA in October 1963. He served as backup pilot for the Gemini 10 mission and worked in the areas of launch operations and crew safety.

Major Williams died on October 5, 1967, near Tallahassee, Florida, in the crash of a T-38 jet.

Chapter Six:

NASA

Payload

Specialists

Dr. John-David F. Bartoe
Research Manager, International Space Station
Payload Specialist

Dr. John-David Bartoe is Research Manager for the International Space Station (ISS) at NASA's Johnson Space Center. He provides oversight for the Program Manager concerning the research capability, research hardware, and research plans of the ISS.

Prior to his present position, Dr. Bartoe was Director of Operations and Utilization in the Space Station Office of NASA Headquarters from 1990 to 1994. He also served as Chief Scientist for the Space Station from 1987 to 1990.

Before coming to NASA Headquarters, he flew on Space Shuttle Mission 51-F (July 29 to August 6, 1985) as a civilian Navy payload specialist. A physicist by training, Dr. Bartoe was co-investigator on two solar physics investigations aboard this mission, designated Spacelab 2, that were designed to study features of the sun's outer layers. In completing this flight, Dr. Bartoe traveled over 2.8 million miles in 126 Earth orbits and logged over 190 hours in space.

From 1966 to 1988, Dr. Bartoe worked as an astrophysicist at the Naval Research Laboratory in Washington, D.C., and published over 60 papers in the field of solar physics observations and instrumentation. He received his B.S. in physics from Lehigh University (1966) and his M.S. and Ph.D. in physics from Georgetown University (1974 and 1976).

Dr. Bartoe is a member of the Association of Space Explorers, and is Chairman of the Space Stations Committee of the International Astronautical Federation. His awards include the NASA Exceptional Achievement Medal, the Navy Distinguished Civilian Service Award, the Flight Achievement Award of the American Astronautical Society, the NASA Space Flight Medal, and the NASA Skylab Achievement Award.

Born November 17, 1944 in Abington, Pennsylvania, he is married to Donna June Bartoe, and has three children.

NAME: Roberta Lynn Bondar, O.C., O.Ont., M.D., Ph.D., F.R.C.P.©
CSA Astronaut (Payload Specialist)

PERSONAL DATA: Born in Sault Ste. Marie, Ontario, Canada. Dr. Bondar has certification in scuba diving, parachuting, and holds a private pilot's license. She enjoys photography, biking, hot air ballooning, roller blading, and flying.

CURRENT STATUS: Distinguished Professor, Centre for Advanced Technology Education (CATE), Ryerson Polytechnic University, Toronto, Ontario; CIBC Distinguished Professor, Faculty of Kinesiology, University of Western Ontario, London, Ontario; Visiting Research Scholar, Department of Neurology, University of New Mexico; Visiting Research Scientist, Universities Space Research Association, Johnson Space Centre, Houston, Texas.

CURRENT ACTIVITIES: Principal investigator, Transcranial Doppler in Patients with Orthostatic Intolerance, University of New Mexico, Deaconess Hospital, Boston; Principal investigator, Transcranial Doppler in Astronauts Before and After Space Flight, Johnson Space Centre, Edwards Air Force Base, and Kennedy Space Centre; Author, Touching the Earth, Key Porter Books, Toronto, Ontario; Chair, Friends of the Environment Foundation (non-profit organization of Canada Trust).

EDUCATION: Attended elementary and secondary school in Sault Ste. Marie, Ontario. Degrees: B.Sc. in zoology and agriculture, University of Guelph, 1968, M. Sc. in experimental pathology, University of Western Ontario, 1971, Ph.D. in neurobiology, University of Toronto, 1974, M.D., McMaster University, 1977. Admitted as a Fellow of the Royal College of Physicians and Surgeons of Canada as a specialist in neurology in 1981.

EXPERIENCE: Dr. Bondar is a neurologist and researcher. After internship in internal medicine at Toronto General Hospital, she completed post-graduate medical training in neurology at the University of Western Ontario; neuro-opthalmology at Tuft's New England Medical Center (Boston) and the Playfair Neuroscience Unit of Toronto Western Hospital; and carotid Doppler ultrasound and transcranial Doppler at the Pacific Vascular Institute (Seattle). She was appointed Assistant Professor of Medicine (Neurology), McMaster University, 1982-84; Scientific staff, Sunnybrook Medical Centre, Toronto, 1988-present; Visiting Research Scholar, Department of Neurology, University of New Mexico, 1993-95; Adjunct Professor, Department of Biology, University of New Mexico, 1992-1994; Distinguished Professor, CATE, Ryerson, 1992-present; Visiting Distinguished Fellow, Department of Medicine, Faculty of Health Sciences, McMaster University, 1993-94; Visiting Distinguished Professor, Faculty of Kinesiology, University of Western Ontario, 1994-present. She was one of the six original Canadian astronauts selected in December, 1983 and began astronaut training in February, 1984. She served as chairperson of the Canadian Life Sciences Subcommittee for Space Station from 1985 to 1989, and as a member of the Ontario Premier's Council on Science and Technology from 1988 to 1989. In early 1990, she was designated a prime Payload Specialist for the first International Microgravity Laboratory Mission (IML-1). Dr. Bondar flew on the space shuttle Discovery during Mission STS-42, January 22-30, 1992 where she performed life science and material science experiments in the Spacelab and on the middeck.

HONORARY DEGREES:D.Sc., Mount Allison University, Sackville, New Brunswick, 1989; D.Hum.L., Mount St. Vincent University, Halifax, Nova Scotia, 1990; Senior Fellowship from Ryerson Polytechnical Institute, Toronto, Ontario, 1990; D.Sc., University of Guelph, Guelph, Ontario, 1990; D.Sc., Lakehead University, Thunder Bay, Ontario, 1991; D.Sc., Algoma College, Laurentian University, Sault Ste.

Marie, Ontario, 1991; D.Sc., Saint Mary's University, Halifax, Nova Scotia, 1992; D.Sc., McMaster University, Hamilton, Ontario, 1992; L.L.D. University of Regina, Regina, Saskatchewan, 1992; L.L.D., University of Calgary, Calgary, Alberta; D.U., University of Ottawa, Ottawa, Ontario, 1992; D.Sc., University of Toronto, Toronto, Ontario, 1992; D.Sc., McGill University, Montreal, Quebec, 1992; D.Sc., York University, Toronto, Ontario, 1992; D.Sc., Carleton University, Ottawa, Ontario, 1993; D.S.L., Wycliffe College, University of Toronto, Toronto, Ontario, 1993; D.Sc., Royal Roads Military College, Victoria, British Columbia, 1993; D.Sc., Memorial University, St. John's, Newfoundland, 1993; D.Sc., Laval University, Laval, Quebec, 1993; D.Sc., University of Montreal, Montreal, Quebec, 1994; D.Sc., University of Prince Edward Island, Charlottetown, Prince Edward Island, 1994; D.Sc., University of Western Ontario, London, Ontario, 1995.

SPECIAL HONORS AND AWARDS: Officer of the Order of Canada; the Order of Ontario; Canada 125 Medal; NASA's Space Medal; Hubertus Strughold Award, Space Medicine Branch, Aerospace Medicine Association; Award of Merit, University of Western Ontario; Medaille de L 'Excellence, L 'Association des Medicins de Langue Francaise du Canada; gLa Personalite de L 'Annee 1992, La Presse; 1995 Women's Intercultural Network International Women's Day Award; 1993 Alumnus of the Year, University of Guelph; Outstanding Canadian, Armenian Community Centre of Toronto; YWCA Woman of Distinction Award, Prince Albert, Saskatchewan, Kurt Hahn Award, Outward Bound; 1992 Paul Harris Recognition Award, Rotary Club of Ancaster, Inductee into the Hamilton Gallery of Distinction, 1995 Women's Intercultural Network International Women's Day Award. Honorary Life Member, Canadian Federation of University Women, Girl Guides of Canada, Federation of Medical Women of Canada, Science North, and Zonta International.

HONORARY APPOINTMENTS: Patron, World Congress of Neurology (Vancover), Canadian Federation of Business and Professional Women's Clubs, Mission Air Transportation Network, Canadian Bushplane Heritage Centre, Young Scientists of Canada, Aphasia Centre (North York), Ontario Parks Association, Earth Observation Theatre - Fort Whyte Centre (Winnipeg); 1995 International Mathematical Olympiad. Honorary Chairperson, Canadian Coalition for Quality Daily Physical Education, Women's Soccer Competition - World Student Games, The Parkinson Foundation of Canada, Marsville Program - Ontario Science Centre. Honorary Colonel, 22 Wing, Canadian Armed Forces, Hornell Heights, Ontario. Honorary Director, Save Our North Atlantic Resources. Member, Canadian Association for Women in Science, l'Association des Medecins de Langue Francaise du Canada, Bootmakers of Canada, Canadian Aviation Historical Society.

HONORS IN NAME OF ROBERTA LYNN BONDAR: Roberta Bondar Public School, Ottawa, Ontario; Dr. Roberta Bondar Public School, Ajax, Ontario; Queen Elizabeth Public School Resource Centre, Sault Ste. Marie; Alex Muir Public School Resource Centre, Sault Ste. Marie; Trophy for Outstanding Male and Female Athlete of the Year, Sir James Dunn Collegiate and Vocational School, Sault Ste. Marie; Roberta Bondar Gymnasium, Sir James Dunn Collegiate and Vocational School, Sault Ste. Marie; Soo College Scholarship, Sault Ste. Marie; Sir James Dunn Collegiate and Vocational School Scholarship, Sault Ste. Marie; Bawating Collegiate and Vocational School Scholarship, Sault Ste. Marie; Girl Guides of Canada Scholarship; Province of Ontario Science and Technology Awards, USS Bondar, The Guelph Trek Club; Roberta Bondar Earth and Space Centre, Seneca College, Toronto, Ontario; Place Roberta Bondar Place - Province of Ontario, Sault Ste. Marie; YWCA Scholarship, Prince Albert, Saskatchewan; Roberta Bondar Rose, Hortico Nurseries; Roberta Bondar Park and Tent Pavilion, Sault Ste. Marie, Ontario.

ORGANIZATIONS: Fellow, Royal College of Physicians and Surgeons of Canada. Member, American Academy of Neurology, Canadian Aeronautics and Space Institute, Canadian Society of Aerospace Medicine, College of Physicians and Surgeons of Ontario, Canadian Stroke Society, Aerospace Medical Association, Albuquerque Aerostat Ascension Association, American Society for Gravitational and Space Biology, Association for Space Explorers, Canadian Society of Aerospace Medicine, Greater Albuquerque Medical Association, Canadian Medical Association, Ontario Medical Association, Canadian Association of Sports Medicine.

NAME: Jay Clark Buckey, Jr. M.D
Payload Specialist

PERSONAL DATA: Born June 6, 1956 in New York, New York. His mother, Jean Buckey, resides in Ft. Myers, Florida. His father, Jay Buckey, Sr., is deceased. Married to the former Sarah Woodroffe Masters of Summit, New Jersey daughter of Parke and Margaret Masters. They have one son and two daughters. Recreational interests include camping, history.

EDUCATION: Graduated from W. Tresper Clarke High School in Westbury, New York, in 1973. Earned a bachelor of science degree in electrical engineering from Cornell University in 1977, and a doctorate in medicine from Cornell University Medical College in 1981. Interned at New York Hospital-Cornell Medical Center, and completed residency at Dartmouth-Hitchcock Medical Center. NASA Space Biology Fellow at University of Texas (UT) Southwestern Medical Center.

ORGANIZATIONS: American Society for Gravitational and Space Biology (Executive Board Member 1991-1994), Aerospace Medicine Association, and American College of Physicians.

SPECIAL HONORS: Meritorious service award from the University of Texas for work on Spacelab Life Sciences-1 (SLS-1) (1991), Outstanding Teacher Award from the Class of 1994 at UT-Southwestern, Distinguished Graduate USAF School of Aerospace Medicine Primary Course (1987), two NASA Certificates of Recognition for hardware developed for SLS-1, NASA Biology Fellowship (1982), Thora Halstead Young Investigator Award (1994), NASA Space Flight Medal (1998).

PUBLICATIONS: Dr. Buckey has over 20 publications in the areas of space physiology, cardiovascular regulation and echocardiographic techniques.

EXPERIENCE: Medical internship, New York Hospital-Cornell Medical Center, New York, 1981-1982; NASA Space Biology Fellow, UT-Southwestern, 1982-1984; Research Instructor, Department of Medicine, UT-Southwestern, 1984-1986; Assistant Professor Medicine, UT-Southwestern, 1986-1994; Associate Professor Medicine, UT-Southwestern, 1995; Medicine Resident, Dartmouth-Hitchcock Medical Center, 1995-1996. Associate Professor of Medicine, Dartmouth Medical School, 1996-present; Flight Surgeon, U.S. Air Force Reserve, 457th Tactical Fighter Squadron at Naval Air Station Joint Reserve Base, Fort Worth, TX, 1987-1995. Dr. Buckey took leave from Dartmouth Medical School to fly as a Payload Specialist on the Neurolab mission, STS-90.

NASA EXPERIENCE: Co-investigator and project manager for the space flight experiment "Cardiovascular Adaptation to Zero-Gravity;" Spacelab Life Sciences-1; Alternate Payload Specialist, Spacelab Life Sciences-2. Most recently, Dr. Buckey served as Payload Specialist-1 on STS-90 Neurolab (April 17 to May 3, 1998). During the 16-day Spacelab flight the seven person crew aboard Space Shuttle Columbia served as both experiment subjects and operators for 26 individual life science experiments focusing on the effects of microgravity on the brain and nervous system. The STS-90 flight orbited the Earth 256 times, covered 6.3 million miles, and logged him over 381 hours in space.

Robert J. Cenker
Aerospace Systems Consultant
Payload Specialist

Mr. Cenker currently consults with various firms in the areas of spacecraft design, assembly, and flight operations, and micro-gravity research. This has included launch vehicle evaluation and systems engineering support for Motorola on Iridium; avionics architecture, generation of performance specification, and generation of performance map for small expendable launch vehicle; and constellation configuration and launch vehicle performance definition for proprietary smallsat communications system. Last two years with RCA were spent as Manager of Payload Accommodations on EOS Platform. Prior assignments at RCA included Integration and Test Manager for the Satcom D & E spacecraft, responsible for implementation of all launch site activities, and Spacecraft Bus Manager on the Spacenet/Gstar programs, responsible for satisfaction of multiple launch vehicle interfaces (Delta, STS and Ariane) by the spacecraft bus design. Other efforts include systems engineering and operations support for INTELSAT on Intelsat K and Intelsat VIII; AT&T on Telstar 401 and 402; Fairchild Matra on SPAS III; and Martin Marietta on Astra 1B, BS3N, ACTS, and Series 7000 communications satellites. Systems engineering and architecture for various spacecraft studies, ranging from individual Smallsats, military communications constellations, and large, assembled-in-orbit platforms. Former member of the technical staff at the RCA/GE Astro Space Division. In 18 years with GE (formerly RCA) he worked in a variety of functions, including satellite attitude control and in-orbit operations; spacecraft assembly, test, and pre-launch operations; and satellite hardware and system design. Approximately two years of this experience were with a Navy navigation satellite program, with the remaining time spent on various commercial communications satellite efforts. Selected by RCA as a Payload Specialist; and approved by NASA to fly on the space shuttle Columbia on Space Shuttle Mission 61-C. During the six day mission, (January 12 to 18, 1986) he performed a variety of physiological tests, observed the deployment of the RCA Satcom Ku-1 satellite, and operated primary experiment, an infrared imaging camera. In completing this flight, Mr. Cenker traveled over 2.1 million miles in 96 Earth orbits and logged over 146 hours in space.

Born November 5, 1948 and raised near Uniontown, Pennsylvania. Mr. Cenker holds Bachelor's and Master's degrees in Aerospace Engineering from Penn State; and a Master's degree in Electrical Engineering from Rutgers. He is an Associate Fellow in the AIAA, a Senior Member of the IEEE, a Life Member of the Penn State Alumni Association, a member of the Association of Space Explorers, and a registered Professional Engineer in the state of New Jersey. He is also a member of TauBeta Pi and Sigma Gamma Tau.

Married to Barbara Ann Cenker. They have two sons and one daughter.

NAME: Roger K. Crouch
  Payload Specialist

PERSONAL DATA: Considers Jamestown, Tennessee, where he was born September 12, 1940, as his hometown. Currently resides in Laurel, Maryland. One daughter, two sons. Hobbies include traveling, photography, basketball, softball, camping, hiking, fishing, and whitewater rafting. His mother, Mrs. Maxine S. Crouch, lives in Jamestown, Tennessee. His father, Willard Crouch is deceased.

EDUCATION: Earned a bachelor of science in physics from Tennessee Polytechnic Institute in 1962, a master of science and a doctor of philosophy in physics from Virginia Polytechnic Institute in 1968 and 1971, respectively. He was a visiting scientist at Massachusetts Institute of Technology in 1979-80.

EXPERIENCE: As the Chief Scientist of the NASA Microgravity Space and Applications Division since 1985 he has served as the manager for a research program that supports materials science, fluid physics, low temperature microgravity physics, combustion science, and biotechnology. He had responsibility for assuring that experiments in the flight program achieved the highest levels of scientific results possible. He served as Program Scientist on Spacelab J, the second International Microgravity Laboratory Program (IML-2), the first United States Microgravity Laboratory (USML-1) and a Program Scientist (Materials Sciences) IML-1. In addition, he helped organize and has served as co-chairman for Microgravity Science Working Groups between NASA and the European Space Agency, France, Germany, Japan and Russia. He was the co-chair of the International Microgravity Science Strategic Planning Group. He was the co-chair for the IML Science Working Group from 1985-1989. He has served on several governmental interagency panels on Materials Science, most recently as a team member assessing the potential for collaborative efforts between the U.S. and China. He was a co-principal investigator on an experiment that flew in the Materials Experiment Apparatus on the D-1 mission. Prior to working in NASA Headquarters, he had been at the Langley Research Center since 1962. His last position there was group leader of a research group investigating the effects of convection on semiconductor properties. He was a principal investigator in the MSAD flight program from 1977-1985. He has done research in various types of semiconductor crystal growth, electrical and optical properties of materials, electronic devices for remote sensing and flat panel displays and heat shield protection for reentry space vehicles. He trained as the Alternate Payload Specialist on STS-42 (First International Microgravity Laboratory).

SPACE FLIGHT EXPERIENCE: Twice flown, Dr. Crouch was a payload specialist on STS-83 (April 4-8,1997) and STS-94 (July 1-17, 1997) and has logged over 471 hours in space. STS-83, the Microgravity Science Laboratory (MSL-1) Spacelab mission, was cut short because of problems with one of the Shuttle's three fuel cell power generation units. Mission duration was 95 hours and 12 minutes, traveling 1.5 million miles in 63 orbits of the Earth. STS-94 was a re-flight of the Microgravity Science Laboratory (MSL-1) Spacelab mission, and focused on materials and combustion science research in microgravity. Mission duration was 376 hours and 45 minutes, traveling 6.3 million miles in 251 orbits of the Earth.

PUBLICATIONS:Published over 40 technical papers and more than 40 technical presentations in various areas of research, concentratingsince 1978 on semiconductor crystal growth and the influence of gravitational forces on materials properties.

SPECIAL HONORS: Floyd Thompson Fellowship 1979; Quality Increase 1972, 1986, 1988; Exceptional Service Award 1989; Outstanding Performance Rating, 1985, 1986, 1987, 1989, Certificates of Recognition 1973, 1975, 1976, 1977, 1979, 1980, 1981, 1984 (2), 1985, 1986, 1987 (3), Special Achievement Award, 1983, Sustained Superior Performance Award, 1989, Superior Accomplishment Award 1992, NASA Exceptional Achievement Medal 1995.

ORGANIZATIONS: Member of American Physical Society, American Association for Crystal Growth, Sigma Pi Sigma, Kappa Mu Epsilon.

NAME: Lawrence J. DeLucas (O. D., Ph.D.)
Payload Specialist

PERSONAL DATA: Born July 11, 1950, Syracuse, New York. Married to the former Katherine Elizabeth Gester. They have three children. Recreational interests include basketball, scuba diving, model airplanes, astronomy and reading.

EDUCATION: Received a bachelor of science degree and a master of science degree in chemistry, University of Alabama at Birmingham, Birmingham, Alabama, 1972 and 1974, respectively; a bachelor of science degree in physiological optics, University of Alabama at Birmingham, Birmingham, Alabama, 1979; a doctorate in optometry in 1981; and a doctorate in biochemistry, University of Alabama at Birmingham, Birmingham, Alabama, 1982.

ORGANIZATIONS: Dr. DeLucas is a member of the American Crystallographic Association, American Diabetes Association, Juvenile Diabetes Association, American Academy of Optometry, American Institute of Aeronautics and Astronautics, Alabama Optometric Association, American Association of Pharmaceutical Scientists, National Aeronautic Association, and Executive Committee and Board of the Helen Keller Eye Research Foundation.

PUBLICATIONS: He has published over 60 research articles in refereed scientific journals, is co-author of 2 books, and co-inventor of 3 patents.

SPECIAL HONORS: Co-Chair, Spacehab Science Advisory Board; Secretary of the Board, Council of Biotechnology Centers, Biotechnology Industry Council; 1st Place in Graduate Student Research Competition sponsored by Sigma Xi.

EXPERIENCE: Research Associate in the Institute of Dental Research, University of Alabama at Birmingham, 1975-1976; Graduate Student, 1977-1982 working on combined doctoral degrees in Optometry and Biochemistry; Member of Vision Science Research Center, 1982-present; Scientist, Research Center in Oral Biology, 1982-present; Member, Graduate Faculty, University of Alabama at Birmingham, 1983-present; Scientist, Comprehensive Cancer Center, University of Alabama at Birmingham, 1984-present; Adjunct Professor, Materials Science, University of Alabama at Huntsville, University of Alabama at Birmingham, University of Alabama, 1989-present; Member, Comprehensive Cancer Center Internal Review Committee, University of Alabama at Birmingham, 1990-present; served on External Review Committee, NASA, 1988; Member of NASA Science Advisory Committee for Advanced Protein Crystal Growth, 1987-present; Adjunct Professor, Laboratory of Medical Genetics, University of Alabama at Birmingham, 1990-present; Adjunct Professor, Department of Biochemistry, University of Alabama at Birmingham, 1990-present; Member, Executive Committee, Helen Keller Eye Research Foundation, 1990-present; Professor, Department of Optometry, University of Alabama at Birmingham, 1989-present; Associate Director, Center for

Macromolecular Crystallography, University of Alabama at Birmingham,. 1986-present; Director, Center for Macromolecular Crystallography, University of Alabama at Birmingham, 1994-present. Dr. DeLucas was a member of the crew of Space Shuttle Columbia for STS-50/United States Microgravity Laboratory-1 (USML-1) Spacelab mission.

NAME: Alexander William Dunlap, D.V.M., M.D.
Payload Specialist

PERSONAL DATA: Born July 15, 1960 in Honolulu, Hawaii. Single. Recreational interests include flying, music, scuba diving, golf, skiing, and photography. His parents, Lt. Col. William L. Dunlap (USAF retired) and Alix E. Dunlap, are deceased.

EDUCATION: Graduated from West Memphis Senior High School, West Memphis, Arkansas in 1978. Received bachelor of science degrees in zoology and in animal science (Cum Laude) from the University of Arkansas, Fayetteville, Arkansas, in 1982 and 1984, respectively, a doctorate in veterinary medicine in 1989 from Louisiana State University, Baton Rouge, Louisiana and a doctorate in medicine in 1996 from the University of Tennessee College of Medicine, Memphis, Tennessee.

ORGANIZATIONS: American Society for Gravitational and Space Biology, American Veterinary Medical Association, Memphis and Shelby County Veterinary Medical Association, American Academy of Family Physicians and Tennessee Academy of Family Physicians.

SPECIAL HONORS: University of Tennessee College of Medicine - Dean's Commendation for Meritorious Achievement, Research Award presented by the American Association for Laboratory Animal Science (outstanding paper published in Laboratory Animal Science, 1990), John Gammon Foundation Scholarship, Student Chapter of the American Association of Equine Practitioners Scholarship and from Louisiana State University he received the Hill's Hospital Design Award and the Hill's Senior Student Award.

PUBLICATIONS: Has published three articles and presented two posters in the areas of animal and human physiology.

EXPERIENCE: In 1984-1985 Dr. Dunlap worked as an Electron Microscopy Research Technician at the University of Tennessee Center for the Health Sciences and as an Electrical Generating Systems Technician for Coleman Engineering, Memphis, Tennessee, in 1986. He was a Student Resident at Louisiana State University School of Veterinary Medicine from 1986-1987 followed by an Externship in Laboratory Animal Medicine at the University of Tennessee Center for the Health Sciences in 1987. After receiving his Doctor of Veterinary Medicine in 1989, he worked as a Veterinarian at Bowling Animal Clinic, Collierville, Tennessee, from 1989-1992. Between 1991-1995 Dr. Dunlap supported five NASA space flights and attended medical school. In 1996 he received his Doctor of Medicine degree and completed his first year of residency through an Accelerated Medical Resident program at the University of Tennessee Department of Family Medicine. He is currently on leave from this program to work on STS-90, Neurolab.

NASA EXPERIENCE: In 1991 he served as a Biospecimen Sharing Program Team Member and a Project Veterinarian during Spacelab Life Sciences-1 (STS-40) and post flight he performed delayed flight profile tests of onboard hardware. He served as the Project Veterinarian, for the Physiological Systems Experiment-02 (STS-52) in 1992. Followed by working as a Dryden Landing Site Biospecimen

Sharing Team Member for the Physiological and Anatomical Rodent Experiment-03 (STS-56) and as a Payload Specialist Finalist/Support Scientist and Veterinarian for Spacelab Life Sciences-2 (STS-58) in 1993. In 1995 he worked as a Veterinarian/Surgeon at the Dryden Landing Site for National Institutes of Health-R2 (STS-70) and post flight he performed biospecimen tests at Kennedy Space Center.

CURRENT ASSIGNMENT: Dr. Dunlap is a Payload Specialist candidate for STS-90, Neurolab. Job responsibilities include training with the principal investigators in the specific experiments to be conducted before, during and post-flight. Specific activities include both task and mission training.

NAME: Samuel T. Durrance (Ph.D.)
NASA Payload Specialist

PERSONAL DATA: Born September 17, 1943, in Tallahassee, Florida, but considers Tampa, Florida his hometown. Married to the former Rebecca Tuggle. Two children. He enjoys going to the beach with his family, scuba diving, flying, running, auto racing, photography, and camping. His parents, Rodney and Leone Durrance, are residents of Lakeland, Florida. Her parents, Tommy and Sue Tuggle, reside in Bossier City, Louisiana.

EDUCATION: Received a bachelor of science degree and a master of science degree in physics (with honors), California State University, Los Angeles, California, 1972 and 1974, respectively; and a doctor of philosophy degree in astro-geophysics, University of Colorado, 1980.

PROFESSION: Dr. Durrance is a Principal Research Scientist in the Department of Physics and Astronomy at The Johns Hopkins University, Baltimore, Maryland. He is a co-investigator for the Hopkins Ultraviolet Telescope, one of the instruments of the Astro Observatory.

ORGANIZATIONS: American Astronomical Society, American Geophysical Union, International Astronomical Union, Association of Space Explorers, Planetary Society, and Phi Kappa Phi.

EXPERIENCE: Dr. Durrance has been involved in the flight hardware development, optical and mechanical design, construction, and integration of the Hopkins Ultraviolet Telescope and the Astro Observatory. He has conducted research and directed graduate students at the Johns Hopkins University for the past 15 years. He has designed and built spectrometers, detectors, and imaging systems, and made numerous spacecraft and ground-based astronomical observations. He conceived and directed a program at Johns Hopkins University to develop adaptive-optics instrumentation for ground based astronomy. He led the team that designed and constructed the Adaptive Optics Coronagraph, which led to the discovery of a cool brown dwarf -- the first unambiguous detection. His research interests include the origin and evolution of the solar system, the search for planets around other stars, and the origin of life. He has published over 60 technical papers about spacecraft operations, planetary astronomy, adaptive optics, aeronomy, and nuclear physics. Dr. Durrance has logged over 615 hours in space as a member of the crew of Space Shuttle Columbia for the STS-35/Astro-1 and Space Shuttle Endeavour for the STS-67/Astro-2 missions.

CURRENT ASSIGNMENT: Dr. Durrance is located at the Johns Hopkins University Center for Astrophysical Sciences in Baltimore, Maryland. He is a member of the research team analyzing ultraviolet data returned from the STS-67/Astro-2 space shuttle flight. He is also President of Earth Systems Technology, a small company developing new technology for the study and management of Earth's resources.

NAME: Jean-Jacques Favier (Ph.D.)
French Payload Specialist

PERSONAL DATA: Born April 13, 1949, in Kehl, Germany. Married to the former Michele Jean. Four children. He enjoys downhill skiing, tennis, wind-surfing, and archeology.

EDUCATION: Attended primary and secondary schools in Strasbourg, France. Received an engineering degree from the National Polytechnical Institute of Grenoble in 1971 and earned a Ph.D. in engineering from the Mining School of Paris and a Ph.D. in metallurgy and physics from the University of Grenoble in 1977.

ORGANIZATIONS: Research Engineer, Commissaniat a l'Energie Atomique (CEA), 1976-1979. Head Solidification Group 1970-1986, Head of Laboratory 1986-1989, Head Solidification and Crystal Growth Service, 1989 to 1993, Cons. European Space Agency (ESA), Centre National D'Etudes Spatiales (CNES), Paris 1983 to present. Astronaut Candidate CNES, Paris 1985 to present. Member of Space Station User Panel of ESA.

SPECIAL HONORS: Recipient Zellidja Association 2nd prize, French Academy Literature 1970, E. Brun Price Award French Academy Sciences. Member of International Organization of Crystal Growth. Member of American Association of Crystal Growth, Societe Francaise de Metallurgie. Groupe Francais de Croissance Cristalline (Committee Chairman). Visiting Professor at University of Alabama in Huntsville (UAH) (1994-95). Member of the Space Science Committee of the European Science Foundation (ESF). Several patents on crystal growth processes, furnaces and insitu diagnosis. Published more than 80 research articles in refereed scientific journals and books.

EXPERIENCE: Dr. Favier is currently the Advisor of the Director of the Material Science Research Center (CEREM) at the French Atomic Energy Commission (CEA) and is presently detached to CNES. He proposed the MEPHISTO program, a collaborative project between the French Space Agency and NASA, and has developed many other scientific projects in collaboration with the United States since 1985. He is the principal investigator (P.I.) for a MEPHISTO materials processing experiment, which made its debut on the United States Microgravity Payload in 1992 and 1994 and is scheduled for subsequent Space Shuttle flights, the next being STS-75 in 1996. He has been a CNES payload specialist candidate since 1985. He has been P.I. of more than 10 space experiments in collaboration with ESA, NASA, and the Russians.

CURRENT ASSIGNMENT: Dr. Favier was assigned as an alternate payload specialist on STS-65/IML-2, the second International Migrogravity Laboratory mission, and supported the mission as a Crew Interface Coordinator (CIC/APS) from the Payload Operations Control Center (POCC) at the Marshall Space Flight Center in Huntsville, Alabama. He is currently assigned as a payload specialist on STS-78/LMS-1, a Life Microgravity Spacelab mission.

NAME: Martin Joseph Fettman (B.S., D.V.M., M.S., Ph.D., Diplomate, ACVP)
Payload Specialist

PERSONAL DATA: Born December 31, 1956, Brooklyn, New York. Single. Recreational interests include scuba diving, amateur radio, flying, bicycling, pistol marksmanship, camping and mountain hiking, photography, travel, reading (mysteries), and music (jazz and classical). His mother, Mrs. Elaine Fettman Peck, resides in Brooklyn, New York, with his stepfather, Mr. Harold Peck. His father, Mr. Bernard P. Fettman, is deceased.

EDUCATION: Graduated from Midwood High School, Brooklyn, New York, in 1973. Received bachelor of science degree in animal nutrition from Cornell University in 1976, doctor of veterinary medicine degree and master of science degree in nutrition from Cornell University in 1980, and doctor of philosophy degree in physiology from Colorado State University in 1982. He received board certification in veterinary clinical pathology in 1984 and is a diplomate of the American College of Veterinary Pathologists.

ORGANIZATIONS: American Academy of Veterinary Nutrition, American Association for Clinical Chemistry, American Association for the Advancement of Science, American College of Veterinary Pathologists, American Dairy Science Association, American Society of Animal Science, American Society of Gravitational and Space Biology, American Veterinary Medical Association, Association of Veterinarians for Animal Rights, New York Academy of Sciences, Shock Society, National Audobon Society (life), National Wildlife Federation (life), Nature Conservancy, Sierra Club.

PUBLICATIONS: He has published over 100 research articles in refereed scientific journals.

EXPERIENCE: Dr. Fettman's first faculty appointment was 1982-1986 in the Department of Pathology of the College of Veterinary Medicine and Biomedical Sciences at Colorado State University, as an Assistant Professor of Clinical Pathology whose duties included teaching, research, and clinical service. From 1983 to the present, he has held a joint appointment in the Department of Physiology at Colorado State University and his research and teaching interests have focused on selected aspects of the Pathophysiology of nutritional and metabolic diseases, with emphasis on the physiological biochemistry of energy, electrolyte, and fluid metabolism. In 1986 he was promoted to Associate Professor, and in 1988 assumed the duties of section chief of Clinical Pathology in the Veterinary Teaching Hospital at Colorado State University. Dr. Fettman spent one year (1989-1990) on sabbatical leave as a Visiting Professor of Medicine at The Queen Elizabeth Hospital and the University of Adelaide, South Australia, where he worked with the Gastroenterology Unit studying the biochemical epidemiology of human colorectal cancer. He was appointed to the Mark L. Morris Chair in Clinical Nutrition at Colorado State University and received a joint appointment in the Department of Clinical Sciences in 1991, and was promoted to Full Professor of Pathology in 1992. Dr. Fettman is a George H. Glover distinguished faculty member of the College of Veterinary Medicine and Biomedical Sciences and was named the 1994 Sigma Xi honored scientist at Colorado State University, the 1994 Spencer T. and Ann W. Olin Lecturer at Cornell University, and a Bard College Distinguished Scientist for 1995.

NASA EXPERIENCE: In his first affiliation with NASA, Dr. Fettman was selected as a payload specialist candidate in December 1991, as the prime payload specialist for Spacelab Life Sciences-2 in October 1992, and flew on STS-58 in October 1993. Sincethe flight, he has made over seventy public appearances representing space life sciences research before higher education, medical, veterinary, and lay organizations, and visited over twenty K-12 schools around the United States and Canada. He is presently a member of the NASA Advisory Council Life and Biomedical Sciences and Applications Advisory Subcommittee.

NAME: Thomas J. Hennen (Chief Warrant Officer 4, U.S. Army, retired)
Payload Specialist

PERSONAL DATA: Born August 17, 1952, in Albany Georgia, but considers Columbus, Ohio to be his hometown. Unmarried. Two sons, one daughter. He enjoys playing basketball, bowling, dancing, snorkeling, scuba diving, sky diving, traveling, and listening to music. His parents, Carl H. (retired USAF CMS) and Antoinette L. Hennen reside in Columbus, Ohio.

EDUCATION: Graduated from Groveport-Madison High School in Groveport, Ohio, in 1970. Attended Urbana College in Urbana, Ohio from 1970-1972 on both an academic and athletic scholarship. Tom has completed the following military courses of instruction: U.S. Army Imagery Interpretation Course, 1973; U.S. Army Administrative Specialist Course, 1973; Distinguished Graduate of the III Corps and Fort Hood Leadership Course, 1974; U.S. Army Automatic Data Processing and System Analysis Course, 1974; Honor Graduate of the 5th U.S. Army Non-Commission Officers Academy, 1975; U.S. Marine Air Ground Intelligence System Operators Course, 1976; Distinguished Graduate of the Defence Sensor Interpretation and Application Training Program, 1976; Distinguished Graduate of the U.S. Air Force Europe (USAFE) Advanced Imagery Interpretation Course, 1978; the Analytical Photogrammetrical Positioning System Operators course, 1978; National Imagery Interpretability Rating System Instructors Course, 1979; U.S. Army Intelligence Analyst Course, 1979; the Computer-Aided Tactical Information System Operator and Supervisor Course, 1980; U.S. Army Pre-Commission Course, 1980; U.S. Army Warrant Officer Orientation Course, 1981; the Advanced Synthetic Aperture Radar Analysis Course, 1981; U.S. Army Infantry Officer Basic Course, 1982; U.S. Army Warrant Officer Senior Course, 1982; U.S. Army Military Intelligence Officer Basic Course, 1983; U.S. Army Military Intelligence Officer Advanced Course, 1984; U.S. Army Armor Officer Basic Course, 1985; the Joint Space Intelligence and Operations Course,1986; U.S. Army Signal Officer Basic Course, 1986; U.S. Army Warrant Officer Advanced Course, 1986; the Tactical Exploitation of National Space Capabilities (TENCAP) Course, 1987; and NASA Payload Specialist Training, 1991.

SPECIAL HONORS: Awarded the Defense Superior Service Medal (DSSM); three U.S. Army Meritorious Service Medals; the U.S. Army Commendation Medal; two U.S. Army Achievement Medals; the NASA Space Flight Medal; Three U.S. Army Good Conduct Medals; the National Defense Service Medal; and two U.S. Air Force Outstanding Unit Awards. Chief Hennen was selected on numerous occasions as Soldier and Non-Commissioned Officer (NCO) of the Quarter/Year by the various commands and agencies to which he was assigned during his enlisted career. Chief Hennen was the first Warrant Officer within the U.S. Army and Department of Defense, to have been selected as a member of a Space Shuttle flight crew.

EXPERIENCE: Chief Hennen served over 24 years in the imagery intelligence field. He received extensive technical training and experience as an operational imagery analyst at both the national and tactical levels; experience as an instructor; training, force, and combat developer; extensive material development and acquisition management experience—all of which combined to make him one of the most qualified imagery intelligence technicians within the Department of Defense (DOD). During 1976 through 1978, Hennen was assigned to the 203rd Military Intelligence Detach ment. While there, he served as Operations NCO and the chief of both the Tactical and Strategic Exploitation Divisions, providing imagery collection, exploitation, and intelligence support to the 1st Calvary Division, the 2nd Armored Division, the 6th Armored Calvary Regiment, and Headquarters III Corps. From 1973 to 1975, he was assigned to the 163rd Military Intelligence Battalion, Fort Hood, Texas. During the assignment he participated in the planning, development, and conduct of major operational and force development tests and evaluations in direct support of U.S. Army and III Corps combat requirements. A small sample of these tests include: the evaluation of the effectiveness of various firing methodologies of the Cobra (AH-1) attack helicopter; the testing and evaluation of new camouflage netting, uniforms, and painted vehicles, now in use throughout the Army; the initial U.S. Army Remotely piloted vehicle testing; phospherous smoke tests; antenna mast tests; and heat loss/energy conservations tests. During 1976 through 1978, Hennen was assigned to the 203rd Military Intelligence Detachment. While there, he served as Operations NCO and the chief of both the Tactical and Strategic Exploitation Divisions, providing imagery collection, exploitation, and intelligence support to the 1st Calvary Division, the 2nd Armored Division, the 6th Armored Calvary Regiment, and Headquarters III Corps. Chief Hennen was assigned to the U.S. Army Intelligence Center, Fort Huachuca, Arizona, from 1981 through 1986. He was the project officer for the Imagery Intelligence (IMINT) Tactical Exploitation of National Space Capabilities Program (TENCAP), responsible for developing all training requirements, concept, and doctrine. His efforts culminated in the production of multi-million dollar training programs, supporting the fielding of a variety of new systems, operating at both the tactical and national intelligence levels. During this assignment, Hennen was appointed as Department of the Army (DA) IMINT subject matter expert. He developed and managed a major project for the Office of the Secretary of Defense (OSD); he authored the U.S. Army Radar Training Plan; participated in the development of the TENCAP Systems Management Model; was selected as a member of a Defense Intelligence Agency (DIA) team that developed the Joint Space Intelligence and Operations Course; and represented DA on the DIA Intelligence Training Equipment (ITE) Subcommittee. In 1986, Hennen was selected by the Commanding General of the U.S. Army Intelligence Center to represent him within the U.S. Army Space Program Office (ASPO) in Washington, D.C., for those matters pertaining to TENCAP requirements, concept development, and the doctrinal and operational employment of TENCAP systems. Additionally, he performed various DA, DOD, and national intelligence community working groups and subcommittees involved in TENCAP program activities. Hennen was personally responsible for managing the development and successful fielding of a state-of-the-art IMINT system to both the European and Pacific Theaters of Operations. Chief Hennen's efforts at ASPO were instrumental in the efficient evolution of 5 major TENCAP systems with a Life Cycle Cost in excess of $2 billion dollars, providing critical and timely intelligence in support of the requirements of the tactical commander on the extended battlefield. Chief Hennen was selected as a payload specialist candidate in September 1988 and moved back to the "Home of Military Intelligence," Fort Huachua, Arizona, during March 1989 to begin Terra Scout payload operations training. During August 1989 he was selected as the primary payload specialist for the Terra Scout experiment manifested on STS-44, and reported to NASA in 1990 to begin Payload Specialist and Space Shuttle Crew Training. CWO Hennen became the first Warrant Officer in space, flying aboard the Space Shuttle Atlantic (STS-44), which launched from Kennedy Space Center Pad 39A at 6:44PM (EST), November 24, 1991. He orbited the Earth 109 times traveling 2.9 million miles, before landing at Edwards Air Force Base, California on December 1, 1991. Mr. Hennen retired from the U.S. Army in December 1995. He is the co-founder and currently serves as the Executive Director of the Atlantis Foundation, a non-profit organization that is both an advocate and a service provider for children with developmental disabilities. The Foundation was a dream and now the reality of his devotion to bring about real change in the special education field, specifically to the severely mentally challenged. Tom, who after viewing our planet from a totally different perspective, has rededicated his life to helping children, especially those who cannot help themselves. He is convinced, now more than ever before, that the future of our planet will be shaped by all our children.

NAME: R. Glynn Holt (Ph.D.)
Payload Specialist

PERSONAL DATA: Born November 28, 1959, in Plainview, Texas. Married to Kathy Anne Lee. They have one daughter. He enjoys tennis, basketball, guitar, and ballroom dancing. His parents, Mr. Jim Holt and Mrs. Wanda Holt, reside in Pecos, Texas.

EDUCATION: Graduated from Greenwood High School, Greenwood, Mississippi, in 1978; received a bachelor of science degree in Physics from the University of Mississippi in 1982, and a doctorate in Physics from the University of Mississippi in 1989.

ORGANIZATIONS: Member of the American Physical Society, Sigma Xi, and the Acoustical Society of America.

EXPERIENCE: After earning his Ph.D. by using optical scattering to observe nonlinear bubble oscillations, Dr. Holt was a visiting scientist at the Institute for Applied Physics, Technical University of Damstadt, West Germany. His research there centered on nonlinear analysis of complex bubble motion series and high-speed photography of bubble oscillations. Later in 1989, he joined the faculty of the Mechanical Engineering Department at Yale University, first as a Postdoctoral Associate (1989-1990), then as Associate Research Scientist (1991-1993) and Lecturer (1993). Dr. Holt maintained a research program involving a variety of phenomena associated with liquid drop dynamics and drop surface rheology. Experiments were performed primarily by using acoustic levitation techniques to isolate, position and oscillate the drops. In the fall of 1993, he joined the Microgravity Research Group at the Jet Propulsion Laboratory. His research there has involved experiments on: 1) nonlinear dynamics of drops in electric fields; 2) nonlinear resonances of acoustically forced shape and volume modes for large bubbles; 3) capillary wave dynamics on acoustically levitated liquid shells; and 4) resonance controlled Faraday bifurcations for small bubbles in an acoustic field, with emphasis on the effects of surface properties on the dynamics of shape oscillations and sonoluminescence.

NASA EXPERIENCE: Dr. Holt served as Co-Investigator on STS-50, directing efforts of the Yale research team on design and implementation of ground-and space-based experiments for the inaugural flight of the Drop Physics Module (DPM) on the first United States Microgravity Laboratory (USML-1) on STS-50. The experiments investigated the dynamic effects of small concentrations of surfactants dissolved in water drops positioned in the DPM using acoustic fields. Dr. Holt served as an Alternate Payload Specialist (APS) on STS-73, the second United Microgravity Laboratory mission (USML-2), which flew October 20 - November 7 aboard Space Shuttle Columbia. He was a Co-Investigator for DPM2. The experiments provided data which clearly showed the effects of mass transport on drop surface visco elastic properties, using drop sizes and shapes which could not be achieved in 1g.

NAME: Millie Hughes-Fulford (Ph.D.)
Payload Specialist

PERSONAL DATA: Born December 21,1945, in Mineral Wells, Texas. Married; her husband, George Fulford is a retired Captain with United Airlines. Her daughter is married and lives in Mill Valley. Recreational interests include scuba diving, swimming, gardening, photography, computer graphics and boating. Her father is deceased, her mother still resides in Mineral Wells, Texas.

EDUCATION: Graduated from Mineral Wells High, in 1962; received a bachelor of science degree in Chemistry and Biology from Tarleton State University in 1968, and a Ph.D. from Texas Womans University in 1972.

ORGANIZATIONS: Member of the American Association for the Advancement of Science, American Society for Gravitational Science and Biology, American Society for Bone and Mineral Research, American Society for Cell Biology and the Association of Space Explorers.

SPECIAL HONORS: 1995 Organizing Committee for the International Conference on Eicosanoids and other active Bio-lipids; 1995-Present Advisory Board for Marine Biological Library Sciences Writing Program, Woods Hole, Mass; 1994 Marin County Woman of the Year, NASA Space Flight Medals (1991); 1987-1990 Member of Committee on Space Biology and Space Medicine, National Research Council; 1986-1989 Board of Regents Embry-Riddle University, Daytona Beach, Florida; I984 Presidential Award for Federal Employee for Western Region; 1972 American Association of university Women's Fellowship; 1968-1971 National Science Foundation Fellow (Graduate), 1965 National Science Foundation Summer Research Fellow (Undergraduate).

EXPERIENCE: Dr. Hughes-Fulford entered college at the age of 16 and earned her BS degree in chemistry and biology from Tarleton State University in 1968. After graduating from Tarleton State University in 1968, Dr.Hughes-Fulford began her graduate work studying plasma chemistry at Texas Woman's University as a National Science Foundation Graduate Fellow from 1968-1971 and an American Association of University Women fellow from 1971-1972. Upon completing her doctorate degree at TWU in 1972, Dr. Hughes-Fulford joined the faculty of Southwestern Medical School, University of Texas, Dallas as a postdoctoral fellow with Marvin D. Siperstein. Her research focused on regulation of cholesterol metabolism. Dr. Hughes-Fulford has contributed over 70 papers and abstracts in the areas of bone and cancer growth regulation. She was named the Federal Employee of the Year Award for the Western Region in 1985, International Zontian in 1992 and Marin County Woman of the Year in 1993. She was a major in the US Army Reserve until 1995. Selected as a payload specialist by NASA in January 1983, Dr. Hughes-Fulford flew in June 1991 aboard STS-40 Spacelab Life Sciences (SLS 1), the first Spacelab mission dedicated to biomedical studies. The SLS-1 mission flew over 3.2 million miles in 146 orbits and its crew completed over 18 experiments during a 9 day period bringing back more medical data than any previous NASA flight. Mission duration was 218 hours, 14 minutes and 20 seconds. Upon her return to Earth, she served as the Scientific Advisor to the Under Secretary of the Department of Veterans Affairs for 3 years. Today, as a Professor at the University of California Medical Center at San Francisco, Dr. Hughes-Fulford continues her research at the Department of Veterans Affairs Medical Center, San Francisco as Director of the Laboratory for Cell Growth and Differentiation and as a principal medical investigator. She is currently the Deputy Associate Chief of Staff at the VA Medical Center, San Francisco. In addition to her duties as the dACOS/E, she is continuing her studies of the control of human colorectal cancer growth with the VA and the regulation of bone growth with NASA. She is also the PI on a series of SpaceHab/Biorack experiments examining the regulation of osteoblast (bone cell) growth regulation. The experiment, OSTEO flew on STS-76, in March of 1996. OSTEOGENE was on STS-81 which flew in January, 1997. OSTEOMARS is manifested on STS-84 scheduled to fly in May, 1997. The experiments are designed to examine the activation of bone cell growth and induction of gene expression in microgravity. These studies should help scientists understand the osteoporosis that occur in astronauts during spaceflight. More information on these studies can be obtained at http://www.spacedu.com.

NAME: Leonid K. Kadenyuk
NSAU Astronaut (NASA Payload Specialist)

PERSONAL DATA: Born January 28, 1951, in the Chernivtsi region of Ukraine. Married to Vera Kadenyuk (nee Kosolapinkova). They have two sons. He enjoys family time, running, athletics.

EDUCATION: Graduated from secondary school in 1967, from the Chernihiv Higher Aviation School in Chernihiv, Ukraine, in 1971, and from GNIKI VVS USSR (State Scientific Research Institute of the Russian Air Forces Center for test pilot training) in 1977, and the Yuri Gagarin Cosmonaut Training Center in 1978. He earned a master of science in mechanical engineering from the Moscow Aviation Institute, Department of Aircraft Construction, Moscow, Russia, in 1989.

EXPERIENCE: Colonel Kadenyuk has been a member of the USSR Cosmonaut Team since 1976. He underwent complete engineering and flight training for Soyuz, Soyuz-TM, orbital station Salyut, orbital complex Mir, including special training as a commander of Buran reentry space vehicle. He has flown 54 different types and modifications of aircraft, has logged more than 2400 hours flying time, and holds the qualifications of Test Pilot, 1st Class, and Military Pilot, 2nd Class, and Test Pilot. As a pilot-instructor he was responsible for the graduation of fifteen students. In 1971, he graduated from Chernihiv Higher Aviation School, Chernihiv, Ukraine, as a pilot-engineer. In 1976 he was selected to join the cosmonaut team at Yuri Gagarin Cosmonaut Training Center, Star City, Moscow, Russia. He attended test pilot training at GNIKI VVS USSR (State Scientific Research Institute of the Russian Air Force). He graduated in 1977, proficient in test aircraft piloting, aerodynamics, aircraft construction and exploitation. The following year, was spent at the Yuri Gagarin Cosmonaut Training Center where he successfully completed general space training. The course included biology, ecology, medicine, meteorology, space geology and geobotany. As a Test Cosmonaut he is trained to perform scientific research, tests and experiments in any of the above-named disciplines, both in-flight and on the ground. From 1978-1983 he served as a Test Cosmonaut/Pilot in the Multiple Usage Space System Group at the Yuri Gagarin Cosmonaut Training Center. While there he underwent advanced training in the conduct of in-flight scientific experiments. He is trained in survival techniques, EVA activities, and work in simulated weightlessness. He was involved in experimental investigations and testing of space technology for the Buran reentry vehicle system. He has performed numerous sky dives including some live, in-flight, reporting. From 1984-1988 he was a Test Pilot at GLIC VVS Russia (former GNIKI VVS USSR) Russian State Test Flight Center, Russian Air Force. During that time, he performed test flights for three State airplane tests on the SU-27, SU-27UB and MIG-25, was promoted to 1st Class Pilot, flight tested the SU-27, MIG-23, MIG-25, MIG-27 and MIG-31 military spacecraft, and performed tests in lowering and landing the "Buran" space ship on MIG-31 and MIG-25. In 1985, he served as Chairman of the State Committee on SU-27M cockpit design.In 1990, following the Ukrainian-USSR State Agreement on a Collaborative Space Program, he was appointed to command the Ukrainian space crew. In the following two years, he trained to command Soyuz-TM-S during its docking with unmanned Buran and Mir station (mission was canceled due to financial difficulties), completed the full course of space training for a commander of the SOYUZ-TM, and also took the full course of manual docking of space ships, using special training equipment. In subsequent years, he underwent engineering and flight training courses as commander of the Buran Space System. Using MIG-31 and MIG-25 he mastered and improved the trajectory for lowering and landing the Buran spacecraft. In 1996, he transferred to the Institute of Botany, National Academy of Sciences of Ukraine, Kyiv, as a scientific investigator developing the collaborative Ukrainian-American experiment in space biology.

NASA EXPERIENCE: Colonel Kadenyuk is one of the first NSAU Astronaut group selected in 1996 by the National Space Agency of Ukraine. In November 1996, NSAU and NASA assigned him to be one of two payload specialists for the Collaborative Ukrainian Experiment (CUE) which was flown on STS-87. He participated in payload specialist training at the Johnson Space Center and was the prime payload specialist aboard Space Shuttle Columbia on STS-87, (November 19 to December 5, 1997). STS-87 was the fourth United States Microgravity Payload flight and focused on experiments designed to study how the weightless environment of space affects various physical processes, and on observations of the Sun's outer atmospheric layers. Two members of the crew performed an EVA (spacewalk) which featured the manual capture of a Spartan satellite, in addition to testing EVA tools and procedures for future Space Station assembly. In completing his first mission Kadenyuk orbited the Earth 252 times, traveled 6.5 million miles and logged a total of 15 days, 16 hours and 34 minutes in space.

NAME: Fred W. Leslie (Ph.D.)
Payload Specialist

PERSONAL DATA: Born December 19, 1951, in Ancon, Panama. Single. He enjoys skydiving and holds a World Record as a participant in the 200 person freefall formation set October 1992. Leslie is an instrument rated commercial pilot with more than 900 hours in various aircraft. He also likes scuba diving, running, and weight training. His father, Grady W. Leslie, resides in Bonham, Texas. His mother, Golden L. Leslie, resides in Kemp, Texas.

EDUCATION: Graduated from Irving High School, Irving, Texas, in 1970; received a bachelor of science degree in engineering science from the University of Texas in 1974, and a masters and Ph.D. degrees in meteorology with a minor in fluid mechanics from the University of Oklahoma in 1977 and 1979, respectively.

ORGANIZATIONS: Served on the American Institute of Aeronautics and Astronautics Fluid Dynamics Technical Committee, Member of the American Meteorological Society, Tau Beta Pi, Chi Epsilon Pi, and the United States Parachute Association.

EXPERIENCE: After Dr. Leslie earned his Ph.D. in 1979, he served as a post doctoral research associate at Purdue University studying fluid vortex dynamics. In 1980, he worked for the Universities Space Research Association as a visiting scientist at the Marshall Space Flight Center (MSFC).

NASA EXPERIENCE: Leslie began work for NASA in 1980 as a research scientist in the Space Science Laboratory at the Marshall Space Flight Center. Since 1983, he has served as a co-investigator for the Geophysical Fluid Flow Cell experiment which examines spherical rotating convection relevant to the atmospheres of stars and planets. The experiment flew on Spacelab 3 and is also a part of the United States Microgravity Laboratory-2 (USML-2) payload. Leslie was a principal investigator for the Fluid Interface and Bubble Experiment examining the behavior of a rotating free surface aboard NASA's KC-135 aircraft flying low-gravity trajectories. He is an author on 27 journal papers, 45 conference papers, and 9 NASA reports involving atmospheric and fluid dynamic phenomena. Leslie also worked in the MSFC Neutral Buoyancy Simulator as a suited subject and safety diver supporting procedure tests for extra-vehicular activity. In 1987, he became chief of the Fluid Dynamics Branch where he directed and conducted research in both laboratory and theoretical investigations along with more than a dozen scientists in the Branch. He was also the mission scientist for Spacelab J (STS-47) coordinating more than 40 domestic and Japanese experiments in fluid dynamics, crystal growth, and life science during the 8-day mission.

SPACE FLIGHT EXPERIENCE: Dr. Leslie flew as a payload specialist on STS-73 launched on October 20, 1995 and landed at the Kennedy Space Center on November 5, 1995. The 16 day mission aboard Columbia focused on materials science, biotechnology, combustion science, and fluid physics contained within the pressurized Spacelab module.

CURRENT ASSIGNMENT: Dr. Leslie is a researcher at the Marshall Space Flight Center, Mail Code: ES71, Huntsville, Alabama 35812. He is a member of the research team analyzing data from the Geophysical Fluid Flow Cell experiment that flew on STS-73/USML-2.

NAME: Gregory T. Linteris (Ph.D.)
Payload Specialist

PERSONAL DATA:Born October 4, 1957, in Demarest, New Jersey, where his parents, Lino Luigi Linteris and Helen Mary Linteris reside. Single. Recreational interests include running, skiing, board sailing, hiking, backpacking, and reading, and was a member of Princeton's wrestling team.

EDUCATION: Graduated from Northern Valley Regional High School at Demarest, New Jersey in 1975; received a bachelor of science degree in chemical engineering from Princeton University in 1979; obtained a master of science degree from the design division of the mechanical engineering department at Stanford University in 1984; and was awarded a doctorate in mechanical and aerospace engineering from Princeton University in 1990.

ORGANIZATIONS: Member of American Institute of Aeronautics and Astronautics, American Physical Society, Combustion Institute, Sigma Xi.

PUBLICATIONS: Dr. Linteris has over 40 publications in the areas of combustion, chemical kinetics, spectroscopy, and heat transfer.

SPECIAL HONORS: Graduated with honors from Princeton University (1979). Awarded a Mechanical Engineering Department Fellowship from Stanford University (1983), and received Fourth Place in the James F. Lincoln National Design Competition (1984). At Princeton, he was the recipient of a Guggenheim Fellowship (1985), a Grumman Prize for excellence in Research (1988), and the Luigi Crocco Award (1988) for outstanding performance as an Assistant in Instruction.

EXPERIENCE: At Princeton from 1985 to 1990, Dr. Linteris studied the high temperature chemical kinetics of combustion reactions in a turbulent chemical kinetic flow reactor using laser induced fluorescence and laser absorption. As a research staff member at the University of California, San Diego, from 1990 to 1992, he studied droplet dynamics and performed numerical and analytical modeling of the chemistry important in the gas-phase reaction region of solid rocket propellants. Since 1992 he has been at the National Institute of Standards and Technology where he has been developing a research program on advanced fire suppressants and studying the inhibition mechanisms of chemical inhibitors. He is Principal Investigator on a NASA microgravity combustion experiment: "Chemical Inhibitor Effects on Diffusion Flames in Microgravity."

SPACE FLIGHT EXPERIENCE: Twice flown, Dr. Linteris was a payload specialist on STS-83 (April 4-8,1997) and STS-94 (July 1-17, 1997) and has logged over 471 hours in space. STS-83, the Microgravity Science Laboratory (MSL-1) Spacelab mission, was cut short because of problems with one of the Shuttle's three fuel cell power generation units. Mission duration was 95 hours and 12 minutes, traveling 1.5 million miles in 63 orbits of the Earth. STS-94 was a re-flight of the Microgravity Science Laboratory (MSL-1) Spacelab mission, and focused on materials and combustion science research in microgravity. Mission duration was 376 hours and 45 minutes, traveling 6.3 million miles in 251 orbits of the Earth.

NAME: Franco Malerba (Ph.D.)
ASI Astronaut (Payload Specialist)

PERSONAL DATA: Born October 10, 1946, in Genova, Italy. Married to the former Marie-Aude Némo. They have one child. Recreational interests include mountaineering, skiing, and tennis. He is fluent in Italian, English, and French.

EDUCATION: 1965 Maturita classica (Lyceum). 1970 University degree, Electronics Engineer, University of Genova, Italy, specializing in the telecommunications field (laurea 110/110 cum Laude). 1974 Doctorate in Physics, University of Genova, (110/110) specializing in Biophysics (after research work at the Italian National Research Council and at the National Institutes of Health, Bethesda, Maryland, USA).

ORGANIZATIONS: Founding Member of the Italian Space Society (ISS).

RESEARCH ACTIVITIES: 1970-75 Research Assistant at the Italian National Research Council (CNR) Laboratorio de Biofisica e Cibernetica (Genova) carrying experimental work on membrane biophysics (using squid axons) and biological membrane modeling with lipid bilayers. 1971 Lecturer of Cybernetics and Information Theory at the Physics Faculty, University of Genova. 1972 Summer Research Assistant at the Nato Saclant Research Center (La Spezia, Italy) working on computer-aided signal detection methodologies for sonar data systems. 1972-74 Research Fellow at the National Institutes of Health (Bethesda, Maryland) designing, developing, testing and using a fast micro-spectrophotometer for research on photoreceptors biophysics (using frog retinas). 1977-80 In 1977, Dr. Malerba was chosen by the European Space Agency (ESA) as one of four European Payload Specialist Candidates for the first Spacelab mission. After this selection he became a staff member at the European Technical Center (ESTEC) of ESA Space Science Department, Space Plasma Physics Division, working in the development, testing, and qualification of ES020 - PICPAB, an experiment in Ionospheric Plasma Physics for the first Spacelab payload, flown in 1983, involving the use of accelerated charged particle beams (cooperation involved French CNRS/CRPE, Norwegian NRDE and ESTEC).

INDUSTRY EXPERIENCE: 1976-89 Held technical and technical management positions with Digital Equipment in Italy and in Europe. He worked mainly in the field of multiprocessor systems (Paris

1976, Milan 1977), computer networks engineering (Geneva 1981-85), and telecommunications technology (Rome 1986-88, and Sophia Antipolis in 1989).

MILITARY STATUS: Reserve Officer, Italian Navy. Served in 1974-75 (Sottotenente Armi Navali); was assigned to the Destroyer San Giorgio as Science Lecturer to the Navy Academy, and then to the Mariperman Technical Center in La Spezia working on ELF transmission systems.

OTHER SKILLS: Obtained scuba diving license from the Calypso Scuba Club, Geneva (1984).

FLYING STATUS: Obtained Private Pilot License (College Park, Washington, D.C., 1973) and then the equivalent Italian flying license.

NASA EXPERIENCE: After the Payload Specialist selection in 1989 by the Italian Space Agency (ASI) and NASA for the TSS-1 mission, he became a staff member of ASI and was assigned to the NASA Johnson Space Center, Houston, Texas, for training. In September 1991, he was designated Prime Payload Specialist for the TSS-1 mission. Dr. Malerba flew as the first Italian citizen in space on STS-46 (July 31, 1992 to August 7, 1992). He is now involved with the Italian Space Agency (ASI) manned space flight program follow-on activities.

NAME: David H. Matthiesen (Ph.D.)
Payload Specialist

PERSONAL DATA: Born August 31, 1958, in Blue Island, Illinois. Married to Mary Manger Matthiesen, Ph.D., of Woodbury, New York. One son. He enjoys golf, racquetball, downhill skiing, and reading. His father, Donald R. Matthiesen is deceased. His mother, Doris A. Flaws later remarried Carl L. Flaws and they reside in Chicago Ridge, Illinois. Her parents, Wendell F. Manger and Jean M. Manger, reside in Woodbury, New York.

EDUCATION: Graduated from Harold L. Richards High School, Oak Lawn, Illinois in 1976; received a bachelor of science degree in Ceramic Engineering from the University of Illinois, Urbana in 1980, a master of science degree in Ceramic Engineering from the University of Illinois, Urbana in 1982; and a doctorate of philosophy in Materials Engineering from the Massachusetts Institute of Technology (MIT) in 1988.

ORGANIZATIONS: Senior Member: American Institute of Aeronautics and Astronautics and member: Space Processing Technical Committee; American Association for Crystal Growth; Materials Research Society; American Ceramic Society; American Society of Metals International (ASM); The Minerals, Metals and Materials Society (TMS); Sigma Xi.

EXPERIENCE: In 1993, Dr. Matthiesen joined the faculty at Case Western Reserve University (CWRU) in Cleveland, Ohio as an assistant professor in the Department of Materials Science and Engineering. He is a Principal Investigator on the NASA funded Crystal Growth Furnace (CGF) for a project to investigate steady state segregation behavior in GaAs. This experiment flew on the first United States Microgravity Laboratory (USML-1/STS-50) and is scheduled to fly again on the USML-2/STS-73 mission. In addition, Professor Matthiesen is Principal Investigator on a NASA funded investigation on the diffusion processes in molten semiconductors (DPIMS).Professor Matthiesen received his Ph.D. from MIT in 1988 for which his thesis was a comparison of the effects of microgravity and high strength magnetic fields on the crystal growth of electronic materials. After graduating from

MIT, Dr. Matthiesen joined the Electronics Materials Department at GTE Laboratories, Incorporated as a Senior Member of the Technical Staff. During this time he was Principal Scientist and then Principal Investigator for a joint US Air Force/GTE Labs/NASA project to investigate the transient growth of gallium arsenide in microgravity. This experiment flew on the first Spacelab Life Sciences (SLS-1/STS-40) and on the first Atmospheric Laboratory for Applications and Science (ATLAS-1/STS-45) as part of the Get-Away-Special program. Professor Matthiesen's teaching responsibilities include heat, mass and momentum transport in materials, thermodynamics, solidification theory and crystal growth. He is the faculty advisor for Senior theses, Special Projects and the CWRU Undergraduate Materials Society. Dr. Matthiesen is responsible for the supervision of undergraduate, graduate and post-doctoral research programs and for the design and construction of the Electronic Materials Crystal Growth Laboratory. His research emphasis is on developing the understanding of and insight to: the heat, mass and momentum transport in processing of materials; growth and characterization of electronic and other inorganic materials, and the development of unique material processing techniques such as applied magnetic fields and growth in the microgravity environment.

NAME: Itzhak Mayo (Lieutenant Colonel, Israel Air Force)
Payload Specialist

PERSONAL DATA: Born September 14, 1954 in Kfar Hittim, a small village in the northern part of Israel. Married to Rinat. They have three children. He likes to swim, enjoys cooking, and reading in any spare time. His parents are deceased.

EDUCATION: Graduated from High School in 1972; received bachelor of science and master of science degrees in physics, specializing in spectroscopy and chemical lasers, from Ben Gurion University, Beer Sheva, Israel, in 1986 and 1988 respectively.

EXPERIENCE: 1972-1974 drafted to the Israel Defense Forces and volunteered to the Israel Air Force (IAF) Academy where he qualified as a Weapons System Operator (WSO) and Navigator. 1974-1979 served as Operational WSO in F-4 Squadron. 1988-1989 conversion to F-16D and operational in F-16D Squadron. 1989-1998 was spent in weapons testing and operational evaluation at the IAF Flight Test Center, where he served as Head of the Avionics Section. Lt. Col. Mayo has accumulated over 3,250 flight hours, mostly on F-4 and F-16, in addition to various fixed wing airplanes like the F-15, D&I models, F/A-18D, and helicopters.

NASA EXPERIENCE: In 1997, Lt. Col. Mayo was selected as a Payload Specialist. He will train as back-up for a Space Shuttle mission with a payload that includes a multispectral camera for recording desert aerosol. In July 1998, he reported for training at the Johnson Space Center, Houston.

NAME: Chiaki Mukai (M.D., Ph.D.)
NASDA Astronaut (Payload Specialist)

PERSONAL DATA: Born May 6, 1952, in Tatebayashi, Gunma Prefecture, Japan. Married to Makio Mukai, M.D., Ph.D. Recreational interests include snow skiing, Alpine competitive skiing, bass fishing, scuba diving, tennis, golf, photography, American Literature, and traveling.

EDUCATION: Graduated from Keio Girls' High School in Tokyo, in 1971. She received her doctorate in Medicine, Keio University School of Medicine, 1977; a doctorate in physiology, Keio University

School of Medicine, 1988; board certified as a cardiovascular surgeon, Japan Surgical Society, 1989.

ORGANIZATIONS: The American Aerospace Medical Association; Japan Society of Microgravity Applications; Japan Society of Aerospace and Environmental Medicine; Japanese Society for Cardiovascular and Thoracic Surgery; Japan Surgical Society.

SPECIAL HONORS: Outstanding Service Award - The Society of Japanese Women Scientist (1996), Special Congressional Recognition -U.S. Congress (1995), Happy Hands Award - Satte Junior Chamber of Commerce (1995), Aeromedical Association of Korea Honorary Membership (1995), Tatebayashi Children's Science Exploratorium Honorary President (1995), Prime Minister's Special Citation for Contributions to Gender Equality (1995), The De La Vaux Medal - The Federation Aeronautique Internationale(1995), The Award for Distinguished Service in Advancement of Space Biology - Japanese Society for Biological Sciences in Space (1995), Prime Minister's Special Citation (1994), Minister of State for Science and Technology's Commendation (1994 & 1992), People of Gunma Prefecture's Certificate of Appreciation (1994), Honorary Citizen of Tatebayashi City (1994), Outstanding Service Award - National Space Development Agency of Japan (1994 & 1992), Award for Distinguished Accomplishments - Tokyo Women's Foundation (1994) and Commendation for Technology - Japan Society of Aeronautical and Space Science (1993).

PUBLICATIONS: Dr. Mukai is credited with approximately sixty publications since 1979.

EXPERIENCE: Board certified for Medicine in 1977. From 1977 through 1978, Dr. Mukai worked as a Resident in General Surgery, Keio University Hospital, Tokyo. She was on the Medical Staff in General Surgery, Shimizu General Hospital, Shizuoka Prefecture in 1978, and on the Medical Staff in Emergency Surgery, Saiseikai Kanagawa Hospital, Kanawaga Prefecture in 1979. Dr. Mukai began her work as a Resident in Cardiovascular Surgery, Keio University Hospital in 1980 and served on the Medical Staff in Cardiovascular Surgery, Saiseikai Utsunomiya Hospital, Tochigi Prefecture in 1982. She returned to Keio University Hospital in 1983 as the Chief Resident in Cardiovascular Surgery, and was later promoted to Assistant Professor of the Department of Cardiovascular Surgery, Keio University. As a NASDA science astronaut, she became a visiting scientist of the Division of Cardiovascular Physiology, Space Biomedical Research Institute, NASA Johnson Space Center from 1987 through 1988. Dr. Mukai remains a Research Instructor of the Department of Surgery, Baylor College of Medicine, Houston, Texas and a visiting associate professor of the Department of Surgery, Keio University School of Medicine, Tokyo, respectively since 1992.

NASA EXPERIENCE: In 1985, Dr. Mukai was selected by the National Space Development Agency of Japan (NASDA), as one of three Japanese Payload Specialist candidates for the First Material Processing Test (Spacelab-J) which flew aboard STS-47. She also served as a back-up payload specialist for the Neurolab (STS-90) mission. Dr. Mukai has logged over 566 hours in space. She flew aboard STS-65 in 1994 and STS-95 in 1998, and is the first Japanese female astronaut to fly twice in spaceIn 1985, Dr. Mukai was selected by the National Space Development Agency of Japan (NASDA), as one of three Japanese Payload Specialist candidates for the First Material Processing Test (Spacelab-J) which flew aboard STS-47. She also flew as a back-up payload specialist for the Neurolab (STS-90) mission. Dr. Mukai has logged over 566 hours in space. She flew aboard STS-65 in 1994 and STS-95 in 1998, and is the first Japanese female astronaut to fly twice in space.

SPACE FLIGHT EXPERIENCE: STS-65 Columbia (July 8-23, 1994) was the second International Microgravity Laboratory (IML-2) flight. The mission consisted of 82 investigations of Space Life

Science (Human Physiology, Space Biology, Radiation Biology, and Bioprocessing) and Microgravity Science (Material Science, Fluid Science and Research on the Microgravity Environment and Countermeasures). IML-2 was also designated as an extended duration orbit mission focusing on medical experiments related to the cardiovascular system, autonomic nerve system, and bone and muscle metabolism. The mission was accomplished in 236 orbits of the Earth, traveling over 6.1 million miles in 353 hours and 55 minutes. STS-95 Discovery (October 29 to November 7, 1998) was a 9-day mission during which the crew supported a variety of research payloads including deployment of the Spartan solar-observing spacecraft, the Hubble Space Telescope Orbital Systems Test Platform, and investigations on space flight and the aging process. STS-95 is scheduled for launch in October 1998. The mission was accomplished in 134 Earth orbits, traveling 3.6 million miles in 213 hours and 44 minutes.

NAME: Ronald A. Parise (Ph.D.)
Payload Specialist

PERSONAL DATA: Born May 24, 1951, in Warren, Ohio. Married to the former Cecelia M. Sokol of Youngstown, Ohio. They have two children. He enjoys amateur radio, flying, scuba diving, sailing, hiking, and camping. His parents, Mr. and Mrs. Henry Parise, reside in Warren, Ohio. Her parents, Mr. and Mrs. Joseph Sokol, reside in Youngstown, Ohio.

EDUCATION: Graduated from Western Reserve High School, Warren, Ohio, 1969; received his bachelor of science degree in physics, with minors in mathematics, astronomy, and geology, Youngstown State University, Ohio, 1973; and a master of science degree and a doctor of philosophy degree in astronomy, University of Florida, 1977 and 1979, respectively.

ORGANIZATIONS: American Astronomical Society, Astronomical Society of the Pacific, Association of Space Explorers, International Astronomical Union, Sigma Xi, and Phi Kappa Phi.

SPECIAL HONORS: NASA Space Flight Medal, 1991, 1995; Distinguished member of Phi Kappa Phi, 1996; Honorary Doctor of Science degree, Youngstown State University, 1996; NASA/GSFC Special Act Award, 1995; Computer Sciences Corp., Space and Earth Technology Systems, Award for Technical Innovation, 1999; NASA Group Achievement Award, 1988, 1991, 1992, 1996, 1998, 2000; NASA/GSFC Community Service Award, 1990; Allied Signal, Quest for Excellence Award, 1997.

EXPERIENCE: Upon graduation in 1979, Dr. Parise accepted a position at Operations Research Inc. (ORI) where he was involved in developing avionics requirements definitions and performing failure mode analyses for several NASA missions. In 1980 he began work at Computer Sciences Corp. in the International Ultraviolet Explorer (IUE) operations center as a data management scientist and in 1981 became the section manager of the IUE hardcopy facility. In 1981 he began work on the development of a new Spacelab experiment called the Ultraviolet Imaging Telescope (UIT). His responsibilities involved flight hardware and software development, electronic system design, and mission planning activities for the UIT project. In 1984 he was selected by NASA as a payload specialist in support of the newly formed Astro mission series. During his twelve years as a payload specialist he was involved in mission planning, simulator development, integration and test activities, flight procedure development, and scientific data analysis, in addition to his flight crew responsibilities for the Astro program. At the completion of the Astro program Dr. Parise assumed an advanced planning and communications engineering support role for a variety of human space flight projects including Mir, International Space Station (ISS), and the X-38. Dr. Parise has engaged in a number of astronomical research projects utilizing data from ground-based observatories, the Copernicus satellite (OAO-3), IUE, and the Astro observatory. His research topics, including circumsteller matter in binary star systems and the evolutionary status of stars in globular clusters, have resulted in several professional publications. A veteran of two space flights, Dr. Parise has logged more than 614 hours and 10.6 million miles in space. He served as a payload specialist aboard STS-35 in 1990 and STS-67 in 1995. Currently, Dr. Parise is supporting the Goddard Space Flight Center, Networks and Mission Services Project, in the area of advanced communications planning for human spaceflight missions. He is also involved with projects in the Advanced Architectures and Automation Branch that are developing the use of standard Internet Protocols (IP) in space data transmission applications.

NAME: James A. (Jim) Pawelczyk (Ph.D.)
Payload Specialist

PERSONAL DATA: Born September 20, 1960, in Buffalo, New York. He identifies Elma, New York as his hometown, where his parents, Joseph and Rita Pawelczyk, continue to reside. Married to the Ruth A. Pawelczyk, M.D. (nee Anderson), daughter of Paul and Barbara Anderson, of State College, Pennsylvania. They have two children. Hobbies include cycling, swimming, woodworking, philately, and outdoor activities.

EDUCATION: Graduated from Iroquois Central High School, Elma, New York, in 1978; Earned two bachelor of arts degrees in biology and psychology from the University of Rochester, New York in 1982; a master of science degree in physiology from the Pennsylvania State University in 1985; and a doctor of philosophy degree in biology (physiology) from the University of North Texas in 1989. He completed a post-doctoral fellowship at the University of Texas Southwestern Medical Center in 1992.

PROFESSIONAL SOCIETIES: American Heart Association, American Physiological Society, American College of Sports Medicine, Society for Neuroscience.

HONORS AND AWARDS: Research Scientist, United States Olympic Swimming Trials, 1984; Predoctoral training award, National Institutes of Health, 1988-1989; Research award, Texas Chapter of the American College of Sports Medicine, 1988; Post-doctoral training award, National Institutes of Health, 1989-1992; Young Investigator Award, Life Sciences Project Division, NASA Office of Life and Microgravity Science Applications, 1994, NASA Space Flight Medal (1998).

SCHOLARLY ACTIVITY: Dr. Pawelczyk is co-editor of Blood Loss and Shock, published in 1994. He has been a principal investigator or co-investigator on 11 federal and state grants and contracts, and has over 20 refereed journal articles and 3 invited book chapters in the areas of cardiovascular regulation and cardiovascular physiology.

EXPERIENCE: Post-doctoral fellowship in cardiovascular neurophysiology, University of Texas Southwestern Medical Center, 1989-1992; Visiting scientist, Department of Anaesthesia, Rigshospitalet, Copenhagen, Denmark, 1990; Assistant Professor of Medicine (Cardiology), University of Texas Southwestern Medical Center, 1992-1995; Director, Autonomic and Exercise Physiology Laboratories, Institute for Exercise and Environmental Medicine, Presbyterian Hospital of Dallas, 1992-1995; Assistant Professor of Bioengineering, University of Texas Southwestern Medical Center, 1995; Assistant Professor of Physiology and Kinesiology, Penn State University, University Park, Pennsylvania, 1995-present. Dr. Pawelczyk took leave from Penn State University to fly as a payload specialist on STS-90 (Neurolab).

NASA EXPERIENCE: User design group, GASMAP (Gas Analysis System for Metabolic Analysis Physiology); Unit principal investigator for the NASA Specialized Center for Outreach, Research and Training (NSCORT) grant in integrative physiology. He received a NASA Young Investigator Award in 1994 for his work in the area of autonomic neurophysiology. Dr. Pawelczyk is a co-investigator for experiments to be flown on the Neurolab mission, and two Shuttle-Mir (Phase 1B) flights. Most recently, Dr. Pawelczyk served as a Payload Specialist on STS-90 Neurolab (April 17 to May 3, 1998). During the 16-day Spacelab flight the seven person crew aboard Space Shuttle Columbia served as both experiment subjects and operators for 26 individual life science experiments focusing on the effects of microgravity on the brain and nervous system. The STS-90 flight orbited the Earth 256 times, covered 6.3 million miles, and logged over 381 hours in space.

NAME: Yaroslav I. Pustovyi (Ph.D.)
NSAU Astronaut (Payload Specialists)

PERSONAL DATA: Born December 29, 1970 in Kostroma, Russia, but considers Kyiv, Ukraine, to be his hometown. Single. Enjoys computers, mathematics, reading, learning new languages, flying, soccer, badminton, basketball, listening to classical and folk music, and singing. His parents, Mr. Ihor V. Pustovyi and Mrs. Oksana Y. Pustovyi (Boichuk), and his brother, Volodymyr I. Pustovyi, reside in Kyiv, Ukraine.

EDUCATION: Graduated from high school in 1988. Received a master of science degree in radio electronics engineering (with honors) from Mozhayskiy Space Engineering Military Academy (Saint-Petersburg, Russia) in 1993. Doctorate in Physics and Mathematics (Radio Physics) from Kharkiv State University, Kharkiv, Ukraine, 1996.

ORGANIZATIONS: Ukrainian Cossack Society.

MILITARY STATUS: Finished 6 years of active duty as the 1st Lieutenant, currently serving in the Ukrainian Air Force Reserve.

PUBLICATIONS: Published 7 articles in the areas of space radio engineering, transient electrodynamics, antennas theory and technology.

EXPERIENCE: Yaroslav Pustovyi studied space avionics and ground control radio equipment in Mozhayskiy Space Engineering Military Academy from 1988 to 1993. After graduation, he entered postgraduate courses in the Mozhayskiy Academy and studied there until November 1994. Since January 1995, Yaroslav Pustovyi worked in the Institute of Magnetism of National Academy of Sciences of Ukraine as a scientific researcher. He investigated non-stationary electrodynamics and defended his thesis on the topic "Radiation of Ultra-Wide-Band Signals by Aperture Antennas" in June 1996. Fluent in Ukrainian, English, and Russian.

NASA EXPERIENCE: Dr. Pustovyi is one of the first NSAU Astronaut group selected in 1996 by the National Space Agency of Ukraine. In November 1996, NSAU and NASA assigned him to be one of two payload specialists for the Collaborative Ukrainian Experiment (CUE) to be flown on STS-87 aboard Space Shuttle Columbia. He currently participates in payload specialist training at the Johnson

Space Center and will serve as the backup payload specialist for STS-87, scheduled for launch in November 1997.

NAME: Ilan Ramon (Colonel, Israel Air Force)
Payload Specialist

PERSONAL DATA: Born June 20,1954 in Tel Aviv, Israel. Married to Rona. They have four children. He enjoys snow skiing, squash. His parents reside in Beer Sheva, Israel.

EDUCATION: Graduated from High School in 1972; bachelor of science degree in electronics and computer engineering from the University of Tel Aviv, Israel, in 1987.

SPECIAL HONORS/AWARDS: Yom Kippur War (1973); Peace of Galilee War (1982); F-16 1,000 Flight Hours (1992).

EXPERIENCE: In 1974, Ramon graduated as a fighter pilot from the Israel Air Force (IAF) Flight School. From 1974-1976 he participated in A-4 Basic Training and Operations. 1976-1980 was spent in Mirage III-C training and operations. In 1980, as one of the IAF's establishment team of the first F-16 Squadron in Israel, he attended the F-16 Training Course at Hill Air Force Base, Utah. From 1981-1983, he served as the Deputy Squadron Commander B, F-16 Squadron. From 1983-1987, he attended the University of Tel Aviv. From 1988-1990, he served as Deputy Squadron Commander A, F-4 Phantom Squadron. During 1990, he attended the Squadron Commanders Course. From 1990-1992, he served as Squadron Commander, F-16 Squadron. From 1992-1994, he was Head of the Aircraft Branch in the Operations Requirement Department. In 1994, he was promoted to the rank of Colonel and assigned as Head of the Department of Operational Requirement for Weapon Development and Acquisition. He stayed at this post until 1998. Colonel Ramon has accumulated over 3,000 flight hours on the A-4, Mirage III-C, and F-4, and over 1,000 flight hours on the F-16.

NASA EXPERIENCE: In 1997, Colonel Ramon was selected as a Payload Specialist. He is designated to train as prime for a Space Shuttle mission with a payload that includes a multispectral camera for recording desert aerosol. In July 1998, he reported for training at the Johnson Space Center, Houston. He is currently assigned to STS-107 scheduled to launch in 2001.

NAME: Paul D. Ronney (Sc.D.)
Payload Specialist

PERSONAL DATA: Born May 1, 1957, in Los Angeles, California, but considers his home town to be Newport Beach, California. Married to Nina Linda Curone. Dr. Ronney enjoys mountaineering and has climbed the highest mountains on 5 continents. He also enjoys marathon running, skiing, backpacking, whitewater kayaking, surfing, guitar playing, and growing tropical fruit.

EDUCATION: Received a Bachelor of Science in Mechanical Engineering from the University of California, Berkley in 1978, a Master of Science in Aeronautics from the California Institute of Technology in 1979, and a Doctor of Science in Aeronautics and Astronautics in 1983 from the Massachusetts Institute of Technology.

ORGANIZATIONS: Dr. Ronney is a member of several professional organizations including the

American Institute of Aeronautics and Astronautics, the American Society of Mechanical Engineers and the Combustion Institute. He is also a member of the Phi Beta Kappa (liberal arts), Tau Beta Pi (engineering), and Pi Tau Sigma (mechanical engineering) honor societies.

PUBLICATIONS: Dr. Ronney has published over 40 journal papers and made over 100 presentations on research in the areas of combustion, microgravity, turbulence, internal combustion engines and control systems, and radiative transfer. One of his recent papers won the 1995 Institution of Mechanical Engineers (U.K.) Starley Premium Award for the best paper published in the Journal of Automobile Engineering in 1994. He also holds one U.S. patent.

EXPERIENCE: Dr. Ronney has been at the University of Southern California since 1993, where he currently holds a joint appointment as an Associate Professor in the Departments of Mechanical Engineering and Aerospace Engineering. Prior to his position at USC, he was an Assistant Professor in the Department of Mechanical and Aerospace Engineering at Princeton University from 1986 to 1993, where he was a recipient of the National Science Foundation Presidential Young Investigator Award. He also held postdoctoral positions at the NASA Lewis Research Center from 1983 to 1985 and the U.S. Naval Research Laboratory from 1985 to 1986. He has 15 years of research experience in the area of microgravity combustion and fluid physics, and has conducted many experimental studies in NASA's drop tower and aircraft facilities.

CURRENT ASSIGNMENT: Dr. Ronney is currently training as an Alternate Payload Specialist (APS) for Spacelab mission MSL-1 (STS-83). The MSL-1 mission will have about 25 experiments in the areas of materials science, combustion and fluid mechanics, including the Structure Of Flame Balls At Low Lewis-number (SOFBALL) experiment on which Dr. Ronney is the Principal Investigator.

NAME: Albert Sacco, Jr. (Ph.D.)
Payload Specialist

PERSONAL DATA: Born on May 3, 1949, in Boston, Massachusetts. Married the former Teran Lee Gardner, of Massachusetts, in November 1971. They have four children. He enjoys jogging, reading, walking, and is an avid scuba diver and a certified scuba instructor. His mother, Sarah Kathleen, and his father, Albert, Sr., reside in Belmont, Massachusetts. Her mother, Marian, and father, Carl, reside in Gilford, New Hampshire.

EDUCATION: Graduated from Belmont Senior High School in 1968; received a bachelor of science degree in Chemical Engineering with honors from Northeastern University, Boston, Massachusetts, in 1973; was awarded a doctorate in Chemical Engineering from the Massachusetts Institute of Technology, Cambridge, Massachusetts, in 1977.

ORGANIZATIONS: Dr. Sacco is a member of the American Institute of Chemical Engineers (Treasurer-Western Section, 1979-1982); past president of the New England Catalysis Society (1983-1985), and the New England representative to the North American Catalysis Society (1985-1989); an Advisory Board member of the American Carbon Society; a member of the American Institute of Aeronautics and Astronautics (AIAA), and serves on the AIAA Technical Committee on Space Processing (1990-1995); and a member of the Association of Space Explorers-USA.

PUBLICATIONS: Dr. Sacco has over 70 publications (including book chapters) in the areas of carbon filament initiation and growth, catalyst deactivation, and zeolite synthesis.

SPECIAL HONORS: One of the four U.S. experts invited to put on a joint U.S./European NATO Advanced Study Institute "Carbon Fibers and Filaments" (1989); was honored in 1984 by the Worcester Engineering Society, receiving the Admiral Earl Awardfor meritorious contributions in applied sciences, specifically in the fields of catalysis and adsorbent deactivation; received a National Science Foundation Young Faculty Initiation Grant (1978); and won the Northeast AIChE student paper contest in 1973.

EXPERIENCE: Since 1977, Professor Sacco has been on the faculty at Worcester Polytechnic Institute in the Department of Chemical Engineering. He has split his time between research and teaching. He was appointed Department Head in July 1989. He has consulted for numerous companies in the fields of catalysis, solid/gas contacting, and equipment design for space applications. Also he, with his father (Al) and brother (Bernard), ran a family restaurant business in Boston for over 20 years.

SPACE FLIGHT EXPERIENCE: Dr. Sacco flew as a payload specialist on STS-73, which launched on October 20, 1995, and landed at the Kennedy Space Center on November 5, 1995. The 16 day mission aboard Columbia focused on materials science, biotechnology, combustion science, and fluid physics contained within the pressurized Spacelab module.

CURRENT ASSIGNMENT: Dr. Sacco is presently a Professor and Head of the Chemical Engineering Department at Worcester Polytechnic Institute. He is also the Principal Investigator on the Zeolite Crystal Growth experiments, which flew on STS-73.

NAME: Robert (Bob) Brent Thirsk (P.Eng., SM, MDCM, MBA)
Payload Specialist

PERSONAL DATA: Born August 17, 1953, in New Westminister, British Columbia. Married to Brenda Biasutti of Montreal, Quebec. They have three children. Bob enjoys spending time with his family as well as flying, hockey, squash, and playing the piano.

EDUCATION: Attended primary and secondary schools in British Columbia, Alberta and Manitoba. Received a bachelor of science degree in mechanical engineering from the University of Calgary in 1976, a master of science degree in mechanical engineering from the Massachusetts Institute of Technology (MIT) in 1978, a doctorate of medicine degree from McGill University in 1982, and a master of business administration degree from the MIT Sloan School of Management in 1998.

ORGANIZATIONS:Member of the Association of Professional Engineers of Ontario, the Canadian College of Family Physicians, the Canadian Aeronautics and Space Institute, the Aerospace Medical Association, and the Colleges of Physicians and Surgeons of Ontario and of British Columbia. He is also a Director of the Canadian Foundation for International Space University.

SPECIAL HONOURS: Won the Association of Professional Engineers, Geologists and Geophysicists of Alberta Gold Medal in 1976. First recipient of the University of Calgary Distinguished Alumni Award (1985). In 1997, was awarded the Gold Medal of the Professional Engineers of Ontario and was awarded honorary membership in the College of Physicians and Surgeons of British Columbia.

EXPERIENCE: Bob was in the family medicine residency program at the Queen Elizabeth Hospital in Montreal when he was selected in December 1983 to the Canadian Astronaut Program. Bob began astronaut training in February 1984 and served as backup payload specialist to Marc Garneau for space shuttle mission 41-G which flew October 5 to 13, 1984. While at MIT and McGill University, Bob did research in biomedical engineering. In the past, Bob led an international team investigating the effect of weightlessness on the heart and blood vessels. He designed and tested an experimental "anti-gravity suit" that may help astronauts withstand the effects of extended spaceflight on the cardiovascular system. Bob has participated in several parabolic flight experiment campaigns on board NASA's KC-135 aircraft and has been involved in various projects (space medicine, space station, mission planning, education) of the Canadian Space Agency. He served as Chief Astronaut of the Canadian Space Agency in 1993 and 1994. In February 1994, he was crew commander for the CAPSULS mission, a simulated 7-day space mission which involved the participation of several international investigators and three other Canadian astronauts. In 1994-95, Bob completed a sabbatical year in Victoria, British Columbia. During this year, he upgraded his skills in clinical practice, space medicine research and Russian language training. On June 20, 1996, Bob flew aboard space shuttle mission STS-78 (the Life and Microgravity Spacelab mission) as a payload specialist. During this 17-day flight aboard the orbiter Columbia, Bob and his six crew mates performed 43 experiments devoted to the study of life and materials sciences. Most of these experiments were conducted within the pressurized Spacelab laboratory module situated in the orbiter's payload bay. The life science experiments investigated changes in plants, animals and humans under spaceflight conditions. The materials science experiments examined protein crystallization, fluid physics and high-temperature solidification of multi-phase materials in a weightless environment. In August 1998, Bob was assigned by the Canadian Space Agency to the Johnson Space Center to pursue advanced astronaut training. This long-term training program involves instruction on both shuttle and space station systems. Within the NASA Astronaut Office, Bob assists with design and operational issues of the space station's Thermal Control System. In Canada, Bob works with various organizations to develop educational projects for students and teachers. One of these projects will provide junior high school students with space technology resources to study the threats to four endangered species.

NAME: Eugene H. Trinh (Ph.D.)
     Payload Specialist

PERSONAL DATA: Born September 14, 1950, in Saigon, Vietnam; was raised from the age of two in Paris, France and has lived in the United States since 1968. Currently a resident of Culver City, California. Married to the former Yvette Fabry. Recreational interests include house remodeling, music, theatre, tennis, swimming, vollyball, soccer, hiking, and photography. His parents, Mr. and Mrs. Trinh, reside in Nice, France. Her parents, Mr. and Mrs. Fabry, reside in Paris, France.

EDUCATION: Secondary education: graduated from Lycee Michelet, Paris, France with a Baccalauret degree in 1968. Received a Bachelor of Science degree in Mechanical Engineering-Applied Physics from Columbia University in 1972; Masters of Science and of Philosophy and a Doctorate of Philosophy in Applied Physics from Yale University in 1974, 1975, and 1977 respectively.

ORGANIZATIONS: Acoustical Society of America, American Institute of Aeronautics and Astronautics, Sigma Xi Research Society, American Society of Mechanical Engineering, American Physical Society.

PUBLICATIONS: Published over 40 reviewed articles and authored as many conference papers in the areas of Fluid Dynamics, Acoustics, Materials Science, and Microgravity science and technology.

SPECIAL HONORS: Full tuition Scholarship (Columbia University), Sheffield Fellowship (Yale University), Group Achievement award NASA for flight experiments,Science Achievement award for Principal Investigator team NASA,NASA Exceptional Scientific Achievement Medal, NASA Flight Medal

RESEARCH ACTIVITIES: 1979 - Present,Physical acoustics, fluid dynamics and containerless materials processing. Development of high intensity acoustic levitation devices and experimental instrumentation and measurement techniques for fluid dynamics experiments as well as high temperature materials processing experiments in ground based laboratory and in low gravity. Development of shuttle flight experiments, and participation in both Spacelab flight mission support activities as well as flight crew training. Alternate Payload Specialist (APS) on Spacelab 3 mission (May 1985). Research Task Manager and Project Scientist for Drop Physics Module flight experiments. NASA investigator in Fluid Physics, Biotechnology, and Materials Science.

OTHER EXPERIENCE: Development and operation of low-gravity experimental apparatuses for tests in the NASA KC-135 airplane. An accumulated low gravity time of about 25 hours (at 0.05 G) has been obtained since 1983. Dr. Trinh was a member of the crew of Space Shuttle Columbia for STS-50/United States Microgravity Laboratory-1 (USML-1) Spacelab mission.

NAME: Luca Urbani (M.D.)
ASI Astronaut (Payload Specialist)

PERSONAL DATA: Born May 11, 1957, in Rome, Italy. He now resides in Rieti, Italy. Married to Cinzia Naccari of Senago (Milan), Italy. They have two sons. Recreational interests include flying (he is a licensed private pilot of airplanes, gliders and ultralights, with about 2,850 hours logged in gliders and single-engine airplanes); gliding (at a competitive level: seven times Italian Gliding Champion in different classes); horseback-riding; skiing; tennis. He is also a licensed amateur radio operator.

EDUCATION: Graduated from Scientific Lyceum "M. Massimo" in Rome in 1975. Received a Doctor of Medicine Degree from the University of Rome "La Sapienza" Medical School in 1981 (Summa cum Laude). Completed residencies in Otorhinolaryngology at the University of Rome "La Sapienza" in 1984 (Summa cum Laude) and in Audiological Medicine at the University of Naples in 1989.

ORGANIZATIONS: Member of: the Aviation Medicine Committee of the Italian Aero Club; the Aerospace Medical Association (AsMA), U.S.A.; the Italian Aerospace Medical Association (AIMAS); the Italian Group on Eye Movements (GIMO); the European Low Gravity Research Association (ELGRA; associate member); the Aerospace Physiology Society, U.S.A.; the Italian Chronobiology Society.

PUBLICATIONS: He has over 50 publications (full papers and abstracts), mostly in the areas of auditory and vestibular pathophysiology and of aerospace physiology and medicine.

SPECIAL HONORS: International FAI (Fédération Aéronautique Internationale) Diamond Badge for Gliding (1985); Italian National Olympic Committee Bronze Medal for Sports Merit (for Gliding: 1989 and 1995); Italian Air Force Long Service Medal (1994).

EXPERIENCE: In 1983-1984, Dr. Urbani served as Medical Officer of the Italian Army, Medical Corps (2nd Lieutenant). Since 1985, he has been serving as Medical Officer in the Italian Air Force, Medical Corps. In 1985-1987 he was Chief of the Medical Service, Vigna di Valle AFB, Rome. Since the late 1987, he has been assigned as a research medical officer at D.A.S.R.S.-Department of Aerospace Medicine, Pratica di Mare AFB, Rome, where his last position has been Chief of the Audio-Vestibular Section. His current rank is Lieutenant Colonel. He qualified as Flight Surgeon at the U.S.A.F. School of Aerospace Medicine, Brooks AFB, Texas, where he was the top graduate of the 1989 AAMIMO Course (Advanced Aerospace Medicine for International Medical Officers). From 1991 to the present, he has held an appointment as instructor of "Aerospace Physiological Techniques" at the Residency Program of Aerospace Medicine, University of Rome "La Sapienza." From 1993 to 1995, he has held an appointment as instructor of "Aerospace Medicine" at the Courses for Air Force Medical Officers, Italian Air Force Health School, Rome. In 1991, Dr. Urbani was selected by the Italian Space Agency (ASI) as one of the five Italian astronaut candidates for the last European Space Agency (ESA) astronaut selection. Eventually, he participated in the ESA selection and was one of the two Italians retained in the group of candidates considered by ESA for the final selection. In 1992, he participated in the ESA project "EXEMSI'92" (Experimental Campaign for the European Manned Space Infrastructure, performed at DLR, Koln, Germany) as a member of the EXPET team (Experimental Programme Execution Team) and as Principal Investigator of the experiment "Oculomotor Performance during Prolonged Isolation," one of the physiological experiments carried out within the project. In February 1994, he took part as crew member to CUS'94 Campaign (Columbus Utilisation Simulation), ESA simulation of a long-term mission increment performed at the Columbus mockup in ESTEC, Noordwijk, The Netherlands.

NASA EXPERIENCE: Following candidature by the Italian Space Agency, Dr. Urbani was selected by the National Aeronautics and Space Administration (NASA) in May 1995 as an Alternate Payload Specialist for the Life and Microgravity Spacelab (LMS) mission, STS-78, and began training for the flight duties of a Payload Specialist Astronaut at the Johnson Space Center in Houston. LMS is an international research mission scheduled for flight on June 1996 aboard the Space Shuttle Columbia. During the mission, Dr. Urbani will act as Crew Interface Coordinator in the Payload Operations Control Center at the Marshall Space Flight Center in Huntsville.

NAME: Scott D. Vangen
Payload Specialist

PERSONAL DATA: Born December 12, 1959, in Granite Falls, Minnesota. Single. His hobbies include music (multi-keyboardist/composition), amateur radio, scuba diving, Nordic/downhill skiing, and soaring. His parents, Orel and Agnes Vangen, are residents of St. Cloud, Minnesota.

EDUCATION: Graduated from Granite Falls High School, Granite Falls, Minnesota, in 1978; received a bachelor of science degree in Electrical Engineering, South Dakota School of Mines and Technology, Rapid City, South Dakota, 1982; and a masters of science degree in Space Technology from the Florida Institute of Technology, Melbourne, Florida, 1986.

NASA EXPERIENCE: Mr. Vangen has been at the Kennedy Space Center, Florida, with the Payloads Operations and Management Directorate since 1982. He has been an experiment engineer and lead mission engineer for multiple domestic and international space shuttle scientific payloads and experiments. He has had extensive hands-on operations experience with various space flight payloads; particularly astrophysics experiments designed to explore the electromagnetic spectrum from cosmic/x-rays through ultraviolet into the infrared. Mr. Vangen has worked extensively preparing experiments to fly aboard spacelab, a scientific research facility carried in the cargo bay of the space shuttle. He was responsible for integration and testing of experiments manifested on Spacelab-1, Spacelab-2, Spacelab-3, Astro-1, D-1, ATLAS-1, and TSS-1. As an experiment engineer he was responsible for preparing the payload elements for launch, including interface and functional testing, troubleshooting, repair, and support activities for launch and landing. He has also supported multiple space flight missions as a member of the experiment science teams for on-orbit operations at the Payload Operations Control Centers located at the Marshall Space Flight Center, Huntsville, Alabama, and the Johnson Space Center, Houston, Texas. Until 1990, he was the lead electrical engineer for the Payload Checkout Unit, the major checkout system used for spacelab testing during experiment integration and checkout. His two most recent assignments, as the space station experiment integration lead electrical engineer and avionics lead, continued his involvement in payload operations as the Kennedy Space Center prepares for the next generation of space science technology, experiments, and payloads.

CURRENT ASSIGNMENT: Mr. Vangen is in flight training as an alternate payload specialist on the crew of STS-67/Astro-2, a spacelab ultraviolet astronomy mission scheduled for January 1995. Payload specialists are normally career scientists and engineers selected for their knowledge of a particular payload. Mr. Vangen's experience with the Astro-1 payload and his contributions to the mission's success contributed to his selection in May of 1993 as the alternate payload specialist for Astro-2.

NAME: Charles D. Walker
MDC Payload Specialist

PERSONAL DATA: Born in Bedford, Indiana, August 29, 1948. Married to the former Susan Y. Flowers, of Joplin, Missouri. They have one daughter and one granddaughter. Recreational interests include photography, running, hiking, scuba diving, reading, collecting books on Space, and bonsai. His mother, Donna Lake Walker, resides in Bedford; his father is deceased.

EDUCATION: Graduated from Bedford High School, Bedford, Indiana, in 1966; received a bachelor of science degree in aeronautical and astronautical engineering from Purdue University in 1971.

SPECIAL HONORS: U.S. Patent No. 4,394,246, Electrophoresis Apparatus with Flow Control, issued 19 July 1983; NASA Space Flight Medal (1984, and twice in 1985); Sagamore of the Wabash, State of Indiana (November 1984); Doctor of Science, honoris causa, St. Louis College of Pharmacy (1985); Aerospace Laurels Award, Aviation Week and Space Technology Magazine (1985); Lindbergh Award, American Institute of Aeronautics and Astronautics - St. Louis Section (1986); NASA Group Achievement Award, as consultant to the 1987-88 Space Station Operations Task Force; Engineering Astronaut Alumnus Award, Purdue University Schools of Engineering (September 1989); Kentucky Colonel, Commonwealth of Kentucky (May 1990).

EXPERIENCE: Following graduation from Purdue University he worked as a civil engineering technician, land acquisition specialist and forest firefighter for the U.S. Forest Service. Subsequently he was a design engineer with the Bendix Aerospace Company where he worked on aerodynamic analysis, missile subsystem design, and flight testing. He also was employed as project engineer with the Naval Sea Systems Command with responsibility for computer-controlled manufacturing systems. Mr. Walker joined the McDonnell Douglas Corporation in 1977 as a test engineer on the Aft Propulsion Subsystem for the Space Shuttle orbiters. He joined the Space Manufacturing (later named Electrophoresis Operations in Space, EOS) team as one of its original members. He shares in a patent for the McDonnell Douglas developed continuous flow electrophoresis (CFES) device. From 1979 to 1986, he was Chief Test Engineer and Payload Specialist for the McDonnell Douglas EOS commercialization project. Mr. Walker led the EOS laboratory test and operations team developing biomedical products. His contributions to the program included engineering planning, design and development, product research, and space flight and evaluation of the CFES device. He was involved with the program support activities at Kennedy Space Center, Florida, and at the Mission Control Center in Houston, Texas. He was responsible for training the NASA astronaut crews in the operation of the CFES payload on STS-4, STS-6, STS-7, and STS-8 shuttle flights during 1982 and 1983. In May 1986, Mr. Walker was appointed Special Assistant to the President of McDonnell Douglas Space Systems Company, working in Washington, D.C. Mr. Walker has been an industry member of the NASA Microgravity Material Science Assessment Task Force, the NASA Space Station Office Quick-is Beautiful/Rapid Response Research Study Group, and the NASA Space Station Operations Task Force. He has been a member of the National Research Council's Space Applications Board. Mr. Walker was Faculty Course Advisor and lecturer for the International Space university 1988 summer session. He was a participant in the 1988 Center for Strategic and International Studies civil Space policy study. He served on the AIAA steering committee formulating the strategic plan for NASA's office of Commercial Programs. Mr. Walkers has served as a board member of the Astronauts Memorial Foundation. He was the organizing committee chairman for the 1992 World Space Congress. He has been a national panel member of the NASA/Industry Manned Flight Awareness Program and the NASA/Industry Education Initiative. Mr. Walker advised the NASA/ Purdue University space life support research center, a NASA/Penn State space commercial development center and a U.S. Department of Education/Ohio State University science education center. He is a board director of the Challenger Center for Space Science Education. Mr. Walker has served as the volunteer chairman of the board of directors of Spacecause, and is past president and a current board director of the National Space Society. He is also currently a board director of the Association of Space Explorers. Walker is a professional engineer registered in California. He has authored several papers and book contributions on the EOS electrophoresis program, space development, commercialization, and space history. Mr. Walker has also written columns and articles appearing in national newspapers and numerous other publications.

NASA EXPERIENCE: While never an employee of NASA, he has been extensively involved in payload preparation and on-pad processing support activities at Kennedy Space Center, Florida, and in flight support at the Mission Control Center, Houston, Texas. He was responsible for training the NASA astronaut crews in the operation of the CFES payload on STS-4, STS-6, STS-7, and STS-8 shuttle flights during 1982 and 1983. Confirmed by NASA in 1983 as the first industrial payload specialist, Mr. Walker accompanied the McDonnell Douglas CFES equipment as a crew member on Space Shuttle missions 41-D, 51-D, and 61-B, accumulating 20 days of experience in space and traveling 8.2 million miles. Aboard these Space Shuttle missions Mr. Walker also performed early protein crystal growth experiments and participated as a test subject in numerous medical studies. Since 1986 Mr. Walker has served in various NASA study and review team capacities including as a member of the NASA Microgravity Material Science Assessment Task Force, the NASA Space Station Office Quick-is-Beautiful/Rapid Response Research Study Group, and the NASA Space Station Operations Task Force. He has served on the national panels of the NASA/Industry Manned Flight Awareness Program and the NASA/Industry Education Initiative.

CURRENTLY: Mr. Walker is Senior Manager of Space Programs Business Development and Marketing with The Boeing Company Washington D.C. Operations.

NAME: S. Christa Corrigan McAuliffe (Deceased)
Teacher in Space Participant
NASA Teacher in Space
Civilian Payload Specialist

PERSONAL DATA: Born in Boston, Massachusetts, September 2, 1948. Her parents, Mr. and Mrs. Edward C. Corrigan, reside in Framingham, Massachusetts.

PHYSICAL DESCRIPTION: Brown hair; brown eyes; height: 5 feet 5 inches; weight: 130 pounds.

EDUCATION: Graduated from Marian High School, Framingham, Massachusetts, in 1966. Received a bachelor of arts degree, Framingham State College, 1970; and a masters degree in education, Bowie State College, Bowie, Maryland, 1978.

MARITAL STATUS: Married to Steven James McAuliffe.

CHILDREN: Scott Corrigan, September 11, 1976; and Caroline Corrigan, August 24, 1979.

RECREATIONAL INTERESTS: Jogging, tennis, and volleyball.

ORGANIZATIONS: Board member, New Hampshire Council of Social Studies; National Council of Social Studies; Concord Teachers Association; New Hampshire Education Association; and the National Education Association.

OUTSIDE ACTIVITIES: Member, Junior Service League; teacher, Christian Doctrine Classes, St. Peters Church; host family, A Better Chance Program (ABC), for innercity students; and fundraiser for Concord Hospital and Concord YMCA.

EXPERIENCE: 1970-1971 Benjamin Foulois Junior High School, Morningside, Maryland. Teacher. American history, 8th grade. 1971-1978 Thomas Johnson Junior High School, Lanham, Maryland. Teacher. English and American history, 8th grade and civics, 9th grade. 1978-1979 Bundlett Junior High School, Concord, New Hampshire. Teacher. English, 7th grade and American history, 8th grade. 1980-1982 Bow Memorial High School, Concord, New Hampshire. Teacher. English, 9th grade. 1982-1985 Concord High School, Concord, New Hampshire. Teacher. Courses in economics, law, American history, and a course she developed entitled "The American Woman," 10th, 11th, and 12th grade.

NASA EXPERIENCE: McAuliffe was selected as the primary candidate for the NASA Teacher in Space Project on July 19, 1985. Christa McAuliffe was the Teacher in Space Participant on STS 51-L, which was launched from Kennedy Space Center, Florida, at 11:38:00 EST on January 28, 1986. The crew on board the Orbiter Challenger included the pilot, Commander M. J. Smith (USN) (pilot), three mission specialist, Dr. R. E. McNair, Lieutenant Colonel E. S. Onizuka (USAF), and Dr. J. A. Resnik, as well as two civilian payload specialist, Mr. G. B. Jarvis and Mrs. S. C. McAuliffe. The STS 51-L crew died on January 28, 1986 after the failed solid rocket booster caused the explosion of STS-51 1 min. 13 sec. after launch.

Late Arrivals

The following entries are due to
information received late for insertion
into the astronaut categories.

NAME: Paul William Richards
      NASA Astronaut

PERSONAL DATA: Born May 20, 1964 in Scranton, Pennsylvania. His hometown is Dunmore, Pennsylvania. Enjoys cycling, golf, sailing, snow skiing, cooking, and home repair/improvement. Married to the former Susan Geiger Palmer, of Flourtown, Pennsylvania. They have three children. His parents are Angela Cordaro Richards and the late James J. Richards. Her parents are Samuel and Joan Geiger of Erdenheim, Pennsylvania.

EDUCATION: Graduated from Dunmore High School, Dunmore, Pennsylvania, in 1982; received a bachelor of science degree in mechanical engineering from Drexel University in 1987 and a master of science degree in mechanical engineering from the University of Maryland in 1991.

ORGANIZATIONS: American Society of Mechanical Engineers, National Society of Professional Engineers, American Institute for Aeronautics and Astronautics, American Society of Naval Engineers, United States Naval Reserves.

AWARDS: NASA Certificate of Recognition for Patent Application (1996). Silver Snoopy Award (1994). NASA Exceptional Achievement Medal (1994). Several Goddard Honor Awards (1994). Several Group Achievement Awards 1994). HST First Servicing Mission Development Team. HST First Servicing Mission Extravehicular Activity Team. HST First Servicing Mission Crew Aids and Tools Development Team. HST First Servicing Mission Integration and Test Team. HST First Servicing Mission Space Support Equipment Team. NASA Manned Flight Awareness Award (1994). NASA Outstanding Performance Awards (1992, 1994, 1995). Quality Increase Award (1993). Certificate of Outstanding Performance (1990, 1993, 1994). Group Achievement Award UARS and GRO MMS and UASE Support Team (1992). NASA Certificate of Recognition for Invention Disclosure (1991). NASA Certificate of Recognition for Technical Brief (1991).

EXPERIENCE: Department of the Navy, Naval Ship Systems Engineering Station, 1983-1987. Transferred to NASA Goddard Space Flight Center (GSFC) in 1987. Worked in the Verification Office, Electromechanical Branch, Robotics Branch, Guidance and Controls Branch, all within the Engineering Directorate. Senior EVA Tool Development Engineer for the Hubble Space Telescope (HST) Servicing Project. Lead Engineer for GSFC HST EVA crew aids and tools. Responsibilities included the design, analysis, fabrication, test, and integration for breadboard, WETF/NBS, engineering, and flight hardware, and the financial tracking, documentation, and review process for these tools. Additional duties included engineering support for the HST WETF/NBS Servicing Mission Simulations as a utility diver and EMU suited subject. Selected by NASA in April 1996, Richards reported to the Johnson Space Center in August 1996. Having completed two years of training and evaluation, he is qualified for flight assignment as a mission specialist. Richards was initially assigned to the Computer Branch working on software for the Space Shuttle and the International Space Station. He next served in the Astronaut Office Shuttle Operations Branch assigned to support Payload and General Support Computers (PGSCs) and the Shuttle Avionics Integration Laboratory (SAIL). He is currently in training for the STS-102 mission, targeted for launch in 2001.

NAME: Anthony W. England (Ph.D.)
NASA Astronaut (former)

PERSONAL DATA: Born May 15, 1942, in Indianapolis, Indiana, but his hometown is West Fargo, North Dakota. His parents, Mr. and Mrs. Herman U. England, reside in Detroit Lakes, Minnesota.

PHYSICAL DESCRIPTION: Brown hair; blue eyes; height: 5 feet 10 inches; weight: 170 pounds.

EDUCATION: Attended primary school in Indianapolis, Indiana, and graduated from high school in North Dakota; received bachelor and master of science degrees in Geology from Massachusetts Institute of Technology (MIT) in 1965, and a doctor of philosophy in Geophysics from MIT in 1970.

MARITAL STATUS: Married to the former Kathleen Ann Kreutz, the daughter of Mr. Howard B. Kreutz of Perham, Minnesota.

CHILDREN: Heidi Lynd, November 5, 1968; Heather Anne, May 15, 1970.

RECREATIONAL INTERESTS: Enjoys sailing and amateur radio.

ORGANIZATIONS: Member of the American Geophysical Union, the Society of Exploration Geophysicists, the Institute of Electrical and Electronics Engineers, and Sigma Xi.

SPECIAL HONORS: Presented the Johnson Space Center Superior Achievement Award (1970). Awarded a NASA Outstanding Scientific Achievement Medal (1973), the U.S. Antarctic Medal (1979), the NASA Space Flight Medal (1985), and the American Astronomical Society Space Flight Award (1986).

EXPERIENCE: He was a graduate fellow at the Massachusetts Institute of Technology for the three years immediately preceding his assignment to NASA. He performed heat flow measurements throughout the southwest; took part in geomagnetic studies in Montana; performed radar sounding studies of glaciers in Washington State and Alaska; performed microwave airborne research in geothermal areas of the Western United States; and participated in and led field parties during two seasons in Antarctica. He was Deputy Chief of the Office of Geochemistry and Geophysics for the U.S. Geological Survey, and was Associated Editor for the Journal of Geophysical Research. He served on the National Academy's Earth Science Panel of the Space Science Board, and on several Federal Committees concerned with Antarctic policy, nuclear waste containment, and Federal Science and Technology. He has logged over 3,000 hours of flying time.

NASA EXPERIENCE: Dr. England was selected as a scientist-astronaut by NASA in August 1967. He subsequently completed the initial academic training and a 53-week course in flight training at Laughlin Air Force Base, Texas, and served as a support crewman for the Apollo 13 and 16 flights. From August 1972 to June 1979, England was a research geophysicist with the U.S. Geological Survey. In 1979 he returned to the Johnson Space Center, as a senior scientist-astronaut (mission specialist), was assigned to the operation mission development group of the astronaut office, and eventually managed that group. Dr. England was a mission specialist on the Spacelab-2 mission (STS 51-F), which launched from Kennedy Space Center, Florida, on July 29, 1985. He was accompanied by Col. Charles G. Fullerton (spacecraft commander), Col. Roy D. Bridges (pilot), fellow mission specialists, Drs. Karl G. Henize, and F. Story Musgrave, as well as two payload specialists, Drs. Loren Acton, and John-David Bartoe. This mission was the first pallet-only Spacelab mission and the first mission to operate the Spacelab Instrument Pointing System (IPS). It carried 13 major experiments of which seven were in the field of astronomy and solar physics, three were for studies of the Earth's ionosphere, two were life science experiments, and one studied the properties of superfluid helium. During the mission Dr. England was responsible for activating and operating the Spacelab systems, operating the Instrument Pointing System (IPS), and the Remote Manipulator System (RMS), assisting with experiment operations, and performing a contingency EVA had one been necessary. After 126 orbits of the earth, STS 51-F Challenger landed at Edwards Air Force Base, California, on August 6,1985. With the completion of this flight England has logged 188 hours in space. Dr. England was Program Scientist for Space Station from May 1986 through May 1987. From June 1987 through December 1987, he taught Remote Sensing Geophysics at Rice University.

Adamson, James C.	President	Honeywell Technology	7000 Columbia Gateway	Columbia, MD 21046
Akers, Thomas D.	Commander-ROTC	1870 Miner Circle	UMR-206 Harris Hall	Rolla, MT 65409
Aldrin, Buzz	10380 Wilshire Blvd	Los Angeles, CA 90024		
Allen, Andrew M.	Technical Operations	United Space Alliance	600 Gemini	Houston, TX 77058
Allen, Joseph P.	Chairman	Veridian	1200 South Hayes Street	Arlington, VA 22202
Altman, Scott D.	Astronaut Office	Code CB Bldg. 4S	2101 NASA Road One	Houston, TX 77058
Anders, William A.	Director	Heritage Flight Museum	PO Box 1630	Eastsound, WA 98245
Anderson, Clayton C.	Astronaut Office	Code CB Bldg. 4S	2101 NASA Road One	Houston, TX 77058
Anderson, Michael P.	Astronaut Office	Code CB Bldg. 4S	2101 NASA Road One	Houston, TX 77058
Antonelli, Dominic A.	Astronaut Office	Code CB Bldg. 4S	2101 NASA Road One	Houston, TX 77058
Apt, Jerome	The Carnegie Museum	Natural History	4400 Forbes Avenue	Pittsburgh, PA 15213
Archambault, Lee J.	Astronaut Office	Code CB Bldg. 4S	2101 NASA Road One	Houston, TX 77058
Armstrong, Neil A.	Chairman	AIL Systems	455 Commack Road	Deer Park, NY 11729
Ashby, Jeffrey S.	Astronaut Office	Code CB Bldg. 4S	2101 NASA Road One	Houston, TX 77058
Bagian, James P.	EPA	OMS-RSPD	2565 Plymouth Road	Ann Arbor, MI 48105
Baker, Ellen S.	Astronaut Office	Code CB Bldg. 4S	2101 NASA Road One	Houston, TX 77058
Baker, Michael A.	Asssitant Director	Code A6	Johnson Space Center	Houston, TX 77058
Barratt, Michael R.	Astronaut Office	Code CB Bldg. 4S	2101 NASA Road One	Houston, TX 77058
Barry, Daniel T.	Astronaut Office	Code CB Bldg. 4S	2101 NASA Road One	Houston, TX 77058
Bartone, John-David	Chief Scientist	Office of Space Station	Johnson Space Center	Houston, TX 77058
Bean, Alan L.	9173 Briar Forest	Houston, TX 77024-7222		
Behnken, Robert L.	Astronaut Office	Code CB Bldg. 4S	2101 NASA Road One	Houston, TX 77058
Blaha, John E.	VP Applied Research	USAA Corporation	9800 Fredericksburg Rd	San Antonio, TX 78288
Bloomfield, Michael J.	Astronaut Office	Code CB Bldg. 4S	2101 NASA Road One	Houston, TX 77058
Bluford, Guion S., Jr.	VP Aerospace Sector	Federal Data Corporation	3005 Aerospace Pkwy	Cleveland, OH 44124
Bobko, Karol J.	VP Product Development	Johnson Engineering	555 Forge River Road	Webster, TX 77598
Boe, Eric A.	Astronaut Office	Code CB Bldg. 4S	2101 NASA Road One	Houston, TX 77058
Bolden, Charles F., Jr.	Commanding General	PO Box 452038	MCAS Miramar	San Diego, CA 92145
Bondar, Roberta	Astronaut Office	Code CB Bldg. 4S	2101 NASA Road One	Houston, TX 77058
Borman, Frank	Chairman	Patlex Corporation	PO Box 1159	Fairacres, NM 88033
Bowen, Stephen G.	Astronaut Office	Code CB Bldg. 4S	2101 NASA Road One	Houston, TX 77058
Bowersox, Kenneth D.	SAIL	Johnson Space Center	Houston, TX 77058	
Brady, Charles E., Jr.	Astronaut Office	Code CB Bldg. 4S	2101 NASA Road One	Houston, TX 77058
Brand, Vance D.	Deputy Director	Aerospace Projects	NASA Dryden Flight Ctr.	Edwards, CA 93523
Brandenstein, Daniel	VP Customer Support	Lockheed Martin Space	595 Gemini Avenue	Houston, TX 77058
Bridges, Roy D., Jr.	Mail Code AA	Director	Kennedy Space Center	FL 32899
Brown, Curtis L., Jr.	19500 E Highway 6	Alvin, TX 77511-7458		
Brown, David M.	Astronaut Office	Code CB Bldg. 4S	2101 NASA Road One	Houston, TX 77058
Brown, Mark N.	Director of Aerospace	General Research Corp.	2940 Presidential Drive	Fairborn, OH 45324
Buchli, James F.	Space Station Manager	United Space Alliance	1150 Gemini Road	Houston, TX 77058-2708
Buckey, Jay Clark	Dartmouth-Hitchcock	1 Medical Center Drive	Lebanon, NH 03756	
Bull, John S.	Aircraft Guidance & Nav	NASA Ames Research	Moffet Field, CA 94035	
Burbank, Daniel C.	Astronaut Office	Code CB Bldg. 4S	2101 NASA Road One	Houston, TX 77058
Bursch, Daniel W.	Astronaut Office	Code CB Bldg. 4S	2101 NASA Road One	Houston, TX 77058
Cabana, Robert D.	ISS Manager Intl. Op.	Bldg. 1 Room 522G	Johnson Space Center	Houston, TX 77058
Cagle, Yvonne D.	Astronaut Office	Code CB Bldg. 4S	2101 NASA Road One	Houston, TX 77058

Caldeiro, Fernando	Astronaut Office	Code CB Bldg. 4S	2101 NASA Road One	Houston, TX 77058
Caldwell, Tracy E.	Astronaut Office	Code CB Bldg. 4S	2101 NASA Road One	Houston, TX 77058
Camarda, Charles J.	Astronaut Office	Code CB Bldg. 4S	2101 NASA Road One	Houston, TX 77058
Cameron, Kenneth D.	Room 3-220	Saab Automobile	3044 West Grand Blvd	Detroit, MI 48202-3091
Carey, Duane G.	Astronaut Office	Code CB Bldg. 4S	2101 NASA Road One	Houston, TX 77058
Carpenter, M. Scott	PO Box 3161	4153 Spruce Way	Vail, CO 81657	
Carr, Gerald P.	President	CAMUS Inc.	PO Box 919	Huntsville, AR 72740
Casper, John H.	Director	Safety/Quality Assurance	Johnson Space Center	Houston, TX 77058
Cenker, Robert	Aerospace Consultant	GORCA, Inc.	155 Hickory Corner	East Windsor, NJ 08520
Cernan, Eugene A.	Chairman	Johnson Eng. Corp.	555 Forge River Road	Webster, TX 77598-4336
Chamitoff, Gregory E.	Astronaut Office	Code CB Bldg. 4S	2101 NASA Road One	Houston, TX 77058
Chang-Diaz, Franklin R.	Code CB-ASPL Bldg 4S	Advance Propulsion Lab.	Johnson Space Center	Houston, TX 77058
Chapman, Philip K.	Chief Scientist	Rotary Rocket Corp.	1250 Bayhill Drive	San Bruno, CA 94066
Chawla, Kalpana	Astronaut Office	Code CB Bldg. 4S	2101 NASA Road One	Houston, TX 77058
Cheli, Maurizio (ESA)	European Astronaut Ctr.	Linder Hohe,	Postfach 90 60 96	D-51127 Koln, Germany
Chiao, Leroy	Astronaut Office	Code CB Bldg. 4S	2101 NASA Road One	Houston, TX 77058
Chilton, Kevin P.	Deputy Director	Politico/Military AffairsJ-5	5104 Jnt. Staff Pentagon	Washington, DC 20318
Chrétien, Jean-Loup	CNES	Direction des Astronaute	2 Place Maurice Quentin	F-75039 Paris, France
Clark, Laurel B.	Astronaut Office	Code CB Bldg. 4S	2101 NASA Road One	Houston, TX 77058
Cleave, Mary L.	Code AS Room 7R86	Deputy Administrator	NASA Headquarters	Washington, DC 20546
Clervoy, Jean-Francois	European Astronaut Ctr.	Linder Hohe,	Postfach 90 60 96	D-51127 Koln, Germany
Clifford, Michael R.	Flight Op. Mgr. Intl.	Boeing Company	2100 Space Park Drive	Houston, TX 77058
Coats, Michael L.	VP Reusable Launch Sy.	Lockheed Martin	PO Box 179	Denver, CO 80201-0179
Cockrell, Kenneth D.	Astronaut Office	Code CB Bldg. 4S	2101 NASA Road One	Houston, TX 77058
Coleman, Catherine G.	Astronaut Office	Code CB Bldg. 4S	2101 NASA Road One	Houston, TX 77058
Collins, Eileen M.	Astronaut Office	Code CB Bldg. 4S	2101 NASA Road One	Houston, TX 77058
Collins, Michael	272 Polynesia Court	Marco Island, FL 34145		
Cooper, L. Gordon, Jr.	President	Galaxy Aerospace Inc.	16303 Waterman Drive	Van Nuys, CA 91406
Covey, Richard O.	VP Houston Operations	Boeing Company	2100 Space Park Drive	Houston, TX 77058
Creamer, Timothy J.	Astronaut Office	Code CB Bldg. 4S	2101 NASA Road One	Houston, TX 77058
Creighton, John O.	Production Test Pilot	Boeing Commercial	PO Box 3707	Seattle, WA 98124
Crippen, Robert L.	President	Cordant Technologies	PO Box 707	Brigham City, UT 84302
Crouch, Roger	ISS Chief Scientist	NASA Office of Life and	Microgravity Sciences	Washington, DC 20546
Culbertson, Frank L., Jr.	Deputy Program Mgr.	Code YA	Johnson Space Center	Houston, TX 77058
Cunningham, Walter	2425 West Loop South	Houston, TX 77027		
Curbeam, Robert L., Jr.	Astronaut Office	Code CB Bldg. 4S	2101 NASA Road One	Houston, TX 77058
Currie, Nancy J.	Astronaut Office	Code CB Bldg. 4S	2101 NASA Road One	Houston, TX 77058
Davis, N. Jan	Mail Code FDOI	Director, Flight Projects	George C. Marshall Ctr.	Huntsville, AL 35812
DeLucas, Lawrence	Ctr. Biophysical Science	University of Alabama	1530 3rd Avenue	Birmingham, AL 35294
Doi, Takao (NASDA)	Astronaut Office	NASDA	2-1-1 Segen, Tukuba-Shi	Ibaraki 305, Japan
Drew, B. Alvin	Astronaut Office	Code CB Bldg. 4S	2101 NASA Road One	Houston, TX 77058
Duffy, Brian	Code AC2 Bldg. 4S	Johnson Space Center	Houston, TX 77058	
Duke, Charles M., Jr.	Duke Ministry for Christ	PO Box 310345	New Braunfels,TX 78131	
Dunbar, Bonnie J.	Astronaut Office	Code CB Bldg. 4S	2101 NASA Road One	Houston, TX 77058
Dunlap, Alexander	Astronaut Office	Code CB Bldg. 4S	2101 NASA Road One	Houston, TX 77058
Duque, Pedro (ESA)	European Astronaut Ctr.	Linder Hohe,	Postfach 90 60 96	D-51127 Koln, Germany

Durrance, Samuel	Director of Technology	Final Analysis Inc.	9701-E Philadelphia Ct.	Lanham, MD 20708
Edwards, Joe F., Jr.	PO Box 1188	Enron Broadband Serv.	1400 Smith Street	Houston, TX 77251-1188
England, Anthony W.	Dept. of Electrical Eng.	University of Michigan	1301 Beal/3228 EECS	Ann Arbor, MI 48109
Engle, Joe H.	PO Box 58386	Houston, TX 77258-8386		
Eyharts, Léopold (ESA)	CNES	Direction des Astronaute	2 Place Maurice Quentin	F-75039 Paris, France
Fabian, John M.	100 Shine Road	Port Ludlow, WA 98365		
Favier, Jean-Jacques	CNES	Direction des Astronaute	2 Place Maurice Quentin	F-75039 Paris, France
Ferguson, Christopher J.	Astronaut Office	Code CB Bldg. 4S	2101 NASA Road One	Houston, TX 77058
Fettman, Martin	Department of Pathology	Colorado State Univ.	Fort Collins, CO 80523	
Feustel, Andrew J.	Astronaut Office	Code CB Bldg. 4S	2101 NASA Road One	Houston, TX 77058
Fincke, E. Michael	Astronaut Office	Code CB Bldg. 4S	2101 NASA Road One	Houston, TX 77058
Fisher, Anna L.	Astronaut Office	Code CB Bldg. 4S	2101 NASA Road One	Houston, TX 77058
Fisher, William F.	Emergency Specialist	Humana Hosp. Clear Lk.	500 Medical Center Blvd	Webster, TX 77598
Foale, C. Michael	Bldg. 1 Room 935A	Assistant Director	Johnson Space Center	Houston, Tx 77058
Ford, Kevin A.	Astronaut Office	Code CB Bldg. 4S	2101 NASA Road One	Houston, TX 77058
Foreman, Michael J.	Astronaut Office	Code CB Bldg. 4S	2101 NASA Road One	Houston, TX 77058
Forrester, Patrick G.	Astronaut Office	Code CB Bldg. 4S	2101 NASA Road One	Houston, TX 77058
Fossum, Michael E.	Astronaut Office	Code CB Bldg. 4S	2101 NASA Road One	Houston, TX 77058
Frick, Stephen N.	Astronaut Office	Code CB Bldg. 4S	2101 NASA Road One	Houston, TX 77058
Fuglesang, Christer	European Astronaut Ctr.	Linder Hohe,	Postfach 90 60 96	D-51147 Koln, Germany
Fulford, Millie	Dept. of Veteran Affairs	VA Medical Center	4150 Clement Street	San Francisco, CA 94121
Fullerton, Charles G.	Bldg. 4800-D/2066	Dryden Flight Rsrch. Ctr.	PO Box 273	Edwards AFB, CA 93523
Garan, Ronald J., Jr.	Astronaut Office	Code CB Bldg. 4S	2101 NASA Road One	Houston, TX 77058
Gardner, Dale A.	Site Manager	TRW	1555 N. Newport Road	Colorado Springs, CO 80916
Gardner, Guy S.	316 S. Taylor Street	Arlington, VA 22204		
Garneau, Marc (CSA)	Canadian Space Agency	6767 route de l'Aeroport	Saint-Hubert, Quebec	J3Y 8Y9, Canada
Garriott, Owen K.	111 Lost Tree Drive	Huntsville, Al 35824		
Gemar, Charles D.	Flight Test Operations	Bombardier Flight Test	1 Learjet Way	Witchita, KS 67209
Gernhardt, Michael L.	2765 Lighthouse Drive	Houston, TX 77058		
Gibson, Edward G.	VP Mgmt. Services	Aviation Mgmt. Syst.	3737 East Bonanza Way	Pheonix, AZ 85034
Gibson, Robert L.	First Officer	Southwest Airlines	7800 Airport Blvd	Houston, TX 77061
Glenn, John H., Jr.	School of Public Policy	Ohio State University	100 Bricker Hall	Columbus, OH 43210
Godwin, Linda M.	Astronaut Office	Code CB Bldg. 4S	2101 NASA Road One	Houston, TX 77058
Good, Michael T.	Astronaut Office	Code CB Bldg. 4S	2101 NASA Road One	Houston, TX 77058
Gordon, Richard F., Jr.	63 Antelope Drive	Sedona, AZ 86336-7150		
Gorie, Dominic L.	Astronaut Office	Code CB Bldg. 4S	2101 NASA Road One	Houston, TX 77058
Grabe, Ronald J.	General Manager	Orbital Sciences Corp.	21700 Atlantic Blvd.	Dulles, VA 20166
Graveline, Duane E.	PO Box 92	Underhill Ctr., VT 05490		
Gregory, Frederick D.	Safety/MissionAssurance	NASA Headquarters	Washington, DC 20546	
Gregory, William G.	Business Development	Honeywell Space Sys.	19019 North 59th Ave.	Glendale, AZ 85308
Grunsfeld, John M.	Astronaut Office	Code CB Bldg. 4S	2101 NASA Road One	Houston, TX 77058
Guidoni, Umberto (ESA)	European Astronaut Ctr.	Linder Hohe,	Postfach 90 60 96	51142 Koln, Germany
Gutierrez, Sidney M.	Mgr. Strategic Planning	Sandia National Labs	PO Box 5800 Dept. 5932	Albuquerque, NM 87185
Hadfield, Chris A. (CSA)	Canadian Space Agency	6767 route de l'Aeroport	Saint-Hubert, Quebec	J3Y 8Y9, Canada
Haise, Fred W., Jr.	CADATT	14316 FM 2354 Road	Baytown, TX 77520	
Halsell, James D., Jr.	Manager Room 3103	Code MK Bldg. M6-0399	Kennedy Space Center	FL 32899

Ham, Kenneth T.	Astronaut Office	Code CB Bldg. 4S	2101 NASA Road One	Houston, TX 77058
Hammond, L. Blaine, Jr.	Dept. 0926	Gulfstream Aircraft Corp.	4150 Donald Douglas Blvd	Long Beach, CA 90808
Harbaugh, Gregory J.	Astronaut Office	Code CB Bldg. 4S	2101 NASA Road One	Houston, TX 77058
Harris, Bernard A., Jr.	Chief Scientist	Spacehab Inc.	1331 Gemini Avenue	Houston, TX 77058
Hart, Terry J.	President	Loral Skynet	500 Hills Drive	Bedminster, NJ 07921
Hartsfield, Henry W., Jr.	NASA Training Operation	Raytheon Systems Co.	2224 Bay Area Blvd	Houston, TX 77058
Hauck, Frederick H.	President	AXA Space	4800 Montgomery Lane	Bethesda, MD 20814
Hawley, Steven A.	Code CA/SAH	Flight Crew Operations	Johnson Space Center	Houston, TX 77058
Helms, Susan J.	Astronaut Office	Code CB Bldg. 4S	2101 NASA Road One	Houston, TX 77058
Hennen, Thomas	Executive Director	The Atlantis Foundation	2800 NASA Road One	Seabrook, TX 77586
Henricks, Terence T.	PO Box 547	Timken Aerospace	Keene, NH 03431-0547	
Herrington, John B.	Astronaut Office	Code CB Bldg. 4S	2101 NASA Road One	Houston, TX 77058
Hieb, Richard J.	Orbital Sciences	21700 Atlantic Blvd	Dulles, VA 20166	
Higginbotham, Joan E.	Astronaut Office	Code CB Bldg. 4S	2101 NASA Road One	Houston, TX 77058
Hilliard Robertson, P.	Astronaut Office	Code CB Bldg. 4S	2101 NASA Road One	Houston, TX 77058
Hilmers, David C.	18502 Point Lookout Dr.	Houston, TX 77058		
Hire, Kathryn P.	Bldg. 2 Unit 3	2023 Enterprise	League City, TX 77573	
Hobaugh, Charles O.	Astronaut Office	Code CB Bldg. 4S	2101 NASA Road One	Houston, TX 77058
Hoffman, Jeffrey A.	NASA Office for Europe	2 Avenue Gabriel	F-75382 Paris Cedex 08	France
Holmquest, Donald L.	Homquist & Associates	109 Marrakech Court	Bellaire, TX 77401-5117	
Holt, R. Glynn	Dept. of Aerospace	Boston University	110 Cummington Street	Boston, MA 02215
Horowitz, Scott J.	Astronaut Office	Code CB Bldg. 4S	2101 NASA Road One	Houston, TX 77058
Hurley, Douglas G.	Astronaut Office	Code CB Bldg. 4S	2101 NASA Road One	Houston, TX 77058
Husband, Rick D.	Astronaut Office	Code CB Bldg. 4S	2101 NASA Road One	Houston, TX 77058
Ivins, Marsha S.	Astronaut Office	Code CB Bldg. 4S	2101 NASA Road One	Houston, TX 77058
Jemison, Mae C.	Rm 306-6182 Steele Hall	The Jemison Institute	Dartmouth College	Hanover, NH 03755
Jernigan, Tamara E.	Astronaut Office	Code CB Bldg. 4S	2101 NASA Road One	Houston, TX 77058
Jett, Brent W.	NASA Office	Yuri Gagarin Centre	141 160 Zvezdny Gorodok	Mosk. Obl, Russia
Johnson, Gregory C.	Astronaut Office	Code CB Bldg. 4S	2101 NASA Road One	Houston, TX 77058
Johnson, Gregory H.	Astronaut Office	Code CB Bldg. 4S	2101 NASA Road One	Houston, TX 77058
Jones, Thomas D.	Astronaut Office	Code CB Bldg. 4S	2101 NASA Road One	Houston, TX 77058
Kadenyuk, Leonid	Ukrainian Space Agency	Academy of Sciences	252 127 Kiev 127	Ukraine
Kavandi, Janet L.	Astronaut Office	Code CB Bldg. 4S	2101 NASA Road One	Houston, TX 77058
Kelly, James M.	Astronaut Office	Code CB Bldg. 4S	2101 NASA Road One	Houston, TX 77058
Kelly, Mark E.	Astronaut Office	Code CB Bldg. 4S	2101 NASA Road One	Houston, TX 77058
Kelly, Scott J.	Astronaut Office	Code CB Bldg. 4S	2101 NASA Road One	Houston, TX 77058
Kerwin, Joseph P.	Life Sciences Systems	Wyle Laboratories	1290 Hercules Drive	Houston, TX 77058-2787
Kilrain, Susan L.	Room 5Y72 Code QS	Office of Space Flight	NASA Headquarters	Washington, DC 20546
Kopra, Timothy L.	Astronaut Office	Code CB Bldg. 4S	2101 NASA Road One	Houston, TX 77058
Kregel Kevin R.	Astronaut Office	Code CB Bldg. 4S	2101 NASA Road One	Houston, TX 77058
Lawrence, Wendy B.	Advanced Syst. & Tech.	Natl. Reconnaissance	14675 Lee Road	Chantilly, VA 20151
Lee, Mark C.	Astronaut Office	Code CB Bldg. 4S	2101 NASA Road One	Houston, TX 77058
Leestma, David C.	Flight Crew Operations	Bldg. 1 Room 920A	Johnson Space Center	Houston, TX 77058
Lenoir, William B.	Booz Allen & Hamilton	World Wide Technology	8283 Greensboro Drive	McLean, VA 22102
Leslie, Fred	Mail Stop 7795, SD 47	Bldg 4481 Room 315A	Marshall Space Flight Ctr.	Huntsville, AL 35812
Lind, Don L.	51 N. 376 E.	Smithfield, UT 84335		

Lindsey, Steven W.	Astronaut Office	Code CB Bldg. 4S	2101 NASA Road One	Houston, TX 77058
Linenger, Jerry M.	550 S. Stoney Point Rd.	Suttons Bay, MI 49682		
Linnehan, Richard M.	Astronaut Office	Code CB Bldg. 4S	2101 NASA Road One	Houston, TX 77058
Linteris, Gregory	Code B356 Bldg. 224	Fire Science Division	Natl. Inst. of Standards	Gaithersburg, MD 20899
Llewellyn, John A.	Bldg. ENB 345 LIB 618	University of So. Florida	4202 East Fowler Ave.	Tampa, FL 33620-5452
Lockhart, Paul S.	Astronaut Office	Code CB Bldg. 4S	2101 NASA Road One	Houston, TX 77058
Lopez-Alegria, Michael	Astronaut Office	Code CB Bldg. 4S	2101 NASA Road One	Houston, TX 77058
Loria, Christopher J.	Astronaut Office	Code CB Bldg. 4S	2101 NASA Road One	Houston, TX 77058
Lounge, John M.	Space Engineering	Spacehab Inc.	555 Forge River Road	Webster, TX 77589
Lousma, Jack R.	The Diamond General	Development Corp.	333 Parkland Plaza	Ann Arbor, MI 48108
Love, Stanley G.	Astronaut Office	Code CB Bldg. 4S	2101 NASA Road One	Houston, TX 77058
Lovell, James A., Jr.	PO Box 49	Lovell Communications	915 South Waukegan Rd	Lake Forest, IL 60045
Low, G. David	Global Data & Message	Orbcomm	2455 Horse Pen Road	Herdon, VA 20171
Lu, Edward T.	Astronaut Office	Code CB Bldg. 4S	2101 NASA Road One	Houston, TX 77058
Lucid, Shannon W.	1622 Gunwale Road	Houston, TX 77062-4538		
MacLean, Steven G.	Canadian Space Agency	6767 route de l'Aeroport	Saint-Hubert, Quebec	J3Y 8Y9, Canada
Magnus, Sandra H.	Astronaut Office	Code CB Bldg. 4S	2101 NASA Road One	Houston, TX 77058
Malerba, Franco	Alenia Spazio SpA	Corso Marche 41	I-10146 Torino, Italy	
Massimino, Michael J.	Astronaut Office	Code CB Bldg. 4S	2101 NASA Road One	Houston, TX 77058
Mastracchio, Richard A.	Astronaut Office	Code CB Bldg. 4S	2101 NASA Road One	Houston, TX 77058
Matthiesen, David	1564 Belle Avenue	Lakewood, OH 44107		
Mattingly, Thomas K., II	Chairman	Universal Space Network	10821 Bloomfield	Los Alamitos, CA 90720
Mayo, Itzhak	Astronaut Office	Code CB Bldg. 4S	2101 NASA Road One	Houston, TX 77058
McArthur, K. Megan	Astronaut Office	Code CB Bldg. 4S	2101 NASA Road One	Houston, TX 77058
McArthur, William S., Jr.	NASA Office	Yuri Gagarin Centre	141 160 Zvezdny Gorodok	Mosk. Obl, Russia
McBride, Jon A.	Suite 901	Image Development Grp.	1018 Kanawha Blvd	Charleston, WV 25301
McCandless, Bruce, II	M/S DC 3005	Lockheed Martin	PO Box 179	Denver, CO 80201-0179
McCool, William C.	Astronaut Office	Code CB Bldg. 4S	2101 NASA Road One	Houston, TX 77058
McCulley, Michael J.	Chief Operating Officer	United Space Alliance	1150 Gemini Avenue	Houston, TX 77058-2708
McDivitt, James A.	9146 Cherry Avenue	Rapid City, MI 49676		
McMonagle, Donald R.	545 Apache Trail	Merritt Island, FL 32953		
Meade, Carl J.	X-33 Program Manager	Lockheed Martin	1011 Lockheed Way	Palmdale, CA 93599
Melnick, Bruce E.	Mail Stop FO 10	Boeing Company	Kennedy Space Center	FL 32815-0233
Melroy, Pamela A.	Astronaut Office	Code CB Bldg. 4S	2101 NASA Road One	Houston, TX 77058
Melvin, Leland D.	Astronaut Office	Code CB Bldg. 4S	2101 NASA Road One	Houston, TX 77058
Michel, F. Curtis	Dept. of Space Physics	Rice University	6100 Main Street	Houston, TX 77005-1892
Mitchell, Edgar D.	PO Box 540037	Lake Worth , FL	33454-0037	
Mohri, Mamoru (NASDA)	Astronaut Office	NASDA	2-1-1 Segen, Tukuba-Shi	Ibaraki 305, Japan
Morgan, Barbara R.	Astronaut Office	Code CB Bldg. 4S	2101 NASA Road One	Houston, TX 77058
Morin, Lee M.	Astronaut Office	Code CB Bldg. 4S	2101 NASA Road One	Houston, TX 77058
Mullane, Richard M.	1301 Las Lomas Rd. NE	Albequerque, NM 87106		
Musgrave, Story	8572 Sweetwater Trail	Kissimmee, FL 34747		
Nagel, Steven R.	Quality Assurance	Code CC4 Bldg 276	Johnson Space Center	Houston, TX 77058
Nelson, George D.	AAAS Project 2061	1333 H Street NW	PO Box 34446	Washington, DC 20005
Nespoli, Paolo (ESA)	Astronaut Office	Code CB Bldg. 4S	2101 NASA Road One	Houston, TX 77058
Newman, James H.	Astronaut Office	Code CB Bldg. 4S	2101 NASA Road One	Houston, TX 77058

Nicollier, Claude (ESA)	Astronaut Office	Code CB Bldg. 4S	2101 NASA Road One	Houston, TX 77058
Noguchi,Soichi (NASDA)	Astronaut Office	NASDA	2-1-1 Segen, Tukuba-Shi	Ibaraki 305, Japan
Noriega, Carlos I.	Astronaut Office	Code CB Bldg. 4S	2101 NASA Road One	Houston, TX 77058
Nowak, Lisa M.	Astronaut Office	Code CB Bldg. 4S	2101 NASA Road One	Houston, TX 77058
Nyberg, Karen L.	Astronaut Office	Code CB Bldg. 4S	2101 NASA Road One	Houston, TX 77058
Ochoa, Ellen	Astronaut Office	Code CB Bldg. 4S	2101 NASA Road One	Houston, TX 77058
Ockels, Wubbo J. (ESA)	Code ADM-RE ESTEC	Postbus 299	NL 2200 AG Noordwijk	Netherlands
O'Connor, Bryan D.	Engineering Department	Futron Corporation	400 Virginia Avenue	Washington, DC 20024
Oefelein, William A.	Astronaut Office	Code CB Bldg. 4S	2101 NASA Road One	Houston, TX 77058
O'Leary, Brian T.	Suite 21-200	1993 S. Kihei Road	Maui, HI 96753	
Olivas, John D.	Astronaut Office	Code CB Bldg. 4S	2101 NASA Road One	Houston, TX 77058
Oswald, Stephen S.	16806 Glenshannon Dr.	Houston, TX 77059		
Parazynski, Scott E.	Astronaut Office	Code CB Bldg. 4S	2101 NASA Road One	Houston, TX 77058
Parise, Ronald	System Science Division	Computer Science Corp.	10210 Greenbelt Road	Seabroke, MD 20706
Parker, Robert A. R.	Director	Jet Propulsion Lab.	4800 Oak Grove Drive	Pasadena, CA 91109
Patrick, Nicholas J. M.	Astronaut Office	Code CB Bldg. 4S	2101 NASA Road One	Houston, TX 77058
Pawelczyk, James	Applied Physiology	Penn State University	University Park Campus	University Park, PA 16802
Payette, Julie (CSA)	Canadian Space Agency	6767 route de l'Aeroport	Saint-Hubert, Quebec	J3Y 8Y9, Canada
Perrin, Philippe (CNES)	CNES	Direction des Astronaute	2 Place Maurice Quentin	F-75039 Paris, France
Peterson, Donald H.	President	Aerospace Operations	427 Pebblebrook	Seabrook, TX 77586
Pettit, Donald R.	Astronaut Office	Code CB Bldg. 4S	2101 NASA Road One	Houston, TX 77058
Phillips, John L.	Astronaut Office	Code CB Bldg. 4S	2101 NASA Road One	Houston, TX 77058
Pogue, William R.	4 Cromer Drive	Bella Vista, AR	72715-5318	
Poindexter, Alan G.	Astronaut Office	Code CB Bldg. 4S	2101 NASA Road One	Houston, TX 77058
Polansky, Mark L.	Astronaut Office	Code CB Bldg. 4S	2101 NASA Road One	Houston, TX 77058
Pontes, Marcos (Brazil)	Astronaut Office	Code CB Bldg. 4S	2101 NASA Road One	Houston, TX 77058
Precourt, Charles J., Jr.	Astronaut Office	Code CB Bldg. 4S	2101 NASA Road One	Houston, TX 77058
Pustovyi, Yaroslav	Ukrainian Space Agency	Academy of Sciences	252 127 Kiev 127	Ukraine
Ramon, Ilan	Payload Specialist Office	Bldg. 4S Room 5803	Johnson Space Center	Houston, TX 77058
Readdy, William F.	Deputy Administrator	Code M-7 NASA Hdqtrs.	Washington, DC 20546	
Reightler, Kenneth S., Jr.	Eng. Analysis & Testing	Lockheed Martin Eng.	2400 NASA Road 1	Houston, TX 77058
Reilly, James F.	Astronaut Office	Code CB Bldg. 4S	2101 NASA Road One	Houston, TX 77058
Reisman, Garrett E.	Astronaut Office	Code CB Bldg. 4S	2101 NASA Road One	Houston, TX 77058
Richards, Paul W.	Astronaut Office	Code CB Bldg. 4S	2101 NASA Road One	Houston, TX 77058
Richards, Richard N.	Reusable Space Sys.	Boeing Company	5301 Bolsa Avenue	Huntington Beach, CA 92647
Ride, Sally K.	California Space Institute	University of California	9500 Gilman Drive	LA Jolla, CA 92093-0524
Robinson, Stephen K.	Astronaut Office	Code CB Bldg. 4S	2101 NASA Road One	Houston, TX 77058
Rominger, Kent V.	Astronaut Office	Code CB Bldg. 4S	2101 NASA Road One	Houston, TX 77058
Ronney, Paul	Mail Code OHE 430L	University So. California	3650 McClintock Avenue	Los Angeles, CA 90089
Ross, Jerry L.	Astronaut Office	Code CB Bldg. 4S	2101 NASA Road One	Houston, TX 77058
Runco, Mario, Jr.	Astronaut Office	Code CB Bldg. 4S	2101 NASA Road One	Houston, TX 77058
Sacco, Albert	Advanced Microgravity	Northeastern University	360 Huntingdon Avenue	Boston, MA 02115-5000
Schirra, Walter M., Jr.	PO Box 73	16834 Via de Santa Fe	Rancho Santa Fe, CA	92067
Schlegel, Hans (ESA)	European Astronaut Ctr.	PO Box 90 60 96	Linder Hohe D-51127	Koln, Germany
Schmitt, Harrison H.	437 Eng. Research Bldg	1500 Engineering Drive	University of Wisconsin	Madison, WI 53706
Schweickart, Russell L.	Low Earth Systems	CTA Commercial System	6116 Executive Blvd	Rockville, MD 20852

Scott, David R.	The Merces Group	Victoria Campbell-Johnson	30 Hackamore Lane	Bell Canyon, CA 91307
Scott, Winston E.	VP Student Affairs	Florida State University	313 Wescott	Tallahassee, FL 32306
Searfoss, Richard A.	24480 Silver Creek Way	Tehachapi, CA 93561		
Seddon, Margaret Rhea	Suite 3601	Vanderbilt Medical Group	Nashville, TN 37130	
Sega, Ronald M.	Eng. & Applied Science	University of Colorado	1420 Austin Bluff's Pkwy	Colorado Springs, CO80933
Sellers, Piers J.	Astronaut Office	Code CB Bldg. 4S	2101 NASA Road One	Houston, TX 77058
Shaw, Brewster H., Jr.	Intl. Space Station	Boeing Company	2100 Space Park Drive	Houston, TX 77058
Shepherd, William M.	Astronaut Office	Code CB Bldg. 4S	2101 NASA Road One	Houston, TX 77058
Shriver, Loren J.	Program Manager	United Space Alliance	1150 Gemini Avenue	Houston, TX 77058
Smith, Steven L.	Astronaut Office	Code CB Bldg. 4S	2101 NASA Road One	Houston, TX 77058
Spring, Sherwood C.	Suite 700	Pacific Sierra Corp.	1400 Key Blvd.	Arlington, VA 22209
Springer, Robert C.	Mail Stop ZA01	Boeing North America	555 Discovery Drive	Huntsville, AL 35806
Stafford, Thomas P.	Stafford, Burke & Hecker	1006 Cameron Street	Alexandria, VA 22314	
Stefanyshyn-Piper, H.	Astronaut Office	Code CB Bldg. 4S	2101 NASA Road One	Houston, TX 77058
Stewart, Robert L.	Canadian Space Agency	6767 route de l'Aeroport	Saint-Hubert, Quebec	J3Y 8Y9, Canada
Stott, Nicole P.	Astronaut Office	Code CB Bldg. 4S	2101 NASA Road One	Houston, TX 77058
Sturckow, Frederick W.	Astronaut Office	Code CB Bldg. 4S	2101 NASA Road One	Houston, TX 77058
Sullivan, Kathryn D.	President	Ctr. of Science / Industry	333 W Broad Street	Columbus, OH 43215
Swanson, Steven R.	Astronaut Office	Code CB Bldg. 4S	2101 NASA Road One	Houston, TX 77058
Tani, Daniel M.	Astronaut Office	Code CB Bldg. 4S	2101 NASA Road One	Houston, TX 77058
Tanner, Joseph R.	Astronaut Office	Code CB Bldg. 4S	2101 NASA Road One	Houston, TX 77058
Thagard, Norman E.	College Rel's FAMU-FSU	Florida State University	2525 Pottsdamer Street	Tallahassee, FL 32310
Thiele, Gerhard (ESA)	European Astronaut Ctr.	PO Box 90 60 96	Linder Hohe D-51127	Koln, Germany
Thirsk, Robert	Canadian Space Agency	6767 route de l'Aeroport	Saint-Hubert, Quebec	J3Y 8Y9, Canada
Thomas, Andrew S. W.	Astronaut Office	Code CB Bldg. 4S	2101 NASA Road One	Houston, TX 77058
Thomas, Donald A.	Astronaut Office	Code CB Bldg. 4S	2101 NASA Road One	Houston, TX 77058
Thornton, Kathryn C.	Dept. Eng. Applied Sci.	University of Virginia	A 237 Thornton Hall	Charlottesville, VA 22903
Thornton, William E.	701 Cowards Creek	Friendswood, TX 77546		
Thuot, Pierre J.	VP Administration	Orbital Sciences Corp.	21700 Atlantic Blvd.	Dulles, VA 20166
Tognini, Michel (ESA)	CNES	Direction des Astronaute	2 Place Maurice Quentin	F-75039 Paris, France
Trinh, Eugene	Microgravity Res. Rm. 8P11	300 E Street SW	Washington, DC 20546	
Truly, Richard H.	Director Code 1731	Natl. Renewable Lab.	1617 Cole Blvd	Golden, CO 80401-3393
Tryggvason, Bjarni V.	Canadian Space Agency	6767 route de l'Aeroport	Saint-Hubert, Quebec	J3Y 8Y9, Canada
Urbani, Luca	Agenzia Spaziale Italiana	Va di Patrizi 13	I-00161 Roma, Italy	
Van Hoften, James D. A.	333/14/C72 Senior VP	Bechtel Corporation	Box 193965	San Francisco, CA 94119
Vangen, Scott	Rm. 3002N Bldg. SSPF	NASA	Kennedy Space Center	FL 32815
Virts, Terry W., Jr.	Astronaut Office	Code CB Bldg. 4S	2101 NASA Road One	Houston, TX 77058
Vittori, Roberto (ESA)	Astronaut Office	Code CB Bldg. 4S	2101 NASA Road One	Houston, TX 77058
Voss, James S.	Astronaut Office	Code CB Bldg. 4S	2101 NASA Road One	Houston, TX 77058
Voss, Janice E.	Astronaut Office	Code CB Bldg. 4S	2101 NASA Road One	Houston, TX 77058
Wakata, Koichi	NASDA Houston Office	Johnson Space Center	2101 NASA Road One	Houston, TX 77058
Walheim, Rex J.	Astronaut Office	Code CB Bldg. 4S	2101 NASA Road One	Houston, TX 77058
Walker, Charles	Information Department	Boeing Company	1200 Wilson Blvd	Arlington, VA 22209
Walz, Carl E.	Astronaut Office	Code CB Bldg. 4S	2101 NASA Road One	Houston, TX 77058
Weber, Mary E.	Astronaut Office	Code CB Bldg. 4S	2101 NASA Road One	Houston, TX 77058
Weitz, Paul J.	3086 N. Tam O'Shatner Dr.	Flagstaff, AZ 86004		

Wetherbee, James D.	Astronaut Office	Code CB Bldg. 4S	2101 NASA Road One	Houston, TX 77058
Wheelock, Douglas H.	Astronaut Office	Code CB Bldg. 4S	2101 NASA Road One	Houston, TX 77058
Whitson, Peggy A.	Astronaut Office	Code CB Bldg. 4S	2101 NASA Road One	Houston, TX 77058
Wilcutt, Terrence W.	Astronaut Office	Code CB Bldg. 4S	2101 NASA Road One	Houston, TX 77058
Williams, David R. (CSA)	Canadian Space Agency	6767 route de l'Aeroport	Saint-Hubert, Quebec	J3Y 8Y9, Canada
Williams, Donald E.	Senior Systems Engr.	SAIC	2200 Space Park Drive	Houston, TX 77058
Williams, Jeffrey N.	Astronaut Office	Code CB Bldg. 4S	2101 NASA Road One	Houston, TX 77058
Williams, Sunita L.	Astronaut Office	Code CB Bldg. 4S	2101 NASA Road One	Houston, TX 77058
Wilmore, Barry E.	Astronaut Office	Code CB Bldg. 4S	2101 NASA Road One	Houston, TX 77058
Wilson, Stephanie D.	Astronaut Office	Code CB Bldg. 4S	2101 NASA Road One	Houston, TX 77058
Wisoff, Peter J. K.	Astronaut Office	Code CB Bldg. 4S	2101 NASA Road One	Houston, TX 77058
Wolf, David A.	Astronaut Office	Code CB Bldg. 4S	2101 NASA Road One	Houston, TX 77058
Woodward III, Neil W.	Astronaut Office	Code CB	Johnson Space Center	Houston, TX 77058
Worden, Alfred M.	PO Box 8065	Vero Beach, FL	32963-8065	
Young, John W.	Associate Director	Mail Code AC5	Johnson Space Center	Houston, TX 77058
Zamka, George D.	Astronaut Office	Code CB Bldg. 4S	2101 NASA Road One	Houston, TX 77058

If you wish to apply for selection as a NASA astronaut, please request an application package in writing to:

Astronaut Selection Office
Mail Code AHX
Johnson Space Center
Houston, TX 77058-3696

Further information on the NASA selection process can be seen on page 4.